Fodor's 96
Scotland

"When it comes to information on regional history, what to see and do, and shopping, these guides are exhaustive."

—*USAir Magazine*

"Usable, sophisticated restaurant coverage, with an emphasis on good value."

—Andy Birsh, *Gourmet Magazine* columnist

"Valuable because of their comprehensiveness."

—*Minneapolis Star-Tribune*

"Fodor's always delivers high quality...thoughtfully presented...thorough."

—*Houston Post*

"An excellent choice for those who want everything under one cover."

—*Washington Post*

Fodor's Travel Publications, Inc.
New York • Toronto • London • Sydney • Auckland

Fodor's Scotland

Editor: Kristen D. Perrault

Area Editor: Gilbert Summers

Editorial Contributors: Rob Andrews, Robert Blake, Beth Ingpen, Linda K. Schmidt, M. T. Schwartzman, Dinah Spritzer, P. D. Williams

Creative Director: Fabrizio La Rocca

Cartographers: David Lindroth, Mapping Specialists

Cover Photograph: Catherine Karnow/Woodfin Camp

Text Design: Between the Covers

Copyright

Special Sales

CONTENTS

ON THE ROAD WITH FODOR'S

A GOOD TRAVEL GUIDE is like a wonderful traveling companion. It's charming, it's brimming with sound recommendations and solid ideas, it pulls no punches in describing lodging and dining establishments, and it's consistently full of fascinating facts that make you view what you've traveled to see in a rich new light. In the creation of *Scotland '96*, we at Fodor's have gone to great lengths to provide you with the very best of all possible traveling companions—and to make your trip the best of all possible vacations.

About Our Writers

The information in these pages is largely the work of Gilbert Summers, a native Scot who has spent the last thirteen years writing numerous guidebooks and articles about his home country. His aim is to make visitors realize that there is a much more diverse nation behind the "haggis and tartan" image (Gilbert has never worn a kilt in his life). He lives out in the barley fields of the rural northeast, within sight of his first love—the sea.

We'd also like to thank the people at Virgin Atlantic Airways for their help and support.

What's New

A New Design

If this is not the first Fodor's guide you've purchased, you'll immediately notice our new look. More readable and easier to use than ever? We think so—and we hope you do, too.

New Takes on the Northern Highlands

Gilbert Summers has added a tour to John o'Groats to this edition. He takes us to Caithness, at the very north of Scotland, a place he describes as "big skies and distant blue hills beyond endless rolling moors."

Travel Updates

In addition, just before your trip, you may want to order a Fodor's Worldview Travel Update. From local publications all over Scotland, the lively, cosmopolitan editors at Worldview gather information on concerts, plays, opera, dance performances, gallery and museum shows, sports competitions, and other special events that coincide with your visit. See the order blank at the back of this book, call 800/799–9609, or fax 800/799–9619.

And in Scotland

Don't automatically think you must go to London to reach Scotland by air. The promoters of business at **Frankfurt and Amsterdam airports** want to get the word out that, in their opinion, it's less of a hassle to make the Scottish connection on mainland Europe. Frankfurt Airport is quoting under 45 minutes' transfer time compared with 75 minutes at London Heathrow. Of course, don't forget you can also fly direct to Glasgow.

In other transportation matters, the Highlands' most recent improvement is the new **Skye road bridge,** which means there is now a hassle-free way to access one of Scotland's most romantic islands. It replaces a short ferry crossing which linked Kyle of Lochalsh on the mainland to Kyleakin on Skye, and has solved the peak-season ferry queues. The bridge is over 1800 feet long, making it one of the longest balanced cantilever bridges in the world.

Following a couple of difficult years for the Scottish tourist industry, operators and entrepreneurs in the accommodations sector are becoming more and more aware of the fierce competition at home, resulting in refurbished hotels, better self-catering accommodations, and more price-conscious, high-quality bed and breakfasts, in an effort to maintain market share. One of the most significant and exciting new properties, to a great extent breaking the mold of conventional accommodation choices, sits in an area of Scotland known as the Borders—only a few miles north of the border between England and Scotland: **Larkhall Burn** is a series of modern terraced cottages with top-class decor and fittings, overlooking the town of Jedburgh. Already given the highest grades possible by the Scottish Tourist Board, Larkhall Burn combines the freedom and flexibility of a self-catering establishment with the service of a hotel—all at a competitive price.

In Grampian, in the northeast of Scotland, an important new museum has just opened that tells the story of Scotland's lighthouses. The **Kinnaird Lighthouse Museum,** perhaps a bit esoteric at first glance, is a major exposition of Scotland's maritime heritage, situated in Fraserburgh on a breezy headland amid all the paraphernalia of a workaday fishing town, and overlooked by a 16th-century castle.

In urban news, Glasgow's new **Gallery of Modern Art** will open in one of the most impressive Georgian buildings in the city center, the former Stirling Library, with its classical columns and facade. It will house works by famous Scots and international artistic innovators.

Glasgow 1996 is the general name for a program of events in which Glasgow celebrates the visual arts. Throughout the summer of 1996, for example, the city's McLellan Galleries will host the largest exhibition to date of the life and work of Charles Rennie Mackintosh, Scotland's most famous 20th-century architect and designer. Late in finding widespread recognition in his homeland, Mackintosh has a distinct and readily recognizable style that has become part of the fabric of the modern age. Also, in September and October 1996, the Glasgow Festival of Design is intended to be a showcase for the best designers working today. Seminars, workshops, and conferences will analyze the contribution they make to our lives and our environment.

Two hundred years ago, a former farmer-turned-customs officer, who found fame as a poet, died in Dumfries. In 1996 the bicentenary of the death of poet Robert Burns, arguably the most famous Scot of all, is being marked by the **Burns International Festival.** It begins with birthday celebrations in January, then runs through a summer-long program. Major concerts plus a range of events organized by Scotland's art organizations, including recitals, concerts, and street theater, are all being put together in and around Ayrshire and Galloway, the homeland of the poet in southwest Scotland.

How to Use This Book

Organization

Up front is the **Gold Guide,** comprising two sections on gold paper that are chock-full of information about traveling within your destination and traveling in general. Both are in alphabetical order by topic. **Important Contacts A to Z** gives addresses and telephone numbers of organizations and companies that offer destination-related services and detailed information or publications. Here's where you'll find information about how to get to Scotland from wherever you are. **Smart Travel Tips A to Z,** the Gold Guide's second section, gives specific tips on how to get the most out of your travels, as well as information on how to accomplish what you need to in Scotland.

Chapters in Scotland, arranged by region, cover exploring, shopping, sports, dining, lodging, and arts and nightlife, and end with a section called Essentials, which tells you how to get there and get around and gives you important local addresses and telephone numbers. At the end of the book you'll find Portraits, wonderful essays about the history of Scotland, with one on Robert Burns, Scotland's most famous poet.

Stars

Stars in the margin are used to denote highly recommended sights, attractions, hotels, and restaurants.

Restaurant and Hotel Criteria and Price Categories

Restaurants and lodging places are chosen with a view to giving you the cream of the crop in each location and in each price range. In all restaurant price charts, costs are per person, excluding value-added tax (VAT) but excluding drinks and tip. In hotel price charts, rates are for standard double rooms excluding city and state sales tax.

Hotel Facilities

Note that in general you incur charges when you use many hotel facilities. We wanted to let you know what facilities a hotel has to offer, but we don't always specify whether or not there's a charge, so when planning a vacation that entails a stay of several days, it's wise to ask what's included in the rate.

Dress Code in Restaurants

The **What to Wear** section at the beginning of the individual chapters' dining sections tells you what's most common in that area. In general, we note a dress code only when men are required to wear a jacket or a jacket and tie.

Credit Cards

The following abbreviations are used: **AE,** American Express; **DC,** Diners Club; **MC,** MasterCard; and **V,** Visa. Discover is not accepted outside the United States.

Please Write to Us

Everyone who has contributed to *Scotland '96* has worked hard to make the text accurate. All prices and opening times are based on information supplied to us at press time, and the publisher cannot accept responsibility for any errors that may have occurred. The passage of time will bring changes, so it's always a good idea to call ahead and confirm information when it matters—particularly if you're making a detour to visit specific sights or attractions.

When making reservations at a hotel or inn, be sure to speak up if you have a disability or are traveling with children, if you prefer a private bath or a certain type of bed, or if you have specific dietary needs or any other concerns.

Were the restaurants we recommended as described? Did our hotel picks exceed your expectations? Did you find a museum we recommended a waste of time? We would love your feedback, positive and negative. If you have complaints, we'll look into them and revise our entries when the facts warrant it. If you've happened upon a special place that we haven't included, we'll pass the information along to the writers so they can check it out. So please send us a letter or postcard (we're at 201 East 50th Street, New York, NY 10022). We'll look forward to hearing from you. And in the meantime, have a wonderful trip!

Karen Cure
Editorial Director

Scotland

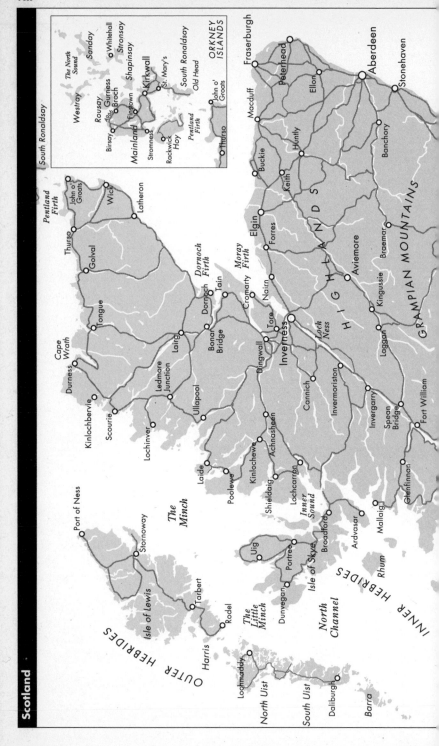

Europe

World Time Zones

Numbers below vertical bands relate each zone to Greenwich Mean Time (0 hrs.).
Local times frequently differ from these general indications,
as indicated by light-face numbers on map.

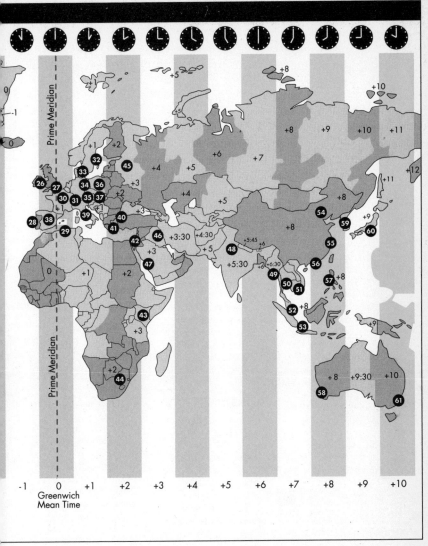

IMPORTANT CONTACTS A TO Z

An Alphabetical Listing of Publications, Organizations, and Companies That Will Help You Before, During, and After Your Trip

No single travel resource can give you every detail about every topic that might interest or concern you at the various stages of your journey—when you're planning your trip, while you're on the road, and after you get back home. The following organizations, books, and brochures will supplement the information in *Fodor's Scotland '96.* For related information, including both basic tips on visiting Scotland and background information on many of the topics below, study Smart Travel Tips A to Z, the section that follows Important Contacts A to Z.

A

AIR TRAVEL

The major gateway to Scotland is **Glasgow Airport** (☎ 0141/887–1111). Flying time is 6½ hours from New York, 7½ hours from Chicago, and 10 hours from Los Angeles.

CARRIERS

Carriers serving Scotland include **American Airlines** (☎ 800/433–7300); **British Airways** (☎ 800/247–9297); **Continental Airlines** (☎ 800/525–0280); **Northwest Airlines** (☎ 800/447–4747); **TWA** (☎ 800/892–4141); **United Airlines** (☎ 800/241–6522); **USAir** (☎ 800/622–1015); and **Virgin Atlantic** (☎ 800/862–8621).

COMPLAINTS

To register complaints about charter and scheduled airlines, contact the U.S. Department of Transportation's **Office of Consumer Affairs** (400 7th St. NW, Washington, DC 20590, ☎ 202/366–2220 or 800/322–7873).

CONSOLIDATORS

Established consolidators selling to the public include **BET World Travel** (841 Blossom Hill Rd., Suite 212-C, San Jose, CA 95123, ☎ 408/229–7880 or 800/747–1476), **Euram Tours** (1522 K St. NW, Suite 430, Washington, DC 20005, ☎ 800/848–6789), **TFI Tours International** (34 W. 32nd St., New York, NY 10001, ☎ 212/736–1140 or 800/745–8000), **Council Charter** (205 E. 42nd St., New York, NY 10017, ☎ 212/661–0311 or 800/800–8222), and **Travac Tours and Charter** (989 6th Ave., 16th Floor, New York, NY 10018, ☎ 212/563–3303 or 800/872–8800; 2601 E. Jefferson, Orlando, FL 32803, ☎ 407/896–0014 or 800/872–8800).

PUBLICATIONS

For general information about charter carriers, ask for the Office of Consumer Affairs' brochure **"Plane Talk: Public Charter Flights."** The Department of Transportation also publishes a 58-page booklet, **"Fly Rights"** ($1.75; Consumer Information Center, Dept. 133-B, Pueblo, CO 81009).

For other tips and hints, consult the Consumers Union's monthly **"Consumer Reports Travel Letter"** ($39 a year; Box 53629, Boulder, CO 80322, ☎ 800/234–1970) and the newsletter **"Travel Smart"** ($37 a year; 40 Beechdale Rd., Dobbs Ferry, NY 10522, ☎ 800/327–3633); *The Official Frequent Flyer Guidebook,* by Randy Petersen ($14.99 plus $3 shipping; 4715-C Town Center Dr., Colorado Springs, CO 80916, ☎ 719/597–8899 or 800/487–8893); *Airfare Secrets Exposed,* by Sharon Tyler and Matthew Wonder (Universal Information Publishing; $16.95 plus $3.75 shipping from Sandcastle Publishing, Box 3070-A, South Pasadena, CA 91031,

☎ 213/255–3616 or 800/655–0053); and *202 Tips Even the Best Business Travelers May Not Know,* by Christopher McGinnis ($10 plus $3.00 shipping; Irwin Professional Publishing, 1333 Burr Ridge Pkwy., Burr Ridge, IL 60521, ☎ 708/789–4000 or 800/634–3966).

B

BETTER BUSINESS BUREAU

For local contacts in the home town of a tour operator you may be considering, consult the **Council of Better Business Bureaus** (4200 Wilson Blvd., Arlington, VA 22203, ☎ 703/276–0100).

BICYCLE TRAVEL

TOURS

Ian Pragnell of **Bespoke Highland Tours** (The Bothy, Camusdarach, Inverness-shire PH39 4NT, ☎ 01687/450272) arranges treks throughout the Highlands and the islands for cyclists of all abilities. **Scottish Border Trails** (Drummore, Venlaw High Rd., Peebles EH45 87RL, ☎ 01721/720336, FAX 01721/723004) runs off-road mountain bike treks in the Borders and vehicle-supported road tours on which your luggage is ferried between stops. **Wildcat Mountain Bike Tours** (15A Henderson St., Bridge of Allan, Stirling FK9 4HN, ☎ and FAX 01786/832321) sells guided, vehicle-supported tours throughout Scotland for novices and experts.

ORGANIZATIONS

Cyclists' Touring Club (National Headquarters, Cotterell House, 69 Meadrow, Godalming, Surrey, GU7 3HS, England, ☎ 01483/417217) actively campaigns for better cyclist facilities throughout the United Kingdom. It publishes a members magazine, route maps, and guides.

Sustrans Ltd (53 Cochrane St., Glasgow G1 1HL, ☎ 0141/552–8241) is a nonprofit organization dedicated to providing environmentally friendly routes for cyclists, notably in and around cities.

PUBLICATIONS

The Scottish Tourist Board's free brochure "Adventure and Special Interest Holidays," published annually, lists prepackaged vacations that may include cycling; its free "**Cycling in Scotland**" brochure has some suggested routes and practical advice. More detailed information on long routes, day trips, and accommodations is given in the guidebook *Cycling in Scotland,* available from Canongate Books Ltd. (14 High St., Edinburgh EH1 1TE, ☎ 0131/557–5111). The Ordnance Survey Landranger series of maps, which shows gradient, is invaluable for cyclists.

BUS TRAVEL

FROM ENGLAND

For timetables, contact **National Express** (Buchanan Bus Station, Killermont St., Glasgow, G2 3NP, ☎ 0141/332–9191).

Travel centers and travel agents also have details, and some travel agents sell tickets.

WITHIN SCOTLAND

For information on the country's bus network contact any bus station or the **Travel Center** (Buchanan Street Bus Station, Glasgow G2 3NP, ☎ 0141/332–9191); **S.M.T.** (St. Andrew Bus Station, Edinburgh EH1 3DU, ☎ 0131/556–8464); and **Edinburgh and Scotland Information Centre** (3 Princes St., Edinburgh EH2 2QP, ☎ 0131/557–1700).

C

CAR RENTAL

Major car-rental companies represented in Scotland include **Alamo** (☎ 800/327–9633, 0800/272–2000 in the U.K.), **Avis** (☎ 800/331–1084, 800/879–2847 in Canada), **Budget** (☎ 800/527–0700, 0800/181–181 in the U.K.), **Hertz** (☎ 800/654–3001, 800/263–0600 in Canada, 0181/679–1799 in the U.K.), and **National** (sometimes known as Europcar InterRent outside North America; ☎ 800/227–3876, 0181/950–5050 in the U.K.). Prices in Glasgow begin at $40 a day and $170 a week for an economy car with unlimited mileage. This does not include tax, which in Scotland is 17.5% on car rentals.

RENTAL WHOLESALERS

Contact **Auto Europe** (Box 7006, Portland, ME 04112, ☎ 207/828–2525 or 800/223–

5555); **Europe by Car** in New York City (write 1 Rockefeller Plaza, 10020; visit 14 W. 49th St.; or call 212/581–3040, 212/245–1713, or 800/223–1516) or Los Angeles (9000 Sunset Blvd., 90069, ☎ 800/252–9401 or 213/272–0424 in CA); **Foremost Euro-Car** (5658 Sepulveda Blvd., Suite 201, Van Nuys, CA 91411, ☎ 818/786–1960 or 800/272–3299); or the **Kemwel Group** (106 Calvert St., Harrison, NY 10528, ☎ 914/835–5555 or 800/678–0678).

THE CHANNEL TUNNEL

For information, contact **Le Shuttle** (☎ 01345/353535 in the U.K., 800/388–3876 in the U.S.), which transports cars, or **Eurostar** (☎ 0171/922–4486 in the U.K., 800/942–4866 in the U.S.), the high-speed train service between London (Waterloo) and Paris (Gare du Nord). Eurostar tickets are available in the U.K. through **Inter-City Europe,** the international wing of BritRail (London, Victoria Station, ☎ 0171/834–2345 or 0171/828–8092 for credit-card bookings), and in the United States through **Rail Europe** (☎ 800/942–4866) and **BritRail Travel** (1500 Broadway, New York, NY 10036, ☎ 800/677–8585).

CHILDREN AND TRAVEL

FLYING

Look into **"Flying with Baby"** ($5.95 plus $1 shipping; Third Street Press, Box 261250,

Littleton, CO 80126, ☎ 303/595–5959), cowritten by a flight attendant. **"Kids and Teens in Flight,"** free from the U.S. Department of Transportation's Office of Consumer Affairs, offers tips for children flying alone. Every two years the February issue of *Family Travel Times* (*see* Know-How, *below*) details children's services on three dozen airlines.

KNOW-HOW

Family Travel Times, published 10 times a year by Travel with Your Children (TWYCH, 45 W. 18th St., New York, NY 10011, ☎ 212/206–0688; annual subscription $55), covers destinations, types of vacations, and modes of travel.

The *Family Travel Guides* catalogue ($1 postage; ☎ 510/527–5849) lists about 200 books and articles on family travel. Also check *Take Your Baby and Go! A Guide for Traveling with Babies, Toddlers and Young Children,* by Sheri Andrews, Judy Bordeaux, and Vivian Vasquez ($5.95 plus $1.50 shipping; Bear Creek Publications, 2507 Minor Ave., Seattle, WA 98102, ☎ 206/322–7604 or 800/326–6566). *Innocents Abroad: Traveling with Kids in Europe,* by Valerie Wolf Deutsch and Laura Sutherland ($15.95 plus $2 shipping; Penguin USA, 120 Woodbine St., Bergenfield, NJ 07621, ☎ 201/387–0600 or

800/253–6476), covers child- and teen-friendly activities, food, and transportation.

TOUR OPERATORS

Contact **Grandtravel** (6900 Wisconsin Ave., Suite 706, Chevy Chase, MD 20815, ☎ 301/986–0790 or 800/247–7651), which has tours for people traveling with grandchildren ages 7 to 17; **Families Welcome!** (21 W. Colony Pl., Suite 140, Durham, NC 27705, ☎ 919/489–2555 or 800/326–0724); or **Rascals in Paradise** (650 5th St., Suite 505, San Francisco, CA 94107, ☎ 415/978–9800 or 800/872–7225).

CRUISING

Cunard Line (555 5th Ave., New York, NY 10017, ☎ 212/880–7500 or 800/528–6273) operates the *Queen Elizabeth (QE2)* on the only regular transatlantic crossings sailing between New York City and Southampton, England, from April through December.

CUSTOMS

U.S. CITIZENS

The **U.S. Customs Service** (Box 7407, Washington, DC 20044, ☎ 202/927–6724) can answer questions on duty-free limits and publishes a helpful brochure, **"Know Before You Go."** For information on registering foreign-made articles, call 202/927–0540.

CANADIANS

Contact **Revenue Canada** (2265 St.

Laurent Blvd. S, Ottawa, Ontario, K1G 4K3, ☎ 613/993–0534) for a copy of the free brochure **"I Declare/Je Déclare"** and for details on duties that exceed the standard duty-free limit.

D

FOR TRAVELERS WITH DISABILITIES

COMPLAINTS

To register complaints under the provisions of the Americans with Disabilities Act, contact the U.S. Department of Justice's **Public Access Section** (Box 66738, Washington, DC 20035, ☎ 202/514–0301, TDD 202/514–0383, FAX 202/307–1198).

GETTING AROUND

Hertz (☎ 800/654–3131) can provide hand controls for individuals with lower-limb disability at its rental offices in Glasgow and Edinburgh. With advance notice, British Rail staff will assist passengers with disabilities; inquire at any British Rail area office.

ORGANIZATIONS

FOR TRAVELERS WITH HEARING IMPAIRMENTS➤ Contact the **American Academy of Otolaryngology** (1 Prince St., Alexandria, VA 22314, ☎ 703/836–4444, FAX 703/683–5100, TTY 703/519–1585).

FOR TRAVELERS WITH MOBILITY IMPAIRMENTS➤ Contact the **Information Center for Individuals with Disabilities** (Fort Point Pl., 27–43 Wormwood St., Boston, MA 02210, ☎ 617/727–5540, 800/462–5015 in MA, TTY 617/345–9743); **Mobility International USA** (Box 10767, Eugene, OR 97440, ☎ and TTY 503/343–1284; FAX 503/343–6812), the U.S. branch of an international organization based in Belgium (*see below*) that has affiliates in 30 countries; **MossRehab Hospital Travel Information Service** (1200 W. Tabor Rd., Philadelphia, PA 19141, ☎ 215/456–9603, TTY 215/456–9602); the **Society for the Advancement of Travel for the Handicapped** (SATH, 347 5th Ave., Suite 610, New York, NY 10016, ☎ 212/447–7284, FAX 212/725–8253); the **Travel Industry and Disabled Exchange** (TIDE, 5435 Donna Ave., Tarzana, CA 91356, ☎ 818/344–3640, FAX 818/344–0078); and **Travelin' Talk** (Box 3534, Clarksville, TN 37043, ☎ 615/552–6670, FAX 615/552–1182).

FOR TRAVELERS WITH VISION IMPAIRMENTS➤ Contact the **American Council of the Blind** (1155 15th St. NW, Suite 720, Washington, DC 20005, ☎ 202/467–5081, FAX 202/467–5085) or the **American Foundation for the Blind** (15 W. 16th St., New York, NY 10011, ☎ 212/620–2000, TTY 212/620–2158).

IN THE U.K.

In Scotland, the nonprofit **Holiday Care Service** (2 Old Bank Chambers, Station Rd., Horley, Surrey RH6 9HW, England, ☎ 01293/774–535) provides a hotel reservation service and free information and advice on holidays for people with special needs. **The Scottish Tourist Board** (23 Ravelston Terr., Edinburgh EH4 3EU, Scotland, ☎ 0131/332–2433) has information on accommodations and transportation. Another useful source is **Disability Scotland** (Princes House, 5 Shandwick Place, Edinburgh EH2 4RG, ☎ 0131/229–8632). A guidebook from the **National Trust for Scotland** (5 Charlotte Sq., Edinburgh EH2 4DU, ☎ 0131/226–5922) details facilities for people with disabilities who visit its various historic houses and monuments.

Main information sources for Great Britain as a whole include the **Royal Association for Disability and Rehabilitation** (RADAR, 12 City Forum, 250 City Rd., London EC1V 8AF, ☎ 0171/250–3222) or **Mobility International** (Rue de Manchester 25, B–1070 Brussels, Belgium, ☎ 00–322–410–6297), an international clearinghouse of travel information for people with disabilities.

PUBLICATIONS

Several free publications are available from the U.S. Information Center (Box 100, Pueblo, CO 81009, ☎ 719/948–3334): **"New Horizons for the Air Traveler with a Disability"** (address to Dept. 355A), describing

THE GOLD GUIDE / IMPORTANT CONTACTS

legally mandated changes; the pocket-size **"Fly Smart"** (Dept. 575B), good on flight safety; and the Airport Operators Council's worldwide **"Access Travel: Airports"** (Dept. 575A).

The 500-page *Travelin' Talk Directory* ($35; Box 3534, Clarksville, TN 37043, ☎ 615/552–6670) lists people and organizations who help travelers with disabilities. For specialist travel agents worldwide, consult the *Directory of Travel Agencies for the Disabled* ($19.95 plus $2 shipping; Twin Peaks Press, Box 129, Vancouver, WA 98666, ☎ 206/694–2462 or 800/637–2256).

TRAVEL AGENCIES AND TOUR OPERATORS

The Americans with Disabilities Act requires that travel firms serve the needs of all travelers. However, some agencies and operators specialize in making group and individual arrangements for travelers with disabilities, among them **Access Adventures** (206 Chestnut Ridge Rd., Rochester, NY 14624, ☎ 716/889–9096), run by a former physical-rehab counselor. In addition, many general-interest operators and agencies (*see* Tour Operators, *below*) can arrange vacations for travelers with disabilities.

FOR TRAVELERS WITH HEARING IMPAIRMENTS➤ One agency is **International Express** (7319-B Baltimore Ave., College

Park, MD 20740, ☎, TDD, and FAX 301/699–8836), which arranges group and independent trips.

FOR TRAVELERS WITH MOBILITY IMPAIRMENTS➤ A number of operators specialize in working with travelers with mobility impairments: **Flying Wheels Travel** (143 W. Bridge St., Box 382, Owatonna, MN 55060, ☎ 507/451–5005 or 800/535–6790), a travel agency that specializes in European cruises and tours; **Hinsdale Travel Service** (201 E. Ogden Ave., Suite 100, Hinsdale, IL 60521, ☎ 708/325–1335 or 800/303–5521), a travel agency that will give you access to the services of wheelchair traveler Janice Perkins; **Nautilus Tours** (5435 Donna Ave., Tarzana, CA 91356, ☎ 818/344–3640 or 800/345–4654); **Wheelchair Journeys** (16979 Redmond Way, Redmond, WA 98052, ☎ 206/885–2210), which can handle arrangements worldwide.

FOR TRAVELERS WITH DEVELOPMENTAL DISABILITIES➤ Contact the nonprofit **New Directions** (5276 Hollister Ave., Suite 207, Santa Barbara, CA 93111, ☎ 805/967–2841).

Options include **Entertainment Travel Editions** (fee $28–$53, depending on destination; Box 1068, Trumbull, CT 06611, ☎ 800/445–4137), **Great American Traveler** ($49.95 annu-

ally; Box 27965, Salt Lake City, UT 84127, ☎ 800/548–2812), **Moment's Notice Discount Travel Club** ($25 annually, single or family; 163 Amsterdam Ave., Suite 137, New York, NY 10023, ☎ 212/486–0503), **Privilege Card** ($74.95 annually; 3391 Peachtree Rd. NE, Suite 110, Atlanta, GA 30326, ☎ 404/262–0222 or 800/236–9732), **Travelers Advantage** ($49 annually, single or family; CUC Travel Service, 49 Music Sq. W, Nashville, TN 37203, ☎ 800/548–1116 or 800/648–4037), and **Worldwide Discount Travel Club** ($50 annually for family, $40 single; 1674 Meridian Ave., Miami Beach, FL 33139, ☎ 305/534–2082).

PASSES

See Rail Travel, *below, in* Important Contacts A to Z *and* Smart Travel Tips A to Z. *See also* Bus Travel, *above, and in* Smart Travel Tips A to Z, *below.*

AUTO CLUBS

If you belong to a motoring organization, look into reciprocal membership benefits, including breakdown assistance, available with the Automobile Association (AA) in Britain. If your auto club doesn't have such an arrangement, consider taking out an associate membership in the **AA** (Fanum House, Basingstoke, Hants, RG2I 2EA, ☎ 01256/20123, FAX 01256/492440) or the **Royal**

Automobile Club (RAC House, Bartlett St., Box 10, Croydon, Surrey CR2 6XW, ☎ 0181/686–2525), available to overseas visitors. Their large touring departments offer a wealth of detailed information about motoring in Britain.

E

Send a self-addressed, stamped envelope to the **Franzus Company** (Customer Service, Dept. B50, Murtha Industrial Park, Box 142, Beacon Falls, CT 06403, ☎ 203/723–6664) for a copy of the free brochure "Foreign Electricity Is No Deep Dark Secret."

F

FERRY TRAVEL

Contact **Caledonian MacBrayne Ltd.** (Ferry Terminal, Gourock PA19 1QP, Renfrewshire, ☎ 01475/650100, FAX 01475/637607), **Western Ferries** (16 Woodside Crescent, Glasgow G3 7UT, ☎ 0141/332–9766), or **P & O Ferries** (Orkney & Shetland Services, Jamieson's Quay, Box 5, Aberdeen AB9 8DL, ☎ 01224/572615, FAX 01224/574411 for Aberdeen-Lerwick; 01856/850655 for Scrabster-Stromness; and 01224/572615 for Aberdeen-Stromness).

G

GAY AND LESBIAN TRAVEL

ORGANIZATION

The **International Gay Travel Association** (Box

4974, Key West, FL 33041, ☎ 800/448–8550), a consortium of 800 businesses, can supply names of travel agents and tour operators.

PUBLICATIONS

The premier international travel magazine for gays and lesbians is **Our World** ($35 for 10 issues; 1104 N. Nova Rd., Suite 251, Daytona Beach, FL 32117, ☎ 904/441–5367). The 16-page monthly **"Out & About"** ($49 for 10 issues; ☎ 212/645–6922 or 800/929–2268), covers gay-friendly resorts, hotels, cruise lines, and airlines.

TOUR OPERATORS

Cruises and resort vacations are handled by **R.S.V.P. Travel Productions** (2800 University Ave. SE, Minneapolis, MN 55414, ☎ 800/328–RSVP) for gays, **Olivia** (4400 Market St., Oakland, CA 94608, ☎ 800/631–6277) for lesbian travelers. For mixed gay and lesbian travel, contact **Toto Tours** (1326 W. Albion, Suite 3W, Chicago, IL 60626, ☎ 312/274–8686 or 800/565–1241), which has group tours worldwide.

TRAVEL AGENCIES

The largest agencies serving gay travelers are **Advance Travel** (10700 Northwest Freeway, Suite 160, Houston, TX 77092, ☎ 713/682–2002 or 800/695–0880), **Islanders/Kennedy Travel** (183 W. 10th St., New York, NY 10014, ☎ 212/242–3222 or 800/988–

1181), **Now Voyager** (4406 18th St., San Francisco, CA 94114, ☎ 415/626–1169 or 800/255–6951), and **Yellowbrick Road** (1500 W. Balmoral Ave., Chicago, IL 60640, ☎ 312/561–1800 or 800/642–2488). **Skylink Women's Travel** (746 Ashland Ave., Santa Monica, CA 90405, ☎ 310/452–0506 or 800/225–5759) works with lesbians.

H

HEALTH ISSUES

MEDICAL-ASSISTANCE COMPANIES

Contact **International SOS Assistance** (Box 11568, Philadelphia, PA 19116, ☎ 215/244–1500 or 800/523–8930; Box 466, Pl. Bonaventure, Montréal, Québec H5A 1C1, ☎ 514/874–7674 or 800/363–0263), **Medex Assistance Corporation** (Box 10623, Baltimore, MD 21285, ☎ 410/296–2530 or 800/573–2029), **Near Services** (Box 1339, Calumet City, IL 60409, ☎ 708/868–6700 or 800/654–6700), and **Travel Assistance International** (1133 15th St. NW, Suite 400, Washington, DC 20005, ☎ 202/331–1609 or 800/821–2828). Because these companies also sell death-and-dismemberment, trip-cancellation, and other insurance coverage, there is some overlap with the travel-insurance policies sold by the companies listed under Insurance, *below.*

I

INSURANCE

Travel insurance covering baggage, health, and trip cancellation or interruptions is available from **Access America** (Box 90315, Richmond, VA 23286, ☎ 804/285–3300 or 800/284–8300), **Carefree Travel Insurance** (Box 9366, 100 Garden City Plaza, Garden City, NY 11530, ☎ 516/294–0220 or 800/323–3149), **Near Services** (Box 1339, Calumet City, IL 60409, ☎ 708/868–6700 or 800/654–6700), **Tele-Trip** (Mutual of Omaha Plaza, Box 31716, Omaha, NE 68131, ☎ 800/228–9792), **Travel Insured International** (Box 280568, East Hartford, CT 06128-0568, ☎ 203/528–7663 or 800/243–3174), **Travel Guard International** (1145 Clark St., Stevens Point, WI 54481, ☎ 715/345–0505 or 800/826–1300), and **Wallach & Company** (107 W. Federal St., Box 480, Middleburg, VA 22117, ☎ 703/687–3166 or 800/237–6615).

L

LODGING

APARTMENT AND VILLA RENTAL

Among the companies to contact are **At Home Abroad** (405 E. 56th St., Suite 6H, New York, NY 10022, ☎ 212/421–9165), **Europa-Let** (92 N. Main St., Ashland, OR 97520, ☎ 503/482–5806 or 800/462–4486), **Interhome** (124 Little Falls Rd., Fair-

field, NJ 07004, ☎ 201/882–6864, **Property Rentals International** (1008 Mansfield Crossing Rd., Richmond, VA 23236, ☎ 804/378–6054 or 800/220–3332), **Rental Directories International** (2044 Rittenhouse Sq., Philadelphia, PA 19103, ☎ 215/985–4001), **Rent-a-Home International** (7200 34th Ave. NW, Seattle, WA 98117, ☎ 206/789–9377 or 800/488–7368), **Vacation Home Rentals Worldwide** (235 Kensington Ave., Norwood, NJ 07648, ☎ 201/767–9393 or 800/633–3284), and **Villas and Apartments Abroad** (420 Madison Ave., Suite 1105, New York, NY 10017, ☎ 212/759–1025 or 800/433–3020). Members of the travel club **Hideaways International** ($99 annually; 767 Islington St., Portsmouth, NH 03801, ☎ 603/430–4433 or 800/843–4433) receive two annual guides plus quarterly newsletters, and arrange rentals among themselves.

FARMHOUSE AND CROFTING HOLIDAYS

A popular option for families with children is a farmhouse holiday, combining the freedom of bed-and-breakfast accommodations with the hospitality of Scottish family life. Information is available from the **British Tourist Authority** (*see* Visitor Info, *below*), from **Scottish Farmhouse Holidays** (5 Drumtenant, Ladybank, Fife, KY7 7UG, Scot-

land, ☎ 01337/830451), and from the **Farm Holiday Bureau** (National Agricultural Centre, Stoneleigh, Warwickshire, England CV8 2LZ, ☎ 01203/696909).

HOME EXCHANGE

Principal clearinghouses include **Intervac International** ($65 annually; Box 590504, San Francisco, CA 94159, ☎ 415/435–3497), which has three annual directories; and **Loan-a-Home** ($35–$45 annually; 2 Park La., Apt. 6E, Mount Vernon, NY 10552-3443, ☎ 914/664–7640), which specializes in long-term exchanges.

M

MONEY MATTERS

ATMS

For specific foreign **Cirrus** locations, call 800/424–7787; for foreign Plus locations, consult the **Plus** directory at your local bank.

CURRENCY EXCHANGE

If your bank doesn't exchange currency, contact **Thomas Cook Currency Services** (41 E. 42nd St., New York, NY 10017, or 511 Madison Ave., New York, NY 10022, ☎ 212/757–6915 or 800/223–7373 for locations) or **Ruesch International** (☎ 800/424–2923 for locations).

WIRING FUNDS

Funds can be wired via **American Express MoneyGram**SM (☎ 800/926–9400 from the U.S. and Canada for locations and information) or **Western Union** (☎ 800/325–6000 for agent locations or to send using MasterCard or Visa, 800/321–2923 in Canada).

P
PASSPORTS AND VISAS

U.S. CITIZENS

For fees, documentation requirements, and other information, call the **Office of Passport Services** information line (☎ 202/647–0518).

CANADIANS

For fees, documentation requirements, and other information, call the Ministry of Foreign Affairs and International Trade's **Passport Office** (☎ 819/994–3500 or 800/567–6868).

PHONE MATTERS

The country code for Scotland is 44. For local access numbers abroad, contact **AT&T** USA-Direct (☎ 800/874–4000), **MCI** Call USA (☎ 800/444–4444), or **Sprint** Express (☎ 800/793–1153).

PHOTO HELP

The **Kodak Information Center** (☎ 800/242–2424) answers consumer questions about film and photography.

R
RAIL TRAVEL

PASSES

If you plan to rack up the miles, rail passes from **Britrail** (1500 Broadway, New York, NY 10036, ☎ 212/575–2667 or 800/677–

8585), which provide unlimited travel over the entire British train network during their period of validity, can be an excellent value. Passes can also be purchased from **Rail Europe** (226–230 Westchester Ave., White Plains, NY 10604, ☎ 914/682–5172 or 800/438–7245 from the East, 800/848–7245 from the West). *See also* Rail Travel *in* Smart Travel Tips, *below.*

SCENIC ROUTES

A luxury private train, the *Royal Scotsman,* does scenic tours, partly under steam power, with banquets en route. Book through Abercrombie & Kent (Sloane Square House, Holbein Pl., London SW1W 8NS, ☎ 0171/730–9600; or 1420 Kensington Rd., Oak Brook, IL 60521, ☎ 312/954–2944 or 800/323–7308); cost ranges from $1,950 for three days to $4,980 for seven days. **Waterman Railways** offers occasional Pullman rail cruises, partly steam-hauled, on the *Cock o' the North* and *Monarch of the Glen* (£399 from London); every passenger gets a window seat, and overnights are in hotels. Details are available from the London (Euston) Travel Center; book through **Waterman Railways** (Box 4472, Lichfield, Staffordshire WS13 6RU, ☎ 01543/254076).

S
SENIOR CITIZENS

EDUCATIONAL TRAVEL

The nonprofit **Elderhostel** (75 Federal St., 3rd Floor, Boston, MA 02110, ☎ 617/426–7788), for people 60 and older, has offered inexpensive study programs since 1975. The nearly 2,000 courses cover everything from marine science to Greek myths and cowboy poetry. Fees for two- to three-week international trips—including room, board, and transportation from the United States—range from $1,800 to $4,500.

For people 50 and over and their children and grandchildren, **Interhostel** (University of New Hampshire, 6 Garrison Ave., Durham, NH 03824, ☎ 603/862–1147 or 800/733–9753) runs 10-day summer programs involving lectures, field trips, and sightseeing. Most last two weeks and cost $2,125–$3,100, including airfare.

LODGING

Scottish Highland Hotels (☎ 0131/557–2368 in Scotland) have a special year-round "Golden Times" package offering one-third off regular rates.

ORGANIZATIONS

Contact the **American Association of Retired Persons** (AARP, 601 E St. NW, Washington, DC 20049, ☎ 202/434–2277; $8 per person or couple annually). Its Purchase

THE GOLD GUIDE / IMPORTANT CONTACTS

THE GOLD GUIDE / IMPORTANT CONTACTS

Privilege Program gets members discounts on lodging, car rentals, and sightseeing.

For other discounts on lodgings, car rentals, and other travel products, along with magazines and newsletters, contact the **National Council of Senior Citizens** (membership $12 annually; 1331 F St. NW, Washington, DC 20004, ☎ 202/347–8800) and **Mature Outlook** (subscription $9.95 annually; 6001 N. Clark St., Chicago, IL 60660, ☎ 312/465–6466 or 800/336–6330).

PUBLICATIONS

The 50+ Traveler's Guidebook: Where to Go, Where to Stay, What to Do, by Anita Williams and Merrimac Dillon ($12.95; St. Martin's Press, 175 5th Ave., New York, NY 10010, ☎ 212/674–5151 or 800/288–2131), offers many useful tips. *"The Mature Traveler"* ($29.95; Box 50400, Reno, NV 89513, ☎ 702/786–7419), a monthly newsletter, covers travel deals.

STUDENTS

CAMPING

Camping is an economical option for young travelers. Consult the free British Tourist Authority booklet *Camping and Caravan Parks in Britain,* or *Forestry Commission Camping and Caravan Sites* (free from the **Forestry Commission,** 231 Corstorphine Rd., Edinburgh EH12 7AT, Scotland, ☎ 0131/334–0303). For help planning a bicycle camping trip, contact the **Camping and Caravanning Club** (11 Lower Grosvenor Pl., London SW1W 0EY, England).

GROUPS

Major tour operators include **Contiki Holidays** (300 Plaza Alicante, Suite 900, Garden Grove, CA 92640, ☎ 714/740–0808 or 800/466–0610) and **AESU Travel** (2 Hamill Rd., Suite 248, Baltimore, MD 21210-1807, ☎ 410/323–4416 or 800/638–7640).

HOSTELING

Contact **Hostelling International–American Youth Hostels** (733 15th St. NW, Suite 840, Washington, DC 20005, ☎ 202/783–6161) in the United States, **Hostelling International–Canada** (205 Catherine St., Suite 400, Ottawa, Ontario K2P 1C3, ☎ 613/237–7884) in Canada, and the **Youth Hostel Association of England and Wales** (Trevelyan House, 8 St. Stephen's Hill, St. Albans, Hertfordshire AL1 2DY, ☎ 01727/855215 and 01727/845047) and the **Scottish Youth Hostels Association** (7 Glebe Crescent, Stirling FK8 2JA, ☎ 01786/451–181) in the United Kingdom. Membership ($25 in the U.S., C$26.75 in Canada, and £9 in the U.K.) gets you access to 5,000 hostels worldwide that charge $7–$20 nightly per person.

I.D. CARDS

To be eligible for discounts on transportation and admissions, get the **International Student Identity Card** (ISIC) if you're a bona fide student or the **International Youth Card** (IYC) if you're under 26. In the United States, the ISIC and IYC cards cost $16 each and include basic travel-accident and illness coverage, plus a toll-free travel hot line. Apply through the Council on International Educational Exchange (*see* Organizations, *below*). Cards are available for $15 each in Canada from **Travel Cuts** (187 College St., Toronto, Ontario M5T 1P7, ☎ 416/979–2406 or 800/667–2887) and in the United Kingdom for £5 each at student unions and student travel companies.

ORGANIZATIONS

A major contact is the **Council on International Educational Exchange** (CIEE, 205 E. 42nd St., 16th Floor, New York, NY 10017, ☎ 212/661–1450) with locations in Boston (729 Boylston St., 02116, ☎ 617/266–1926), Miami (9100 S. Dadeland Blvd., 33156, ☎ 305/670–9261), Los Angeles (1093 Broxton Ave., 90024, ☎ 310/208–3551), 43 other college towns nationwide, and the United Kingdom (28A Poland St., London W1V 3DB, ☎ 0171/437–7767). Twice a year, it publishes *Student Travels* magazine. The CIEE's Council Travel Service is the exclusive U.S. agent for several student-discount cards.

Campus Connections (325 Chestnut St., Suite

1101, Philadelphia, PA 19106, ☎ 215/625–8585 or 800/428–3235) specializes in discounted accommodations and airfares for students. The **Educational Travel Centre** (438 N. Frances St., Madison, WI 53703, ☎ 608/256–5551) offers rail passes and low-cost airline tickets, mostly for flights departing from Chicago. For air travel only, contact **TMI Student Travel** (100 W. 33rd St., Suite 813, New York, NY 10001, ☎ 800/245–3672).

In Canada, also contact **Travel Cuts** (*see above*).

PUBLICATIONS

See the *Berkeley Guide to Great Britain and Ireland* ($17.50; Fodor's Travel Publications, 800/533–6478 or from bookstores).

UNIVERSITY HOUSING

For information on staying in college and university domitories, contact the **Scottish Universities Accommodation Consortium** (SUAC, Box 808, Edinburgh EH14 4AS, ☎ 0131/449–4034), **British Universities Accommodation Consortium** (BUAC, Box 1188, University Park, Nottingham NG7 2RD, England, ☎ 0114/950–4571), or the **Higher Education Accommodation Consortium** (HEAC, 36 Collegiate Crescent, Sheffield S10 2BP, England, ☎ 0114/268–3759).

T

TAXES

VAT

Details on how to get a VAT refund and a list of stores offering tax-free shopping are available from the **British Tourist Authority,** 40 West 57th St., New York, NY 10019; and the British Travel Centre, 12 Regent St., London SW1Y 4PQ.

TOUR OPERATORS

Among the companies selling tours and packages to Scotland, the following have a proven reputation, are nationally known, and offer plenty of options.

GROUP TOURS

Super-deluxe escorted tours are available from **Abercrombie & Kent** (1520 Kensington Rd., Oak Brook, IL 60521-2141, ☎ 708/954–2944 or 800/323–7308) and **Travcoa** (Box 2630, Newport Beach, CA, 92658, ☎ 714/476–2800 or 800/992–2003). For deluxe tours, try **Tauck Tours** (11 Wilton Rd., Westport CT 06881, ☎ 203/226–6911 or 800/468–2825) or **Maupintour** (Box 807, Lawrence, KS 66044, ☎ 913/843–1211 or 800/255–4266). Another operator falling between deluxe and first-class is **Globus** (5301 South Federal Circle, Littleton, CO 80123-2980, ☎ 303/797–2800 or 800/221–0090). For first-class and first-class superior tours, try **British Airways** (800/247–9297), **Caravan Tours** (401 N. Michigan Ave.,

Chicago, IL 60611, ☎ 312/321–9800 or 800/227–2826), **CIE Tours** (108 Ridgedale Ave., Morristown, NJ 07960, ☎ 201/292–3438 or 800/243–8687), **Trafalgar Tours** (21 E. 26th St., New York, NY 10010, ☎ 212/689–8977 or 800/854–0103), **Brendan Tours** (15137 Califa St., Van Nuys, CA 91411, ☎ 818/785–9696 or 800/421–8446), and **Insight International** (745 Atlantic Ave., Boston MA 02111, ☎ 617/482–2000 or 800/582–8380).

PACKAGES

Just about every airline that flies to Scotland sells packages that include roundtrip airfare and hotel accommodations. Carriers to contact include **American Airlines Fly AAway Vacations** (☎ 800/321–2121), **British Airways** (*see above*), **Continental Airlines' Grand Destinations** (☎ 800/634–5555), **Delta Dream Vacations** (☎ 800/872–7786), and **United Airlines' Vacation Planning Center** (☎ 800/328–6877). Other packagers include: **Certified Vacations** (Box 1525, Ft. Lauderdale, FL 33302, ☎ 305/522–1414 or 800/233–7260), **CIE Tours** (108 Ridgedale ave., Box 2355, Morristown, NJ 07962, ☎ 201/292–3899 or 800/243–8687), **DER Tours** (11933 Wilshire Blvd., Los Angeles, CA 90025, ☎ 310/479–4140 or 800/782–2424), and **Jet Vacations** (1775 Broadway, New York, NY 10019, ☎ 212/474–

8740 or 800/538–2762).

THEME TRIPS

Travel Contacts (45 Idmiston Rd., London SE27 9HL, England, ☎ 011/44–81766–7868, FAX 011/44–81766–6123), with 135 member operators, can satisfy virtually any special interest in Scotland. **Journeys Thru Scotland** (21799 Finn Rd., Sheridan, OR 97378, ☎ 800/828–7583, FAX 503/843–4557) arranges tours that focus on golf, castles and gardens, and weaving, spinning, and knitting.

ADVENTURE➤ **All Adventure Travel** (5589 Arapahoe #208, Boulder, CO 80303, ☎ 800/537–4025) can book hiking, walking, kayaking, and skiing programs in Scotland. For strictly hiking, try **Above the Clouds Trekking** (Box 398, Worcester, MA 01602, ☎ 800/233–4499 or 508/799–4499) or **Himalayan Travel** (112 Prospect St., Stamford, CT 06901, ☎ 800/225–2380, FAX 203/359–3669).

BARGE CRUISES➤ For barge tours of Scotland, contact **Abercrombie & Kent** (1520 Kensington Rd., Oak Brook, IL 60521-2141, ☎ 708/954–2944 or 800/323–7308) and **Le Boat** (215 Union St., Hackensack, NJ 07601, ☎ 201/342–1838 or 800/922–0291). **Premier Selections** (The Kemwel Group, 106 Calvert St., Harrison, NY 10528, ☎ 800/234–4000) has luxury barge tours in Scotland with gourmet

cuisine and visits to private manor houses.

FISHING➤ For fishing packages throughout Scotland, try **Rod and Reel Adventures** (3507 Tully Rd., Modesto, CA 95356, ☎ 209/524–7775 or 800/356–6882). **Francine Atkins' Scotland/Ireland, Inc.** 2 Ross Ct., Trophy Club, TX 76262, ☎ 817/491–1105 or 800/742–0355) combines golf and fishing on its tours with stays in castles and stately homes. Upscale golf holidays with gourmet dining are available from **Fenwick & Lang** (900 Fourth Ave., Suite 1201, Seattle, WA 98164, ☎ 206/382–1384 or 800/243–6244). The **Scottish Golf and Travel Service** (12 Rutland Square, Edinburgh, EH1 2BB, Scotland, ☎ 800/847–8064, FAX 011/44–31–221–1400) arranges fishing and golf holidays throughout Scotland.

GOLF➤ A wide array of packages are sold by **GolfTrips** (Box 2314, Winter Haven, FL 33883-2314, ☎ 813/324–1300 or 800/428–1940) and **Golfpac** (Box 162366, Altamonte Springs, FL 32716-2366, ☎ 407/260–2288). Also see **Scottish Golf and Travel Service,** above.

LEARNING VACATIONS➤ **Earthwatch** (680 Mount Auburn St., Watertown, MA 02272, ☎ 617/926–8200 or 800/776–0188) recruits volunteers to serve in its EarthCorps as short-term assistants to scientists on research expeditions. **The Smith-**

sonian Institution (1100 Jefferson Dr. SW, Room 3045, Washington, DC 20560, ☎ 202/357–4700) has a myriad of tours that showcase Europe's natural history and culture.

WALKING➤ **English Lakeland Ramblers** (18 Stuyvesant Oval #1A, New York, NY 10009, ☎ 212/505–1020 or 800/724–8801) arranges walking and hiking tours that focus on literature, culture, and natural history. **Walking the World** (Box 1186, Fort Collins, CO 80522, ☎ 303/225–0500) roams the Highlands, the Cairngorm Mountains, and Loch Ness with travelers 50 years-old and over.

ORGANIZATIONS

The **National Tour Association** (546 E. Main St., Lexington, KY 40508, ☎ 606/226–4444 or 800/682–8886) and **United States Tour Operators Association** (USTOA, 211 E. 51st St., Suite 12B, New York, NY 10022, ☎ 212/750–7371) can provide lists of member operators and information on booking tours.

PUBLICATIONS

Consult the brochure **"Worldwide Tour & Vacation Package Finder"** from the National Tour Association (*see above*) and the Better Business Bureau's **"Tips on Travel Packages"** (publication No. 24-195, $2; 4200 Wilson Blvd., Arlington, VA 22203).

TRAVEL AGENCIES

For names of reputable agencies in your area,

contact the **American Society of Travel Agents** (1101 King St., Suite 200, Alexandria, VA 22314, ☎ 703/739–2782).

U
U.S. GOVERNMENT TRAVEL BRIEFINGS

The U.S. Department of State's Overseas Citizens Emergency Center (Room 4811, Washington, DC 20520; enclose SASE) issues **Consular Information Sheets,** which cover crime, security, political climate, and health risks as well as embassy locations, entry requirements, currency regulations, and other routine matters. For the latest information, stop in at any U.S. passport office, consulate, or embassy; call the interactive hot line (☎ 202/647–5225, FAX 202/647–3000); or, with your PC's modem, tap into the Bureau of Consular Affairs' computer bulletin board (☎ 202/647–9225).

V
VISITOR INFORMATION

IN THE U.S.➤ British Tourist Authority, 551 5th Ave., Suite 701, New York, NY 10176, ☎ 212/986-2200, FAX 212/986-1188; 625 N. Michigan Ave., Suite 1510, Chicago, IL 60611, ☎ 312/787-0490, FAX 312/787-7746; World Trade Center, Suite 450, 350 S. Figueroa St., Los Angeles, CA 90071, ☎ 213/628-3525; 2580 Cumberland Pkwy., Suite 470, Atlanta, GA 30339, ☎ 404/432-9635, FAX 404/432-9641.

IN CANADA➤ British Tourist Authority, 111 Avenue Rd., Suite 450, Toronto, Ontario M5R 3S5B, ☎ 416/925-6326.

IN THE U.K.

Scottish Tourist Board, 23 Ravelston Terr., Edinburgh EH4 3EU, ☎ 0131/332–2433; 19 Cockspur St., London SWIY 5BL, ☎ 0171/930–8661.

W
WEATHER

For current conditions and forecasts, plus the local time and helpful travel tips, call the **Weather Channel Connection** (☎ 900/932–8437; 95¢ per minute) from a touch-tone phone.

THE GOLD GUIDE / IMPORTANT CONTACTS

SMART TRAVEL TIPS A TO Z

*Basic Information on Traveling in Scotland and
Savvy Tips to Make Your Trip a Breeze*

The more you travel, the more you know about how to make trips run like clockwork. To help make your travels hassle-free, Fodor's editors have rounded up dozens of tips from our contributors and travel experts all over the world, as well as basic information on visiting Scotland. For names of organizations to contact and publications that can give you more information, *see* Important Contacts A to Z, *above.*

A

AIR TRAVEL

If time is an issue, **always look for nonstop flights,** which require no change of plane. If possible, **avoid connecting flights,** which stop at least once and can involve a change of plane, although the flight number remains the same; if the first leg is late, the second waits.

CARRIERS

FROM THE U.K.➤ Together British Airways and British Midland operate some 20 flights to Edinburgh and 20 to Glasgow each weekday from London Heathrow. British Midland, Gill Air, Knight Air, ATS Vulcan, British Airways Ex-

press, BusinessAir, and Air U.K. also connect Scotland with English airports, including London Gatwick.

WITHIN SCOTLAND➤ Although a small country, Scotland has a significant internal air network. The major carrier is **British Airways** (operating some services as **British Airways Express.**

CUTTING COSTS

The Sunday travel section of most newspapers is a good source of deals.

MAJOR AIRLINES➤ The least-expensive airfares from the major airlines are priced for round-trip travel and are subject to restrictions. You must usually **book in advance and buy the ticket within 24 hours** to get cheaper fares, and you may have to **stay over a Saturday night.** The lowest fare is subject to availability, and only a small percentage of the plane's total seats are sold at that price. It's good to **call a number of airlines, and when you are quoted a good price, book it on the spot**—the same fare on the same flight may not be available the next day. Airlines generally allow you to change your return date for a $25 to

$50 fee, but most low-fare tickets are nonrefundable. However, if you don't use it, you can apply the cost toward the purchase price of a new ticket, again for a small charge.

CONSOLIDATORS➤ Consolidators, who buy tickets at reduced rates from scheduled airlines, sell them at prices below the lowest available from the airlines directly—usually without advance restrictions. Sometimes you can even get your money back if you need to return the ticket. Carefully read the fine print detailing penalties for changes and cancellations. If you doubt the reliability of a consolidator, **confirm your reservation with the airline.**

ALOFT

AIRLINE FOOD➤ If you hate airline food, **ask for special meals when booking.** These can be vegetarian, low-cholesterol, or kosher, for example; commonly prepared to order in smaller quantities than standard catered fare, they can be tastier.

JET LAG➤ To avoid this syndrome, which occurs when travel disrupts your body's natural cycles, try to maintain a normal routine. At night, **get some sleep.** By day, move about the cabin to **stretch your legs, eat light meals, and drink water—not alcohol.**

SMOKING➤ Smoking is banned on all flights within the U.S. of less than six hours' duration and on all Canadian flights; the ban also applies to domestic segments of international flights aboard U.S. and foreign carriers. On U.S. carriers flying to Scotland and other destinations abroad, a seat in a no-smoking section must be provided for every passenger who requests one, and the section must be enlarged to accommodate such passengers if necessary as long as they have complied with the airline's deadline for check-in and seat assignment. If smoking bothers you, request a seat far from the smoking section.

Foreign airlines are exempt from these rules but do provide no-smoking sections (British Airways has banned smoking, as has Virgin Atlantic on most international flights); some nations have banned smoking on all domestic flights, and others may ban smoking on some flights. Talks continue on the feasibility of broadening no-smoking policies.

B

BICYCLE TRAVEL

Because Scotland's main roads are continually being upgraded, **it is easier than ever for** **bicyclists to access the network of quieter rural roads** in such areas as Dumfries and Galloway, the Borders, and much of eastern Scotland, especially Grampian. Still, care must be taken in getting from some town centers to rural riding areas, so if in doubt, ask a local. In a few areas of the Highlands, notably in northwestern Scotland, the rugged nature of the terrain and limited population have resulted in the lack of side roads, making it more difficult—sometimes impossible—to plan a minor-road route in these areas.

The best months for cycling in Scotland are May, June, and September, when the roads are often quieter and the weather is usually better. Winds are predominantly from the southwest, so plan your route accordingly.

A variety of agencies are now promoting "safe routes" for recreational cyclists in Scotland. These routes are signposted, and the agencies have produced maps or leaflets showing where they run. Perhaps best known is the Glasgow–Loch Lomond–Killin Cycleway, which makes use of former railway track beds, forest trails, quiet rural side roads, and some main roads. The Glasgow to Irvine Cycle Route runs south and west of Glasgow and links with the Johnstone and Greenock Railway Path. In Edinburgh there is the Innocent Railway Path from Holyrood Path to St. Leonards. Contact the relevant tourist board for more information.

BIKES ON BUSES

Although some rural bus services will transport cycles if space is available, you usually can't count on getting your bike on a bus. Be sure to check well in advance with the appropriate bus company.

BIKES ON FERRIES

Bicycles can be taken without any restrictions on car and passenger ferries in Scotland, and it is not generally necessary to book in advance. The three main ferry service operators (*see* Ferry Travel *in* Important Contacts A to Z, *above*) are Caledonian MacBrayne and Western Ferries, both of which carry accompanied bicycles free, and P & O Ferries, which charges from £6 to £10 in addition to the cost of a passenger ticket and requires cycles to be checked in early so that they can be loaded through the boat's cargo entrance.

BIKES ON TRAINS

The business of transporting bikes by rail has become less straightforward in the past few years, with limitations placed on both luggage and cycle space. Scotrail strongly advises making a reservation for you and your bike at least a month in advance. On several trains, reservations are compulsory. A leaflet containing the latest information is available through Scotrail and can be picked up at most manned train stations within Scotland.

CYCLING OFF-ROAD

People in Scotland were cycling off-road long before the mountain bike was invented. Sometimes they cycled over rights of way in the Highlands; sometimes they biked cross-country to shorten the time taken to climb less accessible high hills. The growing popularity of mountain biking, however, has forced the Scots to focus on the suitability and availability of routes.

Scotland's legal position on off-road cycling is complex. Cycling is covered by road traffic laws because a bike is classified as a vehicle. In a strict legal sense, cycling off-road is only possible on specifically designated cycle tracks, routes that have a common-law right of way for cycles, or routes that have the consent of the landowner. Legally, cyclists are not allowed on pedestrian rights of way, but many landowners don't mind if cyclists use them. Nevertheless, it is best for off-road cyclists to seek local advice when planning routes.

BUSINESS HOURS

BANKS

Except on public holidays, **banks are open weekdays 9:30–3:30, some days to 4:45.** Some banks have extended hours on Thursday evenings, and a few are open on Saturday mornings. Some also close for an hour at lunchtime. The major airports operate 24-hour banking services seven days a week.

SHOPS

Usual business hours are Monday–Saturday 9–5:30. Outside the main centers, most shops observe an early closing day once a week, often Wednesday or Thursday—they close at 1 PM and do not reopen until the following morning. In small villages, many also close for lunch. Department stores in large cities stay open for late-night shopping (usually until 7:30 or 8) one day a week. Apart from some newsstands and small food stores, almost all shops are closed on Sunday except in larger towns and cities, where main shopping malls may be open.

BUS TRAVEL

FROM ENGLAND

Coaches (as long-distance and touring buses are usually called) provide the cheapest way to travel between England and Scotland; fares are approximately one-third of the rail fares for comparable trips. About 20 companies operate service between major cities, including National Express. Journey time between London and Glasgow or Edinburgh is 8 to 8½ hours, and the coaches run day and night. Most are quite comfortable; some have food service and videos on board.

The main London terminal is Victoria Coach Station, but some Scottish companies use Gloucester Road Coach Station in west London, near the Penta Hotel. Many people travel to Scotland by coach; in summer a reservation three or four days ahead is advisable.

PASSES

On bus routes, **Tourist Trail Pass** offers complete freedom of travel on any **National Express** or **Scottish Citylink** services throughout the mainland UK. Four different permutations give up to 15 days travel in 30 consecutive days. It is available from Scottish Citylink offices, most bus stations, and any National Express appointed agent.

WITHIN SCOTLAND

The country's bus network is extensive. Bus service is comprehensive in cities, less so in country districts. Express service links main cities and towns, connecting, for example, Glasgow and Edinburgh to Inverness, Aberdeen, Perth, Skye, Ayr, Dumfries, and Carlisle; or Inverness with Aberdeen, Wick, Thurso, and Fort William. These express services are very fast, and fares are quite reasonable.

For town, suburban, or short-distance journeys, you normally buy your ticket on the bus, from a paybox or the driver. Sometimes you need exact change. For longer journeys—for example, Glasgow–Inverness—it is usual to reserve and pay at the bus station booking office.

C

LAPTOPS

Before you depart, **check your portable computer's battery,** because you may be asked at security to turn on the computer to prove that it is what it appears to be. At the airport, you may prefer to **request a manual inspection,** although security X-rays do not harm hard-disk or floppy-disk storage. Also, **register your foreign-made laptop with U.S. Customs.** If your laptop is U.S.-made, call the consulate of the country you'll be visiting to find out whether or not it should be registered with local customs upon arrival. You may want to **find out about repair facilities at your destination** in case you need them.

PHOTOGRAPHY

If your camera is new or if you haven't used it for a while, **shoot and develop a few rolls of film** before you leave. Always **store film in a cool, dry place**—never in the car's glove compartment or on the shelf under the rear window.

Every pass of your film through an X-ray machine increases the chance of clouding. To protect it, carry it in a clear plastic bag and **ask for hand inspection at security.** Such requests are virtually always honored at U.S. airports, and are usually accommodated abroad. Don't depend on a lead-lined bag to protect film in checked luggage—the airline may increase the radiation to see what's inside.

VIDEO

Before your trip, **test your camcorder, invest in a skylight filter to protect the lens, and charge the batteries.** (Airport security personnel may ask you to turn on the camcorder to prove that it's what it appears to be). The batteries of most newer camcorders can be recharged with a universal or worldwide AC adapter charger (or multivoltage converter), usable whether the voltage is 110 or 220. All that's needed is the appropriate plug.

Videotape is not damaged by X-rays, but it may be harmed by the magnetic field of a walk-through metal detector, so **ask that videotapes be hand-checked.** Videotape sold in Scotland is based on the PAL standard, which is different than the one used in the United States. You will not be able to view your tapes through the local TV set or view movies bought there in your home VCR. Blank tapes bought in Scotland can be used for camcorder taping, but they are pricey. Some U.S. audiovisual shops convert foreign tapes to U.S. standards; contact an electronics dealer to find the nearest.

The Channel Tunnel provides the fastest route across the Channel—25 minutes from Folkestone to Calais, or 60 minutes from motorway to motorway. It consists of two large 50-kilometer-long (31-mile-long) tunnels for trains, one in each direction, linked by a smaller service tunnel running between them.

Le Shuttle, a special car, bus, and truck train, operates continuously, with trains departing every 15 minutes at peak times and at least once an hour through the night. No reservations are necessary, although tickets may be purchased in advance from travel agents. Most passengers travel in their own car, staying with the vehicle throughout the "crossing," with progress updates via radio and display screens. Motorcyclists park their bikes in a separate section with its own passenger compartment, while foot passengers must book passage by coach. At press time, prices for a one-day roundtrip ticket began at £107–£154 for a car and its occupants. Prices for a five-day roundtrip ticket began at £115.

Eurostar operates high-speed passenger-only trains, which whisk riders between stations in Paris (Gare du Nord) and London (Waterloo) in 3 hours and between London and Brussels (Midi) in 3¼ hours. At press time, fares were $154 for a one-way, first-class ticket and $123 for an economy fare.

The Tunnel is reached from exit 11a of the M20/A20. Tickets for either Tunnel service can be purchased in advance (*see* Important Contacts A to Z, *above*.)

CHILDREN AND TRAVEL

BABY-SITTING

For recommended local sitters, **check with your hotel desk.**

DRIVING

If you are renting a car, **arrange for a car seat when you reserve.** Sometimes they're free.

FLYING

Always **ask about discounted children's fares.** On international flights, the fare for infants under age 2 not occupying a seat is generally either free or 10% of the accompanying adult's fare; children ages 2 through 11 usually pay half to two-thirds of the adult fare. Some routes are considered neither international nor domestic and have still other rules.

BAGGAGE➤ In general, the adult baggage allowance applies for children paying half or more of the adult fare. Before departure, **ask about carry-on allowances** if you are traveling with an infant. In general, those paying 10% of the adult fare are allowed one carry-on bag, not to exceed 70 pounds or 45 inches (length + width + height) and a collapsible stroller; you may be allowed less if the flight is full.

SAFETY SEATS➤ According to the FAA, it's a good idea to **use safety seats aloft.** Airline policy varies. U.S. carriers allow FAA-approved models, but airlines usually require that you buy a ticket, even if your child would otherwise ride free, because the seats must be strapped into regular passenger seats. Foreign carriers may not allow infant seats, may charge the child's rather than the infant's fare for their use, or may require you to hold your baby during takeoff and landing, thus defeating the seat's purpose.

FACILITIES➤ When making your reservation, **ask for children's meals and a freestanding bassinet** if you need them; bassinets are available only to those with seats at the bulkhead, where there's enough legroom. If you don't need a bassinet, **think twice before requesting bulkhead seats**—the only storage for in-flight necessities is in the inconveniently distant overhead bins.

LODGING

Most hotels allow children under a certain age to stay in their parents' room at no extra charge, while others charge them as extra adults; be sure to **ask about the cut-off age.**

Although there is no general policy regarding hotel rates for children in Scotland, Milton Hotels allow children under 14 to stay for free in their parents' room. Many also have adjoining family rooms. Embassy Hotels allow up to two children under 16 to stay free when sharing their parents' room and offer a 25% discount for children occupying their own rooms.

CRUISES

Many of the crossings from North America to Europe are repositioning sailings for ships that cruise the Caribbean in winter and European waters in summer. Sometimes rates are reduced, and fly/cruise packages are usually available.

Check the travel pages of your Sunday newspaper or contact a travel agent for lines and sailing dates.

To get the best deal on a cruise, **consult a cruise-only travel agency.**

CUSTOMS AND DUTIES

IN SCOTLAND

Entering the United Kingdom, a traveler 17 or over can take in (1) 200 cigarettes or 100 cigarillos or 50 cigars or 250 grams of tobacco; (2) one liter of alcohol over 22% volume or two liters of alcohol under 22% volume or two liters of fortified or sparkling wine; (3) two liters of still table wine; (4) 60 ml of perfume and 250 ml of toilet water; (5) other goods to a value of £136 (no pooling of exemptions is allowed).

BACK HOME

IN THE U.S.➤ You may bring home $400 worth of foreign goods duty-free if you've been out of the country for at least 48 hours and haven't already used the $400 exemption, or any part of it, in the past 30 days.

Travelers 21 or older may bring back one liter of alcohol duty-free, provided the beverage laws of the state through which they reenter the United States allow it. In addition, 100 non-Cuban cigars and 200 cigarettes are allowed, regardless of your age. Antiques and works of art more than 100 years old are duty-free.

Duty-free, travelers may mail packages valued at up to $200 to themselves and up to $100 to others, with a limit of one parcel per addressee per day (and no alcohol or tobacco products or perfume valued at more than $5); outside, identify the package as being for personal use or an unsolicited gift, specifying the contents and their retail value. Mailed items do not count as part of your exemption.

IN CANADA➤ Once per calendar year, when you've been out of Canada for at least seven days, you may bring in C$300 worth of goods duty-free. If you've been away less than seven days but more than 48 hours, the duty-free exemption drops to C$100 but can be claimed any number of times (as can a C$20

duty-free exemption for absences of 24 hours or more). You cannot combine the yearly and 48-hour exemptions, use the C$300 exemption only partially (to save the balance for a later trip), or pool exemptions with family members. Goods claimed under the C$300 exemption may follow you by mail; those claimed under the lesser exemptions must accompany you.

Alcohol and tobacco products may be included in the yearly and 48-hour exemptions but not in the 24-hour exemption. If you meet the age requirements of the province through which you reenter Canada, you may bring in, duty-free, 1.14 liters (40 imperial ounces) of wine or liquor *or* 24 12-ounce cans or bottles of beer or ale. If you are 16 or older, you may bring in, duty-free, 200 cigarettes, 50 cigars or cigarillos, and 400 tobacco sticks or 400 grams of manufactured tobacco. Alcohol and tobacco must accompany you on your return.

An unlimited number of gifts valued up to C$60 each may be mailed to Canada duty-free. These do not count as part of your exemption. Label the package "Unsolicited Gift—Value Under $60." Alcohol and tobacco are excluded.

D

DINING

In a country so involved in the tourism industry, "all day" meal places

are becoming quite widespread. The normal lunch period, however, is 12:30–2:30. A few places offer "high tea"—one hot dish and masses of cakes, bread and butter, and jam, served with tea only, around 5:30–6:30.

FOR TRAVELERS WITH DISABILITIES

In Scotland, many hotels offer facilities for wheelchair users, and special carriages are beginning to appear on intercity and long-distance trains. However, since much of Scotland's beauty is found in hidden hills and corners "off the beaten track," renting a car is probably a better option.

When discussing accessibility with an operator or reservationist, **ask hard questions.** Are there any stairs, inside *or* out? Are there grab bars next to the toilet *and* in the shower/tub? How wide is the doorway to the room? To the bathroom? For the most extensive facilities, meeting the latest legal specifications, **opt for newer accommodations,** which more often have been designed with access in mind. Older properties or ships must usually be retrofitted and may offer more limited facilities as a result. Be sure to **discuss your needs before booking.**

DISCOUNT CLUBS

Travel clubs offer members unsold space on airplanes, cruise ships, and package tours at as much as 50% below regular prices. Membership may include a regular bulletin or access to a toll-free hot line giving details of available trips departing from three or four days to several months in the future. Most also offer 50% discounts off hotel rack rates. Before booking with a club, **make sure the hotel or other supplier isn't offering a better deal.**

DRIVING

FUEL AVAILABILITY AND COSTS

Though costs have been remarkably stable in recent years, **you can expect to pay a good deal more for gasoline than in the United States,** about £2.50 a gallon (55p a liter) for 4-star—up to 10p a gallon higher in remote rural locations. Remember, too, that the British Imperial gallon is about 20% more in volume than the U.S. gallon. What you may find confusing is that although service stations advertise prices by the gallon (mainly for the benefit of the conservative British who continue to resist metrification), pumps actually measure in liters. A British gallon is approximately 4.5 liters.

Most gas stations stock 4-star (97 octane), unleaded and super unleaded, plus diesel. Service stations are located at regular intervals on motorways and are usually open 24 hours a day, though stations elsewhere usually close from 9 PM to 7 AM, and in country areas many close at 6 PM and all day on Sunday.

RULES OF THE ROAD

The most noticeable difference for the visitor is that when **in Britain, you drive on the left.** This takes a bit of getting used to, but it doesn't take very long, particularly if you're driving a British car where the steering and mirrors will be adjusted for U.K. conditions. You should be particularly careful if you have picked up your car at the airport, to give yourself time to adjust to driving on the left—especially if you have jet lag.

One of the most complicated questions facing visitors to Britain is that of speed limits. In urban areas, except for certain freeways, it is generally 30 miles per hour (mph), but it is 40 mph on some main roads, as indicated by circular red signs. In rural areas the official limit is 60 mph on ordinary roads and 70 mph on motorways—and traffic police can be hard on speeders, especially in urban areas. In other respects procedures are similar to those in the United States.

TYPES OF ROADS

A very good network of superhighways, known as motorways, and divided highways, known as dual carriageways, extends throughout Britain, though in the remoter areas of Scotland where the motorway has not penetrated, travel is noticeably slower. Motorways shown with the prefix "M" are mainly two or three lanes in each direction, without any right-hand turns. If you'll be covering longer distances, these are the roads to use, though inevitably you'll see less of the countryside. Service areas are at most about an hour apart. Dual carriageways, usually shown on a map as a thick red line (often with a black line in the center) and the prefix "A" followed by a number perhaps with a bracket "T" (for example, A304[T]), are similar to motorways, except that right turns are sometimes permitted and you'll find both traffic lights and traffic circles on them.

The vast network of other main roads, which typical maps show as either single red "A" roads, or narrower brown "B" roads, also numbered, are for the most part the old coach and turnpike roads built for horses and carriages in the last century or earlier. Travel along these roads is much slower because passing is more difficult, and your trip may take twice the time it would take along a motorway. On the other hand, you'll see much more of Scotland.

Minor roads (shown as yellow or white on most maps, unlettered and unnumbered) are the ancient lanes and byways of Britain, roads that are not only living history but a superb way of discovering the real Scotland. You have to drive along them slowly and carefully—sometimes there isn't even room for two vehicles to pass, and you must reverse into a passing place if you meet an oncoming car or tractor.

F
FERRY TRAVEL

With so many islands, plus the great Firth of Clyde waterway, ferry services in Scotland are of paramount importance. Most of these now transport vehicles as well as foot passengers, although a number of the smaller ones are passengers only.

The main operator is Caledonian MacBrayne Ltd. known generally as Calmac. Services extend from the Firth of Clyde, where there is an extremely extensive network, right up to the northwest of Scotland and all of the Hebrides. Calmac offers an **Island Rover** runabout ticket, which is ideal for touring holidays in the islands, as well as an island-hopping scheme called **Island Hopscotch**, and inclusive holidays under the name **Hebridean Driveaway** which include ferries, accommodation and some meals.

The Dunoon–Gourock route on the Clyde, as well as a run from Islay (Port Askaig) to Jura is served by Western Ferries.

P & O Ferries operates a car ferry for Orkney between Scrabster (near Thurso) or Aberdeen

and Stromness (on the main island of Orkney, called Mainland) and for Shetland between Aberdeen and Lerwick. The main ferries, the *St. Clair* and the *St. Sunniva,* have cabin accommodations and sail five times a week in each direction.

I
INSURANCE

Travel insurance can protect your investment, replace your luggage and its contents, or provide for medical coverage should you fall ill during your trip. Most tour operators, travel agents, and insurance agents sell specialized health-and-accident, flight, trip-cancellation, and luggage insurance as well as comprehensive policies with some or all of these features. Before you make any purchase, **review your existing health and homeowner's policies** to find out whether they cover expenses incurred while traveling.

BAGGAGE

Airline liability for your baggage is limited to $1,250 per person on domestic flights. On international flights, the airlines' liability is $9.07 per pound or $20 per kilogram for checked baggage (roughly $640 per 70-pound bag) and $400 per passenger for unchecked baggage. However, this excludes valuable items such as jewelry and cameras that are listed in your ticket's fine print. You can buy additional insurance from the

airline at check-in, but first **see if your homeowner's policy covers lost luggage.**

FLIGHT

You should **think twice before buying flight insurance.** Often purchased as a last-minute impulse at the airport, it pays a lump sum when a plane crashes, either to a beneficiary if the insured dies or sometimes to a surviving passenger who loses eyesight or a limb. Supplementing the airlines' coverage described in the limits-of-liability paragraphs on your ticket, it's expensive and basically unnecessary. Charging an airline ticket to a major credit card often automatically entitles you to coverage and may also embrace travel by bus, train, and ship.

HEALTH

If your own health insurance policy does not cover you outside the U.S., **consider buying supplemental medical coverage.** It can pay from $1,000 to $150,000 worth of medical and/or dental expenses incurred as a result of an accident or illness during a trip. These policies also may include a personal-accident, or death-and-dismemberment, provision, which pays a lump sum ranging from $15,000 to $500,000 to your beneficiaries if you die or to you if you lose one or more limbs or your eyesight, and a medical-assistance provision, which may either reimburse you for the cost of referrals, evacuation, or repatriation and other services, or may automatically enroll you as a member of a particular medical-assistance company.

L
LANGUAGE

"Much," said Doctor Johnson, "much may be made of a Scotchman *if he be caught young.*" This quote sums up—even today—the attitude of some English people to the Scots language. They simply assume that their English is superior. Since they speak the language of Parliament and much of the media, their arrogance is understandable. The Scots have long been made to feel uncomfortable about their mother tongue and have only themselves to blame, being actively encouraged—at school, for example—to ape the dialect of the Thames Valley ("Standard English") in order to "get on" in life. The Scots language (that is, Lowland Scots, not Gaelic) was a northern form of Middle English and in its day was the language used in the court and in literature. It borrowed from Scandinavian, Dutch, French, and Gaelic. After a series of historical body blows—such as the decamping of the Scottish Court to England after 1603 and the printing of the King James Bible in English but not in Scots—it declined as a literary or official language. It survives, in various forms, virtually as an underground language spoken at home, in shops, on the playground, the farm, or the quayside among ordinary folk, especially in its heartland, in northeast Scotland. (There they describe Scots who use the brayed diphthongs of the English Thames Valley as speaking with a *bool in the mou*—marble in the mouth!) Plenty of Scots speak English with only an accent and virtually all will "modulate" either unconsciously or out of politeness into understandable English when conversing with a nondialect speaker. As for Gaelic, that belongs to a different Celtic culture and, though threatened, hangs on in spite of the Highlands depopulation.

LODGING

In many small towns and villages there are inns and hotels that offer central heating, rooms with bath or shower and telephone and television, and other comforts at competitive prices. But **rural Scotland is bed-and-breakfast land,** and, because Scottish breakfasts are nothing if not hearty, these lodging places represent a very good value. Indeed, they can be hard to beat, especially since most offer genuinely warm hospitality, as well as home cooking and comforts. The Scottish Tourist Board's *Scotland: Hotels and Guest Houses* (£8.50 by mail) and *Scotland Bed and Breakfast* (£5.90) together give details of more than 4,000 bed-and-breakfasts.

APARTMENT AND VILLA RENTALS

If you want a home base that's roomy enough for a family and comes with cooking facilities, **consider a furnished rental.** It's generally cost-wise, too, although not always—some rentals are luxury properties (economical only when your party is large). Home-exchange directories do list rentals—often second homes owned by prospective house swappers—and some services search for a house or apartment for you (even a castle if that's your fancy) and handle the paperwork. Some send an illustrated catalogue and others send photographs of specific properties, sometimes at a charge; up-front registration fees may apply.

HOME EXCHANGE

If you would like to find a house, an apartment, or other vacation property to exchange for your own while on vacation, **become a member of a home-exchange organization,** which will send you its annual directories listing available exchanges and will include your own listing in at least one of them. Arrangements for the actual exchange are made by the two parties to it, not by the organization.

HOTELS

Hotels in the larger cities are generally also good. Glasgow and Edinburgh boast a number of superior establishments, as well as an extensive range of good hotels in all other price categories.

If you are touring around, you are not likely to be stranded: In recent years, even in the height of the season—July and August—hotel occupancy has run at about 80%. On the other hand, if you arrive in Edinburgh at festival time or some place where a big Highland Gathering or golf tournament is in progress, your choice of accommodations will be extremely limited, and your best bet will be to try for a room in a nearby village. To secure your first choice, **it's always a good idea to reserve in advance,** either through a travel agent at home, directly with the facility, or through local Information Centres (see the individual city or regional chapters), making use of their "Book-a-Bed-Ahead" services. Telephone bookings made from home should be confirmed by letter, and country hotels expect you to turn up by about 6 PM.

RATINGS

Scotland was the first part of the United Kingdom to run a national "Classification and Grading Scheme" to take some of the guesswork out of booking accommodations. Though Fodor's does not use this rating system, you will see it in Scottish publications, and when you are considering a hotel, guest house, or bed-and-breakfast, make sure that you pay close attention to its classification and its grading. The classification part is easy. The number of crowns from zero to five tells you the range of the establishment's facilities. Zero crowns (confusingly described as "Listed") is basic, five crowns luxury. The grading part is actually more important. It purports to assess the quality of the place objectively. Very roughly, the ordinary is "Approved," the good "Commended," the very good "Highly Commended," and the "De Luxe" the best of all. Thus a two-crown "Highly Commended" is probably better value all around than a four-crown "Approved." The awards are part of the accommodations listing in the Where to Stay guides distributed at most tourist information centers. Not all establishments participate, but the scheme is becoming popular.

M
MAIL

POSTAL RATES

Airmail letters to the United States and Canada cost 41p, postcards 35p, aerograms 36p. Letters and postcards to Europe under 20 grams cost 30p (25p to other European Union member countries). Within the U.K. first-class letters cost 25p, second-class letters and postcards 19p.

RECEIVING MAIL

If you're uncertain where you'll be staying, you can arrange to have your mail sent to American Express. The service is free to cardholders; all others pay a small fee. You can also collect letters at Edinburgh's main post office; address them Poste Restante, Head Post Office, 2 Waterloo Place, Edinburgh, Scotland.

MONEY AND EXPENSES

Britain's currency is the pound sterling, which is divided into 100 pence (100p). Notes are issued to the values of £50, £20, £10, and £5 (also £1 in Scotland). Coins are issued to the values of £1, 50p, 20p, 10p, 5p, 2p, and 1p. Scottish coins are the same as English ones, but Scottish notes are issued by three banks: the Bank of Scotland, the Royal Bank of Scotland, and the Clydesdale Bank. They have the same face values as English notes, and English notes are interchangeable with them in Scotland. Scottish £1 notes are no longer legal tender outside Scotland. English banks and post offices will exchange them for you, but fewer and fewer English shops are accepting them.

ATMS

Cirrus, Plus and many other networks connecting automated-teller machines operate internationally. Chances are that you can **use your bank card at ATMs** to withdraw money from an account and get cash advances on a credit-card account if your card has been programmed with a personal identification number, or PIN. Before leaving home, **check in on frequency limits** for withdrawals and cash advances. Also **ask whether your card's PIN must be reprogrammed** for use in Scotland. Four digits are commonly used overseas. Note that Discover is accepted only in the United States.

On cash advances you are charged interest from the day you receive the money, whether from a teller or an ATM. Although transaction fees for ATM withdrawals abroad may be higher than fees for withdrawals at home, Cirrus and Plus exchange rates are excellent because they are based on wholesale rates only offered by major banks.

COSTS

A man's haircut will cost £4 and up; a woman's anywhere from £10 to £20. It costs about £1.50 to have a shirt laundered, from £4.20 to dry-clean a dress, and from £7 to dry-clean a man's suit. A local newspaper will cost you about 30p and a national daily, 40p. A pint of beer is around £1.50, and a serving of whisky about the same. A cup of coffee will run from 50p to £1, depending on where you drink it; a ham sandwich, £2; lunch in a pub, £4 and up (plus your drink).

A theater seat will cost from £5 to £20 in Edinburgh and Glasgow, less elsewhere. Nightclubs will take all they can get from you. For dining and lodging

costs, *see* each chapter under that heading.

EXCHANGING CURRENCY

For the most favorable rates, **change money at banks.** You won't do as well at exchange booths in airports, rail, and bus stations, or in hotels, restaurants, and stores, although you may find their hours more convenient. To avoid lines at airport exchange booths, **get a small amount of currency before you leave home.**

At press time, the exchange rate for the pound sterling was £.63 to the dollar.

TAXES

VAT➤ The British sales tax, VAT (Value Added Tax), is 17.5%. The tax is almost always included in quoted prices in shops, hotels, and restaurants. Overseas visitors to Scotland can reclaim the VAT on goods by using the Foreign Exchange Tax-Free Shopping arrangements, available only in participating shops. To **get a VAT refund,** you must complete a Tax-Free Shopping form at the shop where the goods are purchased (take your passport with you) and then present the form and the goods to HM Customs and Excise as you leave Great Britain.

TRAVELER'S CHECKS

Whether or not to buy traveler's checks depends on where you are headed; **take cash to rural areas and small towns, traveler's checks to cities.** The most widely recognized are

American Express, Citicorp, Thomas Cook, and Visa, which are sold by major commercial banks for 1% to 3% of the checks' face value—it pays to **shop around.** Both American Express and Thomas Cook issue checks that can be counter-signed and used by you or your traveling companion. So you won't be left with excess foreign currency, **buy a few checks in small denominations** to cash toward the end of your trip. Record the numbers of the checks, cross them off as you spend them, and keep this information separate from your checks.

WIRING MONEY

You don't have to be a cardholder to send or receive funds through MoneyGram^{SM} from American Express. Just go to a MoneyGram agent, located in retail and convenience stores and in American Express Travel Offices. Pay up to $1,000 with cash or a credit card, anything over that in cash. The money can be picked up within 10 minutes in the form of U.S. dollar traveler's checks or local currency at the nearest MoneyGram agent, or, abroad, the nearest American Express Travel Office. There's no limit, and the recipient need only present photo identification. The cost runs from 3% to 10%, depending on the amount sent, the destination, and how you pay.

You can also send money using Western

Union. Money sent from the United States or Canada will be available for pickup at agent locations in 100 countries within 15 minutes. Once the money is in the system, it can be picked up at any one of 25,000 locations. Fees range from 4% to 10%, depending on the amount you send.

P
PACKAGES AND TOURS

A package or tour to Scotland can make your vacation less expensive and more convenient. Firms that sell tours and packages purchase airline seats, hotel rooms, and rental cars in bulk and pass some of the savings on to you. In addition, the best operators have local representatives to help you out at your destination.

A GOOD DEAL?

The more your package or tour includes, the better you can predict the ultimate cost of your vacation. Make sure you know exactly what is included, and **beware of hidden costs.** Are taxes, tips, and service charges included? Transfers and baggage handling? Entertainment and excursions? These can add up.

Most packages and tours are rated deluxe, first-class superior, first class, tourist, or budget. The key difference is usually accommodations. If the package or tour you are considering is priced lower than

in your wildest dreams, **be skeptical.** Also, **make sure your travel agent knows the hotels** and other services. Ask about location, room size, beds, and whether the facility has a pool, room service, or programs for children, if you care about these. Has your agent been there or sent others you can contact?

BUYER BEWARE

Each year consumers are stranded or lose their money when operators go out of business—even very large ones with excellent reputations. If you can't afford a loss, take the time to **check out the operator**—find out how long the company has been in business, and ask several agents about its reputation. Next, **don't book unless the firm has a consumer-protection program.** Members of the United States Tour Operators Association and the National Tour Association are required to set aside funds exclusively to cover your payments and travel arrangements in case of default. Nonmember operators may instead carry insurance; look for the details in the operator's brochure—and the name of an underwriter with a solid reputation. Note: When it comes to tour operators, **don't trust escrow accounts.** Although there are laws governing those of charter-flight operators, no governmental body prevents tour operators from raiding the till.

Next, **contact your local Better Business Bureau and the attorney general's office** in both your own state and the operator's; have any complaints been filed? Last, **pay with a major credit card.** Then you can cancel payment, provided that you can document your complaint. Always **consider trip-cancellation insurance** (see Insurance, above).

BIG VS. SMALL➤ An operator that handles several hundred thousand travelers annually can use its purchasing power to give you a good price. Its high volume may also indicate financial stability. But some small companies provide more personalized service; because they tend to specialize, they may also be experts on an area.

USING AN AGENT

Travel agents are an excellent resource. In fact, large operators accept bookings only through travel agents. But it's good to **collect brochures from several agencies,** because some agents' suggestions may be skewed by promotional relationships with tour and package firms that reward them for volume sales. If you have a special interest, **find an agent with expertise in that area;** the American Society of Travel Agents can give you leads in the United States. (Don't rely solely on your agent, though; agents may be unaware of small-niche operators, and some special-interest travel companies only sell direct).

SINGLE TRAVELERS

Prices are usually quoted per person, based on two sharing a room. If traveling solo, you may be required to pay the full double occupancy rate. Some operators eliminate this surcharge if you agree to be matched up with a roommate of the same sex, even if one is not found by departure time.

PACKING FOR SCOTLAND

Travel light. Porters are more or less wholly extinct these days (and very expensive where you can find them).

In Scotland **casual clothes are de rigueur,** and very few hotels or restaurants insist on jackets and ties for men in the evenings. If you expect to attend some gala occasion, you may need evening wear. For summer, lightweight clothing is usually adequate, except in the evenings, when you'll need a jacket, sweater, or cardigan. A waterproof coat or parka is essential. Drip-dry and crease-resistant fabrics are a good bet, since only the most prestigious hotels have speedy laundering or dry-cleaning service.

Many visitors to Scotland appear to think it necessary to adopt a Scottish costume. It is not. Scots themselves do not wear tartan ties or Balmoral "bunnets," and only an enthusiastic minority prefer the kilt for everyday wear.

Bring an extra pair of eyeglasses or contact lenses in your carry-on luggage, and if you have a health problem, **pack enough medication** to last the trip or have your doctor write a prescription using the drug's generic name, because brand names vary from country to country (you'll then need a prescription from a local doctor, **Don't put prescription drugs or valuables in luggage to be checked,** for it could go astray. To avoid problems with customs officials, carry medications in original packaging. Also don't forget the addresses of offices that handle refunds of lost traveler's checks.

ELECTRICITY

To use your U.S.-purchased electric-powered equipment, **bring a converter and an adapter.** The electrical current in Scotland is 220 volts, 50 cycles alternating current (AC); wall outlets take plugs with two round oversize prongs and plugs with three prongs.

If your appliances are dual voltage, you'll need only an adapter. Hotels sometimes have 110-volt outlets for low-wattage appliances marked "For Shavers Only" near the sink; don't use them for high-wattage appliances like blow-dryers. If your laptop computer is older, carry a converter; new laptops operate equally well on 110 and 220 volts, so you need only an adapter.

LUGGAGE

REGULATIONS➤ Free airline baggage allowances depend on the airline, the route, and the class of your ticket; ask in advance. In general, on domestic flights and on international flights between the United States and foreign destinations, you are entitled to check two bags—neither exceeding 62 inches, or 158 centimeters (length + width + height), or weighing more than 70 pounds (32 kilograms). A third piece may be brought aboard; its total dimensions are generally limited to less than 45 inches (114 centimeters), so it will fit easily under the seat in front of you or in the overhead compartment. In the United States, the Federal Aviation Administration gives airlines broad latitude to limit carry-on allowances and tailor them to different aircraft and operational conditions. Charges for excess, oversize, or overweight pieces vary.

If you are flying between two foreign destinations, note that baggage allowances may be determined not by piece but by weight—generally 88 pounds (40 kilograms) in first class, 66 pounds (30 kilograms) in business class, and 44 pounds (20 kilograms) in economy. If your flight between two cities abroad *connects* with your transatlantic or transpacific flight, the piece method still applies.

SAFEGUARDING YOUR LUGGAGE➤ Before leaving home, **itemize your bags' contents** and their worth, and label them with your name, address, and phone number. (If you use your home address, cover it so that potential thieves can't see it.) Inside your bag, **pack a copy of your itinerary.** At check-in, **make sure that your bag is correctly tagged** with the airport's three-letter destination code. If your bags arrive damaged or not at all, file a written report with the airline before leaving the airport.

PASSPORTS AND VISAS

If you don't already have one, **get a passport.** While traveling, **keep one photocopy of the data page** separate from your wallet and leave another copy with someone at home. If you lose your passport, promptly call the nearest embassy or consulate, and the local police; having the data page can speed replacement.

U.S. CITIZENS

All U.S. citizens, even infants, need a valid passport to enter Scotland for stays of up to six months. New and renewal application forms are available at any of the 13 U.S. Passport Agency offices and at some post offices and courthouses. Passports are usually mailed within four weeks; allow five weeks or more in spring and summer.

CANADIANS

You need a valid passport to enter Scotland for stays of up to three months. Application forms are available at 28 regional passport offices as well as post offices and travel agencies. Whether for a first or a renewal passport, you must apply in person. Children under 16 may be included on a parent's passport but must have their own to travel alone. Passports are valid for five years and are usually mailed within two to three weeks of application.

R
RAIL TRAVEL

FROM ENGLAND

There are two main rail routes to Scotland from the south of England. The first, the west coast main line, runs from London Euston to Glasgow Central via Rugby, Crewe, Preston, and Carlisle; it takes four or five hours to make the 400-mile trip to central Scotland, and service is frequent and reliable, with one train every two hours on average. Some trains have portions for Edinburgh that are detached at Carstairs. Useful for daytime travel to the Scottish Highlands, and equipped with an excellent restaurant car, is the direct train to Stirling and Aviemore, terminating at Inverness. For a restful route to the Scottish Highlands, take the overnight sleeper service, with air-conditioned, soundproof sleeping carriages, which runs from Lon-don Euston, departing in late evening, to Perth, Stirling, Aviemore, and Inverness, where it arrives the following morning; family compartments are available.

The second route is the east coast main line from London King's Cross to Edinburgh via Newcastle and Durham, crossing into Scotland at Berwick-upon-Tweed; it provides the quickest trip to the Scottish capital, and between 8 AM and 6 PM there are 16 trains to Edinburgh, three of them through to Aberdeen. Limited-stop expresses like the *Flying Scotsman* make the 393-mile London to Edinburgh journey in around four hours. Connecting services to most parts of Scotland—particularly the Western Highlands—are often better from Edinburgh than from Glasgow.

Trains from elsewhere in England are good: There is regular service from Birmingham, Manchester, Liverpool, and Bristol to Glasgow and Edinburgh. From Harwich (the port of call for ships from Holland, Germany, and Denmark), you can travel to Glasgow via Manchester. But it is faster to change at Peterborough for the east coast main line to Edinburgh.

Reservations for all sleeper services are essential.

WITHIN SCOTLAND

Scotland has a good rail network extending all the way to Thurso and

Wick, the most northerly stations in the British Isles. Lowland services, most of which originate in Glasgow or Edinburgh, are generally fast and reliable. A shuttle makes the 50-minute trip between the cities every half hour. (For information about Edinburgh's and Glasgow's train stations, *see* Chapters 3 and 4, respectively.)

Some lines in Scotland—all suburban services and lines north and west of Inverness—operate on one class only (standard). Long-distance services carry buffet and refreshment cars.

DISCOUNT PASSES

To save money, **look into rail passes.** But be aware that if you don't plan to cover many miles, you may come out ahead by buying individual tickets. Standard passes are available for eight days ($299 in first class and $219 in second class), for 15 days ($489 and $339), and one month ($715 and $495). **Britrail Flexipasses** allow you to travel for 4 days in an 8-day period, 8 days in a 15-day period, or 15 days of a 30 day period. You pay $249, $389, and $575 for the Flexipass in first class, $189, $269, and $395 for second class. Britrail passes must be purchased before you leave home. The **BritFrance Rail Pass** covers both France and Britain (and hovercraft Channel crossings); cost for unlimited travel on any 5 days of a 15-day

period is $359 in first class, $259 in second class; $539 and $399 for any 10 days in a 30-day period. The **Britrail Youth Pass** and **Britrail Youth Flexipass** are available for second-class travel for those under 26 on their first travel day; fares for the Youth Pass are $179, $269, $339 and $395 for 8, 15, 22, and 30 days. The Youth Flexipass is $155 for 4 days of travel in an 8 day period, $219 for 8 days in a 15 day period, and $309 for 15 days in a two-month period. Or, try the **Freedom of Scotland Travel Pass,** for 8, 15, and 22 days of consecutive travel for $145, $205, and $259, respectively; with the pass you also travel free on Caledonian MacBrayne's west coast ferries (except to Raasay and Scalpay), and for 33% less on many bus routes. The **Freedom of Scotland Flexipass,** good for 8 days out of 15, costs $185. All these passes must be purchased stateside and are sold by travel agents as well as **Britrail** or **Rail Europe** (*see* Important Contacts A to Z, *above*). Still other passes may be purchased in Scotland. EurailPasses are not valid in Great Britain. *See also* Senior-Citizen Discounts, *below*.

Many travelers assume that rail passes guarantee them seats on the trains they wish to ride. Not so. You need to **book seats ahead even if you are using a rail pass;** seat reservations are required on some European trains, partic-

ularly high-speed trains, and are a good idea on trains that may be crowded—particularly in summer on popular routes. You will also need a reservation if you purchase overnight sleeping accommodations.

FARES

Train fares vary according to class of ticket purchased and distance traveled. The fare system is complex. Before you buy your ticket, be sure to stop at the Information Office/Travel Centre first and request the lowest fare to your destination and information about any special offers. Find out about **InterCity Saver** and about the **Family Railcard** if children are with you. Note that your ticket does *not* guarantee you a seat. For that you need a seat reservation, which must be made and paid for separately at a cost of £1 *per train* on your itinerary (that is, £2 if you need to book seats on two trains). You can opt to sit facing toward or away from the engine, and in a smoking or no-smoking compartment.

SCENIC ROUTES

Although many routes in Scotland run through extremely attractive countryside, several stand out: from Glasgow to Oban via Loch Lomond; to Fort William and Mallaig via Rannoch (ferry connection to Skye); from Edinburgh to Inverness via the Forth Bridge and Perth; from Inverness to Kyle of Lochalsh and to Wick; and from Inverness to Aberdeen. One word of caution: There are very few trains in the Highlands on Sundays.

If you're traveling to more than one country, make sure your rental contract permits you to take the car across borders and that the insurance policy covers you in every country you visit. Remember that unlike cars in the United States or the rest of Europe, British cars have the steering wheel on the right. Therefore, you may want to leave your rented car in Britain and pick up a left-side drive when you cross the Channel.

CUTTING COSTS

If you're flying to Scotland and plan to spend some time first in Edinburgh, don't pick up your car until you're ready to leave the city; otherwise, arrange to pick up and return your car at the airport. And carefully weigh the convenience of renting a car from a major company with an airport branch against the savings to be had from a local company with offices in town.

To get the best deal, **book through a travel agent and shop around.** When pricing cars, **ask where the rental lot is located.** Some off-airport locations offer lower rates—even though their lots are only minutes away from the terminal via complimentary shuttle. You may also want to **price local car-rental compa-**

nies, whose rates may be lower still, although service and maintenance standards may not be up to those of a national firm. Also **ask your travel agent about a company's customer-service record.** How has it responded to late plane arrivals and vehicle mishaps? Are there often lines at the rental counter, and, if you're traveling during a holiday period, does a confirmed reservation guarantee you a car?

Always **find out what equipment is standard** at your destination before specifying what you want; **do without automatic transmission or air-conditioning** if they're optional. In Europe, manual transmissions are standard and air-conditioning is rare and often unnecessary.

Also in Europe, **look into wholesalers**—companies that do not own their own fleets but rent in bulk from those that do and often offer better rates than traditional car-rental operations. Prices are best during low travel periods, and rentals booked through wholesalers must be paid for before you leave the United States. If you use a wholesaler, **know whether the prices are guaranteed** in U.S. dollars or foreign currency, and if unlimited mileage is available; find out about required deposits, cancellation penalties, and drop-off charges; and confirm the cost of any required insurance coverage.

INSURANCE

When you drive a rented car, you are generally responsible for any damage or personal injury that you cause as well as damage to the vehicle. Before you rent, **see what coverage you already have** under the terms of your personal auto-insurance policy and credit cards. For about $14 a day, rental companies sell insurance, known as a collision damage waiver (CDW), that eliminates your liability for damage to the car; it's always optional and should never be automatically added to your bill.

REQUIREMENTS

In Scotland your own driver's license is acceptable. An International Driver's Permit, available from the American or Canadian Automobile Association, is a good idea.

SURCHARGES

Before picking up the car in one city and leaving it in another, **ask about drop-off charges or one-way service fees,** which can be substantial. Note, too, that some rental agencies charge extra if you return the car before the time specified on your contract. To avoid a hefty refueling fee, **fill the tank just before you turn in the car.**

S

Scotland offers a wide variety of discounts and travel bargains for men over 65 and women 60

THE GOLD GUIDE / SMART TRAVEL TIPS

and over. **The Senior Citizen Railcard, available in all major railway stations, offers one-third off all rail fares.** Travelers over 60 are eligible for the Discount Coach Card, which provides one-third off all long-distance National Express or Scottish Citylink coach fares in Britain.

Many hotels advertise off-season discounts for senior citizens, and some offer year-round savings. Budget-minded seniors may also consider overnight accommodations at a university or college residence hall (*see* SUAC *under* Students *in* Important Contacts A to Z, *above*).

For discounted admission to hundreds of museums, historic buildings, and attractions throughout Britain, senior citizens need show only their passport as proof of age. Reduced-rate tickets to theater and ballet are also available.

To qualify for age-related discounts, **mention your senior-citizen status up front** when booking hotel reservations, not when checking out, and before you're seated in restaurants, not when paying your bill. Note that discounts may be limited to certain menus, days, or hours. When renting a car, **ask about promotional car-rental discounts**—they can net lower costs than your senior-citizen discount.

STUDENTS ON THE ROAD

To save money, **look into deals available through student-oriented travel agencies.** To qualify, you'll need to have a bona fide student I.D. card. Members of international student groups also are eligible. *See* Students *in* Important Contacts A to Z, *above*.

GETTING AROUND

A Student Coach Card from National Express, available to full-time students aged 17 and older, provides one-third off all long-distance coach fares in Britain; contact any National Express agent in Britain. Those 16–23 are eligible for the same reduction via the National Express Discount Coach Card.

UNIVERSITY HOUSING

Many universities and colleges throughout Britain open their halls of residence to visitors during vacation periods—that is, from mid-March to mid-April, from July to September, and during the Christmas holidays. Campus accommodations—usually single rooms with access to lounges, libraries, and sports facilities—include breakfast and generally cost about $30 per night. Locations vary from city centers to bucolic lakeside parks.

T

TELEPHONES

The public telephone system in Britain is generally reliable, and

an ongoing modernization program ensures continuing improvement. Public telephone boxes use coins or convenient phone cards, which can be purchased at post offices and at newsstands and other shops.

LONG-DISTANCE

Area codes in England, Northern Ireland, Scotland, and Wales were changed at press time, in order to increase the United Kingdom's telephone-system capacity. The number 1 was added after the initial 0 of all area codes. For example, Glasgow's 041 area code became 0141. To call Scotland from the United States you do not dial the initial 0, but when calling city to city within Scotland, you must dial the 0. The new codes are listed in this book. Keep this in mind when using phone numbers from other sources, which may not reflect the change. Cellular phone numbers and the 0800 toll-free code are not affected.

To make international calls *from* Scotland, you must use the international access code, which has also changed—from 010 to 00. To call North America, dial 00–1–area code–number.

The long-distance services of AT&T, MCI, and Sprint make calling home relatively convenient and let you avoid hotel surcharges; typically, you dial an 800 number in the United States and a local number abroad). Before you go, **find out the local access codes** for your destinations.

TIPPING

Some restaurants and most hotels add a service charge of 10%–15% to the bill. In this case you are not expected to tip. If no service charge is indicated, add 10% to your total bill, but always check first. Taxi drivers should also get 10%, hairdressers and barbers 10%–15%. You are not expected to tip theater or movie theater ushers, elevator operators, or bartenders in pubs.

TRAVEL AGENTS

If you want a travel agent to make all the arrangements, make sure he or she is a SCOTS—an acronym which stands for Special Counsellor on Tourism in Scotland. The North American market is important enough to the Scottish Tourist Board to run a special training program for travel agents working in the United States and Canada.

W

WHEN TO GO

The Scottish climate has been much maligned (sometimes with justification). You can be unlucky: You may spend a summer week in Scotland and experience nothing but low clouds and drizzle. But on the other hand, you may enjoy calm Mediterranean-like weather even in early spring and late fall.

Generally speaking, Scotland is three or four degrees cooler than southern England. The east is drier and colder than the west; Edinburgh's rainfall is comparable to Rome's, while Glasgow's is more like that in Vancouver—yet the cities are only 44 miles apart.

All visitors comment on the long summer evenings, which grow longer still as you travel north. Dawn in Orkney and Shetland in June is at around 1 AM, no more than an hour or so after sunset. Winter days are very short.

Scotland has few thunderstorms and little fog, except for local mists near coasts. But there are often variable winds that reach gale force even in summer. They blow away the hordes of gnats and midges, the curse of the western Highlands.

CLIMATE

What follows are average daily maximum and minimum temperatures for major cities in Scotland.

THE GOLD GUIDE / SMART TRAVEL TIPS

Climate in Scotland

ABERDEEN

Jan.	43F	6C	May	54F	12C	Sept.	59F	15C
	36	2		43	6		49	9
Feb.	43F	6C	June	61F	16C	Oct.	54F	12C
	36	2		49	9		43	6
Mar.	47F	8C	July	63F	17C	Nov.	47F	8C
	36	2		52	11		40	4
Apr.	49F	9C	Aug.	63F	17C	Dec.	45F	7C
	40	4		52	11		36	2

EDINBURGH

Jan.	43F	6C	May	58F	14C	Sept.	61F	16C
	34	1		43	6		49	9
Feb.	43F	6C	June	63F	17C	Oct.	54F	12C
	34	1		49	9		45	7
Mar.	47F	8C	July	65F	18C	Nov.	49F	9C
	36	2		52	11		40	4
Apr.	52F	11C	Aug.	65F	18C	Dec.	45F	7C
	40	4		52	11		36	2

GLASGOW

Jan.	41F	5C	May	59F	15C	Sept.	61F	16C
	34	1		43	6		49	9
Feb.	45F	7C	June	65F	18C	Oct.	56F	13C
	34	1		49	9		43	6
Mar.	49F	9C	July	67F	19C	Nov.	49F	9C
	36	2		52	11		38	3
Apr.	54F	12C	Aug.	67F	19C	Dec.	45F	7C
	40	4		52	11		36	2

HIGHLANDS

Jan.	43F	6C	May	58F	14C	Sept.	61F	16C
	32	0		43	6		49	9
Feb.	45F	7C	June	63F	17C	Oct.	56F	13C
	34	1		49	9		43	6
Mar.	49F	9C	July	65F	18C	Nov.	49F	9C
	36	2		52	11		38	3
Apr.	52F	11C	Aug.	65F	18C	Dec.	45F	7C
	40	4		52	11		34	1

ORKNEY ISLANDS

Jan.	43F	6C	May	54F	12C	Sept.	58F	14C
	36	2		43	6		49	9
Feb.	43F	6C	June	58F	14C	Oct.	52F	11C
	36	2		47	8		45	7
Mar.	45F	7C	July	61F	16C	Nov.	47F	8C
	38	3		50	10		41	5
Apr.	49F	9C	Aug.	61F	16C	Dec.	45F	7C
	40	4		50	10		38	3

1 Destination: Scotland

THE PRIDE OF SCOTLAND

N SOME OLD RECORDINGS of Scottish songs still in circulation you may run across *Roamin' in the Gloamin'* or *I Love a Lassie* or one of the other comic ditties of Harry Lauder, a star of the music halls of the 1920s. With his garish kilt, short crooked walking stick, rich rolling *R*s and *pawky* (cheerfully impudent) humor, chiefly based on the alleged meanness of the Scots, he impressed a Scottish character on the world. But his was, needless to say, a false impression and one the Scots have been trying to stamp out ever since.

How, then, do you characterize the Scots? Temperamentally, they are a mass of contradictions. They have been likened, not to a Scotch egg, but to a soft-boiled egg: a dour hard shell, a mushy middle. The Scots laugh and weep with almost Latin facility, but to strangers they are reserved, noncommittal, in no hurry to make an impression. Historically, fortitude and resilience have been their hallmarks, and there are streaks of both resignation and pitiless ferocity in their makeup, warring with sentimentality and love of family. Very Scottish was the instant reaction of an elderly woman of Edinburgh 200 years ago, when news arrived of the defeat in Mysore in India and of the Scottish soldiers being fettered in irons, two by two: "God help the puir chiel that's chained tae oor Davie."

The Scots are in general suspicious of the go-getter. "Whizz kid" is a term of contempt. But they are by no means plodders, though it is true to say that they are determined and thorough, respecting success only when it has been a few hundred years in the making. Praise of some bright ambitious youngster is quenched with the sneer: "Him? Ah kent (knew) his faither."

Yet this is the nation that built commerce throughout the British Empire, opened wild territories, and was responsible for much of mankind's scientific and technological advancement, a nation boastful about things it is not too good at and shamefacedly modest about genuine achievements. Con-sider the following extract from a handout about the Edinburgh School of Medicine: "If one excepts a few discoveries such as that of 'fixed air' by Black, of the diverse functions of the nerve-roots by Bell, of the anaesthetic properties of chloroform by Simpson, of the invention of certain powerful drugs by Christison and of the importance of antiseptic procedures by Lister, the influence of Edinburgh medicine has been of a steady constructive rather than a revolutionary type."

Among things that strike most newcomers to Scotland are the generosity of the Scots; their obsession with respectability; their satisfaction with themselves and their desire to stay as they are; and, above all, their passionate love of Scotland. An obstinate refusal to go along with English ideas has led to accusations that the nation has a head-in-the-sand attitude toward progress. But the Scots have their own ideas of progress, and they jealously guard the institutions that remain unique to them.

When it comes to education, Scotland has a proud record. The nation boasted four universities—St. Andrews, Aberdeen, Glasgow, and Edinburgh—when England had only two: Oxford and Cambridge. The *lad o' pairts* (man of talents)—the poor child of a feckless father and a fiercely self-sacrificing mother, sternly tutored by the village *dominie* (schoolmaster) and turned loose at the age of 13 with so firm a base of learning that he rose to the very top of his profession—this type of lad is a phenomenon of Scottish social history. The sacrifices that boys made as a matter of course to further their education are an old Scottish tradition. "Meal Monday," the long midsemester holiday at a Scottish university, is a survivor of the long weekend that once enabled students to return to their distant homes—on foot—and replenish the sack of "meal" (oatmeal) that was their only subsistence.

It is a British cliché that an English education teaches you to think and a Scottish education stuffs your head with information. The average Scot does appear to be better informed than his English neighbor and to discuss facts rather than ideas. Scots pride themselves on their international outlook and on being better linguists than the English. The Scots get on well with foreigners, and they offer strangers a kindly welcome and a civility not often found in the modern world.

Just as the Scots have their own traditions in education, so is their legal system distinct from England's. In England the police both investigate crime and prosecute suspects. In Scotland there is a public prosecutor directly responsible to the Lord Advocate (equivalent to England's Attorney General), who is himself accountable to Parliament.

FOR THE MOST PART, HOWEVER, you will notice few practical differences except in terminology. The barrister in England becomes an advocate in Scotland. Law-office nameplates designate their occupants "S.S.C." (Solicitor to the Supreme Court) or "W.S." (Writer to the Signet); cases for prosecution go before the "procurator fiscal" and are tried by the "sheriff" or "sheriff-substitute." The terms are different in England, and procedures are slightly different, too, for Scotland is one of the few countries that still bases its legal system on the old Roman law.

Crimes with picturesque names from ancient times remain on the statute book: *hamesucken,* for example, means assaulting a person in his home. In criminal cases Scotland adds to "Guilty" and "Not Guilty" a third verdict: "Not Proven." This, say the cynics, signifies "Don't do it again."

The Presbyterian Church of Scotland—the "Kirk"—is entirely independent of the Church of England. Until the 20th century it was a power in the land and did much to shape Scottish character. There are still those who can remember when the minister visited houses like an inquisitor and put members of the families through their catechism, punishing or reprimanding those who were not word-perfect. On Sunday morning the elders patrolled the streets, ordering people into church and rebuking those who sat at home in their gardens.

Religion in Scotland, as elsewhere, has lost much of its grip. But the Kirk remains influential in rural districts, where Kirk officials are pillars of local society. Ministers and their wives are seen in all their somber glory in Edinburgh in springtime, when the General Assembly of the Kirk takes place, and, for a week or more, Scottish newspapers devote several column-inches daily to the deliberations.

The Episcopalian Church of Scotland has bishops, as its name implies (unlike the Kirk, where the ministers are all equal), and a more colorful ritual. Considered genteel, Episcopalianism in Scotland has been described rather sourly by the Scottish novelist Lewis Grassie Gibbon as "more a matter of social status than theological conviction . . . , a grateful bourgeois acknowledgment of anglicisation."

Of the various nonconformist offshoots of the established Kirk, the Free Kirk of Scotland is the largest. It remains faithful to the monolithic unity of its forefathers, promoting the grim discipline that John Knox promoted long ago. The Free Kirk is strong in parts of the Outer Hebrides—Lewis, Harris, and North Uist. On Sunday in these areas no buses run, all the shops are shut, and there is a general atmosphere of a people cowering under the wrath of God. Among the fishing communities, especially those of the Northeast from Buckie to Peterhead, evangelical movements, such as the Close Brethren and Jehovah's Witnesses, have made impressive inroads.

Other than religion, Scotland on the whole is mercifully free of the class consciousness and social elitism that so often amuse or disgust foreign residents in England. But its turbulent history has left Scotland a legacy of sectarian bigotry comparable to that of Northern Ireland. Scotland's large minority population of Roman Catholics is still to some extent underprivileged. Catholics tend to stick together, Protestants to mix only with Protestants. Even the two most famous soccer teams in Scotland—Rangers and Celtic—are notorious for their sectarian bias.

A word, finally, is needed on the vexed subject of nomenclature. A "scotchman" is a nautical device for "scotching," or clamping, a running rope. It is not a native of Scotland. Though you may find some rather more conservative people refer to themselves as Scotchmen and consider themselves Scotch, most prefer Scot or Scotsman and call themselves Scottish or Scots.

There are exceptions to this rule. Certain internationally known Scottish products are Scotch. There is Scotch whisky, Scotch wool, Scotch tweed, Scotch mist (persistent drizzling rain). A Scotch snap is a short accented note followed by a longer one—a phrase that is characteristic of Scottish music, though certainly not unique to it. A snack food of a hard-boiled egg wrapped in sausage-meat and rolled in crumb coating, then fried, is a Scotch egg.

Y OU MAY INCLUDE THE SCOTS in the broader term British, but they dislike the word *Brits,* and nothing infuriates them more than being called English. Nonetheless, there are a lot of Anglo-Scots, that is, people of Scottish birth who live in England or are the offspring of marriages between Scottish and English people. The term Anglo-Scots is not to be confused with Sassenachs, the Gaelic word for Saxon, which is applied facetiously or disdainfully to all the English. But at the same time, English people who live in Scotland remain English to their dying day, and their children after them. Similarly, the designation of North Britain for Scotland, which crept in during Victorian times, has now crept out again. It survives only in the names of a few North British hotels. Scots feel that it denies their national identity, and there are some who, on receiving a letter with "N.B." or "North Britain" in the address, will cross it out and return the envelope to the sender.

WHAT'S WHERE

Edinburgh

Scotland's capital makes a strong first impression—Edinburgh Castle looming from the crags of an ancient volcano; the Royal Mile stretching from the castle to the Palace of Holyroodhouse; the neoclassical monuments perched on Calton Hill; Arthur's Seat, a small mountain with steep slopes, little crags, and spectacular vistas over the city and the Firth of Forth. Like Rome, Edinburgh is built on seven hills, and it has an Old Town district that retains striking evidence of a colorful history. Medieval Old Town, with its winding closes (narrow, stone-arched walkways) contrasts sharply with the Georgian New Town and its planned squares and streets. But Edinburgh offers more than just a unique architectural landscape—it's a cosmopolitan capital, rich in museums, pubs, and culture. It's the site of the famous International Festival, when tourists and performers descend upon the city in late summer to celebrate the arts. Even more obvious to the casual stroller during this time is the refreshingly irreverent Edinburgh Festival Fringe, unruly child of the official festival, which spills out of halls and theaters all over town.

Glasgow

Glasgow, Scotland's largest city, suffered gravely from the industrial decline of the 1960s and '70s, but recent efforts at commercial and cultural renewal have restored much of the style and grandeur it had in the 19th century at the height of its economic power. Now it is again a vibrant metropolitan center with a thriving artistic life—so much so that it was selected as Europe's Cultural Capital for 1990. Glasgow is a very convenient touring center, too, in easy reach of the Clyde coast to the south and with excellent transportation links to the rest of Scotland.

The Borders and the Southwest

The Borders area comprises the great rolling hills, moors, wooded river valleys, and farmland that stretch south from Lothian, the region crowned by Edinburgh, to England. All the distinctive features of Scotland—paper currency, architecture, opening hours of pubs and stores, food and drink, and accent—start right at the border; you won't find the Borders a diluted version of England. The Dumfries and Galloway region south of Glasgow is a hilly and sparsely populated area, divided from England by the Solway Firth; it's a region of somber forests and radiant gardens, where the palm, in places, is as much at home as the pine. The county seat is Dumfries, associated with Robert Burns (he spent the last years of his life here) in much the same way as the Borders are with Sir Walter Scott.

Fife and Angus

Fife, northwest of Edinburgh, has the distinction of being the sunniest and driest part of Scotland. This area is one of sandy beaches, fishing villages, and windswept cliffs, hills, and glens. The industrial west may hold little interest, but the east coast is home to the ancient university and golf town of St. Andrews, with its romantic stone houses and seaside ruins. Angus, whose main city, Dundee, is an industrial port, stretches to the northeast into the North Sea. The Angus glens provide scenic hikes through secluded plateaus surrounded by hills and mountains.

Aberdeen and the Northeast

Aberdeen, Scotland's third largest city, is a sophisticated city built largely of glittering granite, and is a main port of North Sea oil operations. The Grampian region spreads out to the west, the terrain changing from coastline—some of the U.K.'s most wild shorelines of high cliffs and sandy beaches—to farmland to forests to hills. Here, the Grampian mountains and the Cairngorms, beautiful regions of heather and forest, granite peaks and deep glens, are popular for hill walking in warm weather and skiing in cold weather. The northeast is also known for its wealth of castles and whisky distilleries.

The Central Highlands

The main towns of Perth and Stirling are easily accessible gateways to the Central Highlands, the rugged and spectacular terrain stretching north from Glasgow. This may not be the famed Highlands of the north, but there's plenty of wild country to be experienced in the Central Highlands; here you'll find lush, green woodlands and lochs. Especially in the Trossachs, deep lochs shimmer at the foot of gently sloping hills covered in birch, oak, and pine. Loch Lomond, Scotland's largest, is here; it's now a big tourist destination due to Sir Walter Scott's poems about the area.

Argyll and the Isles

Argyll, a remote, sparsely populated group of islands in western Scotland, forming part of the Inner Hebridean archipelago, is a transitional area between the Highlands and Lowlands, an environment ranging from lush landscapes to treeless islands, sea lochs to wooded hills. Oban, the hub of transportation for Argyll, is the main sea gateway for Mull and the Southern Islands. The Island of Mull has a rolling green landscape and its capital, Tobermory, has brightly painted houses giving it a Mediterranean look. Iona, near Mull, is Scotland's most important Christian site, with an abbey and a royal graveyard. The Isle of Islay is synonymous with whisky—it produces seven malts. Jura is covered with wild mountains. Sweeping southward, the long Kintyre peninsula is a wonderland of sea views, spectacular sunsets, and prehistoric monuments. Arran is more developed than most southern isles, with mist-shrouded mountains in the north and farmland in the south.

Around the Great Glen

The Great Glen cuts through the Southern Highlands from Inverness to Fort William and is surrounded by Scotland's tallest mountains and greatest lochs; it is considered by many to be the most dramatic, captivating landscape in Scotland. Of its lochs, the most famous is Loch Ness. Inverness, on the Moray Firth, is a major shipping port and the last substantial outpost as you head north. East of Fort William, Glen Nevis is home to Ben Nevis, Britain's highest peak. Serious climbers come from far and wide to scale it.

The Northern Highlands

The Highlands, a remote and wild area of Scotland, are the source of the country's most breathtaking scenery. The great surprises to unprepared visitors are the changing terrain and the stunning effects of light and shade, cloud, sunshine, and rainbows. In a couple of hours you may pass from heather, bracken, and springy turf to granite rock and bog, to serrated peak and snow-water lake, to the red Torridon sandstone of Wester Ross, and the flowery banks of Loch Ewe and Loch Maree. Sea inlets are deep and fjordlike. The black shapes of the isles cluster like basking whales on the skyline. Cliffs where quartzite gleams above crescents of hard sand lead around a northern shore that looks from the air as though it had been trimmed by an axe. Gaelic-speaking natives on the Isle of Skye live in villages along the coast; the varied interior has forested glens, hills of heather, rocky waterfalls, and the Cuillin Mountains. The Outer Hebrides, also known as the Western Isles, arc outward to the Atlantic; this is possibly the most rugged part of Scotland, with constant wind and rain, and an often inhospitable landscape where anything that grows seems a gift. In between are hidden coves with awe-striking white sand beaches and turquoise waters. Westward, the next stop is North America.

The Northern Isles

The nearly unceasing wind and rain in the Northern Isles create a challenging climate that contributes to the feeling that you've reached the end of the world. Orkney, a grouping of almost 70 islands, 20 of them inhabited, has the greatest concentration of prehistoric sites in Scotland. The treeless Mainland, Orkney's major island, strikes a peculiar mix between farmland and prominent stone-age relics, including phenomenally well-preserved standing circles, brochs, and tombs. Shetland's islands, with their dramatic vertical cliffs on the coastline and barren moors in the interior, aren't as rugged as you might think; the harshest winter weather is kept in check by the Gulf Stream. Winter days are sometimes no more than five hours long, while beautiful summer days last almost 20 hours, with a persistent twilight known as the "summer dim." There are no trees to be found, and no spot is farther than 3 miles from the blue-black sea. North Sea oil has brought great wealth to the Shetlands: some of Scotland's best roads are here, the buses are modern, and most homes are recently built.

PLEASURES & PASTIMES

Cultural Festivals

The Edinburgh International Festival is the spectacular flagship of mainstream cultural events, from theater to comedy skits. In fact, the capital suffers from Festival "overkill" in late August, partly due to the size of the Fringe, the less formal and more unruly part of the "official" Festival. This huge grab bag of performances spreads out of halls and theaters onto the streets of the capital. Also adding to the throng are the Edinburgh Military Tattoo and a range of smaller events such as the

Book Festival and the Jazz Festival. Earlier in the year, rival Glasgow holds the increasingly influential MayFest. This broad-based festival is international and eclectic in content, and delivered with all the panache and local support now associated with the city. Folk festivals are also held in many places at various times of the year, as are themed festivals. One example is the Fife Festival of Food and Wine, bringing cheer to bleak March.

Cycling and Hiking

Cycling is an ideal way to see the country. A mountain bike with street tires is as good a touring bike as the traditional, slouch-forward road bikes. But a good bike does not a successful tour make: You will need to build up your endurance for longer rides, and outfit and equip yourself appropriately. Don't forget that while some terrain may be flat, as in the Northern Isles, the conditions may be hazardous—strong winds or thick mist.

If you prefer to use your own two feet, hiking is a superb pursuit for getting to know Scotland's varied landscape of low-lying glens and major mountains. From Edinburgh's Arthur's Seat to Ben Nevis, Britain's tallest peak, Scotland offers an unlimited number of walking and hiking possibilities.

Dining

Scottish restaurants are noted for helpful attention and modest prices, rather than for their exotic or imaginative cuisine. City Scots usually take their midday meals in a pub, wine bar, bistro, or department store restaurant (which may be nonalcoholic and nonsmoking). When traveling, the Scot generally eats inexpensively and quickly at a country pub or village tearoom. Places like Glasgow, Edinburgh, and Aberdeen, of course, offer restaurants of cosmopolitan character and various price levels; of these, the more notable tend to open only in the evening. You will come across restaurants that offer "A Taste of Scotland" menu, full of oddly named traditional dishes often cooked and served in traditional pots and pans. The Taste of Scotland scheme, initiated by the Scottish Tourist Board, has helped—almost by accident—to preserve some of the Scots language, especially the names for a variety of traditional dishes. Most smaller towns and many villages have at least one restaurant where—certainly if a local is in charge—the service is a reminder of a Highland tradition that ensured that no stranger could travel through the country without receiving a welcome.

To start the day with a full stomach, try a "traditional Scottish breakfast," which consists of bacon and fried eggs, served with sausage, fried mushrooms and tomatoes, and, often, fried bread or potato scones. Most places also serve kippers (smoked herring). All this is in addition to juice, porridge, cereal, toast, and other bread products. It is possible to eat a healthier breakfast—fruit, for example, is on most hotel menus—but the high-cholesterol temptations are conventional in Scotland.

Distillery Tours

The process of producing whisky is closely monitored by the British government. It is strictly commercially licensed and takes place only in Scotland's distilleries (and, in Scotland, the product is most definitely spelled "whisky," without an "e"). Many distilleries place strong emphasis on visitor facilities and attempt to inject some drama and excitement into a process that is visually undramatic but nevertheless requires skill, method, and large-scale investment. A typical visit includes some kind of audiovisual presentation, and a tour, and then a dram is usually offered. No tour of Speyside is complete without taking in at least one distillery.

Golf

Scotland is often called the "home of golf" and, brushing aside any suggestion that the game probably originated in the Low Countries, claims it for her own. Certainly, Scotland has a number of very old established courses, often lying close to town centers, where, had it not been for the early rights of golfers, the land would have been swallowed up by developments long ago. Now, with over 400 golf courses—some world-famous—Scotland is a destination for golfers the world over. St. Andrews is such a popular spot for golfers that reservations need to be made up to a year in advance for summer play. Courses are also located in the major urban centers: twenty courses are within or close to Edinburgh, while seven courses are within Glasgow.

Pubs

The Scots enjoy their pub culture. Whether you join in a lively political discussion in a bar in Glasgow or enjoy folk music and dancing in a rural pub in the Highlands, you'll find that a public house is the perfect site to experience the Scottish spirit and, of course, enjoy a pint or a wee dram. Most bars sell two kinds of beer—lager and ale. Lager (try Tennent's or McEwan's), most familiar to American drinkers, is light-colored, heavily carbonated, and served cold. Ale (try McEwan "80 Shilling" and Caledonian "80") is dark, semi-carbonated, and served just below room temperature. All pubs also carry any number of single-malt and blended whiskies.

Scenic Drives

One of the best ways to see Scotland is to rent a car and drive. The following are some of our favorite scenic routes: the road west of Aberdeen into Royal Deeside, on either bank of the River Dee (Aberdeen); the east bank of Loch Ness, from Fort Augustus to Inverness via Dores (Around the Great Glen); the route between Brig o' Turk and Aberfoyle in the Trossachs (Central Highlands); and the Drumbeg road, north of Lochinver (Northern Highlands). For planned routes, *see* Great Itineraries, *below*.

Shopping

The best buys in Britain in general are antiques, craft items, woolen goods, china, men's shoes, books, confectionery, and toys. In Scotland, many visitors go for tweeds, designer knitwear, Shetland and Fair Isle woolens, tartan rugs and fabrics, Edinburgh crystal, Caithness glass, malt whisky, Celtic silver, and pebble jewelry. The Scottish Highlands bristle with old *bothies* (farm buildings) that have been turned into small craft workshops where visitors are welcome—but not pressured—to buy attractive handmade items of bone, silver, wood, pottery, leather, and glass. Handmade chocolates, often with whisky or Drambuie fillings, and the traditional "petticoat tail" shortbread in tin boxes are popular; so, too, at a more mundane level, are boiled sweets in jars from particular localities—Berwick cockles, Jethart snails, Edinburgh rock, and similar crunchy items. Dundee cake, a rich fruit mixture with almonds on top, and Dundee marmalades and heather honeys are among the other eatables that visitors take home from Scotland.

FODOR'S CHOICE

Buildings and Monuments

★ **The facade of Marischal College, Aberdeen.** This ornate facade was built in 1891, and is part of the second-largest granite building in the world.

★ **The Black House at Arnol, the Isle of Lewis in the Outer Hebrides (Northern Highlands).** Built without mortar and thatched on a timber framework without eaves, this house is a good example of a rare type of traditional Hebridean home.

★ **The Georgian House, Edinburgh.** In New Town's Charlotte Square, this house is decorated in period style to demonstrate the lifestyle of an affluent family living in the late 18th century.

★ **Traquair House, near Walkerburn (Borders).** This is said to be the oldest continually occupied house in Scotland. Be sure to sample the ale that is brewed on site in an 18th-century brewhouse.

★ **The Standing Stones of Callanish, Lewis (Northern Highlands).** This series of monoliths is considered second only to Stonehenge in England, and is thought to have been used for astronomical observations.

★ **Torosay Castle, Isle of Mull (Argyll and the Isles).** One of Mull's best-known castles, Torosay has a friendly air and gives visitors the run of much of the house.

★ **Blair Castle, Perthshire (Central Highlands).** A few minutes north of the Pass of Killiecrankie, Blair Castle, one of Scotland's most highly acclaimed, was the former home of several dukes. Inside are military artifacts and a fine collection of furniture and paintings.

Lodging

★ **Auchterarder House, Auchterarder (Central Highlands).** This secluded Victorian country mansion offers bedrooms with original furnishings and views of the Perthshire countryside. $$$$

★ **Channings, Edinburgh.** This elegant hotel is made up of five Edwardian terraced houses; those facing north provide wonderful views of Fife. $$$

★ **Clifton House, Nairn (Great Glen).** This unique hotel has original works of art, antique furnishings, and famed cuisine. $$$

★ **Roman Camp, Callander (Central Highlands).** A former hunting lodge set on 20 acres of gardens with river frontage (fishing available) is the setting for antique-filled rooms and an excellent restaurant. $$$$

★ **Cringletie House, Peebles (Borders).** Turrets and crow-step gables lend a traditional Scottish baronial style to this hotel, whose accommodations are simple and comfortable; the food is its major achievement. $$

★ **Kildrummy Castle, Kildrummy (Aberdeen and the Northeast).** An old Victorian country house is the peaceful setting for attentive service and award-winning cuisine.

Museums and Visitor Centers

★ **Auchindrain Museum (Argyll).** This 18th-century communal tenancy farm has been restored to illustrate early farming life in the Highlands.

★ **Burrell Collection (Glasgow).** Pollock County Park is the setting for one of Scotland's finest art collections, with exhibits ranging from Egyptian, Greek, and Roman artifacts to stained glass and French Impressionist paintings.

★ **Paisley Museum and Art Gallery (Glasgow).** Paisley, part of the Greater Glasgow suburban area, is home to this museum that tells the story of the woolen Paisley Shawl, and describes the famous Paisley pattern and weaving techniques.

★ **Scottish Fisheries Museum (Fife).** In Anstruther, this museum illustrates the life of Scottish fishermen through documents, artifacts, paintings, and quayside floating exhibits.

★ **Highland Folk Museum, Kingussie, near Aviemore (Around the Great Glen).** This 18th-century former shooting lodge houses exhibits of 18th-century furniture, clothing, and implements; in summer, local weavers and other artisans demonstrate Highland crafts.

★ **Carnegie Birthplace Museum (Edinburgh and the Lothians).** In Dunfermline, the birthplace of Andrew Carnegie tells his life story.

Dining

★ **Auchterarder House, Auchterarder (Central Highlands).** This dining room filled with sparkling glassware is attached to a fine hotel (see above) and serves excellent cuisine. $$$$

★ **The Ubiquitous Chip, Glasgow.** With one of the best wine cellars in the city, this unique restaurant is set in a courtyard with a fountain, a pleasant spot for fresh Scottish game and produce. $$

★ **The Atrium, Edinburgh.** This restaurant is a good place to go for pre- or post-theater dinner (the Traverse Theatre is next door) to sample Scottish ingredients combined in unusual ways; the menu changes daily. $$$

★ **The Cellar, Anstruther (Fife).** The fact that this place is popular with locals is a good sign. Come here for top-quality fish, beef, and lamb, cooked in a simple, straightforward fashion. $$$

★ **The Old Monastery, Buckie (Aberdeen).** The setting is a Victorian former religious establishment, and the theme is ever present, from the Cloisters Bar to the Chapel Restaurant. Local specialties include fresh river fish and Aberdeen Angus beef. $$–$$$$

GREAT ITINERARIES

Scottish tourist authorities have developed numerous tourist trails that encompass everything from Scotland's brooding castles to its pungent whisky distilleries. However, you should probably avoid these thematic trails during the height of summer, when crowds and buses tend to swarm the best-known sights. The following recommended itineraries, conceived independently of the Tourist Board, are offered as a guide in planning individual travel.

The Seaways of the West

From Glasgow, you and your rental car can escape into the Western Highlands in under two hours, using a short ferry crossing to save time. Then, if it isn't raining, you'll discover why the romantic landscapes of the west, with their vanished clans and tales of Bonnie Prince Charlie, continue to hold an intense fascination for visitors.

DURATION➤ Four to nine days

THE MAIN ROUTE➤ **One to two nights:** Go west from Glasgow on the A8 along the south bank of the meandering River Clyde to reach Wemyss Bay on the A78. Catch the ferry for the old-fashioned holiday resort of Rothesay on the island of Bute. Tour the hinterland and leave the island via the five-minute Rhubodach–Colintraive ferry and enjoy the typical western scenery around Cowal.

One night: Go south to Lochgilphead, take a quick peek at the Caledonian Canal, then head for Tarbert and the peninsular Mull of Kintyre. If you crave island scenery, you can hop across to the tiny island of Gigha. Otherwise, continue south toward Campbeltown.

One to three nights: Return north through Lochgilphead and head for Oban, a busy ferryport where tartan kitsch and tour buses form the backdrop. Cross from Oban to the dramatic Isle of Mull, eventually arriving at the tiny Isle of Iona, the ancient burial place of Scottish kings. Leave Iona and Mull via the Fishnish–Lochaline ferry, then loop north toward Acharacle for magnificent views of the small isles of Rhum, Eigg, and Muck.

One to three nights: If time permits continue west to Mallaig, a ferryport with connections to the rugged and wild Isle of Skye. Otherwise, head east to Fort William, taking the A82 southwards toward the famous Loch Lomond before returning to Glasgow.

Border Byways

If the bustle of Edinburgh makes you yearn for rural tranquility, discover the romance of the villages and rolling hills that perch on the English–Scottish border. In terms of scenery it's a far cry from the remote Highlands, but there are still plenty of castles and abbeys to explore.

DURATION➤ Three to five days

THE MAIN ROUTE➤ **One to two nights:**
Leave Edinburgh via the A1, then abandon the A1 in favor of more scenic rural roads at the pleasant little town of Haddington. Head cross-country for Gifford, an attractive village tucked into the well-kept East Lothian countryside. Follow the B6355 through the Lammermuir Hills—peaceful, lonely slopes with a strong hint of the Highland moors—before dropping into the small town of Duns.

One to two nights: From Duns you can either divert to Berwick-upon-Tweed, which is, strictly speaking, on the English side of the border; or go south to Kelso, which has a ruined abbey. Continue on the A698 to Jedburgh, an older border town with a well-preserved abbey.

One to two nights: From Jedburgh continue south on the B6375 (via Newcastleton) to Liddesdale, scene of many an ancient cross-border raid. The road eventually reaches Annan and the large, tourist-friendly town of Dumfries.

One to two nights: Take the A701 from Dumfries to Moffat, where you can pick up the A708 for St. Mary's Loch and the waterfall at Grey Mare's Tail. Souvenir hunters will want to make a brief stop in the tidy town of Peebles before returning to Edinburgh.

Anything but the Main Route

If you're on a whirlwind tour of Scotland, this driving tour offers discriminating adventurers the chance of skirting the tourist horde while still experiencing some of the country's better-known sights. A car is indispensable, as is a good road map and a love of driving. This nearly circular tour starts in Dunfermline and ends in either Perth or Edinburgh, but it could be done in either direction.

DURATION➤ Four to seven days

THE MAIN ROUTE➤ **One to two nights:**
From Dunfermline, the ancient capital of Scotland and the birthplace of Andrew Carnegie, take the A823 northwest. This soon cuts through the green and rounded Ochil Hills, giving good views of the nearby Highlands. You can browse for antiques in Auchterarder before continuing to the pleasant Highland-edge town of Crieff (another good spot for bargain hunters).

One to two nights: From Crieff follow the A822 north into the Highlands through the Sma'Glen, but keep your eyes open for a sign marked GLEN QUAICH and KENMORE. This route rises through moors before zigzagging steeply down to the east end of Loch Tay. Head to Fortigall to join, a little way east, the B846. Take this high road over the hills to Tummel Bridge, then go east to join the main and busy A9 (there is no other option here). At Dalwhinnie take the A86 (via Loch Laggan) to cosmopolitan Fort William.

One night: From Fort William take the A82 north past Loch Lochy to Fort Augustus. Leave the busy A82 and keep to the scenic east bank of Loch Ness—home to the fabled and feared Loch Ness Monster (locals call her Nessie). Continue to Inverness.

One to three nights: From Inverness take the A96 and then the A939 to Cawdor Castle, the haunting ground of Shakespeare's Macbeth. Continue south on the A939 and cross the wilds of Dava Moor to reach handsome Grantown-on-Spey. Continue toward Tomintoul and the Royal Deeside region (also known as Castle Country), stopping off at one of the region's many dramatic keeps—perhaps the castles at Corgarff, Balmoral, or Braemar. You can detour along the A93 to Aberdeen, a pleasant but commercial port city. Otherwise, rejoin the A9 and head south to Pitlochry, home to the Edradour Distillery, which claims to be the smallest single-malt distillery in Scotland. Head south along the banks of the River Tummel, joining the B867 at Dunkeld. Continue south for Perth and Edinburgh.

The Highlands and Islands by Bike

Happiness is zooming down a steep coastal hill with horizon-wide views of the rugged Highlands. Biking the eastern side of Scotland, around Aberdeen, is saner since the landscape is mostly soft and gentle. But in the coastal Highlands, from Oban to the Isle of Skye to Inverness, the country turns raw and wild. Cycling in this environment requires more than a little stamina, though dining and lodging facilities are generally closely spaced. The following itinerary starts in Glasgow and ends in Inverness. Some sections take advantage of specially designated cycle routes; others follow main and secondary roads where you must be wary of vehicular traffic. No matter what time of year you visit, bring a rain suit.

DURATION➤ Eight to 14 days

THE MAIN ROUTE➤ **One night:** From Glasgow take the train to Paisley to link with the Glasgow–Irvine Pedestrian and Cycle Route (maps available from Tourist Information Centers). From Paisley via Lochwinnoch and Kilwinning, the next 30 miles lead through tame countryside to Androssan, where you can catch a summer ferry to Brodick, on Arran island.

One to two nights: From Brodick follow the A841 clockwise around the island; or, if you're short on time, turn north toward Lochranza, where there's a frequent summer-only ferry to Claonaig. Continue to the quiet town of Kennacraig or larger Tarbert.

One to two nights: If time permits, follow the B8024 clockwise around Knapdale for outstanding views of the Hebridean islands. Otherwise, continue north from Tarbert along the western bank of Loch Gilp. Your final destination in either case is the small, very pleasant town of Lochgilphead.

One to two nights: Take the minor road (B840) northeast to Ford at the southern end of Loch Awe, Scotland's longest loch. You can make a quick detour to Carnasserie Castle, just off the A816, or continue along the loch's northwestern side to the B845 junction. Follow the B845 to Taynuilt, where there's an unlabeled backroad to Oban via Glen Lonan.

One night: North of Oban there are summer ferries to Craignure, on the Isle of Mull. On Mull, follow the A849 south past Torosay and Duart castles, then circle northward on the B8035 to reach Fishnish Pier, connected by ferry during summer with Lochaline. On the mainland, follow the A884 north to Strontian or Salen.

One night: Continue north along the coast, past Loch Ailort, to the A830 junction. Head west, either to Arisaig or Mallaig.

One to three nights: Summer ferries connect Mallaig with the rugged Isle of Skye. If you're pressed for time, head north on the A851, then east on the A850 for Kyle of Lochalsh—a five-minute ferry ride from the mainland. Otherwise, the A850 leads northwest to the lovely town of Portree and to the wild, spectacular seascapes of northern Skye. When you're ready, backtrack to the Kyle of Lochalsh ferry.

One to two nights: Continue northeast via the villages of Plockton and Stromeferry. It's a demanding uphill ride around the banks of Loch Carron, but there's plenty of accommodation in Lochcarron, and the subsequent ride between Ardarroch and Shieldaig is spectacular. So, too, is the short ride between Shieldaig and Torridon. From Torridon, bike 20 miles to Achnasheen and continue by bike or train to Inverness. The following are the main events on the Scottish calendar.

FESTIVALS AND SEASONAL EVENTS

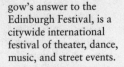

WINTER

JAN. 25➤ Burns Night dinners and other entertainments are held in memory of Robert Burns in Glasgow, Ayr, Dumfries, Edinburgh, and many other towns and villages.

gow's answer to the Edinburgh Festival, is a citywide international festival of theater, dance, music, and street events.

MID-MAY➤ The **Perth Festival of the Arts** (☎ 01738/21031) offers orchestral and choral concerts, drama, opera, recitals, and ballet throughout Perth, Tayside.

☎ 0131/226–4001), which runs for three weeks, is the world's largest festival of the arts. After dark is the **Edinburgh Military Tattoo** (22 Market St., Edinburgh EH1 1DF, ☎ 0131/225–1188), a display of military expertise.

SPRING

MAY➤ **Glasgow Mayfest** (Festival Dir., 18 Albion St., Glasgow G1 1LH, ☎ 0141/552–8000), Glas-

SUMMER

MID-AUG.–EARLY SEPT.➤ The **Edinburgh International Festival** (21 Market St., Edinburgh EH1 1BW,

AUTUMN

SEPTEMBER➤ The **Braemar Royal Highland Gathering** (Princess Royal and Duke of Fife Memorial Park, Braemar, Grampian, ☎ 01339/755377) hosts kilted clansmen from all over Scotland.

2 Scotland: The Home of Golf

Golfing Throughout the Country

By John
Hutchinson

John
Hutchinson
worked for
many years
with the
Scottish Tourist
Board and is
an expert on
the history and
lore of sport in
Scotland.

THERE ARE MORE THAN 400 GOLF COURSES in Scotland and only 5 million local residents, so the country has probably the highest concentration of courses to people anywhere in the world. Some of these courses are world famous as venues for major championships, and any golfer coming to Scotland will probably want to play the "famous names" sometime in his career. Telling your friends in the clubhouse back home that you got a birdie at the Road Hole on the Old Course in St. Andrews, where Lyle, Faldo, and Jacklin have played, somehow carries more weight in terms of prestige than an excellent round at an obscure but delightful little course that no one has ever heard of.

So, by all means, play the championship courses and get your prestige, but remember they are championship courses and, therefore, they are difficult; you may enjoy the actual game itself much more at an easier, if less well-known, location. Remember, too, that everyone else wants to play them, so booking can be more of a problem, particularly on peak days during the summer. Do book early, or, if you are staying in a hotel attached to a course, get them to book for you.

There has always been considerable debate as to who invented golf, but there is no doubt that its development into one of the most popular games in the world stems from Scotland. Like many other games that involve hitting a ball with a stick, golf evolved during the Middle Ages and gradually took on its present form.

The first written reference to golf, variously spelled as "gowf" or "goff," was as long ago as 1457, when James II of Scotland declared that both golf and football should be "utterly cryit doune and nocht usit" because they were distracting his subjects from their archery practice. Mary Queen of Scots, it seems, was fond of golf. When in Edinburgh, she played on Leith Links and on Bruntsfield Links, perhaps the oldest course in the world where the game is still played. When in Fife, she played at Falkland near the palace and St. Andrews itself.

Golf must surely rank as one of Scotland's earliest cultural exports. In 1603, when James VI of Scotland also became James I of England, he moved his court to London. With him went his golf-loving friends, and they set up a course on Blackheath Common, then on the outskirts of London.

Golf clubs as we know them today first began in the middle of the 18th century. The earliest written evidence of the existence of a club is of the Honourable Company of Edinburgh Golfers, now residing at Muirfield, in 1744, and of the Royal and Ancient at St. Andrews in 1754. From then on, clubs sprang up all over Scotland: Royal Aberdeen (1780), Crail Golfing Society (1786), Dunbar (1794), and the Royal Perth Golfing Society (1824).

By the early years of the 19th century, golf clubs had been set up in England, and the game had begun to be carried all over the world by enthusiastic Scots. With them, these Scottish golf missionaries took their knowledge not only of golf, but of golf courses. Scotland is fortunate in that large parts of its coastline are natural golf courses, and the origins of bunkers and the word *links* are to be found in the sand dunes of the Scottish shore. But other countries were not so fortunate. The natural terrain did not exist, and courses had to be designed and created. Willie Park of Musselburgh (who laid out Sunningdale), James

Braid, and C. K. Hutchison (whose crowning glory is at Gleneagles Hotel) are some of the best known of Scotland's golf architects.

Golf has always had a peculiar classlessness in Scotland. It is a game for everyone, and for centuries towns and cities in Scotland have had their own golf courses for the enjoyment of the citizens. The snobbishness and exclusivity of golf clubs in some parts of the world have few echoes here.

Many of the important changes in the design and construction of balls and clubs were pioneered by the professional players who lived and worked around these town courses and who made the balls and clubs themselves. The original balls, called "featheries," were leather bags stuffed with boiled feathers. When, in 1848, the gutta percha ball, called a *guttie,* was introduced, there was considerable friction, particularly in St. Andrews, between the makers of the two rival types of ball. The gutta percha proved superior and was in general use until the invention of the rubber-core ball in 1901.

Clubs were traditionally made of wood: shafts of ash, later hickory, and heads of thorn or some other hardwood like apple or pear. Heads were spliced then bound to the shaft with twine. Players generally managed with far fewer clubs than today. About 1628 the marquis of Montrose, a great golf enthusiast, had a set of clubs made for him in St. Andrews that illustrate the range of clubs used in Stuart times: "Bonker clubis, a irone club, and twa play clubs."

Caddies—the word comes from the French *cadet,* a young boy, and was used, particularly in Edinburgh, for anyone who ran messages—carried the players' clubs around, usually under the arm. Golf carts did not come into fashion in Britain until the 1950s.

The technology of golf may change, but its addictive qualities are timeless. Toward the end of the 18th century, an Edinburgh golfer called Alexander McKellar regularly played golf all day and refused to stop even when it grew dark. One night his wife carried his dinner and nightcap on Bruntsfield Links where he was playing in an attempt to shame him into changing his ways. She failed.

And the addiction continues.

Where to Play

Scotland's courses are well spread throughout the country in all areas but the far northern Highlands and some of the islands. So finding a holiday golf course is never a problem. The country's main golfing areas are outlined below. Some suggestions are also given for the things nongolfers could do in an area. For more information region by region, *see* Sports and Fitness in Chapters 3 through 12.

The Stewartry
Starting at the very southern border, the first of these areas is a delightful part of Scotland set in the rich farmlands around Dumfries, a golfing holiday area since Victorian times.

Powfoot and Southerness are excellent links courses with magnificent views over the Solway Firth, while inland, Dumfries and Moffat have long-established courses that provide excellent golf in a clean invigorating environment. There are also several fine 9-hole courses in the area.

Ayrshire and the Clyde Coast

Lying just an hour to the south of Glasgow either by car or by train, Ayrshire and the Clyde Coast has been a holiday area for Glaswegians for generations. Few people need an introduction to the famous names of Turnberry, Royal Troon, Prestwick, or Western Gailes, all excellent links courses along this coast. In addition, there are at least 20 courses in the area within an hour's drive. Remember, too, that at major locations, such as Turnberry, Troon, and Ayr, there are several different courses to play from the same base.

East Lothian

The sand dunes that stretch eastward from Edinburgh along the southern shore of the Firth of Forth made an ideal location for some of the earliest golf courses in the world. Muirfield is perhaps the most famous course in the area, but around it are over a dozen more, at Gullane, North Berwick, Dunbar, and Aberlady and, nearer Edinburgh, at Longniddry, Prestonpans, and Musselburgh. All are links courses, many with views to the island of the Firth of Forth and northward to Fife, and if you weary of the East Lothian courses, just 20 or so miles away there are nearly 30 more within the city of Edinburgh.

Fife

Few would dispute the claim of St. Andrews to be the Home of Golf, holding as it does the Royal and Ancient, the organization that governs the sport worldwide. Golf has been played in the area since the very beginning, and to play in Fife is for most golfers a cherished ambition. St. Andrews itself has a wide range of full 18-hole courses in addition to the famous Old Course, and along the shores of the Firth of Forth is a string of ancient villages, each with its harbor, ancient red-roofed buildings, and golf course. In all, there are about 30 in the area.

Perthshire

The first inland golfing area to be considered, Perthshire has a variety of really excellent courses developed specifically for holiday golf and for visitors, rather than for large numbers of local club members. Gleneagles Hotel is, of course, the most famous of these golf resort hotels. Its facilities are considered outstanding when compared with anywhere in the world. But other courses in the area, set on the edges of beautiful Highland scenery, will delight any golfer. Crieff, Taymouth, and other courses are in the mountains; Blairgowrie and Perth are set amid the rich farmlands nearer the sea.

Angus

East of Perthshire, north of the city of Dundee, is a string of excellent courses along the shores of the North Sea and inland into the foothills of the Grampian Mountains. The most famous course in Angus is probably Carnoustie, one of several British Open Championship venues in Scotland, but there are many more along the same stretch of coast from Dundee northward as far as Stonehaven. Golfers who excel in windy conditions will particularly enjoy the breezes blowing eastward from the sea. Inland Edzell, Forfar, Brechin, and Kirriemuir all have courses nestling in the farmlands of Strathmore.

Aberdeenshire

The city of Aberdeen, Scotland's third largest, is particularly known for its sparkling granite buildings and the amazing displays of roses each summer. It also offers a good range of courses for the golfer. Aberdeen itself has four major courses, and to the north, as far as Fraserburgh and Peterhead, there are five others, including the popular Cruden Bay. Royal Deeside has three, and in the rich farmlands to the north are three more with at least six 9-hole courses as well.

Speyside

Set on the main A9 road an hour south of Inverness amid the Cairngorm Mountains, the valley of the River Spey is one of Scotland's most attractive all-year sports centers, with winter skiing and in summer, sailing and canoeing, pony-trekking, fishing, and some excellent golf. The main courses in the area are Newtonmore, Grantown on Spey, and Boat of Garten, all fine inland courses with wonderful views of the surrounding mountains and challenging golf provided by the springy turf and the heather. For a change of pace, the Moray Firth courses, with their seaside attractions, are only an hour's drive away.

Moray Coast

No one can say that the Lowlands of Scotland have a monopoly of Scotland's fine seaside golf courses. The Moray Coast, stretching eastward from Inverness, has some spectacular sand dunes, and these have been adapted to create stimulating and exciting links courses.

The two courses at Nairn have long been known to golfers famous and unknown. Charlie Chaplin regularly played here. But in addition there are a dozen courses looking out over the sea from Inverness as far along as Banff and Macduff and several inland amid the fertile Moray farmland.

Dornoch Firth

North of Inverness, the east coast is deeply indented with firths along whose shores are to be found some excellent and relatively unknown golf courses. Royal Dornoch has recently been "discovered" by international golf writers, but knowledgeable golfers have been making the northern pilgrimage for well over a hundred years. There are half a dozen excellent links courses around Dornoch and inland, another Victorian golfing holiday center, Strathpeffer, preserves much of the atmosphere these gentlemen of a past age set out to achieve.

Courses Around the Country

Most courses welcome visitors with the minimum of formalities and often at surprisingly low cost. (Out of season, a few clubs still use the "honest box," in which you drop your fees!) Admittedly, there are at least a few clubs that have always been noted for their exclusive air, and there are newer golf courses emerging as part of exclusive leisure complexes. These are exceptions to the long tradition of recreation for all. Golf in Scotland is usually a very democratic game, played by ordinary folk as well as the rich and leisured. Here is a selection of clubs that welcome visitors. Just three short pieces of advice (particularly for North Americans): 1) in Scotland the game is usually played fairly quickly, so please don't hang about if others are waiting, 2) caddy carts are hand-pulled carts for your clubs, not the electric golf carts that are more familiar to U.S. golfers and rarely available in Scotland, and 3) when they say "rough" they really mean "rough."

Balgownie, Royal Aberdeen Golf Club. This old, established club (1780) is the archetypal Scottish links course: long and testing over uneven ground with the frequently added hazard of a sea breeze. Prickly gorse is inclined to close in and form an additional hurdle. The course is tucked behind the rough, grassy sand dunes, and there are surprisingly few views of the sea. One historical note: In 1783, this club originated the five-minute-search rule for a lost ball. ☎ 01224/702221. *18 holes. Yardage: 6,372. Par 70. Fees: £37/round, £48 daily. Weekend restrictions, letter of introduction required. Advance reservations. Facilities: practice area, catering.*

Ballater. This club has a holiday atmosphere and a course laid out along the river flats of the River Dee. Originally opened in 1906, the club makes maximum use of the fine setting between river and woods and is ideal for a relaxing round of vacation golf. The variety of shops and pleasant walks in nearby Ballater make this a good place for nongolfing partners. ☎ 013397/55567 or 012297/55658. *18 holes. Yardage: 5,638. Par 67. Fees: weekdays, £16/round, £24 daily; weekends, £19/round, £29 daily. Visitors welcome daily. Advance reservations. Facilities: practice area, caddy carts, catering.*

Banff, Duff House Royal Gold Golf Club. Although it is within moments of the sea, this club is a curious blend of a coastal course with a parkland setting. The course, which is only minutes from Banff center, lies within the parkland grounds of Duff House, an Adam mansion that was donated to the town. The club has inherited the ancient traditions of seaside play (golf records here go back to the 17th century). Mature trees and gentle slopes create a pleasant playing atmosphere. ☎ 01261/812075. *18 holes. Yardage: 6,161. Par 69. Fees: weekdays, £13/round, £17 daily; weekends, £19/round, £25 daily. Advance reservations. Facilities: practice area, caddy carts, catering.*

Boat of Garten. Possibly one of the greatest "undiscovered" courses in Scotland, Boat of Garten was designed by famous golf architect James Braid. Each of the 18 holes is individual: Some cut through birchwood and heathery rough, most have long views to the Cairn-gorms and a strong Highland ambience. An unusual feature is the preserved steam railway that runs along part of the course. The occasional puffing locomotive can hardly be considered a hazard. ☎ 01479/831282. *18 holes. Yardage: 5,837. Par 69. Fees: on application. Starting sheet used on weekends. Advance reservations. Facilities: caddies, caddy carts, catering.*

Callander. Another course well worth seeking out, Callander was designed by Tom Morris and has a scenic upland feel. Pine and birchwoods and hilly fairways offer fine views, and the tricky moorland layout demands accurate hitting off the tee. ☎ 01877/330090. *18 holes. Yardage: 5,125. Par 66. Fees: on application. Facilities: practice area, caddies, caddy carts, catering.*

Carnoustie. Home in former days of the British Open Championship, the extensive coastal links around Carnoustie have been played for generations. Carnoustie was also once a training ground for golf coaches, many of whom went to the United States. The choice municipal course here is therefore full of historical snippets and local color, as well as being tough and full of interest. ☎ 01241/853789. *18 holes. Yardage 6,936. Par 74. Fees: £40/round, £120 3 days, £180 5 days. Visitors welcome except Sat. morning, Sun. before 11:30 AM. Advance reservations. Facilities: caddies, caddy carts (May–Oct.), catering.*

Cruden Bay. Another east-coast Lowland course sheltered behind the extensive sand hills, this one offers a typical Scottish golf experience. Runnels and valleys, among other hazards, on the challenging fairways ensure plenty of excitement, and some of the holes are rated among the finest anywhere in Scotland. Like Gleneagles and Turnberry, this course owes its origins to an association with the grand railway hotels that were built in the heyday of steam. Unlike the other two, however, Cruden Bay's railway hotel and the railway itself have gone, though the course has only gotten better. ☎ *01779/812285. 18 holes. Yardage: 6,370. Par 71. Fees: weekdays, £25 daily; weekends, £35 daily; £100 weekly; £160 for 2 weeks. Visitors welcome weekdays, restricted weekends. Advance reservations. Facilities: practice area, caddy carts, catering.*

Dornoch. This course, which was laid out by Tom Morris in 1886 on a sort of coastal shelf behind the shore, has matured to become one of the world's finest. Its location in the north of Scotland, though less than an hour's drive from Inverness Airport, means that it is far from over-run even in peak season. It may not have the fame of a Gleneagles or a St. Andrews, but if time permits, Dornoch is a memorable golfing experience. The little town of Dornoch, behind the course, is both sleepy and charming. ☎ *01862/810219. 18 holes. Yardage 6,581. Par 70. Fees: on application. Advance reservations. Max handicap: men 24, women 35. Facilities: practice area, caddies, caddy carts, catering.*

Dunbar. This ancient golfing site by the sea even has a lighthouse at the 9th hole. It's a good choice for a typical east-coast Lowland course within easy reach of Edinburgh. ☎ *01368/862317. 18 holes. Yardage: 6,426. Par 71. Fees: weekdays, £28 daily; weekends, £40 daily. Visitors welcome after 9:30 AM except Thurs. Advance reservations. Facilities: practice area, caddies (by reservation), catering.*

Fraserburgh. A northeast town with extensive links and dunes that seem to have grown up around the course rather than the other way around. Be prepared for a hill climb and a tough finish. ☎ *01346/518287. 18 holes (4 additional for warm-up). Yardage: 6,279. Par 70. Fees: weekdays, £12 daily; weekends, £16 daily; £40 weekly. Facilities: practice area, catering.*

Girvan. An old established course with play along a narrow coastal strip and a more lush inland section beside the Water of Girvan—the neighborhood river that constitutes a particular hazard at the 15th, unless you are a big hitter. This is quite a scenic course, with good views of the Clyde estuary. ☎ *01465/714272. 18 holes. Yardage: 5,078. Par 65. Fees: weekdays, £10/round, £18 daily. Visitors welcome daily. Facilities: caddy carts, catering.*

Killin. A splendidly scenic course, typically Highland, with a roaring river, woodland bird song, and backdrop of high green hills. There are a few surprises, including two blind shots to reach the green at the 4th. The village of Killin is very attractive, almost alpine in feel, especially in spring when the hilltops may still be white. ☎ *01567/820312. 9 holes. Yardage: 2,410. Par 65. Fees: weekdays, £10/round, £13 daily; £40/5-day ticket. Facilities: caddy carts, club hire catering.*

Ladybank. Fife is famous for its choice of coastal courses, but this one offers an interesting contrast: Though Ladybank is laid out on fairly level ground, the firwoods, birches, and heathery rough give it a Highland flavor among the gentle Lowland fields. Qualifying rounds of the British Open are played here when the main championship is played at St. Andrews. ☎ *01337/830814. 18 holes. Yardage: 6,641. Par 71. Fees: Nov.–Apr., weekdays, £16/round, £23 daily; weekends, £19/round, £27 daily. May–Sept., weekdays, £25/round, £34 daily; weekends, £27/round, £37 daily. Oct., weekdays, £19/round, £27 daily; weekends, £22/round, £30 daily. Visitors welcome daily. Advance reservations essential. Facilities: practice area, caddy carts, catering.*

Leven. Another fine Fife course used as a British Open qualifier, this one also feels like the more famous St. Andrews, with hummocky terrain and a tang of salt in the air. The 1st and 18th share the same fairway. ☎ *01333/428859. 18 holes. Yardage: 6,436. Par 71. Fees: on application. Visitors welcome except Sat. Advance reservations. Facilities: catering.*

Lossiemouth, Moray Golf Club. Discover the mild airs of the "Moray Riviera," as Tom Morris did in 1889 when he was inspired by the lie of the natural links. There are two courses plus a 6-hole minicourse. There is lots of atmosphere here, with golfing memorabilia in the clubhouse, as well as the tale of the British prime minister, Lord Asquith, who took a holiday in this out-of-the-way spot, yet still managed to be attacked by a crowd of militant suffragettes at the 17th. All other hazards on these testing courses are entirely natural. ☎ *01343/813330. 18 holes each (6 separate). Yardage: 6,643, 6,005. Par 71, 69. Fees: Old Course, weekdays, £21/round, £26 daily; weekends, £30/round, £35 daily. New Course, weekdays, £15/round, £20 daily; weekends, £20/round, £25 daily. Facilities: practice area, caddy carts, catering.*

Machrihanish, by Campbeltown. This is a western course that many enthusiasts discuss in hushed tones—a kind of out-of-the-way golfers' Shangri-La. It was laid out in 1876 by Tom Morris on the links around the sandy Machrihanish Bay. The drive of the first tee is across the beach to reach the green—an intimidating start to a memorable series of very individual holes. If you are short on time, consider flying from Glasgow to nearby Campbeltown, the last town on the long peninsula of Kintyre. ☎ *01586/810277. 18 holes. Yardage: 6,228. Par 70. Fees: weekdays, £18/round, £28 daily; weekends £32 daily; £112 weekly. Advance reservations. Facilities: practice area, caddy carts, catering.*

Nairn. Widely regarded in golfing circles as a truly great course, Nairn dates from 1887 and is the regular home of Scotland's Northern Open. Huge greens, aggressive gorse, a beach hazard for five of the holes, a steady prevailing wind, and distracting views across the Moray Firth to the northern hills make play here a memorable experience. ☎ *01667/453208. 18 holes. Yardage: 6,722. Par 72. Fees: weekdays, £30/round, £40 daily; weekends, £35/round, £50 daily. Advance reservations. Facilities: practice area, caddy, caddy carts, catering.*

Rosemount, Blairgowrie Golf Club. Well known to native golfers looking for an exciting challenge, Rosemount's 18 are laid out in the fir-woods, which certainly bring a wild air to the scene. You may encounter a browsing roe deer if you stray too far. There are also, however, wide fairways and at least some large greens. ☎ *01250/872622. 18 holes. Yardage: 6,556. Par 72. Fees: on application. Visitors welcome Mon., Tues., Thurs. Facilities: practice area, caddies, caddy carts, catering.*

3 Edinburgh and the Lothians

Scotland's capital makes a strong first impression—Edinburgh Castle looming from the crags of an ancient volcano; neoclassical monuments perched on Calton Hill; Arthur's Seat, a small mountain with steep slopes, little crags, and spectacular vistas over the city and the Firth of Forth. Like Rome, Edinburgh is built on seven hills, and it has an Old Town district that retains striking evidence of a colorful history. But Edinburgh offers more than just a unique historical and architectural landscape—it's a cosmopolitan capital, rich in museums and culture.

By Gilbert
Summers

Updated by
P. D. Williams

THE FIRST-TIME VISITOR TO SCOTLAND may be surprised that the country still has a capital city at all, thinking perhaps that the seat of government was drained of all its resources and power after the union with England in 1707. Far from it. The Union of Parliaments brought with it a set of political partnerships—such as separate legal, ecclesiastical, and educational systems—that Edinburgh (-*burgh* is always pronounced *burra* in Scots), as former seat of the Scottish parliament, assimilated and integrated with its own surviving institutions. In the trying decades after the union, many influential Scots, both in Edinburgh and beyond, went through an identity crisis, but out of the 18th-century difficulties grew the Scottish Enlightenment, during which great strides were made by educated Scots in medicine, economics, and science.

By the mid-18th century, it had become the custom for wealthy Scottish landowners to spend the winter in town houses in the Old Town of Edinburgh, huddled between the high castle rock and the Royal Palace below. In the tall crowded buildings—called, in Scots, *tenements*—of old Edinburgh, the well-to-do tended to have their rooms on the middle floors, while the "lower orders" occupied dwellings on the top and ground floors. Such an overcrowded arrangement bred plenty of unsavory and odorous hazards (more on this later), but it also bred ideas. Uniquely cross-fertilized in the coffeehouses and taverns, intellectual notions flourished among a people determined to remain Scottish yet deprived of their identity in a political sense. One result was a campaign to expand and beautify the city, to give it a look worthy of its subsequent nickname, Athens of the North. Thus was the New Town of Edinburgh built, with broad streets and gracious buildings creating a harmony that even today's throbbing traffic cannot obscure.

Edinburgh today is the second-most-important financial center in the United Kingdom. Its residents come from all over Britain—not least of all because the city regularly ranks near the top of surveys that measure "quality of life"—and New Town apartments in fashionable streets sell for considerable amounts of money. In some senses the city is showy and materialistic, but Edinburgh still supports several learned societies, many of which have their roots in the Scottish Enlightenment: The Royal Society of Edinburgh, for example, established in 1783 "for the advancement of learning and useful knowledge," is still an important forum for interdisciplinary activities, both in Edinburgh and in Scotland as a whole, publishing scientific papers, holding academic symposia and meetings, and administering research fellowships in many Scottish universities. Hand in hand with the city's academic and scientific life is a rich cultural life, with the Edinburgh International Festival attracting lovers of all the arts. Running for three weeks from late August into September, this is simply one of the top cultural and artistic festivals in the world. It attracts talent from all parts of the globe: top orchestras and conductors, international dance troupes and ballet companies, and leading opera and theater performers.

Thousands of years ago, an eastward-grinding glacier encountered the tough basalt plug or core of an ancient volcano. It swept around the core, scouring steep cliffs and leaving a trail of material like the tail of a comet. This material formed a ramp, gently leading down from the rocky summit. On this "crag and tail" would grow the city of Edinburgh. The lands that rolled down to the sea were for centuries open country, between Castle Rock and the tiny community clustered by the shore that grew into Leith, Edinburgh's seaport. By the 12th century Edinburgh had become a walled town, still perched on the hill. Its shape was becoming clearer: like a fish with its head at the castle, backbone running down the ridge, with "ribs" leading briefly off on either side. The backbone gradually became the continuous thoroughfare now known as the Royal Mile, and the ribs became the "closes" (alleyways), some still surviving, which were the scene of many historic incidents. By the early 15th century Edinburgh had become the undisputed capital of Scotland. The bitter defeat of Scotland at Flodden in 1513 (when Scotland aligned itself with France against England) caused a new defensive wall to be built there, and, though the castle escaped, the city was burned by the English earl of Hertford under the orders of King Henry VIII of England. By the time that Mary, Queen of Scots, returned already widowed from France, in 1561, the guest house of the Abbey of Holyrood had grown to become the Palace of Holyroodhouse. Mary's legacy to the city included the destruction of most of the earliest buildings of Edinburgh Castle, held by her supporters after she was forced to flee her homeland.

By the end of the 18th century the grand New Town was taking shape, though it never was taken as far as the sea at Leith, which had been the original intention. Victorian suburbs added to the gradual sprawl. Despite the expansion, the guardian castle remained the focal point. Princes Street—a master stroke in city planning—was built up only on one side, allowing magnificent views of the great rock on which the fortress stands. The result for today's visitor is a skyline of sheer drama and an aura of grandeur. Edinburgh Castle watches over the city, frowning down on Princes Street, now the main downtown shopping area, as if disapproving its modern razzmatazz. Its ramparts still echo with gunfire each day when the traditional one o'clock gun booms out over the city, startling unwary shoppers. To the east, the top of New Town's Calton Hill is cluttered with sturdy, neoclassical structures, somewhat like an abandoned set for a Greek tragedy.

These theatrical elements give a unique identity to downtown, but turn a corner, say, off George Street, and you will see, not an endless cityscape, but blue sea and a patchwork of fields. This is the county of Fife, beyond the inlet of the North Sea called the Firth of Forth—a reminder, like the Highlands to the northwest glimpsed from Edinburgh's highest points, that the rest of Scotland lies within easy reach.

EXPLORING

The Old Town, which bears a great measure of symbolic weight as the "heart of Scotland's capital," is for lovers of atmosphere and history. The New Town, by contrast, is for those visitors who appreciate the unique architectural heritage of Edinburgh's Enlightenment. If you belong in both categories, don't worry—the Old and the New Towns are only yards apart. For visitors with more time, a wider Edinburgh lies beyond (*see* Off the Beaten Track and Shopping, *below*). Remember that Edinburgh, as cities go, is compact, and much of the interesting city-center environment can be covered on foot.

Time and progress (of a sort) have swept away some of the narrow "closes" (alleyways) and tall tenements of the Old Town, but enough remain for the visitor to imagine the original shape of Scotland's capital. The Old and the New are the essence of Edinburgh, even if, away from this central core, Victorian expansion and urban sprawl have greatly increased the city's dimensions. The following tours bring out the contrasts between the two facets of the city. The first samples the flavor of the Old Town, with a leisurely stroll down the Royal Mile; the second takes in the best of New Town architecture.

Tour 1: The Old Town

Numbers in the margin correspond to points of interest on the Edinburgh map.

★ **❶** Probably every visitor to the city tours **Edinburgh Castle,** which is more than can be said for many of the city's residents. Its popularity as an attraction is due not only to the castle's historic and symbolic value, but to the outstanding views offered from its battlements.

Recent archaeological investigations have established that the rock was inhabited as far back as AD 1000, in the latter part of the Bronze Age. There have been fortifications here since the mysterious people called the Picts first used it as a stronghold in the 3rd and 4th centuries BC. The Picts were dislodged by Saxon invaders from northern England in 452 BC, and for the next 1,300 years the site saw countless battles and skirmishes.

The castle has been held by Scots and Englishmen, Catholics and Protestants, soldiers and royalty; during the Napoleonic Wars it even contained French prisoners of war, whose carvings can still be seen on the vaults under the great hall. In the 16th century, Mary, Queen of Scots, gave birth in the castle to the future James VI of Scotland, who was also to rule England, as James I. In 1573 the castle defended Mary as rightful Catholic queen of Scotland; it was her last stronghold and was virtually destroyed by English artillery.

The oldest surviving building in the complex—in fact, in the entire city—is the tiny 11th-century **St. Margaret's Chapel,** named in honor of Saxon Queen Margaret, who had persuaded her husband, King Malcolm, to move his court from Dunfermline to Edinburgh because the latter's environs—the Lothians—were occupied by Saxon settlers with whom she felt more at home, or so the story goes. (Dunfermline was surrounded by Celts.) The chapel was the only building spared when the castle was razed in 1313 by the Scots, having won it back from their English foes. Also worth seeing are the **crown room,** which contains the **regalia of Scotland—**the crown, scepter, and sword that once graced the Scottish monarch; the **old parliament hall;** and **Queen Mary's apartments,** where she gave birth to James. The **great hall** features an extensive collection of arms and armor and has an impressive vaulted, beamed ceiling.

There are several military features of interest, including the **Scottish National War Memorial,** the **Scottish United Services Museum,** and the famous 15th-century Belgian-made cannon *Mons Meg.* This enormous piece of artillery has been silent since 1682, when it exploded while firing a salute for the duke of York; it now stands in an ancient hall behind the Half-Moon Battery, the curving ramparts that give Edinburgh Castle its distinctive appearance from miles away. Contrary to what you may hear from locals, it is not *Mons Meg* but the battery's time gun that goes off with a bang every weekday at 1, frightening visitors and reminding Edinburghers to check their watches.

The **Esplanade,** the huge forecourt of the castle, was built in the 18th century as a parade ground, using earth from the foundation of the Royal Exchange to widen and level the area. Although it now serves as the castle parking lot, it comes alive with color each year during the festival, when it is used for the Tattoo, a magnificent military display and pageant. *Edinburgh Castle,* ☎ *0131/244–3101.* ☞ *£5.50 adults, £1.50 children, £3.50 senior citizens.* ⊙ *Apr.–Sept., daily 9:30–5; Oct.–Mar., daily 9:30–4:15.*

TIME OUT At the castle, **Mills Mount Restaurant** serves coffee, light lunches, and afternoon teas in a bright premise with panoramic views over the city.

★ ❷ The **Royal Mile,** looking splendid after its multi-million-dollar renovation to reduce traffic, it starts immediately below the Esplanade. It runs roughly west to east, from the castle to the Palace of Holyroodhouse (*see below*), and changes its name as it progresses, from Castlehill to Lawnmarket, High Street, and Canongate. On your stroll downhill from the castle, note on Castlehill the bronze plaque recalling the burning of witches here in the late 16th century. Notice also the cannonball imbedded in the west gable of **Cannonball House.** Legend says it was fired from the castle during the Jacobite rebellion in 1745 led by Bonnie Prince Charlie, the most romantic of the Stuart pretenders to the British throne. Most authorities agree on a more prosaic explanation, however, saying it was a height marker for Edinburgh's first piped water-supply system, installed in 1681.

❸ On your left, the **Camera Obscura** in **Outlook Tower** offers armchair views of the city. This 17th-century building was significantly altered in the 1840s and 1850s with the installation of the present system of lenses, which, on a clear day, project an image of the city onto a white, concave table. *Castlehill,* ☎ *0131/226–3709.* ☞ *£3.20 adults, £1.60 children, £2.50 students, £2 senior citizens, £8.70 family ticket.* ⊙ *Apr.–Oct., weekdays 9:30–6, weekends 10–6; Nov.–Mar., weekdays 10–5 (last admission 4 PM), weekends 10–3:30 (shop open until 5 PM).*

❹ Opposite, the **Scotch Whisky Heritage Centre** reveals the mysterious process that turns malted barley and spring water into one of Scotland's most important exports. Although the process of making whisky is not in itself packed with drama, the center manages an imaginative presentation using models and tableaux viewed while riding in low-speed barrel-cars. At one point visitors find themselves inside a huge vat surrounded by bubbling sounds and malty smells. A gift shop offers a variety of malt whiskies. *358 Castlehill,* ☎ *0131/220–0441.* ☞ *£3.80 adults, £2 children, £2.30 senior citizens, £3.20 students, £10.60 family ticket.* ⊙ *Daily 10–5 (extended hours in summer).*

❺ Farther down on the right the Gothic **Tolbooth Kirk,** built in 1842–44 for the General Assembly of the Church of Scotland (*kirk* means *church*), boasts the tallest spire in the city—240 feet.

Continuing down to the intersection at the end of Castlehill, look for
❻ the **Upper Bow** on the right, immediately east of where Johnston Terrace joins the Lawnmarket. This was once the main route westward from town and castle. Before Victoria Street was built, in the late 19th century, Upper Bow led down into a narrow dark thoroughfare canyoned with tenements. All traffic struggled up and down this steep slope from the Grassmarket, which joins the now-truncated West Bow at its lower end.

From **Lawnmarket** you can start your discovery of the **Old Town closes,** alleyways that are like ribs leading off the Royal Mile backbone.

TIME OUT There are a number of atmospheric pubs and restaurants in this section of the Royal Mile. Try the **Jolly Judge** (James Ct.), a friendly pub where bright firelight brightens the dark-wood beams.

Edinburgh

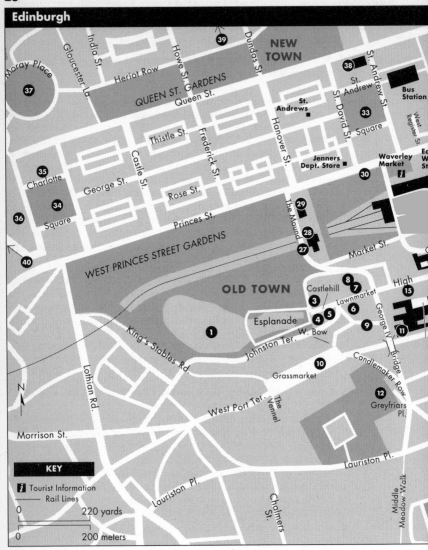

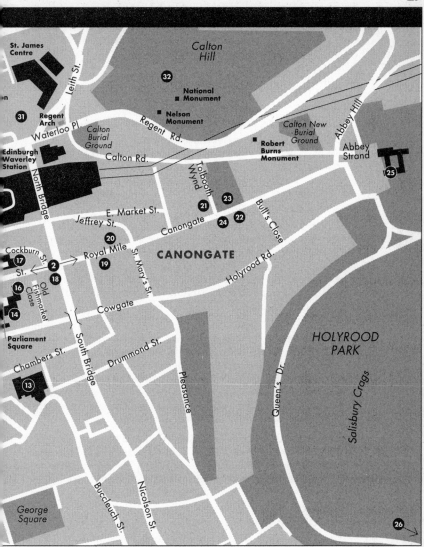

Royal Museum of
Scotland, **13**

Royal Scottish
Academy, **29**

St. Andrew Square, **33**

Scotch Whisky
Heritage Centre, **4**

Scott Monument, **30**

Scottish National
Gallery of Modern
Art, **40**

Scottish National
Portrait Gallery/
Museum of
Antiquities, **38**

Tolbooth Kirk, **5**

Tron Kirk, **18**

Upper Bow, **6**

Victoria Street, **9**

West Register
House, **36**

The Writers'
Museum, **8**

7 The narrow six-story tenement known as **Gladstone's Land,** just beside the Assembly Hall on the left, is a survivor from the 17th century, demonstrating typical architectural features, including an arcaded ground floor and an entrance at second-floor level (livestock sometimes inhabited the ground floor). It is furnished in the style of a 17th-century merchant's house. *Lawnmarket,* ☎ *0131/226–5856.* ✆ *£2.50 adults, £1.30 children, students, and senior citizens.* ☉ *Apr.–Oct., Mon.–Sat. 10–5, Sun. 2–5. Last admission 4:30 PM.*

8 Close by Gladstone's Land, down yet another close, is **The Writers' Museum,** housed in a building known as Lady Stair's House, a good example of 17th-century urban architecture. Built in 1622, it evokes Scotland's literary past with exhibits on Sir Walter Scott, Robert Louis Stevenson, and Robert Burns. *Off Lawnmarket,* ☎ *0131/225–2424, ext. 4901.* ✆ *Free.* ☉ *June–Sept., Mon.–Sat. 10–6, Sun. during festival 2–5; Oct.–May, Mon.–Sat. 10–5.*

For a worthwhile shopping diversion, turn right down George IV **9** Bridge, then down **Victoria Street** to the right, a 19th-century addition to the Old Town. Its shops offer antiques, new designer clothing, and **10** high-quality giftware. Down in the **Grassmarket,** which for centuries was, as its name suggests, an agricultural market, the shopping continues, and there are numerous bars and restaurants which make this a hub of activity at night.

Sections of the Old Town wall can be approximately traced on the north (castle) side by a series of steps that runs steeply up from Grassmarket to Johnston Terrace above. By far the best-preserved section of the wall, however, is to be found by crossing to the south side and climbing the steps of the lane called **The Vennel.** Here you can see a section of the 16th-century **Flodden Wall,** which comes in from the east and turns southward at Telfer's Wall, a 17th-century extension. From here there are outstanding views northward to the castle.

On your way back across Grassmarket to the Royal Mile, note the cobbled cross set in the ground and railed off. This was the site of the town gallows. Among those hanged here were many 17th-century Covenanters (*see below*). Judges were known to issue the death sentence for these religious reformers with the words, "Let them glorify God in the Grassmarket."

Walk from the Grassmarket back along Victoria Street to George IV **11** Bridge, where you'll see the **National Library of Scotland** straight ahead. ☎ *0131/226–4531. Admission to exhibitions free.* ☉ *Mon., Tues., Thurs., Fri. 9:30–8:30, Wed. 10–8:30, Sat. 9:30–1.*

Turn right, walk over the bridge, and a little farther down, on the right, **12** is the **Kirk of the Greyfriars,** built on the site of a medieval monastery. Here, in 1638, the National Covenant was signed, declaring the independence of the Presbyterian Church in Scotland from government control. The covenant plunged Scotland into decades of civil war. *Greyfriars Pl.,* ☎ *0131/225–1900.* ✆ *Free.* ☉ *Easter–Sept., weekdays 10:30–4:30, Sat. 10:30–2; Oct.–Easter, Thurs. 1:30–3:30 only.*

At the corner of George IV Bridge and Candlemaker Row, near the Greyfriars church, stands one of the most-photographed sculptures in Scotland, *Greyfriars Bobby.* This famous West Highland terrier kept vigil beside his master's grave in the churchyard for 14 years, leaving only for a short time each day to be fed at a nearby pub after the one-o'clock salute from the castle.

Before returning to Lawnmarket, you might detour down Chambers Street, which leads off from George IV Bridge. Here, in an imposing **13** Victorian building, the **Royal Museum of Scotland** displays a broad collection drawn from natural history, archaeology, and scientific and industrial history. The great Main Hall, with its soaring roof, is architecturally interesting in its own right but will be enhanced by a major extension, to be completed in 1998. *Chambers St.,* ☎ *0131/225–7534.* ☛ *Free.* ☉ *Mon.–Sat. 10–5, Sun. 12–5.*

Return to High Street via George IV Bridge, and, near Parliament Square, look on the right for a heart set in cobbles. This marks the site of the vanished **Tolbooth,** the center of city life from the 15th century until the building's demolition in 1817. This ancient civic edifice, formerly housing the Scottish parliament and used as a prison from 1640 onward, inspired Scott's novel *The Heart of Midlothian.* Nearly every city and town in Scotland once had a tolbooth. Originally a customs house where tolls were gathered, the name came to mean "town hall" and later "prison" because detention cells were located in the basement.

14 **Parliament House**—the seat of Scottish government until 1707, when the crowns of Scotland and England were united—is partially hidden by the bulk of St. Giles's. It's now the home of the Supreme Law Courts of Scotland. Parliament Hall inside is remarkable for its hammer beam roof and its display of portraits by major Scottish artists. *Parliament Sq.,* ☎ *0131/225–2595.* ☛ *Free.* ☉ *Weekdays 9:30–4:30.*

15 The **High Kirk of St. Giles,** originally the city's parish church, became a cathedral in 1633 and is now often called **St. Giles's Cathedral.** There has been a church on the site since AD 854, although most of the present structure dates from 1829. The spire, however, was completed in 1495. The **Chapel of the Order of the Thistle,** bearing the belligerent national motto NEMO ME IMPUNE LACESSIT ("No one provokes me with impunity"), was added in 1911. *High St.,* ☎ *0131/225–4363. Kirk admission free. Thistle Chapel admission: 50p.* ☉ *Mon.–Sat. 9–5 (until 7 in summer), Sun. 2–5 (services 8 AM, 10 AM, 11:30 AM, 8 PM).*

Another landmark in Old Town life can be seen just outside Parliament House. The **Mercat Cross** (*mercat* means *market*), a focus of **16** public attention for centuries, is still the site of royal proclamations. The cross itself is modern, but part of its shaft is as old as the city.

TIME OUT **Le Sept,** a popular bistro-style restaurant, does a brisk business at lunchtime, with reasonably priced French dishes; try the crêpes, omelets, or roast lamb. *7 Old Fishmarket Close.* ☉ *Daily noon–2:15 and 6–10:30.*

17 Across High Street from St. Giles's are the **City Chambers,** now the seat of local authority. Designed by John Adam in 1753, the building brings a flavor of the New Town's neoclassicism to the Old Town's severity. The chambers were originally known as the Royal Exchange and intended to be a place where merchants and lawyers could conduct business. Note that the building drops 12 stories to Cockburn Street on its north side.

18 Farther down on the right is the **Tron Kirk.** A "tron" is a weigh beam used in public weigh houses, and the church was named after a salt tron that used to stand nearby. The kirk itself was built after 1635, when St. Giles's became an Episcopal cathedral for a brief time. In this church in 1693 a minister offered an often-quoted prayer for the local government: "Lord, hae mercy on aa [every] fool and idiot, and particularly on the Magistrates of Edinburgh."

19 On the right, two blocks past the North Bridge–South Bridge junction, is the not-to-be-missed **Museum of Childhood,** a celebration of toys that even adults will enjoy. *42 High St.,* ☎ *0131/225–2424.* ☞ *Free.* ☺ *June–Sept., Mon.–Sat. 10–6, Sun. during festival 2–5; Oct.–May, Mon.–Sat. 10–5.*

20 Opposite is **John Knox House.** It is not certain that Scotland's severe religious reformer (1514–72) lived here, but mementos of his life are on view inside. This distinctive dwelling offers a glimpse of what Old Town life was like in the 16th century. The projecting upper stories were once commonplace along the Royal Mile, darkening and further closing in the already narrow passage. Look for the initials of former owner James Mossman and his wife, carved into the stonework on the "marriage lintel." Mossman was goldsmith to Mary, Queen of Scots, and was hanged in 1573 for his allegiance to her. *45 High St.,* ☎ *0131/ 556–2647.* ☞ *£1.25 adults, 75p children, £1 senior citizens.* ☺ *Mon.–Sat. 10–4:30.*

Beyond this point you would once have passed out of the safety of the town walls. A plaque outside the **Netherbow Arts Centre** depicts the **Netherbow Port,** a gate that once stood on the site. Look for the brass studs in the street cobbles that mark its location.

Below is the **Canongate,** named for the canons who once ran the abbey at Holyrood, now the site of Holyrood Palace. In Scots, "gate" means "street." Canongate itself was originally an independent "burgh," another Scottish term used to refer to a community with trading rights granted by the monarch. This explains the presence of the handsome **21** **Canongate Tolbooth,** on the left, where the town council once met. Now the tolbooth houses a museum called The People's Story, which focuses on the lives of "ordinary" people from the 18th century to today; special displays include a reconstruction of a cooper's workshop and a 1940s kitchen. *Canongate Tolbooth,* ☎ *0131/225–2424, ext. 4057.* ☞ *Free.* ☺ *June–Sept., Mon.–Sat. 10–6, Sun. during festival 2–5; Oct.–May, Mon.–Sat. 10–5.*

22 Opposite the tolbooth is gable-fronted **Huntly House** (1570), now a museum of local history. The exhibits include collections of Scottish pottery and Edinburgh silver and glass. *142 Canongate,* ☎ *0131/225–2424, ext. 4143.* ☞ *Free.* ☺ *June–Sept., Mon.–Sat. 10–6, Sun. during festival 2–5; Oct.–May, Mon.–Sat. 10–5.*

23 In the graveyard of **Canongate Kirk** are buried some notable Scots, including Adam Smith, author of *The Wealth of Nations* (1776), who once lived in 17th-century Panmure House nearby. Here you can also visit the grave of the undervalued Scots poet Robert Fergusson. The fact that Fergusson's grave is even marked is due to the efforts of the much more famous Robert Burns. On a visit to the city Burns was dismayed to find the grave had no headstone, so he commissioned an architect—by the name of Robert Burn—to design one. (Burn reportedly took two years to complete the commission, so Burns, in turn, took two years to pay.) Burn also designed the Nelson Monument, the tall column on Calton Hill to the north, which you can see from the churchyard.

Before you leave the cemetery, look for the monument to Robert Burns himself, also on Calton Hill and visible from the churchyard; it is the circular temple below Regent Road (*see* Tour 2: The New Town, *below*). Devotees of Burns will want to visit one other grave. Against the eastern wall of the churchyard is a bronze sculpture of the head of Mrs. Agnes McLehose, "Clarinda" of the copious correspondence

Burns engaged in while confined to his lodgings with an injured leg in 1788. Burns and Mrs. McLehose—an attractive and talented woman who had been abandoned by her husband—exchanged passionate letters for some six weeks that year, Burns signing his name "Sylvander"; Mrs. McLehose, "Clarinda." The missives were dispatched across town by a postal service that delivered them for a penny an hour. The curiously literary affair ended when Burns left Edinburgh to take up a farm tenancy and marry Jean Armour.

㉔ Opposite the churchyard is **Acheson House** (c. 1633), once a fine town mansion, which, like so much of the property in the Canongate, fell on hard times. It has been restored, as has Moray House, which dates from 1628, a little farther up the street.

TIME OUT You can get a good cup of tea and a sticky cake (a quintessentially Scottish indulgence) from **Clarinda's** (69 Canongate) or the **Abbey Strand Tearoom** (The Sanctuary, Abbey Strand), near the palace gates.

★ **㉕** Facing you at the end of Canongate are the elaborate wrought-iron gates of the **Palace of Holyroodhouse,** official residence of the queen when she is in Scotland.

The palace came into existence originally as a guest house for the Abbey of Holyrood, which was founded in 1128 by Scottish king David I. Before you enter the gates, look for the brass letters "SSS" set into the road at the beginning of Abbey Strand (the continuation of the Royal Mile beyond the traffic circle). The letters stand for "sanctuary" and recall the days when the former abbey served as a retreat for debtors (until 1880, when the government stopped imprisoning people for debt). Curiously, the area of sanctuary extended across the former royal hunting forest, now Holyrood Park, so debtors could get some fresh air without fear of being caught by their creditors. Oddest of all, however, was the agreement that after debtors checked in at Holyrood they were able to go anywhere in the city on Sunday. This made for great entertainment on Sunday evening as midnight approached: the debtors raced back to Holyrood before the stroke of 12, often hotly pursued by their creditors. The poet Thomas de Quincey and the comte d'Artois, brother of the deposed King Louis XVIII of France, were only two of the more exotic of Holyrood's denizens.

After the Union of the Crowns in 1603, when the Scottish Royal Court packed its bags and decamped for England, the building fell into decline. Oliver Cromwell, the Protestant Lord Protector of England, who had conquered Scotland, ordered the palace rebuilt after a fire in 1650, but the work was poorly carried out and lasted only until the restoration of the monarchy, after Cromwell's death. When Charles II ascended the British throne in 1660, he ordered Holyrood rebuilt in the architectural style of the French "Sun King," Louis XIV, and that is the palace that visitors see today.

In 1688 an anti-Catholic faction ran riot within the palace, and in 1745 the palace was occupied by Prince Charles Edward Stuart, during the last Jacobite campaign. After the 1822 visit of King George IV, in more peaceable times, the palace sank into decline once again. However, Queen Victoria and her grandson King George V renewed interest in the palace, and the buildings were once more refurbished and made suitable for royal residence.

When the royal family is not in residence, you can go inside for a conducted tour. The highlights include the **King James Tower,** the oldest surviving section, which contains the rooms of Mary, Queen of Scots, on the second floor, and Lord Darnley's rooms below. Though much has been altered, there are fine fireplaces, paneling, plasterwork, tapestries, and 18th-century furniture throughout the structure. Along the front of the palace, between the two main towers, are the duchess of Hamilton's room and the Adam-style dining room.

Along the southern side of the palace are the **Throne Room** and other drawing rooms now used mainly for social and ceremonial occasions. Among the rooms at the back of the palace is the **King's Bedchamber.** Another notable attraction is the **Picture Gallery,** which has a huge collection of portraits of Scottish monarchs (some of the royal figures honored here are actually purely fictional, and the likenesses of others are purely imaginary). All the portraits were painted by a Dutch artist, Jacob De Witt, who, in 1684, signed a contract with the Queen's Cashkeeper Hugh Wallace that bound De Witt to deliver 110 pictures within two years, for which he received an annual stipend of £120. Surely one of the most desperate scenes in the palace's history is that of the Dutch artist feverishly turning out potboiler portraits at the rate of one a week for two years. ☎ 0131/556–7371. *Recorded information* ☎ 0131/556–1096. ☛ *£3.50 adults, £3 senior citizens, £1.80 children, £9 family ticket.* ☺ *Apr.–Oct., Mon.–Sat. 9:30–5:15, Sun. 10:30–4:30; Nov.–Mar., Mon.–Sat. 9:30–3:45, Sun. 10–3:45; closed during royal and state visits.*

㉖ Behind the palace lie the open grounds and looming crags of Holyrood Park, which enclose Edinburgh's mini-mountain, **Arthur's Seat** (822 ft.). The park was the hunting ground of early Scottish kings. The views of the city and the surrounding area from the top of Arthur's Seat are breathtaking.

Tour 2: The New Town

At the dawn of the Scottish Enlightenment, in the 18th century, the city fathers busied themselves with various schemes to improve the capital. By that time Edinburgh's unsanitary ambience—created primarily by the crowded conditions in which most people lived—was becoming notorious. The well-known Scots fiddle tune "The Flooers (flowers) of Edinburgh" was only one of many ironic references to the capital's unpleasant atmosphere, which greatly embarrassed the Scot James Boswell, biographer and companion of the English lexicographer Dr. Samuel Johnson. In his *Journal of a Tour of the Hebrides,* Boswell recalled that on retrieving the newly arrived Johnson from his grubby inn in the Canongate, "I could not prevent his being assailed by the evening effluvia of Edinburgh. . . . Walking the streets at night was pretty perilous and a good deal odoriferous. . . ."

To help remedy this sorry state of affairs, in 1767 the city's Lord Provost (Scots for mayor), James Drummond, urged the town council to hold a civic competition to design a new district for Edinburgh. The winner was an unknown young architect named James Craig. His plan was for a grid of three main east–west streets, balanced at either end by two grand squares. These streets survive today, though some of the buildings that line them were altered by later development. Princes Street is the southernmost, with Queen Street to the north and George Street as the axis, punctuated by St. Andrew and Charlotte squares. A look at the map will show you the district's symmetry, unusual in Britain.

㉗ Start your walk on **The Mound,** the sloping street that joins the Old and New towns. The Mound originated in the need for a dry-shod crossing of the muddy quagmire that was left behind when Nor' Loch, the body of water below the castle, was drained (the railway now cuts through this area). The work is said to have been started by a local tailor, George Boyd, who tired of struggling through the mud en route from his New Town house to his Old Town shop. The building of a ramp was under way by 1781, and by the time of its completion, in 1830, "Geordie Boyd's mud brig" (bridge), as the street was first known, had been built up with an estimated 2 million cartloads of earth dug from the foundations of the New Town.

Two galleries immediately east of this great linking ramp are the work of W. H. Playfair (1789–1857), an architect whose neoclassical buildings contributed greatly to Edinburgh's title, the Athens of the North. ★ ㉘ The **National Gallery of Scotland,** immediately east of The Mound, has a wide selection of paintings, from the Renaissance to the Post-Impressionist period, with works by Velázquez, El Greco, Rembrandt, Turner, Degas, Monet, and Van Gogh, among others, as well as a fine collection of Scottish art. The rooms of the gallery are attractively decorated, and it is a pleasure to browse. *The Mound,* ☎ *0131/556–8921.* ☛ *Free.* ☉ *Mon.–Sat. 10–5 (extended during festival), Sun. 2–5. Print Room, weekdays 10–noon and 2–4, by arrangement.*

㉙ The other gallery, the **Royal Scottish Academy,** its imposing, columned facade overlooking Princes Street, holds an annual exhibition of students' work. *Princes St.,* ☎ *0131/225–6671. Admission charges vary depending on exhibition.* ☉ *Late-Apr.–July, Mon.–Sat. 10–5, Sun. 2–5.*

The north side of **Princes Street** is now one long sequence of chain stores whose unappealing modern fronts can be seen in almost any large British town. Luckily the other side of the street is occupied by well-kept gardens, which act as a wide green moat to the castle on its rock. Walk east until you reach the unmistakable 200-foot-high Gothic spire of ㉚ the **Scott Monument,** built in 1844 in honor of Scotland's most famous author, Sir Walter Scott (1771–1832), author of *Ivanhoe, Waverley,* and many other novels and poems. (Note the marble statue of Scott and his favorite dog.) On the death of Sir Walter Scott, public sentiment demanded a grand acknowledgment of the work of the then wildly popular writer. After much delay the committee supervising the construction of a suitable memorial announced a competition for its design. (If in doubt about how to proceed with any civic development, the burghers of Edinburgh usually hold a competition.) After the Gothic structure that you now see was chosen, the committee was somewhat dismayed to learn that the design, submitted under a pseudonym, turned out to be not the work of a prestigious architect, but rather that of a carpenter and self-taught draughtsman, George Meikle Kemp. A well-traveled man, Kemp incorporated elements of France's Rheims Cathedral into his design for the monument. *Princes St.,* ☎ *0131/225–2424.* ☛ *£1.* ☉ *Apr.–Sept., Mon.–Sat. 9–6 (last admission 5:45); Oct.–Mar., Mon.–Sat. 9–3.*

Just opposite is **Jenners**—Edinburgh's equivalent of London's Harrod's department store. Jenners is noteworthy not only for its high-quality wares and good restaurants, but also because of the building's interesting architectural detail—baroque on the outside, with a mock-Jacobean central well inside. By way of a contrast, Edinburgh's newest shopping district is just beyond, on the other side of the road in the **Waverley Market.** This mall includes designer-label boutiques, and shops selling Scottish woolens and tweeds, whisky, and confections. There is another mall—the **St. James Centre**—farther on, beyond Register House.

㉛ Register House, opposite the main post office, marks the end of Princes Street. This was Scotland's first custom-built archives depository and was partly funded by the sale of estates forfeited by Jacobite landowners, following their last rebellion in Britain (1745–46). Work on the building, designed by Robert Adam, Scotland's most famous neoclassical architect, started in 1774. The statue in front is of the Duke of Wellington. *Princes St.,* ☎ *0131/556–6585.* ☛ *Free.* ☼ *Weekdays, legal collection 9:30–4:30, historical collection 9–4:30.*

TIME OUT   Immediately west of Register House is the **Café Royal** (17 W. Register St.), one of the city's most interesting pubs. It has good beer and lots of character, with ornate tiles and stained glass contributing to the atmosphere.

㉜ The monuments on **Calton Hill,** growing ever more noticeable ahead as you walk east along Princes Street, can be reached by first continuing along Waterloo Place, the eastern extension of Princes Street. There is some fine neoclassically inspired architecture on this street, all designed as a piece by Archibald Elliott. The Regent Bridge or, more precisely, the **Regent Arch**—a simple, triumphal, Corinthian-column conceit on top of the bridge, was intended as a war memorial. The road then continues in a single sweep through the **Calton Burial Ground** to the screen walling at the base of Calton Hill. On the left you'll see steps that lead to the hilltop. This was Robert Louis Stevenson's favorite view of his beloved city. Drivers—or walkers who don't feel up to the steep climb—can take the road farther on to the left, which loops up the hill at a more leisurely pace.

The architectural styles represented on Calton Hill include the Gothic—the Old Observatory, for example—and the neoclassical. Under the latter heading fall William Playfair's monument to his talented uncle, the philosopher and mathematician John Playfair, as well as his cruciform **New Observatory.** The piece that commands the most attention, however, is the so-called **National Monument,** often referred to as "Edinburgh's [or Scotland's] Disgrace." Intended to copy Athens's Parthenon, this monument for the dead of the Napoleonic Wars was started in 1822 to the specifications of a design by the ubiquitous Playfair. In 1830, however, only 12 columns later, money ran out, and the columned facade became a monument to high aspirations and poor fund-raising. The tallest monument on Calton Hill is the 100-foot-high **Nelson Monument,** completed in 1814 in honor of Britain's naval hero. ☎ *0131/556–2716. Admission Nelson Monument: £1.* ☼ *Apr.–Sept., Mon. 1–6, Tues.–Sat. 10–6; Oct.–Mar., Mon.–Sat. 10–3.*

After leaving Calton Hill you may wish to continue east along Regent Road, perhaps as far as the **Robert Burns Monument,** to admire the views westward of the castle and of the facade of the former Royal High School (directly above you). Then retrace your steps to the Waterloo Place traf-
㉝ fic lights and make your way to **St. Andrew Square** by cutting through the St. James Centre shopping mall, across Leith Street, and then through the bus station.

On St. Andrew Square, immediately south of the bus station, is the headquarters of the **Royal Bank of Scotland;** take a look inside at the lavish decor of the central banking hall. In the distance, at the other end of George Street, on Charlotte Square, you can see the copper dome of the former St. George's Church. In Craig's symmetrical plan for the New Town, a matching church was intended for the bank's site, but Sir Lawrence Dundas, a wealthy and influential baronet, somehow managed to acquire the space for his town house. The grand mansion was later converted into the bank. The church originally intended for the site, St. Andrew's, is a little farther down George Street on the right.

Walk west along George Street, with its variety of shops, noting on the way the statue of King George IV, at the intersection of George and Hanover streets. George IV visited Scotland in 1822; he was the first British monarch to do so since King Charles II, in the 17th century. By the 19th century Scotland was perceived at Westminster, distant English seat of Parliament, as being almost civilized enough for a monarch to visit in safety.

TIME OUT Hanover Street has a good choice of eateries. Try **La Lanterna** (83 Hanover St.), situated in a wood-panel basement, for value, cheerful service, and no-nonsense Italian home cooking.

The ubiquitous Sir Walter Scott turns up farther down the street. It was at a grand dinner in the Assembly Rooms (between Hanover and Frederick streets on the left) that Scott acknowledged having written the *Waverley* novels (the name of the author had hitherto been a secret.) You'll meet Scott once again, in the form of a plaque just downhill to your right, at 39 Castle Street, where he lived from 1797 until his death.

34 The essence of the New Town spirit survives in **Charlotte Square,** at the western end of George Street. Note the palatial facade of the square's north side, designed by Robert Adam—it is considered one of Europe's finest pieces of civic architecture. Here you will find the ★ **35** **Georgian House,** which the National Trust for Scotland has furnished in period style to show the elegant domestic arrangements of an affluent family of the late 18th century. The hallway was designed to accommodate sedan chairs, in which 18th-century grandees were carried through the streets. *7 Charlotte Sq.,* ☎ *0131/225–2160.* ☛ *£3 adults, £1.50 senior citizens and children.* ☼ *Apr.–Oct., Mon.–Sat. 10–5, Sun. 2–5 (last admission 4:30).*

Also in the square, the former St. George's Church, mentioned above **36** as part of the New Town Plan, now fulfills a different role, as **West Register House,** an extension of the original Register House. *Charlotte Sq.* ☛ *Free.* ☼ *Weekdays 10–4 (exhibitions) and 9–4:45 (research room).*

TIME OUT Try **Bianco's** (9–11 Hope St.), close to the Georgian House, for coffee and croissants. You never have to wait in line; the atmosphere is relaxed; the seats are comfortable; and the coffee, by Edinburgh standards, is very good.

37 To explore further in the New Town, choose your own route northward, down to the wide and elegant streets centering on **Moray Place,** a fine example of an 1820s development, with imposing porticoes and a central, secluded garden (for residents only).

★ **38** A neo-Gothic building on Queen Street houses the **Scottish National Portrait Gallery** and the **Museum of Antiquities.** The gallery contains a magnificent Gainsborough and portraits by the Scottish artists Ramsay and Raeburn. In the museum, don't miss the 16th-century Celtic harps and the Lewis chessmen—mysterious, grim-face chess pieces carved from walrus ivory in the Middle Ages. *Gallery and museum, Queen St.,* ☎ *0131/225–7534.* ☛ *Free.* ☼ *Mon.–Sat. 10–5, Sun. 2–5.*

39 Another attraction within reach of the New Town is the **Royal Botanic Garden.** Walk down Dundas Street, the continuation of Hanover Street, and turn left across the bridge over the Water of Leith, Edinburgh's small-scale river. These 70-acre gardens have the largest rhododendron and azalea collection in Britain. There is also a convenient cafeteria and a shop on the premises. *Inverleith Row,* ☎ *0131/552–7171,* FAX *0131/552–0382.* ☛ *Free (voluntary donation for greenhouses).* ⊙ *Mar., Apr., Sept., and Oct., daily 10–6; May–Aug., daily 10–8; Nov.–Feb., daily 10–4. Shop, café, and exhibition areas, Mar.–Oct., daily 10–5, Nov.–Feb., daily 10–3:30, closed Christmas and New Year's Day.*

㊵ The **Scottish National Gallery of Modern Art,** also close to the New Town, occupies a former school building on Belford Road and features paintings and sculpture, including works by Picasso, Braque, Matisse, and Derain. *Belford Rd.,* ☎ *0131/556–8921.* ☛ *Free.* ⊙ *Mon.–Sat. 10–5, Sun. 2–5 (extended during the festival).*

What to See and Do with Children

Edinburgh emphasizes its history and architecture to such a great degree that children's facilities have to be hunted down. The Tourist Centre above Waverley Market offers up-to-date listings of facilities and activities for children.

Leisure Centers and Activities

The **Brass Rubbing Centre,** near John Knox House on the Royal Mile, provides all the materials children (and adults) need to create do-it-yourself replicas from original Pictish stones and markers, rare Scottish brasses, and medieval church brasses. No experience is needed for this pastime, which children find quite absorbing. *Trinity Apse, Chalmers Close,* ☎ *0131/225–2424, ext. 4143.* ☛ *Free but a charge (40p–£10.50) is made for every rubbing.* ⊙ *June–Sept., Mon.–Sat. 10–6 (Sun. during festival 2–5); Oct.–May, Mon.–Sat. 10–5.*

Dalkeith Park is the nearest boisterous woodland-adventure playground (offering some cause for anxiety for the nervous parent). The more sedate will enjoy the woodland walks and 18th-century bridge. It is not suitable for toddlers. *Dalkeith Park, east end of Dalkeith High St., Dalkeith (10 mi south of Edinburgh; regular bus service from St. Andrew Sq. Bus Station),* ☎ *0131/663–5684.* ☛ *£2 for adult-and-child ticket.* ⊙ *Easter–Oct., daily 10–6.*

Hillend Ski Centre operates a ski school throughout the year that offers group and individual tuition on an artificial surface. All equipment can be rented, although there is nothing available for children under six years. *Biggar Rd. (south of the city),* ☎ *0131/445–4433. Charge for chair lift: £1.45 adults, 95p children and senior citizens.* ⊙ *July–Aug., weekdays 9:30–6, weekends 10:30–7; Sept.–June, weekdays 9:30–9, weekends 9:30–7.*

Little Marco's Leisure Centre is an indoor play area with slides, mazes, crawling tunnels, bouncy castles, and other paraphernalia for energetic toddlers. *51–59 Grove St.,* ☎ *0131/228–2341. Admission for 1½ hrs of supervised play: £3.50 children 4–10, £3 children under 4.* ⊙ *Weekdays 9:30–7, weekends 9:30–8.*

Museums

The **Museum of Childhood** (*see* Tour 1, *above*) appeals to both adults and children. The museum offers a collection of childhood memorabilia, vintage toys, and dolls, as well as a reconstructed schoolroom, street scene, fancy-dress party, and nursery. This often (cheerfully) noisy museum was the first in the world to be devoted solely to the history of childhood.

Zoos

Deep Sea World. This aquarium on the Firth of Forth offers a fascinating view of underwater life. Go down an acrylic see-through tunnel for a diver's eye look at over 5,000 fish, including nine recently acquired 8-foot sharks, and visit the exhibition hall with displays and an audiovisual presentation on local marine life. Ichthyophobes will feel more at ease in the adjacent café and gift shop. *North Queensferry,* ☎ *01383/411411.* ☛ *£4.50 adults, £3.25 children (and senior citizens on weekdays only), £13.50 family ticket.* ☉ *Apr.–Oct., daily 9–6; Nov.–Mar., weekdays 10–4, weekends and holidays 10–6, closed Christmas and New Year's Day.*

Edinburgh Butterfly and Insect World is a breath of the tropics—a sticky and humid, indoor, walk-through, junglelike experience filled with brightly colored butterflies and other creepy-crawlies. *Melville Nurseries, near Dalkeith,* ☎ *0131/663–4932.* ☛ *£3.25 adults, £1.90 children, £2.55 senior citizens and students, £9.30 family ticket.* ☉ *Mar.–Dec., daily 10–5 (last entry 4:30).*

Edinburgh Zoo offers traditional zoo delights plus animal contact and handling sessions in the main season, as well as its ever-popular Penguin Parade (held daily in summer). *Corstorphine Rd., beside Post House Hotel (4 mi west of city),* ☎ *0131/334–9171.* ☛ *£5 adults, £3.20 senior citizens, £2.70 children, £13 family ticket.* ☉ *Apr.–Sept., Mon.–Sat. 9–6, Sun. 9:30–6; Mar. and Oct., Mon.–Sat. 9–5, Sun. 9:30–5; Nov.–Feb., Mon.–Sat. 9–4:30, Sun. 9:30–4:30.*

Off the Beaten Path

Duddingston. Tucked behind Arthur's Seat—about an hour's walk from Princes Street via Holyrood Park—this little community (formerly of brewers and weavers) has an interesting church with a Norman doorway and a watchtower that was built to keep body snatchers out of the graveyard. The church overlooks Duddingston Loch, popular with birdwatchers, and moments away is an old-style pub called the Sheep's Heid Inn, which offers a variety of beers and the oldest skittle-alley in Scotland. *LRT Bus 42 or 46.*

Cramond. This compact settlement on the coast west of the city is the place to watch summer sunsets over the Firth of Forth, with the Cramond Inn nearby offering refreshment. The River Almond joins the main estuary here. Its banks, once the site of mills and works, now offer pleasant leafy walks and plenty to interest the industrial archaeologist. *LRT Bus 40 or 41 (41A in evening and on Sun.).*

Swanston. In the shadow of the Pentland Hills, this conservation village is in sight of, but a world apart from, the southern suburbs and bypass road. There are picturesque white-washed cottages and walks into the hills. Information boards explain the Robert Louis Stevenson connection—his family had a summer cottage here. *LRT Buses 4, 32, or 52 to Fairmilehead, then walk along the footpath leading west along the edge of the golf course. Also LRT Buses 11 and 15 to Comiston. Ask the conductor where to get off for Swanston.*

Leith. Edinburgh's ancient seaport has been revitalized in recent years, with the restoration of those fine commercial buildings that survived an earlier, and insensitive, redevelopment phase. It is worth exploring the lowest reaches of the Water of Leith, an area where pubs and restaurants now proliferate. *LRT Buses 7, 10, 14, 16, 17, 22, 25, 32, 34, 35, 52, or 87, or circle route 2/12.*

Colinton. Here you can sample the flavor of a leafy Edinburgh suburb on the banks of the Water of Leith. Tall trees shelter a riverside walkway that leads to (and beyond) Colinton's Parish Church, another site associated with Robert Louis Stevenson (his grandfather was the local minister). *LRT Buses 32, 45, 47, or 52, then look for signs to Colinton Dell.*

The Pentlands. This unmistakable range of hills immediately south of the city has the longest artificial ski slope in Britain, at Hillend, and an all-year chair lift offering magnificent views (even to nonskiers). There are several other access points along the A702 running parallel to the hills—the best is Flotterstone (where there is a parking lot, pub, and easy, quiet road-walking). *LRT Bus 4 or Edinburgh Transport 315 to Hillend, or 101/102 to Flotterstone (SMT service).*

SHOPPING

To make the most of shopping in Edinburgh you will need at least two days, in part because the town's most interesting shops are distributed among several districts. In Edinburgh's downtown are the High Street–type chain stores, lined up shoulder to shoulder and offering identical goods. But within a few yards, down some of the side streets, you'll find shops offering more exclusive wares, such as designer clothing, unique craft items, 18th-century silverware, and wild-caught, smoked Scottish salmon.

As the capital city and an important tourist center, Edinburgh features a cross section of Scottish specialties, such as tartans and tweeds, rather than products peculiar to the Edinburgh area. Once you venture into Edinburgh's "villages"—perhaps Stockbridge, Bruntsfield, Morningside, or even the Old Town itself—you will find many unusual stores specializing in single items, such as brushes, antique clocks, and designer knitwear using the finest Scottish wool and cashmere. In many cases the goods sold in these stores are unavailable elsewhere in Scotland.

If you are interested in antiques, Edinburgh should be a productive hunting ground. Scotland has a strong tradition of distinctive furniture makers, silversmiths, and artists; top-quality examples of their work can still be found, at a price. Most reputable dealers are able to arrange transport abroad for your purchases if you buy something too bulky to fit into your luggage. Antiques dealers tend to cluster together, so it may be easier to concentrate on one area—St. Stephen Street, Bruntsfield Place, Causewayside, or Dundas Street, for example—if you are short of time. Suggestions for particular shops are made below.

In most shops the prices quoted include the 17½% value-added tax (VAT), if applicable. For certain goods the VAT is not included in the price but will be added to the bill. In any case VAT may be reclaimed once you're home, and most shops that are accustomed to handling foreign customers will supply the necessary forms. Keep your receipt as proof of purchase—refunds will be refused without it.

Shopping hours are generally 9 to 5 or 5:30; many shops stay open until 7 or 8 on Thursday evening. Some of the more specialized shops, such as antiques dealers, may have shorter opening hours. Laws passed in Scotland (not in England) several years ago allow stores to open their doors on Sunday; though this practice has by no means been universally embraced by Scottish shopkeepers, you will find shops with Sunday hours, especially in the main tourist season.

Shopping Districts

Princes Street

Despite its renown as a shopping street, Princes Street in the New Town may disappoint many visitors with its dull, anonymous modern architecture, average chain stores, and fast-food outlets. It is, however, one of the best spots to shop for tartans, tweeds, and knitwear—especially if your time is limited—and the view upward toward the castle is still magnificent.

Holding their ground amid more ordinary stores are a few gems, the most noteworthy being **Jenners** (4 Princes St., ☎ 0131/225–2442), Edinburgh's last surviving independent department store, opposite the Scott Monument. Claiming to be the world's oldest department store (established in 1838), Jenners is housed in a handsome Victorian (and later) building, graced outside with caryatids, which emphasize the importance of women to the business. Although you can buy almost anything here, the store does specialize in china and glassware and in upmarket tweeds and tartans. Its Food Hall features Scottish products—shortbreads and Dundee cakes, honeys and marmalades, many available in attractive gift packs—as well as a range of high-quality groceries. **The Scotch House** (39–41 Princes St., ☎ 0131/556–1252) is popular with overseas visitors for its top-quality (if top-price) clothing and accessories.

Rose Street

One block north of Princes Street, Rose Street has many smaller specialty shops; part of the street is a traffic-free pedestrian zone, so it's a pleasant place to browse. **Alistir Tait** (116a Rose St., ☎ 0131/225–4105) offers a collection of high-quality antique and fine jewelry, silver, clocks, and crystal. If you plan on doing a lot of hiking or camping in the Highlands or the Islands once you leave Edinburgh, you may want to look over the selection of outdoor clothing, boots, jackets, and heavy- and lightweight gear at **Tiso** (121 Rose St., ☎ 0131/225–9486).

George Street

The shops here tend to be fairly upscale. London names, such as Laura Ashley, Liberty, and Waterstones bookshop, are prominent, though some of the older independent stores continue to do good business. Try **Waterstons** (35 George St., ☎ 0131/225–5690), not to be confused with Waterstones bookshop, not only for stationery but for an excellent selection of small gift items. **Grays** (89 George St., ☎ 0131/225–7381) is a long-established ironmonger and hardware store that believes in old-fashioned service. The jeweler **Hamilton and Inches** (87 George St., ☎ 0131/225–4898), established in 1866, is a silver- and goldsmith, worth visiting not only for its modern and antique gift possibilities, but also for its late-Georgian interior, designed by David Bryce in 1834—all gilded columns and elaborate plasterwork.

The streets crossing George Street—Hanover, Frederick, and Castle—are also worth exploring. **Dundas Street,** the northern extension of Hanover Street, beyond Queen Street Gardens, features several antiques shops. **Howe Street** (beyond Frederick St.) has Touch Wood (No. 19) for hand-crafted pine; Linens Fine (No. 22) for a wonderful selection of embroidered and embellished bed linen, tablecloths, cushion covers, and such; and In House (No. 30) for designer furnishings and collectibles at the forefront of modern design. At the foot of the street, Rowland's (No. 42) delicatessen will tempt you with excellent cheeses (try the Lanark Blue—a local specialty). **Thistle Street,** originally George

Street's "back lane," or service area, has several boutiques and more antiques shops, including Joseph Bonnar (No. 72) a specialist in antique jewelry. **South St. Andrew Street,** at the east end of George Street, is home to the oldest hatters in Scotland, Cunningham and Co. (No. 15) founded in 1817; this is the place to go for a genuine Scottish tammie or a length of tweed or cashmere.

The Royal Mile

As may be expected, many of the shops along the Royal Mile in the Old Town sell what may be politely or euphemistically described as tourist-ware. Careful exploration, however, will reveal some worthwhile establishments. For example, **Aika** (60 High St., ☎ 0131/556–3343) specializes in hand-knit garments in natural fibers—wool, cotton, angora, alpaca, mohair, silk, and linen. **Geoffrey (Tailor) Highland Crafts** (57–59 High St., ☎ 0131/557–0256) can clothe you in full Highland dress, with kilts made in its own workshops.

In addition to offering a good selection of whiskies, tartans, and tweeds, shops on the Royal Mile cater to some highly specialized interests and hobbies. For example, one store offers a large selection of playing cards, and another is devoted to doll houses and doll furniture.

Victoria Street/West Bow/Grassmarket

Close to the castle end of the Royal Mile, just off George IV Bridge, the specialty shops of Victoria Street are contained within a small area. If you aren't overwhelmed by the choices here, follow the tiny West Bow to Grassmarket for more of the same. The interior design shop **Ampersand** (18 Victoria St., ☎ 0131/226–2734) stocks a large selection of sundry collectibles, mostly jugs, plates, lamps, and vases, as well as unusual fabric by the meter. **Kinnels** (36 Victoria St., ☎ 0131/220–1150) combines a specialty coffee and tea shop with a relaxed, old-world coffee house, complete with a display of newspapers dating back to the early 1800s. **Robert Cresser's** (40 Victoria St., ☎ 0131/225–2181) brush shop features brushes of all kinds, every one handmade. **Bill Baber** (66 Grassmarket, ☎ 0131/225–3249) is one of the most imaginative of the many Scottish knitwear designers, and a long way from the conservative pastel "woollies" stocked by some of the large mill shops. Back up Victoria Street, try **Byzantium** (9A Victoria St., ☎ 0131/225–1768) for an eclectic mix of antiques, crafts, clothes—and an excellent coffee shop on the top level.

Stockbridge

North of Princes Street, on the way to the Botanic Gardens, this is an oddball shopping area of some charm, particularly on St. Stephen Street. Look for **Hand in Hand** (3 North West Circus Pl., ☎ 0131/226–3598) for beautiful antique textiles; there are also several antique furniture shops. To get to Stockbridge, walk down Frederick Street and Howe Street north away from Princes Street, then turn left onto North West Circus Place.

Stafford Street/William Street

This is a small, upscale shopping area in a Georgian setting. **Studio One** (10–16 Stafford St., ☎ 0131/226–5812) has a well-established and comprehensive inventory of kitchen goods and gift articles. **Something Simple** (10 William St., ☎ 0131/225–4650) stocks clothes for all occasions, including some designer names. **The Extra Inch** (16 William St., ☎ 0131/226–3303) stocks a full selection of clothes European size 38 and over. To get to this neighborhood, walk to the west end of Princes

Street and along its continuation, Shandwick Place, then turn into
Stafford Street. William Street crosses Stafford halfway down.

Department Stores

In contrast to other major cities, Edinburgh has few true department
stores. However, in the city center you will find **Jenners** (4 Princes St.,
☎ 0131/225–2442), Edinburgh's oldest department store, which specializes in traditional Scottish clothing and has a justly famous food
hall. **Frasers** (West End, Princes St., ☎ 0131/225–2472) is a part of
Britain's largest chain of department stores. The ubiquitous **John Lewis**
(69 St. James Centre, ☎ 0131/556–9121), specializing in furniture and
household goods, pledges that they are "Never Knowingly Under-
sold." Unlike Jenners, Frasers and John Lewis are not local, indepen-
dently owned firms, and the goods are similar to those stocked in other,
United Kingdom–wide branches. The High Street multiples, **Marks and
Spencer** (54 Princes St., ☎ 0131/225–2301), **Littlewoods** (91 Princes
St., ☎ 0131/225–1683), **British Home Stores** (64 Princes St., ☎
0131/226–2621), and so on, are also represented on Princes Street.
However, even given the competition, if you plan a morning or a
whole day wandering from department to department, trying on beautiful clothes, buying crystal or china, or stocking up on Scottish food
specialties, with a break for lunch at an in-store restaurant, then Jenners is the store to choose.

Arcades and Shopping Centers

Like most large towns Edinburgh has succumbed to the fashion for
"under one roof" shopping. If you dislike a breath of fresh air (or a
wonderful view) between shops—or if it's raining—try **Waverley Market** (east end of Princes St.), which offers three floors of shops and a
fast-food area. The **St. James Centre** (east end of Princes Street), has
recently undergone extensive refurbishment. **Cameron Toll** (bottom of
Dalkeith Rd.) shopping center, on the south side of the city, caters to
local residents, with food stores and High Street brand names. The newest
shopping center at **South Gyle** (on the outskirts of the city near the airport) is based on a typical US-style shopping mall. Here you will find
the High Street brand names again, including a huge Marks and
Spencer.

Clothing Boutiques

Edinburgh is home to several top-quality designers (although, it must
be said, probably not as many as are found in Glasgow, the country's
fashion center), some of whom make a point of using Scottish materials in their creations, such as **Bill Baber** and **Aika** (*see above*). Well-
heeled Edinburgh also has a branch of **Droopy and Brown** (37–39
Frederick St., ☎ 0131/225–1019), whose distinctive clothing—from
silk ball gowns and wedding dresses to flowing cord skirts and matching jackets, and pretty cotton print summer dresses—is guaranteed to
make the wearer stand out from the crowd. Equally unusual items can
be found at **Judith Glue** (64 High St., ☎ 0131/556–5443), which
stocks brilliantly patterned Orkney knitwear, as well as crafts, cards,
and candles.

If you are shopping for children, especially those who fit the tousled-
tomboy mold, try **Baggins** (12 Deanhaugh St., Stockbridge, ☎
0131/315–2011) for practical, reasonably priced clothes made from
natural fibers. All the clothes here are made to the owner's design in
the store-cum-workshop. **Sprogs** (45 William St., ☎ 0131/220–0320)

is a children's boutique offering end-of-season lines at 50%–70% off normal prices; designs tend to be modern.

Scottish Specialties

If you want to identify a particular tartan, several of the shops in Princes Street will be pleased to assist. The **Clan Tartan Centre** (70–74 Bangor Rd., Leith, ☎ 0131/553–5100) has extensive displays of various aspects of tartanry. For craftware, use as your quality guide the **Royal Mile Living Craft Centre** (12 High St., ☎ 0131/557–9350). Here, crafts are made on the premises, and you can talk to the craftspeople as they work. The range of items available includes hand-woven tartan, kilts, bagpipes, silver, pottery, and Aran knitwear; there is also the Taste of Scotland coffee shop. **Edinburgh Crystal** (Eastfield, Penicuik, ☎ 01968/675128) makes fine glassware that is stocked by many large stores and gift shops in the city center, but you can also visit its premises (visitor center, restaurant, and shop) at Penicuik, just south of the city. The complex is open Monday through Saturday from 9 to 5 and Sunday from 11 to 5. Tours are given weekdays 9:15–3:30. Admission runs £2 for adults, 50p for children, and £1 for senior citizens.

Bookstores

As a university city and cultural center, Edinburgh is well endowed with excellent bookshops, some of the most central being **James Thin, The Edinburgh Bookshop** (57 George St., ☎ 0131/225–4495; and 53 South Bridge, ☎ 0131/556–6743), and **Waterstones** (83 George St., ☎ 0131/225–3436, and 13/14 Princes St., ☎ 0131/556–3034). All stock a wide range of guides and books giving information about every aspect of Edinburgh life, and all have extended opening hours (until 10 PM on certain nights), including Sunday.

SPORTS AND FITNESS

Edinburgh has shared in the fitness boom of the past decade, as can be noted in **Holyrood Park,** where at almost any time of day or night joggers run the circuit around Arthur's Seat. The **Royal Commonwealth Pool** (nearby on Dalkeith Rd., ☎ 0131/667–7211), the largest swimming pool in the city, is part of a complex that includes a fitness center and a cafeteria. **Meadowbank Stadium** (northeast of the city center, ☎ 0131/661–5351) has facilities for more than 30 different track and indoor sports.

Some of the larger Edinburgh hotels have their own fitness centers. Examples include the **Calton Highland** (North Bridge; swimming pool, snooker, squash, gymnasium, massage), **Capital** (Clermiston Rd.; pool, gymnasium), **Edinburgh Sheraton** (Lothian Rd., pool, gymnasium), **Swallow Royal Scot** (Glasgow Rd.; pool, gymnasium), **Forth Bridges Moat House** (South Queensferry; pool, gymnasium, snooker, squash). Most facilities are free to guests, although there may be a charge for snooker and squash. The facilities are generally open to nonguests only through private membership.

Bicycling

Edinburgh is a fairly compact, if hilly, city, and **bicycling** is a good way of getting around, though careful route planning may be needed to avoid traffic. The East Lothian countryside, with its miles of twisting roads and light traffic, is within cycling distance of the city. Cycles may be hired from **Sandy Gilchrist Cycles** (1 Cadzow Pl., ☎ 0131/652–1760),

Secondhand Bike Shop (31–33 Iona St., Leith, ☎ 0131/553–1130), and **Central Cycle Hire** (13 Lochrin Pl., ☎ 0131/228–6333). Rates in summer are about £35 per week for a 3-speed, £50 for a 10-speed, and £50–£60 for a mountain bike. The Secondhand Bike Shop runs a sell-and-buy-back scheme for longer periods (say, more than two weeks), which can save you money.

Golf

Golf courses abound—there are about 20 courses within or close to the city (not including the easily accessible East Lothian courses), many of which welcome visitors. The Tourist Centre will provide local details, and the Scottish Tourist Board offers a free leaflet on golf in Scotland, available from the Edinburgh and Scotland Information Centre (*see* Important Addresses and Numbers in Essential Information, *above*). "SSS" indicates the "standard scratch score," or average score.

The following courses are open to visitors:

Braids (3 mi south of Edinburgh, ☎ 0131/447–6666). Course 1: 18 holes, 5,731 yards, SSS 68. Course 2: 18 holes, 4,832 yards, SSS 63. **Carrick Knowe** (5 mi west of Edinburgh, ☎ 0131/337–1096). 18 holes, 6,229 yards, SSS 70. **Craigentinny** (3 mi east of Edinburgh, ☎ 0131/554–7501). 18 holes, 5,418 yards, SSS 68. **Liberton** (Kingston Grange, 297 Gilmerton Rd., ☎ 0131/664–8580). 18 holes, 5,229 yards, SSS 66. **Lothianburn** (Biggar Rd., ☎ 0131/445–2206). 18 holes, 5,750 yards, SSS 69. **Portobello** (Stanley St., ☎ 0131/669–4361). 9 holes, 2,410 yards, SSS 32. **Silverknowes** (Silverknowes Pkwy., ☎ 0131/336–3843). 18 holes, 6,210 yards, SSS 70. **Swanston** (Swanston Rd., ☎ 0131/445–2239). 18 holes, 4,825 yards, SSS 64. **Torphin Hill** (Torphin Rd., ☎ 0131/441–1100). 18 holes, 5,025 yards, SSS 66.

For information on golfing throughout Scotland, *see* Chapter 2.

Skiing

At Hillend on the southern edge of the city is the longest artificial ski slope in the United Kingdom—go either to ski (equipment can be hired on the spot) or to ride the chair lift for fine city views. *Biggar Rd.,* ☎ *0131/445–4433. Charge for chair lift: £1.45 adults, 95p children and senior citizens.* ☉ *Apr.–June, Mon. and Fri. 9:30–6; Tues., Wed., and Thurs., 9:30–9, weekends 10:30–7; July and Aug., weekdays 9:30–6, weekends 10:30–7; Sept.–Mar., Mon.–Sat. 9:30–9, Sun. 9:30–7.*

Soccer and Rugby

The **Heart of Midlothian Football Club** (soccer) is based at Tynecastle (☎ 0131/337–6132) and its rival club **Hibernian** at Easter Road (☎ 0131/337–2346). **Murrayfield Stadium** (☎ 0131/337–8993) is the venue for international rugby matches. Crowds of good-humored rugby fans from Ireland and Wales add greatly to the atmosphere in the streets of Edinburgh during the early spring, when Scotland plays its international matches at Murrayfield.

DINING

Edinburgh is a sophisticated city, and its restaurants offer an interesting, diverse mix of traditional and exotic cuisines, from Scottish to Mexican, Thai, Chinese, Greek, and Russian.

Be sure, particularly at festival time, to make reservations well in advance. Also, be warned that there is an element of "it'd be fun to open a restaurant" about Edinburgh's eating scene; restaurants can open and close with the passing of a season.

Also note that it is possible to eat well in Edinburgh without spending a fortune. Even those restaurants that are ranked in the **$$$$** category could be squeezed into the top of the **$$$** range, depending on how one picks and chooses from the menu. A service charge of 10% may be added to your bill, though this practice is not adhered to uniformly. If no charge has been added and you are satisfied with the service, a 10% tip is appropriate.

Dining hours in Edinburgh are much the same as in the rest of Great Britain, with the main rush at lunchtime, from 1 to 2, and at dinner, from 8 to 9.

What to Wear
Restaurants in Edinburgh tend to be casual. Generally, the more expensive places prefer a jacket and/or tie; we tell you where this is advisable.

CATEGORY	COST*
$$$$	over £30
$$$	£20–£30
$$	£15–£20
$	under £15

per person for a three-course meal, including VAT and excluding drinks and service

$$$$ **The Grill Room.** Set in the Edwardian splendor of the Balmoral Hotel, the Grill Room has established itself at the top end of Edinburgh's dining scene. The room has a luxurious ambience created by a green marble floor, Chinese lacquer wall panels, an abundance of silver and crystal, and an Oriental theme. The seating is particularly comfortable, and the tables are widely spaced, which makes it a great place for a private conversation or romantic dinner. The service is formal but relaxed, with no pressure to finish up. As its name suggests, the restaurant specializes in grills, which you can see being cooked on the open grill, but there is also an extensive à la carte menu. ✕ *Princes St., ☎ 0131/557–6727. Reservations required. Jacket and tie. AE, DC, MC, V.*

$$$$ **L'Auberge.** A number of Edinburgh restaurants take the best Scottish food and prepare it French style, but L'Auberge is French through and through. A large number of tables are set for two—the French are so romantic here in the heart of reserved Edinburgh. The menu is all in French with only a cursory translation; owner-manager Monsieur Daniel will be glad to explain the recipes to you in detail. The menu changes frequently, but you may be able to choose, for example, the terrine of seafood, the guinea fowl with mushrooms and claret sauce, or venison with Armagnac. The impressive wine list is French (unsurprisingly) and includes—unusual in Edinburgh—excellent dessert wines. ✕ *58 St. Mary St., ☎ 0131/556–5888. Reservations advised. Jacket and tie. AE, DC, MC, V. Closed Christmas Day, Dec. 26, New Year's Day.*

$$$$ **Pompadour.** Insulated by arched windows and lilac drapes from the
★ bustle of west-end Princes Street, the Pompadour aims to impress. The
decor, with its subtle plasterwork and rich murals, is inspired by the
court of Louis XV, as may be expected in a restaurant named after the
king's mistress, Madame de Pompadour. The cuisine is also classic French,
with top-quality Scottish produce completing the happiest of alliances.
The extensive well-chosen wine list complements such dishes as sea bass
with crispy leeks and caviar butter sauce, whole lobster with mustard
and cheese, or loin of venison with potato pancakes. This is the place
to go if you want a festive night out. It's more relaxed and informal
at lunchtime. ✕ *Caledonian Hotel, Princes St.,* ☎ *0131/225–2433.
Reservations advised. Jacket and tie. AE, DC, MC, V. No weekend lunch.*

$$$ **The Atrium.** With its cream-color tented fabric ceiling, smart cream cot-
ton chair covers, and wrought-iron candlesticks and candelabra of
most unusual design, the Atrium is a distinctive setting for pre- or post-
theater dinner (the Traverse Theatre is right next door). The chef-pro-
prietor Andrew Radford uses typical Scottish ingredients in very untypical
combinations: Curly kale, once the staple of every Scottish rural home,
may be married with beef, bacon, and shallots, and salmon might be
presented with zucchini, red pepper, and Parmesan. The menu changes
daily, but there is always a vegetarian option. The wine list has recently
been extended to include dessert wines. ✕ *10 Cambridge St. (beneath
Saltire Ct.),* ☎ *0131/228–8882. Reservations advised. Jacket and tie.
AE, MC, V.*

$$$ **Beehive Inn.** One of the oldest pubs in the city, the Beehive snuggles
in the Grassmarket, under the majestic shadow of the castle. Some 400
years ago the Beehive was a coaching inn, and outside the pub's doors
once stood the main set of city gallows, where over the centuries numerous executions were held. The upstairs **Rafters** restaurant lies hidden in an attractive and spacious attic room, crammed with weird and
wonderful junk. The menu features mostly steaks and fish: try the char-
coal-grilled trout with Drambuie and oregano sauce, or veal panfried
with thyme and mushrooms. ✕ *18/20 Grassmarket,* ☎ *0131/225–7171.
Reservations advised on weekends. AE, MC, V.*

$$$ **Kelly's.** This Scottish restaurant with a French influence is slightly off
the beaten track on the south side of the city but still only a short taxi
ride or 20-minute walk from the center. The entrance to this former
bakery, difficult to spot in a line of residential properties, leads into a
pine-furnished, peach-tinted dining room with only 9 or 10 tables. The
ambience is intimate, ideal for a quiet discussion over an unhurried meal.
Among the fine choices here are smoked Scottish salmon with mush-
rooms in Pernod sauce and Border lamb cutlets with a Grand-Marnier-
and-rosemary glaze. ✕ *46 W. Richmond St.,* ☎ *0131/668–3847.
Reservations advised. AE, MC, V. Lunch during festival only. Closed
Sun., Mon.*

$$$ **Martins.** Don't be put off by the look of this restaurant from the out-
★ side. It's tucked away in a little back alley between Frederick and Cas-
tle streets and has a typically forbidding northern facade. All's well inside,
though, and the menu emphasizes organically grown local products.
The best Scottish salmon, venison, fish, and west-coast shellfish appear in various forms—poached, baked, roasted, and in casseroles—
usually with inventive sauces. Starters may include rabbit liver and
mushrooms with wild-mushroom sauce or terrine of rabbit and chicory
with orange. There's also a far-famed cheese board. This is the place
for serious eating in an unstuffy atmosphere, and lunches are an excellent value. The wine list is serious but affordable and includes an
excellent choice of half-bottles. Smoking is not permitted. ✕ *70 Rose*

Edinburgh Dining and Lodging

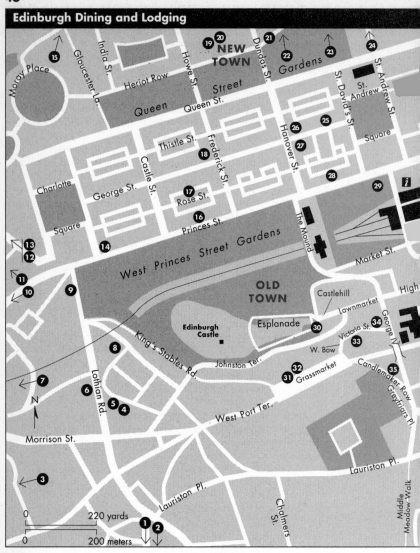

Dining

The Atrium, **8**
L'Auberge, **47**
Beehive Inn, **31**
Buntoms Thai
Restaurant, **23**
The Doric Tavern, **36**
The Grill Room, **29**
Hendersons, **27**
Howie's, **57**
Jackson's, **37**

Kalpna, **49**
Kelly's, **48**
Kweilin, **21**
Lancers, **15**
La Lanterna, **26**
Loon Fung, **4**
Martins, **17**
Merchants, **35**
Old Orleans, **5**
Peter's Cellars, **11**

Pierre Victoire, **32,
34, 41, 42**
Pompadour, **28**
Spices, **33**
Vito, **18**
Waterfront Wine
Bar and Bistro, **43**
The Witchery by
the Castle, **30**
Xian City Chinese
Restaurant, **38**

Lodging

Albany, **44**
Ashdene House, **50**
Balmoral Hotel, **29**
Caledonian, **9**
Channings, **12**
Classic Guest
House, **51**
Crannoch
But & Ben, **13**
Drummond House, **24**

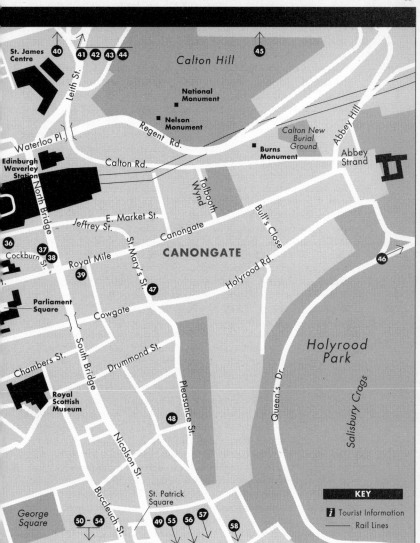

Edinburgh Grand Sheraton, **6**

Ellesmere Guest House, **2**

George Intercontinental, **25**

Howard Hotel, **22**

Lodge Hotel, **10**

Mount Royal Hotel, **16**

Mrs. Coleman, **52**

Mrs. Graham, **53**

Mrs. Valerie Livingstone, **46**

Norton House, **3**

Roselea House, **54**

Roxburghe, **14**

Royal Terrace, **45**

Scandic Crown, **39**

Sibbet House, **19**

Silverburn Steading, **1**

Stakis Grosvenor Hotel, **7**

Stuart House, **40**

Teviotdale House, **56**

Thrums Private Hotel, **55**

Turret Guest House, **58**

28 Northumberland Street, **20**

St. North La., ☎ *0131/225–3106. Reservations required. Jacket and tie. AE, DC, MC, V. No Sat. lunch. Closed Sun., Mon.*

$$$ **Merchants.** On a street running below George IV Bridge and only moments from the Grassmarket and looming Edinburgh Castle, Merchants is competent and reliable. The decor is gently understated, with pinewood flooring, crisp white tablecloths, cane chairs, and exposed beams. The light jazz music playing in the background is definitely not intrusive. A sophisticated fixed-price menu (lunch £9.50, dinner £15.50–£18.50) in French and English, has such adventurous moments as veal in dill and coriander; lamb chops with raspberry-and-mint sauce; and herb roulade filled with prawns and avocado mousse, with orange-and-tarragon vinaigrette. ✕ *17 Merchant St.,* ☎ *0131/225–4009. Reservations required. AE, DC, MC, V.*

$$$ **Spices.** As its name implies, this restaurant specializes in spicy foods drawn from places like India, Persia, Zanzibar, and Goa. Try the Murgh Reshmee Kebab (barbecue chicken breast), the Lamb Pukhraj with pistachios, or the Jhinga Imlidhar (king prawns with tamarind and spices). Don't be afraid to experiment with Spice's phenomenal menu—all dishes have individually chosen and freshly ground spices, a world away from the usual restaurant "curry." The stylish russet decor with black chairs is complimented with carved wooden screens and attentive service. Health-conscious people will appreciate Spice's no-smoking dining area. ✕ *110 West Bow,* ☎ *0131/225–5028. Reservations advised. MC, V. Closed Sun.*

$$$ **Vito.** Like La Lanterna (*see below*), this is a basement restaurant, but here you'll find a whitewashed wine cellar with vaulted ceiling, arches, and nooks and crannies for intimate meals. The vaguely rustic Italian decor complements the genuinely Italian cuisine (there's a southern Italian owner and northern Italian chef, so all regions are featured on the menu). Dishes include king prawns in a sauce of tomato, cream, and brandy, and veal stuffed with cheese and ham. The separate bar area is a good place for a quiet drink before dinner. ✕ *53A Frederick St.,* ☎ *0131/225–5052. Reservations advised. AE, DC, MC, V.*

$$$ **The Witchery by the Castle.** As the name indicates, a somewhat eerie ambience—complete with flickering candlelight—reigns here. There are, in fact, supposed to be three ghosts in the place, one of whom haunts the refrigerator! The lugubrious, cavernous interior is festooned with cauldrons and broomsticks and decorated with cabalistic insignia. The inspiration for this spooky haunt derives from the fact that some 300 years ago hundreds of witches were executed on the Castlehill, barely a few dozen yards from where you will be seated. There's nothing spooky about the food, however, with fine venison, duck, lamb, salmon, and fillet steak among the specialties. There's a £19.90 prix fixe dinner menu. ✕ *352 Castlehill, Royal Mile,* ☎ *0131/225–5613. Reservations required. AE, DC, MC, V.*

$$ **Buntoms Thai Restaurant.** A room in the Linden Hotel was converted into this authentic-looking Thai restaurant by the addition of genuine Thai wall coverings and antiques. You can leave Georgian New Town at the door and be transported halfway around the world with such savory delights as hot-and-sour squid and mushroom salad, seafood cooked with broccoli in oyster sauce, or spiced chicken fried with cashew nuts and onions (one of this restaurant's best offerings). Don't come here if you're on a tight schedule—each dish is prepared fresh, but it's definitely worth the wait, and you'll want to savor each bite. ✕ *Linden Hotel, 9–13 Nelson St.,* ☎ *0131/557–4344. Reservations required. AE, DC, MC, V. Closed Sun. lunch.*

$$ Jackson's. Intimate and candlelit in a historic Old Town close, Jackson's offers good Scots fare, including excellent Aberdeen Angus steaks and Border lamb. Seafood and vegetarian specialties are always on the menu. The decor is rustic, with lots of greenery, stone walls, pine farmhouse-style tables and chairs, and fresh flowers. The wine list includes 60 malt whiskies and some Scottish country wines to complete the Scottish experience. ✕ *2 Jackson Close, 209–213 High St., Royal Mile,* ☎ *0131/225–1793. Reservations advised. AE, MC, V. Closed for lunch Sat. and Sun.*

$$ Kweilin. This pleasant family-run restaurant in Edinburgh's sedate New Town is popular with the city's Chinese community, as well as with tourists. The decor is traditional Chinese, with several large paintings depicting scenes from the Kwangsi province, of which Kweilin is the capital. There are always several suggested menus for two, three, or four diners, which are recommended; but you can, of course, select your own combinations of dishes. The fixed-menu offerings are a good value, starting at £13.50 per person and going up to £21.50 a head for the Executive Choice menu. ✕ *19–21 Dundas St.,* ☎ *0131/557–1875. Reservations advised. MC, V.*

$$ La Lanterna. This inconspicuous basement-level trattoria serves whole-
★ some and straightforward pastas—among them tagliatelle carbonara and spaghetti mare—and other Italian dishes, all in the best of humor. The family who runs the business can afford to be cheerful—their straightforward approach is popular and packs in the customers. The decor is pine-walled and postcard-pinned. Seats are comfortable, though tables are set close. The restaurant is well located in center city, two minutes from Princes Street. ✕ *83 Hanover St.,* ☎ *0131/226–3090. Reservations advised. AE, MC, V. Closed Sun.*

$$ Lancers. This intimate Indian restaurant, decorated with rosewood tables and chairs, is located in the Stockbridge area of Edinburgh, just a short taxi ride from city center. It's on a fairly busy road, but external distractions are blocked out by window blinds, which add to the sense of intimacy. The feel of this place is a little like that of an officers' mess in Bengal, which is entirely appropriate, since it was named after the famed Bengal Lancers, who fought with such distinction alongside the British army in every quarter of the globe. As a simple introduction to Bengali cuisine, you could try the vegetarian (or non-vegetarian) *thali* (a sampler tray including rice, lentils, curries, and more); those already initiated to the delights of this cuisine can pick and choose among varieties of *pasandas, kurmas, tikkas,* and *bhundas.* ✕ *5 Hamilton Pl.,* ☎ *0131/332–3444 or 0131/332–9559. Reservations advised. AE, MC, V.*

$$ Old Orleans. A first in Edinburgh: Cajun cooking, served with real Southern panache, plus Mexican and American dishes that include red snapper and alligator. Choose the spareribs and you are thoughtfully provided with a large bib and finger bowl of hot water. Decor is typical New Orleans: trellis and metalwork, brass instruments, and travel-related items; the music is blues and jazz. There is also a large, mirrored, American-style bar. ✕ *30 Grindlay St.,* ☎ *0131/229–1511. Reservations advised. AE, MC, V.*

$–$$ The Doric Tavern. Do not be put off by the rather tatty entrance staircase plastered with posters and playbills: Inside this café–bistro bar, the stripped wood floor, dark wood tables, and navy velvet curtains create a superbly subdued, languid atmosphere. The menu always features a daily special—like roast pigeon salad with raspberry vinegar dressing—and a selection of fresh fish poached with basil and cream. Lunch can be anything from a large salad, perhaps with strips of venison, to chicken with tarragon or a wild mushroom stir-fry. If you still can't decide, try the fixed-price lunch (£8.50–£11.50) or dinner (£11.50–£16.75), both excellent values. ✕ *15/16 Market St.,* ☎ *0131/ 225–1084. Reservations advised Fri. and Sat. nights. AE, MC, V. Closed Sun. Restaurant closes 11 PM (last orders 10:30), wine bar open until 1 AM weekdays, 2 AM weekends.*

$–$$ Hendersons. This was Edinburgh's original vegetarian restaurant, long before it was fashionable to offer wholesome, meatless creations. If you haven't summoned the courage to try an authentic haggis while in Scotland, come here to sample a vegetarian version. ✕ *94 Hanover St.,* ☎ *0131/225–2131. Reservations not required. AE, DC, MC, V. Closed Sun. except during festival.*

$–$$ Howie's. This simple neighborhood bistro doesn't have a liquor license, but you can bring your own bottle. The steaks are tender Aberdeen beef, the Loch Fyne herring are sweet-cured to Howie's own recipe, and the clientele is lively. ✕ *75 St. Leonard's St.,* ☎ *0131/668–2917 (also at 63 Dalry Rd.,* ☎ *0131/313–3334). Reservations advised. MC, V.* ☼ *Lunch Tues.–Sun., dinner daily.*

$–$$ Kalpna. This vegetarian Indian restaurant is on the city's south side,
★ close to the university. Don't be put off by the unremarkable facade among an ordinary row of shops, or by the low-key decor enlivened by Indian prints and fabric pictures: The food is unlike anything you are likely to encounter elsewhere in the city. If you can't decide what you want to eat, order an Anapurna Thali, a sampler tray that generally comes with curried vegetables or meats complimented with coconut, peas, melt-in-the-mouth halva, fresh coriander, and a touch of garlic. Kalpna tends to fill up as the evening progresses, so book ahead if you want to eat after 8. At lunchtime and in the early evening (except perhaps at festival time) you can usually just drop in. ✕ *2/3 St. Patricks Sq.,* ☎ *0131/667–9890. Reservations advised for dinner. MC, V. Closed Sun., Christmas Day, Dec. 26, New Year's Day.*

$–$$ Loon Fung. Seafood is the specialty of this Cantonese restaurant. Delicious dishes include jumbo king prawns with garlic sauce and black pepper, fresh mussels with ginger and black bean sauce, and fried oysters with ginger and spring onions. The Loon Fung is small, friendly, and candlelit, with rapid service. The green and pink decor is relaxing, although tables are quite closely spaced. For two or more people, the set menu banquets are a good value. A take-out menu is available. ✕ *32 Grindlay St.,* ☎ *0131/229–5757. Reservations advised. AE, MC, V.*

$–$$ Peter's Cellars. With a traditional "country cottage" look, complete with wooden booths, flowered curtains, and well-spaced tables, this cellar wine bar-cum-restaurant is a relaxing venue where you are not expected to dress up. The food, though not elaborate, is carefully cooked with some imaginative touches. Try the seafood ragout, pork kebabs with plum sauce, or supreme of chicken stuffed with pineapple and cream cheese. The fixed-price lunch (£7) and dinner (£15) are a good deal. ✕ *11–13 William St.,* ☎ *0131/226–3161. Reservations advised. AE, MC, V.*

$–$$ Pierre Victoire. Edinburgh has four branches of this very popular bistro chain. All are fairly chaotic, enjoyable eateries serving healthy portions of French country cooking at low prices. The fish is fresh and especially good. Try the baked oysters with bacon and hollandaise. ✕ *38 Grassmarket,* ☎ *0131/226–2442 (open daily); 10 Victoria St.,* ☎ *0131/225–1721 (closed Sun.); 8 Union St.,* ☎ *0131/557–8451 (closed Mon.); and 5 Dock Pl., Leith,* ☎ *0131/556–6178 (closed Sun.). Reservations advised. MC, V.*

$–$$ Waterfront Wine Bar and Bistro. In the heart of Leith, Edinburgh's port, and one of the city's longest-established wine bars, the Waterfront is always busy with a local crowd in their twenties and thirties: Don't come here if you want a quiet meal *à deux*. Blackboards listing wines and daily specials hang on the stone walls, surrounded by shipping memorabilia. Grilled sardines with rosemary butter, wild mushrooms (in season), pan-fried pigeon breasts with strawberry and orange sauce, and fillets of sea bass in white wine and cream sauce are examples of the food on offer. ✗ *1a Dock Pl., Leith,* ☎ *0131/554–7427. Reservations advised (essential on weekends). MC, V.*

$–$$ **Xian City Chinese Restaurant.** Named after the fabled home of Chinese warriors, the Xian City specializes in Cantonese fare and provides a wealth of choices: The menu runs to five pages, offering a selection of duck, chicken, beef, pork, and vegetarian creations, in addition to the seafood dishes that head the list. The walls are adorned with backlit Chinese scenes, and a large fish tank stands proudly in the middle of the restaurant, dividing it into two pleasant, comfortably sized dining rooms. Fixed-menu dinners are priced at around £15 per person for five courses. ✗ *217 High St., Royal Mile,* ☎ *0131/225–2999. Reservations advised. AE, MC, V.*

LODGING

Edinburgh offers a variety of accommodations, many in traditional Georgian properties, some even in the New Town, only a few minutes from downtown. There are also a number of upscale hotels in the downtown area, each with an international flavor. If you are planning to stay in the area during the festival, be sure to reserve several months in advance. Also note that weekend rates in the larger hotels are always much cheaper than midweek rates, so if you want to stay in a plush hotel, come on the weekend.

CATEGORY	COST*
$$$$	over £120
$$$	£100–£120
$$	£80–£100
$	under £80

All prices are for a standard double room, including service, breakfast, and VAT.

$$$$ **Balmoral Hotel.** The attention to detail in the elegant rooms and the
★ sheer élan that has re-created the Edwardian heyday of this former grand railroad hotel all contribute to the Balmoral's growing popularity. Staying here, below the impressive clocktower marking the east end of Princes Street, gives a strong sense of being at the center of Edinburgh life. The hotel's main restaurant is the plush and stylish Grill Room (*see* Dining, *above*). ☎ *Princes St., EH2 2EQ,* ☎ *0131/556–2414,* ℻ *0131/557–8740. 189 bedrooms, 21 suites. 2 restaurants, bar, wine bar, indoor pool, health club. AE, DC, MC, V.*

$$$$ **Caledonian.** A conspicuous block of red sandstone beyond the west
★ end of Princes Street Gardens, "the Caley" was built as the flagship hotel of the Caledonian Railway, and its imposing Victorian decor has been faithfully preserved. The public area has marbled green columns and an ornate stairwell with a burnished-metalwork balustrade. Rooms are exceptionally large and well appointed, and the generous width of the corridors reminds guests that this establishment was designed in a more sumptuous age. ☎ *Princes St., EH1 2AB,* ☎ *0131/225–2433,* ℻ *0131/225–6632. 239 rooms with bath. 2 restaurants, in-room VCRs. AE, DC, MC, V.*

$$$$ **Edinburgh Grand Sheraton.** Built in 1985, this property underwent a major refurbishment in 1993, when two new restaurants were added: the brasserie-style **Terrace,** overlooking Edinburgh Castle and Festival

Square, and the intimate **Grill Room,** serving fine fish, game, and Scottish beef. Bedrooms are well above average size, and many of them are decorated in traditional style with tartan furnishings and prints of old Edinburgh. The grandest rooms face the castle. You can enjoy piano music in the bar and lounge area, and there's a shopping gallery to browse in. A ground floor reception area features a sweeping grand staircase. The hotel's popularity with locals, especially after work and in the evening before and after concerts at Usher Hall, across the street, testifies to its continuing part in Edinburgh's social life. ⌨ *1 Festival Sq., EH3 9SR,* ☎ *0131/229–9131,* ℻ *0131/228–4510. 264 rooms with bath. 2 restaurants, bar, in-house movies, indoor pool, health club. AE, DC, MC, V.*

$$$$ **Royal Terrace.** Over 150 years ago, the renowned Edinburgh architect
★ Playfair designed the street called Royal Terrace as a tribute to King George IV. Most of the impressive Georgian homes on this block were owned by merchants, and the upper floors command a view across the Firth of Forth to Fife. The present hotel consists of a half dozen of these original merchant houses, combined to create one of the most luxurious lodgings in the city. The exterior is unassuming, giving no hint of the sybaritic interior. That this is a hotel devoted to comfort, however, becomes immediately apparent as one enters the reception area, which is deeply carpeted and adorned with a massive pair of chandeliers and an eclectic collection of objets d'art. All rooms are furnished to an equally high standard and even include telephones in the marble bathrooms. The best rooms—commanding the view across the city to the Forth— are on the top floors at the front. ⌨ *18 Royal Terr., EH7 5AQ,* ☎ *0131/557–3222,* ℻ *0131/557–5334. 97 rooms with bath. Restaurant, bar, pool, health club, in-house movies. AE, DC, MC, V.*

$$$ **Channings.** Five Edwardian terraced houses make up this elegant hotel
★ in an upscale neighborhood just minutes from the west end of Princes Street. Quiet rooms with restrained colors, antiques, and great views of Fife (from those facing north) set an elegant and refined tone. The **Brasserie** restaurant offers excellent value, especially at lunchtime; try the crab cakes with crayfish bisque. ⌨ *South Learmonth Gardens, EH4 IEZ,* ☎ *0131/315–2226,* ℻ *0131/332–9631. 48 rooms with bath. Restaurant. AE, DC, MC, V.*

$$$ **George Intercontinental.** Part of this hotel served as an insurance-com-
★ pany office during the 19th century, and the splendidly ornate business hall remains intact as the Carvery Restaurant, the less expensive of the two dining rooms. The hotel's modern extension, added in 1972, is carefully blended with the original structure (1881), and the George retains a more intimate feeling than you'd expect from a rather large hotel. Major renovations throughout 1994–5 helped make the guest rooms with reproduction-antique furnishings, light, airy, and immaculate; sizes range from adequate to spacious, and the desks are unusually large. The best rooms are at the back of the hotel, high up and looking north over the New Town roofs to the Firth of Forth and to Fife beyond. However, even rooms overlooking George Street southward are quiet, and they have bird's-eye views of the 18th-century surroundings. The central location, only yards from the financial center of St. Andrew Square, has only one disadvantage: difficult parking. The pricey French-style Le Chambertin restaurant has excellent food, and its sommelier is one of only two members of the Guild of Master Sommeliers in Scotland. ⌨ *19–21 George St., EH2 2PB,* ☎ *0131/225– 1251,* ℻ *0131/226–5644. 195 rooms with bath. 2 restaurants, bar, minibars. AE, DC, MC, V.*

$$$ **Howard Hotel.** The Howard, close to Drummond Place, is a good example of a New Town building, elegant and superbly proportioned. It

is also small enough to offer personal attention. All bedrooms are spacious and well equipped—you'll find trouser presses, hairdryers, and tea- and coffee-making equipment, for example—and some overlook the garden. ☎ *32 Great King St., EH3 6QH,* ☎ *0131/557–3500,* FAX *0131/557–6515. 16 rooms with bath. Restaurant. AE, DC, MC, V.*

$$$ **Mount Royal Hotel.** Perched above the ground-floor shops on Princes Street and overlooking Edinburgh Castle and the Princes Street Gardens, the entrance to the Mount Royal is almost hidden between two of the city's major stores (Jenners and Marks & Spencer) and could easily be overlooked at first. Bedrooms have wood furnishings and pastel color schemes; the best views are from the rooms at the front of the hotel. ☎ *52 Princes St., EH2 2DQ,* ☎ *0131/225–7161,* FAX *0131/220–4671. 159 rooms with bath. Restaurant. AE, DC, MC, V.*

$$$ **Norton House.** This magnificent 1861 manor house was once the home of the Usher brewing family and still has the feeling of a private country home. Situated on idyllic grounds on the outskirts of Edinburgh, the Norton House provides a lovely alternative to downtown lodgings, yet is easily accessible from center city. The elegant and recently refurbished reception area is graced by marble pillars, and there is a striking wooden staircase leading to the upper floors. The airy guest rooms are decorated with modern furniture and delicate pastel shades. Guests can choose between two restaurants—the elegant main dining room inside, which offers decent Continental food, or the Conservatory, with its fine views of the gardens. ☎ *Ingliston, EH28 8LX,* ☎ *0131/333–1275; fax 0131/333–5305. 47 rooms with bath. 2 restaurants, bar, free parking, airport shuttle. AE, DC, MC, V.*

$$$ **Scandic Crown.** Although it was built late in the 1980s, this modern hotel blends into its surroundings among the ancient buildings on the Royal Mile. Its location is a good reason to stay here. Bedrooms are spacious, neat, and plain—practical rather than luxurious. The restaurant serves some Scandinavian dishes, including a smorgasbord. ☎ *80 High St., Royal Mile, EH1 1TH,* ☎ *0131/557–9797,* FAX *0131/557–9789. 238 rooms with bath. Restaurant, indoor pool, health club, meeting rooms. AE, DC, MC, V.*

$$$ **Stakis Grosvenor Hotel.** This attractive, comfortable hotel in the West End comprises several converted terrace houses and is distinguished by an elegant Victorian facade. Guests are pampered as soon as they enter the large reception area, which is furnished with ample Chesterfield armchairs. The single rooms are fairly small, and the doubles are just adequate. All are brightly decorated with peach curtains and floral bedspreads; the furniture is made of dark wood. First- and second-floor bedrooms have high ceilings with attractive plaster cornices. Just a short walk from the West End's shopping district, the hotel is convenient to the Haymarket railway station. ☎ *Grosvenor St., EH12 5EA,* ☎ *0131/226–6001,* FAX *0131/220–2387. 136 rooms with bath. Restaurant, 2 bars. AE, DC, MC, V.*

$$ **Albany.** Three fine Georgian houses with many original features have been carefully converted into this comfortable city-center hotel. Rooms have high ceilings, neutral color schemes, and plain brown furnishings. Multicolored bedspreads match the curtains, a pleasant compliment to the furniture. There's a good restaurant in the basement and a bar with piano. ☎ *39 Albany St., EH1 3Q4,* ☎ *0131/556–0397,* FAX *0131/557–6633. 20 rooms with bath. Restaurant, bar. MC, V.*

$$ **Roxburghe.** As you sit in a deep leather armchair, the ticking of an antique clock in the background, and look out over the trees of Charlotte Square, it is easy to forget you are half a minute from Princes Street and in the heart of Edinburgh's financial center. The furniture, which includes many antique pieces, has the sheen of generations of polish.

In the rooms, Adam fireplaces and ornate plasterwork complement the hotel's harmonious Georgian architecture. This country-house-come-to-town moves nearer modern times with its busy bar and informal ground-floor restaurant, **The Melrose Room,** but becomes positively overdone in its excessively draped, main dining room downstairs. (The food, unlike the decor, is forgettable.) Not as expensive as the Sheraton or the Caledonian, the Roxburghe is hard to beat for a convenient location, though it can be a little noisy. ⊠ *38 Charlotte Sq., EH2 4HG,* ☎ *0131/225–3921,* ﬀ *0131/220–2518. 75 rooms with bath. Restaurant, bar, coffee shop. AE, DC, MC, V.*

$ **Ashdene House.** On a quiet residential street on the south side of Edinburgh, yet only 10 minutes from the city center by bus, this Edwardian house is a first-class bed-and-breakfast where smoking is not permitted. Bedrooms are decorated without frills or flounces—just modern furnishings and floral fabrics—but in the downstairs public areas, deep, rich color schemes complement the age of the house. The owners are particularly helpful in arranging tours and evening theater entertainment, and they will recommend local restaurants. There is ample parking on the street and in a lot. ⊠ *23 Fountainhall Rd., EH9 2LN,* ☎ *0131/667–6026. 5 rooms with shower. Free parking. No credit cards.*

$ **Classic Guest House.** It is easy to find this Victorian terraced house, on a main route from the south into Edinburgh. The decor is modern classic: stripped pine floors throughout, elegant chinoiserie in the dining room, and pastel florals in the warm bedrooms. Smoking is not permitted. ⊠ *50 Mayfield Rd., EH9 2NH,* ☎ *0131/667–5847. 4 rooms, 3 with en suite shower, 1 with private bath. Dining room. MC, V.*

$ **Crannoch But & Ben.** This is a top-of-the-range bed-and-breakfast offering private facilities, a comfortable residents' lounge, and excellent fried breakfasts. Located only 3 miles from the city and on a good bus route, it's also particularly convenient for the airport. ⊠ *467 Queensferry Rd., EH4 7ND,* ☎ *0131/336–5688. 2 rooms with bath. No credit cards.*

$ **Drummond House.** Many hotels would be put to shame by the ac-
★ commodations at this top-of-the-range guest house in the heart of the New Town, within walking distance of the city center. The Georgian terraced house has spacious rooms, sumptuously decorated and furnished with swagged curtains, canopied beds, and antique furniture—all in elegant taste to suit the age of the house. Dinner (for guests only) is of Cordon Bleu standard. Smoking is not permitted inside Drummond House, but guests can smoke while strolling through the several acres of private gardens open only to Drummond Place residents and guests. ⊠ *17 Drummond Pl, EH3 6PL,* ☎ *and fax 0131/557–9189. 3 rooms with shower. Dining room. MC, V.*

$ **Ellesmere Guest House.** Yet another Victorian terraced house, this bed-and-breakfast is close to the King's Theatre and several good restaurants. Its first-class rooms have modern furniture with pleasant pastel floral bedspreads and curtains; one room has a four-poster bed. Guests can relax in the comfortable sitting room, but the owners prefer that they not smoke. Ellesmere is stocked with brochures covering things to do in Edinburgh. ⊠ *11 Glengyle Terr., EH3 9LN,* ☎ *0131/229–4823,* ﬀ *0131/229–5285. 6 rooms, 2 with bath, 2 with shower. No credit cards.*

$ **Lodge Hotel.** This stone detached Georgian house is easy to find on
★ the main A8 Edinburgh–Glasgow road, a 15-minute walk from Princes Street. It is furnished in period style, with swagged curtains and canopied beds. The spacious bedrooms are stocked with fresh flowers and fruit as well as a decanter of sherry. Downstairs, there is a cocktail bar and peaceful pink-and-gray sitting room. The dining room has

well-spaced tables covered with crisp white cloths and a menu that features fresh Scottish produce. ⌂ *6 Hampton Terr., West Coates EH12 5JD,* ☎ *0131/337–3682,* 𝔽𝔸𝕏 *0131/313–1700. 12 rooms with bath or shower (most rooms are reserved for nonsmokers). Dining room. MC, V.*

$ **Mrs. Coleman.** This bed-and-breakfast is an elegant Victorian detached house, which still has many period trimmings, such as the original plaster cornices in many of the spacious rooms. The decor is marked by cheerful colors and floral fabrics, and the furnishings are modern. The owners are particularly friendly and helpful. ⌂ *54 Craigmillar Park, EH16 5PS,* ☎ *0131/668–3408. 3 rooms with shower. No credit cards.*

$ **Mrs. Graham.** It may be difficult to find a parking space on the quiet
★ back street where this Victorian terraced house is situated, but it's easy enough to take Bus 3, 31, 69, 80, or 81 here, south from the city center. The spotlessly clean bed-and-breakfast has antique furniture complemented by beautiful kilim rugs and wall hangings. ⌂ *18 Moston Terr., EH9 2DE,* ☎ *0131/667–3466. 2 rooms share 1 bathroom. No credit cards.* ☉ *May–Oct.*

$ **Mrs. Valerie Livingstone.** This is a modern terraced villa close to Arthur's Seat, with fine views over the Firth of Forth. Mrs. Livingstone maintains a high standard of accommodation and meals. Smoking is not permitted. ⌂ *50 Paisley Crescent, EH8 7JQ,* ☎ *0131/661–6337. 2 rooms. Dining room. No credit cards.* ☉ *Apr.–Oct.*

$ **Roselea House.** Another south-side bed-and-breakfast guest house, on the main route from the south, the Roselea is easy to find. The Victorian house is decorated in pink-and-blue floral swags and wallpaper, and there is a sitting room for guests. ⌂ *11 Mayfield Rd., EH9 2NG,* ☎ *0131/667–6155,* 𝔽𝔸𝕏 *0131/667–3556. 7 rooms, 2 with bath, 5 with shower. AE, MC, V.*

$ **Sibbet House.** The late-18th-century Georgian elegance of this small
★ terraced town house in Edinburgh's New Town has been enhanced by careful attention to drapery, decor, and period antique furniture. Prices are reasonable, and breakfasts are traditionally Scottish and sustaining, to say the least. You must eat out in the evenings, but all kinds of restaurants are only a few minutes' stroll away. This establishment also offers a facility that few others can match—the host plays the bagpipes (but only on request). ⌂ *26 Northumberland St., EH3 6LS,* ☎ *0131/ 556–1078,* 𝔽𝔸𝕏 *0131/557–9445. 4 rooms, 3 with shower, 1 with bath. MC, V.*

$ **Silverburn Steading.** Just outside Edinburgh in a rural setting at the foot of the Pentland Hills, this bed-and-breakfast makes a relaxing base to return to after a day sightseeing in the city center, only 20 minutes away by car. Ask for a room at the back if traffic noise bothers you. ⌂ *Silverburn, Penicuik, Midlothian EH26 9LJ,* ☎ *01968/78420. 3 rooms, 2 with bath. No credit cards.*

$ **Stuart House.** Within 15 minutes' walk of the city center, this bed-and-
★ breakfast is in a Victorian terraced house with some fine plasterwork. The decor suits the structure: Bold colors, floral fabrics, and generously curtained windows combine with antique and traditional-style furniture and chandeliers to create an opulent ambience. A light supper can be served in guests' rooms in the evening, if required. Smoking is not permitted. ⌂ *12 E. Claremont St., EH7 4JP,* ☎ *0131/557–9030. 7 rooms with bath or shower. No credit cards.*

$ **Teviotdale House.** This is a small, family-run and -owned hotel in Edinburgh's genteel south side. The hosts, the Covilles, are friendly, and the house is a warm retreat on a tree-lined street away from but within reach of center-city bustle (a 30-minute walk from Charlotte Sq.). Individually decorated rooms and innovative, appetizing home cooking make this a pleasant, reasonable budget alternative to center-city hotels. The establishment is entirely no-smoking. ☒ *53 Grange Loan, EH9 2ER, ☎ and fax 0131/667–4376. 7 rooms, 5 with en suite bath, 2 with private bath. Dining room. AE, MC, V.*

$ **Thrums Private Hotel.** There is a pleasing mix of the modern and traditional in this detached Victorian house. It is small, cozy, and quiet, yet surprisingly close to downtown Edinburgh. ☒ *14 Minto St., EH9 1RQ, ☎ 0131/667–5545. 14 rooms, 12 with bath. Restaurant, bar. MC, V. Closed Christmas Day, New Year's Day, and 1 week Jan.*

$ **Turret Guest House.** On a quiet residential street on the south side, this bed-and-breakfast is close to bus routes as well as the Commonwealth Pool and Holyrood Park. Cheerful and cozy, it has modern furnishings, but many of the building's Victorian cornices, paneled doors, and high ceilings remain. ☒ *8 Kilmaurs Terr., EH16 5DR, ☎ 0131/667–6704. 6 rooms, 3 with shower. No credit cards.*

$ **28 Northumberland Street.** An exceptional standard is set at this bed-
★ and-breakfast in the center of the New Town. The Georgian terraced house has shuttered windows and antique furniture and rugs (some used as wall hangings). One single bedroom has been transformed into an Indian-style tent with fabric-covered walls and ceiling. The host, a keen golfer, and the hostess, a lawyer, both enjoy meeting guests and are very helpful. ☒ *28 Northumberland St., EH3 6LS, ☎ 0131/557–8036, FAX 0131/558–3453. 3 rooms with bath or shower. Dining room. DC, MC, V.*

THE ARTS AND NIGHTLIFE

The Arts

Edinburgh is world renowned for its flagship arts event, the **Edinburgh International Festival,** and there is no escaping a sense of theater if you visit the city from August to early September. The annual festival has attracted all sorts of international performers since its inception in 1947. Even more obvious to the casual stroller during this time is the refreshingly irreverent Edinburgh Festival Fringe, unruly child of the official festival, which spills out of halls and theaters and onto the streets all over town. At other times throughout the year professional and amateur groups alike offer a range of cultural options appropriate to a capital city, even if Edinburgh's neighbor and rival city, Glasgow, has the reputation of being more lively.

The List, available from newsagents throughout the city, and *What's On in Edinburgh,* available from the Information Centre (*see* Important Addresses and Numbers in Edinburgh Essentials, *below*) carry the most up-to-date details about cultural events. *The Scotsman,* an Edinburgh daily, also carries reviews in its arts pages on Monday and Wednesday. Tickets are generally available from the relevant box office in advance; in some cases, from certain designated travel agents; or at the door, although concerts by national orchestras often sell out long before the day of the performance.

The **Edinburgh International Festival** (1996: August 11–31), the premier arts event of the year, has for nearly 50 years attracted performing artists of international caliber to a celebration of music, dance, and drama. *Advance information, programs, tickets, and reservations available from the Edinburgh Festival Office, 21 Market St., Edinburgh EH1 1BW, ☎ 0131/226–4001.*

The **Edinburgh Festival Fringe** offers many theatrical and musical events, some by amateur groups (you have been warned) and is more of a grab bag than the official festival. During festival time it's possible to arrange your own entertainment program from morning to midnight and beyond, if you do not feel overwhelmed by the variety available. *Information, programs, and tickets available from Edinburgh Festival Fringe, 180 High St., Edinburgh EH1 1QS, ☎ 0131/226–5257 or 0131/226–5259.*

The **Edinburgh Film Festival** (1996: August 10–25) is yet another aspect of this busy summer festival logjam. *Advance information and programs available from the Edinburgh Film Festival, at the Filmhouse, 88 Lothian Rd., Edinburgh EH3 9BZ, ☎ 0131/228–4051. Box office, ☎ 0131/228–4051.*

The **Edinburgh Military Tattoo** (1996: August 2–24) may not be art, but it is certainly entertainment. It is sometimes confused with the festival itself, partly because the dates overlap. This celebration of martial music and skills is set on the castle esplanade, and the dramatic backdrop augments the spectacle. Dress warmly for late-evening performances. Even if it rains the show most definitely goes on. *Tickets and information available from Edinburgh Military Tattoo, 22 Market St., Edinburgh, EH1 1QB, ☎ 0131/225–1188.*

Away from the August-to-September festival overkill, the **Edinburgh Folk Festival** (Box 528, Edinburgh, EH10 4DU, ☎ 0131/556–3181) usually takes place around Easter each year. This 10-day event blends performances by Scottish and international folk artists of the highest caliber.

Traditional Theater
Edinburgh's three main theaters are the **Royal Lyceum** (Grindlay St., ☎ 0131/229–9697) and the **King's** (Leven St., ☎ 0131/229–1201), both of which offer contemporary and traditional dramatic works, and **Edinburgh Festival Theatre,** (Nicolson St., ☎ 0131/529–6000), which hosts a variety of theatrical and musical entertainment.

The Playhouse (Greenside Pl., ☎ 0131/557–2692) hosts mostly popular artists and has a Christmas pantomime. At Musselburgh, on the eastern outskirts of Edinburgh, the **Brunton Theatre** (Brunton Hall, High St., Musselburgh, ☎ 0131/665–2240) offers a regular program of performances. At the **Church Hill Theatre** (Morningside Rd., ☎ 0131/447–7597), local dramatic societies mount productions of a high standard.

Modern Theater
The **Traverse Theatre** (Cambridge St., ☎ 0131/228–1404) has developed a solid reputation as a venue for stimulating new work—though it has toned down its previously avant-garde approach.

The **Netherbow Arts Centre** (43 High St., ☎ 0131/556–9579) includes modern plays in its program of music, drama, and cabaret, as does the **Theatre Workshop** (34 Hamilton Pl., ☎ 0131/225–7942), which hosts fringe events during the Edinburgh Festival and modern, community-based theater all year.

Music
The **Usher Hall** (Lothian Rd., ☎ 0131/228–1155) is Edinburgh's grandest concert hall, venue for the Scottish National Orchestra during its winter season (October–March). More intimate in scale and used generally for smaller recitals and chamber music is the **Queen's Hall** (Nicolson St., ☎ 0131/668–3456). You can find popular artists at the **Playhouse** (*see above*).

For jazz enthusiasts the main focus of entertainment is the **International Jazz Festival** (116 The Canongate, Edinburgh, EH8 8DD, ☎ 0131/557–1642), held in August each year, but live jazz can also be found in the city throughout the year. Consult *The List* for information.

Dance
Edinburgh has no ballet or modern-dance companies of its own, but visiting companies perform from time to time at the King's Theatre or Royal Lyceum (*see above*).

Film
Apart from cinema chains, Edinburgh has the excellent **Filmhouse** (88 Lothian Rd., ☎ 0131/228–6382; box office, 0131/228–2688), which is the best venue for modern, foreign-language, offbeat, or simply less-commercial films. A copy of its diverse monthly program is available from the box office and at a variety of other locations throughout the city (at the Tourist Centre, for example, or in theater foyers).

Of the other cinemas, the **Cameo** (38 Home St., ☎ 0131/228–4141), with three extremely comfortable theaters, a bar, and late-night specials (Thurs.–Sat., 11:30 PM), and the family-owned and -run **Dominion** (Newbattle Terrace, ☎ 0131/447–2660) offer the most pleasant alternative to the larger commercial theaters.

Nightlife

Edinburgh's nightlife is quite varied and includes discos, Scottish musical evenings, and *ceilidhs* (pronounced *kay-lees*). The Edinburgh and Scotland Information Centre above Waverley Market (*see* Important Addresses and Numbers in Edinburgh Essentials, *below*) can supply information on various categories of nightlife, especially on spots offering dinner-dances. Jazz and folk music in general are wide ranging, though pub and hotel venues change. *The List* gives much information on the music scene. In quiet-living Edinburgh, there are no nightclubs of the cabaret-and-striptease variety.

Casinos
Berkeley Casino Club (2 Rutland Pl., ☎ 0131/228–4446) is a private club that offers free membership on 48 hours' notice, as do **Casino Martell** (7 Newington Rd., ☎ 0131/667–7763), the **Stanley** (5b York Pl., ☎ 0131/556–1055), and **Stakis Regency Casino** (14 Picardy Pl., ☎ 0131/557–3585), whose restaurant is highly rated.

Pubs/Bars
Abbotsford (3 Rose St., ☎ 0131/225–1894) offers five real ales (changing all the time), bar lunches, and lots of Victorian atmosphere.

Drum and Monkey (80 Queen St., ☎ 0131/538–8111), with cozy dark wood booths and a maroon color scheme, is just the place for soup and sandwich lunches with a pint of Old Wallop beer.

Milne's Bar (21–25 Rose St., ☎ 0131/225–6738) is known as the poets' pub because of its popularity with the Edinburgh literati. Pies and baked potatoes go well with seven real ales and varying guest beers. The place was made to look old with Victorian advertisements and photos of old Edinburgh.

Tiles (1 St. Andrew Sq., ☎ 0131/558–1507), a converted banking hall, gets its name from the wealth of tiles covering the walls. The ceiling is elaborate plasterwork. The 10 to 15 real ales are complemented by an à la carte bistro menu.

Discos/Nightclubs

Many Edinburgh discos offer reduced admission and/or less expensive drinks for early revelers. Consult *The List* for special events.

Buster Browns (25–27 Market St., ☎ 0131/226–4224) offers mainstream chart sounds Friday–Sunday 10:30 PM–2 AM.

The Citrus Club (Grindlay St., ☎ 0131/229–6977) offers a variety of music, usually spun by good quality DJs, on Wednesday, Friday, and Saturday nights from 10 PM–3 AM.

Minus One (Carlton Highland Hotel, North Bridge, ☎ 0131/556–7277) has live music and a DJ on Friday and Saturday and a DJ only on Thursday. The sounds here are mainstream, for groovers of all generations. It's open Thursday–Saturday 10 PM–3 AM.

Red Hot Pepper Club (3 Semple St., ☎ 0131/229–7733) moves to mainstream music Friday and Saturday 10 PM–4 AM.

Folk Clubs

There are always folk performers in various pubs throughout the city. **Edinburgh Folk Club** (Cafe Royal, 17 W. Register St., ☎ 0131/339–4083) features folk music every Wednesday at 8 PM.

Scottish Evenings and Ceilidhs

Several hotels feature traditional Scottish-music evenings in the summer season, including the **Carlton Highland Hotel** (North Bridge, ☎ 0131/556–7277) and **George Hotel** (George St., ☎ 0131/225–1251). Contact the individual hotels for information.

Other well-established Scottish entertainments include **Jamie's Scottish Evening** (King James Hotel, Leith St., ☎ 0131/556–0111) and **The Scottish Experience** (12 High St., ☎ 0131/557–9350).

Cocktail Bars

Harry's Bar (7b Randolph Pl., ☎ 0131/539–8100) is in a basement and decorated with Americana. Despite the disco music, it is hugely popular with locals. Harry's is open daily noon–1 AM.

L'Attache (beneath the Rutland Hotel, 1 Rutland Pl., ☎ 0131/229–3402), another basement bar, has live folk and rock music Sunday–Thursday 8 PM–1:30 AM, Friday and Saturday 8 PM–2 AM.

Madogs (38A George St., ☎ 0131/225–4308) was one of Edinburgh's first all-American cocktail bar-restaurants. It's popular with professionals after work and has live music most weeknights. It's open Sunday 6:30 PM–2 AM, Monday–Wednesday noon–2 AM, Thursday–Saturday noon–3 AM. No sneakers.

EXCURSIONS FROM EDINBURGH

Tour 3: West Lothian and the Forth Valley

Numbers in the margin correspond to points of interest on the West Lothian and the Forth Valley map.

The Lothians is the collective name given to the swath of countryside surrounding Edinburgh. This driving tour of West Lothian explores the Forth Valley west of Edinburgh, as well as some of the territory north of the River Forth. In a round-trip of about 70 miles, it is possible to see plenty of the central belt of Scotland and to skirt the edge of the Central Highlands. The river Forth snakes across a widening floodplain on its descent from the Highlands, and by the time it reaches the western extremities of Edinburgh, it has already passed below the mighty Forth bridges and become a broad estuary.

This is the route to take if your interests incline toward castles and stately homes because they sprout thickly on both sides of the Forth. Note that it is possible to visit some of the places included in this excursion by train: Dalmeny, Linlithgow, and Dunfermline all have rail stations. Bus services link most areas as well, but working out a detailed itinerary by bus would be best left to your travel agent or guide. **Historic Scotland** (☎ 0131/244–3101) runs many of the destinations described here.

Leave Edinburgh by Queensferry Road—the A90—and follow signs for the Forth Bridge. Beyond the city boundary at **Cramond** (*see* Off the Beaten Track, *above*) take the slip road, B924, for South Queensferry, watching for signs to **Dalmeny House,** the first of the stately homes clustered on the western edge of Edinburgh. Home of the Earl and Countess of Rosebery, this 1815 Tudor Gothic pile displays among its sumptuous contents the best of the family's famous collection of 18th-century French furniture. (Much of this collection was formerly displayed at Mentmore, the country seat 40 miles north of London, which belonged to the present earl's grandfather, Baron Mayer de Rothschild.) Highlights include the library; the drawing room, with its tapestries and highly wrought French furniture; the Napoleon Room; and the Vincennes and Sevres porcelain collections. *B924, by South Queensferry (7 mi west of Edinburgh),* ☎ *0131/331–1888.* ☛ *£3.50 adults, £1.80 children, £2.80 students.* ☉ *May–Sept., Mon. and Tues. noon–5:30, Sun. 1–5:30. Last admission 4:45.*

★ ❷ Follow the B924 for the descent to South Queensferry and views of the **Forth bridges.** The **Forth Rail Bridge,** which looms over the former Forth ferry port, was opened in 1890 and is 2,765 yards long, except on a hot summer's day when it expands by about another yard! Its neighbor is the 1,993-yard-long **Forth Road Bridge,** opened in 1964.

The B924 continues westward under the approaches to the suspension bridge and then meets the A904. On turning right, onto A904, you'll ❸ see signs for **Hopetoun House.** These palatial premises, home of the marquesses of Linlithgow, are considered to be among the Adam family's finest designs. The pile was started in 1699 to the original plans of Sir William Bruce, then enlarged between 1721 and 1754 by William Adam and his son Robert. There is a notable painting collection, and the house has decorative work of the highest order, plus all the paraphernalia to amuse visitors: nature trail, restaurant, stables, museum, garden center. Much of the wealth that created this sumptuous building came from the family's mining interests. *West of South Queensferry,* ☎ *0131/331–2451.* ☛ *£4 adults, £2 children, £3.30 students and senior citizens, £10.50 family ticket.* ☉ *Apr.–Sept., daily 10–5:30 (last admission 4:45).*

❹ On this Forth Valley castle trail you can also visit the **House of the Binns,** signed from the A904. Here the 17th-century General Tam Dalyell transformed a fortified stronghold into a gracious mansion. The present exterior dates from around 1810 and shows a remodeling into a kind of mock fort with crenellated battlements and turrets. Inside there are magnificent plaster ceilings in Elizabethan style. *Off A904, 4 mi east of Linlithgow,* ☎ *0131/226–5922.* ☛ *£3 adults, £1.50 children, stu-*

West Lothian and the Forth Valley

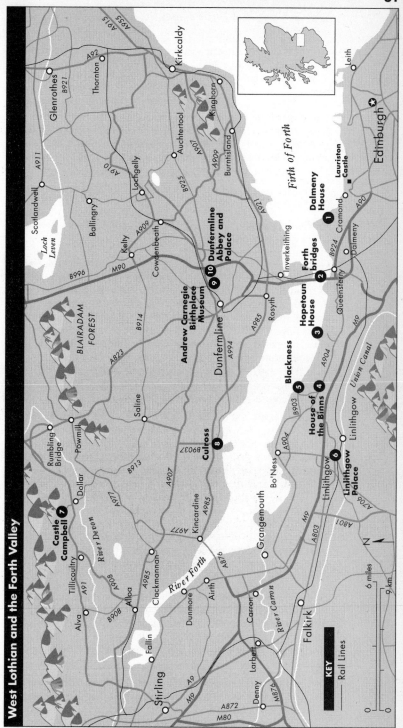

dents, and senior citizens. ☺ *June–Sept., Sat.–Thurs. 1:30–5:30 (last tour 5 PM).*

⑤ For a look at a more austere fortress, follow signs off the A904 to **Blackness.** The castle here stands like a grounded gray hulk on the very edge of the Forth. A curious 15th-century structure, it has had a varied career as a strategic fortress, state prison, powder magazine, and youth hostel. The countryside is gently green and cultivated, and open views extend across the blue Forth to the distant ramparts of the Ochil Hills (seen in close-up later on the route). *B903, 4 mi northeast of Linlithgow,* ☎ *0131/244–3101.* ☛ *£1.50 adults, £1 senior citizens, 75p children.* ☺ *Apr.–Sept., Mon.–Sat. 9:30–6:30, Sun. 2–6:30; Oct.–Mar., Mon.–Wed. and Sat. 9:30–4, Thurs. 9:30–noon, Sun. 2–4.*

From Blackness, take the B903 to its junction with the A904. Turn left for Linlithgow on the A803.

TIME OUT   The **Four Marys** (67 High St., Linlithgow) specializes in uncomplicated but wholesome pub lunches.

⑥ On the edge of Linlithgow Loch stands the splendid ruin of **Linlithgow Palace,** birthplace of Mary, Queen of Scots (1542). Burned, perhaps by accident, by Hanoverian troops during the last Jacobite rebellion in 1746, this impressive shell stands on a site of great antiquity, though nothing for certain survived an earlier fire in 1424. The palace gatehouse is from the early 16th century, and the central courtyard's elaborate fountain dates from around 1535, but the halls and great rooms are cold stone echoing husks. *South shore of Linlithgow Loch,* ☎ *0131/244–3101.* ☛ *£2 adults, £1.25 senior citizens, 75p children.* ☺ *Apr.–Sept., Mon.–Sat. 9:30–6, Sun. 2–6; Oct.–Mar., Mon.–Sat. 9:30–4, Sun. 2–4.*

At this point it's best to join the M9, which will speed you westward. From the M9 you will begin to gain tempting glimpses of the Highland hills to the northwest and the long humped wall of the Ochil Hills, across the river-plain to the north. The **River Carron,** which flows under the M9, gave its name to the *carronade,* a kind of cannon manufactured in Falkirk, a few minutes to the southwest. On your right you'll notice the apocalyptic complex of Grangemouth Refinery (impressive by night), which you may also smell if the wind is right (or wrong!). The refinery processes North Sea crude, but was originally sited here because of the now extinct oil-shale extraction industry of West Lothian, pioneered by a Scot, James "Paraffin" Young. This short section may not be the most scenic in Scotland, but it has certainly played its role in the nation's industrial history.

Follow Kincardine Bridge signs off the motorway, cross the Forth and take the A977 north from Kincardine, formerly a trading port and distillery center. Take the A985 to Alloa, get on the A908 (signed Tillicoultry) for a short stretch, and then pick up the B908 (signed Alva). At this point you'll be leaving the industrial northern shore of the Forth behind.

The scarp face of the **Ochil Hills** looms unmistakably ahead, an old fault line, bearing up the harder volcanic rocks in contrast to the softer coal measures through which you have just traveled. The steep Ochils provided grazing land and water power for Scotland's second-largest textile area. Some mills still survive in the so-called Hillfoots towns on the scarp edge east of Stirling. You can explore this region by following the A91 eastward at **Alva.** Several walkers' routes run into the narrow chinks of glens here. Behind Alva is **Alva Glen** (park near the converted Strude Mill, at the top and eastern end of the little town). A little farther east is the **Ochil Hills Woodland Park,** which provides access to Silver Glen. The **Mill Glen,** behind Tillicoultry (pronunced *tilly-COOT-ree*), and its giant quarry, fine waterfalls, and interesting plants is another option for energetic explorers. The tourist information center at Tillicoultry can provide further information, as well as a *Mill Trail* brochure, which can lead you to a variety of mill shops offering bargain woolen and tweed goods.

The main road, squeezed between the gentle River Devon and the steep slopes above, continues to **Dollar.** This *douce* (Scots for *well-mannered* and *gentle*) and tidy town below the slopes lies at the mouth of Dollar Glen. At first sight, the tilting slopes seem an unlikely terrain for wheeled vehicles. By following signs for **Castle Campbell,** however, you will find a road that angles sharply up the east side of the wooded defile. The narrow road ends in a parking lot from which it's only a short walk to Castle Campbell, high on a great sloping mound in the center of the glen. With the green woods below, bracken hills above, and a view that on a clear day stretches right across the Forth Valley to the tip of Tinto Hill near Lanark, this is certainly the most atmospheric fortress within easy reach of Edinburgh. Formerly known as Castle Gloom, Castle Campbell stands out among Scottish castles for the sheer drama of its setting. The sturdy square of the tower house survives from the 15th century, when this site was first fortified by the Earl of Argyll. Other buildings and enclosures were subsequently added, but the sheer lack of space on this rocky eminence ensured that there were never any drastic changes. The castle is associated with the earls of Argyll, as well as with John Knox, the fiery religious reformer, who preached here. It also played a role in the religious wars of the 17th century, having been captured by Oliver Cromwell in 1654 and garrisoned with English troops. *Dollar Glen, 1 mi north of Dollar,* ☎ *0131/244–3101.* ☛ *£2 adults, £1.25 senior citizens, 75p children.* ☉ *Apr.–Sept., Mon.–Sat. 9:30–6, Sun. 2–6; Oct.–Mar., Mon.–Wed. and Sat. 9:30–4, Thurs. 9:30–noon, Sun. 2–4.*

From the castle, retrace your route to A91 and turn left. Just a few minutes outside Dollar, turn right onto a minor road (signed Rumbling Bridge). Then turn right onto the A823. Follow A823 through Powmill (signs for Dunfermline); turn right off of A823, following the signs for Saline (a pleasant if undistinguished village), and take an unclassified road due south to join the A907. Turn right, and then within a mile go left on the B9037, which leads down to **Culross.** On the muddy shores of the Forth, this is one of the most remarkable little towns in all Scotland. It once had a thriving industry and export trade in coal and salt (the coal was used in the salt-panning process). It also had, curiously, a trade monopoly in the manufacture of baking *girdles* (griddles). But as local coal became exhausted, the impetus of the Industrial Revolution passed it by and other parts of the Forth Valley prospered. Culross became a backwater town, and the merchants' houses of the 17th and 18th centuries were never replaced by Victorian developments or modern architecture. In the 1930s, the very new and then very poor National Trust for Scotland started to buy up the decaying properties. With the help of a variety of other agencies, these buildings were conserved and brought to life, and Culross is now a vigorous community, even if it has the air of a film set. With its mercat cross, cobbled streets, tolbooth, and narrow wynds, Culross is a living museum of a 17th-century town. *7½ mi west of Dunfermline,* ☎ *0131/226–5922. Admission to Palace, Study, and Town House £3.50 adults, £1.80 children.*

⊗ *Easter and May–Sept. daily, Study and Town House 11–5:30 (Oct. 1–5:30); Palace 1:30–5:30.*

Take the B9037 east to join the A994, which leads to **Dunfermline,** once the world center for the production of damask linen; the **Dunfermline District Museum** on Viewfield Terrace, ☎ 01383/721–814, tells the full story. Today the town is better known as the birthplace of millionaire philanthropist Andrew Carnegie. Undoubtedly Dunfermline's most famous son, Carnegie endowed the town with a library, health and fitness center, spacious park, and, naturally, a Carnegie Hall, still the focus of culture and entertainment. The 1835 weaver's cottage in which

❾ Carnegie was born is now the **Andrew Carnegie Birthplace Museum.** Don't be misled by the cottage's exterior. Inside it opens into a larger hall, where documents, photographs, and artifacts tell Carnegie's fascinating life story. You will learn such obscure details as the fact that Carnegie was only the third man in the United States to be able to translate Morse code by ear as it came down the wire! *Moodie St.,* ☎ *01383/724–302. Admission £1.50 adults, 75p students and senior citizens, children under 15 free.* ⊗ *Apr.–Oct., Mon.–Sat. 11–5, Sun. 2–5; Nov.–Mar., daily 2–4.*

❿ Also of note in the town are the **Dunfermline Abbey and Palace** complex. The abbey was founded by Queen Margaret, the English wife of the Scots King Malcolm Canmore (1057–93). Some Norman work can be seen in the present church, where Robert the Bruce lies buried. The palace grew from the abbey guest house and was the birthplace of Charles I. Dunfermline was the seat of the Royal Court of Scotland until the end of the 11th century, and its central role in Scottish affairs is explored by means of display panels dotted around the drafty but hallowed buildings. *Monastery St.,* ☎ *0131/244–3101.* ☞ *£1.50 adults, £1 senior citizens, 75p children.* ⊗ *Apr.–Sept., Mon.–Sat. 9:30–6, Sun. 2–6; Oct.–Mar., Mon.–Wed., Fri., and Sat. 9:30–4, Thurs. 9:30–noon, Sun. 2–4.*

From Dunfermline, follow Edinburgh signs to the A823 and return via the Forth Road Bridge (toll: 40p).

Tour 4: Midlothian and East Lothian

Numbers in the margin correspond to points of interest on the Midlothian and East Lothian map.

In spite of the finest stone carving in Scotland (at Rosslyn Chapel), associations with Sir Walter Scott, outstanding castles, and miles of varied rolling countryside, Midlothian, the area south of Edinburgh, for years remained off the beaten tourist path. Perhaps a little in awe of sophisticated Edinburgh to the north and the well-manicured charm of the stockbroker belt of nearby upmarket East Lothian, Midlothian remained quietly preoccupied with its own workaday little towns and dormitory suburbs. Now Midlothian has decided it is at least as interesting as several other parts of Scotland that are fervently marketing themselves as tourism destinations. Judge for yourself in this tour.

As for East Lothian, it started with the advantage of golf courses of world-rank, most notably Muirfield, plus a scattering of stately homes and interesting hotels. Red pantiled and decidedly middle class, East Lothian is an area of glowing grainfields in summer and quite a few discreetly polite, "strictly private" signs at the end of driveways. It nevertheless has plenty of interest for the visitor, including photogenic villages, active fishing harbors, and vistas of pastoral Lowland Scotland, a world away (but much less than an hour by car) from bustling Edinburgh.

The tour described here can certainly be driven in one day, although it could be split into two separate excursions if you want to budget more time for some individual sights. Public transport is available to many of the venues described. Inquire at the St. Andrew Square bus station for bus services.

★ ❶ Leave Edinburgh via the A701 (Liberton Rd.). At the not-very-picturesque community of Bilston, look for signs left for **Rosslyn Chapel** (signed Roslin B7006). Conceived by Sir William Sinclair and dedicated to St. Matthew in 1450, the chapel is famous for the quality and variety of the stone carving inside. Human figures, animals, and plants are all included, covering almost every square inch of stonework. The chapel was actually never finished. The original design called for a cruciform structure, but only the choir and parts of the east transept walls were completed. *Roslin, off A703, 7½ mi south of Edinburgh,* ☎ *0131/440–2159.* ☛ *£2 adults, £1.50 senior citizens, 75p children.* ☼ *Apr.–Oct., Mon.–Sat. 10–5, Sun. noon–4:45.*

❷ From Roslin return to the A703 for **Penicuik.** There are fine views of the Pentland Hills beyond the town, but its chief attraction for the tourist is the **Edinburgh Crystal Visitor Centre.** You may have seen this distinctive style of glassware in Edinburgh's upscale shops. Guided tours reveal the stages involved in the manufacture of cut crystal. In addition, groups of 6–12 people can pre-book a VIP tour (adults over 18 only). This includes the chance to blow a glass bubble and also to cut your own piece of glass, which will then be polished and given to you as a keepsake. Advance booking is essential for this tour. The Visitor Centre itself has crystal pieces on display, as well as an audiovisual exhibition on the production of crystal. *Eastfield, Penicuik, 10 mi south of Edinburgh,* ☎ *01968/675128. Admission to center free. Cost of tours: £2 adults, £1 senior citizens, 50p children. VIP tour: £20.* ☼ *Center, restaurant, and shop Mon.–Sat. 9–5, Sun. 11–5. Tours weekdays 9:15–3:30.*

TIME OUT The **Old Bakehouse** (☎ 01968/660830) at West Linton, southwest of Penicuik on the A702, serves home-cooked fare in quaint, wood-beamed rooms. Danish open sandwiches are the specialty, but home-made soups and a hot main course are also included on the menu. Tuesday through Sunday, lunch is served noon–2:30, dinner 6–9. On weekends between 3 and 4:30 you can also take afternoon tea.

After pausing to admire the Pentland Hills arching along the skyline to the southwest, from West Linton follow the B7059 and the A701 to Leadburn and then Howgate. Get onto the A6094 for a few minutes, then turn right onto the B6372 and continue past Temple, an attractive village on the edge of the Moorfoot Hills, toward Gorebridge.

❸ At the junction of B6372 with A7, just before Gorebridge, you have a choice. If your interests tend toward social history, turn left and drive 2 miles to reach the **Scottish Mining Museum** at **Newtongrange.** Here, in the buildings of a now-closed colliery, you can learn something about the history of Scotland's coal miners. You can visit various buildings in the complex and view the giant winding engine, as well as the ranks of rusty, coal-dusty boilers that supplied the steam to turn it. The mine's former offices now relate, by means of realistic tableaux, the power that the mining company had over the lives of the individual workers in a frighteningly autocratic system that survived well into

Midlothian and East Lothian

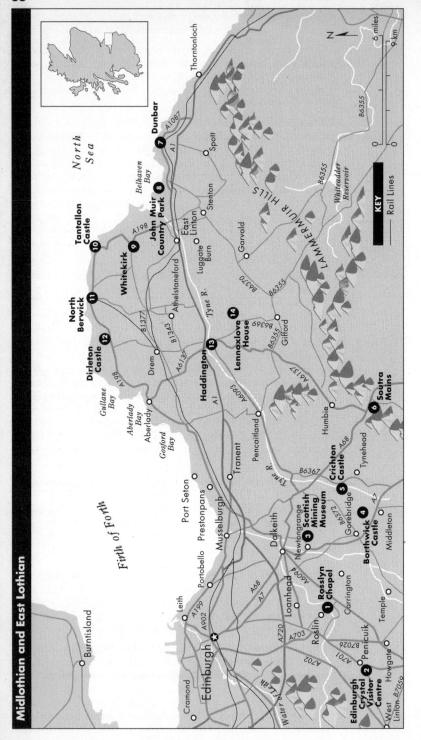

North Sea

Firth of Forth

KEY
— Rail Lines

LAMMERMUIR HILLS

Thorntonloch

Dunbar **7**

Belhaven Bay

Tantallon Castle **10**

John Muir Country Park **8**

Whitekirk **9**

North Berwick **11**

Dirleton Castle **12**

Whiteadder Reservoir

Spott

Stenton

East Linton

Athelstaneford

Luggate Burn

Garvald

Gifford

Lennoxlove House **14**

Haddington **13**

Drem

Gullane Bay

Aberlady Bay

Aberlady

Gosford Bay

Pencaitland

Humbie

Soutra Mains **6**

Tyne R.

Tynehead

Crichton Castle **5**

Scottish Mining Museum **3**

Gorebridge

Borthwick Castle **4**

Middleton

Tranent

Port Seton

Prestonpans

Musselburgh

Dalkeith

Newtongrange

Portobello

Leith

Cramond

Burntisland

Loanhead

Rosslyn Chapel **1**

Carrington

Roslin

Temple

Edinburgh

Penicuik **2**

Edinburgh Crystal Visitor Centre

Howgate

West Linton

the 1930s. The mining company owned the houses, shops, and even the pub. Newtongrange was in fact the largest planned mining village in Scotland. The scenery is no more attractive than you would expect around a former mining community, though the green Pentland Hills are still in view in the distance. ☎ *0131/663–7519.* ☛ *£1.95 adults, £1 children.* ⊘ *Apr.–Sept., daily 10–4.*

If you instead turn right at the Gorebridge junction (A7/B6372), a few moments' travel takes you a world away from gloomy thoughts of worker exploitation by the mine-owning aristocracy. Follow the A7 south to a sign for **Borthwick.** Take a left onto an unclassified road off A7, and a few minutes later, in green countryside with scattered woods and lush ❹ hedgerows, you can see **Borthwick Castle.** Dating from the 15th century and still occupied (it is now a hotel), this stark, tall twin-towered fortress is associated with Mary, Queen of Scots. She came here on a kind of honeymoon with her ill-starred third husband, the Earl of Bothwell. Their already dubious bliss was interrupted by Mary's political opponents, often referred to as the Lords of the Congregation, a confederacy of powerful nobles who were against the queen's latest liaison and who instead favored the crowning of her young son James. Rather insensitively, they laid siege to the castle while the newlyweds were there. The history books relate that Mary subsequently escaped "disguised as a man." She was not free for long, however. It was only a short time before she was defeated in battle and imprisoned. She languished in prison for 21 years before Queen Elizabeth of England signed her death warrant (1587). Bothwell's fate was equally gloomy: He died insane in a Danish prison.

❺ From Borthwick, you can reach the next destination—**Crichton Castle**— by taking a peaceful walk through the woods (there are signposts along the way) or by doubling back by car to the B6372 and turning right onto the A68. Crichton Castle is just beyond the village of Pathhead (you'll see signs on A68). This was a Bothwell family castle. Queen Mary attended the wedding here of Bothwell's sister, Lady Janet Hepburn, to Mary's natural brother, Lord John Stewart. Of particular interest in the extensive ruin is the curious arcaded range with its diamond faceted stonework. This particular geometric pattern cut into the stone is unique in Scotland and is thought to have been inspired by Renaissance styles on the Continent, particularly Italy. The oldest part of the work is the 14th-century keep (square tower). Like Borthwick Castle, Crichton is set in attractive, rolling Lowland scenery, interrupted here and there with patches of woodland. *B6367, 7 mi southeast of Dalkeith,* ☎ *0131/244–3101.* ☛ *£1.20 adults, 75p children.* ⊘ *Apr.–Sept., Mon.–Sat. 9:30–6, Sun. 2–6.*

If the attractive setting of Crichton has beguiled you, you may want to end this section of the tour to explore the countryside and then return to Edinburgh via the A68 and Dalkeith. To continue the tour into East Lothian, follow the A68 south, away from Edinburgh, to the very edge of the Lammermuir Hills. Just beyond the junction with the ❻ A6137 you'll come to a spot called **Soutra Mains.** There's a small parking lot here, from which you can enjoy glorious unobstructed views extending northward over the whole of the Lothian plain.

Make your way back to the A6137 and turn right onto it; turn right again onto the B6355, and head east for the junction with the B6370, which leads to Dunbar.

TIME OUT   The **Goblin Ha'Hotel** (☎ 0162081/244) in Gifford, a peaceful backwater town on the B6355, offers a wholesome afternoon tea that is very popular with day-trippers from Edinburgh. Gifford itself, with its 18th-century kirk and mercat cross, is a good example of a tweedily respectable, well-scrubbed, red-pantile-roofed East Lothian village.

In the days before tour companies started offering package deals to the Mediterranean, **Dunbar** was a popular holiday resort. Now a bit faded, the town is of interest primarily because of a number of spacious Georgian-style properties, characterized by the astragals, or fan-shaped windows, above the doors; the symmetry of the house fronts; and the parapeted roof lines. Though not the popular seaside playground it once was, Dunbar does still have an attractive beach and a picturesque harbor, as well as opportunities for golf and sailing.

West of Dunbar, on the way back to Edinburgh, the A1087 leads to the sandy reaches of **Belhaven Bay,** signposted from the main road, and to the **John Muir Country Park,** which takes in the estuary of the River Tyne winding down from the Moorfoot Hills. The country park offers varied coastal scenery: rocky shoreline, golden sands, and the mixed woodlands of Tyninghame, teeming with wildlife. Dunbar-born John Muir (whose family emigrated to the United States when he was a child) founded the U.S. National Park system. Only recently has the work of this early conservationist been acknowledged in his native Scotland.

From the park, drive north on the A198 (a right turn off the A1), to reach **Whitekirk.** The unmistakable red sandstone church, with Norman tower, stands on a site occupied since the 6th century. It was a place of pilgrimage in medieval times because of its healing well. Behind the kirk, in a field, stands a tithe barn. Tithe barns originated in the practice of giving to the church a proportion of local produce, which then required storage space. At one end of the structure is a 16th-century tower house, which at one point in its history accommodated visiting pilgrims. The large three-story barn was added to the tower house in the 17th century. *St. Mary's Parish Church, A198.* ☛ *Free.* ☺ *Early morning to late evening.*

Only minutes farther on, grim and battered **Tantallon Castle** rises on a cliff beyond the flat fields. This substantial ruin defends a headland with the sea on three sides. The red sandstone is pitted and eaten by time and sea-spray, with the earliest surviving stonework dating from the late-14th century. The fortress was besieged in 1529 by the cannons of King James V. (Rather inconveniently, the besieging forces ran out of gunpowder.) Cannons were used again, to deadlier effect, in a later siege during the Civil War in 1651. Twelve days of battering with the heavy guns of Cromwell's General Monk greatly damaged the flanking towers. However, much of the curtain wall of this former Douglas stronghold survives. *A198, 3 mi east of North Berwick,* ☎ *0131/244–3101.* ☛ *£2 adults, £1.25 senior citizens, 75p children.* ☺ *Apr.–Sept., Mon.–Sat. 9:30–6, Sun. 2–6; Oct.–Mar., Mon.–Wed. and Sat. 9:30–4, Thurs. noon–4, Sun. 2–4.*

The seaside resort of **North Berwick,** a few minutes west on the A198, is a pleasant little place that manages to retain a small-town personality even when it's thronged with city visitors on warm summer Sunday afternoons. Munching on ice cream, the city folk stroll on the beach and in the narrow streets or gape at the sailing craft in the small harbor.

Dirleton Castle is a 12th-century castle surrounded by a high outer wall. Within the wall you'll find a 17th-century bowling green, set in the shade of yew trees and surrounded by a herbaceous flower border that comes ablaze with color in high summer. Dirleton Castle was once occupied by King Edward I of England, in 1298, as part of his campaign for the continued subjugation of the unruly Scots. *A198, 8 mi west of North Berwick,* ☎ *0131/244–3101.* ✆ *£2 adults, £1.25 senior citizens, 75p children.* ☉ *Apr.–Sept., Mon.–Sat. 9:30–6, Sun. 2–6; Oct.–Mar., Mon.–Sat. 9:30–4, Sun. 2–4.*

Very noticeable along this coastline are the golf courses of East Lothian on every available links space. Next to Dirleton is **Gullane,** which is respectable and clad mostly in expensive golfing sweaters. **Muirfield,** venue for the Open Championship, is nearby, as is **Greywalls,** now a hotel, but originally a private house designed by Sir Edwin Lutyens. Away from the golf, Gullane's beach, well within driving distance of the city, offers opportunities for restful summer evening strolls.

⑬ A198 eventually leads to Aberlady, from which you take the A6137 south to the former county town of **Haddington,** one of the best-preserved medieval street plans in the country. Among the many buildings of architectural or historical interest is the Town House, which was designed by William Adam in 1748 and enlarged in 1830. A wall plaque at the Sidegate recalls the great heights of floods from the River Tyne. Beyond is the medieval Nungate footbridge, with the Church of St. Mary a little way upstream.

⑭ Just to the south of Haddington, by way of the B6369, is **Lennoxlove House,** which displays items associated with Mary, Queen of Scots. A turreted country house, part of it dating from the 15th century, Lennoxlove is a cheerful mix of family life and Scottish history. Housed in the beautifully decorated rooms are collections of portraits, furniture, and porcelain. *B6369, 1 mi south of Haddington,* ☎ *0162/082–3720.* ✆ *£3 adults, £1.50 children.* ☉ *May–Sept., Wed., Sat., and Sun. 2–5.*

Return to the A1 at Haddington and head west back to Edinburgh. From Haddington it's about 15 miles back to center city.

EDINBURGH ESSENTIALS

Arriving and Departing

By Bus

Scottish Citylink Coaches (Bus Station, St. Andrew Sq., ☎ 0131/556–8464; recorded timetable, ☎ 0131/556–8414) and **NationalExpress** (Walnut Grove, Perth, ☎ 01738/33481) provide bus service to and from London. The main terminal, St. Andrew Square Station, is only a couple of minutes (on foot) north of Waverley rail station, immediately east of St. Andrew Square. Long-distance coaches must be booked in advance from the booking office in the terminal. Edinburgh is approximately eight hours by bus from London.

By Car

Downtown Edinburgh centers on Princes Street, which runs east–west. Drivers from the east coast will come in on A1, Meadowbank Stadium serving as a landmark. The highway bypasses the suburbs of Musselburgh and Tranent; therefore, any bottlenecks will occur close to downtown. From the Borders the approach to Princes Street is by A7/A68 through Newington, an area offering a wide choice of accommodations. From Newington the east end of Princes Street is reached by North Bridge and South Bridge. Approaching from the southwest, drivers will join the west end of Princes Street (Lothian Rd.), via A701 and A702, and those coming west from Glasgow or Stirling will meet Princes Street from M8 or M9, respectively. A slightly more complicated approach is via M90—from Forth Road Bridge/Perth/east coast; the key road for getting downtown is Queensferry Road, which joins Charlotte Square close to the west end of Princes Street.

By Plane

At present, Edinburgh Airport offers no transatlantic flights. **Glasgow Airport** (☎ 0141/887–1111, ext. 4552), 50 miles west of Edinburgh, is now the major point of entry into Edinburgh for transatlantic flights (*see* Arriving and Departing in Chapter 5). **Edinburgh Airport** (☎ 0131/333–1000), 7 miles west of the city, has airlinks throughout the United Kingdom—London Heathrow/Gatwick/Stansted/London City, Birmingham, Aberdeen, Bristol, Kirkwall (Orkney), Shetland, Manchester, Leeds/Bradford, Norwich, Southampton, East Midlands, Humberside, and Belfast in Northern Ireland—as well as with a number of European cities, including Amsterdam, Dublin, and Brussels. There are flights to Edinburgh Airport virtually every hour from London's Gatwick and Heathrow airports; it's usually faster and less complicated to fly through Gatwick, which has excellent rail service from London's Victoria Station. Airlines serving Edinburgh include **British Airways, British Midland, Air UK, Enterprise, BusinessAir, Servisair, Sabena, Aer Lingus,** and **Air France.**

BETWEEN EDINBURGH AIRPORT AND CITY CENTER

There are no rail links to center city, despite the fact that the airport sits between two main lines. By bus or car you can usually make it to Edinburgh in a comfortable half hour, unless you hit the morning or evening rush hours (7:30–9 AM and 4–6 PM).

By Bus: Two companies, **Lothian Regional Transport** (☎ 0131/220–4111) and **Guide Friday** (☎ 0131/556–2244), run buses between Edinburgh Airport's main terminal building and Waverley Bridge, in center city and within easy reach of several hotels. The buses run every 30 minutes on weekdays (9–5) and less frequently (roughly every hour) during off-peak hours and on weekends. The trip takes about 30 minutes (about 45 minutes during rush hour). Single fare for Lothian Regional Transport is £2.80, for Guide Friday, £3.20.

By Limousine: The following Edinburgh firms provide chauffeur-driven limousines to meet flights at Edinburgh Airport: **David Grieve Chauffeur Drive** (8 Merchiston Mews, ☎ 0131/229–8666; cost, about £30), **Scothire Chauffeur Drive** (46 Ladywell Ave., ☎ 0131/334–9017; cost, £25), and **Sleigh Ltd.** (6 Devon Pl., ☎ 0131/337–3171; cost, about £40).

By Rental Car: There is a good choice of car rental companies operating from the terminal building. The cost is from £40 a day, depending on the firm. If you choose to plunge yourself into Edinburgh's traffic system, take care on the first couple of traffic circles (called roundabouts) you encounter on the way into town from the airport—even the most experienced drivers find them challenging. By car the airport is about 7 miles west of Princes Street downtown and is clearly marked from A8. The usual route to downtown is via the suburb of Corstorphine. The following rental firms have booths at the airport: **Avis** (☎ 0131/333–1866), **Alamo** (☎ 0131/344–3250), **Europcar** (☎ 0131/344–3114), and **Hertz** (☎ 0131/344–3260).

By Taxi: These are readily available outside the terminal. The trip takes 20–30 minutes to center city, 15 minutes longer during morning and evening rush hours. The fare is roughly £12. Note that because of a local regulation, airport taxis picking up faires from the terminal are any color, not the typical black cabs, although these do take fares going to the airport.

BETWEEN GLASGOW AIRPORT AND EDINBURGH

By Bus and Train: Scottish Citylink Coaches (☎ 0141/332–9191) buses leave Glasgow Airport every hour at five minutes to the hour for Buchanan Bus Station in downtown Glasgow (a 20-minute trip) and then continue to St. Andrew Bus Station in downtown Edinburgh. The trip takes one hour and 40 minutes, including the stop in Glasgow, and costs about £6. A somewhat more pleasant option is to take a cab from Glasgow Airport to Glasgow's Queen Street Train Station (15 minutes, £11) and then take the train to Waverley Station in Edinburgh. Trains leave about every 30 minutes; the trip takes 50 minutes and costs £6. Another, less expensive alternative—best for those with little luggage—is to take the bus from Glasgow Airport to Glasgow's Buchanan Bus Station, walk five minutes to the Queen Street train station, and catch the train to Edinburgh.

By Taxi: Taxis to downtown Edinburgh take about 70 minutes and cost around £70.

By Train

Edinburgh's main train station, **Waverley,** is downtown, below Waverley Bridge and around the corner from the unmistakable spire of the Scott Monument. Recorded information on services to King's Cross Station in London is available over the telephone for weekday service (☎ 0131/557–3000), Saturday service (☎ 0131/557–2737), and Sunday service (☎ 0131/557–1616). For information on all other destinations or for other inquiries, call 0131/556–2451. King's Cross Station can be reached by dialing 0171/278–2477. Travel time from Edinburgh to London by train is as little as 4½ hours for the fastest services.

Edinburgh's other main station is **Haymarket,** about four minutes (by rail) west of Waverley. All Glasgow and other western and northern services stop here. Haymarket can be slightly more convenient for visitors staying in hotels beyond the west end of Princes Street.

Getting Around

By Bus

Lothian Regional Transport, operating dark-red-and-white buses, is the main operator within Edinburgh. The **Edinburgh Freedom Ticket** (£2), allowing unlimited one-day travel on the city's buses, can be purchased in advance. More expensive is the **Tourist Card** (£4.80 for 2 days, £1.40 each additional day), available in units of 2 to 13 days, which gives unlimited access to buses (except Airlink) and includes vouchers for savings on tours and entrance fees. *27 Hanover St.,* ☎ *0131/220–4111.* ☼ *Mar.–Oct., Mon.–Sat. 8 AM–7 PM, Sun. 9–4:15; Nov.–Feb., Mon.–Sat. 8–6, closed Sun.*

S.M.T. (St. Andrew Sq., ☎ 0131/556–8464), operating green buses, provides much of the service into Edinburgh and offers day tours around and beyond the city. You will also see other bus companies, including **Lowland Scottish** and **Fife Scottish,** which generally operate routes into and out of Edinburgh to other parts of Scotland.

By Car

Driving in Edinburgh has its quirks and pitfalls, but competent drivers should not be intimidated. Metered parking in center city is scarce and expensive, and the local traffic wardens are alert. When parking, note that illegally parked cars are routinely wheel-clamped and towed away. Getting your car back will be expensive. After 6 PM, however, the parking situation improves considerably, and you may manage to find a space quite near your hotel, even downtown. But if you park on a yellow line or in a resident's parking bay, be prepared to move your car by 8 AM the following morning, when the rush hour gets under way.

Princes Street is usually considered the city center. The street runs east–west; motorists using the A1 east-coast road enter the city from the east end of Princes Street. Using the bypass, it is possible to reach key points to the west, such as the airport or the Forth Road Bridge (gateway to the north), from many parts of the outskirts and from East Lothian without getting tangled up in downtown traffic.

By Taxi
Taxi stands can be found throughout the downtown area; the following locations are the most convenient: the west end of Princes Street, South St., David Street, and North St. Andrew Street (both just off St. Andrew Sq.), Waverley Market, Waterloo Place, and Lauriston Place. Alternatively, hail any taxi displaying an illuminated "For Hire" sign.

By Train
Edinburgh has no urban or suburban rail systems.

Maps
Several excellent city maps are available at bookshops. The *Bartholomew Edinburgh Plan,* with a scale of approximately 4 inches to 1 mile, by the once-independent and long-established Edinburgh cartographic company John Bartholomew and Sons Ltd., is particularly recommended.

Guided Tours

Orientation
Scottish Tourist Guides (contact Bob Motion, 14 East Court, Thistle Foundation, Niddrie Mains Rd., Edinburgh EH16 4ED, ☎ and fax 0131/661–7977), endorsed by the Scottish Tourist Board, offers knowledgeable guides appropriate for an individual or a group. The tours are wide ranging and flexible.

Lothian Regional Transport's Edinburgh Classic Tour provides a worthwhile introduction to the Old Town and the New Town. The tour doesn't offer the most in-depth commentary, but it is useful for orienting new visitors to the city. The ticket is quite a bargain because it is valid on any other Lothian bus (except Airlink and night buses) for the remainder of the day. There are frequent departures from Waverley Bridge (outside the rail station) and other points around the city. Open-top buses operate in suitable weather. This is a flexible, show-up-and-hop-on service, meaning that you can get off the bus at any attractions you may want to see more closely. Allow an hour for the complete tour. You can buy tickets from the Lothian Regional Transport office on Hanover Street (*see* Getting Around, *above*), or you can buy them from the driver. *Cost: £4.50 adults, £1 children.*

Scotline Tours' City Tour offers a comprehensive introduction to the city, as well as visits to Edinburgh Castle, the High Kirk of St. Giles, and the Palace of Holyroodhouse. (Note that the fees quoted below include admission to the castle and palace.) Allow at least four hours for the entire tour. Scotline also offers a range of day tours to points beyond the city. *87 High St.,* ☎ *0131/557–0162. Call 8 AM–11 PM for reservations. Cost: £16.50 adults, £7.50 children.*

Guide Friday, Ltd., also offers an orientation tour. It runs less frequently than Lothian Regional Transport's equivalent, but you may enjoy riding through the streets of Edinburgh on one of Guide Friday's cheerful open-top, double-decker buses. The commentaries provided tend to be more colorful than accurate. The minimum tour time is one hour. *Reception Centre, Waverley Station,* ☎ *0131/556–2244. Cost: £5.50 adults, £1.50 children 5–12, £4 senior citizens.*

The Cadies and Witchery Tours, fully qualified members of the Scottish Tourist Guides Association, have since 1983 steadily built a reputation for combining entertainment and historical accuracy in their lively, enthusiastic, and varied walking tours through the Old Town. ☎ *0131/225–6745. Cost: £5.*

Special-Interest
Scottish Tourist Guides (*see* Orientation Tours, *above*) will design tours tailored to your interests; it also offers a special Nightlife Tour. **The Cadies and Witchery Tours** (*see above*) operates a Ghosts and Ghouls tour through the narrow Old Town alleyways and closes with costumed guides and other theatrical characters showing up en route.

Robin's Edinburgh Tours, run by an Edinburgh native, offers a number of tours built around specific themes, such as Georgian Edinburgh, Robert Burns in Edinburgh, and Holyrood Royal Park, as well as a range of talks and slide shows. *66 Willowbrae Rd.,* ☎ *0131/661–0125. Cost: from £4.*

Tours from Edinburgh
Both **Lothian Regional Transport** and **Scotline Tours** (*see* Orientation Tours, *above*) offer day trips to destinations such as St. Andrews and Fife or the Trossachs and Loch Lomond.

Personal Guides
Scottish Tourist Guides (☎ 0131/661–7977) can supply guides (in 19 languages) who are fully qualified and will meet clients at any point of entry into the United Kingdom or Scotland.

Important Addresses and Numbers

Consulate
American Consulate General (3 Regent Terr., ☎ 0131/556–8315).

Emergencies
For **police, ambulance,** or **fire,** dial 999. No coins are needed for emergency calls made from pay phones.

Hospital
Edinburgh Royal Infirmary (51 Lauriston Pl., ☎ 0131/229–2477) is south of the city center—down George IV Bridge and then to the right.

Where to Change Money
Most city-center banks have a **bureau de change** (usual banking hours are weekdays 9:30–4:45). The bureau de change at the Tourist Centre, Waverley Market is open on Sunday from May to September. There are also bureaux de change at **Waverley Rail Station, Edinburgh Airport,** and **Frasers** department store (west end of Princes Street).

Late-Night Pharmacies

You can find out which pharmacy is open late on a given night by look-ing at the notice posted on every pharmacy-shop door. A pharmacy—or "dispensing chemist"—is easily identified by its sign, showing a green cross on a white background.

Boots (48 Shandwick Pl., west end of Princes St., ☎ 0131/225–6757) is open weekdays 8:30–9, Saturday 8:45–9, Sunday 10–5.

Travel Agencies

American Express (139 Princes St., ☎ 0131/225–7881) is near Frasers department store, at the west end of Princes Street. **Thomas Cook** (79a Princes St., ☎ 0131/220–4039) is near Littlewoods department store, in the center of Princes Street.

Lost and Found

To retrieve lost property, try the **Lothian and Borders Police Headquarters** (Fettes Ave., ☎ 0131/311–3131).

Post Offices

The **Head Post Office** is at 2 Waterloo Place, at the east end of Princes Street (☎ 0131/550–8232; open weekdays 9–5:30, Sat. 9 AM–12:30 PM). Main post offices in the city center are at 40 Frederick Street, 33 Forrest Road, and 7 Hope Street. Many newsagents also sell stamps.

Visitor Information

Visitors arriving in Edinburgh can get expert advice on what to see and do, where to go, and what's going on throughout Scotland at the **Edinburgh and Scotland Information Centre,** adjacent to Waverley Station. Follow the TIC signs in the station and throughout the city. In addition to free information and literature, its comprehensive range of services also includes an accommodations service (Book-A-Bed-Ahead), coach tour tickets, theater reservations, route planning, a Scottish bookshop, and currency exchange. Visitors can also buy National Trust, Historic Scotland, and Great British Heritage passes here. For 24-hour recorded information call 01891/775770; the charge is 48p per minute. *3 Princes St., ☎ 0131/557–1700. ☺ May, June, Sept., Mon.–Sat. 9–7, Sun. 11–7; July, Aug., Mon.–Sat. 9–8, Sun. 11–8; Nov.–Mar., Mon.–Sat. 9–6, closed Sun.; Oct. and Apr., Mon.–Sat. 9–6, Sun. 11–6.*

Complete information is also available at the tourist-information desk at **Edinburgh Airport.** ☎ *0131/333–1000. ☺ Apr.–Oct., Mon.–Sat. 8:30 AM–9:30 PM, Sun. 9:30–9:30; Nov.–Mar., weekdays 8:30–6, weekends 9–5.*

The List, a publication available from city-center bookshops and newsagents, and **What's On in Edinburgh,** from the Edinburgh and Scotland Information Centre, both list information about all types of events, from movies and theater to sports. **The Scotsman,** a national newspaper published in Edinburgh, is good for both national and international news coverage, as well as for reviews and notices of upcoming events in Edinburgh and elsewhere in Scotland.

4 Glasgow

Recent efforts at commercial and cultural renewal have restored much of the style and grandeur Glasgow had in the 19th century, at the height of its economic power. Now it is again a vibrant metropolitan center with a thriving artistic life: The city was selected as Europe's Cultural Capital for 1990. Glasgow is a convenient touring center, too, in easy reach of the Clyde coast to the south and with excellent transportation links to the rest of Scotland.

By John
Hutchinson

Updated by
Gilbert
Summers

IN THE DAYS WHEN BRITAIN still had an empire, Glasgow pronounced itself the Second City of the Empire. The people of Glasgow were justifiably proud of their city, since it was there that Britain's great steamships (including the 80,000-ton *Queen Elizabeth*) were built. The term *Clydebuilt* (from Glasgow's River Clyde) became synonymous with good workmanship and lasting quality. It was also the Glaswegians who built the railway engines that opened up the Canadian prairies, the South African veldt, the Australian plains, and the Indian subcontinent. Scots engineers were to be found wherever there were engines (and so it was perhaps no coincidence that even Captain Kirk on the Starship *Enterprise* had to say, "Beam me up, Scottie" to his engineer).

Scholars have argued for years about what the name Glasgow means (pronounce it to rhyme with *toe* and put the stress on the first syllable), but, generally, "dear green place" is the interpretation that finds most favor today. Most suitable it is, too, for a town that, despite industrialization, has more city parks than anywhere else in Britain, and even the famous River Clyde is now clean enough for trout and salmon.

Glasgow first came into prominence in Scottish history somewhere around 1,400 years ago, and typically for this rambunctious city it was all to do with an argument between a husband and his wife. One of the local chieftains suspected, with some justification, that his wife had been having an affair, so he crept up on the suspect, one of his knights, and took from him a ring that she had rather foolishly given her lover—foolishly, because it had originally been given to her by her husband. The furious husband flung the ring into the River Clyde, then told his wife the next day that he wanted her to wear it that evening. The lady was distraught and called on the local holy man, Mungo, to help. Clearly a useful man to have in a tricky situation, Mungo sent a monk out fishing, and the first bite the monk had was a salmon with the ring in its mouth. Whether the lady learned her lesson or called on Mungo's services regularly after that, history does not relate.

Mungo features in two other legends: one of a pet bird that he nursed back to life and another, of a bush or tree, the branches of which he used to relight a fire. Tree, bird, and the salmon with a ring in its mouth are all to be found on the city of Glasgow's coat of arms, together with a bell that Mungo brought from Rome. Mungo is now the city's patron saint. His tomb is to be found in the mighty medieval cathedral that bears his name.

Glasgow led a fairly quiet existence in the Middle Ages. Its cathedral was the center of religious life, and although the city was made a Royal Burgh in 1175 by King William the Lion, its population was never more than a few thousand. What changed Glasgow irrevocably and laid the foundations for its immense prosperity was the Treaty of Union between Scotland and England in 1707. This allowed Scotland to trade with the essentially English colonies in America, and with their expansion Glasgow prospered. In came cotton, tobacco, and rum; out went various Scottish manufactured goods and clothing. The key to it all in the early days was tobacco, and the prosperous merchants were known as the Tobacco Lords. It was they who ran the city, and their wealth laid the foundation stone for the manufacturing industries of the 19th century.

As Glasgow prospered, so her population grew. The "dear green place" became built over. The original medieval city around the cathedral and the High Street expanded westward. The 18th-century Merchant City, today the subject of a great deal of refurbishment, lies just to the south and west of George Square, and the houses of the merchants are even farther westward, along the gridiron pattern of Glasgow's streets up the hill toward Blytheswood Square.

But the city is not known as an 18th-century city; that honor is left to Edinburgh, in the east. Rather, Glasgow is known as one of the greatest Victorian cities in Europe. The population grew from 80,000 in 1801 to over 700,000 in 1901, and with this enormous growth there developed also a sense of exuberance and confidence, which is reflected in its public buildings. The City Chambers, built in 1888, are an extravaganza of marble and red sandstone, a clear symbol of the Victorian merchants' hopes for the future.

Yet, always at the forefront of change, Glasgow boasts, side by side with the overtly Victorian, an architectural vision of the future in the work of Charles Rennie Mackintosh. The Glasgow School of Art, the Willow Tearoom, and the churches and school buildings he designed point clearly to the clarity and simplicity of 20th-century lines.

Today, Glasgow has taken the best of the past and adapted it for the needs of the present day. The "dear green places" still remain in the city-center parks, to be enjoyed by citizens and visitors alike; the medieval cathedral stands proud, as it has done for 800 years; the Merchant City is revived and thriving; the Victorian splendor has been cleaned of its grime and will look good for many years to come; and the cultural legacy of museums and performing arts lives on stronger than ever (Glasgow was crowned European City of Culture in 1990, throughout 1996 "Glasgow 1996" celebrates the visual arts with special exhibitions in many of the city's galleries, and Glasgow is to be named the "City of Architecture" in 1999). To cap it all, its superb location also makes it an ideal base from which to enjoy day tours of the Scottish countryside. Burns Country, the gardens of Galloway, the islands of the Clyde, Loch Lomond, the Trossachs, and Argyll are only about an hour or so from the city center, as is Edinburgh.

EXPLORING

The first walking tour is relatively flat and almost entirely on city streets; it includes the ancient cathedral, the oldest house in Glasgow, the High Street, and the center of medieval activity—the Merchant City— which developed as Glasgow prospered. Included, too, is the River Clyde, on which Glasgow's trade across the Atlantic developed. The river is always at the center of the city, cutting it in half and offering often surprising views across to the buildings on the other side. In this central part of the city are some of the best examples of the confidence and exuberance in architecture that so characterized the Glasgow of 100 years ago and that today are experiencing a renaissance and a newfound appreciation.

The second tour goes westward and encompasses the University of Glasgow and that other "forgotten" side of Glasgow, unjustly perceived as a grimy center of heavy industry. The University of Glasgow was founded in 1451, making it the third-oldest in Scotland after St. Andrews and Aberdeen, and at least 130 years ahead of the University of Edinburgh. It has thrived as a center of educational excellence, particularly in the sciences. The university buildings are set in parkland, reminding the vis-

itor that Glasgow is a city with more green space per citizen than any
other in Europe. It is also a city of museums and art galleries, having
benefited from the generosity of industrial and commercial philan-
thropists and from the deep-seated desire of the city fathers to place Glasgow at the forefront of British cities. The second walk is quieter and less
bustling, though there are some gentle slopes to walk up.

Tour 1: Medieval Glasgow and the Merchant City

*Numbers in the margin correspond to points of interest on the Glas-
gow map.*

①   **George Square,** the focal point of Glasgow's business district, is the
natural starting point for any walking tour. It's in the very heart of Glasgow and convenient to the Buchanan Street bus and underground stations and parking lot, as well as to the Queen Street railway station.
The tourist information center of the Greater Glasgow Tourist Board
is also close by on St. Vincent Place. The square itself is lined with an
impressive array of statues of worthies from days gone by: Queen Victoria; Scotland's national poet Robert Burns; the inventor and devel-
oper of the steam engine, James Watt; Prime Minister William Gladstone;
and towering above them all, Scotland's foremost writer, Sir Walter Scott.
The column was intended for George III, after whom the square is named,
but his statue was not erected after he was found to be insane toward
the end of his reign. A statue of Sir Walter Scott stands in its place.

★ **②**   The magnificent Italian Renaissance-style **City Chambers** on the east
side of the square was opened by Queen Victoria in 1888. Among the
outstanding features of the interior are the vaulted ceiling of the entrance hall, marble and alabaster staircases, and the banqueting hall,
as well as a number of the smaller suites, each furnished in different
woods. *George Sq.,* ☎ *0141/227–4017. Free guided tours weekdays
at 10:30 and 2:30 (may be closed for occasional civic functions).*

Leave George Square by the northeast corner and head eastward
through a not particularly pretty part of the city along George Street,
past the University of Strathclyde. Turn left at High Street, then go up

★ **③**   the hill to **Glasgow Cathedral,** an unusual double church, one above
the other. Dedicated to St. Mungo, Glasgow's patron saint, the cathedral was begun in the 12th century and completed about 300 years
later. It was spared the ravages of the Reformation, which destroyed
so many of Scotland's medieval churches, because the trade guilds of
Glasgow regarded it as their own church and defended it. In the lower
church is the splendid crypt of St. Mungo, who is sometimes also
called St. Kentigern. (*Kentigern* means "chief word," while *Mungo* is
perhaps a nickname meaning "dear name.") The site of the tomb has
been revered since the 6th century, when St. Mungo founded a church
here. *Cathedral St.,* ☎ *0131/244–3101.* ☛ *Free.* ☸ *Services Apr.–Sept.,
Mon.–Sat. 9:30–6, Sun. 2–5; Oct.–Mar., Mon.–Sat. 9:30–4, Sun. 2–
4.*

Take time to visit the St. Mungo Museum and Cathedral Visitor Center, opened in 1993. On display is material covering the many religious
groups who've settled throughout the centuries in Glasgow and the west
of Scotland. The centerpiece is Salvador Dali's magnificent painting,
Christ of St. John of the Cross. Inside there's a gift shop, toilets, and
a café. *2 Castle St.,* ☎ *0141/553–2557.* ☛ *Free.* ☸ *Mon.–Sat. 10–5,
Sun. 11–5. Closed Christmas, New Year's.*

One fascinating if macabre place just off Cathedral Square is the
④   **Necropolis,** a burying ground since the beginning of recorded history,

with some extraordinarily elaborate Victorian graves, watched over by a statue of John Knox. It includes the tomb of 19th-century Glasgow merchant William Miller, author of the "Wee Willie Winkie" nursery rhyme. *Behind Glasgow Cathedral,* ☎ *0141/333–0800.*

5 Opposite the cathedral, across Castle Street, is **Provand's Lordship,** Glasgow's oldest house. It was built in 1471 by Bishop Andrew Muirhead as a residence for churchmen. Mary, Queen of Scots, is said to have stayed here. After her day, however, the house fell into decline and was used alternately as a sweet shop, a soft-drink factory, the home of the city hangman, and a junk shop. It was eventually rescued by the city and turned into a museum. Exhibits show the house as it might have looked in its heyday. *Castle St.,* ☎ *0141/552–8819.* ☛ *Free.* ☉ *Mon.–Sat. 10–5, Sun. 11–5.*

Retrace your steps down Castle Street and High Street. Look for the Greek goddess Pallas on top of the imposing gray sandstone building on the right, the former Bank of Scotland building, before reaching the
6 Tolbooth Steeple at **Glasgow Cross.** This was the very center of the medieval city. The mercat cross, topped by a unicorn, marked the spot where merchants met, where the market was held, and where criminals were executed. Here, too, was the *tron,* or weigh beam, used to check merchants' weights, installed in 1491. The Tolbooth Steeple itself dates from 1626 and served as the civic center and place where travelers entering the city paid tolls.

Continue east along London Road (under the bridge) about a quarter
7 of a mile and you'll come to **The Barras** ("barrows", or pushcarts), Scotland's largest indoor market, a mecca for those addicted to searching through piles of junk for bargains. Open only on weekends, this is probably the nearest Scotland gets to a flea market. The atmosphere is always good humored, and you can find just about anything here, in any condition, from old model railroads to cheese rolls. ☎ *0141/552–7258.* ☛ *Free.* ☉ *Weekends 9–5.*

8 Turn down Greendyke Street from London Road to reach **Glasgow Green** by the River Clyde. Glasgow's oldest park has a long history as a favorite spot for public recreation and political demonstrations. Note the Nelson Column, erected long before London's; the Arch, now the finish line for the thousands of runners of the Glasgow Half Marathon; and the Templeton Business Centre, once a carpet factory, built in the late 19th century in the style of the Doge's Palace in Venice. The most
★ **9** significant building in the park is the **People's Palace,** an impressive Victorian red sandstone building that houses an intriguing museum dedicated to the city's social history; included among the exhibits is one devoted to the ordinary folk of Glasgow, called "The People's Story." Also on show are the writing desk of John McLean, the "Red Clydeside" political activist who came to Lenin's notice, and the famous "banana boots" worn on stage by Billy Connolly. Behind the museum are the well-restored Winter Gardens, a relatively sheltered spot favored by visitors who want to escape the often-chilly winds whistling across the green. ☎ *0141/554–0223.* ☛ *Free.* ☉ *Mon.–Sat. 10–5, Sun. 11–5.*

Go back to Greendykes Street, past the new St. Andrew's Square development—with the magnificent St. Andrew's Church (1750) as its centerpiece—then via Saltmarket northwards to Tolbooth Steeple. Continue westward along Trongate. This is where the powerful "tobacco barons" who traded with the Americas presided. On the right, down Albion Street, are the offices of Glasgow's daily papers, the *Herald* and the *Evening Times.* On the left, jutting out into Trongate, is

Glasgow

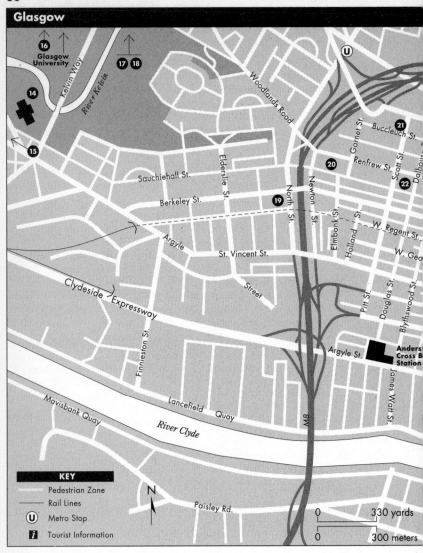

The Barras, **7**
Botanic Gardens, **18**
City Chambers, **2**
George Square, **1**
Glasgow Cathedral, **3**
Glasgow Cross, **6**
Glasgow Gallery of
Modern Art, **12**

Glasgow Green, **8**
Glasgow School of
Art, **22**
Hunterian Art
Gallery, **17**
Hunterian
Museum, **16**
Hutcheson's Hall, **10**
Kelvingrove, **14**

Mitchell Library, **19**
Museum of
Transport, **15**
Necropolis, **4**
People's Palace, **9**
Provand's Lordship, **5**
Regimental Museum
of the Royal
Highland Fusiliers, **20**

Scottish Stock
Exchange, **13**
Tenement House, **21**
Virginia Court, **11**

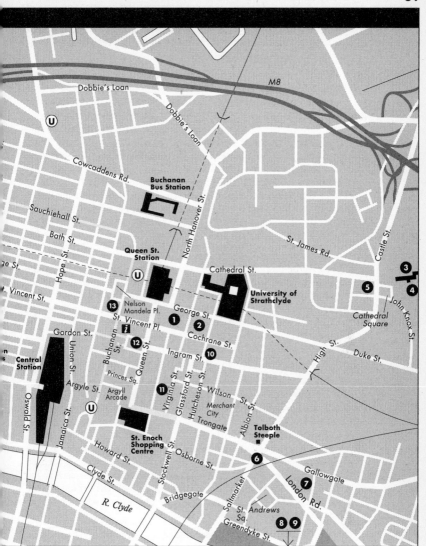

Dobbie's Loan

M8

Dobbie's Loan

U

Cowcaddens Rd.

Buchanan
Bus Station

Sauchiehall St.

Bath St.

St. James Rd.

North Hanover St.

Queen St.
Station

U

Cathedral St.

University of
Strathclyde

Castle St.

3

5

4

John Knox St.

Cathedral
Square

ge St.

Hope St.

Vincent St.

Nelson
Mandela Pl.

St. Vincent Pl.

13

George St.

1

2

Cochrane St.

Duke St.

High St.

Gordon St.

Union St.

Central
Station

12

Buchanan St.

Queen St.

Ingram St.

10

Princes Sq.

Argyle St.

Argyll
Arcade

11

Virginia St.

Glassford St.

Hutcheson St.

Wilson

Merchant
City

Albion St.

St.

U

St. Enoch
Shopping
Centre

Jamaica St.

Oswald St.

Howard St.

Stockwell St.

Osborne St.

Trongate

Tolboth
Steeple

6

Gallowgate

Clyde St.

Bridgegate

Saltmarket

7

London Rd.

R. Clyde

St. Andrews
Sq.

Greendyke St.

8

9

the Tron Steeple, all that remains of a church burned down in 1793 when a joke by the local chapter of the Hell-Fire Club (young aristocratic troublemakers) got a little out of hand. The rebuilt church has now been converted into the Tron Theatre.

Continue down the Trongate then turn right into Hutcheson Street. This is Glasgow's **Merchant City,** a once run-down area but now renovated. Among the preserved Georgian and Victorian buildings are elegant designer boutiques. The City and County Buildings, on your right, were built in 1842 to house civil servants; note the impressive arrangement of bays and Corinthian columns. At the end of the street, ★ ❿ just south of George Square, look for **Hutcheson's Hall,** a visitor center, shop, and regional office for the National Trust for Scotland. This elegant, neoclassical building was designed by David Hamilton in 1802. The hall was originally a hospice founded by two brothers, George and Thomas Hutcheson; you can see their statues in niches in the facade. *158 Ingram St., ☏ 0141/552–8391. ☛ Free. ☉ Weekdays 9:30–5, Sat. 10–4. Shop open Mon.–Sat. 10–5.*

Turn west onto Ingram Street and left down Glassford Street to see the **Trades House** on the right, which has a facade built in 1791 to designs by Robert Adam. Turn right along Wilson Street to reach Virginia Street, another favorite haunt of Glasgow's tobacco merchants. At No. 33, a former tobacco exchange survives, now an indoor shopping center. ⓫ Nearby, **Virginia Court,** somewhat faded now, also echoes those far-off days. Peer through the bars of the gates and note the wagon-wheel ruts still visible in the roadway. Close by is a good range of antiques shops, notably the Virginia Galleries with its pleasant indoor café.

Walk northward up Virginia Street back to Ingram Street. To the left you'll have a good view down to the elegant Royal Exchange Square and the **Royal Exchange** itself. Designed by David Hamilton and finished in 1829, the Exchange was a meeting place for merchants and traders. It later became Stirling's Library, but in April 1996 opens as ⓬ the **Glasgow Gallery of Modern Art.** It incorporates the mansion built in 1780 by William Cunningham, one of the wealthiest of the tobacco lords. Royal Exchange Square leads, for pedestrians, westward to the pedestrian-zone shopping area of Buchanan Street. The Princes Square shopping mall on the east side has a particularly good selection of specialty shops.

Make your way down to Argyle Street. Looking to the west, you'll see the large railway bridge supporting the tracks going into **Central Station.** The depot is known as the Heilanman's Umbrella, because it was the point of meeting and shelter for so many Highlanders who had moved to Glasgow in search of better economic opportunities in the last century. Pause to look at the lovely iron arcading of **Gardner's Warehouse** at 36 Jamaica Street. Head north up Union Street and note the extraordinary architecture of Nos. 84–100, the so-called **Egyptian Halls,** designed and built in 1871 by Alexander "Greek" Thomson.

From here continue north to St. Vincent Street and turn right to reach ⓭ Nelson Mandela Place, also called St. George's Place. Here is the **Scottish Stock Exchange,** worthwhile for the exterior alone: It was built in 1877 in an ornate "French Venetian" style.

Pause briefly at the handsome **Merchants' House** on the corner of West George Street and George Square (now the home of Glasgow's Chamber of Commerce) to look at the golden sailing ship against the sky, a reminder of the importance of trade to Glasgow's prosperity. *West side*

*of George Sq., ☎ 0141/221–8272. ☛ Free. Hall and anterooms may
be seen by arrangement. ☉ May–Sept., weekdays 2–4.*

Tour 2: The West End

You can use the suggested route here to acquaint yourself with the rich
legacy of education, culture, art, and parkland that is to be found in
Glasgow's West End. Included are a number of museums and galleries,
each of which could take up an enjoyable day in itself, so you could
think of this as the basis of several walks.

★ ⑭ A good place to start is at the city's main art gallery and museum, **Kelvingrove**—looking like a combination of cathedral and castle—in Kelvingrove Park, west of the M8 beltway, at the junction of Sauchiehall
and Argyle streets (note that Sauchiehall is pronounced *socky-hall*). There
are parking facilities, and plenty of buses go there from downtown.
The building is a magnificently ornamented red sandstone edifice dating from the early part of this century. There has always been debate
as to which facade is the front and which is the back. However you
enter, Kelvingrove houses what is claimed to be Britain's finest civic
collection of British and Continental paintings, with 17th-century
Dutch art, a selection from the French Barbizon school, French Im-
pressionism, Scottish art from the 17th century to the present, silver,
ceramics, European armor, even Egyptian archaeological finds. ☎
0141/357–3929. ☛ Free. ☉ Mon.–Sat. 10–5, Sun. 11–5.

★ ⑮ Across Argyle Street in the Old Kelvin Hall exhibition center is the **Museum of Transport.** Here Glasgow's history of locomotive building is
dramatically displayed with full-size exhibits. The collection of Clydebuilt ship models is world famous. Anyone who remembers Britain in
the 1950s will be able to wallow in nostalgia at the re-created street
scene from that era. *Kelvin Hall, 1 Bunhouse Rd., ☎ 0141/357–3929.
☛ Free. ☉ Mon.–Sat. 10–5, Sun. 11–5.*

Kelvingrove Park takes its name from the River Kelvin, which flows
through it. Lord Kelvin, the scientist who pioneered a great deal of work
in electricity, is remembered by a statue in the park. The city purchased
the land for the park in 1852, and, apart from the abundance of statues of prominent Glaswegians, the park is graced by a massive fountain commemorating a Lord Provost of Glasgow from the 1850s, a duck
pond, a play area, a small open-air theater, and lots of exotic trees. It
can be a charming retreat from the noise and bustle of the city.

As you walk up Kelvin Way through the trees, the skyline to your left
is dominated by the Gilbert Scott building, the University of Glasgow's
main edifice. Built just over a century ago, the building is a good example of the Gothic Revival style. The **University of Glasgow Visitor
Centre** has exhibits on the university, a coffee bar, and a gift shop, and
is the starting point for walking tours of the campus. *University Ave.,
☎ 0141/330–5511. ☛ Free. ☉ Mon.–Sat. 9:30–5; also Sun. 2–5 from
May–Sept.*

Turn left up University Avenue, past the Memorial Gates, which were
erected in 1951 to celebrate the university's 500th birthday. On either
side of the road here are two important galleries, both maintained by
the university. They house the collections of William Hunter, an 18th-
century Glasgow doctor who assembled a staggering quantity of extremely valuable material. On the south side of University Avenue, in
⑯ the Victorian part of the university, is the **Hunterian Museum,** the city's
oldest (1807), which displays Hunter's hoards of coins, manuscripts,

scientific instruments, and archaeological artifacts in a striking Gothic building. *Glasgow University,* ☎ *0141/330–4221.* ☛ *Free.* ⊘ *Mon.–Sat. 9:30–5.*

★ ⑰ Even more interesting is the **Hunterian Art Gallery,** in an unremarkable building from the 1970s across the road. The gallery houses the doctor's collection of paintings, together with prints and drawings by Reynolds, Rodin, Rembrandt, and Tintoretto, as well as a major collection of paintings by James McNeill Whistler, who had a great affection for the city that bought one of his earliest paintings. Also in the gallery is a replica of Charles Rennie Mackintosh's town house, which used to stand nearby. The rooms are all furnished with Mackintosh's distinctive Art Nouveau chairs, tables, beds, and cupboards, and the walls are decorated in the equally distinctive style devised by him and his wife, Margaret. *Glasgow University, Hillhead St.,* ☎ *0141/330–5431.* ☛ *Free.* ⊘ *Mon.–Sat. 9:30–5. Mackintosh House closed 12:30–1:30.*

At this point you can either make a small detour to the Botanic Gardens and return along the banks of the River Kelvin to Kelvingrove Park or go directly through some of Glasgow's elegant 19th-century districts to the extreme northwest of the downtown area, where the rest of the tour resumes.

⑱ The walk from the university to the **Botanic Gardens** is unfortunately not very exciting, but it's worth the effort. Continue along University Avenue and turn right at Byres Road, going as far as Great Western Road and the Grosvenor Hotel. The 40 acres of gardens are across the busy Great Western Road. Begun by the Royal Botanical Institute of Glasgow in 1842, the displays here include an herb garden, a wide range of tropical plants, and a world-famous collection of orchids. The most spectacular building in the complex is the **Kibble Palace,** built in 1873; it was originally the conservatory of a Victorian eccentric named John Kibble. Its domed, interlinked greenhouses contain tree ferns, palm trees, temperate plants, and the Tropicarium, where you can experience the lushness of a tropical rain forest. Elsewhere on the grounds are more conventional greenhouses, as well as well-maintained lawns and colorful flower beds. *Great Western Rd.,* ☎ *0141/334– 2422.* ☛ *Free. Gardens open daily 7–dusk; Kibble Palace open Mon.– Sat. 10–4:45, Sun. 12–4:45; other greenhouses open daily 1–4:45 (all close at 4:15 in winter).*

After leaving the Botanic Gardens, cross the River Kelvin on St. Margaret Drive just past the BBC Scotland building. Turn right, then right again down the steps to the Kelvin Walkway on the north bank of the river. (Farther upstream the Kelvin Walkway connects with the West Highland Way, an official long-distance footpath leading to Fort William, approximately 100 miles away.) The walkway headed downstream back toward the city center first crosses a foot-bridge, then passes old mill buildings and goes under Belmont Street and the Great Western Road at Kelvinbridge before passing Kelvinbridge underground station and going under the Gibson Street bridge and back into Kelvingrove Park.

At this point, you can choose to take one of the paths up the hill and explore the stately Victorian crescents and streets of the park area or you can take the lower road past the fountain and head directly back to Sauchiehall Street. Whichever way you choose, you should end up, having walked eastward, at the point where Sauchiehall Street crosses the M8 motorway. Down North Street to your right (southward) you'll

⑲ see the front of **Mitchell Library,** the largest public reference library in

Europe; it houses over a million volumes, including what is claimed to be the largest collection on Robert Burns in the world. The library's founder, Stephen Mitchell, who died in 1874 (the same year the library was founded), is commemorated by a bust in the entrance hall. Minerva, goddess of wisdom, looks down from the library's dome, encouraging the library's users and frowning at the drivers thundering along the motorway just in front of her. The western facade (at the back) is particularly beautiful. *North St.,* ☎ *0141/305–2999.* ☛ *Free.* ⊘ *Weekdays 9–9, Sat. 9–5.*

Cross the M8 motorway, and continue down Sauchiehall Street to the **②⓿ Regimental Museum of the Royal Highland Fusiliers,** which displays the history of this famous regiment and the men who served in it. Exhibits include medals, badges, and uniforms. *518 Sauchiehall St.,* ☎ *0141/332–0961.* ☛ *Free.* ⊘ *Mon.–Thurs. 9–4:30, Fri. 9–4.*

★ **㉑** Turn up Garnet Street and go to the top, then right on Buccleuch (pronounced *buck-LOO*) Street. On the left is the **Tenement House,** a very special find tucked away from normal tourist routes. This is an ordinary, simple city-center apartment that was occupied from 1911 to 1965 by the same lady, Miss Agnes Toward, who never seemed to throw anything away. What is left is a fascinating time capsule, painstakingly preserved with her everyday furniture and belongings. The red sandstone tenement building itself dates from 1892. *145 Buccleuch St.,* ☎ *0141/ 333–0183.* ☛ *£2 adults, £1 children.* ⊘ *Mar.–Oct., daily 1:30–5 (last admission 4:30).*

★ **㉒** Coming out of the Tenement House, turn east on Buccleuch Street to Scott Street. Turn south on Scott Street, noticing the mural that reflects the name of the area, Garnethill, then turn left onto Renfrew Street to reach Charles Rennie Mackintosh's masterpiece, the **Glasgow School of Art.** The building—exterior and interior, structure, furnishings, and decoration—forms a unified whole, reflecting the inventive genius of this man, who was only 28 years old when he won the competition for the design of the building. Architects and designers from all over the world come to admire it, but because it is a working school of art, general visitor access is sometimes limited. Conducted tours are available, and there is always the chance that you can have a quick look inside. It's best to call ahead for more information. *167 Renfrew St.,* ☎ *0141/353–4500.*

TIME OUT The **Willow Tearoom** (above a jeweler's shop at 217 Sauchiehall St.) is restored to its original archetypal Art Nouveau design by Charles Rennie Mackintosh, right down to the decorated tables and chairs. The building was designed by Mackintosh in 1903 for Miss Kate Cranston, who ran a chain of tearooms. The tree motifs are echoed in the street address, since *sauchie* is an old Scots word for *willow*.

To return to the city center you can either continue down Sauchiehall Street or turn south down Blythswood Street, noting the elegant Blythswood Square (1823–29).

What to See and Do with Children

Many of Glasgow's attractions are also suitable for children, in small doses. The tourist board (*see* Important Addresses and Numbers in Glasgow Essentials, *below*) can provide detailed information and can tell you about swimming pools and sports centers. Most of Glasgow's parks have tennis, lawn-bowling, and putting facilities. In addition, individual parks have boating, dry ski slope, windsurfing, croquet, trampolines, and table tennis. Check with the Parks Department (☎ 0141/227–5064) for details.

Eastwood Butterfly Kingdom, set in lovely Rouken Glen Park not far from the city center, offers a touch of the exotic, with free-flying butterflies and moths in a tropical setting. There is also a tearoom and gift shop. *Rouken Glen Park,* ☎ *0141/620–2084.*

Haggs Castle, an ancient house of the Maxwell family, has been given over entirely to children. Adults are tolerated if they behave themselves. Many of the rooms are designed to illustrate what life was like for children in days gone by; during school holidays the museum runs an extensive interactive program aimed at helping children experience history firsthand. *100 St. Andrews Dr.,* ☎ *0141/427–2725.* ☞ *Free.* ⊙ *Mon.–Sat. 10–5, Sun. 11–5.*

The **Museum of Education** is of great interest to children (even though some profess to hate it), but also to adults. Located in Scotland Street School, one of Charles Rennie Mackintosh's elegant buildings (1906), the museum's classrooms are fitted out in the styles of different historical periods (Victorian, World War II, and the 1950s and 1960s) and the staff is dressed in appropriate costume. There is a permanent exhibition on the history of education in Scotland, and temporary exhibition on a variety of themes. *225 Scotland St.,* ☎ *0141/429–1202.* ☞ *Free.* ⊙ *Mon.–Sat. 10–5, Sun. 2–5.*

People's Palace (*see* Tour 1)

Tenement House (*see* Tour 2)

Victoria Park has a pleasant boating lake and an arboretum, as well as a remarkable Fossil Grove, where the fossilized stumps of trees said to be over 330 million years old have been preserved. (Glasgow has obviously been laying out excellent parks for a long time.) *Victoria Park Dr. N, off Airthrey Ave.,* ☎ *0141/959–2128.* ☞ *Free.* ⊙ *Mon.–Sat. 8–dusk, Sun. 10–dusk; Fossil Grove open by appointment.*

Off the Beaten Path

Pollok Country Park

★ **Pollok Country Park** provides a peaceful green oasis off Paisley Road, just 3 miles southwest of the city center. (You can get there by taxi or car, by city bus, or by a train from Glasgow Central Station to Pollokshaws West Station.) The key attraction here is the **Burrell Collection,** Scotland's finest art collection. A custom-built, ultra-modern yet elegant building houses 8,000 exhibits of all descriptions, from ancient Egyptian, Greek, and Roman artifacts to Chinese ceramics, bronzes, and jade to medieval tapestries, stained glass, Rodin sculptures, and exquisite French Impressionist paintings—all from the magpie collection of an eccentric millionaire, Sir William Burrell, who donated his treasures to the city in 1944. The building was designed with large glass walls so that the items on display could relate to their surroundings: art and nature, supposedly, in perfect harmony. It does, however, seem an incongruous setting for Chinese porcelain and the reconstruction of medieval castle rooms. ☎ *0141/649–7151.* ☞ *Free.* ⊙ *Mon.–Sat. 10–5, Sun. 11–5.*

★ Also located in Pollok Country Park is **Pollok House,** which dates from the mid-1700s and contains the Stirling Maxwell Collection of paintings, including works by El Greco, Murillo, Goya, Signorelli, and William Blake. Fine 18th- and early 19th-century furniture, silver, glass, and porcelain are also on display. The house has fine gardens and looks over the White Cart River and Pollok Park, where, amid mature trees and abundant wildlife, the City of Glasgow's own highland cattle peacefully graze. ☎ 0141/632–0274. ☛ *Free.* ☉ *Mon.–Sat. 10–5, Sun. 11–5.*

Paisley

Once a distinct burgh in its own right, Paisley is now part of the Greater Glasgow suburban area. If your taste runs toward the urban rather than the rural, this town offers plenty of gritty character, largely because of vestiges of its industrial heritage. Paisley can be easily reached by taxi, car, or bus. Trains also run regularly from Glasgow Central to Paisley Gilmour Street Station. Town trail leaflets are available from the tourist information center.

Paisley's industrial prosperity came from textiles and, in particular, from the woolen Paisley shawl. The internationally recognized Paisley pattern is based on the shape of a palm shoot, an ancient Babylonian fertility symbol brought to Britain by way of Kashmir. The full story of the pattern and of the innovative weaving techniques introduced in Paisley is told in the **Paisley Museum and Art Gallery,** which has a world-famous shawl collection. *High St.,* ☎ 0141/889–3151. ☛ *Free.* ☉ *Mon.–Sat. 10–5; closed public holidays.*

The life of the workers in the textile industry is brought to life in **Sma' Shot Cottages,** re-creations of mill workers' houses with displays of linen, lace and Paisley shawls. An 18th-century weaver's cottage is also open to visitors. *11/17 George Pl.,* ☎ 0141/889–1708. ☛ *Free.* ☉ *Apr.–Sept., Wed. and Sat. 1–5 or by appointment.*

Paisley's 12th-century Cluniac **Abbey** dominates the town center. Almost completely destroyed in 1307 and then rebuilt after the Battle of Bannockburn, the abbey is traditionally associated with Walter Fitzallan, the High Steward of Scotland, who gave his name to the Stewart monarchs of Scotland. Outstanding features include the fine stone-vaulted roof and stained glass of the choir. Paisley Abbey is today a busy parish church. ☎ 0141/889–7654. ☛ *Free; group visits by arrangement.* ☉ *Mon.–Sat. 10–3:30, and for Sunday services at 11, 12:15 and 6:30.*

SHOPPING

The old image of industrial Glasgow has changed considerably in recent times as the city has strenuously shrugged off its poor-cousin-to-Edinburgh label. This is evidenced by the many stores, individual shops, and malls that have enhanced Glasgow's style without sacrificing its undoubted character.

Department Stores

The main department stores are **Debenham's** (*see* Argyle Street, *below*) and **Frasers** (*see* Buchanan Street, *below*); other names—**Littlewoods** (56 Argyle St., ☎ 0141/248–3713), **British Home Stores** (67–81 Sauchiehall St., ☎ 0141/332–0401), **C&A** (218 Sauchiehall St., ☎ 0141/333–9441), and **Marks and Spencer** (2/12 Argyle St., ☎ 0141/552–4546)—are also represented. Frasers is the store most worth visiting, not only for its exceptional interior and display, but also for its variety of designer names and helpful, friendly staff.

Shopping Districts

Argyle Street/St. Enoch Square

Start at St. Enoch Square (which is also the main underground station); it houses the St. Enoch Shopping Centre. Walk east toward the main pedestrian area of Argyle Street and you will find all the usual High Street chain stores. The recently much-improved **Debenham's** (87 Argyle St., ☎ 0141/221–0088) department store has been refitted and redecorated, and the upgraded stock includes china and crystal as well as women's and men's clothing (it can also be entered from the St. Enoch Centre). The pedestrian zone on Argyle Street is invariably overcrowded, especially on Saturday, and is certainly not for the impatient shopper. An interesting diversion off Argyle Street is **Argyll Arcade,** a covered street which has the largest collection of jewelers under one roof in Scotland. This L-shape arcade, built in 1904, houses several locally based jewelers and a few shops specializing in antique jewelry. To be recommended are Saul Bercott Ltd. (No. 56) and the arcade branch of Laing the Jeweller (No. 48) for handmade and contemporary designs. Mr. Harold and Son (No. 33) and Michael James (No. 4) have good collections of antique and reproduction designs. Because these shops are privately owned, it is not unheard of to get a cash discount (try asking, you may be lucky). The other end of the Argyll Arcade leads to Buchanan Street.

St. Enoch Square/Argyle Street can be reached on the underground system and directly by the internal rail system. Many buses run along either part of Argyle Street or streets nearby.

Buchanan Street

This is probably Glasgow's premier shopping street and is almost totally pedestrianized. Immediately opposite the exit of the Argyll Arcade is **Frasers** (45 Buchanan St., ☎ 0141/221–3880), Glasgow's largest and most interesting department store. Frasers is a Glasgow institution, and its wares reflect much of Glasgow's new and traditional images, leading European designer clothes and fabrics combining with home-produced articles, such as tweeds, tartans, glass, and ceramics. The magnificent interior is itself worth a visit, set off by the grand staircase rising to various floors and balconies.

Other shops to look out for in Buchanan Street include **R. G. Lawrie Ltd.** (110 Buchanan St., ☎ 0141/221–0217), which specializes in highland outfitting, Scottish gifts, woolens, and cashmere, and **Henry Burton** (corner of Gordon St., ☎ 0141/221–7380), a traditional gentleman's outfitter. You will find excellent outerwear at **Tiso Sports** (129 Buchanan St., ☎ 0141/248–4877). Household names like Laura Ashley, Burberry's, Liberty, Jaeger, and Roland Cartier are found here as well. Buchanan Street also sports the entrances to the excellent **Princes Square** (48 Buchanan St., ☎ 0141/221–0324) development. Elegant and stylish, this houses many of the finest specialty stores.

For another shop worthy of mention, follow Buchanan Street to St. Vincent Street, turn to your left, and you will find **Robert Graham** (71 St. Vincent St., ☎ 0141/221–6588) tobacconist. This shop has a tremendous variety of tobaccos and pipes. Much of Glasgow's wealth was generated by the Tobacco Lords during the 17th and 18th centuries; at Graham's you will experience a little of that colorful history. Also on St. Vincent Street is **John Smith & Son (Glasgow) Ltd.** (57 St. Vincent St., ☎ 0141/221–7472), founded in the mid-18th century, which prides itself on being a thoroughly Scottish bookshop, with an excellent selection of books about Scotland. Buchanan Street runs perpendicular to Argyle Street. At one end are Buchanan Street underground and Scotrail Queen Street stations.

Merchant City

This area on the edge of the city center is a recent upscale development consisting of some new buildings and old warehouses converted into living space. It is home to many of Glasgow's young and upwardly mobile. Shopping here is expensive, but the area is certainly worth visiting for those who are seeking the young Glasgow style.

Ichi Ni San (26 Bell St., ☎ 0141/552–2545) is a glitzy fashion shrine with the latest looks from the hottest designers. **The Hat Shop** (30 Wilson St., ☎ 0141/553–2469) has some really unusual concoctions. **Alexandra Stewart** (54 Wilson St., ☎ 0141/552–2002) is an interior design store full of tempting furnishings and decorative knickknacks. Also worth a visit is **In House** (24–26 Wilson St., ☎ 0141/552–5902), with its top quality designer Italian furniture as well as glassware, china, and textiles. **Casa Fina** (2 Wilson St., ☎ 0141/552–6791) stocks stylish and modern furniture and giftware. Wander around **Stockwell China Bazaar** (67–77 Glassford St., ☎ 0141/552–5781) for a huge array of fine china and earthenware, glass, and ornaments. While in this area you will also find the **National Trust for Scotland**'s shop (Hutcheson's Hall, 158 Ingram St., ☎ 0141/552–8391). Many items for sale are designed exclusively for National Trust properties and are generally handmade.

The Merchant City is close to ScotRail's High Street station or can be easily reached by walking eastward from ScotRail's Argyle Street station.

The Barras

This is Glasgow's famous weekend street market and should certainly not be missed during your visit. Apart from the excellent opportunity to pick up a bargain while you browse among the stalls, you will enjoy the lively and colorful surroundings. Stalls sell antique (and not-so-antique) furniture, bric-a-brac, student-designed jewelry and textiles—you name it, it's here. The **Barras** (☎ 0141/552–7258) is approximately 80 years old and is made up of nine markets—the largest indoor market in Europe. It prides itself on selling everything "from a needle to an anchor."

You can reach the Barras by walking from Scotrail's Argyle Street station, or take any of the various buses to Glasgow Cross at the foot of the Gallowgate.

West Regent Street/Blythswood Square

For antiques connoisseurs and art lovers, a walk along West Regent Street is highly recommended. Your first stop should be the **Victorian Village** (57 West Regent St.), a complex of small antiques shops. Of particular interest among the jewelry, coins, and bric-a-brac are stores specializing in antiquarian books, army memorabilia, 1920s clothing, and Victorian pastimes. Farther along West Regent Street are various galleries and antiques shops, some specializing in Scottish antiques and paintings. **Cyril Gerber** (148 West Regent St., ☎ 0141/221–3095 or 0141/204–0276), specialists in 20th-century British paintings, will export, as will most galleries. The **Compass Gallery** (178 West Regent St., ☎ 0141/221–6370) usually has interesting exhibitions on view.

In this area you are not far from **Glasgow School of Art** (167 Renfrew St., ☎ 0141/353–4526), and apart from the famous Charles Rennie Mackintosh building itself, there is a shop selling various books, cards, jewelry, and ceramics. There are also guided tours during the summer months. Students often sell their work, if you are lucky enough to be visiting during the degree shows in June.

West Regent Street can be reached by walking from Renfield Street (parallel to Buchanan St.); most buses from the West End coming into town travel along this street or one running parallel to it. Renfrew Street can be reached by walking to the right along Pitt Street at the end of West Regent Street.

The West End/Byres Road

This part of the city is dominated by the university, and the shops cater to local and student needs. One place of interest is **De Courcey's** antiques and crafts arcade (5–21 Cresswell La.). There are quite a few shops to visit, and a variety of goods, including paintings and jewelry, are regularly auctioned here. De Courcey's is in one of the cobblestone lanes to the rear of Byres Road. **Peckham's Delicatessen** (100 Byres Rd., ☎ 0141/357–1454; Clarence Rd., ☎ 0141/357–2909; Central Station, ☎ 0141/248–4012) is a Glasgow institution for continental sausages, cheeses, and everything for a delicious picnic. **The Californian Gourmet** (293 Byres Rd., ☎ 0141/337–1642) has everything edible for homesick Americans: bagels, pecan pie, and Ben & Jerry's ice cream. **Papyrus** (374 Byres Rd., ☎ 0141/334–6514; 296–298 Sauchiehall St., ☎ 0141/353–2182) has a wide range of designer cards, small gifts, and a good selection of books.

Byres Road is reached on the underground system: Get off at Hillhead station. By bus from the city center, numbers 44 and 59 pass by the university and cross over Byres Road (get off at the first stop on Highburgh Rd. and walk back).

Arcades and Shopping Centers

As in many other major cities and towns, various centers can be found in and around the city. **St. Enoch's Shopping Centre** (55 St. Enoch Sq., ☎ 0141/204–3900) is relatively new and is Europe's largest glass-roof shopping center (eye-catching if not especially pleasing). It houses various stores, but most could be found elsewhere. There is, however, an indoor ice-skating rink where equipment can be rented, an interesting diversion during a day's shopping. Other centers include **Sauchiehall Street Centre** (177 Sauchiehall St., ☎ 0141/332–0726) and **The Forge Shopping Centre** (1221 Gallowgate, ☎ 0141/556–6661) at Parkhead, which both offer a variety of shopping. By far the best complex, however, is **Princes Square** (48 Buchanan St.), high-quality shops in an art-nouveau setting, with cafés and restaurants. Look particularly for the Scottish Craft Centre, which has an outstanding collection of work created by some of the best craftspeople in Scotland.

Specialty Stores

Clothing

Glasgow has a very fashion-conscious image in Scotland, and a variety of both local and international fashion houses can be visited. The Merchant City area (*see above*) is popular with young people. At Princes Square there are famous designer names like **Katherine Hamnett** (Unit 38 Princes Sq., ☎ 0141/248–3826), selling pricey women's and men's clothing in classic and modern styles. **Ted Baker** (Unit 25 Princes Sq., ☎ 0141/221–9664) sells men's designer clothing—lots of shirts, ties, and accessories, but no suits—at designer prices. The West End has a number of shops where you may find items of local design. Worth a special mention is **Strawberry Fields** (517 Great Western Rd., ☎ 0141/339–1121), housing a colorful array of children's wear. At **Riah Harvey** (4 Eaglesham Rd., Clarkston, ☎ 0141/644–5566), on the south side of the city, there is a good selection of fashion for women 5'2" and under.

Gifts

All the usual Scottish-theme gifts can be found in various locations in Glasgow. Gift items here tend to be a little more interesting and of a higher quality than those found in other, more tourist-oriented areas of the country.

MacDonald MacKay Ltd (105 Hope St., ☎ 0141/204–3930) makes and sells Highland dress and accessories, ladies' kilts, and skirts made to measure and offers an export service.

Glasgow has a definite place in the history of art and design, being most famous for its association with Charles Rennie Mackintosh. For high-quality giftware in his style, **Catherine Shaw** (24 Gordon St., ☎ 0141/204–4762 and in the Argyll Arcade, ☎ 0141/221–9038) offers a unique selection.

Glasgow Environs

Both Ayr and Troon can be reached easily from Glasgow by train from Central Station; trains run every half hour during the week.

Ayr

Ayr has a good mixture of traditional and new shops. Queen's Court, Sandgate, combines small crafts and gift shops. The **Diamond Factory** (27 Queen's Ct., ☎ 01292/280476) is a jewelry workshop where visitors are invited to view craftsmen at work. All jewelry is designed and made on the premises. Ask about rings that can be engraved with a family crest and about seal engraving. The store will export your purchases if you do not have time to wait for completion of the work. The **Mill Shop, Begg of Ayr** (Viewfield Rd., ☎ 01292/267615) has a good selection of scarves, stoles, plaids, and travel rugs that are handmade on the premises. **Acanthus** (11–15 Old Bridge St., ☎ 01292/287585), specialists in china and crystal, will export any purchase worldwide.

Troon

This small coastal town north of Ayr is famous for its international golf course, Royal Troon. Many Glaswegians frequent **Regalia** (44–48 Church St., ☎ 01292/312162) for its unusual collection of designer outfits.

SPORTS AND FITNESS

Bicycling and Jogging

The tourist board (*see* Important Addresses and Numbers in Glasgow Essentials, *below*) can provide a list of cycle paths and of the many parks and gardens in Glasgow with facilities for these sports; many of the parks also have tennis courts and/or bowling greens.

Fishing

With loch, river, and sea fishing available, the area is a mecca for fishermen. Details of fishing permits and locations are available from the tourist board.

Golf

Seven courses are operated within Glasgow proper by the local authorities. Bookings are relatively inexpensive and can be made with ease, especially during the week. A comprehensive list of contacts, facilities, and charges of the 30 or so other courses nearby the city is available from the Greater Glasgow Tourist Board.

Alexandra Park (Alexandra Parade, ☎ 0141/556–3991). 9 holes, 2,281 yards, par 31.
King's Park (Croftfoot, ☎ 0141/637–1066). 9 holes, 2,103 yards, SSS 32.
Knightswood (Lincoln Ave., ☎ 0141/959–2131). 9 holes, 2,717 yards, SSS 33.
Lethamhill (Cumbernauld Rd., ☎ 0141/770–6220). 18 holes, 6,081 yards, SSS 69.
Linn Park (Simshill Rd., ☎ 0141/637–5871). 18 holes, 4,814 yards, SSS 64.
Littlehill (Auchinairn Rd., ☎ 0141/772–1916). 18 holes, 6,199 yards, SSS 69.
Ruchill (Brassey St., ☎ 0141/946–9728). 9 holes, 2,208 yards, SSS 32.

Health and Fitness Clubs

There are some 40 clubs throughout the city. Most include a swimming pool and gymnasium, and some have squash, karate, horseback riding, shooting, badminton, or sailing facilities. See the brochure available from the tourist board for details. The larger hotels in the city also offer a variety of sports and leisure facilities, usually free of charge, to their guests. Currently, the following hotels have at least a pool and gym: **Central** (☎ 0141/221–9680), **Moat House** (☎ 0141/204–0733), **Marriott** (☎ 0141/226–5577), **Jury's Pond** (☎ 0141/334–8161), **Hilton** (☎ 0141/204–5555), and **Swallow** (☎ 0141/427–3146).

Sailing and Water Sports

The Firth of Clyde and Loch Lomond both offer water-sports facilities with full equipment rental. Details are available from the tourist board.

Soccer

The city has been sports-mad, especially for football (soccer), for over 100 years, and the rivalry between its two main clubs, Rangers and Celtic, is legendary. Rangers wear blue, are predominantly Protestant, and play at **Ibrox** (pronounced *EYE-brox*; ☎ 0141/427–8500) to the west of the city; Celtic wear green, are predominantly Roman Catholic, and play in the east at Parkhead (☎ 0141/552–8591). Matches are played usually on a Saturday in winter, and Glasgow has in total nine different teams playing in the Scottish Leagues. Admission prices start at about £5. Do not go looking for the family-day-out atmosphere of many American football games; soccer remains a man's game played in relatively primitive surroundings, though Ibrox is an exception to this.

DINING

The restaurants of Glasgow have diversified over the past several years; as a result, this is one of the cities in Scotland where you'll find Chinese, Italian, and Indian food in addition to the usual French and Scottish offerings. Glasgow also has a strong café culture: visit one or two to get a feel for this important part of the city. Pubs are also good bets for cheap bar lunches.

What to Wear

In the majority of Glasgow's restaurants, almost anything goes—T-shirts and jeans included. However, a few up-market establishments encourage more formal attire (jacket, or jacket and tie), and this is noted.

CATEGORY	COST*
$$$$	over £40
$$$	£30–£40
$$	£15–£30
$	under £15

per person for a three-course meal, including VAT, excluding drinks and service

$$–$$$ **Rogano.** This restaurant's art deco interior, modeled after the style of
★ the *Queen Mary* liner—bird's eye maple paneling, chrome trim, and dramatic ocean murals—is enough to recommend it; the excellent food in the sumptuous main restaurant, the lively downstairs diner, and the oyster bar near the entrance is a bonus. Portions are generous in the main restaurant, where specialties include game terrine and classic seafood dishes that are impeccably prepared though predictable. The vegetables can be disappointing. Downstairs, where the menu changes monthly, the brasserie-style food is more modern and imaginative; the menu might list clam chowder or Mediterranean grilled swordfish. The theater menu provides early-evening and late-night bargains, and the fixed-price lunch menu is popular upstairs. Rogano is patronized by the Glasgow establishment and visiting glitterati, who appreciate, as you will, the extremely good service. ✕ *11 Exchange Sq.,* ☎ *0141/248–4055. Reservations advised. Jacket and tie. AE, DC, MC, V. Closed bank holidays.*

$$ **Buttery.** This restaurant's exquisite Victorian–Edwardian surroundings
★ are echoed by the staff's period uniforms. The best Scottish fish, beef, and game is on the menu, as well as excellent vegetarian dishes. Try the grilled fillet of brill with peppercorn butter. Service is friendly and the ambience relaxed. ✕ *652 Argyle St.,* ☎ *0141/221–8188. Reservations advised. AE, DC, MC, V. Closed Sat. lunch, Sun.*

$$ **Drum and Monkey.** This spectacular bar–restaurant in relaxed Victorian surroundings is a popular lunch and after-work meeting place. Snacks and bar meals are appetizing, and the bistro serves exceptional Scottish–French cuisine; try the lamb cutlets, pan-fried with herbs, and the carrot and orange soup. ✕ *93–95 St. Vincent St.,* ☎ *0141/221–6636. Reservations advised. AE, MC, V.*

$$ **Loon Fung.** There is plenty of space in this popular Cantonese restaurant, which was once a cinema and now seats 200. The pleasant and efficient staff guides you enthusiastically through the house specialties, including the famed dim sum. If you like seafood, try the deep-fried won ton with prawns, crispy stuffed crab claws, or lobster in garlic and cheese sauce. The business lunch and fixed-price dinner are reasonably priced. ✕ *417 Sauchiehall St.,* ☎ *0141/332–1240. AE, MC, V.*

Glasgow Dining and Lodging

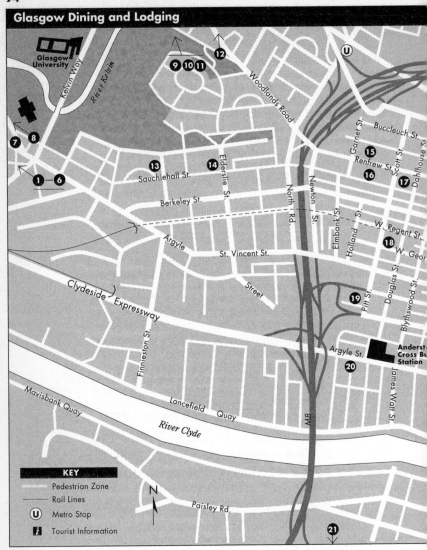

Dining

Ali Baba's Balti Bar, **23**

Ashoka West
End, **4**

The Bay Tree, **12**

Buttery, **20**

Café Gandolfi, **27**

CCA Café/Bar, **17**

Cottier's, **8**

Drum and Monkey, **24**

Fazzi Café Bar, **22**

Janssens
Café Restaurant, **7**

Loon Fung, **16**

Malmaison Café Bar
and Brasserie, **18**

Rogano, **25**

Two Fat Ladies, **5**

The Ubiquitous
Chip, **2**

Lodging

Angus, **13**

Babbity Bowster's, **28**

Cathedral House, **29**

Devonshire Hotel, **6**

Glasgow Hilton, **19**

Kirklee Hotel, **9**

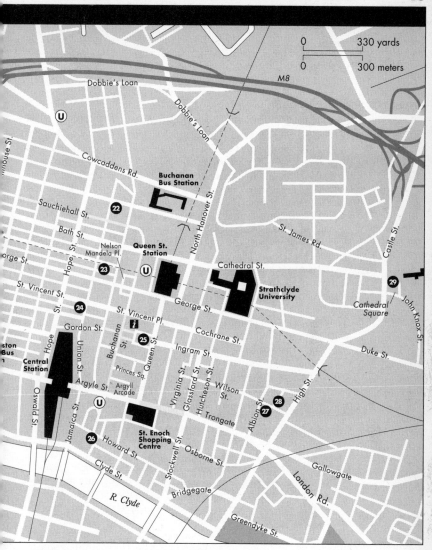

The Malmaison Glasgow, **18**

One Devonshire Gardens, **1**

The Sandyford, **14**

Sherbrooke Castle Hotel, **21**

St. Enoch Hotel, **26**

The Town House, **11**

The Victorian House, **15**

The White House, **10**

Wickets, **3**

$$ **Malmaison Café Bar and Brasserie.** A hotel basement (*see* Lodging, *below*) fitted with wooden booths provides a quiet, relaxed environment to appreciate a varied British–Continental menu. Traditional favorites like grilled liver and bacon with caramelized onion, or Cumberland sausage and mash, appear alongside classic French coq au vin. For dessert try the creamed rice pudding with Armagnac prunes. ✕ *278 W. George St.,* ☎ *0141/221–6401. Reservations advised. Jacket and tie. AE, DC, MC, V.*

$$ **Two Fat Ladies.** It's easy to mistake this restaurant for an all-night grocery because the kitchen is seen through the window. Inside there is no ornamentation of any sort, just Formica tables, nicotine-yellow walls, and a vinyl floor. The cooking, however, compensates for the austere, institutional decor. Fish predominates: fresh and prepared with imagination and skill. Squad lobster, turbot, John Dory, and monkfish are a typical selection. Portions are generous; the salads, colossal. Desserts are less interesting—tiramisù, apple tart, and chocolate mousse—and the wine list is like the decor, minimalist. Unforgettable, nevertheless. ✕ *88 Dumbarton Rd.,* ☎ *0141/339–1944. DC, MC, V. Closed lunch, Sun. and 2 weeks at Christmas.*

$$ **The Ubiquitous Chip.** Set in a courtyard inside a Victorian mews (once used for stables) with a fountain and lots of plants, this is one of the most interesting locales in which to relax over a meal. The menu changes daily but usually includes seafood from the West Coast, roe-deer steaks, and lamb. For traditionalists there is braised venison and silverside, and for the more adventurous, pigeon with wild mushroom sauce or turbot with a crust of pine kernels. The cellar here is the best in the city, with a comprehensive wine list and a huge selection of single malts. Lunches are informal; a large variety of salads and one or two hot dishes are served. The clientele is steady—executives from the nearby BBC headquarters and academics from Glasgow University. ✕ *12 Ashton La.,* ☎ *0141/334–5007. Reservations advised. AE, DC, MC, V.*

$–$$ **Café Gandolfi.** Once a Victorian pub, this café's location and decor reflect its trend-setting aspirations. On the edge of the Merchant City, it is now a haven for the design-conscious under-thirty crowd. Wooden tables and chairs carved by Scottish artist Tim Stead are so fluidly shaped it is hard to believe they're inanimate. The café opens early for breakfast, serving croissants, eggs en cocotte, and espresso. The rest of the day is filled with interesting soups, salads, local specialties, and Mediterranean favorites. Don't miss the smoked venison or the finnan haddie. Homemade ice cream and good pastries ensure busy afternoons, and evenings are livened up with good beers but less compelling wines. ✕ *64 Albion St.,* ☎ *0141/552–6813. Reservations advised. MC, V.*

$–$$ **Cottier's.** A converted Victorian church with interior decor by Glasgow artist Daniel Cottier is the unusual setting for this theater bar and restaurant (the Arts Theatre is attached). Red walls warm the downstairs bar with its beamed ceilings. Chicken in pumpkin-seed sauce or Colombian beef and dried fruit stew might be among the South American dishes on the menu. ✕ *93 Hyndland St.,* ☎ *0141/357–5825. MC, V. Closed Christmas, New Year's.*

$–$$ **Janssens Café Restaurant.** Described as "Amsterdam in Glasgow," this restaurant has spare but pleasantly relaxing surroundings in which to enjoy a Continental menu served by a friendly Dutch staff. Pita bread filled with grilled lamb, or gratinéed mussels are typical of the dishes served, and there are lots of fresh salads. ✕ *1355 Argyle St.,* ☎ *0141/ 334–9682. MC, V.*

$ **Ali Baba's Balti Bar.** Balti—a kind of Indian stir-fry served in the pan in which it is cooked—has become very popular in Glasgow in recent years; this was the first Balti restaurant in the city. There's a comfortable sofa to sprawl in for pre-dinner drinks, and spacious dining areas decorated à la "Arabian Nights." Try the *pakora,* lamb *kofta,* or delicious *aloo sag* (potato and spinach) balti. The service is fast and efficient. ✕ *54 W. Regent St.,* ☎ *0141/332–6289. AE, MC, V.*

$ **Ashoka West End.** This Punjabi restaurant consistently outperforms its many competitors in quality, range, and taste. Its extensive menu is split into popular and gourmet sections, but all portions are large enough to please the ravenous. There is nothing heavy-handed about the cooking here: Vegetable samosas are crisp and light; the spicing for the lamb, chicken, and prawn dishes is fresh and fragrant; and the milder kormas are pleasantly creamy. The selection of breads is superb. The eclectic Eastern decor, involving a bizarre mixture of plants, murals, rugs, and brass lamps, and inappropriate Western music simply emphasize the Ashoka's idiosyncracy. ✕ *1284 Argyle St.,* ☎ *0141/339–0936. AE, DC, MC, V. Closed lunch.*

$ **The Bay Tree.** A small vegetarian haven in the university area of the city, this no-smoking café serves hearty fare such as peanut and paprika soup or vegetable and bean hotchpotch. The modern paintings on the walls are often for sale. ✕ *403 Great Western Rd.,* ☎ *0141/334– 5898. Reservations not accepted. No credit cards. Closed Mon., Christmas, and New Year's.*

$ **CCA Café/Bar.** Attached to the Centre for the Contemporary Arts, this warehouse-style café with oil cloths on the tables, bentwood chairs, and plants and posters galore, offers a particularly good choice of vegetarian dishes, although meat and fish entrées are also served. Try the spinach dumplings with tomato sauce and cheese-and-chive topping, or the wild mushroom loaf with apple-and-ginger chutney. There's a good wine and beer list, chalked up on the blackboard. ✕ *350 Sauchiehall St.,* ☎ *0141/332–7864. AE, DC, MC, V (minimum charge £7). Closed Sun., Christmas, and New Year's.*

$ **Fazzi Café Bar.** This inexpensive Italian café–bar (with a delicatessen at one end), with its red-and-white checked tablecloths and bentwood chairs set on a tiled floor, is a cheerful place for a quick plateful of *gnocci a la pomarda* (gnocci with tomato sauce), or spinach and ricotta ravioli. ✕ *65–67 Cambridge St.,* ☎ *0141/332–0941. AE, MC, V.*

LODGING

Glasgow is now better equipped with hotels of all categories than it has ever been. The city has become a major business destination in the past several years, with the Scottish Conference and Exhibition Centre serving as the focal point. There are now some big city-center hotels (including the Hilton and Marriott) of both expensive and moderate character, and some good and reasonable small hotels and guest houses in the suburbs (in most cases, transportation into town is quick and dependable). All the larger hotels have restaurants open to nonguests.

CATEGORY	COST*
$$$$	over £110
$$$	£80–£110
$$	£45–£80
$	under £45

All prices are for a standard double room, including service, breakfast, and VAT.

$$$$ **Devonshire Hotel.** This upscale hotel occupies an elegant terraced mansion, and the native Glasgow hospitality and friendliness contrast sharply with the formality of the sumptuous decor—elegant drapes, marbled pillars, stained glass, and four-poster beds. Frequented by stars

when they're in town (Whitney Houston and Bruce Springsteen among them), the hotel strives for excellence in every department, including the modern British cuisine that makes the most of Scotland's fish and game. ⊞ *5 Devonshire Gardens, G12 0UX,* ☎ *0141/339–7878,* ℻ *0141/339–3980. 16 rooms with bath and shower. Restaurant. AE, DC, MC, V.*

$$$$ **Glasgow Hilton.** You'll be struck by the professionalism at this typical international hotel; Glasgow friendliness permeates the very upscale image. Three themed restaurants, **Cameron's,** a highland shooting lodge; **Minsky's,** a New York–style deli and carvery; and **Raffles,** a colonial-themed bar complete with waiters in safari suits, serve superb food. ⊞ *1 William St., G3 8HT,* ☎ *0141/204–5555,* ℻ *0141/204–5004. 319 rooms with bath. 3 restaurants, 2 bars, meeting rooms, beauty salon, health club. AE, DC, MC, V.*

$$$$ **One Devonshire Gardens.** This hotel is comprised of a group of Vic-
★   torian houses on a sloping tree-lined street to the west of the city, only 10 minutes from the center. Such celebrities as Luciano Pavarotti and Elizabeth Taylor name it as their favorite. The sophisticated ivory-walled drawing room has comfortable navy sofas. Each individually decorated bedroom has rich wallpaper, heavy drapes, and French mahogany furniture; three rooms have four-poster beds. The restaurant is equally stylish with a menu that changes daily and specialties including fillet of venison with potato and turnip gratin, or terrine of chicken and bacon with Cumberland sauce. The staff, appropriately garbed in long white aprons, provides impeccable service. The wine list is commanding, as are the prices. ⊞ *1 Devonshire Gardens, G12 0UX,* ☎ *0141/339–2001,* ℻ *0141/337–1663. 24 rooms with bath, 3 with shower. Restaurant. AE, DC, MC, V.*

$$–$$$$ **Sherbrooke Castle Hotel.** Come to the Sherbrooke for a flight of Gothic fantasy. Its cavernous rooms hark back to grander times when the south side of Glasgow was home to the immensely wealthy tobacco barons, whose homes were built with turrets and towers. The spacious grounds are far from the noise and bustle of the city, yet only 10 minutes' drive from the city center. Like the tobacco barons, the hotel's proprietor insists on tasteful decor and good traditional cooking. The busy bar is well patronized by locals. ⊞ *11 Sherbrook Ave., Pollokshields, G41 4PG,* ☎ *0141/427–4227,* ℻ *0141/427–5685. 25 rooms with bath and/or shower. AE, DC, MC, V.*

$$$ **The Malmaison Glasgow.** Set in a converted church, the Malmaison prides itself on being a "small, personal service hotel. " The modern decor is plain, but there's a splendid staircase with a wrought-iron balustade illustrating Napoleon's exploits (the hotel takes its name from the French emperor's home). In the basement is a café–bar serving delicious traditional British–Continental favorites (*see Dining, above*). ⊞ *278 W. George St., G2 4LL,* ☎ *0141/221–6400,* ℻ *0141/221–6411. 21 rooms with bath. AE, DC, MC, V.*

$$$ **The White House.** This is an unusual Glasgow hotel insofar as it has no dining room. All accommodations at the White House are in self-contained suites, and guests can either cook their own food in the fully appointed kitchen or have food delivered to their suites. The larger suites comprise several linked rooms, and the less expensive have a kitchen area in the sitting room. Stays can be as short as one night or as long as one year. ⊞ *11–13 Clevedon Crescent, G12 0PA,* ☎ *0141/339–9375,* ℻ *0141/337–1430. 31 suites. AE, DC, MC, V.*

$$ **Angus.** Another privately run city-center hotel on Sauchiehall Street, the Angus is intimate yet spacious. Its biggest plusses are the friendly staff and their eye for detail. All rooms have been tastefully decorated creating a Victorian ambience. ⊞ *966 Sauchiehall St., G3 7TQ,* ☎ *0141/*

357–5155, FAX *0141/339–9469. 17 rooms with bath/shower. AE, DC, MC, V.*

$$ **Babbity Bowster's.** There's a lively atmosphere at this small, intimate hotel in a restored 18th-century town house designed by Robert Adam. In addition to a gallery on the first floor that features many works by Glaswegian artists, the hotel offers a bar, restaurant, and café. ☎ *16– 18 Blackfriars St., G1 1PE,* ☎ *0141/552–5055,* FAX *0141/552–5215. 6 rooms with shower. Restaurant, bar, café, lighted boules court. AE, MC, V.*

$$ **Cathedral House.** In the heart of old Glasgow, near the cathedral, this small, friendly, freshly decorated hotel is convenient for sight-seeing. The café–bar offers a fixed-price lunch, and there's also a restaurant with an à la carte menu listing interesting Icelandic dishes among more usual fare. ☎ *28–32 Cathedral Sq., G4 0XA,* ☎ *0141/552–3519,* FAX *0141/552– 2444. 7 rooms with bath. Restaurant, bar. AE, DC, MC, V.*

$$ **Kirklee Hotel.** Located in a quiet district of Glasgow near the univer-
★ sity, this hotel is small and cozy. Its owners take pride in being friendly and helpful and in keeping the hotel spotless and comfortable. ☎ *11 Kensington Gate, G12 9LG,* ☎ *0141/334–5555,* FAX *0141/339–3828. 9 rooms with bath and shower. MC, V.*

$$ **The Town House.** A handsome old terraced house in a quiet cul-de-sac, the Town House thrives on repeat business from satisfied guests. The owners are particularly welcoming. The high ceilings, plasterwork, and other original architectural features of the house are complemented by restrained cream-and-pastel–striped decor, stripped pine doors, and plain fabrics. Evening meals are served on request. There is a comfortable sitting room with books and information leaflets to browse through. ☎ *4 Hughenden Terrace, G12 9XR,* ☎ *0141/357–0862,* FAX *0141/339– 9605. 10 rooms with shower. MC, V.*

$$ **Wickets.** In the heart of Billy Connolly's neighborhood, Partick, this hotel dominates one of the area's few green spaces—the West of Scot-land cricket ground. It is a handsome white mansion house with an airy, continental feel. Its glass-fronted restaurant looking onto an ex-tensive garden is a rare pleasure in the city. The bar areas are split be-tween the traditional and the artfully Parisienne. Since cricket is not Glasgow's premier sport, Wickets enjoys a tranquil, leafy setting. The rooms are furnished with a cheerful bravado. ☎ *52 Fortrose St., G11 5LP,* ☎ *and fax 0141/334–9334. 10 rooms with bath or shower. AE, DC, MC, V.*

$–$$ **St. Enoch Hotel.** A location right in the city center makes this hotel a good base for sight-seeing. Recently completely refurbished, the hotel is decorated throughout in an unimaginative modern style with few pretensions, but the low room rates compensate for the lack of atmo-sphere. There is a café–bar serving inexpensive, quick meals. ☎ *St. Enoch Sq., 44 Howard St., G1 4EE,* ☎ *and fax 0141/221–2400. 45 rooms with shower. AE, MC, V.*

$ **The Sandyford.** With a fine Victorian exterior, this hotel on the west end of famous Sauchiehall Street is convenient to all city-center facil-ities, including the Scottish Exhibition Centre and many art galleries. The Sandyford is more an upscale bed-and-breakfast than a hotel, al-though its rooms are somewhat spartan, with stark white interiors and pine furniture. ☎ *904 Sauchiehall St., G3 7TF,* ☎ *0141/334–0000,* FAX *0141/337–1812. 25 rooms with bath/shower. AE, DC, MC, V.*

$ **The Victorian House.** Centrally located, but on a quiet residential street, this "overgrown bed-and-breakfast" is one block down from the Charles Rennie Mackintosh–designed Glasgow School of Art. The plain bed-rooms are rather disappointing after the dramatic, dark red decor of the entrance hall and reception area. The staff is welcoming. No meals are served other than breakfast, but there are plenty of restaurants on nearby Sauchiehall Street. ⌑ *212 Renfrew St., G3 6TX,* ☎ *0141/332–0129,* FAX *0141/353–3155. 37 rooms with shower. MC, V.*

THE ARTS AND NIGHTLIFE

Glasgow was the 1990 European City of Culture, the first British city to be so designated, and has chosen the City of Architecture and Design for 1999. It's clear just how strong Glasgow's international reputation is when it comes to cultural events. That reputation has grown from the strong base developed by the city authorities in the 19th century and has continued in the remarkable renaissance the city has enjoyed in the past 10 years.

The Arts

Theater

Glasgow offers a plethora of live theater. One of the most exciting is the internationally renowned **Citizen's Theatre** (119 Gorbals St., ☎ 0141/429–0022), where productions, and their sets, are often of hair-raising originality. More contemporary works are staged at **Cottier's Arts Theatre** (93 Hindland St., ☎ 0141/339–5868), in a converted church. The **Centre for the Contemporary Arts** (350 Sauchiehall St., ☎ 0141/332–7521) stages not only modern plays, but also has exhibitions, films, and musical performances. The **King's Theatre** (Bath St., ☎ 0141/227–5511) stages drama, light entertainment, variety shows, musicals, and amateur productions. The **Mitchell** (Mitchell Library, North St., ☎ 0141/227–5511) mostly accommodates amateur productions, but also hosts lectures and meetings. The **Pavilion** (Renfield St., ☎ 0141/332–1846) offers family variety entertainment along with rock and pop concerts. The **Royal Scottish Academy of Music and Drama** (100 Renfrew St., ☎ 0141/332–5057) stages a variety of international and student performances. The **Tramway** (25 Albert Dr., ☎ 0141/227–5511), the city's old museum of transport, is now an exciting venue for opera, drama, and dance. The **Tron** (63 Trongate, ☎ 0141/552–4267) houses Scottish and international theater. The **Arches** (Midland St., ☎ 0141/221–9736) stages serious and controversial drama from around the world. **Theatre Royal** (Hope St., ☎ 0141/332–9000) also has performances of major drama, including an occasional season of plays by international touring companies.

Tickets for performances can be purchased at theater box offices or at the **Ticket Center** (Candleriggs, ☎ 0141/227–5511).

Concerts

Glasgow's **Royal Concert Hall** (2 Sauchiehall St., ☎ 0141/227–5511) was opened for the City of Culture celebrations in 1990. It has 2,500 seats and is the permanent home of the Royal Scottish Orchestra, which performs a winter series of concerts and a summer proms series. Other concert halls include **City Halls** (Candleriggs, ☎ 0141/227–5511); the **Henry Wood Hall** (Claremont St., ☎ 0141/332–3868), a former church now used for classical concerts; and the **Scottish Exhibition and Conference Centre** (Finnieston, ☎ 0141/248–3000), which is a regular venue for pop concerts.

Film

The **Glasgow Film Theatre** (Rose St., ☎ 0141/332–6535) is an independent public cinema screening the best nonmainstream films from all over the world. The **MGM Film Centre** (Sauchiehall St., ☎ 0141/332–9513), the **Grosvenor** (West End, ☎ 0141/339–4298), and the **Odeon Film Centre** (Renfield St., ☎ 0141/332–8701) show all the latest releases. For details of programs, consult the daily newspapers.

Opera and Ballet

Glasgow is home to the Scottish Opera and Scottish Ballet, both of which perform at the **Theatre Royal** (Hope St., ☎ 0141/332–9000). Visiting dance companies from many countries perform here also.

Nightlife

Glasgow's pubs were once famous for hard drinkers who demanded few comforts. Times have changed and many pubs have been turned into smart wine bars. For a taste of an authentic Glasgow pub with some traditional folk music occasionally thrown in, go to the Stockwell Street area and search out **Scotia Bar, The Victoria Bar,** or **Clutha Vaults.** Real ale enthusiasts should visit the **Brewery Tap** (1055 Sauchiehall St., ☎ 0141/339–8866) or the **Bon Accord** (153 North St., ☎ 0141/248–4427). If you visit only one pub in Glasgow, make it the **Horseshoe Bar** (17–21 Drury St., ☎ 0141/221–3051), which offers a sepia-tinted sentimental glimpse of all the friendlier Glasgow myths, and serves that cheerful distillation over what is purported to be the world's longest bar. Refurbishment would be a curse on its original tiling, stained glass, and deeply polished woodwork. Almost as intriguing as the decor is the clientele—a complete cross section of the city's populace. The upstairs lounge serves the steak pie Britain became famous for, and the waitress will ask some pretty stiff questions if you don't finish. In the center of town try the **Drum and Monkey** (93 St. Vincent St.), a trendy pub with a classic Victorian look and live music during the week. **Nico's** (375 Sauchiehall St.), designed along the lines of a Paris café, is a favorite with the nearby art school students and young Glaswegian professionals. The best Gaelic pub is **Uisge Beatha** (232–246 Woodlands Rd., ☎ 0141/332–0473), pronounced *oos-ka-va-hah* and meaning the "water of life," a euphemism for scotch. It serves beer from its own Glaschu Brewery, nearby; try the Fraoch (heather beer) in season. There is good live music in the **Halt** (106 Woodlands Rd.), which has a mixed-age clientele. In the city center, close to the River Clyde, the **Riverside Club** (Fox St., off Clyde St.) features traditional ceilidh bands on Friday and Saturday evenings; arrive early—it's very popular.

Any tourist office (*see* Important Addresses and Numbers in Glasgow Essentials, *below*) provides up-to-date listings, as does the fortnightly magazine, *The List.*

Among the city's large number of dancing hot spots are **Volcano** (Benalder St., off corner of Dumbarton and Byres Rds., ☎ 0141/334–8292; open 11 PM–2:30 AM; admission £4–£6), dark and spartan, with a different mood and music nightly; **Cleopatra's** (508 Great Western Rd., ☎ 0141/334–0560, open 11 PM–1 or 3 AM; admission £5), favored by Glasgow University students as well as trendy young professionals; and **The Tunnel** (84 Mitchell St., ☎ 0141/204–1000; open 10:30 PM–3 AM; admission £5–£7), unpredictable yet fashionable.

SHORT EXCURSIONS FROM GLASGOW

Glasgow is well placed as a touring base for excursions northward to the Highlands or south to the fertile farmlands of Ayrshire and the Clyde Valley. Here are two one-day itineraries you could do by car or, in a modified form, by public transportation. You will find details of places to visit in the north covered in the Central Highlands section of this book.

Tour 1: Ayrshire and the Clyde Coast

Numbers in the margin correspond to points of interest on the Glasgow Excursions: Ayrshire and the Clyde Valley map.

Robert Burns is Scotland's national and well-loved poet. His birthday is celebrated with speeches and dinners, drinking and dancing (Burns Suppers) on January 25, in a way in which few other countries celebrate a poet. He was born in Alloway, just an hour or so to the south of Glasgow, and the towns and villages where he lived and loved make an interesting day out from the city.

Ideally, you need a car, but if not, you can go by bus or train (*see* Getting Around in Glasgow Essentials, *below*, for excursion-ticket details) Take the bus or train to Largs for Cumbrae; Ardrossan for Arran; Ayr and Kilmarnock for the Burns Heritage Trail; and Troon, Prestwick, and Ayr to play golf. Bus companies also operate one-day guided excursions to this area. The Scottish Tourist Guides Association provides guides.

If you travel by car, begin your trip from Glasgow city center westbound on the M8, signposted for Glasgow Airport and Greenock. You will pass the Erskine Bridge and look across to **Dumbarton** and its Rock, a nostalgic farewell point for emigrants leaving Glasgow. Note, too, how narrow the river is here and remember that the *Queen Elizabeth 2* and the other *Queens* and great ocean liners sailed these waters from the place of their birth.

Join the A8 and follow it from Greenock to Gourock and around the coast past the Cloch lighthouse. The views north and west to Loch Long, the Holy Loch, and the Argyll Forest Park are outstanding on a clear day—and may make you want to abandon your plans and take the ferry across the estuary to Dunoon. Head south on the A78, having resisted the temptation, to the old Victorian village of **Wemyss Bay,** where the station and especially the covered walkway between platform and steamer pier, with its exuberant wrought-ironwork, are a reminder of the grandeur and style of the Victorian era and the generations of visitors who used trains and ferries for their summer holidays. From here there is a ferry service to the Isle of Bute, a favorite holiday spot for Glaswegians earlier this century. South of Wemyss Bay, the island of Arran, another Victorian holiday favorite, comes into view and then the island of Great Cumbrae (a weighty name for a tiny island) and its ferryport, Largs. At Largs is **Vikingar,** the Viking Heritage Centre, telling the story of the Viking influence on Scotland, with film, tableaux, and displays (details from the local Tourist Information Centre).

South of Largs is **Kelburn Castle and Country Park,** the historic estate of the Earl of Glasgow. There are walks and trails through the mature woodlands, including the maze-like Secret Forest, which leads deep into the thickets. The visitor center explains it all, and the adventure center and commando-assault course will wear out overexcited children. (They tell a tale here of rescuing an elderly lady from halfway around the assault course, who commented, "Well, I did think it was rather a *hard* nature trail." Make sure you read the signposts.) *Fairlie, Ayrshire KA2Q ORE,* ☎ *01475/568685.* ☛ *£3.50 adults, £2 senior citizens and children.* ☉ *Late Mar.–late Oct., daily 10–6; grounds only, Nov.–Mar., daily 11–5.*

Follow the A78 ever southward through Ardrossan to Irvine (pronounced *Irvin*), where the Magnum Leisure Centre, Sea World Exhibition, and Scottish Maritime Museum are all of interest. Robert Burns puts in an appearance at Irvine. He came here to learn to dress flax (the raw material for linen), and the heckling (flax-dressing) shed where he worked and the house where he lived are museums. The Irvine Burns Club is possibly the oldest in the world.

Continue on A78 past Troon and Prestwick, two holy places for golfers, particularly since the first British Open was played at Prestwick. You can easily see why golf is so popular here. The whole Ayrshire coast, 60 miles long, seems one endless golf course. Go past Prestwick airport to reach **Ayr,** a peaceful and elegant town with an air of prosperity and some good shops. Burns was baptized in the Auld Kirk (Old Church) in the town and wrote a humorous poem about the Twa Brigs (two bridges) that cross the river nearby. He described Ayr as a town unsurpassed "for honest men and bonny lasses." The Tam o'Shanter Museum has plenty of Burns relics and reminders of one of his most famous poems, "Tam o'Shanter."

⑤ The poet was born at **Alloway** on the B7024 about 2 miles south of town. The thatched whitewashed cottage (and adjacent museum), which his father built, is a shrine to Burns's memory. ☎ *01292/441215.* ☛ *£2.50 adults, £1.25 children and senior citizens, £6 family ticket (includes admission to Burns Monument).* ☉ *June–Aug., Mon.–Sat. 9–6, Sun. 10–6; Apr., May, Sept., Oct., Mon.–Sat. 10–5, Sun. 1–5; Nov.–Mar., Mon.–Sat. 10–4.*

Down the road from Burns's Cottage and around the corner from Alloway's ruined church, is the new **Tam o' Shanter Experience.** "Tam o' Shanter," one of Burns's most famous poems, is brought to life in a three-screen theatrical set, which transports the audience to 18th-century Ayr. There is also a restaurant and gift shop. ☎ *01292/443700 or contact local tourist information center for opening times and charges.*

Nearby **Auld Alloway Kirk** (old Alloway church) is where Tam o' Shanter, hero of Burns's poem unluckily passed a witches' revel—with Old Nick himself playing the bagpipes—on his way home from a night of drinking. Close by is the **Brig o' Doon** ("brig" is Scots for "bridge"), which Tam, in flight from the witches, managed to cross just in time. His gray mare, Meg, lost her tail to the closest witch. (Any resident of Ayr will tell you that witches cannot cross running water.) The **Burns Monument** (entrance fee included in charge for Burns Cottage) overlooks the Brig o' Doon.

TIME OUT The **Tam o'Shanter Experience** in Alloway (Mill Rd., ☎ 01292/ 443700) serves food and drinks in an attractive setting. In Ayr, **Fouter's Bistro** (2A Academy St., ☎ 01292/261391) serves French fare.

⑥ If you have time, continue south from Ayr and Alloway to **Culzean Castle and Country Park.** This magnificent mansion was built by Robert Adam on a dramatic clifftop setting. It stands just off the A719, and you could easily spend a whole day here walking around the classically elegant rooms, the gardens, and the estate. The people of Scot-

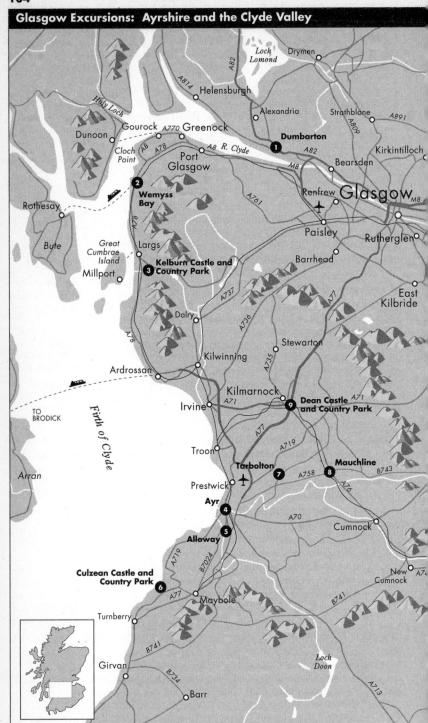

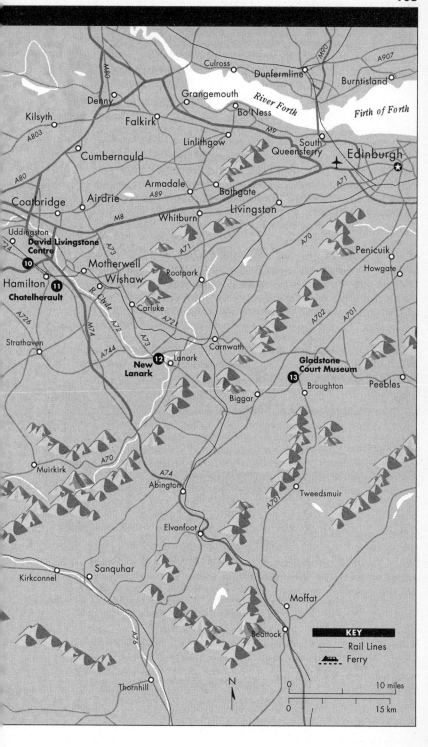

KEY
——— Rail Lines
🚂 Ferry

0 ———————— 10 miles

0 ———————— 15 km

land made a gift of a flat in the castle to President Eisenhower. Also inside is the Eisenhower Presentation, an exhibition of memorabilia. ☎ 01655/760269. ☛ *County park and castle £5.50 adults, £3 senior citizens and children; country park only £3 adults, £1.50 senior citizens and children. Park open year-round, daily 9:30–sunset (grounds only). Castle open Apr.–Oct., daily 10:30–5:30 (last admission 5 PM).*

❼ You'll return to Ayr, then turn eastward on the A758, the Mauchline Road, but before you get there, turn left on a little road to **Tarbolton,** where you will find the **Bachelors' Club,** a 17th-century house where Burns learned to dance, founded a debating and literary society, and became a Freemason. ☎ 01292/541940. ☛ *£1.50 adults, 80p children.* ☺ *Easter–Sept., daily 1:30–5:30; Oct., weekends 1:30–5:30.*

❽ **Mauchline** also has strong connections with the poet. There is a Burns House here; four of his daughters are buried in the churchyard; and Poosie Nansie's pub, where he used to drink, is still in use today. The village is also famous for making curling stones.

❾ Head north on A76 to Kilmarnock, an industrial town, home of Johnny Walker whisky, where again Burns enthusiasts will enjoy the Burns Museum and the Dick Institute. If you are looking for something different by now, go to **Dean Castle and Country Park** off Glasgow Road to enjoy a 14th-century castle with a wonderful collection of medieval arms and armor. Burns also inevitably gets a mention. Glasgow is only half an hour away on the fast A77. *Dean Castle and Country Park,* ☎ 01563/522702. ☛ *£2 adults, £1 senior citizens, 50p children.* ☺ *Daily noon–5. (Closed Christmas, New Year's).*

Tour 2: The Clyde Valley

The River Clyde is (or certainly was) famous for its shipbuilding and heavy industries, yet its upper reaches flow through some of Scotland's most fertile farmlands, which concentrate on growing tomatoes. It is an interesting area, with ancient castles as well as industrial and social museums that tell the story of manufacturing and mining prosperity.

❿ Take A724 out of Glasgow, south of the river through Rutherglen toward Hamilton. It is not a very pretty road, but in Blantyre look for signs to the **David Livingstone Centre,** a park area around the tiny (tenement) apartment where the great explorer of Africa was born in 1813. Displays tell of his journeys, of his meeting with Stanley ("Doctor Livingstone, I presume"), of Africa, and of the industrial heritage of the area. ☎ 01698/823140. ☛ *£2.50 adults, £1.50 senior citizens, £1.25 children, £6.50 family ticket.* ☺ *Year-round Mon.–Sat. 10–6, Sun. 1–6.*

Close by in Uddingston is **Bothwell Castle,** dating from the 13th century. Its walls are well preserved and stand above the River Clyde.

⓫ The Hamilton Mausoleum, in Strathclyde Country Park near the industrial town of Hamilton, was built in the 1840s as an extraordinary monument to the lavish eccentricities of the dukes of Hamilton (who had more money than sense). Also nearby is **Chatelherault** (pronounced *SHAT-lerro*), a unique one-room-deep facade, part shooting lodge, part glorified dog kennel, designed in elegant Georgian style by William Adam, also for the dukes of Hamilton. Within Chatelherault is an exhibition describing life on the estate in all its former glory. ☎ 01698/426213. ☛ *Free to grounds, small fee for Visitor Centre.* ☺ *Apr.–Sept.,* *daily 10:30–5:30; Oct.–Mar., daily 10:30–4:30; occasionally closed for functions.*

TIME OUT **Hamilton Old Parish Church,** built by William Adam, Robert's father, in 1734, is open in the morning and contains an ancient cross, a Covenanters Memorial, and fine embroideries.

From Hamilton, take the A72 toward **Lanark,** a pleasant agricultural town. You pass the ruins of medieval Craignethan Castle, lots of greenhouses for tomatoes, plant nurseries, and gnarled old orchards running down to the Clyde. Before reaching Lanark, follow the signs ⑫ down a long winding hill, to **New Lanark,** one of the world's most important industrial heritage sites—though in this wooded river valley, the ambience is hardly industrial. Here in 1785 a "model" village was set up to house the workers employed in cotton mills, which were powered by the fast-flowing waters of the Clyde. After many changes of fortune the mills eventually closed, but the site has been saved and has a new lease on life with renovated housing. The refurbishment was excellent, and the arty-types who bought the houses seem to lead normal lives despite having tourists peering in all day. One of the mills has been converted into an interpretation center, which tells the story of this brave social experiment. Upstream, the Clyde flows through some of the very finest river scenery anywhere in Lowland Scotland, with woods and spectacular waterfalls. ☎ *01555/665876.* ☛ *£2.95 adults, £1.95 children, £8.50 family ticket.* ☼ *Daily 11–5.*

⑬ A72 continues south of Lanark to join A702 near Biggar. The **Gladstone Court Museum** offers a fascinating portrayal of life in the town, with reconstructed Victorian shops, a bank, a telephone exchange, and a school. *Gladstone Ct., Biggar,* ☎ *01899/21050.* ☛ *£1.50 adults, 80p children, £4 family ticket.* ☼ *Apr.–Oct., Mon.–Sat. 10–12:30 and 2–5, Sun. 2–5.*

Just down the street is the **Gasworks,** built in 1839, a fascinating reminder of the efforts once needed to produce gas for light and heat. ☛ *Free.* ☼ *June–Sept., daily 2–5.*

By the time you get to Biggar, you are near the headwaters of the Clyde, on the moors in the center of southern Scotland. The Clyde flows west toward Glasgow and the Atlantic Ocean, while the Tweed, only a few miles away, flows eastward toward the North Sea. There are fine views around Biggar: to Culter Fell and to the Border Hills in the south.

TIME OUT Outside Biggar, the **Shieldhill Hotel** (☎ 01899/20035), near the curiously named village of Quothquan, is an excellent bed-and-breakfast, in luxurious surroundings.

At the end of a full day of touring you can return to Glasgow the quick way by joining the M74 from the A744 west of Lanark (the Strathaven road). Or take a more scenic route through Strathaven (pronounced *STRA-ven*) itself, A726 to East Kilbride, and enter Glasgow from south of the river.

GLASGOW ESSENTIALS

Arriving and Departing

By Bus
Glasgow's bus station is at **Buchanan Street** (☎ 0141/332–7133 or 0141/332–9191), and serves a wide variety of towns and cities in

Scotland, Wales, and England, including London (journey time from London is approximately 8 hours); it also has services to Glasgow Airport and Edinburgh. Buchanan Street is close to the underground station of the same name and to Queen Street station.

By Car

Visitors who come to Glasgow from England and the south of Scotland will probably approach the city from the M6, M74, and A74. The city center is clearly marked from these roads. From Edinburgh the M8 leads to the city center and is the motorway that cuts straight across the city center and into which all other roads feed. From the north either the A82 from Fort William or the A/M80 from Stirling also feed into the M8 in Glasgow city center. From then on, you only have to know your exit: exit 16 serves the north of the city center, exit 17/18 leads to the northwest and Great Western Road, and exit 18/19 takes you to the hotels of Sauchiehall Street, the Scottish Exhibition Centre, and the Anderston Centre.

By Plane

Glasgow Airport, about 7 miles west of the city center on the M8 to Greenock, offers internal Scottish and British services, European and transatlantic scheduled services, and vacation-charter traffic. Most major European carriers fly into Glasgow, offering frequent and convenient connections (some via airports in England) to Amsterdam, Berlin, Brussels, Copenhagen, Dusseldorf, Frankfurt, Hanover, Munich, and Reykjavík. There are frequent shuttle services from London, as well as regular flights from Birmingham, Bristol, East Midlands, Leeds/Bradford, Manchester, Southhampton, Isle of Man, and Jersey. There are also flights from Wales (Cardiff) and Ireland (Belfast, Carrickfinn, Dublin, and Londonderry).

Local Scottish connections can be made to Aberdeen, Barra, Benbecula, Campbeltown, Edinburgh, Inverness, Islay, Kirkwall, Shetland (Sumburgh), Stornoway, and Tiree. There is an airport information desk (☎ 0141/887–1111) and a tourist information desk and accommodations-booking service (☎ 0141/848–4440).

Airlines operating through Glasgow Airport to Europe and the rest of the United Kingdom include **Aer Lingus** (☎ 0141/248–4121), **Air UK** (☎ 01345/666777), **British Airways** and **British Airways Express** (☎ 01345/222–111), **British Midland** (☎ 0141/204–2436), **Business Air** (☎ 0500/340146), **Manx** (☎ 0141/221–0162), **Icelandair** (☎ 0181/388–5599), and **Sabena** (☎ 01345/056341).

Scheduled services to and from North America are provided by **Air Canada** (☎ 0800/181–313), **American Airlines** (☎ 0800/0101–51), and **British Airways** (☎ 0141/226–4175).

BETWEEN THE AIRPORT AND CENTER CITY

Though there is a railway station (Paisley Gilmour St.) about 2 miles from Glasgow airport, most people travel the short distance to the city center by bus or taxi. Journey time is about 20 minutes except at rush hour.

By Bus: Express buses run from Glasgow Airport to the Central railway station (☎ 0141/204–2844) and to the Buchanan Street bus station (☎ 0141/332–7133 or 0141/332–9191). There is service every 30 minutes throughout the day. The fare is about £2.

By Limousine: Most of the companies that provide chauffeur-driven cars and tours will also do limousine airport transfers. Companies that are currently members of the Greater Glasgow Tourist Board are **Charlton** (☎ 0140/427–1155), **Charter** (☎ 0141/942–4228), **Kingston** (☎ 0141/554–6066), **Little's** (☎ 0141/883–2111), **Peter Holmes** (☎ 0141/954–4455), and **Robert Neil** (☎ 0141/641–2125).

By Rental Car: All the usual rental companies, including **Alamo** (☎ 0141/848–1166), **Avis** (☎ 0141/221–2827), **Eurodollar** (☎ 0141/887–7915), **Europcar** (☎ 0141/423–5661), and **Hertz** (☎ 0141/887–2451), have offices within the terminal building. Costs vary according to the size of the cars, but average about £20–£30 per day.

By Taxi: Metered taxis are available at the terminal building. The fare should be about £12.

The drive from Glasgow Airport into the city center is normally quite easy even for visitors who are used to driving on the right. The M8 motorway runs beside the airport (junction 29) and takes you straight into Glasgow city center (and offers excellent views of the city and the River Clyde). Thereafter Glasgow's streets follow a grid pattern, at least in the city center, but a map is useful and can be supplied by the rental company.

By Train

Glasgow has two main rail stations: **Central** and **Queen Street.** Central is the arrival and departure point for trains from London Euston (journey time is approximately 5 hours), which come via Birmingham, Crewe, and Carlisle in England, as well as via Edinburgh from Kings Cross. It also serves other cities in the northwest of England and towns and ports in the southwest of Scotland. These include Kilmarnock, Dumfries, Ardrossan (for the island of Arran), Gourock (for Dunoon), Wemyss Bay (for the island of Rothesay), and Stranraer (for Ireland). Queen Street Station has connections to Edinburgh (journey time 50 minutes) and onward on the east coast route to Aberdeen or south via Edinburgh to Newcastle, York, and London Kings Cross. Other services from Queen Street go to Stirling, Perth, and Dundee; northward to Inverness, Kyle of Lochalsh, Wick, and Thurso; along the Clyde to Dumbarton and Balloch (for Loch Lomond); and on the scenic West Highland line to Oban, Fort William, and Mallaig. Oban and Mallaig have island ferry connections. The passenger-information line (☎ 0141/204–2844) for both Central and Queen Street stations operates 24 hours.

A regular bus service links Queen Street and Central stations. Both of these are close to stations on the Glasgow Underground (subway). At Queen Street go to Buchanan Street, and at Central go to St. Enoch. Black city taxis are available at both stations.

Getting Around

Glasgow city center—the area defined by the M8 motorway to the north and west, the River Clyde to the south, and Glasgow Cathedral to the east—is relatively compact, and visitors who are staying in this area should make some of their excursions on foot. Glaswegians themselves walk a good deal and the streets are designed for pedestrians (some are for pedestrians only). The streets are relatively safe even at night (but you should be sensible), and good street maps are available from bookstores and the excellent tourist-information center (*see* Important Addresses and Numbers, *below*). Most of the streets follow a grid plan; if you get lost, though, just ask a local—they are famous for being friendly.

To go farther afield, to the West End (the university, the Transport Museum, Kelvingrove Museum and Art Gallery, or the Hunterian Museum) or to the south (for example, the Burrell Collection), some form of transportation is required.

By Bus

The many different bus companies cooperate with the underground and ScotRail to produce the Family Day Tripper Ticket (£6 or £11), which is an excellent way to get around the whole area from Loch Lomond to Ayrshire. Tickets are a good value and are available from the PTE and at main railway and bus stations.

By Car

A car is not necessary in the city center. Though most of the newer hotels have their own parking lots, parking in the city center can be very trying. More convenient are the park-and-ride schemes at underground stations (Kelvinbridge, Bridge St., and Shields Rd.) that will bring you into the city center in a few minutes. The West End museums and galleries have their own parking lots, as does the Burrell, so there are no problems there. Remember, parking wardens are constantly on patrol, and you will be fined if you park illegally. Multistory parking garages are open 24 hours a day at the following locations: Anderston Centre, George Street, Waterloo Place, Mitchell Street, Cambridge Street, and Buchanan Street. Rates at the individual garages vary between £1 and £2 per hour.

By Limousine

Several chauffeur-driven limousine companies (*see* Between the Airport and City Center, *above*) also provide tours of the city center and beyond.

By Subway

As befits the Second City of the Empire, Glasgow is the only city in Scotland that has a subway, or underground, as it's called here. It was built at the end of the last century and takes the simple form of two circular routes, one going clockwise and the other counterclockwise. All trains will eventually bring you back to where you started, and the complete circle takes 24 minutes. This extremely simple and effective system operated relatively unchanged in ancient carriages (cars) until the 1970s when it was entirely modernized. The tunnels are relatively small, so the trains themselves are tiny (by London standards) and this, together with the affection in which the system is held and the bright orange paintwork of the trains, gives it the nickname the Clockwork Orange.

Flat fares (50p) and the **Heritage Trail** one-day pass (£1.60) are available. Trains run regularly Monday to Saturday, with a limited Sunday service, and connect the city center with the West End (for the university) and the city south of the River Clyde. Look for the orange "U" signs marking the 15 stations. Further information is available from the Strathclyde Passenger Transport Executive Travel Centre, St. Enoch Square (☎ 0141/226–4826).

By Taxi

Metered taxis (usually black and of the London type) can be found at taxi ranks all over the city center. Most are radio controlled, so they can be called very easily. Some have also been specially adapted to take wheelchairs. In the street, a taxi can be hailed if it is displaying its illuminated FOR HIRE sign. Taxi firms also arrange tours of the city. They vary from one to three hours, usually at a fixed price. They can be booked in advance, and you can be picked up and dropped off where you like. Contact the **Taxi Owners Association** (☎ 0141/332–7070) or the **Taxi Cab Association** (☎ 0141/332–6666).

By Train

In addition to the underground, the Glasgow area has an extensive network of suburban railway services. They are still called the Blue Trains by local people, even though most of them are now orange. Look for signs to LOW LEVEL TRAINS at Queen Street and Central stations. For further information and a free map, call Strathclyde PTE (☎ 0141/226–4826) or ScotRail (☎ 0141/204–2844). Details are also available from the tourist board.

Guided Tours

Orientation

Discovering Glasgow bus tours leave daily in summer from the west side of George Square. The Greater Glasgow Tourist Board (*see* Important Addresses and Numbers, *below*) can give further information and arrange reservations. **Strathclyde Buses Ltd.** (operating orange buses) follows a similar route from George Square. (Tickets may be purchased on the bus, or call 0141/226–4826 for information.) Details of longer tours northward to the Highlands and Islands can be obtained from the tourist board.

Special-Interest

The Scottish Tourist Guides Association (☎ and FAX 0141/776–1052) can tailor a tour to suit you. Standard fixed fees apply. **Classique Sun Saloon Luxury Coaches** (☎ 0141/889–4050) operates restored coaches from the '50s, '60s, and '70s on tours to the north and west. Car-and-driver tours tailored to your personal interests and needs are offered by **Little's Chauffeur Drive** (☎ 0141/883–2111) and **Man Friday Services** (☎ 01475/633151).

BOAT TOURS

There are cruises on the Clyde, starting from the Broomielaw, the traditional departure pier for over 100 years for vacationers on the river. Services are operated by the *Waverley* (☎ 0141/221–8152, prices £9.95–£19.95), the world's last oceangoing paddle steamer, which sails down the Clyde to Largs, Dunoon, Rothesay, and elsewhere during the day and evening in summer. You can make reservations through the tourist board or call direct. Cruises are also available on Loch Lomond and to the islands in the Firth of Clyde; details are available from the tourist board.

HELICOPTER TOURS

Clyde Helicopters (☎ 0141/226–4261) swoop over downtown Glasgow and the immediate environs, taking off from the helipad at the Scottish Exhibition Centre. Trips normally last 10 to 30 minutes and cost between £30 and £70.

PERSONAL GUIDES AND WALKING TOURS

In each case your first contact should be the tourist board, where you can find out about special walks on a given day. The **Scottish Tourist Guides Association** (☎ and FAX 0141/776–1052) also offers an all-around service.

Important Addresses and Numbers

Emergencies
For fire, police, or ambulance, dial 999 from any telephone. No coins are needed for emergency calls from public phone booths.

Hospitals
Twenty-four-hour accident and emergency services are provided at **Glasgow Royal Infirmary** (Castle St., ☎ 0141/552–3535). The hospital is by the cathedral. Facilities are also available at **Glasgow Western Infirmary** (Dumbarton Rd., ☎ 0141/211–2000), near the university.

Dentists
Most dentists will treat visitors by appointment. A full list can be found in the Yellow Pages telephone directory. Emergency dental treatment can be obtained from the **Glasgow Dental Hospital** (378 Sauchiehall St., ☎ 0141/211–9600 weekdays from 9–3).

Late-Night Pharmacies
Pharmacies in Glasgow operate on a rotating basis for late-night opening (hours are posted in storefront windows), but **R. H. Brown** (693 Great Western Rd., ☎ 0141/339–0012) is open daily 9–9.

Post Office
The **head post office** is at 1–5 George Sq. (☎ 0141/248–2882); there are many smaller post offices around the city.

Visitor Information
The **Greater Glasgow Tourist Board** (☎ 0141/204–4400) offers an excellent tourist-information service from its headquarters at 35 St. Vincent Place, which is just around the corner from George Square and Queen Street Station. At this location there is also an accommodations-booking service, bureau de change, and ticket office for the theater, city bus tours, guided walks, boat trips, and extended coach tours around Scotland. Books, maps, and souvenirs are sold. The office is open Monday–Saturday 9 AM–6 PM and, in summer, Monday–Saturday 9 AM–8 PM and Sunday 10 AM–6 PM. The tourist board's branch office at the airport is open daily 7:30–6.

Information about goings-on around town can be found in the Greater Glasgow Tourist Board's own publications, as well as in *The List* and the *Herald* and *Evening Times* newspapers.

5 The Borders and the Southwest

Dumfries, Galloway

The Borders area comprises the great rolling hills, moors, wooded river valleys, and farmland that stretch south from Lothian, the region crowned by Edinburgh, to England. The Dumfries and Galloway region south of Glasgow is a hilly and sparsely populated area, divided from England by the Solway Firth; it's a region of somber forests and radiant gardens, where the palm, in places, is as much at home as the pine.

By Gilbert
Summers

IF YOU ARE COMING TO SCOTLAND from any point south of the border in England, then the Borders is the first region of Scotland you will encounter. Let it be said straightaway that although the border has no checkpoints or customs outposts, the Scottish tourist authorities firmly promulgate the message that it is indeed Scottish land you are on once you cross the border. All the idiosyncrasies that distinguish Scotland—from the myriad names for beer, to the seemingly unpredictable Monday local holidays—start as soon as one reaches the first Scottish signs by the main roads north.

Although most visitors inevitably pass this way, the Borders and especially Galloway to the west are unfortunately overlooked. So strong is the tartan-ribboned call of the Highlands that many visitors rush past, pause for breath at Edinburgh, then plunge northward, thus missing a scenic portion of upland Scotland. This area never possessed the high romance of the Gaelic-speaking clans in the Highlands to the north, but it did have (and still has) powerful Border families, whose ancestry is soaked in the bloodshed that occurred along this once very real frontier between Scotland and her more opportunist neighbor to the south.

The Borders folk take great pride in the region's heritage as Scotland's main woolen-goods manufacturing area. And to this day the residents possess a marked determination to defend their towns and communities. The changing times, however, have thankfully allowed them to reposition their priorities: Instead of guarding against southern raiders, they now concentrate on maintaining a fiercely competitive rugby team for the popular intertown rugby matches. The Borders are a stronghold of this European counterpart to American football.

Border communities are also reestablishing their identities through the curious affairs known as the Common Ridings. Long ago it was essential that each town be able to defend its area, and over the centuries this need has become formalized in mounted gatherings to "ride the boundaries." The observance of the tradition lapsed in certain places but has been revived. Leaders and attendants are solemnly elected each year, and Borderers who now live away from home make a point of attending their own event. (You are welcome to watch and enjoy the excitement of clattering hooves and banners proudly displayed, but this is essentially a time for the native Borderers.) The Common Ridings possess as much, if not more, authenticity and historic significance as the concocted Highland Games, so often taken to be the essence of Scotland. The little town of Selkirk, in fact, claims its Common Riding to be the largest mounted gathering anywhere in Europe.

Both the Borders and the Dumfries and Galloway regions have as broad a selection of stately homes and fortified castles as you will encounter in Scotland (with the possible exception of Grampian). Galloway, the area west of Dumfries, has the advantage of a coastline facing south, made even more appealing by the North Atlantic Drift (Scotland's part of the Gulf Stream), which bathes the coastal lands with warmer water. With its coastal farmlands giving way to woodlands, high moors, and some craggy hills, Galloway may not be the Highlands, but it gives a convincing impression to those seeking the authentic Scotland.

EXPLORING

If you are coming by car from the south, you can choose from a number of routes into Scotland. Starting from the east, the A1 brings you from the English city of **Newcastle** to the border in about an hour. The A1 has the added attraction of Berwick-Upon-Tweed, on the English side of the border. Moving west, the A697, which leaves the A1 beside **Alnwick** (in England) and crosses the border at **Coldstream,** is a leisurely back-road option with an attractive view of the countryside. The A68 offers probably the most scenic route to Scotland: after climbing to **Carter Bar,** it reveals a view of the rolling blue Border hills and windy skies before dropping into the ancient town of **Jedburgh,** with its ruined abbey.

The fast-flowing M6 becomes the A74 (currently being upgraded) when it arrives at Scotland's border. The M6 gives car-borne visitors the choice of the leisurely A7 northeastward toward Edinburgh or the A75 and other parallel routes westward into Galloway and to the ferry ports of **Stranraer** and **Cairnryan.** If you choose to get off one of these main arteries and explore some back roads on your way west, you may occasionally be delayed by a herd of cows on their way to the milking parlor, but this is often far more pleasant than tussling with heavy-goods vehicles rushing to make the Irish ferries.

Tour 1: The Borders—Towns, Towers, and Countryside

Numbers in the margin correspond to points of interest on the Borders map.

❶ The town of **Jedburgh** (*-burgh* is always pronounced *burra* in Scots) on the A68 makes a good starting point for a circle through the best sights of the Borders—a route that also encompasses all four of the great ruined abbeys. The monks in these long-abandoned religious foundations were the first to work the fleeces of their sheep flocks, hence laying the foundation for what is still the area's main industry. It should be noted that this route will certainly take more than one day. To travel it in a leisurely way and spend time at some of the grand mansions noted, one could easily allow three days, although the total driving distance is not great. In the Borders there are several points of interest located quite close to one another.

Jedburgh was for centuries the first major Scottish target of invading English armies. In more peaceful times it developed textile mills, most of which have since perished. The large landscaped area around the town's tourist-information center was once a mill but now provides an encampment for the modern armies of tourists. The past still clings to this little town, however. The ruined abbey dominates the skyline and is compulsory visiting for anyone interested in acquiring a feeling of the former role of the border abbeys.

★ Still impressive, though it is now only a roofless shell, **Jedburgh Abbey** was destroyed by the English earl of Hertford's forces in 1544–45, during the destructive time known as "the Rough Wooing." This was the English King Henry VIII's armed attempt to persuade the Scots that it was a good idea to unite the kingdoms by the marriage of his young son to the infant Mary, Queen of Scots. (The Scots disagreed and sent Mary to France instead.) The full story is explained in vivid detail at the Jedburgh Abbey Visitor Centre, which provides information on interpreting the ruins. Only ground patterns and foundations remain of the once-powerful religious complex. *High St.,* ☎ *0131/244–3101.* ☛ *£2.50 adults, £1.50 senior citizens, £1 children.* ⊙ *Apr.–Sept., Mon.–Sat. 9:30–6, Sun. 2–6; Oct.–Mar., Mon.–Sat. 9:30–4, Sun. 2–4.*

There is much else to see in Jedburgh, including the **Mary, Queen of Scots House.** This *bastel* (from the French *bastille*) was the fortified town

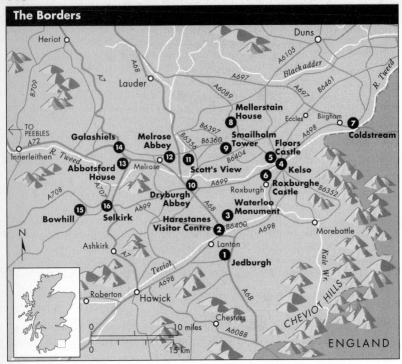

house in which, some say, Mary stayed before embarking on her famous 20-mile ride to visit her wounded lover, the earl of Bothwell, at **Hermitage Castle** (*see* Off the Beaten Track, *below*). An interpretative center in the building relates the tale. *Queen St.,* ☎ *01835/863331.* ☛ *£1.20 adults; 60p children, students, and senior citizens.* ☉ *Mar.–mid Nov., daily 10–5.*

2 Just a few miles to the north along the A68 you'll encounter signs for the **Harestanes Visitor Centre,** where you can learn about the role that the Borders estates—major landholdings with woodland and tenanted farms—played in shaping the Borders landscapes. The center is on the estate of the marquis of Lothian and conveys life in the Borders through a custom-built interpretative center which contains audiovisuals and displays on the themes of the countryside and wildlife. Outside there is a play area and nature trail. *Monteviot, at the junction of A68 and B6400,* ☎ *01835/830306.* ☛ *Free.* ☉ *Apr.–Oct., daily 10–5.*

3 You can then navigate eastward on the A698, keeping the **Waterloo Monument** on your left. This pencil-thin tower is another reminder of the whims and power of the landowning gentry: An earlier marquis of Lothian built the monument in 1815, with the help of his tenants, in celebration of the victory of Wellington at Waterloo. If you have time, you can walk to the tower from the Harestanes Visitor Centre. *Off B6400, 5 mi north of Jedburgh.*

4 **Kelso,** about 5 miles to the northeast, is one of the most attractive Borders burghs. Often described as having a Continental flavor—some visitors think it resembles a Belgian market town—the town has a broad, paved square and accurate examples of Scots town architecture. **Kelso**

Abbey is the least intact ruin of the four great Border abbeys—just a gaunt fragment of what was once the largest of the group. The last monks (and the townsfolk who had taken refuge with them) died leaping from the turrets onto English spikes and spears in 1545, after which the structure was reduced to its present fragmentary—but highly atmospheric—state. *Bridge St.,* ☎ *0131/244–3101.* ☛ *Free.* ☉ *Apr.–Sept., Mon.–Sat. 9:30–6, Sun. 2–6; Oct.–Mar., Mon.–Sat. 9:30–4, Sun. 2–4.*

Just across the road from the abbey is **Kelso Museum and the Turret Gallery.** Housed in one of the town's oldest buildings, this museum includes displays of a Victorian schoolroom, a 19th-century marketplace, a reconstructed skinner's workshop, and an interpretation of Kelso Abbey and its importance, as well as an arts-and-crafts gallery. *Abbey Court,* ☎ *01573/225470.* ☛ *80p adults, 40p senior citizens and children.* ☉ *Easter–late Oct., Mon.–Sat. 10–noon and 1–5, Sun. 2–5.*

★ ❺ Just 2 miles northwest of Kelso, on the bank of the River Tweed, stands the palatial mansion of **Floors Castle.** Ancestral home of the duke of Roxburghe, the castle was built by William Adam in 1721 and modified with mock-Tudor touches by William Playfair in the 1840s. A holly tree in the deer park marks the place where King James II was killed in 1460 by cannon-shot. *A6089,* ☎ *01573/223333.* ☛ *£3.80 adults, £3 senior citizens, £1.90 children, £10 family ticket, grounds £1.80.* ☉ *Easter–Oct., daily 10:30–5:30.*

❻ Do not confuse the comparatively youthful Floors Castle with **Roxburghe Castle,** nearby, off the A699. Only traces of rubble and earthworks remain of this ancient pile. The modern-day village of **Roxburgh** is young; the original Roxburgh, one of the oldest burghs in Scotland, has virtually disappeared, though its name lives on not only in the duke's title, but also in the name of the old county of Roxburghshire.

❼ Follow the A698 eastward about 5 miles along the north bank of the Tweed to **Coldstream,** perched on the English border. This stretch of the Tweed is lined with dignified houses and gardens, the best known of which is **The Hirsel,** the estate of former British prime minister Sir Alec Douglas Home (Lord Home of The Hirsel). A complex of farmyard buildings now serves as a craft center and museum, and there are interesting walks in the extensive grounds. It's a favorite spot for birdwatchers, and superb rhododendrons bloom here in late spring. The house itself is not open to the public. *A697, immediately west of Coldstream,* ☎ *01890/882834.* ☛ *Free (small parking charge). Grounds open year-round, daily during daylight hrs; museum and craft center open weekdays 9–5, weekends noon–5.*

Three miles above Coldstream the England-Scotland border extends down from the hills and runs beside the Tweed for the rest of its journey to the sea. Coldstream itself, like Gretna, was once a marriage place for runaway couples from the south (a plaque on the former bridge tollhouse recalls this fact). It is also celebrated in military history: In 1659, General Monck raised a regiment of foot guards here on behalf of his exiled monarch Charles II. Known as the Coldstream Guards, the successors to this regiment have become an elite corps in the British army. The **Coldstream Museum,** situated in the guards' former headquarters, investigates the history of the community of Coldstream, past and present. A special exhibition recalls the history of the Coldstream Guards. *Market Sq., Coldstream,* ☎ *01890/882630.* ☛ *£1 adults, 50p children.* ☉ *Easter–Oct., Mon.–Sat. 10–1 and 2–5, Sun. 2–5.*

If you are spending a lot of time in the area, you could tour even farther east, certainly as far as **Berwick-Upon-Tweed, Paxton House,** and

Manderston House (*see* Off the Beaten Track, *below*). Otherwise circle westward on any of a number of minor routes west of the A697 to reach **Mellerstain House,** 7 miles northwest of Kelso. Devotees of ornate country houses are well served in the Borders. Begun in the 1720s, Mellerstain was finished in the 1770s by Robert Adam and is considered to be one of his finest creations. Sumptuous plasterwork covers almost all interior surfaces, and there are outstanding examples of 18th-century furnishings. The beautiful terraced gardens are as renowned as the house. *Off A6089,* ☎ *01573/410225.* ☛ *£3.50 adults, £3 senior citizens, £1.50 children.* ☺ *Easter, May, June, and Sept., Sun., Wed., and Fri. 12:30–5; July and Aug., Sun.–Fri. 12:30–5.*

★ ⑨ South of Mellerstain, off the B6404, sits a characteristic Borders structure that certainly contrasts with the luxury of Mellerstain House. **Smailholm Tower** stands gaunt and uncompromising on top of a barren, rocky ridge. Built solely for defense, this 16th-century Border *peel* (small fortified towers common to this region) offers memorable views. If you let your imagination wander in this windy spot, you can almost see the flapping pennants and rising dust of an advancing raiding party and hear the anxious securing of doors and bolts. Sir Walter Scott found this an inspiring spot. His grandfather lived at nearby Sandyknowe Farm (not open to the public), and the young Scott visited the tower often during his childhood. *Off B6404.* ☛ *£1.50 adults, £1 senior citizens, 75p children.* ☺ *Apr.–Sept., Mon.–Sat. 9:30–6, Sun. 2–6.*

★ ⑩ Sir Walter's final resting place, **Dryburgh Abbey,** is another 5 miles to the southwest. Situated on gentle parkland in a loop of the Tweed, Dryburgh is certainly the most peaceful and secluded of the abbeys on this excursion. The abbey suffered from English raids until, like Melrose, it was abandoned in 1544. The style is Transitional, a mingling of rounded Romanesque and pointed Early English. The side chapel, where the Haig and Scott families lie buried, is lofty and pillared, detached from the main buildings. *Off A68.* ☛ *£2 adults, £1.25 senior citizens, 75p children.* ☺ *Apr.–Sept., Mon.–Sat. 9:30–6, Sun. 2–6; Oct.–Mar., Mon.–Sat. 9:30–4, Sun. 2–4.*

★ ⑪ There is no escaping Sir Walter in this part of the country: Four miles from Dryburgh is **Scott's View,** possibly the most photographed rural view in the south of Scotland. (Perhaps the only view that is more often used to summon a particular interpretation of Scotland is Eilean Donan Castle, far to the north.) You arrive at this peerless vista by taking the B6356 north from Dryburgh. A poignant tale is told of the horses of Scott's funeral cortege: On their way to Dryburgh Abbey they stopped here out of habit as they had so often in the past. The sinuous curve of the River Tweed, the gentle landscape unfolding to the triple peaks of the **Eildons,** then rolling out into shadows beyond, is certainly worth seeking—and costs nothing to enjoy.

⑫ Cross the main A68 to reach Melrose, another 5 miles to the west. **Melrose Abbey,** last of the four Borders abbeys in the tour, is in the center of this handsome community. "If thou would'st view fair Melrose aright, go visit it in the pale moonlight," wrote Scott in *The Lay of the Last Minstrel,* and so many of his fans took the advice literally that a sleepless custodian begged him to rewrite the lines. Today the abbey is still impressive: a red sandstone shell with slender windows in the Perpendicular style and some delicate tracery and carved capitals, carefully maintained. Among the carvings high on the roof is one of a bagpipe-playing pig, a figure you are not likely to encounter elsewhere in your travels. *Main Sq., Melrose,* ☎ *0131/244–3101.* ☛ *£2.50 adults,*

£1.50 senior citizens, £1 children. ☼ *Apr.–Sept., Mon.–Sat. 9:30–6, Sun. 2–6; Oct.–Mar., Mon.–Sat. 9:30–4, Sun. 2–4.*

Next to the abbey is the National Trust for Scotland's **Priorwood Gardens,** which specializes in flowers for drying. There is also an orchard adjacent to the gardens with a variety of old apple species. ☛ *£1.* ☼ *Apr.–Dec. 24, Mon.–Sat. 10–5:30, Sun. 1:30–5:30.*

Also in the main square—which is really a triangle—is the renovated **Melrose Station,** the only surviving station of the old **Waverley Route,** which until 1969 ran between Edinburgh and Carlisle. It is now used as offices, with a restaurant on the ground floor.

TIME OUT The **Melrose Station Restaurant** (☎ 01896/822546) serves morning coffee and light lunches as well as complete evening meals.

Also in the center of Melrose at the Ormiston Institute is the **Trimontium Exhibition,** which reveals the fact that the largest Roman settlement in Scotland was at nearby Newstead and displays artifacts discovered there. Tools and weapons, a blacksmith's shop, pottery, and scale models of the fort are included in the display. ☎ *01896/822463.* ☛ *£1 adults, 50p children.* ☼ *Apr.–Oct., daily 10:30–4:30.*

Other attractions in Melrose include **Teddy Melrose,** a teddy bear museum, which tells the story of British teddy bears from the early 1900s. There's a collector's bear shop. *High St.,* ☎ *01896/822464.* ☛ *£1.50 adults, 50p children.* ☼ *Mon.–Sat. 10–5, Sun. 2–5.*

Melrose Motor Museum is the place for automotive historians to view early products of Scottish manufacture, including a 1909 Albion and an Arrol Johnston from 1926. *Annay Rd.,* ☎ *01896/822624 or 01835/822356.* ☛ *£2 adults, £1.50 senior citizens and students, 50p children.* ☼ *May–Oct., daily 10:30–5:30.*

★ ⑬ Two miles west of Melrose stands one of the Borders' most visited attractions, **Abbotsford House,** home of Sir Walter Scott. In 1811, already an established writer, Scott bought a farm on this site named Cartleyhole, which was a euphemism for the real name, Clartyhole (*clarty* means muddy or sticky in Scots). The name was surely not romantic enough for Scott, who renamed the property and eventually had it entirely rebuilt in the Romantic style, emulating several other Scottish properties. The resulting pseudo-monastic, pseudo-baronial mansion became the repository for the writer's collection of Scottish memorabilia and historic artifacts. The library holds some 9,000 volumes. Scott died here in 1832. Today the house is owned by his descendants. *B6360,* ☎ *01896/752043.* ☛ *£3 adults, £1.50 children.* ☼ *Late Mar.–Oct., Mon.–Sat. 10–5, Sun. 2–5.*

⑭ **Galashiels,** a gray and busy Borders town a few miles farther northwest, is still active with textile mills and knitwear shops. At the **Peter Anderson Woollen Mill** is a museum of the town's history and industry; visitors can go on a mill tour and learn about the manufacture of tartans and tweeds. *Nether Mill, Galashiels,* ☎ *01896/752091.* ☛ *£1.75 adults, children free.* ☼ *Year-round, Mon.–Sat. 9–5; June–Sept., also Sun. 12–5. Guided tours Mon.–Thurs. 10:30, 11:30, 1:30, 2:30; Fri. 10:30 and 11:30.*

If time permits, head west on A72 to Innerleithen, then south on B709 to reach **Traquair House,** said to be the oldest continually occupied house in Scotland; ale is still brewed in the 18th-century brewhouse here, and is recommended! *Near Innerleithen,* ☎ *01896/830323.* ☛ *£3.75 adults,*

£3.20 senior citizens, £1.75 children, £10 family ticket. ⊙ Mid-Apr.–June, and Sept., daily noon–5:30; July and Aug., daily 10:30–5:30 (last admission 5 PM); Oct., Fri.–Sun. 2–5.

From Traquair, head south to join A707 and travel east to reach
🟢 **Bowhill.** Another of the stately homes in the Borders, this 19th-century building houses an outstanding collection of works by Gainsborough, Van Dyck, Canaletto, Reynolds, and Raeburn, as well as porcelain and period furniture. *Off A708, 3 mi west of Selkirk, ☎ 01750/20732. Admission to house: £4 adults, £3.50 senior citizens, £1 children; admission to grounds: £1 adults, children under 5 free. House open July, daily 1–4:30; grounds and playground open May–Aug., Sat.–Thurs. noon–5:30 (open Fri. in July).*

🟢 **Selkirk** is a hilly outpost with a smattering of antiques shops and an assortment of bakers selling the Selkirk Bannock and other cakes—evidence of Scotland's incurable sweet tooth. Sir Walter Scott was sheriff (county judge) of Selkirkshire from 1800 until his death in 1832, and his statue stands in Market Place, outside the **courthouse** where he presided. A display within the courtroom examines Scott's life, his writings and his time as sheriff, and includes an audiovisual presentation. *Sir Walter Scott's Courtroom, ☎ 01750/20096. ☛ Free. ⊙ Apr.–Oct., weekdays 10–12:30 and 1:30–4, Sat. 10–2, Sun. 2–4.*

Halliwell's House Museum is tucked off the main square in Selkirk. The building was once an ironmonger's shop, which has been recreated downstairs, while upstairs tells the story of the town. (There is useful background information on the Common Ridings, with an audiovisual presentation.) *Market St., ☎ 01750/20096. ☛ Free. ⊙ Late Mar.–Oct., Mon.–Sat. 10–5, Sun. 2–4 (July and Aug., daily until 6); Nov.–mid-Dec., daily 2–4.*

The main A7 then switchbacks gently southward to **Hawick,** the largest of the Borders towns but not necessarily the most interesting. From Hawick it's just a short drive back to Jedburgh.

Tour 2: The Galloway Highlands

Numbers in the margin correspond to points of interest on the Dumfries and Galloway map.

Galloway is the name given to the southwest portion of Scotland, west of the main town of Dumfries. This tour takes in a number of the area's diverse scenic options—from its gentle coastline and breezy uplands to places that are gradually disappearing below blankets of conifers. Use caution when negotiating the various side roads off the A75 that are mentioned in this tour: Although the main trunk road has been improved in recent years, dawdling visitors are liable to find aggressive trucks tailgating them as these commercial vehicles race for the Irish ferries at Stranraer and Cairnryan. (Anything as environmentally sensible as a direct east–west railway link was closed years ago.) Trucks notwithstanding, Galloway offers some of the most pleasant touring roads in Scotland. The local folk are also quite friendly; the area has not yet been overrun by tourists.

🟢 The M6 deteriorates into the A74 before reaching **Gretna** (though it is currently being upgraded). Gretna and **Gretna Green** are, quite simply, an embarrassment to native Scots. What else can you say about a place that advertises "amusing joke weddings," as does one of the visitor centers here? The reason for all these strange goings-on is tied to the reputation the community received as a refuge for runaway couples from

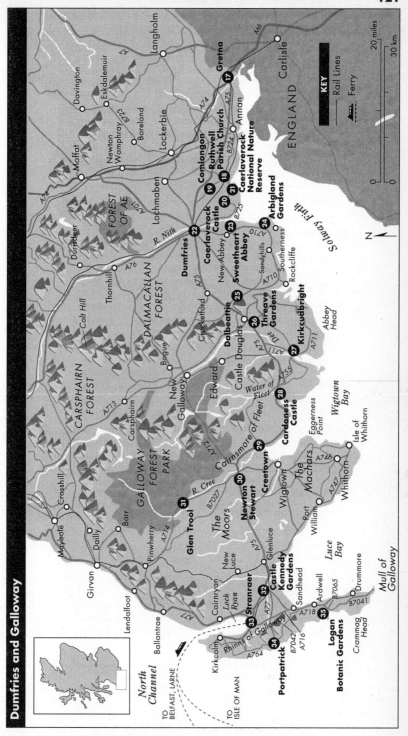

Dumfries and Galloway

KEY
Rail Lines
Ferry

20 miles
30 km

ENGLAND

Carlisle

Langholm

Davington

Eskdalemuir

Gretna

17

Moffat

Boreland

Lockerbie

Newton
Wamphray

Comlongon **18**

Ruthwell
Parish Church

Annan

Caerlaverock
National Nature
Reserve

19

Lochmaben

21
20

FOREST
OF AE

Durisdeer

R. Nith

22

Caerlaverock
Castle

23

New Abbey

Sweetheart
Abbey

24

Arbigland
Gardens

Solway Firth

Thornhill

Colt Hill

DALMACALLAN
FOREST

Dumfries

Crocketford

New Abbey

Sandyhills

Southerness

Rockcliffe

N

25

Dalbeattie

Threave
Gardens

26

Abbey
Head

Kirkcudbright

27

CARSPHAIRN
FOREST

Bogue

New
Galloway

Carsphairn

Edward

Castle Douglas

Water of
Fleet

28

Cardoness
Castle

Eggerness Point

Wigtown
Bay

Isle of
Whithorn

Crosshill

GALLOWAY
FOREST
PARK

Cairnsmore of Fleet

29

Creetown

The
Machars

A746

Whithorn

Barr

R. Cree

30

Newton
Stewart

Wigtown

Port
William

Maybole

Glen Trool

31

The
Moors

Dailly

Pinwherry

New
Luce

Glenluce

Castle
Kennedy
Gardens

Luce
Bay

Girvan

Cairnryan

32

Sandhead

Ardwell

Drummore

Mull of
Galloway

Lendalfoot

Loch
Ryan

Stranraer

33

35

Crammag
Head

Ballantrae

North
Channel

Kirkcolm

Rhinns of Galloway

34

Portpatrick

Logan
Botanic Gardens

ISLE OF MAN

TO
BELFAST, LARNE

TO
ISLE OF MAN

England, who once came north to take advantage of Scotland's less strict marriage laws. At one time anyone could perform a legal marriage in Scotland. Often the village blacksmith did the honors, presumably because he was conveniently situated near the main road.

The landscape is not very impressive around the flat fields of the **Upper Solway Firth.** You'll find more of interest as you continue west beyond the town of Annan. Inside **Ruthwell Parish Church,** 4 miles west of Annan, is the 8th-century **Ruthwell Cross,** an Anglican Christian sculpture admired for the quality of its carving. Considered an idolatrous monument, it was destroyed by the Scottish authorities in 1640 but was later reassembled. Nearby is the **Savings Bank Museum,** which tells the story of the savings-bank movement, founded by the Reverend Doctor Henry Duncan in 1810. *Ruthwell, 6½ mi west of Annan,* ☎ *01387/870640.* ☛ *Free.* ⊙ *Daily 10–1 and 2–5; closed Sun. and Mon. Oct.–Mar.*

Less obscure perhaps is what may be the first Scottish castle you'll see, **Comlongon,** on the B724. A more recent mansion house adjoins this well-preserved 15th-century border keep. Visitors can also enjoy the accommodations of a bed-and-breakfast at the castle. *B724, midway between Dumfries and Annan,* ☎ *01387/870283,* FAX *01387/870266.* ☛ *£3 adults, £1.50 children.* ⊙ *Mar.–Nov., Sun. 10–6.*

★ ⓴ Farther along, on a coastal loop of the B725, is **Caerlaverock Castle,** moated and built in a triangular design unique in Britain. This 13th-century fortress has solid-sandstone masonry and an imposing double-tower gatehouse. King Edward of England besieged the castle in 1300, when his forces occupied much of Scotland as the Wars of Independence commenced. The castle suffered many times in Anglo-Scottish skirmishes. *Off B725, 9 mi south of Dumfries,* ☎ *0131/244–3101.* ☛ *£2 adults, £1.25 senior citizens, 75p children.* ⊙ *Apr.–Sept., Mon.–Sat. 9:30–6, Sun. 2–6; Oct.–Mar., Mon.–Sat. 9:30–4, Sun. 2–4.*

ⓤ Also on the B725 is the **Caerlaverock National Nature Reserve,** a treat for bird-watchers, who can observe wintering wildfowl from blinds and a visitor center. *B725, by Caerlaverock Castle,* ☎ *01387/770275.* ☛ *Free.* ⊙ *Year-round.*

ⓥ The nearby town of **Dumfries,** where Robert Burns spent the last years of his short life, is a no-nonsense, red-sandstone community. The **River Nith** meanders through Dumfries, and the pedestrian-only town center makes shopping a pleasure (the A75 now bypasses the town). The town also contains Robert Burns's favorite pub (the Globe Inn), the house he lived in, and his mausoleum.

Not surprisingly, in view of its close association to the poet, Dumfries has a **Robert Burns Centre,** housed in a sturdy former mill overlooking the river. The center has an audiovisual program and an extensive exhibit on the life of the poet. *Mill Rd.,* ☎ *01387/253374.* ☛ *Free (small charge for audiovisual show).* ⊙ *Apr.–Sept., Mon.–Sat. 10–8, Sun. 2–5; Oct.–Mar., Tues.–Sat. 10–1 and 2–5.*

As you travel westward again, the real Galloway begins. Cross the River Nith and head out of town by the A710, another coastal loop. Within a few minutes you reach the village of **New Abbey. Sweetheart Abbey,** which provides a mellowed red and roofless backdrop to the village, was founded in 1273 by Devorgilla Balliol, in memory of her husband, John. The couple's son, also named John, was the puppet king installed in Scotland by Edward of England, when the latter claimed sovereignty over Scotland. After John's appointment the Scots gave him a scathing nickname that would stay with him for the rest of his life: *Toom*

Tabard, meaning "Empty Shirt." *A710 at New Abbey,* ☎ *0131/244–3101.* 🖝 *£1 adults, 50p children.* ☉ *Apr.–Sept., Mon.–Sat. 9:30–6, Sun. 2–6; Oct.–Mar., Mon.–Wed. and Sat. 9:30–4, Thurs. 9:30–noon, Sun. 2–4.*

Continue south through bright-green landscape along the A710 to the **24** sign for **Arbigland Gardens.** Here pops up another of Galloway's curious tales: The son of the former gardener of Arbigland, whose name was John Paul, left Scotland and became the founder of the U.S. Navy. This seafaring son, John Paul Jones, returned to his native coast in a series of daring raids in 1778. The gardens tended by Jones's father are typical of the area: lush and sheltered, with blue water visible through the protecting trees. You are only moments from the coast. *Off A710, by Kirkbean,* ☎ *01387/880283.* 🖝 *£2 adults, £1.50 senior citizens, 50p children.* ☉ *May–Sept., Tues.–Sun. and bank holidays.*

The road to **Southerness** (A710) ends in a welter of caravan holiday homes in the shadow of one of Scotland's earliest lighthouses, built in 1749 by the port authorities of Dumfries, anxious to make the treacherous River Nith approaches safer.

The road then turns west and becomes faintly Riviera-like. You can take a brisk walk from **Rockcliffe** to **Sandyhills,** two of the sleepy coastal communities overlooking the creeping tides and endless shallows of the **Solway coast.** Eventually the road turns north to **Dalbeattie. 25** Like the much larger Aberdeen far to the northeast, Dalbeattie's buildings were built with local granite from the town's quarry. Granite has a well-scrubbed gray glitter, but Dalbeattie is not typical of Galloway towns, whose house fronts are predominantly painted in pastels.

Castle Douglas lies just a few minutes west, away from the coast. Although it is a pleasant town with a long main street where the home bakeries vie for business, Castle Douglas's main attraction is its prox-★ **26** imity to **Threave Gardens.** As Scotland's best-known charitable conservation agency, the National Trust for Scotland cares for several garden properties. This horticultural undertaking demands the employment of many gardeners—and it is at Threave that the gardeners train, thus ensuring there is always some fresh development or experimental planting here. This gives lots of vigor and interest to the sloping parkland around the mansion house of Threave. There is a good visitor center as well. *South of A75, 1 mi west of Castle Douglas,* ☎ *01556/502575.* 🖝 *£3.50 adults, £1.80 senior citizens and children. Gardens open daily 9:30–sunset; walled garden and greenhouses open daily 9:30–5. Visitor Centre and shop open Apr.–Oct., daily 9:30–5:30.*

Threave Castle (not to be confused with the mansion house in Threave Gardens) is a few minutes away by car and is signposted from the main road. To get there you must leave your car in a farmyard (trying to pretend you don't have the feeling you're intruding) and walk the rest of the way. Reassured by the Historic Scotland signs (because Threave is being cared for by the national government), you make your way down to the reeds by the river on an occasionally muddy path. At the edge of the river you can then ring a bell, and, rather romantically, a boatman will come to ferry you across to the great, gaunt tower looming from a marshy island in the river. Threave was an early home of the Black Douglases, the earls of Nithsdale, and lords of Galloway. The castle was dismantled in the religious wars of the mid-17th century, though enough of it remains to have housed prisoners from the Napoleonic Wars of the 19th century. *North of A75, 3 mi west of Castle Douglas,* ☎ *0131/*

244–3101. ☛ *£1.50 adults, £1 senior citizens, 75p children (includes ferry). ⊙ Apr.–Sept., Mon.–Sat. 9:30–6, Sun. 2–6.*

From Threave you can make your way from **Castle Douglas** southwest to **Kirkcudbright,** an 18th-century town of unpretentious houses, some of them color washed in pastel shades and roofed with the blue slates of the district. For much of this century it has been known as an artists' town, and its L-shaped main street is full of crafts and antiques shops. Conspicuous in the town center is **Maclellan's Castle,** the shell of a once-elaborate castellated mansion dating from the early 16th century. *Off High St., ☎ 0131/244–3101. ☛ £1.20 adults, 75p children. ⊙ Apr.–Sept., Mon.–Sat. 9:30–6, Sun. 2–6; Oct.–Mar., Sat. 9:30–4, Sun. 2–4.*

Nearby is the 17th-century **Broughton House,** once the home of the artist E. A. Hornel (he was one of the "Glasgow Boys" of the early 20th century). Many of his paintings hang in the house, which is furnished in period style, and contains an extensive library, specializing in local history. There is also a Japanese garden to enjoy. *12 High St., ☎ 01557/330437. ☛ £2 adults, £1 children. ⊙ Apr.–mid-Oct., daily 1–5:30.*

The delightfully old-fashioned **Stewartry Museum,** stuffed with all manner of local paraphernalia, allows you to putter and absorb as much or as little as takes your interest in the mahogany display cases. *St. Mary St., ☎ 01557/331643. ☛ £1.50 adults, 75p senior citizens and students, children free if accompanied. ⊙ Mar., Apr., and Oct., Mon.–Sat. 11–4; May, Mon.–Sat. 11–5; June and Sept., Mon.–Sat. 11–5, Sun. 2–5; July and Aug., Mon.–Sat. 10–6, Sun. 2–5; Nov.–Feb., Sat. 11–4.*

The **Tolbooth Arts Centre,** in the old tolbooth, gives a history of the town's artists' colony and its leaders E.A. Hornel, Jessie King, and Charles Oppenheimer and displays some of their paintings as well as work by modern artists and craftspeople. *High St., opening times as for Stewartry Museum, above.*

You can twist your way westward by the A755, across the bridge to reach **Gatehouse of Fleet,** a peaceful, pleasant backwoods sort of place, with a castle guarding its southern approach from the A75. **Cardoness Castle** is a typical Scottish tower house, severe and uncompromising. The 15th-century structure once was the home of the McCullochs of Galloway, then later the Gordons. *A75, 1 mi southwest of Gatehouse of Fleet, ☎ 0131/244–3101. ☛ £1.20 adults, 75p children. ⊙ Apr.–Sept., Mon.–Sat. 9:30–6, Sun. 2–6; Oct.–Mar., Sat. 9:30–4, Sun. 2–4.*

If you single-mindedly pursue the suggested policy of avoiding the A75, then your route will loop to the northwest. Take a right by the Anwoth Hotel in Gatehouse of Fleet, where the signpost points to Gatehouse Station. This route will provide you with a taste of the Galloway hinterland. Beyond the wooded valley where the **Water of Fleet** runs (local rivers are often referred to as "Water of . . ."), dark hills and conifer plantings lend a brooding, empty air to this lonely stretch. Soon the road circles left, returning to the low-ground community of **Creetown,** noted for its **Gem Rock Museum.** The museum has an eclectic mineral collection and is the perfect place to pick up a pair of earrings or another rocky trinket. *A75, ☎ 01671–820357. ☛ £2.25 adults, £1.75 senior citizens, £1.25 children, £5.75 family ticket. ⊙ Easter–Sept., daily 9:30–6; Oct.–Christmas, daily 10–4; mid-Jan.–Feb., weekends 10–4; Mar.–Easter, daily 10–4 (last admission 30 minutes before closing); and by appointment.*

③⓪ The solid and bustling little town of **Newton Stewart** makes a good touring base with the far western region of Galloway (*see* The Machars in Off the Beaten Track, *below*). One possible excursion to the north from Newton Stewart takes you to the **Galloway Forest Park** (open at all times, admission free). Take the A714 north from town along the wooded valley of the **River Cree** (there is a nature reserve, the Wood of Cree, on the far bank). After about 10 miles turn right at the signpost

★ ③① for **Glen Trool**. This road leads you toward the hills that have thus far been the backdrop for the woodlands. Watch for another sign for Glen Trool. Follow this little road through increasingly wild woodland scenery to its terminus at a car park. Only after you have left the car and climbed for a few minutes onto a heathery knoll does the full, rugged panorama become apparent. With high, purple-and-green hilltops shorn rock-bare by glaciers, a dark, winding loch, and thickets of birch trees sounding with birdcalls, the setting almost looks more highland than the real Highlands to the north. Glen Trool is one of Scotland's best-kept secrets. Note **Bruce's Stone,** just above the car park, marking the site where Scotland's champion Robert the Bruce (King Robert I) won his first victory, in 1307, in the Scottish Wars of Independence.

If this excursion has whetted your appetite for the wilder side of Galloway, retrace your route to the A714, then cross over to the B7027 farther westward, taking a road west at **Glassoch Bridge** (on the B7027). Once you escape the thick conifers, this passage leads high into the moorland. If in doubt, follow signs for the moor community of **New Luce.** You can drop down to the green valleys of the Lowlands from

★ ③② there to visit **Castle Kennedy Gardens,** a high point of the area. The original Castle Kennedy is the gaunt shell seen on the grounds. It was burned out in 1716. The present property owners, the Earl and Countess of Stair, live on the grounds, at **Lochinch Castle,** built in 1864. Pleasure grounds dispersed throughout the property were built by the second earl of Stair in 1733. The Earl was a field marshal and used his soldiers to help with the heavy work of constructing banks, ponds, and other major landscape features. When the rhododendrons are in bloom, the effect is kaleidoscopic. *North of A75, 3 mi east of Stranraer,* ☎ *01776/702024.* ☛ *£2 adults, £1.50 senior citizens, £1 children.* ⊙ *Easter–Sept., daily 10–5.*

TIME OUT There is a pleasant **tearoom** at the Castle Kennedy Gardens, but if a more substantial meal is required, try the **Eynhallow Hotel** (☎ 01581/400256) nearby, for its homecooked bar food.

③③ The green and rolling countryside of the western end of Galloway affords dairy herds plenty of pasture. **Stranraer** is the main ferry port (if you happen to make a purchase in one of its shops, you may wind up with some Irish coins in your change). More scenic, perhaps, is the hol-

③④ iday town of **Portpatrick,** a few miles west on the A77, across the Rhinns of Galloway. Once an Irish ferry port, Portpatrick's exposed harbor eventually proved too risky for larger vessels. Today the village is the starting point for Scotland's longest official long-distance footpath, the **Southern Upland Way,** which runs a switchback course for 212 miles to **Cockburnspath,** on the eastern side of the Borders. Just south of Portpatrick are the lichen-yellow ruins of 16th-century **Dunskey Castle,** accessible by a clifftop path.

Portpatrick is halfway down the **Rhinns of Galloway,** and this area's southern portion has a number of interesting places to visit. Take the B7042/A716 to **Ardwell House Gardens,** a pleasant garden on a domestic scale. *Ardwell, 11 mi southeast of Stranraer.* ☎ *01776/860227.*

☛ *£1.50 adults, 75p senior citizens and children.* ۞ *Mar.–Oct., daily 10–6 (walled garden 10–5).*

★ ㉟   More spectacular for garden lovers are the **Logan Botanic Gardens,** an outstation of Edinburgh's **Royal Botanic Garden.** The Logan Gardens feature plants that enjoy the prevailing mild climate: especially tree ferns, cabbage palms, and other southern-hemisphere exotica. *Off B7065, 14 mi south of Stranraer.* ☎ *01776/860231,* FAX *01776/860333.* ☛ *£2 adults, £1.50 senior citizens, 50p children, £4.50 family ticket.* ۞ *Mar. 15–Oct., daily 10–6.*

If you wish to continue to the southern tip of the Rhinns, to the **Mull of Galloway,** follow the B7065/B7041 until you run out of land. The cliffs and seascapes here are rugged, and there is a lighthouse and a bird reserve.

What to See and Do with Children

Biggar Puppet Theatre regularly presents performances by Purves Puppets. The theater also has games and a picnic area. *B7016, east of Biggar,* ☎ *01899/220631.* ☛ *£4 adults, £3 children.* ۞ *Year-round, Mon., Tues., and Thurs.–Sat 10–5; also Easter–Sept., Sun. 2–5. (Telephone for additional opening times and details.)*

Castle Douglas's **Blowplain Open Farm** provides guided tours showing the area's daily life on a small hill farm. *Balmaclellan, Castle Douglas,* ☎ *01644/420206.* ☛ *£2 adults, £1 children.* ۞ *Easter–Oct., Mon.–Fri., tour at 2 PM (lasts 2 hrs).*

Bowhill Adventure Playground, Bowhill (*see* Tour 1). *Off A708, 3 mi west of Selkirk,* ☎ *01750/20732. Admission to grounds and playground: £1.* ۞ *May–Aug., Sat.–Thurs. noon–5 (also Fri. noon–5 in July).*

Drumlanrig Castle adventure playground (*see* Off the Beaten Track, below).

Little Wheels Museum, Portpatrick (*see* Tour 2).

Robert Smail's Printing Works, a fully operational restored print shop with reconstructed waterwheel, will fascinate older children, who can try their hand at typesetting. *7/9 High St., Innerleithen,* ☎ *01896/830206.* ☛ *£2 adults, £1 children.* ۞ *Easter–Oct., Mon.–Sat. 10–1 and 2–5, Sun. 2–5 (last admission 45 minutes before closing).*

Teviotdale Leisure Centre, one of the best-equipped centers in the area, has all manner of recreational facilities, including a swimming pool, squash courts, indoor bowls hall and Turkish steam room. *Mansfield Rd., Hawick,* ☎ *01450/374440.* ۞ *Sat.–Mon., Wed., Thurs. 10–9, Tues., Fri. noon–9.*

Tweedhope Sheepdogs (*see* Off the Beaten Track, *below*).

At the children's nursery in **Thirlestane Castle,** children are allowed to play with Victorian-style toys and masks and to dress up in costumes. The nursery is one of myriad rooms in the 17th-century castle. *Lauder, 28 mi south of Edinburgh,* ☎ *01578/722430.* ☛ *£3.50 adults, £9 family ticket; grounds only, £1.* ۞ *Easter week, May, June, and Sept., Mon., Wed., Thurs., and Sun. 2–5; July–Aug., Sun.–Fri. 2–5 (grounds open noon–6). Last admission to house and grounds 4:30.*

Off the Beaten Path

Drumlanrig Castle is an ornate red-sandstone structure built on the site of an earlier Douglas stronghold about 15 miles northwest of Dumfries in Nithsdale. The 17th-century castle contains Louis XIV furniture and a valuable collection of paintings by Leonardo da Vinci, Holbein, Rembrandt, and others. There's also a bird of prey center with falconry displays, craft workshops, and visitor center on the grounds. *Off A76, ☎ 01848/330248. ☛ £4 adults, £2.50 senior citizens, £2 children, £10 family ticket; park only £2. Castle open May–mid-June, Mon.–Wed. and Fri. 1–5, Sat. and Sun. 11–5; mid-June–Aug., Fri.–Wed. 11–5; last entry 4. Grounds open May–mid-Sept., daily 11–6.*

Grey Mare's Tail waterfall, on the wild road to Selkirk (A708), makes a dramatic 220-foot plunge as it drops down a cataract from Loch Skene. The short path to the cascade is treacherous in wet weather, but after heavy rain a close-up view is impressive. (Heed the warnings at the information kiosk on the site.) The area around the falls is noted for its wildflowers. *Off A708, 10 mi north of Moffat, ☎ 0141/552–8391 (the National Trust for Scotland).*

Hermitage Castle is the most complete remaining example of the gaunt and grim medieval border castles. Restored in the early 19th century, it was built in the 14th century (replacing an earlier structure) to guard what was at the time one of the important routes from England into Scotland. The original owner, Lord Soulis, notorious for diabolical excess, was captured by the local populace, who wrapped him in lead and boiled him in a cauldron, or so the tale goes. The castle lies on an unclassified road between the A7 and B6399, about 10 miles south of Hawick. *Liddesdale, ☎ 0131/244–3101. ☛ £1.20 adults, 75p children. ⊘ Apr.–Sept., Mon.–Sat. 9:30–6, Sun. 2–6; Oct.–Mar., Sat. 9:30–4, Sun. 2–4.*

Manderston House is a good example of the grand, no-expense-spared Edwardian country house. The family who built it made its fortune selling herring to Russia. An original 1790s Georgian house on the site was completely rebuilt to the specifications of John Kinross. The staircase is silver plated (thought to be unique) and was modeled after the Petit Trianon at Versailles. There is also much to see downstairs in the kitchens, and outdoors, among a cluster of other buildings, is the one-of-a-kind marble dairy. *Off A6105, 2 mi east of Duns, ☎ 01361/883450. Telephone for admission charges. ⊘ Mid-May–Sept., Thurs. and Sun. 2–5:30.*

The **Museum of Scottish Lead Mining,** which can be reached from the A76 (the main Dumfries–Kilmarnock road) by taking the Mennock Pass through rounded moorland hills, tells the story of one of Scotland's lesser-known industries. There are underground trips for the stout-hearted. The museum is at Wanlockhead, a fairly bleak spot and Scotland's highest elevated village. *B797, ☎ 01659/74387. ☛ £3 adults, £2.50 senior citizens and students, £1.50 children, £8.50 family tickets. ⊘ Apr.–Oct., daily 11–4:30 (last guided tour at 4). ⊘ In winter by appointment only.*

Paxton House, west of Berwick-upon-Tweed, is a handsome Palladian mansion with interiors designed by Adam, and Chippendale and Trotter furniture. The splendid Regency picture gallery is an outstation of the National Galleries of Scotland and contains a magnificent collection of paintings. *Paxton, ☎ 01289/386291. ☛ £3.50 adults, £1.75 children, £3 senior citizens. Garden only: £1.50 adults, 75p children. ⊘ Easter–Oct., daily noon–5. Tearoom open daily, 10–5.*

Tweedhope Sheepdogs demonstrate their skills twice a day; the sheepdog is an essential aid to the Scottish hillfarmer as he manages his flock over difficult terrain. There is also a craft shop and, adjacent, a fishery and fish smoker which welcomes visitors. The fishery also has a pleasant tearoom. *Moffat Fisheries, Hammerlands,* ☎ *01683/21471.* ☛ *£2 adults, £1 children.* ⊙ *Easter–Oct., Mon.–Fri. 10:30–4:30. Sheepdog demonstrations at 11 AM and 3 PM.*

The Machars

The Machars is the name given to the triangular promontory south of the main east–west route (A75) in western Galloway, roughly 10 miles from the Rhinns of Galloway (*see* Tour 2). This is an area of gently rolling farmlands, yellow gorse hedgerows, rich grazings for dairy cattle, and a number of stony prehistoric sites. Most of the glossy, green expanse is used for dairy farming. Fields are bordered by dry stane dykes (dry walling) of sharp-edge stones; and small hills and hummocks give the area its characteristic frozen-wave look, a reminder of the glacial activity that shaped the landscape.

Places of interest in the Machars include the sleepy hamlet of **Wigtown,** which has a broad main street and colorful housefronts. Down by the muddy shores of Wigtown Bay there's a monument to the Wigtown Martyrs, two women who were tied to a stake and left to drown in the incoming tide during the anti-Covenant witch-hunts of 1685. Much of Galloway's history is linked with Border feuds, but even more with the ferocity of the so-called Killing Times, when the Covenanters were persecuted for their belief that the king should be second to the church, and not vice versa. Wigtown, like several other places in the region, is dominated by a hilltop Covenanters' Monument, a reminder of the old persecutions.

The Machars are well known for their early Christian sites. The A746 was a pilgrim's way and a royal route. It ends at **Isle of Whithorn** (which is not in fact quite an island), a place that early Scottish kings and barons sought to visit at least once in their lives. The pilgrimage was often prescribed as a penance, but these pleasant shores impose no penance today. The goal was St. Ninian's chapel, the 4th-century cell of Scotland's premier saint. Some pilgrims made for Whithorn village and others for the sandspit "isle." Both places claimed to be the site of the original "Candida Casa" of the saint. As you approach Whithorn's 12th-century priory, observe the royal arms of pre-1707 Scotland (that is, Scotland before the Union with England) carved and painted above the arch of the Pend (covered way). The **Whithorn Dig and Visitor Centre** explains the significance of what is claimed to be the site of the earliest Christian community in Scotland. *45–47 George St., Whithorn,* ☎ *01988/500508.* ☛ *£2.70 adults, £1.50 senior citizens and children, £7.50 family ticket.* ⊙ *Easter–Oct., daily 10:30–5 (last tour 4:30).*

Near the visitor center stands the **Whithorn Museum,** *which includes a collection of early-Christian crosses and the shell of a 12th-century priory. Main St., Whithorn,* ☎ *0131/244–3101.* ☛ *£1.20 adults, 75p children.* ⊙ *Apr.–Sept., Mon.–Sat. 9:30–6, Sun. 2–6; Oct.–Mar., Sat. 9:30–4, Sun. 2–4.*

SHOPPING

As with other, more rural areas of Scotland away from the Central Belt, shopping in the Borders and Galloway area centers on the larger towns; stores in the smaller towns and villages usually fulfill only day-to-day requirements. The Borders in particular has a fairly affluent population, which is reflected in the variety of upscale shops in Peebles, for example, where there are more deluxe stores than might be expected. If you want to spend a morning shopping, Peebles is the place to do it. Below are a few of the interesting shops to be discovered on your travels.

The Borders

As the center of Scotland's woolen-goods industry, this area provides the country's widest choice of ready-made items. **Peter Anderson Woollen Mill** (Nether Mill, Galashiels, ☎ 01896/2091) has a wide selection of woolens and tweeds. **Tom Scott Knitwear Shop** (Kirkside, Denholm, Hawick, ☎ 0145087/283) specializes in cashmere and lambswool. The **Scottish Museum of Woollen Textiles** (Walkerburn, ☎ 0189/687–281) has a large mill shop offering a wealth of styles.

Throughout the Borders region look for the specialty sweets indigenous to the area—Jethart Snails, Hawick Balls, Berwick Cockles, and Soor Plums—which, with tablet (a solid caramellike candy) and fudge, are available from most local confectioners.

PEEBLES

You can easily spend a day browsing on Peebles High Street and in the courts and side streets leading off it, where you will find temptation at every turn. **Scott's Hardware Store** (50 High St., ☎ 01721/720262), which modern merchandising methods have thankfully not yet penetrated, has every kind of tool, implement, fixture, fitting, and garden requirement (and mousetraps) spread in glorious array over floors and walls—and even hanging from the ceiling. **Head to Toe** (43 High St., ☎ 01721/722752) stocks natural beauty products of all descriptions; dried flowers and porcelain display dishes are also available. Craftspeople and jewelers are also well represented on the street. **Keith Walter** (28 High St., ☎ 01721/720650) is a gold and silversmith making items on the premises and stocking jewelry made by other local designers. **The Country Shop** (56 High St., ☎ 01721/720630) is an upscale gift store with plenty of souvenirs; if you need a rest after all that shopping, The Country Shop has a coffee shop upstairs, with views over the town and bustling High Street.

Dumfries and Galloway

In the western half of the area covered in this chapter, **Dumfries** is the main shopping center, with all the big-name chain stores as well as specialty shops. **Greyfriars Crafts** (56 Buccleuch St., ☎ 01387/264050) has mainly Scottish goods, including Edinburgh Crystal, Caithness Glass, and Ettrick Valley textiles. For a souvenir that's easier to pack, try **David Hastings** (Marying, Shieldhill, Amisfield, Dumfries, ☎ 01387/710451; visitors by appointment; approval service offered), which has more than 80,000 old postcards.

If you are visiting Drumlanrig Castle (*see* Off the Beaten Track, *above*), do not miss the **crafts center** (north of Dumfries at Thornhill, ☎ 01848/331555) in the stable block, chock full of all types of crafts work, including stainless steel jewelry and cutlery, leathercraft, blown-glass pieces, paintings, and origami greetings cards, among others. To the northeast, at Moffat, **The Corner Gallery** (Churchgate, ☎ 01683/21010) stocks Scottish designer knitwear from the smaller producers; here you are likely to see a more original selection of goods than in the larger knitwear outlets. Farther west, at Castle Douglas, **The Posthorn** (26–30 St. Andrew St., ☎ 01556/502531) consists of two shops specializing in gift items, including the figurines made by Border Fine Art; export facilities are provided. **Galloway Gems** (130–132 King St., ☎ 01556/503254) not only has gold and silver jewelry, but also stocks mineral specimens and polished stone slices. At Gatehouse of Fleet, there is a well-stocked gift and crafts shop (and a tearoom with delicious home-baked goods) at the **Mill on the Fleet** heritage center (High St., ☎ 01557/814099). Also in the town is **Galloway Lodge Preserves** (24–28 High St., ☎ 01557/814357), whose Marmalade, Mustard, and Merchandise Shop stocks the complete line of the company's locally made produce, plus Scottish pottery.

At Kirkcudbright, the **Harbour Cottage Art Gallery** (The Harbour, ☎ 01557/330073) may be just the place to find a painting of the part of Scotland that is dearest to you; prices vary, depending on the artist exhibiting. Pictures of a different sort can be found at **Benny Gillies Books, Maps and Prints** (31 Victoria St., Kirkpatrick Durham, ☎ 01556/650412), which stocks an outstanding selection of hand-colored antique maps and prints featuring areas throughout Scotland.

Finally the **Creetown Gem Rock Museum** (Creetown, ☎ 01671/820357; *see also* Tour 2 in Exploring the Borders and the Southwest, *above*) sells extraordinary mineral and gemstone crystals in its gift shop—both loose and in settings.

SPORTS AND FITNESS

Bicycling
This is an essentially farming, rural area with some upland stretches but with a wide choice of quiet side roads to avoid the heavy traffic on "A" routes. The Craik Forest is typical of Forestry Commission properties with mountain bike routes and trails in the network of forestry access roads.

Bicycles may be rented in the Borders from **Hawick Cycle Centre** (45 N. Bridge St., Hawick, ☎ 01450/373352), **Glentress Bike Centre** (Glentress, Peebles, ☎ 01721/722934), and **Scottish Border Trails** (Bowhill, Selkirk, ☎ 01750/22515). In Dumfries and Galloway, you can rent from **Ace Cycles** (11 Church St., Castle Douglas, ☎ 01556/504542), **Greirson and Graham** (10 Academy St., Dumfries, ☎ 01387/259483), and **Nithsdale Cycle Centre** (Rosefield Mills, Dumfries, ☎ 01387/254870).

Fishing
The **Solway Firth** is noted for sea angling, notably at **Isle of Whithorn, Port William, Portpatrick, Stranraer,** and **Loch Ryan.** Game fishing far exceeds the reputation (and the expensive salmon beats) of the River Tweed, sometimes called the Queen of Scottish Rivers. A comprehensive guide, *Angling in the Scottish Borders,* is the only way to find your way around the many Borders waterways. The *Castabout Anglers Guide to Dumfries and Galloway* covers the southwest. The tourist boards for Galloway and the Borders (*see* Important Addresses and Numbers in The Borders and the Southwest Essentials, *below*) carry these and other publications (including a comprehensive information pack). In short, finding suitable water in this area is quite easy.

Golf
There are 23 courses in Galloway and 17 in the Borders. Both tourist boards (*see* Important Address and Numbers in The Borders and the Southwest Essentials, *below*) supply comprehensive leaflets.

Health and Fitness Clubs
The **Teviotdale Leisure Centre** (Mansfield Rd., Hawick, ☎ 01450/374440), one of the best-equipped centers in the area, has a swimming pool, squash

courts, indoor bowls hall, Turkish steam room, and locker-room facilities. ⊙ *Tues. 10–9, Fri. noon–9.*

Horseback Riding

The Borders and Galloway have a strong tradition of horseback riding, sustained partly through the Common Ridings, a popular annual rite. There are many riding and trekking centers, including **Pony Trekking Centre** (Brighouse Bay Holiday Park, Borgue, Kirkcudbright, ☎ 01557/870267), **Barend Properties Riding School and Trekking Centre** (Sandyhills, by Dalbeattie, Kirkcudbright, ☎ 01387/780663), **Westertoun Riding Centre** (Westruther, Gordon, Berwickshire, ☎ 01578/740270), and **Hazeldean Riding Centre** (Hassendean Burn, Hawick, ☎ 01450/870419).

Water Sports

The **Galloway Sailing Centre** (Loch Ken, ☎ 01644/420626) rents dinghies, windsurfing equipment, and canoes, and runs sailing courses.

DINING AND LODGING

The Borders region is reasonably well served by hotels ranging from the budget to the luxury categories. Being slightly off the beaten tourist track, Dumfries and Galloway offer a good selection of relatively inexpensive options for accommodations and food.

Dining

CATEGORY	COST*
$$$$	over £40
$$$	£30–£40
$$	£15–£30
$	under £15

per person for a three-course meal, including VAT, excluding drinks and service.

WHAT TO WEAR

Dress in this region is more conservative than in Glasgow. Although jeans, shorts, and T-shirts would be frowned upon in any even vaguely up-market hotel restaurant, smaller cafés and restaurants accept almost anything—except swimwear.

Lodging

CATEGORY	COST*
$$$$	over £110
$$$	£80–£110
$$	£45–£80
$	under £45

All prices are for a standard double room, including service, breakfast, and VAT.

Boreland

LODGING

$ **Nether Boreland.** A member of the Farm Holiday Bureau, Nether Boreland offers an insight into Scottish farming, combined with spacious accommodations and fresh local produce at meals. Golf, fishing, and pony trekking are close by. ⌖ *Boreland, Lockerbie, Dumfriesshire,* ☎ *01576/610248. 2 rooms with shower, 1 with bath. No credit cards. Closed Nov.–Feb.*

Dalbeattie
LODGING

$ **Auchenskeoch Lodge.** This quaint and informal Victorian shooting lodge,
★   now a country-house hotel, has five bedrooms and delicious food (for
residents only). Guests are urged to help themselves to each of the
delectable puddings on offer. Many of the vegetables and herbs are home
grown on the 20 acres of gardens and woodland surrounding the
house. The furnishings have a comfortable, faded, chintzy elegance;
there is a full-size billiards table in the game room. The sitting room
offers crammed bookshelves and an open fire. A private loch, turf and
gravel maze, and croquet lawn provide outdoor entertainment. ⌖
Auchenskeoch, by Dalbeattie, ☎ *01387/780277. 4 rooms with bath,
1 with shower. MC, V. Closed Nov.–Easter.* $

Galashiels
DINING AND LODGING

$$ **Woodlands House Hotel.** This Gothic revival–style hotel, chintz-hung
and traditionally furnished, has stunning views over Tweeddale. The
main restaurant specializes in fresh seafood and hearty Scottish cui-
sine, while Sanderson's Steakhouse is named after a former owner of
the house whose portrait gazes down on diners. ⌖ *Windyknowe Rd.,
TD1 1RG,* ☎ *and fax 01896/754722. 9 rooms with bath. 2 restau-
rants, golf privileges, horseback riding, fishing. MC, V.*

Gatehouse-of-Fleet
DINING AND LODGING

$$$ **Cally Palace.** This hotel was once a private mansion (built in 1759),
and many of the public rooms in the Georgian building retain their
original grandeur, which includes elaborate plaster ceilings and marble fireplaces. The bedrooms are individually decorated and well
equipped. The house is surrounded by 150 acres of gardens, loch, and
parkland, including an 18-hole golf course, and has an indoor leisure
center with pool, solarium, and sauna. Scottish produce stars in the
French-influenced restaurant in such dishes as poached salmon with
hollandaise sauce. The staff is exceptionally friendly and prepared to
spoil you. ⌖ *Gatehouse-of-Fleet, Galloway,* ☎ *01557/814341,* FAX
*01557/814522. 56 rooms with bath. Restaurant, bar, indoor pool, hot
tub, sauna, 18-hole golf course, putting green, tennis court, croquet,
fishing. MC, V. Closed Jan. and Feb.*

$ **High Auchenlarie Farmhouse.** This working beef farm, set high on a
hillside overlooking Wigtown Bay, offers bed-and-breakfast and, for
a small additional charge, evening meals. It's an excellent place to come
to enjoy the throaty call of moo-cows. ⌖ *Gatehouse-of-Fleet, DG7
2DW,* ☎ *01557/840231. 2 rooms with shower, 1 with bath and shower.
No credit cards.* ☙ *Mar.–Oct.*

Jedburgh
LODGING

$–$$ **Larkhall Burn.** Your accommodations in this new development will be
★   in one of a series of modern terraced cottages set on a sunny hillside,
high above the rooftops of the attractive town of Jedburgh. The interiors of these units are decorated in pastel shades and floral fabrics.
You can order your meals to be delivered from a restaurant in town,
or utilize the well-equipped kitchen. You also have the option of maid
service. Larkhall Burn provides more comfort than many hotels, and
at a competitive price. The minimum stay is two nights. Prices include
everything except phone charges. ⌖ *Larkhall Burn, Jedburgh, Rox-*

burghshire TD8 6AX, ☎ and ℻ 01835/862040. 4 2-bedroom and 2 3-bedroom cottages available at press time. MC, V.

$ **Spinney Guest House.** Made up of unpretentiously converted and
★ modernized farm cottages, this is a bed-and-breakfast offering the highest standards for the price. ☎ *Langlee, TD8 6PB, ☎ and fax 01835/863525. 1 room with bath, 2 with shower. No credit cards. Closed Dec.–Feb.*

Kelso

DINING AND LODGING

$$–$$$ **Ednam House Hotel.** This large, attractive hotel is on the banks of the
★ River Tweed, close to Kelso's grand abbey and the many fine Georgian and early Victorian buildings in the old Market Square. Ninety percent of the guests are return visitors, and the open fire in the hall, sporting paintings, and cozy armchairs give the place a homey feeling. The restaurant's three glass walls afford views of the garden and river; the fare here includes fresh local vegetables, salmon from the River Tweed, Aberdeen Angus beef, and homemade ice cream and traditional puddings. ☎ *Bridge St., TD5 7HT, ☎ 01573/224168, ℻ 01573/226319. 32 rooms with bath or shower. Restaurant, golf privileges, horseback riding, fishing. MC, V. Closed Christmas–early Jan.*

Melrose

DINING

$ **Marmion's Brasserie.** This cozy restaurant has outstanding country-
★ style cuisine. It is a great place to stop for lunch after a visit to nearby Abbotsford or Dryburgh Abbey. Try the honey-and-orange lamb, or the Stilton-stuffed mushrooms. ✗ *Buccleuch St., ☎ 01896/822245. Reservations advised. MC, V. Closed Sun.*

DINING AND LODGING

$$ **Burts Hotel.** Built in 1772, this quiet hotel in the center of Melrose retains a considerable amount of its period style, updated with modern conveniences. It has a particularly welcoming bar, with a cheerful open fire and a wide selection of fine malt whiskies, ideal for a quiet dram before or after a meal in the elegant dining room, which has dark-green striped wallpaper, high-back upholstered chairs, and white linen tablecloths. Saddle of venison and roast duck terrine are typical entrées. The bedrooms and public areas are individually decorated with reproduction antiques and floral pastels. ☎ *Market Sq., Melrose, TD6 9PN, ☎ 01896/822285, ℻ 01896/822870. 14 rooms with bath, 7 with shower. Restaurant (reservations advised), fishing can be arranged. AE, DC, MC, V.*

Moffat

DINING AND LODGING

$$ **Wellview.** Set in beautiful gardens and overlooking both the town and the nearby hills, this Victorian house offers the highest standard of accommodation, "Taste of Scotland" cuisine, and a wide-ranging wine list. ☎ *Ballplay Rd., Moffat DGIO 9JU, ☎ 01683/20184. 6 rooms with bath or shower. Restaurant (reservations advised). MC, V.*

North Middleton

LODGING

$$$$ **Borthwick Castle.** There are hotels named after castles, there are hotels occupying castles, and then there is Borthwick, which is firstly a castle and secondly a hotel. Nowhere else in Scotland offers the extraordinary experience of staying in a 15th-century fortress that was

welcoming guests half a century before Columbus discovered the Americas. Your "bedchamber," be reassured, is comfortable and fully equipped—the plumbing is not 15th-century. No two rooms are alike; your's may have dark antique furniture, a four-poster bed, and heavy drapes. Fine food is served in a magnificent vaulted room—the Great Hall—by candlelight and the glow of a log fire. This property is a 20-minute drive from central Edinburgh. ⊞ *North Middleton, Midlothian EH23 4QY, ☎ 01875/820514, FAX 01875/821702. 6 rooms with bath or shower. AE, DC, MC, V. Closed Jan.–mid-March.*

Peebles
DINING AND LODGING

$$$–$$$$
★ **Peebles Hydro.** This is one of those rare places that not only has something for everyone, but has it in abundance: Archery, snooker, pony trekking, squash, a whirlpool, and a sauna are just a few of the diversions the hotel offers. The elegant Edwardian building, reminiscent of a French château, is set on 30 acres. Bedrooms are comfortably furnished, though inevitably in a hotel of this size, room sizes and decorative standards can vary. In the public areas the high ceilings emanate an airy, spacious ambience. The restaurant features a Scottish menu, with local salmon, lamb, and beef. ⊞ *Peebles, ☎ 01721/720602, FAX 01721/722999. 137 rooms with bath. Restaurant (reservations advised, jacket and tie), pool, tennis court, health club, bicycles, baby-sitting, children's programs (0–16), playground, laundry service. AE, DC, MC, V.*

$$$ **Park Hotel.** This hotel, on the banks of the River Tweed at the northern tip of the Ettrick Forest, offers comfort and tranquility. Rooms have striped or floral wallpaper and pastel fabrics. The restaurant serves superior Scottish cuisine, many of the dishes based on local salmon and trout. ⊞ *Innerleithen Rd., EH45 8BA, ☎ 01721/720451, FAX 01721/723510. 24 rooms with bath. Restaurant (reservations advised). AE, DC, MC, V.*

$$
★ **Cringletie House.** Surrounded by grounds that include an old-fashioned walled garden whose produce is used in the hotel, this privately owned property, personally supervised by the owners and their family, is well worth seeking out. There are turrets and crow-step gables in traditional Scottish baronial style, and the spacious first-floor drawing room has an elaborate ceiling and pretty views of the valley. The simple yet comfortably furnished bedrooms are a prelude to the hotel's major achievement: its food. The restaurant is popular with locals (especially for Sunday lunch) for its straight-forward, delicious home-cooked meals, such as roast duckling with red currant-and-Cassis sauce. Afternoon tea served in the conservatory is especially recommended. ⊞ *Eddleston, by Peebles, EH45 8PL ☎ 01721/730233, FAX 01721/730244. 13 rooms with bath. Restaurant (reservations required), putting green, tennis court, croquet. AE, MC, V.*

LODGING

$ **Drummore.** This hillside bed-and-breakfast, set in an acre of wild gardens full of bird life, is well-positioned both for touring the Borders and for visiting Edinburgh. The house is modern and clean, and the guest lounge has a vast picture window which overlooks the River Tweed. ⊞ *Venlaw High Rd., EH45 8RL, ☎ 01721/720336, FAX 01721/723004. 2 rooms. No credit cards. ☺ Apr.–Oct.*

Port William
DINING AND LODGING

$$$ **Corsemalzie House.** This attractive 19th-century mansion is set on 40 acres of peaceful grounds behind the fishing village of Port William.

Sporting pursuits are the hotel's main attraction, with shooting, sea and game fishing, and golf on tap. The restaurant features a "Taste of Scotland" menu, and the public rooms and bedrooms are in keeping with the country-house style of the hotel. ⌖ *Corsemalzie, Port William, Newton Stewart, Wigtownshire,* ☎ *01988/860254,* ℻ *01988/860213. 15 rooms with bath. Golf privileges, fishing. AE, MC, V. Closed late-Jan.–Feb.*

Quothquan
DINING AND LODGING
$$$ **Shieldhill.** This foursquare Norman manor has stood on this spot since 1199 (though it was greatly enlarged in 1560). It is in an ideal location for touring the Borders—just 27 miles from Edinburgh and 31 from Glasgow. The rooms are named after great Scottish battles—Culloden, Glencoe, Bannockburn—and are furnished with great comfort (miles of Laura Ashley fabrics and wallpaper). ⌖ *Quothquan, near Biggar, ML12 6NA,* ☎ *01899/20035,* ℻ *01899/21092. 11 rooms with bath or shower. Restaurant. AE, DC, MC, V.*

St. Boswells
DINING AND LODGING
$$$–$$$$ **Dryburgh Abbey Hotel.** Right next to the abbey ruins, this civilized hotel is surrounded by beautiful scenery and has a restaurant (no smoking) specializing in traditional Scottish fare. The restrained decor and earthy, muted colors throughout create a peaceful atmosphere in keeping with the location. ⌖ *St. Boswells TD6 0RQ,* ☎ *01835/822261,* ℻ *01835/823945. 26 rooms with bath. Restaurant (reservations advised, jacket and tie), golf privileges. MC, V.*

Selkirk
DINING AND LODGING
$$$ **Philipburn House.** An 18th-century house set on 4 acres of gardens, Philipburn is an ideal place for families. The property has deluxe accommodations; rooms and the dining room have an Austrian feeling, all pine and floral prints. Poolside suites and a pine lodge are also available. A bit of advice: The hotel is renowned for its food, so work up a good appetite in the heated swimming pool and do not gorge yourself on the superb home-baked afternoon teas. Venison, Borders lamb, and, of course, salmon and trout from the nearby River Tweed are featured on Philipburn's imaginative menu, which is also enlivened with Alpine specialties such as Rosti, Swiss, grated pan-fried potatoes, often with onions or cheese. ⌖ *Linglie Rd., Selkirk, TD7 5LS,* ☎ *01750/20747,* ℻ *01750/21690. 16 rooms with bath or shower. Restaurant, pool. DC, MC, V.*

Swinton
DINING AND LODGING
$$–$$$ **Wheatsheaf Hotel and Restaurant.** A country inn on the main street, the Wheatsheaf offers outstanding food in both the black-beamed bar and the restaurant. The sheer class of the cuisine, whether the meal is beef, salmon, or venison, has won widespread praise, yet neither the food nor the small but carefully chosen wine list is overpriced. If you do not want to leave after your meal, stay in one of the four attractive bedrooms decorated in country style. ⌖ *Wheatsheaf Hotel, Swinton,* ☎ *01890/860257. 4 rooms, 3 with shower. Restaurant (reservations required, jacket and tie). V.*

THE ARTS AND NIGHTLIFE

The Arts

Some of the Borders area approaches the sphere of Edinburgh and its artistic life. Farther afield, **Gracefield Arts Centre** (Edinburgh Rd., Dumfries, ☎ 01387/262084) has public art galleries and studios with a constantly changing exhibition program. **The Dumfries and Galloway Arts Festival** is usually held at the end of May, at several venues throughout the region.

Some of the major towns have movie houses showing films on general release. Note also the **Robert Burns Centre Film Theatre** (Mill Rd., Dumfries, ☎ 01387/264808), which features special-interest, foreign, and other films that are not widely released.

Nightlife

Small towns in a rural hinterland generally do not offer a wild, urban-style nightlife. Overall, there is a wide choice of hotel bars and pubs.

BORDERS AND THE SOUTHWEST ESSENTIALS

Arriving and Departing

By Bus

From the south the main bus services use the M6 or A1, with appropriate feeder services into the hinterland; contact **Citylink** (☎ 0141/332–9191). There are also bus links from Edinburgh and Glasgow. Contact **Lowland Omnibuses** (☎ 01896/752237) or **Stagecoach Western Scottish** (☎ 01563/525192, 01387/253496, or 01776/704484).

By Car

Route A68, in the east, makes an attractive border crossing from England into Scotland. (The A1 along the east coast is not recommended north of the border because of the high volume of traffic.) However, the main route into both the Borders and Galloway from the south is the M6, which deteriorates into the less well-maintained A74 north of the Border (it is currently being upgraded). The A7 through Hawick makes an attractive although slow alternative to the A74.

By Ferry

There are no ferry services into Edinburgh or other east coast ports in this area. However, it is possible to travel from Northern Ireland to Scotland: **P&O European Ferries** runs a service from **Larne** to **Cairnryan** several times daily, with a crossing time of 2 hours, 15 minutes. Details are available from P&O at Cairnryan, Stranraer, Wigtownshire DG9 8RF, ☎ 01581/200276. **Seacat** operates a fast-speed catamaran service four times a day, taking only 90 minutes to cross from **Belfast** to **Stranraer.** For details and bookings, ☎ 0345/523523.

By Plane

The nearest Scottish airports are at **Edinburgh** and **Glasgow.** *See* Chapters 4 and 5 for details.

By Train

Visitors can use the Intercity services from **London Euston,** in England, to **Glasgow;** these trains stop at **Carlisle,** just south of the border, and some stop at **Lockerbie.** There are also direct trains from Carlisle to **Dumfries,** stopping at **Gretna Green.** On the east coast some Intercity services stop at **Berwick-Upon-Tweed,** just south of the border. The Borders are not well served by rail. For more information, call Glasgow's Central Station (☎ 0141/204–2844).

Getting Around

By Bus

Bus service in the area includes **Citylink** (☎ 0141/332–9191) long-distance coaches that call at main towns along the A75, including **Annan, Dumfries, Castle Douglas, Kirkcudbright, Twynholm, Gatehouse-of-Fleet, Creetown, Newton Stewart,** and **Glenluce.** Western Scottish (☎ 01776/704484) serves towns and villages in Dumfries and Galloway, while **Lowland Omnibuses** (☎ 01896/752237) offers Reiver Rover and Waverley Wanderer flexible tickets, which provide considerable savings for travel in the Borders.

By Car

A solid network of rural roads allows you to avoid the A1 in the eastern borders, as well as the A75, which runs along the Solway coast east to west, linking **Dumfries** and **Stranraer.** Both roads carry heavy traffic, partly because of the poor rail connections.

By Train

Train travel is not very practical in the Borders. In fact the **Scottish Borders Rail Link** is nothing of the kind: it's actually a bus service linking **Hawick, Selkirk,** and **Galashiels** with Intercity rail services at **Carlisle.** In Galloway there are connecting trains from Carlisle to **Stranraer,** which also has a direct link to Ayr and Glasgow. There is also a direct service twice daily between **Dumfries** and Stranraer. (Both the Borders and Galloway suffered badly in the shortsighted contraction of Britain's rail network in the 1960s.) Contact **British Rail** (☎ 01228/44711) for further details.

Guided Tours

Orientation

The bus companies mentioned above also run a variety of orientation tours in the area. In addition, tours are run by **Galloway Heritage Tours** (Rosemount Guest House, Kippford, ☎ 01556/620214) and **Nelson's Coaches** (107 S. Drumlanrig St., Thornhill, ☎ 01848/330376).

Special-Interest

The area is primarily covered through Edinburgh- or Glasgow-based companies (*see* Chapters 4 and 5 for details). The following local companies offer chauffeur-driven tours tailored to customers' requirements: **Ramtrad Holidays** (54 Edinburgh Rd., Peebles, ☎ 01721/720845), which also offers golf packages, and **James French** (Coldingham, ☎ 01890/771283).

Important Addresses and Numbers

Emergencies

For **police, fire,** or **ambulance,** dial 999 from any telephone. No coins are needed for emergency calls from public telephone booths.

Late-Night Pharmacies

All towns in the region have at least one pharmacy. Pharmacies are not found in rural areas, where general practitioners often dispense medicines. The police will provide assistance in locating a pharmacist in an emergency.

Visitor Information

The main tourist-information centers in the area are open all year. They are **Gretna Gateway** (off the M74 northbound at Gretna (☎ 01461/338500), the **Tourist Information Centre** at Whitesands, Dumfries (☎ 01387/253862), the **Tourist Information Centre** at the Murray's Green, Jedburgh (☎ 01835/863435), and the **Tourist Information Centre** at Drumlanrig's Tower, High Street, Hawick (☎ 01450/372547). Seasonal information centers are located at Castle Douglas, Coldstream, Dalbeattie, Eyemouth, Galashiels, Gatehouse-of-Fleet, Gretna Green, Kelso, Kirkcudbright, Langholm, Melrose, Moffat, Newton Stewart, Peebles, Sanquhar, Selkirk, and Stranraer.

6 Fife and Angus

St. Andrews, Dundee

Fife, northwest of Edinburgh, has the distinction of being the sunniest and driest part of Scotland. This area is one of sandy beaches, fishing villages, and windswept cliffs, hills, and glens. The industrial west may hold little interest, but the east coast is home to the ancient university and golf town of St. Andrews, with its romantic stone houses and seaside ruins. Angus, whose main city, Dundee, is an industrial port, stretches to the northeast into the North Sea. The Angus glens provide scenic hikes through secluded plateaus surrounded by hills and mountains.

THE REGIONS OF FIFE AND ANGUS sandwich Scotland's fourth-largest—and often overlooked—city, Dundee. This is typical eastern-seaboard country: open beaches, fishing villages, and breezy cliff-top walkways. Scotland's east coast has only light rainfall throughout the year; northeastern Fife, in particular, may claim the record for the most sunshine and the least rainfall in all Scotland. Though the hills that attract so many visitors to Scotland may seem a long way west when you're touring the East Neuk of Fife (*neuk,* pronounced *nyook,* is Scots for *corner*), the particular charm of Angus is its variety: In addition to its seacoast and pleasant Lowland market centers, there's also a hinterland of lonely rounded hills with long glens running into the typical Grampian Highland scenery beyond.

By Gilbert
Summers

Fife stretches far up the Forth Valley (which is west and a little north of Edinburgh). In these western parts the region still bears the scars of heavy industry, especially coal mining. Yet these signs are less evident as you move farther east: Northeastern Fife, around the university-and-golf town of St. Andrews, seems to have played no part in the industrial revolution; the residents instead earned a livelihood from the grain fields or from the sea. Fishing has been a major industry, and in the past a string of Fife ports traded across the North Sea. Today the legacy of Dutch-influenced architecture—crow-step gables and distinctive town houses, for example—is still plain to see and gives these East Neuk villages a distinctive charm.

St. Andrews is unlike any other Scottish town. Once Scotland's most powerful ecclesiastical center, seat also of the country's oldest university, and then, much later, the very symbol and spiritual home of golf, the town has a comfortable, well-groomed air, sitting almost smugly apart from the rest of Scotland.

Angus—Dundee's hinterland—provides considerable attractions and diversions, though they're often overlooked by travelers who are driving between Fife or Perth and the Grampian countryside to the north. One of Angus's interesting features, which it shares with the eastern Lowland edge of Perthshire, is its fruit-growing industry. Seen from roadside or railway, what at first sight appear to be sturdy vineyards on field-length wires, turn out to be soft-fruit plants, mainly raspberries. The chief fruit-growing area is Strathmore, the broad vale between the northwesterly Grampian mountains and the small coastal hills of the Sidlaws behind Dundee. Striking out from this valley—the heart of the Angus region—visitors can make a number of day trips to uplands or seacoast.

EXPLORING

Tour 1: Around Fife

Numbers in the margin correspond to points of interest on the Fife Area and St. Andrews maps.

❶ This tour starts in **St. Andrews,** Scotland's golf mecca and possibly the most visited town in the country after Edinburgh. The center of this compact city retains its original medieval street plan of three roughly parallel streets—North Street, Market Street, and South Street—leading away from the city's earliest religious site, near the cathedral. The local legend regarding the founding of St. Andrews has it that a certain St. Regulus, or Rule, acting under divine guidance, carried relics of St. Andrew by sea from Patras in Greece. He was shipwrecked on this Fife head-

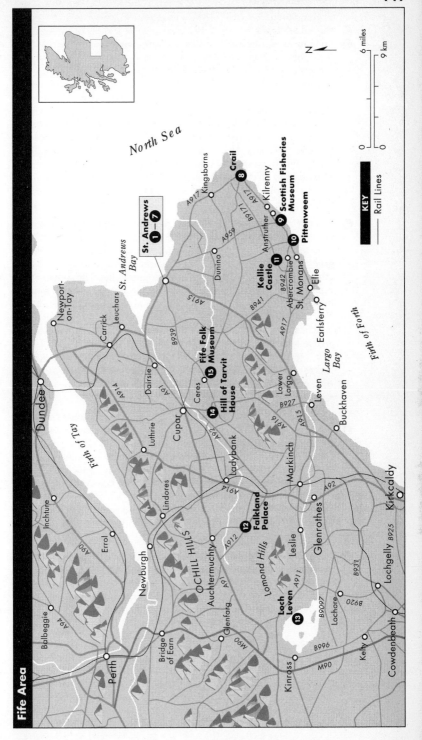

Fife Area

North Sea

St. Andrews
1 — 7

Crail 8

Scottish Fisheries Museum 9

Pittenweem 10

Kellie Castle 11

Fife Folk Museum 15

Hill of Tarvit House 14

Falkland Palace 12

Loch Leven 13

Kingsbarns
Kilrenny
Anstruther
St. Monans
Abercrombie
Elie
Earlsferry
Dunino
Ceres
Lower Largo
Leven
Buckhaven
Dairsie
Cupar
Luthrie
Ladybank
Markinch
Glenrothes
Leslie
Lindores
Auchtermuchty
Glenfarg
Bridge of Earn
Kinross
Lochore
Kelty
Cowdenbeath
Lochgelly
Kirkcaldy
Newburgh
Errol
Inchture
Balbeggie
Perth
Dundee
Newport-on-Tay
Carrick
Leuchars

St. Andrews Bay
Firth of Tay
Firth of Forth
Largo Bay
OCHIL HILLS
Lomond Hills

KEY
Rail Lines

N

6 miles
9 km

land and founded a church. The holy man's name survives in the square-
shaped **St. Rule's Tower,** consecrated in 1126 and the oldest surviving
building in St. Andrews. Nearby is the city **cathedral,** today only a ruined, poignant fragment of what was formerly the largest and most magnificent church in Scotland. Work on it began in 1160, and consecration
was finally celebrated in 1318, after several setbacks. The cathedral was
subsequently damaged by fire and repaired, but finally fell into decay
during the Reformation, in the 16th century. Only ruined gables, parts
of the nave south wall, and other fragments survive, although you can
still enjoy dizzying views of town from St. Rule's Tower, accessed via
a steep set of stairs. The on-site museum helps visitors interpret the remains and gives a sense of what the cathedral must once have been like.
Museum and St. Rule's Tower, ☎ *0131/244–3101.* ☛ *£1.50 adults, £1
senior citizens, 75p children.* ☉ *Apr.–Sept., Mon.–Sat. 9:30–6, Sun. 2–
6; Oct.–Mar., Mon.–Sat. 9:30–4, Sun. 2–4.*

Directly north of the cathedral on the shore stands **St. Andrews Castle,** which was started at the end of the 13th century. Although now a
ruin, the remains include a rare example of a bottle dungeon, cold and
gruesome, in which many prisoners spent their last hours. Even more
atmospheric is the castle's mine and countermine. The former was a
tunnel dug by besieging forces in the 16th century; the latter, a tunnel
dug by castle defenders in order to meet and wage battle below ground.
You can stoop and crawl into this narrow passageway—an eerie experience, despite the addition of electric light. The Visitor Centre has
a good audiovisual presentation on the castle's history. ☎ *0131/244–
3101.* ☛ *£2 adults, £1.25 senior citizens, 75p children. Joint ticket to
cathedral and castle: £3 adults, £1.75 senior citizens, £1 children.* ☉
*Apr.–Sept., Mon.–Sat. 9:30–6, Sun. 2–6; Oct.–Mar., Mon.–Sat. 9:30–
4, Sun. 2–4.*

After visiting the castle, you can walk west along the street called The
Scores to reach the **Royal & Ancient Golf Club of St. Andrews.** This is
the ruling house of golf worldwide, and the spiritual home of all who
play or follow the game. Its clubhouse on the dunes—a building of some
dignity, more like a town hall than a clubhouse and open to club members only—is adjacent to St. Andrew's famous **Old Course.** The town
of St. Andrews prospers on golf, golf schools, and golf equipment (the
manufacture of golf balls has been a local industry for more than 100
years), and the Old Course is associated with the greatest players of
the game.

Just opposite the Royal & Ancient Golf Club is **The British Golf Museum,** which explores the centuries-old relationship between St. Andrews
and golf, and displays a variety of golf memorabilia. *Golf Pl.,* ☎ *01334/
478880.* ☛ *£3.50 adults, £2.50 senior citizens and students, £1.50
children, £9 family ticket.* ☉ *Mid-Apr.–mid-Oct., daily 10–5:30; mid-
Oct.–mid-Apr., Thurs.–Mon. 11–3 (closed Christmas, New Year's).*

St. Andrews is also the home of Scotland's oldest university. Founded
in 1411, **St. Andrew's University** now consists of two stately old colleges in the middle of town and some attractive modern buildings on
the outskirts. A third weather-worn college, originally built in 1512,
has become a fashionable girls' school. The handsome university buildings can be explored on guided walks, sometimes led by students in
scarlet gowns. ☎ *01334/462110. Tours twice daily in July and Aug.*

Having sampled the religious, academic, and sporting ambience of St.
Andrews, leave town by Route A917, which leads to the east and then
south past the numerous East Neuk fishing communities along the Fife

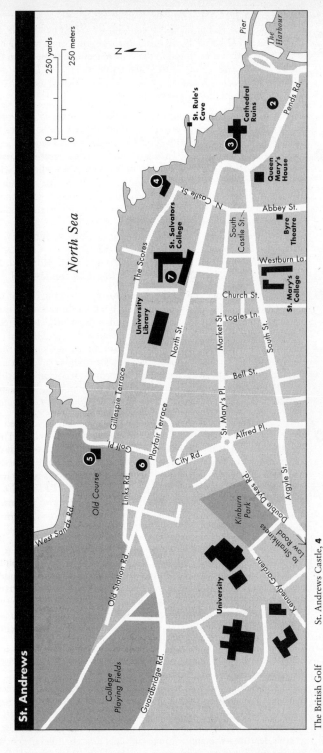

St. Andrews

The British Golf
Museum, 6
Cathedral, 3
Royal & Ancient
Golf Club of
St. Andrews, 5

St. Andrews Castle, 4
St. Andrew's
University, 7
St. Rule's Tower, 2

★ ⑧ coast. Stop in the town of **Crail** to see its picturesque Dutch-influenced Town House, or Tolbooth, which contains the oldest bell in Fife, cast in Holland in 1520. Full details on the heritage and former trading links of this tiny port can be found in the **Crail Museum and Heritage Center.** *62 Marketgate, Crail,* ☎ *01333/450869.* ☞ *Free.* ☉ *Easter week and June–mid-Sept., Mon.–Sat. 10–12:30 and 2:30–5, Sun. 2:30–5; Apr., May, and late Sept., weekends 2:30–5.*

A few minutes farther along A917 to the southwest is **Anstruther,** which boasts an attractive waterfront (larger than Crail's) with a few shops brightly festooned with children's buckets and spades as a ges-
★ ⑨ ture to seaside vacationers. Facing the harbor is the **Scottish Fisheries Museum,** housed in a colorful cluster of buildings, the earliest of which dates from the 16th century. This museum illustrates the difficult life of Scottish fishermen, past and present, through documents, artifacts, paintings, and tableaux. (These displays, complete with the reek of tarred rope and net, have been known to induce nostalgic tears in not a few old deckhands.) There are also floating exhibits at the quayside. *Anstruther harbor,* ☎ *01333/310628.* ☞ *£2.50 adults, £1.50 senior citizens and children, £7.50 family ticket.* ☉ *Apr.–Oct., Mon.–Sat. 10–5:30, Sun. 11–5; Nov.–Mar., Mon.–Sat. 10–4:30, Sun. 2–4:30.*

⑩ About 1½ miles down the road is **Pittenweem,** a working harbor with many examples of East Neuk architecture. Look for the crow-step gables (the stepped effect on the ends of the roofs), the white *harling* (Scots for *rough-casting,* the rough mortar finish on walls), and the red pantiles (S-shaped in profile). The "weem" part of the town's name comes from the Gaelic *uaime,* or *cave.* This town's particular cave is at Cove Wynd up a close (alleyway) behind the waterfront. It contains the shrine of St. Fillan, a 6th-century hermit who lived therein. *Cove Wynd, near harbor,* ☎ *01333/311495 (St. John's Episcopal Church).* ☞ *40p adults, children free.* ☉ *Tues.–Sat. 10–5, Sun. noon–5.*

⑪ For a break from this nautical atmosphere follow B942 inland to **Kellie Castle.** Dating from the 16th and 17th centuries and restored in Victorian times, the castle stands among the grain fields and woodlands of northeastern Fife. The castle is surrounded by 4 acres of attractive gardens. *B9171 (3 mi northwest of Pittenweem),* ☎ *01333/720271.* ☞ *Castle and gardens, £3 adults, £1.50 children; gardens only, £1 adults. Castle open Easter–mid-Oct., daily 1:30–5:30 (last admission 4:45). Garden and grounds open all year, 9:30–sunset.*

You could continue along the coast to take in **St. Monans,** with its working harbor and ancient church by the sea, as well as the twin communities of Elie and Earlsferry, whose sheltered waters are appreciated by sailboard enthusiasts. Alternatively, rejoin the A917 and pass through **Lower Largo,** birthplace of Alexander Selkirk, the Scottish sailor who was the prototype for Daniel Defoe's Robinson Crusoe. Follow signs for **Glenrothes,** a modern town with a selection of sporting facilities that is also notable for its public murals and sculptures.

From Glenrothes take the A92 north then the A912 northwest to reach **Falkland,** one of the most attractive communities in all Fife. A royal burgh of twisting streets and crooked stone houses, the town is
★ ⑫ dominated by **Falkland Palace,** a former hunting lodge of the Stuart monarchs and one of the earliest examples in Britain of the French Renaissance style. Overlooking the main street is the palace's most attractive feature—the south range of walls and chambers, rich with Renaissance buttresses and stone medallions, built for James V in the 1530s by French masons. James V died here in 1542, and the palace

was a favorite resort of his daughter, Mary, Queen of Scots. Behind the palace are gardens that contain a most unusual survivor: a "royal" tennis court (not at all like its modern counterpart) built in 1539 and still in use. *A912 (11 mi north of Kirkcaldy, ☎ 01337/857397. ☛ £4 adults, £2 children and senior citizens; gardens only, £2 adults, £1 senior citizens and children. ☉ Apr.–mid-Oct., Mon.–Sat. 11–5:30, Sun. 1:30–5:30 (last admission to palace 4:30, to garden 5).*

⑬ Farther to the west as you follow A911 is Scotland's largest Lowland loch, **Loch Leven,** famed for its fighting trout. The area is also noted for its birdlife, particularly its wintering wildfowl. You can find out more about the ecology of the loch at the **Vane Farm Nature Reserve,** a well-equipped visitor center run by the Royal Society for the Protection of Birds, on the southern shore overlooking the loch. *Vane Farm, Rte. B9097, just off M90 and B996, ☎ 01577/862355. ☛ £2 adults, £1 senior citizens, 50p children. ☉ Apr.–Dec. 20, daily 10–5; Jan.–Mar., daily 10–4.*

⑭ Your next destination is **Cupar,** a busy market town with a variety of shops. On rising ground south of town (take Route A916) is the National Trust for Scotland's **Hill of Tarvit House.** A 17th-century mansion, the house was later altered in the high-Edwardian style at the turn of the 20th century by the Scottish architect Sir Robert Lorimer. Inside the house are fine collections of antique furniture, Chinese porcelain, bronzes, tapestries, and Dutch paintings. *A916 (2 mi south of Cupar), ☎ 01334/653127. ☛ £3 adults, £1.50 children, students, and senior citizens; gardens only, £1 adult, 50p children. ☉ Easter–mid-Oct., daily 1:30–5:30 (last admission 4:45); garden open daily 9:30–sunset.*

TIME OUT   In summer the National Trust operates a **tearoom** inside Hill of Tarvit House, which is always stocked with tasty homemade Scottish baked goods.

⑮ Before making your way back to St. Andrews, you can learn more about the history and culture of rural Fife by visiting the **Fife Folk Museum** at Ceres, reached by going south on A916 and east on B939. The life of local rural communities is reflected in artifacts and documents, all housed in suitably authentic buildings that include a former weigh house and adjoining weavers' cottages. *☎ 01334/828250. ☛ £1.60 adults, £1.30 senior citizens, 50p children. ☉ Easter and May–Oct., Sat.–Thurs. 2–5.*

Tour 2: Dundee and Angus

Numbers in the margin correspond to points of interest on the Angus Area map.

⑯ This tour starts with a walk through **Dundee** and continues with a drive up the coast as far as Montrose. The return loop leads you along peaceful back roads as far as Kirriemuir. Most of the roads in this area are uncluttered, with the exception of the main road from Perth/Dundee to Aberdeen—the A90—on which special care is needed.

Dundee's urban-renewal program—its determination to shake off its grimy industrial past—was motivated in part by the arrival of the **RRS (Royal Research Ship)** *Discovery,* the vessel used by Captain Robert Scott on his polar explorations. The steamer was originally built and launched in Dundee; now it's a permanent tourist exhibit. A new Visitor Centre and on-board exhibition allows visitors to sample life as it was aboard the intrepid *Discovery. Discovery Point, Discovery Quay, Dundee, ☎ 01382/201245. ☛ £4 adults, £2.90 senior citizens, children, and stu-*

Angus Area

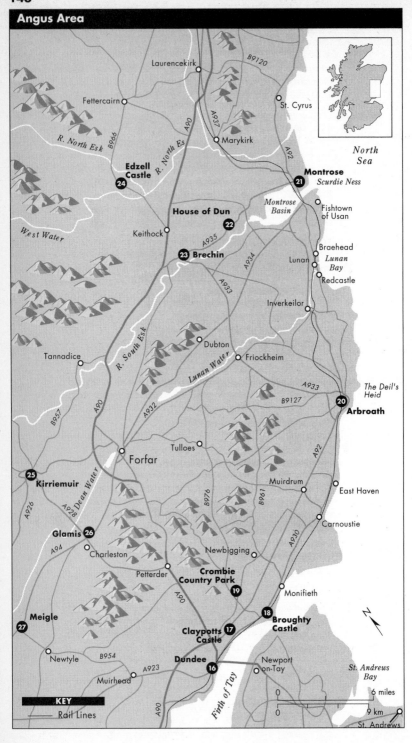

KEY

— Rail Lines

North Sea

Montrose Basin

Scurdie Ness

Lunan Bay

The Deil's Heid

St. Andrews Bay

6 miles

9 km

Laurencekirk

Fettercairn

R. North Esk

B9120

St. Cyrus

Marykirk

A937

A90

B966

R. North Esk

A92

Edzell Castle 24

Montrose 21

Fishtown of Usan

West Water

House of Dun 22

Keithock

A935

Braehead

Lunan

Redcastle

23 **Brechin**

A934

A933

R. South Esk

Inverkeilor

Tannadice

Dubton

Lunan Water

Friockheim

A933

B9127

20 **Arbroath**

A932

B957

Tulloes

A90

Forfar

Dean Water

Muirdrum

East Haven

25 **Kirriemuir**

B976

B961

A92

Carnoustie

A926

A928

Glamis 26

A94

Charleston

Newbigging

A930

Petterder

Crombie Country Park 19

Monifieth

Meigle 27

A90

18 **Broughty Castle**

Claypotts Castle 17

Newport on-Tay

Newtyle

B954

A923

Dundee 16

Muirhead

Firth of Tay

St. Andrews

dents, £11–£13.50 family ticket. ⊙ Mon.–Sat. 10–5, Sun. 11–5; daily until 4 in winter.

At nearby Victoria Dock is another historic vessel, the frigate **Unicorn,** a 46-gun wooden warship. The *Unicorn* has the distinction of being the oldest British-built warship afloat (the fourth-oldest in the world), having been launched at Chatham, England, in 1824. Onboard models and displays offer a glimpse into the history of the Royal Navy. *Victoria Dock (just east of Tay Rd. Bridge),* ☎ 01382/200900. ☞ *£3 adults, £2 children, students, and senior citizens.* ⊙ *Mid-Mar.–Sept. daily 10–5 (telephone for winter opening hours).*

Dundee's principal museum and art gallery is **The McManus Galleries,** which has displays—many of them new—on a range of subjects, including local history, trade, and industry. *Albert Sq.,* ☎ 01382/223141. ☞ *Free.* ⊙ *Mon. 11–5, Tues.–Sat. 10–5.*

The **Barrack Street Museum** specializes in natural history, with exhibitions on the wildlife and geology of Angus and the Highlands. The museum also displays the skeleton of the famous Tay Whale, immortalized by Scotland's worst poet, William MacGonagall, born in Dundee in 1830. His consistently dire poems caused him to be lionized by Edinburgh's legal and student fraternity. The stranding of a whale locally was one of many incidents that moved him to verse. *Barrack St. and Meadowside,* ☎ 01382/223141, ext. 65152. ☞ *Free.* ⊙ *Mon. 11–5, Tues.–Sat. 10–5.*

The **University Botanic Gardens** are a well-landscaped collection of native and exotic plants. Also on the premises are tropical and temperate greenhouses and a visitor center. *Riverside Dr.,* ☎ 01382/566939. ☞ *£1 adults, 50p senior citizens and children.* ⊙ *Mar.–Oct., Mon.–Sat. 10–4:30, Sun. 11–4; Nov.–Feb., Mon.–Sat. 10–3, Sun. 11–3.*

In the eastern suburbs of Dundee, away from the surviving Victorian architecture of the city center, are two castles of interest. **Claypotts Castle** is a well-preserved 16th-century tower house laid out on a Z-plan. *South of A92 (3 mi east of city center),* ☎ 0131/244–3101. ☞ *£1.20 adults, 75p children.* ⊙ *Apr.–Oct. Mon.–Sat., 9:30–6, Sun. 2–6.*

Approximately 1 mile farther east is **Broughty Castle.** This former fortress guarding the Tay estuary is now a museum with displays on fishing, ferries, and the history of the town's whaling industry. There is also a display of arms and armor. *Broughty Ferry (4 mi east of city center),* ☎ 01382/776121. ☞ *Free.* ⊙ *Mon. 11–1 and 2–5; Tues.–Thurs. and Sat. 10–1 and 2–5; also Sun. 2–5 from July–Sept.*

Dundee is ringed by country parks that offer ample sports and leisure activities. **Crombie Country Park** has a reservoir with extensive woodlands in 250 acres, as well as wildlife blinds, nature trails, a children's play park, picnic areas, and a display-and-interpretation center staffed by a ranger. *Off Rte. B961 (7 mi from Newbigging),* ☎ 01241/860360. ☞ *Free.* ⊙ *Daily 10–dusk.*

Leave Dundee by the A92 coast road, which leads to **Arbroath** (15 mi north of Dundee), a holiday resort and fishing town where traditional boat-building can still be seen. Arbroath has several small curers and processors, with shops offering the town's most famous delicacy, "Arbroath smokie"—whole haddock gutted and lightly smoked.

Arbroath Abbey, founded in 1178, in the center of town, is unmistakable and seems to straddle whole streets, as if the town was simply ignoring the redstone ruin in its midst. Surviving today are remains of the church, as well as one of the most complete examples in existence of an abbot's residence. From here in 1320, a passionate plea was sent by King Robert the Bruce and the Scottish church to Pope John XXII in far-off Rome. The pope had until then sided with the English kings, who adamantly refused to acknowledge Scottish independence. The Declaration of Arbroath stated firmly, "For as long as but a hundred of us remain alive, never will we on any conditions be brought under English rule. It is in truth not for glory, nor riches, nor honours that we are fighting, but for freedom—for that alone, which no honest man gives up but with life itself." Some historians describe this plea (originally drafted in Latin) as the single most important document in Scottish history. The pope advised English King Edward to make peace, but warfare was to break out along the border from time to time for the next 200 years. *Arbroath town center,* ☎ *0131/244–3101.* ☛ *£1.20 adults, 75p children.* ☉ *Apr.–Sept., Mon.–Sat. 9:30–6, Sun. 2–6; Mar.–Oct., Mon.–Sat. 9:30–4, Sun. 2–4.*

Also notable in the town is the **Signal Tower Museum.** Arbroath was the shore base for the construction of the Bell Rock lighthouse, on a treacherous, barely exposed offshore rock in the early 19th century. This signal tower was built to facilitate communication between the mainland and the builders working offshore. The museum in the tower now tells the story of the lighthouse, built by Robert Stevenson in 1811. (The name Stevenson is strongly associated with the building of lighthouses throughout Scotland, though the most famous son of that family is remembered for another talent. In fact, Robert Louis Stevenson gravely disappointed his family by choosing to become a writer instead of an engineer.) The museum also houses a collection of items related to the history of the town, its folk life, and the local fishing industry. *Ladyloan (west of harbor),* ☎ *01674/673232.* ☛ *Free.* ☉ *Mon.–Sat. 10–5; also Sun. 2–5 in July and Aug.*

A 15- to 20-minute drive to the north, along the coast via the A92, is
㉑ Montrose, a handsome, unpretentious town with a museum and a selection of shops. The town is also noted for its attractive beach. Behind Montrose the River Esk forms a wide estuary known as the Montrose basin. The Scottish Wildlife Trust operates a nature reserve here, with a good number of geese, ducks, and swans.

From Montrose head west on the A935. Signs will direct you to the Na-
★ ㉒ tional Trust for Scotland's leading attraction in this area, the **House of Dun,** overlooking the Montrose Basin. This 1730s mansion, built by architect William Adam, is particularly noted for its ornate plasterwork. *A935 (4 mi west of Montrose),* ☎ *01674/810264.* ☛ *£3 adults, £1.50 children; garden only, £1.* ☉ *Easter–June and Sept., daily 1:30–5:30; July and Aug., daily 11:30–5:30; early Oct., Sat. and Sun. 1:30–5:30 (last admission 5). Garden and grounds, daily 9:30–sunset.*

㉓ Farther west is **Brechin,** a small market town in Strathmore. Its cathedral was founded in about 1200 and contains an interesting selection of antiquities. Also nearby is the 10th-century **Round Tower,** one of only two on mainland Scotland (they are more frequently found in Ireland). It was originally built for the local Culdee monks.

Make your way due north by the B966, north of Edzell (which most Scots now associate with the U.S.-run military listening post nearby).
★ ㉔ **Edzell Castle,** an impressive ruin from the 16th century, is nestled among the Grampian foothills. This structure was originally a typical Scottish fortified tower, but was later transformed into a house that gave some degree of domestic comfort as well as protection from the

Reality check. Call home.

—— *AT&T USADirect® and World Connect®. The fast, easy way to call most anywhere.* ——

Take out AT&T Calling Card or your local calling card.** Lift phone. Dial AT&T Access Number for country you're calling from. Connect to English-speaking operator or voice prompt. Reach the States or over 200 countries. Talk. Say goodbye. Hang up. Resume vacation.

Austria*†††.....................022-903-011	Luxembourg 0-800-0111	Turkey* 00-800-12277
Belgium* 0-800-100-10	Netherlands*..................06-022-9111	United Kingdom................0500-89-0011
Czech Republic* 00-420-00101	Norway 800-190-11	
Denmark 8001-0010	Poland†♦¹ ....0◊010-480-0111	
Finland 9800-100-10	Portugal† 05017-1-288	
France.................................19-0011	Romania* ¹01-800-4288	
Germany...........................0130-0010	Russia*†(Moscow)................155-5042	
Greece* 00-800-1311	Slovak Rep.* 00-420-00101	
Hungary*.....................00◊-800-01111	Spain● 900-99-00-11	**AT&T**
Ireland 1-800-550-000	Sweden 020-795-611	Your True Choice
Italy* 172-1011	Switzerland* 155-00-11	

For a free wallet sized card of all AT&T Access Numbers, call: 1-800-241-5555.

elements. The simple "L" shape of the original building was extended, and a pleasance, or walled garden, was added in 1604. This formal garden, along with unique heraldic and symbolic sculptures, survives today. *Off B966 (6 mi north of Brechin),* ☎ *0131/244–3101.* ☛ *£2 adults, £1.25 senior citizens, 75p children.* ☉ *Apr.–Sept., Mon.–Sat. 9:30–6, Sun. 2–6; Oct.–Mar., Mon.–Wed. and Sat. 9:30–4, Thurs. 9:30– noon, Sun. 2–4.*

You can rejoin the hurly-burly of the A90 for the journey back to Dundee, though the more pleasant route leads southwestward using minor roads (there are several options) along the face of the Grampians, following the fault line that separates highland and lowland at this point.

❷❺ At the intersection of Routes B957 and A926 is **Kirriemuir,** heart of Angus's red sandstone countryside and birthplace of the writer and dramatist Sir James Barrie (1860–1937), most well known abroad as the author of *Peter Pan.* Barrie's house, now in the care of the National Trust for Scotland, has upper floors furnished as they might have been in Barrie's time, with manuscripts and personal mementoes displayed. The outside washhouse is said to have been Barrie's first theater. Next door, at 11 Brechin Road, is an exhibition on "The Genius of J. M. Barrie" giving literary and theatrical background. *9 Brechin Rd., Kirriemuir,* ☎ *01575/572646 or 01575/572353.* ☛ *£1.50 adults, 80p children.* ☉ *Easter–Sept., Mon.–Sat. 11–5:30, Sun. 1:30–5:30; early Oct., Sat. 11:30–5:30, Sun. 1:30–5:30 (last admission 5).*

★ ❷❻ About 6 miles due south on the A928, across pleasantly rolling countryside, is the village of **Glamis,** site of the **Angus Folk Museum.** This museum village is made up of a row of 19th-century cottages with unusual stone-slab roofs; exhibits focus on the crafts and tools of domestic and agricultural life in the region over the past 200 years. *Off A94 (5 mi southwest of Forfar),* ☎ *01307/840288.* ☛ *£2 adults, £1 children.* ☉ *Easter–Sept., daily 11–5; early Oct., Sat. and Sun. 11–5 (last admission 4:30).*

★ Approximately another mile to the southwest is **Glamis Castle,** one of Scotland's best-known castles because of its association with the present Royal Family. This was the childhood home of the current Queen Mother and the birthplace of Princess Margaret. The property of the earls of Strathmore and Kinghorne since 1372, the castle was largely reconstructed in the late-17th century; the original keep, which is much older, is still intact. One of the most famous rooms in the castle is Duncan's Hall, the legendary setting for Shakespeare's *Macbeth.* Guided tours offer visitors a look at fine collections of china, tapestries, and furniture. Other visitor facilities include shops, a produce stall, and licensed restaurant. *A94 (6 mi southwest of Forfar),* ☎ *01307/840242.* ☛ *£4.50 adults, £3.50 senior citizens and students, £2.40 children, £13 family ticket.* ☉ *Apr.–mid-Oct, daily 10:30–5:30 (last tour at 4:45).*

❷❼ The local museum at **Meigle,** on the A94 in the wide swathe of Strathmore, has a magnificent collection of some 25 sculptured monuments from the Celtic Christian period (8th to 10th centuries), nearly all of which were found in or around the local churchyard. This is one of the most notable collections of medieval work in Western Europe. *A94 in Meigle (12 mi west/southwest of Forfar),* ☎ *0131/244–3101.* ☛ *£1.20 adults, 75p children.* ☉ *Apr.–Sept., Mon.–Sat. 9:30–6, Sun. 2–6.*

From Meigle you can take Route B954 back to Dundee, just 15 miles east.

What to See and Do with Children

Craigtoun Country Park. Here children can choose from among a miniature railway, a re-created Dutch village, boating, bowling, putting, trampolines, an adventure play area, bouncy castles, and guided country walks. *Off A915 (2½ mi southwest of St. Andrews),* ☎ *01334/ 473666.* ☛ *£2 adults, £1 children under 5, senior citizens, and students.* ☺ *Easter–early Oct., daily 10:30–6:30 (last admission 5:30).*

Kerr's Miniature Railway. Established in 1935 and hauled by steam and diesel engines, this railway has a real old-time feel to it. Tunnel, footbridge, turntable, and locomotive shed are all in scale. *Sea front, Arbroath,* ☎ *01241/879249. For admission charges and opening times, contact the tourist information center.*

Scottish Deer Centre. Here children can see red deer at close quarters on ranger-guided tours. There are also nature trails, a winery, falconry displays, an adventure playground, a shop, and a restaurant. *A91, near Rankelour Farm (3 mi west of Cupar),* ☎ *01337/810391. Admission £4 adults, £3 senior citizens and students, £2.50 children, £11 family ticket.* ☺ *Apr.–Oct., daily 10–5.*

Sea Life Centre. Sea lions, penguins, and many other forms of marine life are displayed here in settings designed to simulate their natural environment. The exhibits include numerous aquariums and pool gardens. *The Scores, West Sands, St. Andrews,* ☎ *01334/474786.* ☛ *£4.25 adults, £3.75 senior citizens and students, £2.95 children 4–14.* ☺ *Daily 10–6 (extended hours in July and Aug.).*

Off the Beaten Path

Fife

Two points of interest are often overlooked by motorists touring rural Fife. Only minutes from the famous Old Course of St. Andrews, on Route A919 at **Leuchars,** is a 12th-century church with some of the finest Norman architectural features to be seen anywhere in Scotland. Note in particular the blind arcading (arch shapes on the wall) and the beautifully decorated chancel and apse.

A few minutes west of St. Andrews on the B939, an unclassified road goes through Strathkinness and about 3 miles later runs by the River Eden. The nearest community is at Dairsie (back on the A91). Stop for a moment at **Dairsie Bridge** over the river. It is 450 years old and has three arches. Above the trees rises the spire of **Dairsie Church,** dating from the 17th century, and the stark ruin of **Dairsie Castle,** often overlooked, stands gloomily over the river nearby. With wild-rose hedges, grazing cattle, and pheasants calling from the woody thickets, this is the very essence of rural, Lowland Fife, yet it's only about 15 minutes from the Old Course.

Angus

The **White and Brown Caterthuns** are the remains of Iron Age hill forts that crown two rounded hills to the west and south of Edzell Castle. Lovers of wild places will enjoy the drive to the Caterthuns from Edzell (if in doubt at junctions, turn left), especially the climb up the narrow road (from Balrownie to Pitmudie) that passes between the two hills; along the way there are magnificent views southward to the patterned fields of Strathmore. Marked paths run up to each fort (both are now officially protected sites) from the main road. The White Caterthun, so called because of the pale quartzite rock that was used to build its now-tumbled ramparts, is the better preserved of the two. After you've explored the Caterthuns, drop southward to rejoin main routes running along Strathmore. ☎ *0131/244–3101.* ☞ *Free.*

The **Glens of Angus** extend north from various points on Route A94. Known individually as the glens of Isla, Prosen, Clova, and Esk, these long valleys run into the high hills of the Grampians and offer a choice of clearly marked walking routes (those in Glen Clova are especially appealing).

SHOPPING

Shopping in this mainly rural region is inevitably concentrated in the larger towns. St. Andrews, with its university and its world-renowned golfing facilities, attracts enough affluent people to sustain some interesting smaller specialty shops. Dundee, as Scotland's fourth-largest city, is an important retail shopping center for the northern part of Angus, but the choices for shoppers here are similar to those found in most large towns (department stores, such as Marks and Spencer, predominate).

Fife

CUPAR

If you're approaching the shopping mecca at St. Andrews from the south and are interested in women's fashion, it's worth stopping in Cupar to visit **Margaret Urquhart** (13–17 Lady Wynd, ☎ 01334/652205), a boutique that attracts customers from as far away as Edinburgh and Glasgow and stocks a wide range of British and international designer names.

ST. ANDREWS

Among the worthwhile specialty shops you'll find in St. Andrews are **Graeme Renton** (72 South St., ☎ 01334/476334), the best place in the region, if not in all Scotland, for Oriental rugs and carpets of all colors, patterns, and sizes—many of them antiques. **Church Square Ceramics and Workshops** (Church Sq., between South St. and Market St., ☎ 01334/477744) offers decorative and domestic stoneware, ceramic, and enameled jewelry. **Bonkers** (80 Market St., ☎ 01334/473919) has a huge selection of clothing, clocks, books, cards, pottery, and gift items. **St. Andrews Fine Art** (84A Market St., ☎ 01334/474080) is the place to go for Scottish paintings from 1800 to the present (oils, watercolors, drawings, and prints are available).

GLENROTHES

In the west of Fife, Glenrothes, Dunfermline, and Kirkcaldy are the main shopping towns for day-to-day needs. The **Balbirnie Craft Centre** (near Balbirnie House, Glenrothes ☎ 01592/758759), in an 18th-century stable mews, is a peaceful setting in which to buy items made by craftspeople who live on the premises: their work includes pottery, fashion design, furniture, silver, jewelry, and leather goods.

Dundee

The modern covered shopping mall in Dundee—the **Wellgate Shopping Centre** (off Panmure Street, ☎ 01382/225454)—is the place to visit if you're looking for the major retail chains. If you search around a little, however, you'll find a scattering of smaller shops that have more character and unusual selections. **The Cookshop** (27 Wellgate Centre, ☎ 01382/221256) stocks an enormous variety of cooking equipment and other kitchenware. A treat for overseas visitors whose own home grocers may only stock tea bags and packaged coffee is **J. Allan Braithwaite** (6 Castle St., ☎ 01382/322693), where you can select from over

30 blended teas (including mango and apricot) and 13 freshly roasted coffees (remember that such specialty teas can usually be taken home without import restriction if you purchase them as gifts). There are also several good jewelers in Dundee; try **Rattrays** (32 Nethergate, ☎ 01382/227258), which has been in business for over 140 years. **Stephen Henderson the Jeweller** (1 Union St., ☎ 01382/221339) has a good selection of silver and pewter Ortak jewelry from Orkney, *skean dhus* (ornamental Highlander daggers), and *quaichs,* a small dish traditionally used for whisky tasting.

SPORTS AND FITNESS

Bicycling
The back roads of Fife make pleasant bicycling terrain, as does the long valley of Strathmore (except for the A94), where some roads run deep into the Angus Glens. The following firms rent bicycles: **East Neuk Outdoors** (Cellardyke Park, Anstruther, ☎ 01333/311929) and **Nicholson's Cycle Centre** (2 Forfar Rd., Dundee, ☎ 01382/461212).

Fishing
As in most of the rest of Scotland, there is a wide choice of fishing in sea, loch, and river. Leaflets giving detailed information are available at tourist information centers (*see* Important Addresses and Numbers in Fife and Angus Essentials, *below*).

Golf
Every golfer's ambition is to play at St. Andrews, and once you are in Fife the ambition is easily realized. The following five St. Andrews courses are open to visitors (all are part of the St. Andrews Club). For details of availability—there is sometimes a waiting list—contact the Reservations Department, Links Management Committee, Golf Place, St. Andrews (☎ 01334/475757).

Old Course (15th century). 18 holes, 6,578 yards, SSS 72, handicap certificate required.
New Course (1894). 18 holes, 6,604 yards, SSS 72.
Jubilee Course (1899). 18 holes, 6,284 yards, SSS 72.
Eden Course (1913). 18 holes, 5,971 yards, SSS 69.
Strathyrum Course (1993). 18 holes, 5,195 yards, SSS 69.

There are more than 40 other courses in the region. Most have refreshment facilities and offer golf to the visitor by the round or the day. Details about locations and opening hours are available from tourist information centers (*see* Important Addresses and Numbers in Fife and Angus Essentials, *below*). Many of the area's hotels offer golfing packages or will arrange a day's golf.

Health and Fitness Clubs
Arbroath Sports Centre (Keptie Rd., Arbroath, ☎ 01241/872999) has a swimming pool, squash courts, games hall, and a gymnasium.

The **Saltire Centre** (Montrose Rd., Arbroath, ☎ 01241/431060) has fitness rooms, sauna, and exercise equipment.

Cupar Sports Centre (Main St., Cupar, ☎ 01334/654793) has a swimming pool, sports hall, fitness rooms, squash, steam bath, and sunbeds.

Dundee Olympia Leisure Centre (Earl Grey Pl., Dundee, ☎ 01382/223141, ext. 4187) has four swimming pools, a diving pool, sauna, water slides, exercise equipment, and a restaurant.

Montrose Sports Centre (Marine Ave., Montrose, ☎ 01674/676211) is an indoor sports center with a gymnasium.

DINING AND LODGING

Dining

In St. Andrews and in some of the West Fife towns, such as Kirkcaldy and Dunfermline, you will find restaurants serving traditional Scottish fare, as well as ethnic food (Italian and Chinese are popular), in addition to numerous small cafés of all kinds. Bar lunches are becoming the rule in large and small hotels throughout the region, and in seaside places the "carry oot" (to go) meal is an old tradition.

WHAT TO WEAR
Dress is, for the most part, casual; that said, some city center establishments might prefer more formal dinner attire, and this is noted.

CATEGORY	COST*
$$$$	over £30
$$$	£20–£30
$$	£10–£20
$	under £10

per person for a three-course meal, including VAT, excluding drinks and service

Lodging

If you're staying in Fife, the obvious base is St. Andrews, where you will find ample accommodations of all kinds. Other towns also offer a reasonable selection, and you will find good hotels and guest houses at Dunfermline and Kirkcaldy. Along the coastal strip and in the Howe of Fife between Strathmiglo and Cupar there are some superior country-house hotels, many with their own restaurants.

CATEGORY	COST*
$$$$	over £110
$$$	£80–£110
$$	£45–£80
$	under £45

All prices are for a standard double room, including service, breakfast, and VAT.

Aberdour
LODGING

$ **Hawkcraig House.** This old ferryman's house offers an interesting accommodation option not only for Fife and Angus, but also for Edinburgh, only 30 minutes away by road or rail. The historic house is set on the waterfront with lovely views of a serene stretch of coast—an ideal place to escape the noisy bustle of cities. Rooms have antique furniture and floral chintz fabrics. Accommodation is bed-and-breakfast with the option for evening meals (the hostess offers a Taste of Scotland menu). ⌂ *Hawkcraig Point, Fife KY3 OTZ,* ☎ *01383/860335. 1 room with bath, 1 with shower. No credit cards.* ☉ *Mid-Mar.–Oct.*

Anstruther
DINING

$$$ **The Cellar.** Specializing in fish, but offering a selection of Scottish beef
★ and lamb as well, the Cellar is devoted to serving top-quality ingredients cooked simply to preserve all the natural flavor. The crayfish-and-

mussel bisque is famous, and the wine list reflects high standards. Entered through a small courtyard, the restaurant is charmingly furnished in an unpretentious, old-fashioned style. It is popular with the locals, and its fame is spreading quickly. Reservations are advised, but you still stand a better chance of getting a table here more quickly than at the Peat Inn (*see below*). ✕ *24 E. Green St., Anstruther, Fife,* ☎ *01333/ 310378. Reservations advised. AE, MC, V.*

Arbroath

DINING

$ **Byre Farm Restaurant.** When touring around the cozy hinterland of Angus, amid the farms and woods, you may stumble upon this unpretentious little establishment on the edge of a tiny village, and wonder how it survives. The answer: its good plain Scottish cooking, and its proximity to the city of Dundee. You'll eat in a long, low room— a barn conversion—at unfussy pine tables. Try the salmon cutlets braised in butter, the pan-fried lamb chops, or the roast beef with roasted potatoes. There's also a Scottish traditional high tea here, a substantial meal served in the late afternoon. ✕ *Redford, Carmyllie, Arbroath, Angus DD11,* ☎ *01241/860245. Reservations advised for high tea and dinner. MC, V.*

Ceres

DINING AND LODGING

$$–$$$$ **The Peat Inn.** This popular inn and eatery is best known for its out-
★ standing restaurant, generally considered one of the finest in Scotland. Mouth-watering entrées like ragout of scallops, monkfish and pork, or roast saddle of venison with lentils and smoked bacon justify the high prices charged for dinner; lunch is slightly cheaper, but for either you may have to book well in advance. In a detached building there are eight comfortable double suites, making the inn into a French-style restaurant with rooms. 🏠 *Junction of B940 and B941, 5 mi south-west of St. Andrews,* ☎ *01334/840206,* 🅵🅰🅇 *01334/840530. 8 rooms with bath. Restaurant (reservations advised), bar. AE, DC, MC, V. Closed Mon. and Sun.*

Dundee

DINING AND LODGING

$$–$$$ **Angus Thistle Hotel.** In the center of Dundee, this hotel offers pleasant views extending in all directions, especially from rooms on the higher floors. Some suites have four-poster beds, whirlpool baths, and private sitting rooms. The decor is modern throughout. The hotel's restaurant serves adequate meals, drawn mostly from the beef and fish categories. 🏠 *101 Marketgait, Dundee DD1 1QT,* ☎ *01382/226874,* 🅵🅰🅇 *01382/ 322564. 58 rooms with bath. Restaurant, bar. AE, DC, MC, V.*

Forfar

DINING

$–$$ **The Drovers Inn.** Set in the heart of the Angus farmlands, the Drovers
★ is a rare find in Scotland, having more of the feeling of an English country pub. Plain but friendly surroundings, decorated with old farm implements and historic photographs, are the setting for simple bar food, homemade pies, and nourishing soups. It's a popular place with locals; on weekends it's best to make reservations, even for bar meals. ✕ *Memus, near Forfar,* ☎ *01307/860322. Restaurant (reservations advised). MC, V. Closed Wed. dinner in winter.*

$–$$ **Forester's Seat.** On a hillside just outside Forfar, Forester's is an airy, oak-furnished conservatory-style restaurant serving a hearty Scottish menu—steaks, lamb, and salmon appear in various guises, with plentiful supplies of vegetables and salad. It's not haute cuisine, but the food is appetizing and the welcome friendly. Afterwards, there is a garden center, delicatessen and wine shop, and winery to explore. ✕ *Forester's Centre, Arbroath Rd., Forfar,* ☎ *01307/818786. Reservations advised. MC, V.*

DINING AND LODGING

$$ **Royal Hotel.** In the center of Forfar, this former coaching inn has been fully modernized and has a leisure complex with swimming pool, gymnasium, and roof garden. The bedrooms are well equipped, though some in the most modern part of the hotel are rather small. All are decorated in an attractive green-and-peach color scheme, with stained wood finishes and floral fabrics. The public rooms have retained their 19th-century charm. This hotel provides an attractive base for exploring or golfing. The two restaurants serve well-cooked, standard fare—fish and chips, lasagne—served by a friendly staff. ⌨ *Castle St., Forfar, Angus DD8 3AE,* ☎ *and fax 01307/462691. 19 rooms with bath or shower. 2 restaurants, indoor pool, sauna. AE, DC, MC, V.*

LODGING

$ **Quarrybank Cottage.** Once a Victorian quarryman's cottage hospital, this property is now a spacious and immaculately kept bed-and-breakfast establishment set among the green fields of Angus just a few minutes' drive from Forfar. The freshly decorated rooms are enlivened with curios from all over the world, collected by the owners on their travels. ⌨ *Balgavies, by Forfar,* ☎ *and fax 01307/830303. 3 rooms with shower and bath. No credit cards.*

St. Andrews
DINING AND LODGING

$$$–$$$$ **Rufflets Country House Hotel.** This ivy-bedecked country house just outside St. Andrews is surrounded by 10 acres of formal and informal gardens. All the rooms are attractively decorated and comfortable, with all the amenities one would expect of a top-class hotel, but at a moderate price. Dinner is served in the roomy Garden Restaurant, famous for its use of local produce to create memorable Scottish dishes. Recommended are the Tay salmon and fillet of Aberdeen Angus beef. ⌨ *Strathkinness Low Rd., St. Andrews, Fife KY16 9TX,* ☎ *01334/472594,* ☰ *01334/478703. 26 rooms with bath. Restaurant, bar. AE, DC, MC, V.*

$–$$ **The Grange Inn.** On a breezy hilltop overlooking St. Andrews, the Grange Inn offers an attractive blend of old-fashioned charm with polished brass, low lights, and open fires. The three dining areas include one (no smoking) with superb views over St. Andrews. The delicious specials might include monkfish with pesto, braised duck with red cabbage, or gravadlax with sweet dill mustard. There is also an extensive wine list. Two guest rooms are plain and on the small side, but they're comfortable (and within stumbling distance of the inn's cozy pub). ⌨ *Grange Rd., St. Andrews, Fife KY16 8LJ,* ☎ *01334/472670,* ☰ *01334/478703. 2 rooms with bath. Restaurant (reservations advised). AE, DC, MC, V.*

$ **University of St. Andrews.** For accommodation within walking distance of all the town's attractions, it's hard to better the university for value and convenience. Room sizes—mainly singles—vary from adequate in the new building to happily spacious in the old building. The newer rooms have private bathrooms (all rooms come equipped with sinks), and all have access to a restaurant, bar, lounge, TV room, and laundry facilities. ⌨ *79 North St.,* ☎ *01334/462000,* ☰ *01334/462500.*

350 rooms, 150 with shower. Restaurant, bar, coin laundry. MC, V.
⊙ Late June–late Sept.

THE ARTS AND NIGHTLIFE

The Arts

Theater

Byre Theatre (Abbey St., St. Andrews, ☎ 01334/476288) has a resident repertory company that performs during the summer months.

Dundee Repertory Theatre (Tay Sq., Dundee, ☎ 01382/223530). This award-winning complex, which includes an exhibition gallery, is home to a resident theater group, as well as a dance company. Both offer diverse programs.

Little Theatre (Victoria Rd., Dundee, ☎ 01382/225835) presents a wide variety of performances, especially modern theatrical works by local and visiting groups.

Whitehall Theatre (Bellfield St., Dundee, ☎ 01382/322684) offers a variety of choices, including Scottish shows, light opera, and variety and musical entertainments.

Music

Bonar Hall (Park Pl., Dundee, ☎ 01382/229450) hosts classical, jazz, and rock concerts, as well as chamber music.

Caird Hall (City Sq., Dundee, ☎ 01382/223141, ext. 4288) is one of Scotland's finest concert halls, staging a wide range of music.

Film

Cannon Film Centre (Seagate, Dundee, ☎ 01382/226865) screens mainstream films.

Odeon Multiplex (Stack Leisure Park, Dundee, ☎ 01382/400855) shows recent releases.

Steps Film Theatre (Wellgate Centre, Dundee, ☎ 01382/434037) screens less-mainstream films, as well as current releases.

Nightlife

Discos

Dundee has several discos in and around the city, including **De Sthils** (S. Ward Rd., Dundee, ☎ 01382/200066), **Fat Sam's Disco** (31 S. Ward Rd., Dundee, ☎ 01382/26836), **Arthur's** (St. Andrews St., ☎ 01382/221061), and **Oscar's** (Brown St., ☎ 01382/201603 or 01382/221176). Brechin offers **Flicks** (High St., ☎ 01356/624313), while Arbroath dances at **Club Metro** (Queen's Dr., ☎ 01241/872338).

Folk Music

The following establishments occasionally offer ceilidhs and/or evening performances of traditional folk music: **Royal Jubilee Arms Hotel** (Dykehead, Cortachy, Angus, ☎ 01575/540381) has a regular Thursday folk night, while **West Port Bar** (Henderson's Wynd, Dundee, ☎ 01382/200993) offers folk music on most Mondays—phone to confirm.

Pubs

In St. Andrews, **Bert's Bar** (South St.) is a spartan, no-nonsense drinking den where leathery old men like to swill pints and swap stories. The crowd is quite friendly, and the decor—even down to the black-and-white television and pickled eggs—is decidedly Scottish. **Chariots** (The Scores), located inside the Scores Hotel, is popular with locals in their thirties and forties. With open fires and dark wood paneling, the **Grange Inn** (*see* St. Andrews Dining and Lodging, *above*) has a pleasant old-style, traditional feel, not to mention an excellent food menu. In Anstruther, the **Dreel Tavern** (High St.) is a 16th-century coaching inn famous for its hand-drawn ales (no gas-powered autopumps here). In Arbroath, seek out the **Foundry Bar** (E. Mary St., ☎ 01241/872524), another spartan bar frequented by locals, which is enlivened by impromptu music sessions: Customers bring along their fiddles and accordions and all join in.

FIFE AND ANGUS ESSENTIALS

Arriving and Departing

By Bus

Two companies, **Lothian Regional Transport** (☎ 0131/220–4111) and **Guide Friday** (☎ 0131/556–2244), run buses between Edinburgh Airport's main terminal building and Waverley Bridge in downtown Edinburgh. The buses run every 15 minutes during the day (9–5) and less frequently (roughly every hour) during off-peak hours and on weekends. The trip from the airport takes about 30 minutes (about 45 minutes during rush hour). From Edinburgh's St. Andrew Square Bus Station, **Scottish Citylink** (☎ 0131/557–5717) buses run to various points throughout Fife and Angus.

By Car

The M90 motorway from Edinburgh takes visitors to within a half hour of St. Andrews and Dundee. Travelers coming from Fife can use the A91 and the A914, then cross the Tay Bridge to reach Dundee, though the quickest way is to use the M90 and the A85. Travel time from Edinburgh to Dundee is about 1 hour, from Edinburgh to St. Andrews, 1½ hours.

By Plane

Glasgow Airport (☎ 0141/887–1111), 50 miles west of Edinburgh, is now a major point of entry for international flights. Passengers landing in Glasgow have easy access to Edinburgh and Fife and Angus. **Edinburgh Airport** (☎ 0131/333–1000), 7 miles west of downtown Edinburgh, has airlinks throughout the United Kingdom, as well as with a number of cities on the Continent.

By Train

ScotRail (☎ 0131/556–2451) stops at Leuchars (for St. Andrews), Dundee, Arbroath, and Montrose.

Getting Around

By Bus

A local network provides service from St. Andrews and Dundee to many of the smaller towns throughout Fife and Dundee. The fare for the Kirkaldy–St. Andrews run is £2.60; St. Andrews–Dundee, £1.55;

Perth–Montrose, £5.50. For information about routes and fares call **Fife Scottish** (☏ 01592/642394) or **Strathtay Scottish** (☏ 01382/228345).

By Car

Fife is an easy area to get around and presents no major obstacles to the traveler. Most of the roads are quiet and uncongested. The most interesting sights are in the east, which is served by a network of cross-country roads. Angus is likewise an easy region to explore, being serviced by a main fast road—the A94/A90—which travels through the middle of the Strathmore valley and then on to Aberdeen; another, gentler road—the A92—that runs to the east near the coast; and a network of rural roads between the Grampians and Route A94/A90.

By Train

The stations listed in Arriving and Departing, above, are the area's only stations.

Guided Tours

Orientation

Tayside Transport (☏ 01382/202655) in late July through early August offers a variety of general orientation tours of the main cities and the region.

Special-Interest

Links Golf Tours (7 Pilmour Links, St. Andrews, ☏ 01334/478639) offers tours tailored to individual requirements.

Important Addresses and Numbers

Emergencies

For police, fire, or ambulance, dial 999 from any telephone. No coins are needed for emergency calls made from public telephone booths.

Doctors and Dentists

Consult your hotel, a tourist information center, or the yellow pages of the telephone directory for listings of local doctors and dentists.

Late-Night Pharmacies

Late-night pharmacies are not found outside the larger cities. In St. Andrews, Dundee, and other larger centers, pharmacies use a rotating system for off-hours and Sunday prescription service. Consult the listings displayed on pharmacy doors for the names and addresses of pharmacies that provide service outside regular hours. In an emergency the police can help you contact a pharmacist. Note that in rural areas general practitioners may also dispense medicines.

Visitor Information

Information is available from the **Tourist Information Centre** in St. Andrews (70 Market St., ☏ 01334/472021, FAX 01334/478422), the **Tourist Information Centre** in Dundee (4 City Sq., ☏ 01382/227723, FAX 01382/226353), **Tourist Information Centre** in Arbroath (Market Pl., ☏ 01241/872609, FAX 01241/878550). Smaller tourist information centers operate seasonally in the following towns: Anstruther, Brechin, Carnoustie, Crail, Cupar, Forfar, Kirriemuir, and Montrose.

7 Aberdeen and the Northeast

Aberdeen, Scotland's third largest city, is a sophisticated city built largely of glittering granite, and is a main port of North Sea oil operations. The Grampian region spreads to the west, the terrain changing from coastline— some of the U.K.'s wildest shorelines of high cliffs and sandy beaches—to farmland, to forests, to hills. The Grampian mountains and the Cairngorms, regions of heather and forest, granite peaks and deep glens, are popular for hill walking and skiing. The northeast is also known for its wealth of castles and whisky distilleries.

By Gilbert
Summers

BECAUSE OF ITS GEOGRAPHIC ISOLATION, Aberdeen has, throughout its history, been a fairly autonomous place. Even now, it is still perceived by many inhabitants of the United Kingdom as lying almost out of reach in the north. In reality, this northeastern locale is only 90 minutes flying time from London or—thanks to recent road improvements—a little more than two hours by car from Edinburgh.

In the 18th century, local granite quarrying produced a durable silver stone that would be used to build the Aberdonian structures of the Victorian era. Thus granite was used boldly—in glittering blocks, spires, columns, and parapets—to build Aberdeen. Downtown Aberdeen remains one of the United Kingdom's most distinctive urban environments, although some would say it depends on the weather and the brightness of the day. The mica chips embedded in the rock are a million mirrors in sunshine. In rain and heavy clouds, however, their sparkle is snuffed out.

The North Sea has always been an important feature of Aberdeen: In the 1850s, the city was famed for its fast clippers, sleek sailing ships that raced to India for cargoes of tea. In the late-1960s, the course of Aberdeen's history was unequivocally altered when oil and gas were discovered in the North Sea. Aberdeen at first seemed destined to become an oil-rich boomtown, and throughout the 1970s the city was overcome by new shops, new office blocks, new hotels, new industries, and new attitudes. Fortunately, some innate local caution has helped the city to retain a sense of perspective and prevented it from selling out entirely.

Yet even if Aberdeen, the country's third-largest city after Glasgow and Edinburgh, vanished from the map of Scotland, an extensive portion of the Northeast would still be worth exploring. Aberdeen's hinterland encompasses the old counties of Aberdeenshire, Kincardineshire to the south, and hanging from the Moray Firth coast to the north, Banffshire and Morayshire.

The area's chief scenic attraction lies in the gradual transition from high mountain plateau—by a series of gentle steps through hill, forest, and farmland—to a coastline where the word *unadulterated* truly applies. The coastline includes some of the United Kingdom's most perfect wild shorelines, both sandy and high cliff. The Grampian Mountains to the west contain some of the highest ground in the United Kingdom, in the area of the Cairngorms. But the Grampian hills have also shaped the character of the folk who live in the Northeast. In earlier times, the massif made communication with the south somewhat difficult. As a result, native Northeasterners still speak the richest Lowland Scottish (*not* Gaelic, which is an entirely different language).

EXPLORING

A major attraction in the Northeast is its wealth of castles. There are so many that in one part of the region a Castle Trail has been assembled, leading you to fortresses like the ruined medieval Kildrummy Castle, which once controlled the strategic routes through the valley of the River Don. Later work, such as Craigievar, a narrow-turreted castle resembling an illustration from a fairy-tale book, reflects the changing times of the 17th century, when defense became less of a priority. Later still, grand mansions, such as Haddo House, with its symmetrical facade and elegant interiors, surrender any defensive need entirely and instead make statements about their owner's status and power. Nowhere else in Scotland is there such an eclectic selection of castles. The Northeast offers visitors an opportunity to touch the fabric of Scotland's story, with the added advantage that the area is slightly off the beaten path.

As a visitor to Scotland, you can be sure of one thing: No matter where you are, a whisky distillery can't be far off, an assessment that would undoubtedly hold true in Morayshire. In this part of Scotland the distilling is centered in the valley of the River Spey and its tributaries. Just as the Loire in France has famous vineyards clustered around it, the Spey has famous single-malt distilleries. Instead of Muscadet, Chinon, Vouvray or Pouilly-sur-Loire, there's Glenfiddich, Glen Grant, Tamdhu, or Tamnavulin. As well as being sweeter and less peaty than some of the island malts, eastern or Speyside malts have the further advantage of having generally easier-to-pronounce brand names.

Union Street is the center of Aberdeen, and through traffic from the north and northwest is signposted through Aberdeen beyond its east end and to the harbor. Through traffic from the south is signposted around Anderson Drive, from where all the main routes into the Grampian hinterland are also signposted: for example, the Deeside and Donside routes, the main Inverness A96, as well as coastal routes to the north. Outside Aberdeen, the Castle and Whisky trails are generally well marked.

Tour 1: Aberdeen—The Silver City Center

Numbers in the margin correspond to points of interest on the Aberdeen map.

1 What Princes Street is to Edinburgh, Union Street is to **Aberdeen:** the central pivot of the city plan and the product of a wave of enthusiasm to rebuild the city in a contemporary style. This tour encompasses some of Aberdeen's best early-19th-century buildings. Some hints of an older Aberdeen have survived and can be noticed while touring. Conversely, this tour will also show you how today's plans are changing the face of Aberdeen, a city of handsome granite buildings that give it a silvery complexion.

★ **2** Start outside the tourist information center on Broad Street. Immediately opposite is **Marischal College,** founded in 1593 by the earl of Marischal as a Protestant alternative to the Catholic King's College in Old Aberdeen (*see* Tour 2, *below*), though the two combined to form Aberdeen University in 1860. (The earls of Marischal held the hereditary office as keepers of the king's mares.) The original university buildings on this site have undergone extensive renovations. What you see in front of you is a facade built in 1891. The spectacularly ornate work is set off by the gilded flags, and this turn-of-the-century creation is still the second-largest granite building in the world. Only the Escorial in Madrid is larger. *Broad St.,* ☎ *01224/632727.* ☛ *Free.* ☉ *Museum weekdays 10–5, Sun. 2–5.*

3 To find a survivor from an earlier Aberdeen, go underneath the concrete supports of St. Nicholas House (of which the tourist information center is a part) to find **Provost Skene's House** (*provost* is Scottish for mayor). Formerly one of a closely packed area of town houses, Provost Skene's House, steeply gabled and rubble-built, survives in part from 1545. It was originally a domestic dwelling house and is now a museum portraying civic life, with restored furnished period rooms and

Royal Deeside

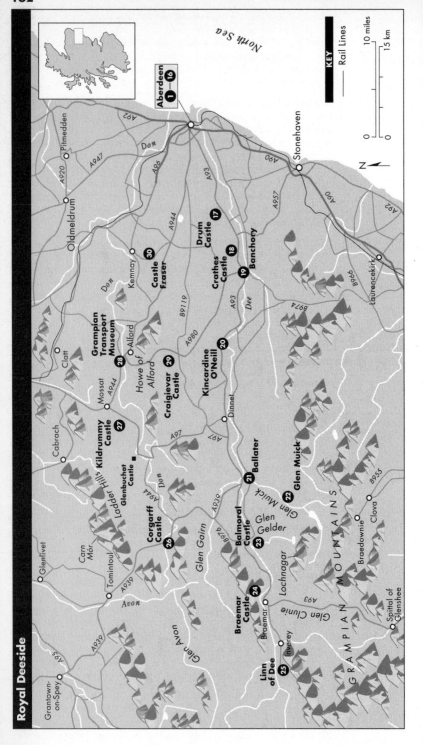

North Sea

Aberdeen ❶ – ⓰

Stonehaven

KEY
—— Rail Lines

10 miles
15 km

N

Plmedden

Oldmeldrum

Drum Castle ⓱

Crathes Castle ⓲

Banchory ⓳

Castle Fraser ㉚

Kemnay

Grampian Transport Museum ㉘

Alford

Howe of Alford

Craigievar Castle ㉙

Kincardine O'Neill ⓴

Clatt

Mossat

Kildrummy Castle ㉗

Cabrach

Ladder Hills

Glenbuchat Castle

Corgarff Castle ㉖

Ballater ㉑

Glen Muick ㉒

Dinnet

Glenlivet

Carn Mòr

Tomintoul

Glen Gairn

Balmoral Castle ㉓

Glen Gelder

Lochnagar

Clova

Braedownie

Braemar Castle ㉔

Braemar

Glen Clunie

Grantown-on-Spey

Avon

Glen Avon

Linn of Dee ㉕

Inverey

Spittal of Glenshee

G R A M P I A N   M O U N T A I N S

Aberdeen Art
Gallery, **5**

Commercial Union
Assurance building, **8**

His Majesty's
Theatre, **6**

King's College, **13**

Marischal College, **2**

Mercat Cross, **10**

Provost Ross's
House, **12**

Provost Skene's
House, **3**

Robert Burns
statue, **7**

Robert Gordon's
University, **4**

St. Machar's
Cathedral, **15**

St. Nicholas Kirk, **9**

Seaton Park, **16**

Tolbooth, **11**

Town House, **14**

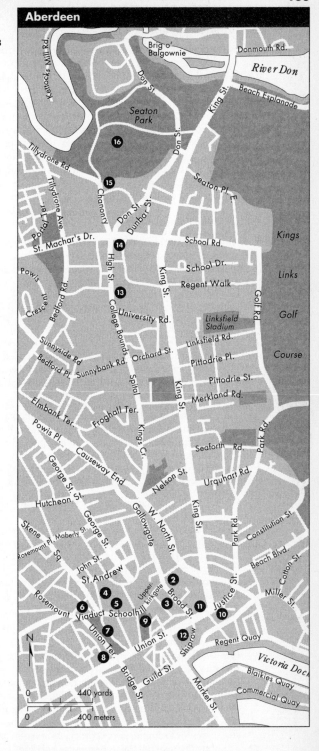

Aberdeen

a painted chapel. *Guestrow, off Broad St.,* ☎ *01224/641086.* ☛ *Free.* ⊙ *Mon.–Sat. 10–5.*

The tour then takes on a more contemporary twist, away from the well-wrought granite and the portion of a 16th-century townscape. Provost Skene's House is close to a 1960s shopping development, the St. Nicholas Centre. Go down Upperkirkgate to the lowest point, where you will see shopping malls—the **St. Nicholas Centre** on the left, the **Bon-Accord Centre** on the right. Until recent years, George Street, at the foot of the hill here, was a bustling shopping street running at right angles. But not even Aberdeen—in its far northern perch—has exempted itself from the British trend toward chain-store anonymity, and it has thus demolished traditional stonework to accommodate the chains. If you do enter the portals of the Bon-Accord Centre, you will eventually emerge at the truncated George Street. Note the spacious John Lewis Store, built in a design closely resembling a double-decker sandwich, with an illuminated filling and the crusts left on.

Although shopping is hard to resist here, try to do so for the moment and continue up Schoolhill, with its range of smaller specialty shops. Opposite is St. Nicholas Kirk, which you can examine on your way back, along Union Street.

On your right, as the slope eases off, is a complex of silver-toned buildings, in front of which stands a statue of General Charles Gordon, the military hero of Khartoum (1885). Interestingly, he is not, how-
❹ ever, the Gordon recalled in **Robert Gordon's University** behind the statue. Built in 1731, the structure was originally called Robert Gordon's Hospital and it was used to educate poor boys. It became an independent school later and then an institute of technology, before gaining university status in 1992.

❺ Adjacent is the **Aberdeen Art Gallery,** which plays an active role in Aberdeen's cultural life and is a popular rendezvous for locals. It houses a wide-ranging collection—from the 18th century to contemporary work. The sculpture court is certainly worth seeing, with its gallery supported by columns of different shades of polished granite. *Schoolhill,* ☎ *01224/ 646333.* ☛ *Free.* ⊙ *Mon.–Sat. 10–5, Thurs. 10–8, Sun. 2–5.*

Cross the street to get a better view of a library, church, and nearby theater, collectively known by all Aberdonians as Education, Salvation, and Damnation. Silvery and handsome, the **Central Library** and **St. Mark's**
❻ **Church** date from the last decade of the 19th century, while **His Majesty's Theatre** (1904–08) has been restored inside to its full Edwardian splendor. If you carry a camera, you can choose an angle that includes the statue of Scotland's first freedom fighter, Sir William Wallace, in the foreground, pointing majestically to Damnation. *Rosemount Viaduct in city center, box office* ☎ *01224/641122.*

Turning left onto Union Terrace, you will see another statue, this one
❼ of **Robert Burns** addressing a daisy. Behind Burns are the **Union Terrace Gardens,** faintly echoing Edinburgh's Princes Street Gardens in that they separate the older part of the city to the east, from the 19th-century development of Union Terrace and points westward (as well as Union Street itself). Most of the buildings on Union Terrace around the grand-looking Caledonian Hotel are late-Victorian, when exuberance and confidence in style was at its height. The results are impressive. Note for example, at the corner of Union Street, the wonderfully
❽ elaborate **Commercial Union Assurance building** (1885). Its Doric portico (plain-column extension) has been a landmark and meeting place

for generations of locals. They call it the "monkey house," though few can tell you why.

Turn left onto Union Street (though there is plenty of this main street to explore should you wish to turn right). Note the smug cats seated primly on the parapet of **Union Bridge.** The bridge was built in the early years of the 19th century, as was much of Union Street. The bridge has a gentle rise—or descent, if you are traveling east—and the street is carried on a series of blind arches. The north side of Union Bridge is the most obvious reminder of the grand thoroughfare's artificial levels. Much of the original work remains.

As you make your way through the main-street crowds, you will also pass, on your left, the colonnaded facade of 1829 that screens the church-
❾ yard of **St. Nicholas Kirk** from the shopping hustle and bustle. Behind the facade is the church itself, already seen from Schoolhill. This is the Mither Kirk, the original burgh church, yet curiously it is not within the bounds of the early settlement that was located to the east, near the end of present-day Union Street. During the 12th century, the port of Aberdeen flourished and room could not be found for the church within the settlement. Its earliest features are the pillars—supporting a tower built much later—and its clerestory windows: Both date from the original 12th-century structure. St. Nicholas was divided into east and west kirks at the Reformation, followed by a substantial amount of renovation from 1741 on. Some early memorials and other works have survived. *Union St.* ⊘ *Weekdays 10–1.*

Arriving at the east end of Union Street you are not only within a few moments of your starting point at the tourist information center, but also within the original old town. This is the **Castlegate.** The actual castle once stood somewhere behind the Salvation Army Citadel of 1896, an imposing baronial granite tower whose design was inspired by Bal-
❿ moral Castle. Just beyond King Street is the impressive **Mercat Cross** (built in 1686 and restored in 1820), always the symbolic center of a Scottish medieval burgh. Note that along its parapet, among its 12 panels are the portraits of the Stewart monarchs. Opposite is the hand-
⓫ some tower of the **Tolbooth,** dating from the 17th century. Also in sight here is the stylishly colonnaded facade of the Atheneum, built as a library, but now serving mainly as offices and eating places.

★ As the final reminder of this older part of Aberdeen, turn away from the Town House and head down to the left to Shiprow, once the main road into town in bygone days. Much has been swept away and re-
⓬ developed, but one building has survived since 1593: **Provost Ross's House,** which now houses **Aberdeen's Maritime Museum,** telling the story of the city's involvement with the sea, from early inshore fisheries by way of tea clippers to the North Sea oil boom (*see* What to See and Do with Children, *below*).

Below is the harbor, which contains some fine architecture from the 18th and 19th centuries. Explore it if time permits and you don't mind the background traffic.

Tour 2: A Short Excursion in Old Aberdeen

Old Aberdeen was once an independent burgh and lies to the north of the city, near the River Don. Although swallowed up by the expanding main city before the end of the 19th century, Old Aberdeen, which lies between **King's College** and **St. Machar's Cathedral,** still retains a certain degree of character and integrity. Reach it by taking a No. 20

bus north from a stop near Marischal College or a No. 1, 2, 3, or 4 up King Street, off the Castlegate.

★ ⑬ Visitors should alight in **College Bounds,** with its handsome 18th- and 19th-century houses, cobbled streets, and paved sidewalks. **King's College,** founded in 1494, can be seen, the flying (or crown) spire of its Chapel unmistakable. The structure was built around 1500, and the fact that it has survived at all was due to the zeal of the principal, who managed to defend his church against the destructive fanaticism that swept through Scotland during the Reformation, when the building was less than a century old. Today's visitor will find a renovated structure with the chapel playing an important role in university life. The tall oak screen that separates nave from choir, along with the ribbed wooden ceiling and stalls, constitutes the finest medieval wood carving to be found anywhere in Scotland.

⑭ Continuing up what is now the High Street of Old Aberdeen, you will see some restored Georgian houses, including the **Town House,** straight ahead. This Georgian work, plain and handsome, uses parts of an earlier building from 1720. Behind the Town House the modern intrusion of St. Machar's Drive destroys some of the old-town ambience, but the atmosphere is restored by a stroll down the **Chanonry,** past the elegant houses once lived in by the officials connected with the cathedral nearby. Today, they house mainly university staff. *High St.,* ☎ *01224/273702.* ☉ *Visitor Centre (with shop and cafeteria) Mon.–Sat. 10–5, Sun. noon–5.*

⑮ It is said that St. Machar was sent by St. Columba to build a church on a grassy platform near the sea, where a river flowed in the shape of a shepherd's crook. This spot fit the bill, and **St. Machar's Cathedral** was built in AD 580. However, nothing remains of the original foundation. Much of the existing building dates from the 15th and 16th centuries. The central tower collapsed in 1688, reducing the building to half its original length. The twin octagonal spires on the western towers date from the first half of the 16th century. The nave is thought to have been rebuilt in red sandstone in 1370, but the final renovation was completed in granite by the middle of the 15th century. Along with the nave ceiling, the twin spires were finished in time to take a battering in the Reformation, when the barons of the Mearns stripped the lead off the roof of St. Machar's and stole the bells. The cathedral suffered further mistreatment—including the removal of stone by Oliver Cromwell's English garrison in the 1650s—until a 19th-century restoration program restored the church to its former grandeur. *Chanonry,* ☎ *01224/485988.* ☉ *Daily 9–5.*

⑯ Beyond St. Machar's Cathedral lies **Seaton Park,** with its spring daffodils, tall trees, and herbaceous borders boldly colored. Until 1827, the only way out of Aberdeen to the north was over the River Don on the Brig o' Balgownie, a single-arch bridge found at the far end of Seaton Park—a 15-minute walk. It dates from 1314 and is thought to have been built by Richard Cementarius, Aberdeen's first provost. After enjoying the scenery of Seaton Park, which today has restored houses at either end, you can return to the city center.

Tour 3: Royal Deeside and Castle Country

Numbers in the margin correspond to points of interest on the Royal Deeside map.

Although basically a car tour, much of this area is accessible either by public transportation or on tours from Aberdeen. Deeside, the valley running west from Aberdeen down which the River Dee flows, earned its "Royal" appellation when discovered by Queen Victoria. To this day, where royalty goes, lesser aristocracy and fastbuck millionaires from across the globe follow. In fact, it is still the aspiration of many to own a grand shooting estate on Deeside. In a sense, this yearning is understandable, since piney hill slope, purple moor, and blue river intermingle most tastefully here, as you will see from the main road. Royal Deeside's gradual scenic change adds a growing sense of excitement as the road runs deeper and deeper into the Grampians.

There are castles along the Dee and to the north. This tour rises out of the river valley to find them, returning to Aberdeen by a route illustrating this gradual geological change: uplands lapped by a tide of farms.

⑰ The first 15 miles toward Banchory by either north or south Deeside roads (leaving the city by the Bridge of Dee) have only a subtle scenic flair. Castle hoppers can explore **Drum Castle,** an ancient foursquare tower dating from the 13th century, with later additions. Note the rounded corners of the tower, said to make battering-ram attacks more difficult. Nearby, fragments of the ancient Forest of Drum still stand, dating from the early days when Scotland was covered by great woodlands of oak and pine. *Off the A93, 10 mi west of Aberdeen,* ☎ *01330/ 811204. Admission to castle and garden: £3.50 adults, £1.80 senior citizens and children; to grounds and garden only: £1.50 adults, 80p children.* ☾ *Daily, Easter–June 1:30–5:30, July–Aug. 11–5:30, Sept. 1:30–5:30; early Oct., weekends 1:30–5:30 (last admission 4:45). Garden of historic roses open Easter–early Oct., daily 10–6. Grounds open daily 9:30–sunset.*

⑱ Perhaps of greater interest is **Crathes Castle,** roughly 4 miles west on the A93. The Burnett family had been keepers of the Forest of Drum for generations but acquired lands here by marriage and later built a new castle, completed in 1596. Crathes is in the care of the National Trust for Scotland; the trust also looks after the grand gardens, with their calculated symmetry and clipped yew hedges. Be careful not to confuse Crathes Castle, near Aberdeen, with Crathie Kirk, near Balmoral, where folk go to gaze at royalty. *Off the A93, 3½ mi east of Banchory,* ☎ *01330/844525.* ☛ *Grounds only £1.50 adults, 80p senior citizens and children; castle, garden, and grounds £4 adults, £2 senior citizens and children.* ☾ *Castle Apr.–mid-Oct., daily 11–5:30 (last admission 4:45), garden and grounds daily 9:30–sunset.*

TIME OUT Sample the excellent National Trust of Scotland's home baking in Crathes Castle's **tearoom** (☎ 01330/844525).

⑲ **Banchory,** a few minutes west on the A93, is an immaculate place with a pinkish tinge to its granite. It is usually bustling with ice cream-eating city strollers, out on a day trip from Aberdeen. If you visit in autumn and have time to spare, drive out to the **Brig o'Feuch** ("Bridge of," then pronounce it "Fyooch" with "ch" as in loch). Here, salmon leap in season, and the fall colors and foaming waters make for an attractive scene.

⑳ If you are pressed for time, continue west on the A93, through a landscape where the mixed farmlands are confined to the valley floor, sheltered by birch thickets and blankets of dark woods. Note, as you pass through, the ruined kirk in **Kincardine O'Neill.** Built in 1233, it was once a shelter for travelers, the last hospice before the Mounth, the name given to the massif that shuts off the south side of the Dee Valley. Beyond Banchory (and the B974), no motor roads run south until you reach Braemar, though the Mounth is crossed by a network of tracks used in former times by Scottish soldiers, invading armies (including the Romans), and cattle drovers.

There are many other intricate features to examine in the area, especially if you have the time. There's the picture-postcard bridge at **Potarch** and the **Braeloine Interpretative Centre** in Glen Tanar beyond Aboyne, which has a display on natural history, a café, a picnic area, and walks. *Glen Tanar,* ☎ *013398/86072.* ☉ *Daily 10–5 (extended hours in summer).*

Back on the main road, look for a large granite boulder on which is carved, YOU ARE NOW ENTERING THE HIGHLANDS. You may find this piece of information superfluous, given the quality of the scenery. Drive an-
㉑ other 5 miles west on the A93 and you will reach **Ballater.** This quaint holiday resort, once noted for the curative properties of its local well, has profited from the proximity of the royals, nearby at Balmoral. Visitors are amused by the array of BY ROYAL APPOINTMENT signs proudly hanging from many of its various shops (even monarchs need bakers and butchers). If you get a chance, take time to stroll around this neat community—well laid out in silver-gray masses. Note that the railway station now houses the tourist information center and a display on the former glories of this Great North of Scotland branch line, closed in the 1960s along with so many others in this country.

Ballater makes a good pausing place, and, if you can afford it, Craigendarroch is an excellent base (*see* Dining and Lodging, *below*). Nearby, visitors have the opportunity to capture the feel of the eastern Highlands—as long as they have their own transportation. Start your ex-
★ ㉒ pedition into **Glen Muick** (pronounced "mick," Gaelic for pig) by crossing the River Dee and turning upriver on the south side, shortly after the road forks into this fine Highland glen. The native red deer are quite common throughout the Scottish Highlands, but Glen Muick is one of the very best places to see them in abundance, with herds grazing the flat valley floor. Beyond the lower glen, the prospect opens to reveal not only grazing herds, but also fine views of the battlement of cliffs edging the mountain called Lochnagar.

However, there is no public transportation into this cul-de-sac glen, and your tour or local coach service will instead take you west again, on the A93. The enormous car park roughly 7 miles ahead is indica-
㉓ tive of the popularity of **Balmoral Castle,** the rebuilt castle modified by Prince Albert in 1855 for his queen. Balmoral's visiting hours depend on whether the royals are in residence. In truth, there are more interesting and historic buildings to explore, as the only part of the castle on view is the ballroom, with an exhibition of Royal artifacts. *On the A93,* ☎ *013397/42334.* ☛ *£2.50 adults, £2 senior citizens, under 16 free.* ☉ *May–July, Mon.–Sat. 10–5.*

Continuing west into Highland scenery, you can get further pine-framed glimpses of the "steep frowning glories of dark Lochnagar," as it was
㉔ described by the poet Byron. About 8 miles farther on the A93 sits **Braemar Castle,** dating from the 17th century, with defensive walls later built in the plan of a pointed star. At Braemar (the braes or slopes of the district of Mar), the standard or rebel flag was first raised at the start of the spectacularly unsuccessful Jacobite rebellion of 1715. Thirty years later, during the last rebellion, Braemar Castle was strengthened and garrisoned by Hanoverian (government) troops. *On the A93, at Braemar,* ☎ *013397/41219, off-season* ☎ *013397/41224.* ☛ *£1.90 adults, £1.50 senior citizens, 90p children.* ☉ *Easter–Oct., Sat.–Thurs. 10–6.*

The village of Braemar is associated with the Braemar Highland Gathering held every September. Although it's one of many such events celebrated throughout Scotland, Braemar's gathering is distinguished by the presence of the royal family. Braemar also has a tricky golf course laden with foaming waters. Erratic duffers take note: The compassionate course managers have installed, near the water, poles with little nets on the end for those occasional shots that may go awry.

★ ㉕ Although the main A93 slinks off to the south from Braemar, a little unmarked road will take you farther west into the hilly heartlands. In fact, even if you do not have your own car, you can still explore the area by catching the post bus that leaves from Braemar Post Office once a day. The road offers you delectable views over the winding river Dee and the blue hills before passing through the tiny hamlet of Inverey and crossing a bridge at the **Linn of Dee.** *Linn* is a Scots word meaning rocky narrows, and the river's rocky gash here is deep and roaring. Park beyond the bridge and walk back to admire the sylvan setting of the river and woodland, replete with bending larch bows and deep, tranquil pools with salmon glinting in them.

Now return to Braemar, retracing the route as far as Balmoral. From Balmoral, there is an interesting way out of Royal Deeside by car. Look for a narrow road going north, signposted B976. Be careful on the first twisting mile through the trees. Soon you will emerge from scattered pines into the open moor in upland Aberdeenshire. Behind is the massif of Lochnagar again, and to the west are snow-tipped domes of the big Cairngorms. Roll down to a bridge and go left on the A939, which comes in from Ballater. Another high moor section follows: As the road leaves the scattered buildings by the bridge, see if you can spot the roadside inscription to the company of soldiers who built the A939 in the 18th century.

㉖ The soldiers paved their military highway roughly 12 miles north to **Corgarff Castle,** a lonely tower house with another star-shaped defensive wall—a curious replica of Braemar Castle. To get there, you will find it signposted left at the next junction. Corgarff was built as a hunting seat for the earls of Mar in the 16th century. After an eventful history that included the wife of a later laird being burned alive in a family dispute, the castle ended its career as a garrison for Hanoverian troops. The troops also had the responsibility of trying to prevent illegal whisky distilling, at one time a popular hobby in these parts. *Off A939,* ☎ *0131/244–3101.* ☛ *£2 adults, £1.25 senior citizens, 75p children.* ☉ *Apr.–Sept., Mon.–Sat. 9:30–6, Sun. 2–6.*

If you return south to the A939/A944 junction and then make a left onto the A944, the excellent castle signposting will tell you that you are on the **Castle Trail.** The A944 meanders along the River Don to the village of Strathdon, where a great mound by the roadside—on the left—turns out to be a *motte,* or the base of a wooden castle, built in the late 12th century. Surviving mottes are significant in terms of confirming the history of Scottish castles, but it is difficult for visitors to become enthusiastic about a great grassed-over heap, no matter what its historic content.

★ ㉗ From here, a sign points to **Glenbuchat Castle,** a plain Z-plan tower house; about 12 miles to the northeast you will encounter the more interesting **Kildrummy Castle.** Visitors can enjoy the ruins of the castle itself, the gardens behind it, and the country house–style Kildrummy Castle Hotel. Kildrummy is significant because of its age (13th century) and because it has ties to the mainstream medieval traditions of

European castle building. It shares features with Harlech and Caernarvon in Wales, as well as with continental sites, such as Château de Coucy near Laon, France. Kildrummy had undergone several expansions at the hands of English King Edward I when, in 1306, back in Scottish hands, the castle was besieged by King Edward I's son. The defenders were betrayed by a certain Osbarn the Smith, who had been promised a large amount of gold by the English besieging forces. They gave it to him after the castle fell, pouring it molten down his throat, or so the ghoulish story goes. Kildrummy's prominence came to an end after the collapse of the 1715 Jacobite uprising. It had been the rebel headquarters and was consequently dismantled. ☎ *0131/244–3101.* ☛ *£1.50 adults, £1 senior citizens, 75p children.* ☉ *Apr.–Sept., Mon.–Sat. 9:30–6, Sun. 2–6; Oct.–Mar., Sat. 9:30–4, Sun. 2–4.*

The **garden** behind the castle—with a separate entrance from the main road—is built in what was the original quarry for the castle. This sheltered bowl within the woodlands has a broad range of shrubs and alpine plants and a notable water garden. If the weather is pleasant, it makes for a nice place to pause and plan the next stage of your journey. *A97, off the A944, Aberdeenshire,* ☎ *019755/71264 or 019755/71277.* ☛ *£1.70 adults, 50p children.* ☉ *Apr.–Oct., daily 10–5 (telephone to confirm opening times late in the season).*

TIME OUT The **Mossat Shop,** 4 miles past Kildrummy, at the junction of the A97 and the A944, is another possible pit stop for tea or some light shopping. If you have more time, however, then visit the **village hall** in the tiny rural community of **Clatt,** 7 miles northeast just off the A97. It has a savory reputation for its home baking; local ladies bake the delicious breads and cakes at this cooperatively run establishment (weekends only). People come from miles around to sample the results. There is also a produce and crafts shop.

If you wish to forego Clatt and its cream cakes, make a right onto the A944 for Alford (pronounced *Ah*-furd) at the A97/A944 junction. Alford, a plain and sturdy settlement in the Howe (Hollow) of Alford, gives those visitors who have grown somewhat weary from castle hopping a break: It has a museum instead. The **Grampian Transport Museum** specializes in road-based means of locomotion. One of its more unusual exhibits is the *Craigievar Express,* a steam-driven creation invented by the local postman to deliver mail more efficiently. *Alford,* ☎ *019755/62292.* ☛ *£2.50 adults, £1.80 senior citizens, £1 children, £5.50 family ticket.* ☉ *Apr.–Oct., daily 10–5.*

★ ㉙ Your return to Aberdeen leads you to two of the finest castles on the trail. The first is **Craigievar.** Located about 5 miles to the south on the A980, this historic structure represents one of the finest traditions of local castle building. It also has the advantage of having survived intact, much as the stonemasons left it in 1626, with its pepper-pot turrets and towers, the whole slender shape covered in a pink-cream pastel. It was built in relatively peaceful times by William Forbes, a successful merchant in trade with the Baltic Sea ports (hence he was also known as Danzig Willie). Centuries of care and wise stewardship have ensured that the experience proffered today's visitor is as authentic as possible. *On the A980,* ☎ *013398/83635.* ☛ *£5 adults, £2.50 senior citizens and children.* ☉ *May–Sept., daily 1:30–5:30 (last admission 4:45). Grounds open daily 9:30–sunset.*

㉚ Your return to Aberdeen could be by way of **Castle Fraser,** a massive structure—in fact, it is the largest of the castles of Mar. While this building shows a variety of styles reflecting the taste of previous owners from the 15th to the 19th centuries, its design is typical of the cavalcade of castles that exist here in the Northeast. It has the further advantages of a walled garden, a picnic area, and a tearoom. *3 mi south of Kemnay off the A944,* ☎ *01330/833463.* ☛ *£3.50 adults, £1.80 senior citizens and children.* ☉ *Mid-Apr.–June, and Sept., daily 1:30–5:30; July and Aug., daily 11–5:30; early Oct., weekends 1:30–5:30 (last admission 4:45).* ☉ *Gardens daily 9:30–6 (or sunset if earlier), grounds daily 9:30– sunset.*

From Castle Fraser, your quickest route back to the city is to turn south to join the A944 or north to the A96.

Tour 4: The Northeast

Numbers in the margin correspond to points of interest on the Northeast map.

Tour 3 covered the immediate hinterland of Aberdeen. This tour ranges more widely to sample the seaboard, including some of the best-preserved coastal scenery in Scotland. The tour also meanders inland, to revisit briefly the malt-whisky theme. Speyside—the valley or strath of the River Spey—is famed for its whisky distilleries, which it promotes in yet another signposted trail. Whisky distilling is not an intrinsically spectacular process. It involves pure water, malted barley, and sometimes peat smoke, then a lot of bubbling and fermentation, all of which causes a range of extremely odd smells. The end result is a prestigious product with a fascinating range of flavors that you either enjoy immensely or not at all.

On this tour, instead of assiduously following the whisky trail, we will dip into it and blend it with some other aspects of the lower end of Speyside—the old county of Moray. Whisky notwithstanding, Moray's scenic qualities, low rainfall, and other reassuring weather statistics are worth remembering when you plan your route.

Because of its convenient transport links to both the coast and the countryside, this tour starts from **Elgin.** As the center of the fertile Laigh (low-lying lands) of Moray, it has been of local importance for centuries. Like Aberdeen, it is self-supporting and previously remote, sheltered by great hills to the south and lying between two major rivers, the Spey and the Findhorn. Beginning in the 13th century, Elgin became an important religious center, a cathedral city with a walled town growing up around the cathedral and adjacent to the original settlement. Left in peace for at least some of its history, Elgin prospered and became, by the early 18th century, a mini-Edinburgh of the north and a place where country gentlemen came to spend the winter. It even echoed Edinburgh in the widescale reconstruction of the early 19th century: Much of the old town was swept away in a wave of rebuilding, giving Elgin the fine neoclassical buildings that survive today.

The old shape of the town survived almost intact until this century, when it succumbed to the modern madness of demolishing great swaths of buildings for the sake of better traffic flow. It suffered from its position on the Aberdeen–Iverness main road. However, the central main street plan and some of the older little streets and wynds (alleyways) remain. Visitors can also recall Elgin's past by observing the arcaded shop fronts—some of which date from the late-17th century—that give the main shopping street its gruffy, aged appeal.

At the center of town, the most conspicuous, positively unavoidable building is **St. Giles Church,** which divides High Street. The grand foursquare

The Northeast

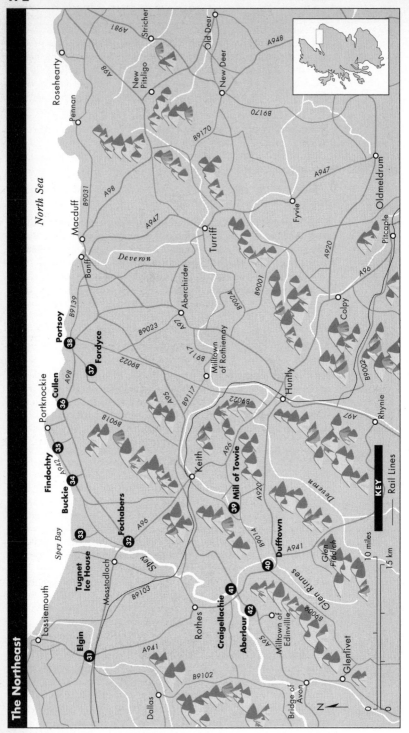

North Sea

Rosehearty

Pennan

Stricher
A981

New Pitsligo
A98

A950

Old Deer

New Deer
A948

A947

B9170

Oldmeldrum

Macduff
B9031

A98

A947

Deveron

Banff

B9139

Portsoy
38

Fordyce
37

B9022

Cullen
36

Porknockie

A98

A95

B9018

Findochty
34
A942

Buckie

Fochabers
32

33

Spey Bay

A96

Tugnet
Ice House

Lossiemouth

Mosstodloch

B9103

Spey

Elgin
31

A941

Rothes

Dallas

B9102

Turriff

Aberchirder

A97

B9023

B9117

B9117

Milltown of
Rothiemay

B9117

Keith
A96

B9022

A96

Mill of Towie
39

A920

B9014

Craigellachie
41

Aberlour
42
A95

Milltown of
Edinville

B9000

Bridge of
Avon

Dufftown
40
A941

Glen
Fiddich

Glen Rinnes

B9009

Glenlivet

Fyvie

A947

B9170

B9001

B9002A

Huntly

A96

A920

Pitcaple

Colpy

B9002

Rhynie

A97

Deveron

KEY
Rail Lines

10 miles

15 km

N

building built in 1828 exhibits the style known as Greek Revival: Note the columns, the pilasters (half-columns attached to the walls), and the top of the spire, surmounted by a representation of the Lysicrates Monument. Farther east, past the arcaded shops, you can see the **Little Cross** (17th century), which marked the boundary between the town and the cathedral grounds.

★ Cooper Park, located a short distance to the southeast across the modern bypass road, is home to a magnificent ruin, the **cathedral** consecrated in 1224. The cathedral's eventful story included devastation by fire: a 1390 act of retaliation by Alexander Stewart, the Wolf of Badenoch. The illegitimate son-turned-bandit of King David II had sought revenge for his being excommunicated by the bishop of Moray. The cathedral was rebuilt but finally fell into disuse after the Reformation in 1560. By 1567, the highest authority in the land at the time, the regent earl of Moray, had stripped the lead from the roof to pay for his army. Thus ended the career of the religious seat known as the Lamp of the North. Some traces of the cathedral settlement survive, although they have been drastically altered: the gateway Pann's Port and the Bishop's Palace.

③② Take the A96 east to **Fochabers.** Just before reaching it, you will see the works of a major local employer, Baxters of Fochabers, a family-run firm with an international reputation for fine foods. From Tokyo to New York, upmarket stores stock their soups, jams, chutneys, and other gourmet products—all of which are made here, close to the River Spey. Factory tours yield glimpses of impeccably attired staff stirring great vats of boiling marmalade and other concoctions. The **Baxters Visitors Centre** also offers a video presentation, a re-creation of the Baxters' first grocery shop, as well as a real shop stocking Baxter's goods (among other products), the Best of Scotland shop (specializing in Scottish goods), and a restaurant offering an assortment of delectables. *1 mi west of Fochabers on the A96,* ☎ *01343/820666,* FAX *01343/821790.* ☛ *Free.* ☉ *Weekdays 9:30–5, weekends 10–5 (extended hours in summer). Guided tours on weekdays only, Mon.–Thurs. 10–4, Fri. 10–2; no tours during factory holiday weeks in April (1 wk), June (2 wks), and Aug. (1 wk).*

After traversing the Spey bridge and entering Fochabers, visitors will find this community has the symmetrical village green typical of the planned village. Perhaps this pleasing, mellow ambience attracts the extraordinary range of antiques dealers in Fochabers, with shops' wares ranging from near-junk to designer pieces. Through one of these shops you can enter the **Fochabers Folk Museum,** which has an excellent display of rural items in a converted church, ranging from carts and carriages to interesting farm implements. ☎ *01343/820362.* ☛ *60p adults, 40p senior citizens and children, £1.50 family ticket.* ☉ *Winter, daily 9:30–1 and 2–5; summer, daily 9:30–1 and 2–6.*

If you have your own car, you may care to divert up the road that runs south directly opposite the museum. Leaving the houses behind for well-hedged country lanes, you will discover a Forestry Commission sign to the **Earth Pillars.** These curious eroded sandstone pillars are framed by tall-trunked pines and overlook a wide prospect of the lower Spey Valley. Another option for motorists is to take the B9108 from Fochabers down to the mouth of the River Spey. Here, by a storm beach with a high stone swell of smooth-washed pebbles, the river enters the sea.

③③ Nearby is the **Tugnet Ice House,** once the centerpiece of the local salmon fishing industry. Before the days of mechanical refrigeration, the salmon were stored in icy chambers. The ice was gathered in the winter and lasted in its insulated cellars throughout the fishing season. Now a museum housed in the Ice House tells the story. *Spey Bay, 5 mi west of Buckie,* ☎ *01309/673701.* ☛ *Free.* ☉ *May–Sept., daily 11–5.*

From Fochabers, take the A98 east for about 3 miles before making a left on the A942, which runs closer to the coast through the fishing port of **Buckie** and its satellite villages. This outpost is gray and workaday, with plenty of Victorian architecture. But don't miss its latest acquisition: the **Buckie Drifter** maritime museum. Housed in premises designed to be reminiscent of an old drifter, this is a hands-on visitor center that tells the story of the herring industry and Buckie's development as a herring port. Upstairs, you enter a 1920s quayside scene, with a replica steam drifter that you can board, barrels you can pack with herring, and a cooper at work. *Freuchny Rd., off Commercial Rd.,* ☎ *01542/834646.* ☛ *£2.50 adults, £1.60 senior citizens and children, £7 family ticket.* ☉ *Apr.–Oct., Mon.–Sat. 10–6, Sun. noon–6.* The **Peter Anson Gallery** shows a selection of watercolor works also related to the development of the fishing industry. *Cluny Pl.,* ☎ *01309/673701.* ☛ *Free.* ☉ *Weekdays 10–8, Sat. 10–12.*

Visitors will find a string of other fishing communities down by the shore, running east. These salty little villages paint a colorful scene with their gable-ended houses and fishing nets set out to dry amid the rocky shoreline.

The residents of **Findochty**—located about 2 miles east of Buckie on the A942—are known for their fastidiousness and creativity in painting their fisher-houses, taking the fine art of housepainting to a new level. Some residents even paint the mortar between the stonework a different color. The small town also has a harbor with a faint echo of the Mediterranean about it.

You will see some wonderfully painted homes again at **Cullen,** a few miles from Findochty on the A98, in the old fishermen's town below the railway viaduct. But the real attractions of this little resort are its white-sand beach and the fine view west toward the Bowfiddle Rock. A stroll along the beach reveals the shape of the fishing settlement below and planned town above. Cullen and its little shops are far enough away from major town superstores to survive on local, intermittent trade; most unusual for a town of its size, Cullen has a full range of speciality shops—ironmongers, butchers, a baker, a haberdasher, and a locally famous ice-cream shop among them.

TIME OUT   **The Seafield Arms,** built as a coaching inn for the new town, serves a friendly pub lunch.

If Cullen represents a neat and planned town, contrast it with the much more ancient layout of **Portsoy,** about 6 miles east along the coast. But travelers with their own means of transportation can make another discovery before they even reach Portsoy. Midway between Cullen and Portsoy, make a right turn, heading south in the direction of the conservation village of **Fordyce,** which lies among the barley fields of Banffshire like a small slice of rural England gone far adrift. You can stroll by the churchyard; picnic on the old bleaching green (an explanatory notice board tells you all about it); or buy stamps from the local post office, where the lady behind the counter still weighs the letters using old-style brass weights. There is also a restored 19th-century carpenter's workshop to visit.

Public transportation will take you straight from Cullen to **Portsoy.** This little town boasts the oldest harbor on the Moray Firth, built in the 17th century. Once a North Sea trading port and later participating in the 19th-century fishing boom, the community thereafter fell into a decline. But thoughtful conservation programs have revitalized much of Portsoy's old fabric.

Although there's a lot more of the coast to explore (*see* Off the Beaten **39** Track, *below*), there are a number of inland routes that lead to the **Mill of Towie,** a fully restored oatmeal mill, dating from a time when the meal mill played a vital role in the local economy. Mill tours are available. *Drummuir, Keith, Banffshire, ☎ 01542/810307.* ☛ *£1.50 adults, £1 senior citizens and children.* ⊙ *Mill daily 8–5, craft shop (☎ 01542/810355) Easter and May–Oct., daily 10:30–4:30.*

TIME OUT   The Mill of Towie's former grain store is now a **restaurant** (☎ 01542/810328) serving morning coffee, lunches, and teas.

★ **40**   **Dufftown,** on one of the Spey tributaries, farther south on the B9014, is a town planned in 1817 by the Earl of Fife. One of the most famous malt whiskies of all, the market leader **Glenfiddich** is distilled here. The independent company of William Grant and Sons Limited was the first distillery to realize the tourist potential of the distilling process. It subsequently built an entertaining visitor center in addition to offering tours. In short, if you do intend to visit a distillery, it may as well be Glenfiddich, especially because it probably offers the most complete range of on-site activities, from floor malting to bottling. In fact, it is the only Speyside distiller that bottles on the premises. The audiovisual show and displays in the visitor center are also worthwhile, and the traditional stone-walled premises with the typical pagoda-roofed malting buildings have a pleasant period ambience. Not all visitors have to like whisky to come away feeling they've learned something about a leading Scottish export. *North of Dufftown on the A941, ☎ 01340/820373.* ☛ *Free.* ⊙ *Weekdays 9:30–4:30, except Christmas and New Year's; Easter–mid-Oct., Sat. 9:30–4:30, Sun. noon–4:30.*

On a mound just above the distillery is a grim, gray, and squat curtain-walled castle, **Balvenie.** This fortress, dating from the 13th century, once commanded the glens and passes toward Speyside and Elgin. *Dufftown, A941, ☎ 0131/244–3101.* ☛ *£1.20 adults, 75p children.* ⊙ *Apr.–Sept., Mon.–Sat. 9:30–6, Sun. 2–6.*

Back in the center of Dufftown, the conspicuous battlemented clock tower—the centerpiece of the planned town and a former jail—houses a local museum open in summer. Down the hill (east), look for a sign to Mortlach Church. Set in a hollow by the Dullan Water, this church is thought to be one of the oldest Christian sites in Scotland, perhaps founded by St. Moluag, a contemporary of St. Columba, as early as AD 566. Note the weathered Pictish cross in the churchyard and the even older stone under cover in the vestibule, with a strange Pictish elephantlike beast carved on it. Though much of the church was rebuilt after 1876, some early work survives, including three lancet windows from the 13th century and a leper's squint (a hole extended to the outside of the church so that lepers could hear the service but be kept away from the rest of the congregation).

41   From Dufftown take the A941 about 4 miles northwest to **Craigellachie,** renowned as an angling resort on the Spey. Like so many Speyside settlements, Craigellachie is sometimes enveloped in the malty reek of the local industry. As you arrive in the village, you will notice the huge cooperage, the place where barrels are made and repaired. The Spey itself is crossed by a handsome suspension bridge, designed by Thomas

Telford in 1814 and now bypassed by the modern road. Go left and
④ upstream by the A95 to **Aberlour** (often marked as Charlestown of Aberlour on maps). This is another handsome little burgh, essentially Victorian in style, though actually founded in 1812 by the local landowner.
While Glenfarclas, Cragganmore, and Aberlour itself are names of noted
local whiskies, for a nonalcoholic change of pace, take a look at the
Village Store. After the owners died the shop was locked away intact,
complete with stock. In the late 1980s, new owners discovered they
had bought a time capsule—a range of products dating from the early
decades of the present century—as well as all the paraphernalia, books
and ledgers, accounts, and notes of a country business.

TIME OUT In Aberlour, **The Old Pantry** (The Square, ☎ 01340/871617) serves
everything from a cup of coffee to a four-course spread.

At this point, you are only about 15 miles south of Elgin, the starting
point of this tour.

What to See and Do with Children

Amusement Centers
The **Adventure Playground** has a fishing-village theme, including model
houses, fishing nets, and a paddling pool. *Beach Esplanade.* ☞ *Free.*
☉ *Daily.*

Codona's Amusement Park, like Adventure Playground, is also located on the shore. *Beach Blvd.,* ☎ *01224/581909.* ☞ *Free, individual tickets for rides.* ☉ *Easter school holidays and June–July, daily;
May–Sept., holiday Mondays.*

Museums
The **Aberdeen Maritime Museum** is a fascinating place for grade-
schoolers, with its ship models, paintings, and equipment associated
with the fishing, local shipbuilding, and North Sea oil and gas industries. *Provost Ross's House, Ship Row,* ☎ *01224/585788.* ☞ *Free.* ☉
Mon.–Sat. 10–5.

Satrosphere is a hands-on exhibition of science and technology that makes
science come alive. Children (and adults) of even the most unscientific
bent will love it. *19 Justice Mill La.,* ☎ *01224/213232.* ☞ *£3 adults,
£1.50 children and senior citizens.* ☉ *Daily, Mon.–Sat. 10–5, Sun.
1:30–5 (until 4 PM in winter). Closed Tues. during the school year.*

The **Rosemount Celebration Centre** has an activities-based heritage
museum and learning center called Jonah's Journey, based on life in a
2,000-year-old Israelite village. The center offers costumes, spinning
and weaving, mosaic making, puppet plays, and jigsaw puzzles. *Rosemount Pl.,* ☎ *01224/647614.* ☞ *£1.50 adults, £3 children, £8 family
ticket.* ☉ *Weekdays 9–3:30 (closed Tues. PM and 3 weeks at Christmas; call ahead).*

Zoos and Parks
All the city's parks have free entry, including the very popular **Winter
Gardens** in **Duthie Park.**

Doonies Farm, run by Aberdeen's Department of Leisure and Recreation, is a model farm with Clydesdale horses, ponies, cattle, sheep,
and small animals, some of which children may handle. *Off A956 from
Aberdeen.* ☉ *Daily dawn–dusk.* ☞ *Free.*

★ **Duthie Park and Winter Gardens.** In addition to being a great place to feed the ducks, Duthie Park has a boating pond and trampolines, carved wooden animals, and playgrounds. In the Winter Gardens children can see fish in ponds, free-flying birds, turtles, and terrapins. *Polmuir Rd., Riverside Dr.* ☛ *Free.* ⊙ *Park and gardens year-round; entertainment in summer only. Gardens open daily 10–dusk.*

Hazlehead Park and Zoo has a potpourri of domestic animals and birds, a free-flight, walk-through aviary, and an aquarium house. A maze (very uncommon in Scotland), electric cars, putting, and trampolines are also available during the summer. *Groats Rd., Hazlehead Ave.* ☛ *Free.* ⊙ *Zoo daily 10–dusk, maze July–Sept., daily 10–dusk, also weekends in early summer.*

Storybook Glen displays a fairy-tale theme in a 20-acre parkland/garden setting: The Jolly Miller, Old MacDonald's Farm, and the Old Woman Who Lived in a Shoe are some of the characters featured in large-scale models. Take care with small children; some of the models are rather decrepit. *Off S. Deeside Rd., B9077, about 4 mi from Aberdeen,* ☎ *01224/732941.* ☛ *£3 adults, £2 senior citizens, £1.50 children.* ⊙ *Mar.–Oct., daily 10–6, Nov.–Feb., weekends 11–4.*

Off the Beaten Path

A unique re-creation by the National Trust for Scotland of a 17th-century garden, **Pitmedden Garden** is best visited in high summer, from July onward, when annual bedding plants form intricate formal patterns of the garden plots. The 100-acre estate also has a variety of woodland and farmland walks, as well as the Museum of Farming Life. ☎ *01651/842352.* ☛ *£3 adults, £1.50 senior citizens and children.* ⊙ *May–Sept., daily 10–5:30 (last admission 5).*

Kinnaird Lighthouse Museum is at the northeasternmost point of Scotland, overlooked by a 16th-century castle. It tells the story of Scotland's lighthouses, vital in the development of the country's maritime history. *Kinnaird Head, Fraserburgh. Call the local tourist information center for admission charges and opening hours.*

Created as the home of the earls and marquesses of Aberdeen, **Haddo House**—designed by William Adam—is now cared for by the National Trust for Scotland. Built in 1723, the elegant mansion has a light and graceful design, with curving wings on either side of a harmonious facade. *Off B99, northwest of Ellon.* ☛ *£3.50 adults, £1.80 senior citizens and children.* ⊙ *House Easter–June, and Sept., daily 1:30–5:30; July, Aug., daily 11–5:30; early Oct., weekends 1:30–5:30 (last admission 4:45); garden and country park, daily 9:30–sunset.*

★ The **Duff House,** in Banff, is a splendid William Adam–designed baroque mansion that has been completely restored as an outstation of the National Galleries of Scotland. Many fine paintings are displayed in rooms furnished to reflect the days when the house was occupied by the Dukes of Fife. *Banff.* ☛ *£2.50 adults, £1 senior citizens and children.* ⊙ *Apr.–Sept., Wed.-Mon. 10–5; Oct.-Mar., Thurs.-Sun. 10–5.*

The Bullers of Buchan, located off the A975 south of Peterhead, is worth seeing for those explorers who like their sites austere and elemental. On a stretch of windy cliff and cove coastline—once used by smugglers—the sea has cut through a cave, collapsing its roof and forming a great rocky cauldron, fearsome in bad weather. The Bullers of Buchan is an impressive site, but not for the vertigo-prone. Approach the cliff edge with great care.

A major element in Aden Country Park, the **Northeast Scotland Agricultural Heritage Centre,** tells the moving story through videos of life on the land and the hard toil of the farming folk. Implements, tableaux, models, and displays create a vivid impression. Aden Country Park is also an important recreational resource for the locals, with countryside trails that meander throughout the park's 230 acres. *Off A92, just west of Mintlaw,* ☎ *01771/622857. Admission to Heritage Centre: £1 adults, children free.* ☉ *May–Sept., daily 11–5; Apr., Oct., and early Nov., weekends noon–5 (last admission 4:30).*

A huddle of houses tucked below a crescent of grassy cliffs, **Pennan** shot to minor fame as the setting for some of the filming of *Local Hero,* which starred Burt Lancaster. The phone box and the hotel featured in the film are still there. Pennan is set in a remote cliff coastline about as far from the tourist trail as is possible. *Off B9031 between Fraserburgh and Macduff.*

In an area rife with castles, many are distinguished within their own categories: Craigievar for untouched perfection, Corgarff for sheer loneliness, Haddo House for elegance. Perhaps **Fyvie** stands out in its own category: most complex. Five great towers built by five successive powerful families turned a 13th-century foursquare castle into an opulent Edwardian (early 20th century) statement of wealth. There's an array of superb paintings on view, including 12 Raeburns, as well as myriad sumptuous interiors and walks on the castle grounds. Fyvie is praised for its sheer impact, if you like your castles oppressive and gloomy. *Off A947 between Oldmeldrum and Turriff,* ☎ *01651/891266.* ☛ *£3.50 adults, £1.80 senior citizens and children.* ☉ *Castle Apr.–June, and Sept., daily 1:30–5:30; July, Aug., daily 11–5:30; early Oct., weekends 1:30–5:30 (last admission 4:45); grounds daily, 9:30–sunset.*

Given the general destruction caused by the 16th-century religious upheaval of the Reformation, abbeys in Scotland tend to be ruinous and deserted sites, but at **Pluscarden Abbey** the way of life of the monks continues. Originally a 13th-century foundation, the religious community abandoned their abbey after the Reformation. The third Marquis of Bute bought the remains in 1897 and initiated a repair and restoration program that continues to this day. Monks from an abbey near Gloucester, England, returned here in 1948, and today the abbey is an active religious community. *Off B9010 from Elgin.* ☛ *Free.* ☉ *Daily 5 AM–8:30 PM.*

SHOPPING

Aberdeen, serving a large and fairly prosperous hinterland, has the widest choice of shopping in the region. Elgin, a smaller center, has a few shops of interest. Because of the fishing and farming prosperity, plus new money from oil and even newer money from people moving from the south, there are a few shopping surprises in some of the smaller towns, as well.

Aberdeen

Aberdeen's shopping scene is in the throes of change. For generations, folk from round about would come into Aberdeen for the day—the city is a kind of large-scale market town—and their chief delight would be to stroll the length of Union Street and perhaps take in George Street as well. Now this pattern is changing, thanks mainly to the modern and faceless shopping developments (pleasant enough in an anonymous way), the Trinity Centre (Union St.), and the St. Nicholas and Bon-Accord centers (George St.), which have taken the emphasis away from Union Street.

However, smaller specialty shops are still to be found, particularly in the Chapel Street/Thistle Street area at the west end of Union Street and on the latter's north side, which has a series of interesting little businesses well worth discovering. **Nova** (20 Chapel St., ☎ 01224/641270), where the locals go for gifts, stocks major U.K. brand names, such as Liberty of London, Dartington Glass, and Crabtree and Evelyn, as well as a wide range of Scottish silver jewelry. **Colin Wood** (25 Rose St., ☎ 01224/643019) is the place to go for antiques and prints. **Harlequin** (65 Thistle St., ☎ 01224/635716) stocks a large selection of embroidery and tapestry kits, designer yarns, and colorful expensive knitwear. **Elizabeth Watt's** (69 Thistle St., ☎ 01224/647232) is the place to look for smaller antiques, especially china and glassware.

Elsewhere in town, **Elliot's** (100 Rosemount Pl., ☎ 01224/630967) is where discriminating, slightly older women go to be looked after and advised in matters of smart dressing. Visitors looking for bargains can try the **Crombie Woollen Mill** (Grandholm Mills, Woodside, off the A96, ☎ 01224/483201) on the edge of town; a particularly good value are the men's overcoats bearing the Crombie name (known for high quality).

At the **Aberdeen Family History Shop** (164 King St., ☎ 01224/646323) you can browse through a huge range of publications related to local history and genealogical research. For a small membership fee, the Aberdeen & North East Family History Society will undertake some research on your behalf.

Aberdeen shops catering to children include **The Toy Bazaar** (45 Schoolhill, ☎ 01224/640021), which stocks a range of toys for children preschool age and up. **Craftplay** (282 Holburn St., ☎ 01224/584784) stocks toys and crafts materials. **The Early Learning Centre** (Bon-Accord Centre, George St., ☎ 01224/624188) specializes in toys with educational value.

Deeside

Farther afield from Aberdeen, the opportunities for shopping are certainly more scattered. The **McEwan Gallery** (on A939, 1 mi west of Ballater, ☎ 013397/55429) displays a good range of fine paintings, watercolors, prints, and books (many with a Scottish theme) in an unusual house built by the Swiss artist Rudolphe Christen in 1902. For a low-cost gift you could always see what is being boiled up at **Dee Valley Confectioners** (Station Sq., Ballater, ☎ 013397/55499).

Also in Ballater (where the royals seem to do much of their Scottish shopping, as evidenced by the many BY APPOINTMENT TO signs), you can buy Scottish designer knitwear at **Goodbrand Knitwear** (1 Braemar Rd., ☎ 013397/55947). **Jane Knitwear** (18 Bridge St., ☎ 01339/755920) has a wide range of Scottish designer knits; there are styles to suit all tastes and color preferences. At either of **Countrywear's** two shops (15 and 35 Bridge St., ☎ 013397/55453) you'll find everything you need for Scottish country living, including fishing tackle, shooting accessories, cashmere, tweeds, and that flexible garment popular in Scotland between seasons: the bodywarmer.

Elsewhere in the Northeast

To the north of the region is Fochabers, the place for antiques hunters, with several antiques shops all within a few yards of each other on the main street. Try **Sylvan Antiques** (23 High St., ☎ 01343/820814) for pottery and bric-a-brac. **Antiques (Fochabers)** (Hadlow House, The Square, ☎ 01343/820838) has kitchenware and furniture. **Pringle Antiques** (High St., ☎ 01343/821204) stocks small furniture, pottery, glassware, and jewelry. **Just Art** (64 High St., ☎ 01343/820500) is a fine art gallery with ceramics and paintings. **Balance** (50 High St., ☎ 01343/821443) stocks homeopathic remedies, potpourris, and the like. Finish your visit at **The Quaich** (85 High St., ☎ 01343/820981), a good place to sit with a cup of tea and a home-baked snack.

In Portsoy, **Portsoy Marble** (at the old harbor, ☎ 01261/842404) stocks not only marble items—eggs, platters, etc.—but also local pottery, books, cards, knitwear, and ornaments. (The greenish or reddish Portsoy marble even found its way to the Palace of Versailles in France.)

Elgin has, in addition to the usual range of High Street stores, **Gordon and MacPhail** (South St., ☎ 01343/545111), an outstanding delicatessen and wine merchant that, in addition to wine, stocks a breathtaking range of otherwise scarce malt whiskies. This is a good place to shop for gifts for those foodies among your friends. **J. D. Yeadon** (32 Commerce St., ☎ 01343/542411) is a dependable bookshop. **Johnstons of Elgin** (Newmill, ☎ 01343/554099, FAX 01343/554055) has a worldwide reputation for its luxury fabrics, including cashmere. The color range is particularly noteworthy because it breaks away from the otherwise slightly predictable pastel blue, pink, yellow, and green of most mill shops.

SPORTS AND FITNESS

Bicycling
Northeast Scotland is excellent biking country, with networks of minor roads and farm roads crisscrossing rolling fields. Tourist information centers can provide lists of suggested cycle tours. Rates for bicycle rentals vary, depending on the type of bike. An average rate for a mountain bike is £10 a day.

You can rent bicycles at **Aberdeen Cycle Centre** (188 King St., Aberdeen, ☎ 01224/644542), **Alpine Bikes** (70 Holburn St., Aberdeen, ☎ 01224/211455), or **Outdoor Gear** (88 Fonthill Rd., Aberdeen, ☎ 01224/573952).

Camping
Most of the population centers in the area have campsites. It is possible to camp on private land, but you must obtain the permission of the landowner first. Except for the more remote upland areas, "wild land" camping is better pursued farther west.

Canoeing
For information on canoeing in the area, contact the **Aberdeen Sports Council** (Room A18, St. Nicholas House, Aberdeen, ☎ 01224/276276, ext. 2838), or the **Scottish Sports Council** (in Edinburgh, ☎ 0131/317–7200).

Fishing
With major rivers, such as the Dee, Don, Deveron, and Ythan, as well as popular smaller rivers, such as the Ugie, plus loch and estuary fishing, this is one of Scotland's leading game-fishing areas. Details of beats, boats, and permit prices can be obtained from local tourist information centers. Some local hotels offer fishing packages or, at least, can

organize permits. Prices vary widely, depending on the fish and individual river beat.

Golf

The Northeast has over 50 golf clubs, some of which have championship courses. All towns and many villages have their nine- and 18-hole municipal links, at which you pay £5–£10 per round. The more prestigious clubs charge up to £40 a day and expect you to book by letter or to bring a letter of recommendation from a member. The following courses in and around Aberdeen are open to visitors.

Balnagask (St. Fitticks Rd., ☎ 01224/876407). 18 holes, 5,986 yards, SSS 69.

Hazlehead (☎ 01224/321830). Course 1: 18 holes, 6,204 yards, SSS 70. Course 2: 18 holes, 5,801 yards, SSS 68.

Murcar (Bridge of Don, ☎ 01224/704345). 18 holes, 6,240 yards, SSS 70.

Westhill (☎ 01224/740159). 18 holes, 5,921 yards, SSS 68.

Health and Fitness Clubs

The major clubs in the area are **Bon-Accord Swimming and Leisure Centre** (Justice Mill La., Aberdeen, ☎ 01224/587920), **Kincorth Sports Centre** (Corthan Dr., Aberdeen, ☎ 01224/879759), **Sheddocksley Sports Centre** (Springhill Rd., Aberdeen, ☎ 01224/692534), **Balmedie Leisure Centre** (Eigie Rd., Balmedie, ☎ 01358/743725), **Fitness n'Fun** (130 High St., Elgin, ☎ 01343/549307), and **Westerdyke Leisure Centre** (4 Westdyke Ave., Skene, ☎ 01224/743098).

Skiing

The area's main skiing development is at **Glenshee** (☎ 013397/41320, FAX 013397/41665), just south of Braemar, though the season can be brief here. Visitors accustomed to long alpine runs and extensive choice will find the runs here short, unlike the lift lines. **The Lecht** (☎ 019756/51440, FAX 019756/51426) lies at even lower altitude, also within easy reach of the area, and is mainly suitable for beginners. The development at **Cairngorm** (☎ 01479/861261, FAX 01479/861207) by Aviemore is also within easy reach (*see* Chapter 11). There is a dry ski slope at **Alford** (☎ 019755/62380).

DINING AND LODGING

Dining

Partly in response to the demands of spendthrift oilmen, the number of restaurants in Aberdeen has grown over the past several years, and the quality of the food has improved. Elsewhere in the region you will never be far from a good pub lunch or a hotel high tea or dinner.

WHAT TO WEAR
In Aberdeen, people tend to dress up when dining out; the same is true at more expensive restaurants outside Aberdeen. Otherwise, casual but smart dress is preferred.

CATEGORY	COST*
$$$$	over £40
$$$	£30–£40
$$	£15–£30
$	under £15

*per person for a three-course meal, including VAT, excluding drinks and service

Lodging

The Northeast has some splendid country hotels with log fires and rich furnishings, where you can also be sure of eating well if you have time for a leisurely meal. Note that in Aberdeen, many hotels offer very competitive room rates on weekends.

CATEGORY	COST*
$$$$	over £110
$$$	£80–£110
$$	£45–£80
$	under £45

*All prices are for a standard double room, including service, breakfast, and VAT.

Aberdeen

DINING

$$$ Gerard's. On a side street moments from the West End, Gerard's is a long-established part of the Aberdeen dining scene. Classic French cuisine is ably prepared with local produce—fish and red meats in particular. Try the Angus fillet steak, stuffed with pâté, ham, and mushrooms, wrapped in bacon and served in a red-wine sauce. The setting is relaxed in both the main dining room, with its eclectic mix of antique pine and mahogany tables and chairs, and in the garden room, with its greenery, tile or marble tables, and flagstone floor. ✕ *50 Chapel St., Aberdeen AB1 1SN,* ☎ *01224/639500. Reservations advised. AE, DC, MC, V.*

$$–$$$ The Silver Darling. Situated right on the quayside, the Silver Darling is
★ one of Aberdeen's most acclaimed restaurants. It specializes, as its name suggests, in fish. The style is French provincial, with an indoor barbecue guaranteeing flavorful grilled fish and shellfish. ✕ *Pocra Quay, Footdee, AB2 1DQ,* ☎ *01224/576229. Reservations advised (essential on weekends). AE, DC, MC, V. Closed weekend lunch, Sun. evening, and 2 weeks at Christmas.*

DINING AND LODGING

$$$$ The Marcliffe at Pitfodels. The Marcliffe at Pitfodels benefits from the
★ skills and experience of leading Scottish hotelier Stewart Spence. This spacious building, in the up-market "west end" of the city, is made up of an old country house, with later additions; the combination of old and new is impressive. Rooms are individually decorated, some with reproduction antique furnishings, others with a more modern style. ☎ *N. Deeside Rd., Pitfodels, Aberdeen AB1 9PN,* ☎ *01224/861000,* FAX *01224/868860. 42 rooms with bath. AE, DC, MC, V.*

$$–$$$$ Caledonian Thistle Hotel. Well situated and offering pleasant views over tidy gardens, the Caledonian, one of the larger hotels in the Granite City, is generally considered to be one of the best hotels in the city. Rooms are redecorated regularly, and the attractive restaurant serves such dishes as chicken breasts with brandy, paprika, and cream. Despite its size, the service here is very friendly. ☎ *Union Terr., AB9 1HE,* ☎ *01224/640233,* FAX *01224/641627. 80 rooms with bath. Restaurant, coffee shop, wine bar. AE, DC, MC, V.*

$$–$$$ Atholl Hotel. One of Aberdeen's many splendid silver granite properties, the Atholl Hotel is turreted and gabled and set within a leafy residential area to the west of the city. Rooms are done in rich, dark colors; the best views are from the top floor; the larger rooms are on the first floor. The restaurant prepares traditional dishes like lamb cutlets and roast rib of beef. ☎ *54 Kings Gate, Aberdeen AB9 2YN,* ☎ *01224/323505,* ₣ₐₓ *01224/321555. 35 rooms with bath or shower. Restaurant. MC, V.*

$$ **Craighaar Hotel.** Don't be fooled by the plain, modern exterior—this is a hotel with character, a refreshing change from the many indistinguishable business hotels in Aberdeen. That said, the Craighaar is popular with businesspeople (it's very convenient to the airport). But what makes this establishment stand out is the personal service—this is the kind of place where the staff remembers your name. The comfortable restaurant serves cuisine with a Scottish slant: Orkney oysters, smoked trout, crab claws, gourmet scampi, and char-grilled steaks. Bedrooms are cheerful with bright floral prints. The gallery suites—split-level rooms—are outstanding. Ask about the great deals on weekend rooms. ☎ *Waterton Rd., Bucksburn, Aberdeen AB2 9HS,* ☎ *01224/ 712275,* ₣ₐₓ *01224/716362. 55 rooms with bath or shower. Restaurant, bar. AE, DC, MC, V.*

Ballater

DINING AND LODGING

$$$–$$$$ **Craigendarroch.** This magnificent country house hotel, just outside Ballater on a hillside overlooking the River Dee, really does manage to keep everyone happy. Hotel guests are cosseted in luxurious surroundings and can use the nearby leisure facilities—pool, squash courts, and beauty salon, to name just a few. An even better value are the pine lodges set among the trees around the hotel. These self-catering cottages are geared for families and fitted with every kind of labor-saving appliance. There is also a solid choice of on-site restaurants, including the top-quality **Oaks** for à la carte dinners. ☎ *Ballater, AB35 5XA,* ☎ *013397/55858,* ₣ₐₓ *013397/55447. 50 rooms with bath. 3 restaurants, 2 indoor pools, wading pool, hot tub, tennis court, exercise room, Ping-Pong. AE, DC, MC, V.*

$$–$$$ **Darroch Learg Hotel.** Amid tall trees on a hillside, the Darroch Learg is everything a Scottish country-house hotel should be, with the added bonus that the charming town of Ballater is moments away. Built in the 1880s as a country residence, the hotel exudes charm. Most bedrooms—decorated with mahogany furniture and designer fabrics in rich colors—enjoy a stunning panoramic view south across Royal Deeside. Food in the conservatory restaurant is sophisticated—delicately flavored terrines and soups—but also substantial, with the rich flavors of local beef and fish produce. ☎ *Braemar Rd., Ballater, Aberdeenshire AB35 5UX,* ☎ *013397/55443,* ₣ₐₓ *013397/55252. 20 rooms with bath. Restaurant. AE, DC, MC, V.*

Banchory

DINING AND LODGING

$$$–$$$$ **Raemoir Hotel.** The core of this large mansion dates from the 18th century, though a number of additions have been built over the years. Central heating has been added as well, so there is no need to fear chilly, windy rooms. All the guest rooms are comfortable and well appointed; many are hung with beautiful tapestries. The hotel is set on spacious grounds and overshadowed by the 1,500-foot-high Hill of Fare. Adjoining the hotel's property are 3,500 acres of land on which fishing, stalking, and shooting can be arranged. Guests who don't want to venture too far away from the hotel can make use of the minigolf course and tennis court. ☎ *Raemoir, Kincardineshire AB3 4ED,* ☎ *01330/ 824884,* ₣ₐₓ *01330/822171. 28 rooms with bath. Restaurant, sauna, 9-hole golf course, tennis court, fishing, baby-sitting, helipad. AE, DC, MC, V.*

$$$ **Banchory Lodge.** With the River Dee running past just a few yards away at the bottom of the garden, the Banchory Lodge, a fine example of a Georgian country house, is an ideal resting place for anglers. The lodge has retained its period charm and is well maintained inside and out. Tranquillity is the keynote here. Rooms, with bold colors and tartan or floral fabrics, are individually decorated. The restaurant has high standards for its Scottish cuisine with French overtones; try the fillet of salmon, roast duckling, or guinea fowl with wild berries. ⊞ *Kincardineshire AB3 3HS,* ☎ *01330/822625,* ℻ *01330/825019. 22 rooms with bath. Restaurant, fishing. AE, DC, MC, V.*

Banff
LODGING

$$ **Eden House.** This Georgian mansion house, set high above the River Deveron has magnificent views and makes a comfortably elegant base from which to explore the Northeast. The rooms are all individually decorated and furnished with antique pieces complementing the age of the house. The sitting room retains its original early 19th-century hand-painted wallpaper. Fishing and shooting can be arranged, while numerous golf courses are within easy reach. Dinner in the river-view dining room might include local seafood, Deveron salmon, game, or Scottish beef. ⊞ *Banffshire, AB45 3NT,* ☎ *01261/821282. 5 rooms; 2 with bath, 1 with shower. Dining room (reservations essential), tennis court, fishing, billiards. No credit cards. Closed Christmas and New Year's.*

Braemar
DINING AND LODGING

$$$ **Invercauld Arms.** A Scottish Baronial hotel in the grand manner, the Invercauld Arms underwent major refurbishment in the early 1990s and has completely thrown off its previously rather drafty and decayed atmosphere. Now its welcoming entrance, with plush sofas and elegant velvet chairs, leads to beautifully restored public rooms with attractive plasterwork and to comfortable bedrooms with floral drapes and reproduction antique furniture. Overlooking the site where the standard was raised for the 1715 Jacobite uprising, the hotel also makes an ideal base for exploring the other historic sites on Royal Deeside. End the day looking out to Braemar Castle from the restaurant's bay windows while enjoying such dishes as Aberdeen Angus steak with tomato and wild mushroom sauce or chicken with bean sprouts and water chestnuts with oyster sauce. ⊞ *Braemar AB35 5YR,* ☎ *01339/741605,* ℻ *01339/741428. 68 rooms with bath or shower. Restaurant (reservations advised, jacket and tie). AE, DC, MC, V.*

Drybridge
DINING

$$–$$$$ **The Old Monastery.** Standing on a broad, wooded slope set back from
★ the coast near Buckie, with westward views as far as the hills of Wester Ross, the Old Monastery was once a Victorian religious establishment. This theme has been preserved and carries through to the restrained decor of the Cloisters Bar and the Chapel Restaurant, with its hand stenciling. The local specialties—the freshest fish from sea and river and Aberdeen Angus beef—make up the major part of the menu, or you can opt for such dishes as chicken breast coated in oatmeal and pan-fried, served with a lemon, mustard, and cream sauce. Homemade soups and delicious puddings are bonuses, as is the no-smoking dining room. This is quite simply the best for miles around. ✗ *Buckie, Banffshire AB5 2JB, tel 01542/832660. Reservations advised. Jacket*

and tie. Closed Sun., Mon., 3 weeks in Jan. and 2 weeks in Nov. AE, DC, MC, V.

Fordyce
LODGING

$ **Academy House.** This top-of-the-range bed-and-breakfast offers accommodation in what was once the headmaster's house for the local secondary school, now closed. Traditional decor and some well-chosen antique furniture decorate the spacious, well-proportioned rooms. Evening meals are served upon request. ☎ *School Rd., AB45 2SJ,* ☎ *01261/842743. 3 rooms (no private facilities). No credit cards.*

Glenlivet
DINING AND LODGING

$$ **Minmore House.** Former home of George Smith, founder of the Glenlivet Distillery, Minmore is now a family-run hotel that retains a strong private-house feel. Faded chintz in the drawing room (where afternoon tea is served to guests) and a paneled library (which now houses a bar with nearly 100 malt whiskies) are complemented by very comfortable bedrooms (one, allegedly, with a ghost) with an eclectic mix of antique furnishings. The restaurant serves exceptionally well-cooked food, including such dishes as Highland lamb with a mint and honey glaze; the menu changes daily. The Speyside Way long-distance footpath passes below the house, providing good walks. The area is famous for birdwatching—you may sight buzzards, peregrines, or maybe even a golden eagle. *Glenlivet, Ballindalloch, Banffshire,* ☎ *01807/590378,* FAX *01807/590472. 10 rooms with bath. Restaurant, bar. MC, V.*

Kildrummy
DINING AND LODGING

$$$$ **Kildrummy Castle.** A grand, late-Victorian country house, this hotel offers an attractive blend of a peaceful setting, attentive service, and sporting opportunities. Oak paneling, beautiful plasterwork, and gentle color schemes create a serene environment, enhanced by the views of Kildrummy Castle Gardens next door. The award-winning cuisine features local game and seafood. ☎ *Kildrummy (by Alford), Aberdeenshire AB33 8RA,* ☎ *01975/571288,* FAX *01975/571345. 15 rooms with bath or shower. Restaurant, golf privileges, fishing. AE, MC, V.*

Old Deer
DINING AND LODGING

$$ **Saplinbrae House.** The restaurant in this country-house hotel is very popular with the locals. As elsewhere in this farming region, with its bounteous salmon rivers, local produce is the basis of the menu. Game pie, roast duck, and hefty steamed puddings require forward planning to ensure that you have the capacity to stay the course (try a healthy breakfast followed by a day's hill walking before booking a meal here). Rooms have traditional decor with dark color schemes. ☎ *Near Mintlaw, Aberdeenshire AB4 8PL,* ☎ *01771/623515,* FAX *01771/622320. 14 rooms with bath. Restaurant (reservations advised). AE, DC, MC, V.*

Sandend
LODGING

$ **Broom Farm.** Set on a hilltop overlooking Sandend Bay, with its beautiful, deserted sandy beach, seals basking on the rocks, and dolphins cruising the Moray Firth, this working farm offers bed-and-breakfast accommodations in a private wing of the main house. Guests have their own bathroom, a bunkroom for children, bedroom, and dressing room, all with traditional pine furniture and pastel color schemes. There is also a large sitting room downstairs for guest use. The owners take great care to ensure that visitors get the most out of their stay in this still undiscovered corner of Scotland. ⌕ *Broom Farm, Sandend, Portsoy Banffshire AB45 2UD,* ☎ *01542/840401. 1 suite for couple or family. No credit cards.*

Udny Station Village
DINING

$–$$ **Muffin and Crumpet Bistro.** Do not be put off by the rather unprepossessing exterior of this restaurant: Inside you will find excellent food served amid an eclectic array of ornaments ranging from dolls' prams to china jugs arranged on shelves around the walls. The cook is Marilyn Rattray, well-known throughout Scotland for her Taste of Scotland menus that feature fresh local beef, chicken, pork, fish, and game, with a wealth of vegetables to choose from; try the roast Aberdeen Angus beef and the sticky toffee pudding—a local favorite. There is a separate cozy bar with comfortable sofas where you can have a drink before or coffee after your meal. ✕ *Udny Station Village, near Aberdeen,* ☎ *01651/842210. Reservations advised. MC, V.*

THE ARTS AND NIGHTLIFE

The Arts

As you would expect, Aberdeen is the main cultural center of the region. The main Aberdeen newspapers—the *Press and Journal* and the *Evening Express*—and *Aberdeen Leopard* magazine can fill you in with what's going on anywhere in the Northeast. Outside Aberdeen a number of small-town local papers list events under the "What's On" heading. Tourist information centers usually print their own listings of events. Aberdeen's tourist information center has a monthly "What's On" with a full calendar, as well as contact telephone numbers.

Theater
His Majesty's Theatre (Rosemount Viaduct, Aberdeen, ☎ 01224/641122) is one of the most beautiful theaters in Britain. Live shows are presented throughout the year, many of them in advance of their official opening in London's West End.

Concerts
The Music Hall (Union St., Aberdeen, ☎ 01224/632080) presents seasonal programs of concerts by the Scottish National Orchestra, the Scottish Chamber Orchestra, and other major orchestras and musicians. Its wide-ranging program of events also includes folk concerts, crafts fairs, and exhibitions.

The Lemon Tree (5 W. North St., ☎ 01224/642230) features an innovative and international program of dance, stand-up comedy, folk, jazz, rock 'n' roll, and art exhibitions.

Aberdeen Arts Centre (King St., ☎ 01224/635208) is a theater and concert venue where experimental theater, poetry readings, exhibitions by local and Scottish artists, and many other arts-based presentations can be enjoyed.

The **Aberdeen International Youth Festival** in August has worldwide recognition and attracts youth orchestras, choirs, dance, and theater companies from many countries. During the festival, many of the companies that appear also take their productions to other venues in the Northeast. For details, contact AIYF Box Office (Music Hall, Union St., Aberdeen, ☎ 01224/641122).

Another arts base in the area is **Haddo House,** 20 miles north of Aberdeen (off B9005 near Methlick, ☎ 01651/851770), where the Haddo House Hall Arts Trust runs a wide-ranging program of events.

Dance
His Majesty's Theatre and **Aberdeen Arts Centre** (*see above*) are regular venues for dance companies. Contact the box offices for details of current productions.

Film
Major theaters in the area include the **Cannon** (Union St., Aberdeen, ☎ 01224/591477), **Capitol** (Union St., Aberdeen, ☎ 01224/583141), **Odeon** (Justice Mill La., Aberdeen, ☎ 01224/587160), **Moray Playhouse** (High St., Elgin, ☎ 01343/542680), **Victoria** (W. High St., Inverurie, ☎ 01467/621436), and the **Playhouse** (Queen St., Peterhead, ☎ 01779/471052).

Opera
Both **His Majesty's Theatre** in Aberdeen and **Haddo House** (*see above*), near Methlick, present operatic performances at certain times throughout the year; telephone for details or inquire at the tourist information center in Aberdeen's St. Nicholas House.

Nightlife

In part because of the oil-industry boom, Aberdeen has a fairly lively nightlife scene, though much of it revolves around pubs and hotels. Visitors interested in trying their luck at the gaming tables can place their bets at the **Stakis Regency Casino** (61 Summer St., ☎ 01224/645273). Several of the larger hotels in the area run dinner dances in the summer season; check with the local tourist information centers for details.

Discos
Two notes of warning about discos in Aberdeen: Most of these establishments do not allow jeans or athletic shoes, and it's advisable to check beforehand that a particular disco is not closed because of a private function. Below is a list of the city's most popular discos.

Cotton Club (491 Union St., Aberdeen, ☎ 01224/581858).
Eagles (120 Union St., Aberdeen, ☎ 01224/640641).
Hotel Metro (17 Market St., Aberdeen, ☎ 01224/583275).
The Ministry (Dee St., Aberdeen, ☎ 01224/211661).
Mr G's (70–78 Chapel St., Aberdeen, ☎ 01224/642112).
The Palace Nightclub (Bridge Pl., Aberdeen, ☎ 01224/581135).
Zig-Zag (2 Diamond St., Aberdeen, ☎ 01224/641580).

Jazz Clubs
There is jazz on Saturday night at the **Masada Continental Lounge** (Rosemount Viaduct, Aberdeen, ☎ 01224/641587). The **Lemon Tree** (*see above*) stages frequent jazz events in its wide-ranging music program.

Rock Club
The Lemon Tree (*see above*) is the main rock venue.

ABERDEEN AND
THE NORTHEAST ESSENTIALS

Arriving and Departing

By Bus

Long-distance coach service operates to and from most parts of Scotland, England, and Wales. Main operators include **Scottish Citylink** (Aberdeen bus station, ☎ 01224/580275) and **National Express** (☎ 01738/633481).

By Car

It is now possible to travel from Glasgow and Edinburgh to Aberdeen on a continuous stretch of the A90/M90, a fairly scenic route that runs up Strathmore, with a fine hill view to the west. The coastal route, the A92, is a more leisurely alternative, with its interesting coastal resorts and fishing villages. The most scenic route, however, is probably the A93 from Perth, north to Blairgowrie and into Glen Shee. The A93 then goes over the Cairnwell Pass, the highest main road in the United Kingdom. (This route is not recommended in the winter months when snow can make driving over high ground difficult.)

By Ferry

There is a summer ferry service between Aberdeen, Lerwick (Shetland), and Bergen (Norway), which means that it is possible to travel from Norway to Aberdeen by boat. It is operated by P&O Ferries (contact via Box 5, Jamieson's Quay, Aberdeen, ☎ 01224/572615, FAX 01224/574411) and is subject to annual review; if you plan to use this route, check carefully that the service will be running.

By Plane

Aberdeen's airport—serving both international and domestic flights—is in Dyce, 7 miles west of the city center on the A96 (Inverness). The terminal building is modern (expanded in recent years because of Dyce's prominent role in North Sea oil-rig communications) and generally uncrowded.

Airlines linking Aberdeen with Europe include **Air U.K.,** with flights to Amsterdam (the Netherlands), Paris (France), and Bergen and Stavanger (Norway); **SAS (Scandinavian Airlines),** serving Stavanger; and **Business Air,** with flights to Esbjerg (Denmark). An extensive network of domestic flights linking Aberdeen with most major U.K. airports is operated by **Air U.K., ATS Vulcan, British Airways, Brymon, Business Air, Eurodirect, Gill Air,** and **Knight Air.** Consult the individual airlines or your travel agent for arrival and departure times (airport information desk, ☎ 01224/722331). Also worth noting is the direct Amsterdam–Aberdeen link enabling transatlantic passengers to visit Scotland's northeast by first flying from the United States to Amsterdam and then flying on to Aberdeen with Air U.K.; this can actually be faster than traveling to Aberdeen from other parts of Scotland or England.

BETWEEN THE AIRPORT AND CITY CENTER

By Bus: Grampian Transport's number 27 bus operates between the airport terminal and Union Street in the center of Aberdeen. Buses (exact fare £1.30) run every 40 minutes, and the journey time is approximately 40 minutes.

By Train: For those interested in train service to the airport, Dyce is on **ScotRail's** Inverness–Aberdeen route. The rail station is a short taxi ride from the terminal building. The ride by rail into Aberdeen from the airport takes 12 minutes. Trains run approximately every 90 minutes (more frequently at peak times, less frequently in the middle of the day). If you are intending to visit the western part of the area first, it is possible to travel northwest, away from Aberdeen, by rail direct to Elgin via Inverurie, Insch, Huntly, and Keith.

By Rental Car: The following car rental firms have desks at Aberdeen Airport: **Avis** (☎ 01224/722282), **Europcar** (☎ 01224/770770), and **Hertz** (☎ 01224/722373). The drive to the center of Aberdeen is very easy via the A96 (which can be busy in the rush hour).

By Train

Travelers can reach Aberdeen directly from Edinburgh (2½ hours), Glasgow (3 hours), and Inverness (2½ hours). See ScotRail time-table for full details. There are also London–Aberdeen routes that go through Edinburgh and the east-coast main line.

Getting Around

Aberdeen is not a large city, and its center is Union Street, the main throughfare running east–west. Anderson Drive is an efficient ring road on the western side of the city; inexperienced drivers should be extra careful on its many traffic circles. In general, road signs are clear and legible, and parking near the center of Aberdeen is no worse than in any other U.K. city, though the park-and-ride facility clearly signposted on the outskirts of Aberdeen is recommended.

By Bus

Grampian Transport operates services throughout the city. There is an inquiry kiosk on St. Nicholas Street, outside Marks and Spencers department store, and timetables are available at the kiosk or from the tourist information center at St. Nicholas House nearby.

By Car

Car rental firms in Aberdeen include **Arnold Clark** (☎ 01224/248842), **Budget Rent a Car** (☎ 01224/488770), **Eurodollar** (☎ 01224/626955), **Europcar** (☎ 01224/631199), **Alamo** (☎ 01224/770955), **Mitchell Self-Drive** (☎ 01224/642642), **Watson's Self-Drive** (☎ 01224/625625), and **Kenning** (☎ 01224/571445). Street maps are available from the tourist information center or from newsagents and booksellers.

By Taxi

Taxi stands can be found throughout the center of Aberdeen: along Union Street, at the railway station at Guild Street, at Back Wynd, and at Regent Quay. Taxis are mostly black, though variations in beige, maroon, or white exist.

Guided Tours

Orientation

City tours are available on most days between June and mid-September. Contact **Grampian Transport** (☎ 01224/637047). **Grampian Coaches** (operated by Grampian Transport), **Bluebird Northern** (☎ 01224/212266), and **McIntyre Coaches** (☎ 01224/493112) all operate tours encompassing the Northeast coastline and countryside. Some of the tours are of general interest, others are based on one of the area's various trails: Malt Whisky, Coastal, Castle, or Royal.

PERSONAL GUIDES

The **Scottish Tourist Guides Association** (contact Mrs. Anne Sinclair, 32 Henderson Dr., Skene, Aberdeen AB32 6RA, ☎ 01224/741314, FAX 01224/644822) can supply experienced personal guides, including foreign-language-speaking guides if necessary.

The following firms offer chauffeur-driven limousines to take clients on tailor-made tours: **Guy Salmon Chauffeur Drive** (☎ 01764/663556) and **Scotland Scene Ltd.** (☎ 01343/541468).

WALKING TOURS

The **Scottish Tourist Guides Association** (*see above*) organizes an "Old Aberdeen" walk from mid-May through August on Wednesday evenings and Sunday afternoons.

Important Addresses and Numbers

Emergencies

For fire, police, or ambulance, dial 999 from any telephone. No coins are needed for emergency calls made from public telephone booths.

Grampian Police (Force Headquarters, Queen St., Aberdeen, ☎ 01224/639111). There is a lost property office here.

Aberdeen Royal Infirmary (Accident and Emergency Department, Foresterhill, Aberdeen, ☎ 01224/681818).

Dr. Gray's Hospital, Elgin (Accident and Emergency Department, at end of High St. on A96, ☎ 01343/543131, ext. 77310.

Doctors and Dentists

The **Grampian Health Board** (Primary Care Department, Woolmanhill, ☎ 01224/681818, ext. 55537) can help you find a doctor or dentist.

Late-Night Pharmacies

The following Aberdeen pharmacies keep longer hours than most:

Anderson Pharmacy (4 Union Grove, ☎ 01224/587148) and **Boots the Chemists Ltd.** (Bon Accord Centre, George St., ☎ 01224/626080). There also is an in-store pharmacist at **Safeway Food Store** (215 King St., ☎ 01224/624398).

Notices on pharmacy doors will guide you to the nearest open pharmacy at any given time. The police can provide assistance in an emergency.

Visitor Information

The **Tourist Information Centre** (St. Nicholas House, Broad St., Aberdeen, ☎ 01224/632727, FAX 01224/620415) provides information on rental cars, tour tickets, and Rail Rovers and sells maps, souvenirs, and tour publications. In fact, this tourist information center supplies information on all Scotland's Northeast. There is also a currency exchange.

The other main tourist information centers covering the region include: the **Tourist Information Centre** in Banff (Collie Lodge, ☎ 01261/812419, FAX 01261/815807), the **Tourist Information Centre** in Banchory (Bridge St., ☎ 01330/822066, FAX 01330/825126) and the **Tourist Information Centre** in Braemar (The Mews, Mar Rd., ☎ 01339/741600). Other tourist board information centers open in the region in the summer season are found in Aboyne, Alford, Ballater, Crathie, Ellon, Fraserburgh, Huntly, Inverurie, Mintlaw, Peterhead, Stonehaven, and Turriff.

In **Elgin** contact the Tourist **Information Center** (17 High St., ☎ 01343/542666; fax 01343/552982). In the Moray District, seasonal offices open generally from Easter through the end of September are found in Buckie, Cullen, Dufftown, Forres, Keith, Lossiemouth, and Tomintoul.

8 The Central Highlands

Stirling, Loch Lomond and the Trossachs, Perthshire

The main towns of Perth and Stirling are easily accessible gateways to the Central Highlands, the rugged and spectacular terrain stretching north from Glasgow. This may not be the famed Highlands of the north, but there's plenty of wild country; here you'll find lush, green woodlands and lochs. In the Trossachs, deep lochs—including Loch Lomond, Scotland's largest—shimmer at the foot of gently sloping hills covered in birch, oak, and pine.

By Gilbert
Summers

THE CENTRAL HIGHLANDS CONSIST of what were once the counties of Perthshire and Stirlingshire. Today the county seats of Perth and Stirling, respectively, still play important roles as the primary administrative centers in the region. Both municipalities lie on the edge of a Highland area that offers reliable road and rail connections to the central belt of Scotland. Just how near the area is to the well-populated Midland Valley can be judged by the visitor who looks out from the ramparts of Edinburgh Castle: The Highland hills—which meander around the Trossachs and above Callander—are clearly visible. Similarly, the high-tower blocks of some of Glasgow's peripheral housing developments are noticeable from many of the higher peaks, notably Ben Lomond.

In fact, the Lowland/Highland contrast is quite pronounced in this region. Geologists have designated a prominent boundary between the two distinct landscapes as the Highland Boundary Fault. This geological barrier, however, also marked the differences between Scotland's two languages and cultures, Gaelic and Scots, with the Gaels ensconced within a mountain barrier. In the Central Highlands the fault line runs through Loch Lomond, close to Callander, to the northeast above Perth, and into the old county of Angus.

As early as 1794 the local minister in Callander, on the very edge of the Highlands, wrote: "The Trossachs are often visited by persons of taste, who are desirous of seeing nature in her rudest and unpolished state." What these early visitors came to see was a series of lochs and hills, whose crags and slopes were hung harmoniously with shaggy birch, oak, and pinewoods. The tops of the hills are high but not too wild (real wilderness would have been too much for these fledgling nature lovers). The Romantic poets, especially William Wordsworth, sang the praises of such locales. Though Wordsworth is most closely associated with the Lake District in England, his travels through Scotland and the Trossachs inspired several poems. But it was Sir Walter Scott who definitively put this Highland-edge area on the tourist map by setting his dramatic verse narrative *The Lady of the Lake,* written in 1810, firmly in the physical landscape of the Trossachs. Scott's verse was an immediate and huge success, and visitors flooded in to trace the events of the poem across the region. Today visitors continue to flock here, though few can quote a line of his poem.

If the Trossachs have long attracted those with discriminating tastes, then much of the same sentimental aura has attached itself to Loch Lomond. This is Scotland's largest loch in terms of surface area. By looking at the map, you will see that the loch is narrow to the north and broad in the south. The hard rocks to the north confine it to a long thin ribbon, and the more yielding Lowland structures allow it to spread out and assume a softer, wider form. Thus Lowland fields and lush hedgerows quickly give way to dark woods and crags (all this just a half hour's drive from the center of Glasgow). The song "The Banks of Loch Lomond," said to have been written by a Jacobite prisoner incarcerated in Carlisle, England, seems to capture a particular style of Scottish sentimentality, resulting in the notoriety of the "bonnie, bonnie banks" around the world, wherever exiled Scots are to be found.

The main towns of Perth and Stirling serve as roadway hubs for the area, but there are also a number of options in many of the area's smaller towns, places like Callander, Crieff, Pitlochry, Dunkeld, and Aberfeldy. There is also a string of small but embracing villages: Killin, Crian-

The Central Highlands

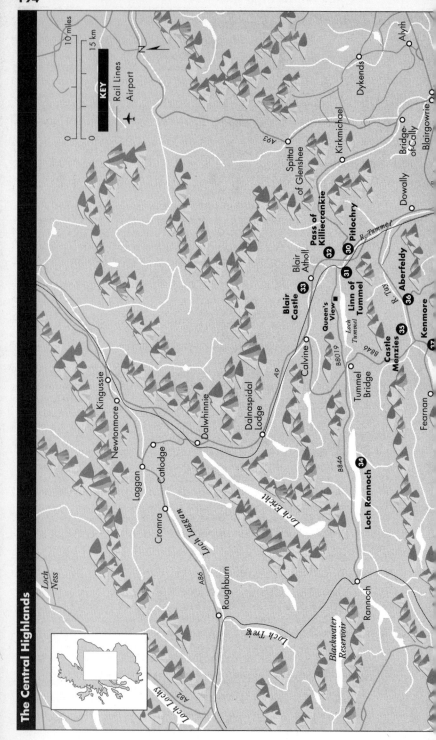

KEY

✈ Rail Lines
Airport

10 miles
15 km

N

Loch Ness

Kingussie
Newtonmore
Laggan
Catlodge
Cromra
Roughburn

A86
Loch Laggan
A82
Loch Lochy

Dalwhinnie
Dalnaspidal Lodge

Loch Ericht

Blackwater Reservoir
Loch Treig
Rannoch

Calvine
A9

B846

B8019
Queen's View

Blair Castle 33
Blair Atholl

Loch Rannoch 34
Tummel Bridge
B846

Fearnan

Castle Menzies 35
Loch Tummel
Pass of Killiecrankie 32
30 Pitlochry
R. Tummel
31 **Linn of Tummel**

Aberfeldy 36
R. Tay
R. Tummel
Kenmore 37

Spital of Glenshee
A93
Kirkmichael

Dowally
Bridge-of-Cally
Blairgowrie
Dykends
Alyth

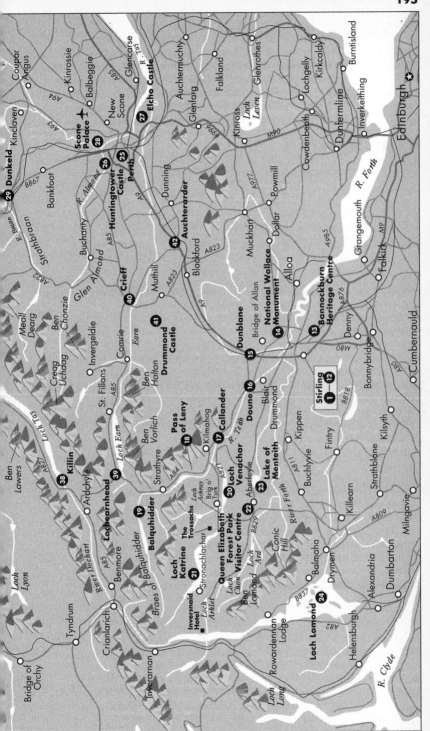

larich, Lochearnhead, Kenmore, and Kinlochrannoch, minor route centers tucked into the hills and covered in the tours described below.

Finally, remember that even though the Central Highlands are easily accessible, there is still much high, wild country in the region. Ben Lawers, near Killin, is the ninth-highest peak in Scotland, and the moor of Rannoch is as bleak and empty a stretch as can be seen anywhere in the northlands. But if the glens and lochs prove to be too lonely or intimidating, it's a short journey to the softer and less harsh Lowlands.

EXPLORING

The main towns of Stirling and Perth are located at the junction of many routes, making both places natural starting points for Highland tours. Stirling itself is worth covering in some detail on foot. The successive waves of development of this important town—from castles and Old Town architecture to Victorian developments and urban and industrial sprawl—can be traced quite easily. There are also peripheral points of interest worth visiting, including the **Bannockburn Heritage Centre,** which recounts how Scotland secured its independence for 400 years in one of its few victories over the English, and the **Wallace Monument,** commemorating Scotland's earliest freedom fighter, William Wallace.

The Trossachs are a short distance from Stirling, and visitors usually cover them in a loop. Those visiting **Loch Lomond** can get there from either Glasgow or Stirling, and there are two other routes available as well. The main road up the west bank (A82) is not recommended for leisurely touring. Do use this road, however, if you are on your way to Oban, Kintyre, or Argyll. Loch Lomond is best seen from one of two cul-de-sac roads: by way of Drymen at the south end, up to Rowardennan or, if you are pressed for time, west from Aberfoyle to reach Loch Lomond near its north end, at Inversnaid. Visitors should note that in the Trossachs, the road that some maps show going all the way around Loch Katrine is a private road belonging to the Strathclyde Water Board and is open only to walkers and cyclists.

Getting around Perthshire is made interesting by the series of looped tours accessible from the A9, a fast main artery. Exercise caution while driving the A9 itself, however. There have been many auto accidents in this area. Although the entire route can be completed in a single day, travelers with some time on their hands who seek a little spontaneity can take their chances on a variety of accommodations in villages along the way.

Tour 1: Around Stirling

Numbers in the margin correspond to points of interest on the Stirling map.

1 In some ways, **Stirling** is like a smaller version of Edinburgh. Its castle, built on a steep-sided plug of rock, dominates the landscape, and its Esplanade offers views of the surrounding valley-plain of the River Forth. To take advantage of its historical heritage (the Stuart monarchs held court here from time to time, as they did in Edinburgh), Stirling maintains a busy tourism calender that includes a summer program of open-air historical tableaux.

Opposite the tourist center on Dumbarton Road, where this tour begins, visitors can see that an impressive proportion of Stirling's town walls remain. Diagonally to the left is Corn Exchange Road, with a modern statue of Rob Roy MacGregor, notorious cattle dealer and drover,

part-time thief and outlaw, and Jacobite (most of the time). Farther along
② Dumbarton Road to the west is the **Smith Art Gallery and Museum,**
founded in 1874 with the bequest of a local collector and now a good
example of a community art gallery offering a varied exhibit program.
☎ 01786/471917. ☛ *Free. ☉ Apr.–Sept., Tues.–Sat. 10:30–5, Sun. 2–
5; Oct.–Mar., Tues.–Fri. noon–5, Sat. 10:30–5, Sun. 2–5.*

Near Rob Roy's statue, a gentle but relentless uphill path known as
③ the **Back Walk** eventually leads to the city's most famous and worthwhile sight—Stirling Castle. The Back Walk will take you along the
outside of the city's walls, past a watchtower and the grimly named
Hangman's entry, cut out of the great whinstone boulders that once
marked the outer defenses of the town.

Walk east, keeping to the outside of the walls, until you reach Academy
Road and the Old High School, built in 1854 on the site of the former
Greyfriars Monastery and now the Stirling Highland Hotel. At the far
end of the street, note two fine examples of Scottish domestic archi-
④ tecture. Now used for private housing, **Darrow House** dates from the
17th century. Look for the characteristically crow-stepped gables,
dormer windows, and a projecting turn-pike stair.

The adjacent **Spittal House** on the right has been restored to match its
handsome partner. Turn left and uphill onto St. John's Street. There is
another typical town house farther up the street, on the left, sometimes
⑤ known as **Bothwell Ha** (Hall), that is said to have been owned by the
Earl of Bothwell, Mary, Queen of Scots' third husband. Behind it, also
on the left, is the former military detention barracks soon to be restored
partly as offices and partly as a visitor center on the theme of crime
and punishment. Adjacent is the **Erskine Marykirk,** a neoclassical
church built in 1824 that now houses a youth hostel (*see* Dining and
Lodging, *below*).

There are a number of points of interest at the top of St. John's Street.
⑥ Most notable among them is the **Church of the Holy Rude,** with part
of the nave surviving from the 15th century. A portion of the original
medieval timber roof can also be seen. The church has the distinction
of being the only church in Scotland still in use that witnessed the coro-
nation of a Scottish monarch: James VI in 1567. Adjacent to the
church is the **Guildhall,** built as Cowane's Hospital in 1639 for *decayed
breithers* (unsuccessful merchants). The ancient facility is now the setting for summer concerts and evenings of participatory song, music,
and dance, called ceilidhs. Above the entrance is a small, cheery statue
of the founder himself, John Cowane, that is said to come alive on Hog-
manay Night (December 31) to walk the streets with the locals and
join in their New Year's revelry. *St. John St.* ☛ *Free. ☉ Weekdays 9–
5 (except when functions are being held).*

You'll encounter some unusual monuments at this point on the Back
⑦ Walk. The most notable are the **Star Pyramid** of 1858 and the curious
macabre glass-walled **Martyrs Monument,** erected in memory of two
Wigtownshire girls who were drowned in 1685 for their Covenanting
faith. At this point, you can't help but see the castle, which dominates
the foreground. From **Ladies' Rock,** a high perch within the churchyard, there are excellent views of the looming fortress.

★ ⑧ **Stirling Castle**'s strategic position made it the grandest prize in the Scots
Wars of Independence in the late-13th and early 14th centuries. The
Battle of Bannockburn in 1314 was fought within sight of its walls,
and the victory by Robert the Bruce (King Robert I) yielded both the

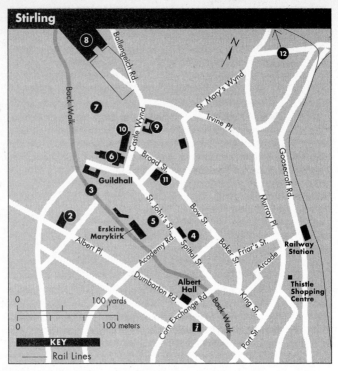

castle and freedom from English subjugation for the Scots for almost four centuries.

King Robert's daughter Marjory married Walter, the High Steward of Scotland, and their descendants included the Stewart dynasty of Scottish monarchs (Mary, Queen of Scots, was a Stewart, though she preferred the French spelling, *Stuart*). The Stewarts were mainly responsible for many of the works that survive within the castle walls today. They made Stirling Castle their court and power base, creating fine Renaissance-style buildings that were not completely obliterated, despite subsequent reconstruction for military purposes.

Before touring the castle, visit the **Royal Burgh of Stirling Visitor Centre,** conspicuous on the Esplanade. After an audiovisual briefing, you will enter the castle from its outer defenses, which consist of a great curtain wall and batteries dating from 1708, built to bulwark earlier defenses by the main gatehouse. From this lower square the most conspicuous feature is the **palace,** built by King James V between 1538 and 1542. This edifice shows the influence of French masons in the decorative figures festooning the ornately worked outer walls. Overlooking the upper courtyard is the **Great Hall,** built by King James IV in 1503. Before the Union of Parliaments in 1707, when the Scottish aristocracy sold out to England, this building had been used as one of the seats of the Scottish Parliament. After 1707 it sank into decline, becoming a riding school, then a barracks. Today, a slow restoration is under way.

Among the later works built for regiments stationed here, the **King's Old Building** stands out; it is a 19th-century baronial revival on the site of an earlier building. The oldest building on the site is the **Mint,** or **Coonzie**

Hoose, perhaps dating as far back as the 14th century. Below is an arched passageway leading to the westernmost section of the ramparts, the **Nether Bailey.** You'll have the distinct feeling here that you are in the bow of a warship sailing up the *carselands* (valley-plain) of the Forth Valley, which fans out before the great superstructure of the castle.

This is the place, among the gun platforms and the crenellations of the ramparts, to ponder the strategic significance of Stirling. To the south lies the hump of the Touch and the Gargunnock Hills (part of the Campsie Hills), diverting would-be direct routes from Glasgow and the south. For centuries all roads into the Highlands across the narrow waist of Scotland led to Stirling, formerly the lowest bridging point of the River Forth. If you look carefully northward, you can still see the Old Stirling Bridge, for centuries the lowest and most convenient place to cross the river. For all these geographic reasons, the castle here was perhaps the single most important fortress in Scotland. *Central Stirling,* ☎ *0131/244–3101.* ☛ *£3.50 adults, £2 senior citizens, £1 children.* ⊙ *Apr.–Sept., daily 9:30–5:15; Oct.–Mar., daily 9:30–4:15.*

Below the castle's Esplanade is the heart of the old town of Stirling, which you passed on the way up. As you walk down from the Esplanade along **Castle Wynd,** the path leads to a series of interesting buildings. In fact, below the Portcullis Hotel is one of the most important buildings surviving from the 16th century. This is **Argyll's Ludging,** built in three phases from the 16th century onward. Notice that the building is actually older than the name it bears—that of Archibald, ninth Earl of Argyll, who bought it in 1666.

Farther down, you will encounter a long and ornate facade, windowless and roofless and constructed in a distinctive Renaissance style. Look for the armorial carved panels, the gargoyles, and the turrets flanking a railed-off *pend* (archway). This is **Mar's Wark** (Work or Building), the stark remains of a palace built in 1570 by Lord Erskine, Earl of Mar, as well as Stirling Castle governor. Mar's Wark was sieged and severely damaged during the 1745 Jacobite rebellion, but its admirably worn shell survives. *At top of Castle Wynd,* ☎ *0131/244–3101. View from outside only.*

When you stand in front of Mar's Wark and look downhill, you are gazing into the heart of the Old Town. One of the Old Town's most notable structures is the **Tolbooth** of 1705 (on the right), which has a traditional Scottish steeple and gilded weathercock. For centuries the Burgh Court handed down sentences here; the jail was next door. The Tolbooth is soon to house a new exhibition on the history of the Royal Burgh of Stirling. Opposite is a row of Scottish tenement-style housing, renovated and full of tenants.

TIME OUT **Darnley's Coffee House** (16–18 Bow St., ☎ 01786/474468) faces you at the foot of Dumbarton Road and serves reasonable coffee and fresh carrot cake, among other sweet treats. The building housing Darnley's is from the late-16th century and derives its name from a popular tale that maintains Lord Darnley generally preferred to stay here rather than at his wife's (Mary, Queen of Scots') residence in the castle.

Farther out is the **Old Stirling Bridge,** by the A9, off the center of town. Dating from the 15th century, the bridge can still be crossed on foot. It was near this site that the Scottish freedom fighter William Wallace and a ragged army of Scots won a major victory in 1297. Their story is told in an exhibition and audiovisual presentation at the **National Wallace Monument** (*see* Tour 2, *below*).

Numbers in the margin correspond to points of interest on the Central Highlands map.

The next year, rising from the uncertainties and timidity of the great lords of Scotland (ever unsure of which way to jump and whether or not to bow to England's demands), Robert the Bruce materialized as the nation's champion, and the last bloody phase of the Wars of Independence began. This tale is recounted at the **Bannockburn Heritage Centre,** hidden among the sprawl of housing and commercial developments on the southern edge of Stirling. This was the site of the famed Battle of Bannockburn in 1314. In Bruce's day, the Forth had a shelved and partly wooded floodplain. He chose the site cunningly, noting the boggy ground on the lower reaches, in which the heavy horses of the English would founder. The atmosphere has been re-created within the center by means of an audiovisual presentation and an arresting mural depicting the battle in detail (look closely for some very unsavory goings-on), as well as models and costumed figures. *Off M80,* ☎ *01786/812664.* ☛ *£2 adults, £1 senior citizens and children. Heritage Centre and shop open Mar., Nov., Dec. 1–23, daily 11–3; Apr.–Oct., daily 10–5:30.*

Tour 2: The Trossachs and Loch Lomond

Inspired by the views of mountainous terrain seen from the ramparts of Stirling Castle, you can now make your way out to the Highland line. Start by navigating out of Stirling on the A9 past the pencil-thin **National Wallace Monument** on the Abbey Craig, from which you can see the Ochil Hills as a rocky moorland beyond. Follow Bridge of Allan signs northward, crossing the River Forth by Robert Stephenson's New Bridge of 1832, next to the historic old one. The National Wallace Monument is signposted at the next traffic circle. Up close, this Victorian shrine to William Wallace, built between 1856 and 1869, becomes less slim and soaring, revealing itself to be a substantial square tower with a creepy spiral stairway. An exhibition and audiovisual presentation tell Wallace's story. *Abbey Craig,* ☎ *01786/472140.* ☛ *£2.50 adults, £1.50 senior citizens and children.* ☺ *Feb. and Nov., Sat. and Sun. 10–4; Mar.–May and Oct., daily 10–5; June and Sept., daily 10–6; July and Aug., daily 9:30–6:30.*

You may wish to detour east for a minute or two on the A91, along the south side of the Abbey Craig, to visit **Cambuskenneth Abbey.** The scanty remains of this 13th-century religious seat lie in a sweeping bend of the River Forth, with the dramatic outline of Stirling Castle as a backdrop. Important meetings of the Scottish Parliament were once held here, and King Edward I of England visited in 1304. The abbey was looted and damaged during the Scots Wars of Independence (1307–14). The reconstructed tomb of King James III (who died in 1488) can be seen near the outline of the high altar.

The road west to **Bridge of Allan** lies along the edge of the Ochil Hills and runs past the campus of Stirling University. Bridge of

Allan was formerly a spa town and has substantial Victorian properties. Rejoin the A9 for a few moments' journey north to **Dunblane.** Its 13th-century **cathedral** has been partly restored, and the oldest part of the community—with its twisting streets and mellow town houses—huddles around the square and churchyard where the cathedral stands.

Turn west onto the A820 and continue west for a few minutes to another Highland-edge community, **Doune.** This was once a center for pistol making. No Highland chief's attire was complete without a prestigious and ornate pair of pistols. Today, Doune is more widely known as the site of one of the best-preserved medieval castles in Scotland. (It is signposted left as you enter the town from the Dunblane road.) It looks like an early castle is supposed to look: grim windowed and high walled, with echoing stone vaults and numerous drafts. Construction of the fortress began in the early 15th century on a now-peaceful riparian tract. The best place to photograph this squat, great-walled fort is from the bridge, a little way upstream, which carries the A9 west from Stirling. *Off A84,* ☎ *0131/244–3101.* 🖝 *£2 adults, £1.25 senior citizens, 75p children.* ◷ *Apr.–Sept., Mon.–Sat. 9:30–6, Sun. 2–6; Oct.–Mar., Mon.–Wed. and Sat. 9:30–4, Thurs. 9:30–1, Sun. 2–4.*

⑰ Rejoin another main road, the A84, and continue to **Callander,** a traditional Highland-edge resort. Callander bustles throughout the year—even on Sunday during off-peak times—simply because it is a gateway to Highland scenery within easy reach of Edinburgh and Glasgow. As a result there is plenty of window-shopping here, plus nightlife in pubs and a good choice of accommodations, from simple bed-and-breakfasts to lavish, sophisticated hotels (*see* Dining and Lodging, *below*).

Callander's **Rob Roy and Trossachs Visitor Centre,** housed in the former St. Kessog's Church, provides visitors yet another encounter with the famed Rob Roy MacGregor. As defender of the down-trodden and scourge of the authorities, MacGregor is known as a tartan Robin Hood. An old-style and much revered Highland hero, Rob Roy died peacefully at his home in 1734. You can learn more about his high jinks in a high-tech account—replete with displays and tableaux—in the modern visitor center. *Ancaster Sq.,* ☎ *01877/330342.* 🖝 *£1.70 adults, £1.35 senior citizens and children.* ◷ *Feb., weekends 10–4; Mar.–Dec., daily 10–5.*

TIME OUT **Pip's Coffee House** (☎ 01877/330470; closed Wed.), just off the main street in the center, is bright and cheerful and has an interesting picture gallery.

Callander's other attractions away from the bustle of the main street are mainly rural in nature: a walk signposted from the east end of the main street to the **Bracklinn Falls,** over whose lip Sir Walter Scott once rode a pony to win a bet, or another walk through the woods up to the **Callander Crags,** with views of the Lowlands as far as the Pentland Hills behind Edinburgh. (This walk is for the fit and well-shod only.)

Callander is the gateway to the Trossachs, but since it is on the main road, the A84, it also attracts overnight visitors on their way to Oban, Fort William, and beyond. All this traffic enters the proper Highlands just north of Callander, where the thickly clad slopes squeeze both the **⑱** road and rocky river into the narrow **Pass of Leny.** An abandoned railway—now a pleasant walking or bicycling path—also goes through the pass. If time permits, go part of the way along this path out of Callander past **Ben Ledi** mountain and Loch Lubnaig.

Beyond Strathyre and its extensive forestry-commission plantings, within a 20-minute drive of Callander, is a road that will take you west **⑲** to **Balquhidder** (pronounced *bal*-whidd-*er*). In this northern extension of the excursion, the first Highland glen that many visitors will see runs westward. Note its characteristics, seen throughout the north: a flat-bottomed, U-shape profile formed by prehistoric glaciers; extensive forestry plantings replacing much of the natural woodlands above; a sprinkling of farms; and farther up the glen, new hill roads bulldozed into the slopes to provide access for shepherds and foresters. Note also the shut-up look of some of the houses, many of which are second homes for affluent residents of the south. The glen is also where **Lochs Voil**

and Doune spread out, adding to the stunning vistas. This area is often known as the Braes (Slopes) of Balquhidder and was once the home of the MacLarens and the MacGregors. Rob Roy MacGregor's grave is signposted beside Balquhidder itself. The site of his house, now a private farm, is beyond the car park at the end of the road.

The glen has no through road, although in earlier times local residents were familiar with hill passes to the north and south. There still exists, for example, a right-of-way from the churchyard where Rob Roy is buried, via the plantings in Kirkton Glen and then on to open windy grasslands and a blue *lochan* (little lake). This path eventually drops into the next valley, Glen Dochart, and rejoins the A84.

The A821 runs west along with the first and gentlest of the Trossachs ⑳ lochs: **Loch Venachar.** The sturdy gray-stone buildings with a small dam at the Callander end control the water fed into the River Teith (and, hence, into the Forth) to compensate for the Victorian tinkerings with the water supply. Within a few minutes the A821 becomes muffled in woodlands and twists gradually down to **Brig o' Turk.** (*Turk* here is Gaelic for *tuirc,* meaning wild boar, a species that sadly has been extinct in this region since about the 16th century.)

TIME OUT   **The Byre** (☎ 01877/376292; limited opening hours in winter, so call ahead) is a well-run pub and restaurant just beyond Brig o' Turk, with dark beams and loosely defined Victorian decor, as well as attentive, friendly service. It's a lunchtime haven, particularly on a wet day in the woodlands, but also offers a full evening menu. A number of signposted walks also start from here.

West of Brig o' Turk stretches **Loch Achray,** dutifully fulfilling expectations of what a verdant Trossachs loch should be: small, green, reedy meadows backed by dark plantations, rhododendron thickets, and lumpy, thickly covered hills. Note the car park on the left, where walkers begin their ascent of the steep, heathery **Ben An.** To enjoy the best Trossachs' views, you will need a couple of hours and your wind. If you don't have much time, continue driving to the end of Loch Achray, following the road (turn right) into a narrow pass. This is the heart of the Trossachs. During the time of Sir Walter Scott, the path was narrow and almost hidden by the overhanging crags and mossy oaks and birches. Today it leads to a slightly anticlimactic car park with a shop, a café, and a visitor center. Not readily visible from the park, the 90-
★ ㉑ year-old steamer, the **S.S. Sir Walter Scott,** embarks on cruises of **Loch Katrine** every summer. To see the finest of the Trossachs lochs or to locate some of the landmarks cited in Scott's *Lady of the Lake,* you must— even for just a few minutes—go westward on foot. The road beyond the car park is open only to Strathclyde Water Board vehicles and is well-paved and level.

After going back through the pass on the main A821, turn right and head south, to higher moorland blanketed with conifer plantations (some of which have near-mature timber planted about 60 years ago by the Forestry Commission). The conifers hem in the views of Ben Ledi and Ben Venue, which can be seen over the spiky green waves of trees as the road snakes around heathery knolls and hummocks. There is another viewpoint at the highest point here, indicated by a small car park on the right.

Soon the road swoops off the Highland edge and leads downhill. Near ㉒ the start of the descent, the **Queen Elizabeth Forest Park Visitor Centre** can be seen on the left. The center features displays on the life of the forest, a summer-only café, some fine views over the Lowlands to the south, and a network of footpaths. *Off A821.* ☿ *Easter–Oct., daily 10–6.*

㉓ The Trossachs end here. The route back east to Stirling gradually leaves the hills behind and is noted mainly for the **Lake of Menteith,** a few minutes east of Aberfoyle. Mary, Queen of Scots, was stowed away at the lake for her own safety as a child in 1547. On a wooded islet the ruined **Inchmahome Priory,** where Mary was supposedly cosseted, can be reached by boat from the Port of Menteith.

㉔ Instead of returning to Stirling (barely half an hour), those visitors who want to cover **Loch Lomond** in one day have a couple of options. To reach Loch Lomond quickly from Aberfoyle, you can choose to see either the southern, wider end of the loch—studded with islands—near the Highland line, or the more enclosed northern portion. The distances to Balmaha, toward the south end, and to Inversnaid farther north, are about the same: approximately 14 miles, though there is an optional extension of about 7 miles to Rowardennan north of Balmaha. These distances will be easier to follow by consulting your map. Both routes are recommended and are briefly described here. Which one you choose depends on your taste. The **Aberfoyle–Inversnaid** trip is bereft of tea shops. In fact, during the off-season, the route has, in certain places, a wild and windswept air when it extends beyond the shelter of trees. The **Aberfoyle–Balmaha** section (via Drymen) offers a wider choice of pubs and hotels—and even a good-quality dress shop in Drymen.

For the Aberfoyle–Inversnaid trip, take the B829 (signposted Inversnaid and Stronachlachar), which runs west from Aberfoyle and offers outstanding views of **Ben Lomond,** especially in the vicinity of **Loch Ard.** The next loch, where the road narrows and bends, is **Loch Chon,** dark and forbidding. Its ominous reputation is further enhanced by the local legend, the presence of a dog-headed monster prone to swallowing passersby. Beyond Loch Chon, the road climbs gently from the plantings to open moor with a breathtaking vista over **Loch Arklet** to the **Arrochar Alps,** the name given to the high hills west of Loch Lomond. Hidden from sight in a deep trench, Loch Arklet is dammed to feed Loch Katrine.

Go left at a road junction (a right will take you to Stronachlachar) and take the open road along Loch Arklet. These deserted green hills were once the rallying grounds of the Clan Gregor. Near the dam on Loch Arklet, on your right, **Garrison Cottage** recalls the days when the government had to billet troops here to keep the MacGregors in order.

From Loch Arklet, the road zigzags down to **Inversnaid,** where you will see a hotel, a house, and a car park, with Loch Lomond stretching out of sight above and below. The long-distance walkers' route, the **West Highland Way,** which runs 95 miles from Glasgow to Fort William, follows the bank here. Take a brief stroll up the path, particularly if you are visiting during the spring, when the oak-tree canopy is filled with birdsong. You may get an inkling why Scots get so romantic about their bonny, bonny banks.

The only return to Aberfoyle is by retracing the same route—except that you may wish to go down to **Stronachlachar** on Loch Katrine. This is where the steamer calls; the town is no more than a pier with neatly clipped hedges and a cluster of houses belonging to Strathclyde Water Board workers. Loch Katrine's water is taken by aqueduct and tunnel to Glasgow—a Victorian feat of engineering that has ensured the purity of the supply to Scotland's largest city for more than a hundred years.

The second way of getting to Loch Lomond from Aberfoyle involves a faster trip on the main road to **Drymen,** a respectable and cozy town in the Lowland fields, with shops and pubs catering to the well-to-do Scots who have moved here from Glasgow.

TIME OUT   Drymen has a solid handful of pubs and tea shops, but try the **Clachan Inn** (☎ 01360/660824), which serves appetizing bar meals.

The B837 from Drymen, signposted Rowardennan and Balmaha, heads northwest, and in a few minutes Loch Lomond comes into view. At the little settlement of **Balmaha,** the versatile recreational role filled by Loch Lomond becomes clearer: Cruising craft are at the ready, hikers appear out of woodlands on the West Highland Way, and day-trippers stroll at the loch's edge. The heavily wooded offshore islands look alluringly near. One of the best ways to explore them is to take a cruise with the boat-hire company **MacFarlane and Son** (Boatyard, Balmaha, Loch Lomond G63 0JG, ☎ 01360/870214). (You can even rent a rowboat from MacFarlane's if you prefer doing your own exploration.) The island of **Inchcailloch** (*Inch-* is really *Innis,* Gaelic for *island*), just offshore, can be explored in an hour or two. There are pleasant pathways through oak woods planted in the 18th century, when the bark was used in the tanning industry.

Behind Balmaha is **Conic Hill,** a wavy ridge of bald heathery domes above the pine trees, and you can note from your map how Inchcailloch and the other islands line up with it. This geographic line is indicative of the Highland Boundary Fault, which runs through the loch and the hill.

If you want to take in even more of Loch Lomond, the cul-de-sac road continues northwest to **Rowardennan,** with the loch seldom more than a field's length away. Where the drivable road ends, in a car park crunchy with pinecones, you can ramble along one of the marked lochside footpaths, or make your way towards not-so-nearby Ben Lomond.

Tour 3: Around Perthshire

㉕   Some say **Perth** took its name from a Roman camp, Bertha, on the shores of the Tay. Whatever the truth, this strategic site has been occupied continuously for centuries, even prior to its becoming a Royal Burgh in 1210. Perth has long been a focal point in Scottish history, and several critical events took place here, including the assassination of King James I in 1437 and John Knox's preaching in St. John's Kirk in 1559. (Knox's sermon undoubtedly stirred his congregation: Afterward, they went rampaging through the town, igniting the Reformation in Scotland.) Later, the 17th-century religious wars in Scotland saw the town occupied first by the marquis of Montrose, then later by Oliver Cromwell's forces. Perth was also occupied by the Jacobites in the 1715 and 1745 rebellions.

Perth has been rebuilt and recast innumerable times, and, sadly, no trace remains of the pre-Reformation monasteries that once dominated the city skyline. In fact, modern Perth has swept much of its colorful history under a grid of bustling shopping streets. The town serves a wide rural hinterland and has a well-to-do air, making it one of the most interesting shopping towns aside from Edinburgh and Glasgow. Yet unlike Stirling, Perth's attractions—with the exception of the shops—are more scattered and take more time to reach on foot. Some, in fact, are far enough away to necessitate the use of a car, bus, or taxi. The following places are near the town center: **St. John's Kirk** (St. John St., ☎ 01738/626159) dating from the 15th century, escaped the worst excesses of the mob and is now restored; **Perth Art Gallery and Museum** (George St., ☎ 01738/632488) has a wide-ranging collection of local history and archaeology, plus a rotating exhibit program.

On the North Inch of Perth look for **Balhousie Castle** and the **Regimental Museum of the Black Watch.** Some will tell you the Black Watch was a Scottish regiment whose name is a reference to the color of their tartan. An equally plausible explanation, however, is that the regiment was established to keep an undercover watch on rebellious Jacobites. The *Black* is the Gaelic word *dubh,* meaning hidden or covert, used in the same way as the English word, *blackmail. Facing North Inch Park (entrance from Hay St.),* ☎ *01738/621281, ext. 8530.* ☛ *Free.* ⏰ *Weekdays 10–4:30 (3:30 in winter). Closed Dec. 23–Jan 3.*

The nearby Round House is home to the **Fergusson Gallery,** displaying a selection of 6,000 works—paintings, drawings, prints—by the Scottish artist, J.D. Fergusson. *Marshall Pl.,* ☎ *01738/441944.* ☛ *Free.* ⏰ *Mon.–Sat. 10–5.*

Off the A9, west of town, is **Caithness Glass,** where, from the viewing gallery, you can watch glassworkers creating smoky-smooth bowls, vases, and other glassware. There is also a small museum, restaurant, and shop. *Inveralmond, Perth,* ☎ *01738/637373.* ☛ *Free.* ⏰ *Factory weekdays 9–4:30, shop Easter–Oct., Mon.–Sat. 9–5, Sun. 11–5; Oct.–Easter, Mon.–Sat. 9–5, Sun. noon–5.*

㉖ A modest selection of castles is also within easy reach. **Huntingtower Castle,** a curious double tower dating from the 15th century, is associated with a political attempt to wrest power from the young James VI in 1582. Some early painted ceilings survive, the vaguest hint of the sumptuous decor once found in many such ancient castles that are now reduced to bare and drafty rooms. *Off A85,* ☎ *0131/244–3101.* ☛ *£1.50 adults, £1 senior citizens, 75p children.* ⏰ *Apr.–Sept., Mon.–Sat. 9:30–6, Sun. 2–6; Oct.–Mar., Mon.–Wed. and Sat. 9:30–4, Thurs. 9–1, Sun. 2–4.*

㉗ Much the same description applies to **Elcho Castle,** a fortified mansion on the east side of Perth. Some fabric and plasterwork still cling to the cold stone in this abandoned 15th-century seat of the earls of Wemyss. The effect is slightly eerie: Instead of a long-dead shell, there are hints of a building barely alive. *On River Tay,* ☎ *0131/244–3101.* ☛ *£1.20 adults, 75p children.* ⏰ *Apr.–Sept., Mon.–Sat. 9:30–6, Sun. 2–6.*

★ **㉘** **Scone Palace** is another story altogether: More cheerful and vibrant, the palace is the present home of the Earl of Mansfield and is open to visitors. Although it incorporates various earlier works, the palace today consists mainly of a 19th-century theme, featuring mock castellations that were fashionable at the time. There is plenty to see for the visitor with an interest in the acquisitions of an aristocratic Scottish family: magnificent porcelain, furniture, ivory, clocks, and 16th-century needlework. Visitor facilities also include a coffee shop, restaurant, gift shop, and play area, as well as extensive grounds that include a pinetum. The palace has its own chapel nearby, on the site of a long-gone abbey. The chapel stands by Moot Hill, the ancient meeting and crowning place of the Scottish kings. *Braemar Rd.,* ☎ *01738/52300.* ☛ *£4.50 adults, £3.70 senior citizens, £2.50 children, £13 family ticket.* ⏰ *Easter–Oct., daily 9:30–5.*

To take in the rest of Perthshire, go north on the A9 into the High- **㉙** lands at **Dunkeld,** where the hills and woodlands converge. Exit from the A9 and cross Thomas Telford's handsome river bridge of 1809 to enter the town. Note **Dunkeld Antiques** (☎ 01350/728832) on the right, facing the river across the bridge; it is well worth a browse. In Dunkeld you will find that the National Trust for Scotland not only cares for grand mansions and wildlands but also actively restores smaller properties. The work it completed under its "Little Houses" scheme can be seen in the square off the main street, just opposite the fish-and-chips shop. All the houses in the square were rebuilt after the 1689 Battle of Killiecrankie (*see below*), when, after its victory, the Jacobite army marched south and was defeated here.

㉚ The A9 continues north to **Pitlochry,** perhaps the typical central-Highland resort. Always full of leisurely hustle and bustle, Pitlochry has wall-to-wall souvenir and gift shops, large hotels recalling even more laid-back days, and a mountainous golf course. One popular attraction is the **Pitlochry Dam and Fish Ladder,** just behind the main street. So that generating needs do not clash with sports interests, most Scottish dams have salmon passes or ladders of some kind, enabling the fish to swim upstream to their spawning grounds. In Pitlochry, the fish ladder leads into a glass-paneled pipe so that they can observe the visitors.

For those with a whisky-tasting bent, Pitlochry also is home to **Edradour Distillery,** which claims to be the smallest single-malt distillery in Scotland (but then, so do others). *2½ mi east of Pitlochry,* ☎ *01796/472095.* ☛ *Free.* ☉ *For tours and tastings Mar.–Oct., Mon.–Sat. 9:30–5, Sun. noon–5; shop also open Nov.–Feb., Mon.–Sat. 10–4.*

㉛ The **Linn of Tummel,** a series of marked walks along the river and through tall, mature woodlands, is a little way north of the town. Above the Linn, the new A9 is raised on stilts and gives an exciting view of the valley. Visitors can pick up a walks booklet at the **Killiecrankie Visitor Centre,** a short distance farther on. To reach the Linn and Killiecrankie from Pitlochry, stay on the old A9, heading north. From the old A9, note the B8019 road heading west. (The tour returns to this point later.) *Off A9,* ☎ *01796/473233.* ☛ *£1 adults, children free.* ☉ *Site all year, visitor centre Apr.–Oct., daily 10–5:30.*

★ **㉜** The **Pass of Killiecrankie,** set among the oak woods and rocky river, was a key strategic point in the Central Highlands: A famous battle was won here in the Jacobite rebellion of 1689. The National Trust for Scotland's visitor center at Killiecrankie explains the significance of this, the first attempt to restore the Stuart monarchy. The battle was noted for the death of the Jacobite leader, James Graham of Claverhouse, also known as Bonnie Dundee, hit by a stray bullet; the rebellion fizzled out after that.

★ **㉝** Only a few minutes farther north from the Pass of Killiecrankie sits **Blair Castle.** Take the A9 to Blair Atholl, where the castle is clearly signposted. Because of its historic contents and its war-torn past, this is one of Scotland's most highly rated castle visits. White painted and turreted, Blair Castle has been home to successive dukes of Atholl and their family, the Murrays. One of the many fascinating details in the interior is a preserved piece of flooring that still bares marks of the red-hot shot fired through the roof during the 1745 Jacobite rebellion—the last occasion in Scottish history that a castle was besieged. The castle holds not only military artifacts—the duke is allowed to keep a private army, the Atholl Highlanders—but also a fine collection of furniture and paintings. Outside, extensive parklands are backed by high rounded hills. ☎ *01796/481207.* ☛ *£5 adults, £4 senior citizens and children, £14 family ticket.* ☉ *Apr.–late Oct., daily 10–6 (last admission at 5).*

From Blair the main A9 heads north over the watershed (by way of the Pass of Drumochter) to Speyside. To stay in Perthshire, return south to the B8019, noted earlier, below Killiecrankie. The B8019 turns into the B846 at Tummel Bridge and continues to Loch Rannoch. Take this section if you have plenty of time and are following this tour

(34) over a few days. **Loch Rannoch,** with its shoreline birch trees and dark pines behind, is the quintessential Highland loch. Continuing westward the road ends at Rannoch, where you meet the West Highland railroad line on its way across Rannoch Moor to Fort William. Fans of Robert Louis Stevenson, especially of *Kidnapped,* will not want to miss the last, lonely section of road. Stevenson describes the setting:

The mist rose and died away, and showed us that country lying as waste as the sea; only the moorfowl and the peewees crying upon it, and far over to the east a herd of deer, moving like dots. Much of it was red with heather, much of the rest broken up with bogs and hags and peaty pools. . . .

Apart from the blocks of alien conifer plantings in certain places, little here has changed.

If you stay on the B846, heading south and then east, you will pass

(35) **Castle Menzies.** This Z-plan 16th-century fortified tower/house is now the setting for the **Clan Menzies' Museum.** ☎ *01887/820982.* ☞ *£2.50 adults, £2 senior citizens, £1 children.* ☉ *Apr.–mid-Oct., Mon.–Sat. 10:30–5, Sun. 2–5 (last admission at 4:30).*

(36) A little farther on, travelers will reach **Aberfeldy** by way of General Wade's Aberfeldy Bridge (1733). This is the most impressive example of an English-built military road, a five-arch, humpback bridge designed by William Adam. Aberfeldy itself is a sleepy town that is popular as a tourist base. If you wish to return to Perth, the A9 is only about a 10-mile drive east on the A827.

(37) The next loop returns west to **Kenmore,** at the eastern end of Loch Tay. **Taymouth Castle** nearby has a famous parkland golf course. However, before continuing west, you should explore an interesting route running southeast from Kenmore. An unclassified road hairpins spectacularly out of the valley, giving superb views over the Ben Lawers mountain range to the north of Loch Tay and back to Schiehallion. After taking that slight detour, take the north-bank road by Loch Tay, the A827. At Fearnan you can divert a few minutes northward to Fortingall to view the **Fortingall yew,** near the Fortingall Hotel, in the churchyard. Wearily resting its great limbs on the ground, this tree is thought to be more than 3,000 years old. Legend has it that Pontius Pilate was born beside it, while his father served as a Roman legionnaire in Scotland.

The A827 offers fine views west along Loch Tay toward Ben More and Stobinian. The sign to Ben Lawers also points toward **Killin,** a village

(38) with an almost-alpine flavor. Known for its modest but surprisingly diverse selection of crafts and woolen wares, Killin is also noted for its scenery. The **Falls of Dochart,** white-water rapids overlooked by a pine-clad islet, are located at the west end of the village. Across the River Dochart and near the golf course sit the ruins of **Finlarig Castle,** built by Black Duncan of the Cowl, a notorious Campbell laird. The castle's beheading pit is certainly the most hair-raising of its surviving features. The castle can be visited at any time.

Southwest of Killin the A827 joins the main A85. By turning south over the watershed, you will see fine views of the hill ridges behind Killin. The road leads into Glen Ogle, "amid the wildest and finest scenery we had yet seen . . . putting one in mind of prints of the Khyber Pass," as Queen Victoria recorded in her diary when she passed this way in 1842.

㊴ The glen drops into the settlement of **Lochearnhead.** Make a left at the intersection, and you will see the **Lochearnhead Watersports Centre** by the shore of Loch Earn; the center offers instruction and equipment rentals for water-sports enthusiasts, from novices to experts. **Loch Earn** is the last of the lochs on this Perthshire loop. Still on the A85 going east you will have good views of the long, gray screes of Ben Vorlich southward across the loch.

You will then drive by the village of **St. Fillans,** through lush Perthshire estates and farmlands, and on to **Comrie.** The countryside east of Comrie looks more lush and is reminiscent of the Lowlands; the higher hills

㊵ can be seen to the north. **Crieff,** the hilly town you will encounter next, offers walks with Highland views from **Knock Hill** above the town, as well as tours of the **Glenturret Distillery,** signposted on the west side of the town. ☎ 01764/656565, ℻ 01764/654366. ☛ *£2.90 adults, £2.50 senior citizens, £1.70 children 12–17, children under 12 free.* ☉ *Mar.–Dec., Mon.–Sat. 9:30–4:30, Sun. 12–4:30; Jan.–Feb., weekdays 11:30–2:30.*

TIME OUT **Glenturret Distillery Visitor Centre** (*see above*) offers a choice of restaurants which serve award-winning "Taste of Scotland" menus.

Just south of Crieff is a paperweight manufacturer, part of a complex called the **Crieff Visitors Centre.** Adjacent to the complex is a small pottery factory and a restaurant. During the week there are surprisingly interesting tours of the factory grounds, where you can see Thistle hand-painted pottery, intricate millefiori glass, and lamp-work Perthshire paperweights being made. *A822, just south of Crieff,* ☎ *01764/654014.* ☛ *Free (small charge for pottery factory tour).* ☉ *Daily 9–6 (restricted hours in winter; call ahead for details).*

Perth is less than half an hour away via the A85, but an equally interesting return can be made by diverting through Auchterarder. On

㊶ the way, the A822 passes **Drummond Castle,** with its unusual formal Italian garden. *Off Crieff/Muthill Rd.,* ☎ *01764/681257. Admission to garden: £3 adults, £2 senior citizens, £1.50 children.* ☉ *Gardens May–Oct., daily 2–6 (last admission at 5 PM).*

㊷ The A823 leads to **Auchterarder,** famous for the **Gleneagles Hotel** and its recreational facilities (*see* Dining and Lodging, *below*). A number of antiques shops have also made a name for themselves at Auchterarder. The nearby **Glenruthven Weaving Mill** has been converted into a heritage center with a Scottish theme. The steam engine that once powered the mill can also be viewed. From Auchterarder, the fast-moving A9 stretches northeast to Perth.

What to See and Do with Children

Other than the sports-and-leisure facilities listed under Sports and Fitness, *below,* attractions for children are limited. There are several bicycle routes suitable for older children, however. And pony trekking is an option throughout the area (check with your local tourist information center for details). Near Perth, **Fairways Heavy Horse Centre** (Glencarse Village, ☎ 01738/632561; ☉ Mar.–Oct.) offers Clydesdale horses for day rides. For £2 (£1 children) you can tour the center's stables and exercise fields.

Most children will enjoy both the **Rob Roy and Trossachs Visitor Centre** (*see* Tour 2), and the **Vane Farm Nature Centre** (near Loch Leven, Kinross, ☎ 01577/862355). The latter is operated under the auspices of the Royal Society for the Protection of Birds and has a visitor center with a screened viewing area, nature trail, shop, picnic area, and two camouflaged shelters for observing wildlife, known as hides.

Off the Beaten Path

If Stirling is your base and you feel like taking a brisk evening walk and have your own transportation, seek out the little road that starts by the campus of Stirling University and climbs toward Sheriffmuir. On the way it passes close to the hill called **Dumyat,** on the breezy moors of the Ochils. A short walk is rewarded by superb views across the midland valley of Scotland, to Stirling and far beyond. The road is signposted Sheriffmuir from the old A9.

The ospreys that frequent Speyside's Loch Garten in summer get so much attention from conservation societies that they sometimes overshadow **Loch of the Lowes,** a Scottish Wildlife Trust reserve behind Dunkeld. Here the domestic routines of the osprey, one of Scotland's conservation success stories, can be observed in relative comfort. The reserve is off the A923 northeast of Dunkeld. ☎ *01350/727337.* ⊙ *Visitor center Apr.–Sept., 10–5. Observation blind open at all times.*

Duncryne Hill has possibly the most outstanding Loch Lomond view from the south end. It takes only a few minutes' clambering up a bracken-covered hill to get there. You may be rewarded by a spectacular sunset. You can't miss this unmistakable dumpling-shaped hill, behind Gartocharn on the Balloch–Drymen road, the A811.

Glen Lyon is worth exploring if you are in the Killin area. Lyon is one of central Scotland's most attractive glens. All the elements of Scottish glens can be found here: a rushing river, forests, high hills on both sides, prehistoric sites complete with legendary tales, and the typical *big hoose* hidden on private grounds. There is even a dam at the head of the loch, as a reminder that little of Scotland's scenic beauty is unadulterated. You can reach the glen either by way of Fortingall (*see* Tour 3) or by a high road from Loch Tay.

SHOPPING

The Central Highlands presents an interesting assortment of shopping choices, ranging from the larger population centers of Perth and Stirling, where High Street stores compete with long-established local firms, to the smaller towns and villages, where the selection is more limited but the relaxed pace makes for a pleasant shopping environment.

Callander

Northwest of Stirling are the bustling shops of Callander. A vast selection of woolens is on display at **Kilmahog Woollen Mill** (☎ 01877/330268). **Trossachs Woollen Mill** (☎ 01877/330178) is to the north of town at the Trossachs turning. The **Callander Woollen Mill** (☎ 01877/330273) is on Main Street. All the stores offer overseas mailing and tax-free shopping. **Presentations** (86 Main St., ☎ 01877/330212) stocks Scottish gifts and crafts and specializes in producing clan crests and badges that can be mailed anywhere in the world. Also uniquely Scottish is the stoneware of **Mounter Pottery** (Ancaster Square La., ☎ 01877/331052), which you can see being made.

Crieff

Like Perth, Crieff is a center for china and glassware. The **Crieff Visitors Centre** (A822, south of Crieff, ☎ 01764/654014) has a gift shop that sells small and large lamp-work paperweights, millefiori glass, and hand-painted pottery. Nearby, at **Stuart Crystal** (Muthill Rd., ☎ 01764/654004), Stuart crystal is engraved; factory tours and a factory shop are also available here. If you want something to put in your new set of crystal glasses, visit **Glenturret Distillery** (just outside Crieff on the road to Comrie, ☎ 01764/656565). The distillery offers guided tours and a free sampling of its product, Glenturret Pure Single Highland Malt.

Dunkeld

The small town of Dunkeld is home to the **Highland Horn and Deerskin Centre** (City Hall, Atholl St., ☎ 01350/727569). Here stag antlers and cow horns are shaped into horn-handled walking sticks, cutlery, and tableware. Deerskin is made into shoes, moccasins, handbags, wallets, and purses. The center offers a worldwide postal service and a tax-free shop.

Loch Lomond

If you are traveling west to Loch Lomond, visit Mr. Macpherson, who has a weaving shed at Tarbet called **Inverhoulin** (☎ 01301/702269), where you can see tartans weaved in a traditional handloom manner. Also in Tarbet, housed in a converted church at Station Road, is **The Black Sheep** (☎ 01301/702685), which specializes in crafts and offers a good cup of coffee and a meal. South of Loch Lomond are some of the larger shopping centers in the towns of Alexandria, Dumbarton, and Helensburgh. Try **R & A Urie** (45 W. Clyde St., Helensburgh, ☎ 01436/672331) for fine china and crystal (it has an export service). **MacGillivrays** (89 W. Clyde St., ☎ 01436/675161) has Scottish gifts including shortbread, tartan-dressed dolls, and pottery. Scottish silver jewelry, including the Charles Rennie Mackintosh Collection, is featured at **Hudsons Jewellers** (101 Main St., Alexandria, ☎ 01389/753738). This part of the Central Highlands also offers an exceptional selection of paintings by contemporary Scottish artists: try **Helensburgh Fine Arts** (78 W. Clyde St., Helensburgh, ☎ 01436/671821) or **The Rowan Gallery** (36 Main St., Drymen, ☎ 01360/660996).

Perth

Perth proffers an unusual buy: Scottish freshwater pearls from the River Tay, in delicate settings that take their theme from Scottish flowers. The Romans coveted these pearls. If you do, too, then you can make your choice at **Cairncross Jewellers and Goldsmiths** (18 St. John St., ☎ 01738/624367), where you can also admire a display of some of the more unusual shapes and colors of pearls found. Antique Scottish jewelry and silver can be found at **Timothy Hardie** (25 St. John St., ☎ 01738/633127). **Whispers of the Past** (George St., ☎ 01738/635472) has a collection of linens and jewelry. A comprehensive selection of sheepskins, leather jackets, and hand-knit Aran sweaters are on sale at **C & C Proudfoot** (104 South St., ☎ 01738/632483). Perth is an especially popular hunting ground for china and glass: **Watson of Perth** (163–167 High St., ☎ 01738/639861) has sold exquisite bone china and cut crystal since 1900 and can pack your purchase safely for shipment overseas. **The Perthshire Shop** (Lower City Mills, W. Mill St., ☎ 01738/627958) sells giftware including rugs, scarves, handbags, and mugs in Perthshire's own tartan. Just outside Perth, at **Caithness Glass** (Inveralmond, off the A9 at the northern town boundary, ☎

01738/637373), you can see glassware being made and then buy the product in the factory shop.

Stirling

In Stirling, Murray Place and the Thistle Centre are the streets where you'll find standard, mainstream shops. Lovers of antiquarian books should trek to the older part of town, where the **Corn Exchange Bookshop** (55 King St., ☎ 01786/473112) will keep them happy for an hour or two with its extensive number of titles, including books on every aspect of Scotland. **R. R. Henderson Ltd.** (6–8 Friars St., ☎ 01786/473681) is a kilt maker established in 1923 (knitwear and tweeds can be sent worldwide). **John M. Hay** (29–31 Friars St., ☎ 01786/473573) is the place to buy a set of bagpipes or a record or cassette of Scottish music (it also offers an overseas-shipment service). Finally, do not miss the medieval fairs held on Broad Street from time to time during the summer season.

South of Stirling, at Larbert, don't miss **Barbara Davidson's pottery studio** (Muirhall Farm, Larbert, ☎ 01324/554430) in a picturesque 18th-century farm setting. Here's a unique opportunity to buy a souvenir from one of the best-known potters in Scotland; in July and August you can even try throwing your own pot (for a small charge).

East of Stirling is **Mill Trail** country, along the foot of the Ochil Hills. A leaflet from a tourist information center will lead you to the delights of a real mill shop and low mill prices—even on cashmere—at **Tillicoultry, Alva,** and **Alloa.**

SPORTS AND FITNESS

Bicycling

The big attraction for cyclists is the dedicated Glasgow–Killin cycleway. This takes advantage of former railroad track-beds, as well as otherwise private roads plus some quiet minor roads, to get well into the Central Highlands by way of the Trossachs and Callander. Details (maps, leaflets, etc.) from Loch Lomond, Stirling, and Trossachs Tourist Board (*see* Central Highlands Essentials, *below*). Away from the cycleway, the main roads can be quite busy with holiday traffic. You can rent bikes from:

Lochside Mountain Bike Hire (Lochside Guest House, Arrochar, ☎ 01301/702467), **Pedlars Mountain Bike Hire** (Main St., Killin, ☎ 01567/820652), **New Heights Mountain Bike Hire** (26 Barnton St., Stirling, ☎ 01786/450809), **Trossachs Cycle Hire** (Trossachs Holiday Park, Aberfoyle, ☎ 01877/382614), **Wheels** (Manse La., Callander, ☎ 01877/331100).

Fishing

There are several fishing options in the area, including course and game fishing, loch and river fishing, and sea angling. Tourist information centers produce annually updated leaflets.

Golf

Blairgowrie (Rosemount, ☎ 01250/872622), 18 holes, 6,556 yards, par 72.
Callander (Aveland Rd., ☎ 01877/330090), 18 holes, 5,125 yards, par 66.

Hiking

Tourist information centers carry information on a variety of local routes. The publications *Walk Loch Lomond and the Trossachs* or *Walk Perthshire* are invaluable for hikers and trekkers and are available at bookshops or tourist information centers.

Horseback Riding

Coilessan Riding Centre (Coilessan House, Ardgarten, Arrochar, ☎ 01301/702523) is an approved riding outfit for beginners and experienced riders alike, offering over 20 routes on hill and seashore tracts.

Water Sports

Lochearnhead Water Sports Centre (Loch Earn, ☎ 01567/830330) has sailboats, canoes, and sailboards for wind surfing.

Loch Tay Boating Centre (Carlin and Brett, Pier Rd., Kenmore, ☎ 01887/830291) has cabin cruisers and canoes.

DINING AND LODGING

Dining

The restaurants of this region have been continually improving over the past several years. Regional country delicacies, such as loch trout, river salmon, mutton, and venison, are now found regularly on modest menus; this was extremely rare just 20 years ago. The urban areas south and southwest of Stirling, in contrast, lack refinement in matters of eating and drinking. There you will find simple low-built pubs, often crowded and noisy but serving substantial food at lunchtime (eaten balanced on your knee, perhaps, or at a shared table). Three heavy courses at one of these pubs will cost you about £10.

WHAT TO WEAR

Dress in the Central Highlands is casual, but you should err on the smart side. Country house hotels require jacket and tie.

CATEGORY	COST*
$$$$	over £40
$$$	£30–£40
$$	£15–£30
$	under £15

*per person for a three-course meal, including VAT, excluding drinks and service

Lodging

In Stirling and Callander, as well as in the small towns and villages throughout the region, you will find a selection of tourist accommodations out of all proportion to the size of the communities. (The industrial towns are the exceptions.) Standards of less-expensive establishments have improved in recent years and are still improving. The grand hotels, though few, were brought into existence by the rich carriage trade of the 19th century, when travel in Scotland was the fashion, and the level of service at these places has, by and large, not slipped. You will also find many country hotels, however, that match the grand hotels in comfort.

CATEGORY	COST*
$$$$	over £110
$$$	£80–£110
$$	£45–£80
$	under £45

All prices are for a standard double room, including service, breakfast, and VAT

Auchterarder

LODGING

$$$$ **Auchterarder House.** This wood-paneled, richly furnished Victorian coun-
★ try mansion is secluded and superbly atmospheric. Once owned by the steam locomotive magnate James Reid, the Auchterarder House still shows all the ebullience of the Victorian railway age. Many of the bedrooms have their original furniture, and all share views of private parkland and the Perthshire countryside. All meals are served at a time suitable to the guest, and breakfast at noon is not unheard of. The plush, exuberantly styled dining room, filled with glittering glassware, is an appropriate setting for the hotel's excellent cuisine. ☎ *B8062, Perthshire PH3 1DZ, ☎ 01764/663646, FAX 01764/662939. 15 rooms with bath. Restaurant (reservations required, jacket and tie), croquet. AE, DC, MC, V.*

$$$$ **Gleneagles Hotel.** One of Britain's most famous hotels, Gleneagles is the very image of modern grandeur. Like a vast, secret palace, it stands hidden in breathtaking countryside amid world-famous golf courses. Recreation facilities are seemingly endless, and there are also three restaurants: the elegant **Strathearn,** the **Dormy Grill** (at the 18th hole of the King's Course), and the **Country Club Brasserie** (by the swimming pool). All this plus a shopping arcade, Champneys Health Spa, Gleaneagles Mark Phillips Equestrian Centre, the British School of Falconry, and Gleneagles Jackie Stewart Shooting School make a stay here a luxurious and unforgettable experience. ☎ *PH3 1NF, ☎ 01764/662231, FAX 01764/662134. Jacket and tie required in formal areas of the hotel after 7 PM; otherwise dress casual. 236 rooms with bath. Restaurant (reservations advised), tennis, pool, sauna, 1 9-hole and 3 18-hole golf courses. AE, DC, MC, V.*

Balloch

DINING AND LODGING

$$$$ **Cameron House.** This luxury hotel offers a mix of top-quality hotel and
★ country-club facilities (including swimming pools, a gymnasium, and squash courts) on the shores of Loch Lomond. Award-winning chef Jef Bland (formerly of the Caledonian Hotel in Edinburgh) oversees Scottish-French cuisine of the highest order, served in rich Victorian surroundings. Bedrooms are decorated in modern pastel shades with high-quality reproductions of antique furniture. ☎ *Loch Lomond, Alexandria, Dumbartonshire G83 8QZ, ☎ 01389/755565, FAX 01389/759522. 68 rooms with bath. Restaurant (reservations advised), bar, 2 pools, health club. AE, DC, MC, V.*

Brig o' Turk

DINING AND LODGING

$$ **Dundarroch Country House and The Byre Restaurant.** This Victorian, antiques-furnished country house, set on 14 acres of grounds, offers first-class guest-house accommodations. The adjoining **Byre Restaurant** serves savory Scottish meals in a Victorian setting. Try the poached Tay salmon with hollandaise sauce. ☎ *Trossachs, Perthshire FK17 8HT, ☎ 01877/376200, FAX 01877/376202 (Dundarroch); ☎ 01877/376292*

(The Byre). 2 rooms with bath, 1 with shower. Restaurant (reservations advised). MC, V.

Callander

DINING AND LODGING

$$$$ **Roman Camp.** This former hunting lodge, dating from 1625, has 20
★   acres of gardens with river frontage, yet is within easy walking distance
of Callander's town center. Private fishing on the River Teith is another
attraction, as are the sitting rooms and the library, which, with their
numerous antiques, are more reminiscent of a stately family home than
a hotel. The restaurant has high standards, with a good reputation for
its salmon, trout, and other seafood cooked in an imaginative, modern Scottish style, and a chef who won't serve the same main course
twice. ☎ *Perthshire FK17 8BG, ☎ 01877/330003; fax 01877/331533.
14 rooms with bath or shower. Restaurant (reservations advised, jacket
and tie). AE, DC, MC, V.*

Crainlarich

DINING AND LODGING

$ **Lodge House.** Few other guest houses in Scotland can match the moun-
tain views from this 100-year-old property. Informal and cozy, the hotel
is successful thanks to what the Scots call "the crack"—conviviality
between host and guests. The food is good Scots fare: haggis, salmon,
and oatcakes. The bedrooms are plain and unfussy, but more than adequate. You may wish to go out for a walk along the riverbank after
dinner, or have a wee dram in the tiny bar instead. ☎ *Lodge House,
Crianlarich, Perthshire FK20 8RU, ☎ 01838/300276. 6 rooms with
bath or shower. MC, V.*

Denny

LODGING

$ **Lochend Farm.** Extensive views, wholesome farm cooking, and a pleas-
antly languid pace are the hallmarks of this peaceful working farm.
It's only 5 miles from the M9/M80, so it also makes a good touring
base. The traditionally furnished (and very comfortable) bedrooms have
washbasins and share a private bathroom. ☎ *Carronbridge, Denny,
Stirlingshire FK6 5JJ, ☎ 01324/822778. 2 rooms. No credit cards.*

Glenfarg

DINING AND LODGING

$$ **Bein Inn.** Once a prosperous drovers' inn, this hotel has an air of leafy,
languid seclusion, bordered as it is by a rippling river and a quiet rural
road. The busy M90 is only 2 miles away, so you're also within easy
reach by car of Edinburgh and Perth. The hotel itself retains the feel
of an old inn with its friendly bar and traditionally furnished lounge
and dining room. The latter features a Taste of Scotland menu and is
popular with both guests and nonguests. All the bedrooms are spacious,
with modern furnishings. ☎ *Perthshire PH2 9PY, ☎ 01577/830216.
13 rooms with bath. Restaurant (reservations advised). MC, V.*

Kinloch Rannoch

LODGING

$$ **Cuilmore Cottage.** This 18th-century croft has been carefully modernized to a very high standard, but it is the superb food (included in the
room rate) which is most memorable: The hostess, Mrs. Steffan, has
been awarded a special prize by the Taste of Scotland organization for
her homegrown fruit and vegetables, and for her home baking. Try the
loin of lamb with redcurrant jelly or saddle of rabbit with herb

dumplings. ✆ *Perthshire PH16 5QB,* ☎ *and fax 01882/632218. 2 rooms with bath. AE, DC, MC, V.*

Perth

DINING AND LODGING

$$–$$$ **Parklands.** A smart Georgian town house overlooking lush woodland—an ideal setting for this top-quality hotel—the Parklands is perhaps best known for its cuisine, featuring Scottish fish, game, and beef. The restrained decor and period furniture is in keeping with the subdued but elegant ambience. ✆ *2 St. Leonards Bank, PH2 8ER,* ☎ *01738/622451,* FAX *01738/622046. 14 rooms with bath. Restaurant. AE, DC, MC, V.*

$$ **Sunbank House.** This early Victorian house, set on its own manicured grounds on the outskirts of Perth, has superb views over the city. Exceptionally high standards of decor, cuisine, and cleanliness are vigilantly maintained. ✆ *50 Dundee Rd., PH2 7BA,* ☎ *01738/624882,* FAX *01738/442515. 5 rooms with bath, 5 with shower. MC, V.*

Stirling

DINING

$$ **Heritage.** This elegant 18th-century establishment is run by a French family. The decor is all fanlights and candles; the menu features such French and Scottish classics as coq au vin and beef escalopes with wild mushrooms. ✕ *16 Allan Park,* ☎ *01786/473660,* FAX *01786/449748. Reservations advised. MC, V. Closed Christmas, Jan. 1.*

$ **Cross Keys Hotel.** A quaint, stone-walled dining room adds atmosphere to this restaurant's varied traditional Scottish menu, which includes roast beef, poached salmon, and game pie. If you have enjoyed your meal so much that you don't want to leave, there are three cozy cottage-style bedrooms upstairs. ✕ *Main St., Kippen (A811, west of Stirling),* ☎ *01786/870293. 3 rooms with shared bath. Reservations advised. Jacket and tie. MC, V.*

DINING AND LODGING

$$$$ **Stirling Highland Hotel.** This hotel occupies a handsome building that was once the Old High School. Many original architectural features, retained during the conversion, add to the historic atmosphere. The decor is old-fashioned in style, with solid wood furnishings, tartan or floral fabrics, and neutral color schemes. ✆ *Spittal St., FK8 IDU,* ☎ *01786/475444,* FAX *01786/462929. 76 rooms with bath, 4 suites. 2 restaurants, piano bar, indoor pool, hot tub, sauna, steam room, exercise room, Ping-Pong, squash. AE, DC, MC, V.*

$$ **Terraces Hotel.** This is a centrally located hotel, useful for exploring Stirling; since there is plenty of parking space, it makes a good base for touring the region, too. It's a Georgian town house that has been comfortably converted, and the service is attentive. The **Melville Restaurant,** part of the hotel, serves something for all tastes: pasta, steak, chicken, salmon, and seafood, all competently prepared and served in relaxing brown- and bronze-tone surroundings. ✆ *4 Melville Terr., FK8 2ND,* ☎ *01786/472268,* FAX *01786/450314. 18 rooms with bath or shower. Restaurant (reservations advised, jacket and tie). AE, DC, MC, V.*

LODGING

$ **Stirling Youth Hostel.** Purpose-built within the shell of a former church, the hostel offers high-grade four- and six-bed rooms (and a few doubles) with en suite facilities. Use of the television room, the dining room, and the self-catering, fully equipped kitchen is included in the bargain price of £10.15 per person, including breakfast. ✆ *Erskine*

Marykirk, St. John's St., FK8 IDU, ☎ 01786/473442, FAX 01786/445715. 128 beds. MC, V.

$ **West Plean.** This handsome house is part of a working farm. It has a walled garden and woodland walks. Well-cooked food and spacious rooms make this bed-and-breakfast an excellent bargain. 🕾 *Denny Rd., FK7 8HA, ☎ 01786/812208. 3 rooms with bath or shower. No credit cards.*

THE ARTS AND NIGHTLIFE

The Arts

Outside the main cities, opportunities for cultural activities are limited, except when communities hold arts festivals—a growing phenomenon in Scotland—or if the community is on the itinerary of one of Scotland's major artistic companies; for example, the Scottish Opera. The following venues have a rotating program of cultural events, but check with local tourist-information centers for schedules of other events at such places as **Alloa Town Hall,** the **Guildhall** in **Stirling,** and **Denny Civic Theatre** in **Dumbarton.**

Theater

The **Macrobert Arts Centre** (Stirling University, ☎ 01786/461081) has a theater, art gallery, and studio with a program that ranges from films to pantomime. The **Perth Repertory Theatre** (High St., Perth, ☎ 01738/621031) is a Victorian theater offering a variety of plays and musicals.

Pitlochry Festival Theatre (Pitlochry, ☎ 01796/472680) presents seven plays each season and features concerts on some Sundays. The theater is open from May to early October.

Nightlife

The nightlife in the area tends toward ceilidhs and Scottish concerts. Folk evenings in a number of hotels are also popular. Consult local tourist information centers for entertainment options. In general, local pubs are friendly and down-to-earth, with patrons who don't mind talking to visitors about what to see and do.

CENTRAL HIGHLANDS ESSENTIALS

Arriving and Departing

By Bus
There is a good network of buses connecting with the central belt via Edinburgh and Glasgow. Express services also link the larger towns in the Central Highlands with all main towns and cities in England.

By Car
Visitors will find an easy access to the area from the central belt of Scotland via the motorway network. The M9 runs within sight of the walls of Stirling Castle, and Perth can be reached via the M90 over the Forth Bridge.

By Plane
Perth and Stirling can be reached easily from **Edinburgh** and **Glasgow** airports (*see* Chapters 4 and 5) by train, car, or bus.

By Train
The Central Highlands are linked to Edinburgh and Glasgow by rail, with through routes to England (some direct-service routes from London take fewer than five hours). A variety of Saver ticket options are available, although in some cases on the ScotRail system, the discount fares must be purchased before your arrival in the United Kingdom.

Getting Around

By Bus
The following companies offer reliable service on a number of convenient routes.

Allander Coaches Ltd. (Unit 19, Cloverfield Estate, Milngavie, Glasgow, ☎ 0141/956–3636).

Scottish Citylink-National Express (Leonard St., bus station, Perth, ☎ 01738/626848).

Midland Bluebird Bus Services (Goosecroft Rd. bus station, Stirling, ☎ 01786/473763).

Stagecoach (Ruthvenfield Rd., Inveralmond Industrial Estate, Perth, ☎ 01738/629339).

By Car
There is an adequate network of roads, and the area's proximity to the central belt speeds road communications. The Scottish Tourist Board's touring map is useful.

By Train
The **West Highland Line** runs through the western portion of the area. Services also run to Stirling, Dunblane, Perth, and Gleneagles; destinations on the Inverness–Perth line include Dunkeld, Pitlochry, and Blair Athol.

Guided Tours

Orientation
The bus companies listed in Getting Around By Bus, *above,* offer a number of general orientation tours. Inquire at the nearest tourist information center, where tour reservations can usually be booked.

Special-Interest
There are many taxi and chauffeur companies offering tailor-made tours by the day or week; the nearest tourist information center is your best source for detailed, up-to-date information. In the eastern portion of the Central Highlands, try **Turpie's Tours** (3 Bridge Rd., Caputh, by Perth, ☎ 01738/710607). Possibilities in the south and west include **Goosecroft Station Taxis** (Cunningham Rd., Springkerse Industrial Estate, Stirling, ☎ 01786/472220), **Ians Taxi and Minibus** (Gargunnock filling station, Gargunnock by Stirling, ☎ 01786/860207), and **Dumbarton and Alexandria T.O.A.** (Main St., Alexandria, ☎ 01389/757171).

Do not miss the opportunity to take a boat trip on a Scottish loch. The S.S. *Sir Walter Scott* sails on Loch Katrine in the summer season; you can book it through the tourist information center at Callander. On Loch Lomond there are a number of cruise possibilities: from Tarbet, **Cruise Loch Lomond** (Shore Cottage, Tarbet, ☎ 01301/702356); from Balloch, the *Lomond Duchess* and *Lomond Maid* (Balloch Marina, Riverside, ☎ 01389/751481); and from Balmaha, **Macfarlane and**

Son operates the **Royal Mail boat** to the islands on the loch and takes passengers (Balmaha Boatyard, ☎ 01360/870214).

Important Addresses and Numbers

Emergencies
For police, fire, or ambulance, dial 999 from any telephone. No coins are needed for emergency calls from telephone booths.

Doctors and Dentists
Local practitioners will usually treat visiting patients. Information is available from tourist information centers, and names of doctors can also be found in the yellow pages of the telephone directory. The main hospital emergency rooms in the region are **Perth Royal Infirmary** (Tullylumb, Perth, ☎ 01738/623311), **Stirling Royal Infirmary** (Livilands Gate, Stirling, ☎ 01786/434000), and **Vale of Leven Hospital** (Main St., Alexandria, ☎ 01389/754121).

Late-Night Pharmacies
Late-night pharmacies are found only in the larger towns and cities. In an emergency, the police will provide assistance in locating a pharmacist. In rural areas, general practitioners may also dispense medicines.

Visitor Information
The **Tourist Information Centre** in Stirling (41 Dumbarton Rd., Stirling FK8 2QQ, ☎ 01786/475019, FAX 0786/471301) and the **Tourist Information Centre** in Perth (45 High St., Perth PH1 5TJ, ☎ 01738/638353, FAX 0738/630416) can provide information on the region. Local tourist information centers can be found throughout the region and are open during the peak season (generally Apr.–Oct.) in the following towns: Aberfeldy, Aberfoyle, Alva, Auchterarder, Balloch, Blairgowrie, Callander, Crieff, Drymen, Dumbarton, Dunblane, Dunkeld, Helensburgh, Inveralmond, Killin, Kinross, Pirnhall, Pitlochry, Tarbet, and Tyndrum. All are clearly marked with the standard i sign in white on a blue background.

9 Argyll and the Isles

Argyll is a remote group of islands in western Scotland. The Island of Mull has a rolling landscape and its capital, Tobermory, has brightly painted houses, giving it a Mediterranean look. Iona, near Mull, is Scotland's most important Christian site. The Isle of Islay, synonymous with whisky, produces seven malts. The Kintyre peninsula is a wonderland of sea views and prehistoric monuments. Arran, more developed, has mist-shrouded mountains and farmland.

THIS POPULAR AND ALLURING REGION in western Scotland, divided in two by the long peninsula of Kintyre, is characterized by a splintered, complex seaboard. The west is an aesthetic delight, though it's regularly drenched by rain. The same soggy saga also holds true in the Great Glen area, but an occasionally wet foray is the price visitors pay for the glittering freshness of oakwoods and bracken-covered hillsides, and for the bright interplay of sea, loch, and rugged green peninsula.

By Gilbert
Summers

Kintyre also separates the islands of the Firth of Clyde (including Arran), from the islands of the Inner Hebrides, the largest of which are Mull, Islay, and Jura. You could spend all your time touring these larger islands, but keep in mind that there are plenty of small islands that can also be explored—Bute in the Clyde estuary or the captivating gem of Colonsay between Islay and Mull, for example. Those visiting the mainland cannot avoid the touring center of Oban, an important ferry port with a main road leading south into Kintyre.

EXPLORING

On mainland-based tours Loch Fyne tends to get in the way. It is a long haul around the end of this fjord-like sea loch to reach Inveraray, a popular destination. Ferry services provided by Caledonian MacBrayne (*see* Getting Around by Car, *above*) make all kinds of inter-island tours possible. From Ardrossan, southwest of Glasgow, you can reach the island of Arran, then exit westward to Kintyre by a short ferry crossing. You can continue to the islands of Islay and Jura, and from there a ferry can take you northeast to Oban. (All the ferries transport cars and pedestrians.) The tours described below begin on the mainland but also highlight the main islands.

Tour 1: Around Argyll

Numbers in the margin correspond to points of interest on the Argyll and the Isles map.

Just as it is impossible to avoid Fort William when touring the north,
❶ it is almost impossible to avoid **Oban** when touring this part of Scotland. Unlike Fort William, however, Oban has a legitimate waterfront and several ferry excursions from which to choose. It also has a more pleasant environment, though it does get busy during the peak season. Oban is a traditional Scottish resort where you can find ceilidhs and tartan kitsch, as well as late-night revelry in pubs and hotel bars. There is an inescapable sense, however, that just over the horizon, on the islands or down Kintyre, loom more peaceful and authentic environs.

Take the main A85 east out of town. After about 2 miles a sign points
❷ north (left) to **Dunstaffnage Castle,** once an important stronghold of the MacDougalls. There are outstanding views from the ramparts across the **Sound of Mull** and the **Firth of Lorne,** a nautical crossroads of sorts once watched over by Dunstaffnage Castle and commanded by the galleys (in Gaelic, *birlinn*) of the Lords of the Isles. ☎ *0131/244–3101. ☛ £1.50 adults, £1 senior citizens, 75p children. ☼ Apr.–Sept., weekdays 9:30–6, Sun. 2–6.*

From the castle keep you should also be able to see **Connel Bridge,** 2 miles farther east. This elegant structure once carried a branch railway along the coast but has since surrendered to the all-conquering automobile. When you reach the bridge, look below the narrows in the shadow of the girders to see if the **Falls of Lora** are running. Upstream is fjord-like **Loch Etive** (with cruises from Oban); the water leaving this deep, narrow loch foams and fights with the sea tides, creating turbulence and curious cascades.

❸ Continue 6 miles on the A85 to Taynuilt. The **Bonawe Iron Furnace** is signposted to the left. No industrial activity takes place there now, but once the peaceful wooded slopes overlooked the smoky glow of furnaces burning local timber to make charcoal. The furnaces played a central role in the iron-smelting industry, which flourished here between 1753 and 1876. Today, Historic Scotland cares for the well-preserved buildings. *Bonawe, 12 mi east of Oban, off A85,* ☎ *0131/244–3101.* ☞ *£2 adults, £1.25 senior citizens, 75p children.* ⊘ *Apr.–Sept., Mon.–Sat. 9:30–6, Sun. 2–6.*

★ ❹ Continue through the narrow Pass of Brander to the **Cruachan Dam Power Station Visitor Centre.** The frequent railway-signal posts on the track above are actually avalanche warnings. **Ben Cruachan** is the mountain that gave you the view from Dunstaffnage Castle; now you have no view at all, since you are almost underneath it. If you want to go farther underneath the mountain, stop at the visitor center for instructions. Actually a horseshoe-shape series of peaks, Ben Cruachan has a dam built within its confines. Water flows down from the dam to Loch Awe, the loch on your right, turning turbines along the way. You can learn about this at the visitor center and on a half-mile minibus trip down a tunnel into a huge cavern-cum-turbine hall. Be sure to take this trip, which will bring you under several cubic miles of mountain. *Off A85, 18 mi east of Oban,* ☎ *01866/822673.* ☞ *£2 adults, 50p children over 8 (under 8 free).* ⊘ *Mar.–mid-Nov. daily 9–4:30.*

By continuing east, you will reach Lochawe Station, where cruises (try the *Lady Rowena*) run from the pier. As an alternative you can visit **★ ❺** **Kilchurn Castle,** a ruined fortress at the eastern end of Loch Awe. The castle was built by Sir Colin Campbell of Glenorchy in the 15th century and rebuilt in the 17th century. The Campbells had their original power base in this area. Park and cross the railway line, then walk across the grassy flats to the airy vantage points, complete with informative signs, amid the towers; from there you'll see more fine panoramas. *Northern tip of Loch Awe, 21 mi east of Oban,* ☎ *0131/244–3101.*

There is also a superb view from the **Duncan Ban Macintyre Monument** near Dalmally (*see* Off the Beaten Track, *below*). After the monument turn right on the A819, signposted Inveraray (possibly the most misspelled place in the Highlands). **Loch Awe** is the longest loch in Scotland; the road soon leaves its pleasant banks, turning south to join the A83. This road is usually busy carrying traffic from Glasgow and Loch Lomond by way of the high pass of the **Rest and Be Thankful.** (Though not covered in this tour, many visitors come up Loch Lomond and head west by the A83. The Rest and Be Thankful is perhaps its most scenic point—an aptly named, almost Alpine pass among high green slopes and gray rocks.)

TIME OUT The simple decor—wood-top tables and fittings—lets you concentrate on the seafood at the **Loch Fyne Oyster Bar** (A83, on the approach to Loch Fyne, ☎ 01499/600236). Local oysters and crisp white wine certainly are a far cry from roadside hamburgers and french fries.

Ardkinglas Woodland Garden, around the head of Loch Fyne (go left at the junction), is home to Scotland's tallest tree, a grand fir stand-

Argyll and the Isles

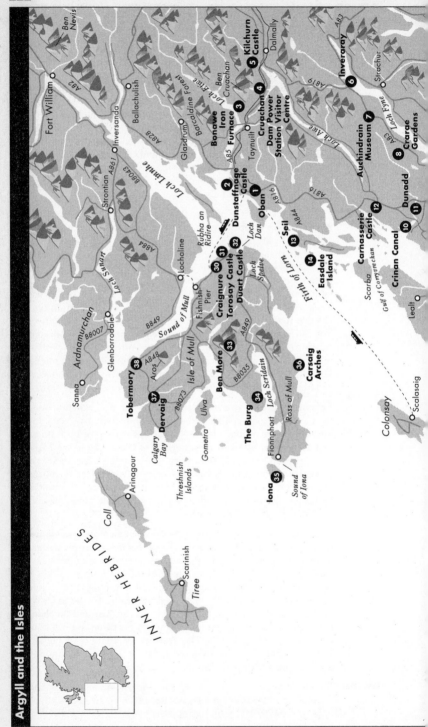

Ben Nevis

Fort William

A82

Ballachulish

Inversanda

A861

Strontian

B8043

Ardnamurchan

Loch Sunart

A884

Glenborrodale

B8007

Sanna

Coll

Arinagour

INNER HEBRIDES

Scarinish

Tiree

Glasdrum

Barcaldine Forest

A828

Loch Linnhe

Lochaline

Rubha an Ridire

Sound of Mull

B849

Fishnish Pier

Fishnish

A848

Aros

Tobermory

Dervaig

37 38

B8073

Isle of Mull

Ulva

Gometra

Threshnish Islands

Calgary Bay

Ben More

The Burg

34

B8035

A849

Loch Scridain

Ross of Mull

Fionnphort

Iona 35

Sound of Iona

Ben Cruachan

Loch Etive

Bonawe Iron Furnace

3

A85

Taynuilt

Cruachan Dam Power Station Visitor Centre

4

Kilchurn Castle

5

Dalmally

Dunstaffnage Castle

2

1 Oban

A816

Loch Awe

A819

Inveraray

6

Strachur

A83

Loch Fyne

Auchindrain Museum

7

Crarae Gardens

8

A83

Loch Feochan

Loch Nell

A844

Seil

13

Firth of Lorn

Easdale Island

14

Craignure

30

Torosay Castle

31 32

Duart Castle

Loch Don

Loch Spelve

33

Carsaig Arches

36

Carnasserie Castle

12

Dunadd

11

10

Crinan Canal

Scarba

Gulf of Corryvreckan

Lealt

Colonsay

Scalasaig

ATLANTIC OCEAN

NORTHERN IRELAND

Firth of Clyde

Wemyss Bay

Sound of Bute

Sound of Jura

Sound of Gigha

KEY
— Rail Lines
- - - Ferry Lines

N

0   10 miles
0   15 km

Maidens

Ardrossan

Largs

Dunoon

Auchenbreck

Wemyss Bay

Rothesay

Millport

Bute

9 Lochgilphead

Loch Gilp

B8000

Knapdale

Tarbert

Kennacraig

Kilberry

Claonaig

Loch Caolisport

B8024

Oronsay

Sound of Jura

Jura

Loch Tarbert

Paps of Jura

Small Isles Bay

29

Feolin Ferry

28 Craighouse

Port Askaig

Loch Finlaggan 27

26

Bridgend

21 Bowmore

A846

Islay

25 Kildalton Cross

Ardbeg

Port Ellen

24 The Oa

Mull of Oa

Kintra

Laggan Bay

Islay Woollen Mill

23 Kilnave

Ardnave Point

Nave Island

22 Port Charlotte

Loch Gorm

B8018

B8017

Rhinns of Islay

A847

Portnahaven

Port Wemyss

Loch Indaal

Lagg

Eigg

Sound of Islay

Kilchenzie

Campbeltown

Southend

Kilmory

A841

Machrie Moor Stone Circles **20**

Drumadoon Point

Blackwaterfoot

Lamlash

Holy Island

Isle Of Arran Heritage Museum 16

15 Brodick

Brodick Castle and Country Park 17

Arran

18

19

Catacol

Lochranza

Gigha Island

Tayinloan

B842

A83

Kintyre

ing 200 feet high. *A83, 12 mi east of Inveraray, ☎ 01499/600263.* ☞ *£1 adults, children free.* ☉ *Daily year-round.*

★ ❻ If neither the oysters nor the tall trees have diverted you, make a right at the A819/A83 junction for **Inveraray.** Note on the approaches to this little town the ornate 18th-century bridgework that carries the road along the lochside. This is the first sign that Inveraray is not just a higgledy-piggledy assembly of houses. In fact much of Inveraray was designed as a planned town for the third Duke of Argyll. The present Campbell duke's seat is **Inveraray Castle,** a grayish-green, turreted stone castle that can be seen through the trees on the right. Like Inveraray, the castle was built around 1743. Plenty of this powerful family's history can be seen on a tour. *½ mi north of Inveraray, ☎ 01499/302203.* ☞ *£3.50 adults, £2.50 senior citizens, £1.75 children, £9 family ticket.* ☉ *Apr.–June and Sept.–mid-Oct., Mon.–Thurs. and Sat. 10–1 and 2–5, Sun. 1–5; July and Aug., Mon.–Sat. 10–5, Sun. 1–5.*

The **Combined Operations Museum** sits nearby, a reminder that this sleepy place among the hills was an important wartime training area. *Cherry Park, ☎ 01499/500218.* ☞ *£1 adults, 80p senior citizens and children.* ☉ *Apr.–June and Sept.–mid-Oct., Mon.–Thurs., Sat. 10–5:30, Sun. 1–5:30; July and Aug., Mon.–Sat. 10–5:30, Sun. 1–5:30 (last admission 5).*

Other attractions include the **Inveraray Jail,** one of the latest generation of visitor centers. The old town jail and courtroom now house realistic courtroom scenes, period cells, and all the other paraphernalia that enable the visitor to glimpse life behind bars in Victorian times. *Inveraray, ☎ 01499/2381.* ☞ *£3.90 adults, £2.50 senior citizens, £2 children, £10.90 family ticket.* ☉ *Apr.–Oct., daily 9:30–6 (last admission 5); Nov.–Mar., daily 10–4 (last admission 3).*

Also in Inveraray is the **Arctic Penguin,** a 1911 lightship and a rare example of a riveted iron vessel. She now houses exhibits and displays on the maritime heritage of the River Clyde and Scotland's west coast. *☎ 01499/302213. Admission £2.85 adults, £1.65 children, £2 senior citizens, £7 family ticket.* ☉ *Apr.–Oct., daily 10–6; Nov.–Mar., daily 10–5.*

★ ❼ Continue along the loch southward beyond Inveraray to reach the **Auchindrain Museum.** Formally a communal tenancy farm, this 18th-century cooperative venture has been restored. The old thatched buildings provide information about early farming life in the Highlands. There is also an interpretation center and shop. *A83, 5½ mi south of Inveraray, ☎ 01499/500235.* ☞ *£2.50 adults, £2 senior citizens, £1.50 children, £7.50 family ticket.* ☉ *Apr.–Sept., daily 10–5 (closed Sat. in Apr.).*

★ ❽ Your next stop may be **Crarae Gardens,** farther south, which are occasionally likened to a wild valley in the Himalayas. Magnolias and azaleas give the area a moist and lush atmosphere, undoubtedly aided by the local rainfall. There are paths through the plantings to suit trekkers of every fitness level. *A83, 10 mi southwest of Inveraray, ☎ 01546/86614 or 01546/86388.* ☞ *£2.50 adults, £1.50 children, £7 family ticket.* ☉ *Daily 9–6 (or sunset if earlier); Visitor Centre open Easter–Oct.*

❾ **Lochgilphead,** the area's main town, is at its aesthetic best when the tide is in: **Loch Gilp,** really a bite out of Loch Fyne, reveals acres of mud at low tide. Where you go from here will depend on how much time you have. If, for example, you're spending only a day in the area, then follow the suggestion for a short looping tour, given here. If you have more time, you can go down Kintyre to take in the little island of Gigha (*see* Off the Beaten Track, *below*) or cross to Islay and Jura from Kennacraig, a short drive to the south.

⑩ Take the A816 Oban road north for 2 miles and turn left for the **Crinan Canal.** This waterway was opened in 1801 to enable fishing vessels to avoid the long haul around the south-stretching peninsula Kintyre and reach the Hebridean fishing grounds more easily. Shortly you will find yourself at the western end of the canal, where it drops to the sea in a series of lochs. This area can be a busy spot, with yachting enthusiasts strolling around and frequenting the coffee shop beside the Crinan Hotel.

⑪ To capture a glimpse of early Scottish history, return to the main road (A816), turn north, and look for a sign to **Dunadd** (4 mi north of Lochgilphead). If you follow the track to a rocky hump that rises out of the levels that lie around Crinan, you will find—by clambering up the rock—a basin, a footprint, and an outline of a boar carved on the smooth upper face of the knoll. This breezy refuge was once the capital of the early kingdom of Dalriada, founded by the first wave of Scots who migrated from Ireland. *West of A816, 4 mi northwest of Lochgilphead,* ☎ *0131/244–3101.* ☛ *Free.*

⑫ A little farther north sits **Carnasserie Castle,** a tower house with the peculiar distinction of having belonged to the writer of the first book printed in Gaelic. The writer was John Carswell, bishop of the Isles, who translated a text by the dour Scottish reformer John Knox into Gaelic and published it in 1567. *Off A816, 9 mi north of Lochgilphead,* ☎ *0131/244–3101.* ☛ *Free.*

TIME OUT The **Cuilfail Hotel** (☎ 01852/200274) at Kilmelford (A816), formerly a coaching inn, offers pleasant bar meals.

⑬ Before you reach Oban, one more side road may divert you. The B844 leads to the island of **Seil** via the Bridge over the Atlantic. This crossing is less spectacular than it sounds—the island is so close to the mainland that a single-span bridge, built in 1791, carries the road across. **⑭** From Seil, visitors are ferried to neighboring **Easdale Island.** Once Easdale and Seil were known as the slate islands: Extensive quarrying for roofing materials was undertaken on both isles.

Tour 2: Arran

Many Scots, especially those from Glasgow and the west, are well disposed toward **Arran,** which reminds them of unhurried childhood holidays. In fact, its cafés and boarding houses exude a 1950s mood, suggesting that this small isle has been caught in a time warp. Only a few decades ago the Clyde estuary was the coastal playground for the majority of the populace living in Glasgow and the Clydeside conurbation. Their annual holiday comprised a trip by steamer to any one of a number of Clyde coast resorts, known as going *doon the watter* (down the water, the estuary of the Clyde). Today the masses go to Spain, but, like other parts of the Clyde, the island of Arran has for a long time been associated with the healthy outdoor life.

To get to Arran, take the ferry from Androssan. During the ride, take a walk on deck and note the number of fellow travelers wearing walking boots. They're ready for the delights of **Goat Fell,** an impressive peak (2,868 ft) that gives the island one of the most distinctive profiles of any in Scotland.

⓯ In less than an hour from Ardrossan, the ferry arrives in **Brodick** with the cone of Goat Fell and its satellites serving as an eye-catching backdrop to the northwest. As you will have seen while crossing, the southern half of the island is less mountainous: The Highland Boundary Fault crosses just to the north of Brodick Bay.

Brodick, the largest township on the island, is really just a village, with a frontage spaciously set back from a promenade and beach. Head south (left) from the pier by the A841, a road that encircles the island and makes it difficult to get lost. A sign to Corriegills moments later indicates the first of many short walks. A walk to Corriegills offers fine views over Brodick Bay.

Beyond dense conifer woods the A841 drops suddenly into **Lamlash,** with views offshore to steep-flanked Holy Island. This entire area has a breezy seaside holiday atmosphere. To reach the highest point accessible by car on the island, go through the village and turn right beside the bridge. This is known as the **Ross Road.** It climbs steeply up a thickly planted valley, yielding fine views of Lamlash Bay.

The narrow road ends east of Sliddery with a return to the A841. Make a left by the church to reach nearby **Lagg.** This little community in a hollow beneath the sheltering trees sits peacefully by the banks of the Kilmory Water.

TIME OUT   The **Lagg Hotel** (☎ 01770/870255; closed Nov.–Feb.), an inn since 1791, is a warm place offering appetizing buffet lunches on Sunday, and excellent bar lunches and evening meals the rest of the week.

Continue east on the A841 along the bottom end of the island past white-painted farmhouses and cottages. There are views across gently tilting fields to the steep hump of **Ailsa Craig,** offshore in the Firth of Clyde. Cheese connoisseurs will be pleased to know the creamery at Torrylinn makes Arran Cheddar from local milk. Beyond Kildonan the road twists north; the trees extend to the sea edge, where gannets seem to dive through the branches. The route soon reaches **Whiting Bay,** a string of hotels and well-kept property along the seafront. From there return to Brodick; on the way back you will enjoy scenic mountain views over the conifer spikes.

⓰ Brodick is the site of the **Isle of Arran Heritage Museum,** which documents the life of the island from ancient times to the present century. A number of buildings, including a cottage and *smiddy* (blacksmith's), have period furnishings and displays on prehistoric life, geology, farming, fishing, and many other aspects of the island's heritage. *Rosaburn, Brodick,* ☎ *01770/302636.* ☛ *£1.50 adults, £1 senior citizens, 75p children, £4.50 family ticket.* ☼ *Apr.–Oct., Mon.–Sat. 10–5.*

Just beyond the museum is a junction where the String Road cuts across the island. Drive up the String Road a short way to find a signpost to the right, for Glen Rosa. The road soon becomes undrivable, but visitors can walk through a long glen that offers a glimpse of the wild ridges that call so many outdoor enthusiasts to the island.

★ **⓱** To find the island's most important draw for those other than the outdoor enthusiasts, return to the A841. **Brodick Castle and Country Park** is on the north side of Brodick Bay, its red sandstone cosseted by trees and parkland. Now under the auspices of the National Trust for Scotland, this former seat of the dukes of Hamilton has a number of rooms open to the public. The furniture, paintings, silver, and sporting trophies are opulent in their own right, but the real attraction is the brilliantly colored rhododendrons, particularly in late spring and early summer. Though there are many unusual species, you will find the ordinary deciduous yellow variety unmatched for its scent: Your initial encounter with them is comparable to hitting a wall of perfume. *1½ mi north of Brodick pier,* ☎ *01770/302202. Admission to castle, gardens, and park: £4 adults, £2 senior citizens and children; admission to gardens and park: £2 adults, £1 children. Castle open Easter–Sept., daily 11:30–5; early Oct., Sat. and Sun. 11:30–5 (last admission 4:30). Park and gardens open year-round, daily 9:30–sunset.*

TIME OUT An important feature of **Brodick Castle** is the award-winning restaurant (open Easter–Sept., daily 10–5; early Oct., weekends 10–5), offering visitors, who may have walked many acres plunging their noses into every blossom, a chance to quench their thirst. The fare includes morning coffee with hot scones, a full lunch menu that changes daily (venison or salmon might be available), and afternoon tea, with everything homebaked, including the bread.

Northward from Brodick the road is built along a raised beach platform, a phenomenon quite common in Scotland and caused by the lifting of the land after its burden of ice melted at the end of the Ice Age. Large, round boulders rest on softer sandstones in certain places on the shore. These stones, called *erratics,* were once carried by glaciers off the granite mountains that loom in the distance to your left as you approach **Corrie.** This brief string of settlements has stores that sell pottery and crafts items, another common find on the island.

Farther along, at **Sannox,** a locale consisting of another cluster of houses, there is a sandy bay of ground granite, washed down from the mountainous interior. There are also outstanding views of the rugged hills of the interior, particularly the steep pyramid of **Cir Mhor.** The road then climbs away from the coast, although there is a good coastal walk from North Sannox.

⑱ The road rejoins the coast at **Lochranza.** This attractively situated settlement is yet one more community that focuses on crafts. The sheltered bay of Loch Ranza, spilling in shallows up the flat-bottomed glacial glen, is set off by a picturesque ruin. Situated on a low sand spit, **Lochranza Castle** is said to have been the landing place of Robert the Bruce, who returned from Rathlin Island in 1307 to start the campaign that won Scotland's independence. ☎ *0131/244–3101.* ☛ *Free.* ☉ *Apr.–Sept., Mon.–Sat. 9:30–6, Sun. 2–6; Oct.–Mar., Mon.–Sat. 9:30–4, Sun. 2–4.*

Beyond Lochranza, the raised beach backed by a cliff continues to make a scenic platform for the road. There are fine views across the sound **⑲** to the long rolling horizon of Kintyre. At **Catacol,** immediately after the Catacol Bay Hotel, sit the **Twelve Apostles,** a row of fishermen's houses identical except for differences in the window shapes (so they can be recognized from offshore).

Near the scattered homesteads of **Machrie**—which has a popular **⑳** beach—look for a Historic Scotland sign to the **Machrie Moor Stone Circles.** The sign says the site is 1 mile farther, but on foot it feels a bit farther than that. A well-surfaced track will take you to a grassy moor by a ruined farm, where you will be able to see small rounded granite-boulder circles and much taller, eerie, red-sandstone monoliths. The Machrie area is littered with these sites: chambered cairns, hut circles, and standing stones dating from the Bronze Age.

Continuing to **Blackwaterfoot,** you can return to Brodick by the String Road, unless you want to drive the only part of the island not otherwise covered in the tour, the main road south as far as the Ross Road. If you decide to take the Ross Road, there are good views of Campbeltown Loch and the end of the Kintyre peninsula. Otherwise, to return to Brodick, turn left by the Kinloch Hotel, up the hill. There are more fine views of the granite complexities of Arran's hills: gray notched ridges beyond brown moor and, beyond the watershed, a vista of Brodick Bay. From this high point you roll down to Brodick, your starting point.

Tour 3: Islay and Jura

Islay

Islay has a personality distinct from that of the rest of the Hebrides. The western half, in particular, has large farms rather than crofts. A number of distilleries—the source of the island's delectable malt whiskies—provide jobs for the locals. Islay is also known for its wildlife, especially its birds, including the rare chough—a crow with red legs and beak—and, in winter, its barnacle geese.

(21) The town of **Bowmore** is compact and about the same size (population 1,000) as the ferry port of Port Ellen, but is perhaps slightly better suited as a base for touring. Bowmore, which gives its name to the whisky made in the distillery (founded 1779) by the shore, is a tidy town. Its grid pattern was laid out in 1768 by the local landowner Daniel Campbell of Shawfield. Bowmore's Main Street stretches from pierhead to the dominating parish church of 1767, built in an unusual circular design—so the devil could not find a corner to hide in. The town has a modest selection of accommodations and restaurants despite its small size.

TIME OUT   Rub elbows with the locals at the **Harbour Inn** (Main St., ☎ 01496/810330), with its cheerfully noisy and cramped public bar frequented by off-duty distillery workers who are happy to exchange island gossip. The excellent restaurant serves lunch 12–2, high tea 5–7, and dinner 7–9 (closed Sun.).

Many of Islay's best beaches—as well as wildlife and historical preserves—are in its western half, contrasting with the southeast area, which is mainly an extension of Jura's inhospitable quartzite hills. Take the A846 north out of Bowmore (signposted Bridgend) to the A847 in order to skirt the sand flats at the head of Loch Indaal. Follow the loch shores all the way to Bruichladdich, which, like Bowmore, is the name of a **(22)** malt whisky, as well as a village with a distillery. You will reach **Port Charlotte** a few minutes later. Above the road on the right, in a converted kirk, is the **Museum of Islay Life,** a haphazard but authentic and informative display of times past. ☎ 01496/850358. ☛ £1.20 adults, 60p children. ۞ Mar.–Oct., Mon.–Sat. 10–5, Sun. 2–5.

For further exploration continue on the A847 into the wilder landscape of the **Rhinns of Islay.** At the southern end are the scattered cottages of **Portnahaven** and its twin, **Port Wemyss.** You can return to Port Charlotte by the bleak unclassified road that loops westward and passes by the recumbent stone circle at Coultoon and the chapel at Kilchiaran before reaching Port Charlotte.

To get a glimpse of Islay's peerless western seascapes, make a left onto the B8018, north of Bruichladdich. After 2 miles turn left again onto a little road that meanders past Loch Gorm and ends close to **Machir**

Bay and its superb (and probably deserted) sandy beach. Soon after you turn around to go back, make a right, which will lead you to the derelict kirk of **Kilchoman.** In the kirkyard are some interesting grave slabs and two crosses of late-medieval date from the Iona school of carving, an excellent introduction to the island's wealth of stone carvings. (There was another Scottish "school" in Kintyre.) From Kilchoman turn right and then left to circle Loch Gorm, pausing as the road all but touches the coast at Saligo. It's worth a stroll beyond the former wartime camp to enjoy the view of some fine seascapes, especially if the westerlies are piling up high breakers on the rock ridges.

On the return journey east, turn right at the B8018, then left on the B8017. Take a left at Aoradh Farm onto a minor road that runs north along the west side of Loch Gruinart. The road soon brings you to **Kilnave** (Cill Naoimh on local maps). Kilnave's ruined chapel is associated with a dark tale in which a group of wounded Maclean clansmen were defeated in a nearby battle with the MacDonalds in 1598. The Macleans sought sanctuary in the chapel; their pursuers set its roof aflame, and the clansmen perished within. In the graveyard is a weathered, 8th-century carved cross.

Visitors are inevitably drawn to viewing the long reaches of **Loch Gruinart.** Dunes flank its sea outlet, and pale beaches rise out of the falling tides. For the best view return to the B8017, cross the flats at the head of the loch, and then go left and up its eastern shore. Park before a gate, where the road deteriorates. Those who appreciate wide skies, crashing waves, and lonely coast should continue on foot, possibly around the headland held together with marram grass. From the far dunes there are views of Colonsay and Oronsay across Hebridean waters, on which plumes and fans of white spray rise from hidden reefs. The priory on the island of Oronsay, with its famous carved cross, is barely distinguishable.

To discover what the south of the island has to offer, take the long straight of the A846 that passes the island airport just inland from the endless sandy curve of Laggan Bay. Before you reach Port Ellen, go straight ahead to a minor road to Imeraval, then make a right at a junction and then a left. This takes you to the southern peninsula of **The Oa,** a region of caves rich in tales of smuggling. Visitors to The Oa usually go as far as the Mull of Oa, the tip, where there is a monument recalling the 650 men who lost their lives when the troopships *Tuscania* and *Otranto* went down nearby in 1918.

Port Ellen is a sturdy community, founded in the 1820s, with much of its architecture still dating from the 19th century. It has a harbor, a few shops, and some inns, but not enough commercial development to mortgage its personality. The A846 continues eastward, passing more names known to the malt-whisky connoisseur: the whisky of the **Laphroaig distillery**—which offers tours—is perhaps one of the most distinctive of the local whiskies, with a tangy, peaty, seaweed/iodine flavor. *1½ mi along road to Ardbeg from Port Ellen,* ☎ *01496/302418 or 01496/302393. Tours by appointment.*

After Ardbeg the A846 becomes narrower and passes through a pleasantly rolling, partly wooded landscape. The reason for taking this route east is not to take a scenic tour of distillery premises, but to see the finest carved cross anywhere in Scotland: the 8th-century **Kildalton Cross.** Carved from a single slab of epidiorite rock, this ringed cross is encrusted on both sides with elaborate designs in the style of the Iona school. Interesting early grave slabs from the 12th and 13th centuries can also be seen in the yard around the chapel, which stands down a lonely side road, signposted from Ardbeg. From Kildalton retrace your route to Bowmore.

From Bowmore take the A846 north (following signs for Port Askaig) through Bridgend. Hardly a mile beyond, you will see a sign for the ★ 26 **Islay Woollen Mill.** Set in a wooded hollow by the river, the mill has a shop selling high-quality products that are woven on site. There is also a fascinating selection of working machinery to inspect.

If time permits, before reaching Port Askaig (a fairly frequent ferry service runs from here to Jura), you may wish to explore a side road (to 27 the left) a mile beyond Ballygrant. To get to **Loch Finlaggan,** make a left and then drive through a gate. At first sight, there is not a great deal to see. But the little island on the loch, with its scanty and overgrown traces of early buildings, was the council seat of the Lords of the Isles. This former western power base of the Clan Donald threatened the sovereignty of the Stuart monarchs of Scotland in its heyday: a reminder of how independent the Highlands were in those times. A cottage interpretative center is located nearby, with an exhibition relating to the ongoing excavations of the island ruins. ☎ 01496/840644. *Small admission charge.* ☉ *Apr.–Sept., Sun., Tues., and Thurs. 2:30–5.*

Return to the main road (A846) and continue driving northeast. Note that just beyond Keills is another side road that will take you for a pleasant ride along the coast until you come to a turning space and parking lot at the **Bunnahabhain Distillery,** which sits on an attractive shore site (☎ 01496/840646, visits by appointment). There are impressive views of Jura on the way. Then retrace the route to the main road, going left then steeply downhill to the tiny ferry community by the pier.

Jura

Although it is possible to meet an Islay native in a local pub, such an event is statistically less likely on **Jura,** with its one road, one distillery, one hotel, and six sporting estates. In fact, visitors have a better chance of bumping into one of the island's 5,000 red deer, which outnumber the human population by at least 20 to one. The island has a much more rugged look than Islay, with its profiles of the Paps of Jura, a hill range at its most impressive when basking in the rays of a west-coast sunset.

Having crossed the Sound of Islay by ferry from Port Askaig (it takes just a few minutes), explorers will find it easy to choose which road to take—Jura only has one. Apart from the initial stretch it is all single-lane. The A846 starts off below one of the many raised beaches then climbs across poor moorland, providing scenic views across the Sound of Jura. Look for the standing stone, right, then note the ruined **Claig Castle** on an island just offshore. The Lords of the Isles built it to control the sound. Beyond the farm buildings of Ardfin, you reach **Jura House** in the woodlands, with its sheltered garden walks and fine views. ☎ 01496/820315. *Admission to gardens: £2 adults, £1 students, under 16 free.* ☉ *Daily 9–5.*

28 Beyond Jura House the road turns northward for **Craighouse,** across open moorland with scattered forestry blocks and the faint evidence, in the shape of parallel ridges, of the original inhabitants' lazy beds or strip cultivation. The original settlements were cleared with the other parts of the Highlands when the island became more of a sheep pasture and deer forest. The road soon drops down to the community of Craighouse, home to the island's only distillery.

TIME OUT The **Jura Hotel** (☎ 01496/820243), in spite of its monopoly, genuinely welcomes its guests and can be relied on for high-quality accommodations and food.

㉙ The aptly named **Small Isles Bay** has a superb strip of beach to the north of Craighouse. As the road climbs away from the bay, the little cottage above the burn is a reminder of the history of this island: The cottage is the only survivor of a village with a population of 56 that was destroyed in 1841. Ironically, a sheep *fank* (fold) farther up the burn shows what happened to the stones of the demolished cottages. Although the landscapes of Jura seem devoid of life, they are in fact populated with many ghosts, most of which are missed by the casual visitor.

Beyond the River Corran the road climbs, offering austere views of the Paps, with their long quartzite screes and of the fine, though usually deserted, anchorage in the scoop of Lowlandman's Bay. The next section of road is more hemmed in and runs to **Lagg,** formerly a ferry-crossing point on the old cattle-driving road between here and Feolin. Beyond Lagg, the sea views are blocked by conifer plantings. Views of fjordlike **Loch Tarbert,** westward to the left, are at their best beside the forestry plantation a little farther on. At this point the road leads through a stretch of rough, uninhabited landscape. A gate and cattle grid by **Ardlussa** to the north mark the start of a Site of Special Scientific Interest in a shady oakwood. The coast here is rocky and unspoiled. Choose your own picnic site, but be sure to park sensibly. Yellow flag (a Scottish iris), bracken, strands of crisp seaweed on the salty grass, and background birdsong from the mossy woods make this an idyllic stretch when the sun shines. Try not to be too loud, so you won't distract the area's resident otter population.

The last house you will see is at **Lealt,** where you cross the river. Only a little way beyond this point the tarmac ends, rather abruptly, with a turning space paved into the hill. Ordinary cars should not attempt to go any farther on the remainder of this trail, though jeeps, rovers, and other high-clearance vehicles can make it through. The track beyond the surfaced road continues for another 5 miles to **Kinuachdrach,** a settlement that once served as a crossing point to Scarba and the mainland. The coastal footpath to Corryvreckan lies beyond, over the bare moors. This area has two enticements: The first, for fans of George Orwell, is the house of **Barnhill,** where the author wrote *1984;* the second, for wilderness enthusiasts, is the whirlpool of the **Corryvreckan** and the unspoiled coastal scenery.

To return to the ferry that will take you to Islay, you have no choice but to retrace your route.

Tour 4: The Isle of Mull

It's possible to spend a long weekend on Mull and not meet a single resident who was born north of Manchester, England. Though Mull certainly has an indigenous population, the island is often referred to as the Officers' Mess because of its popularity with retired military men. It has a thriving tourist industry, with several thousand visitors per year making their way across the Ross of Mull to Iona, cradle of Scottish Christianity and ancient burial site of the kings of Scotland.

㉚ Most visitors arrive at **Craignure** by way of Oban, but you should also consider the short ferry crossing from Lochaline on a beautiful part of the mainland to **Fishnish,** a little west of Craignure. This summer-only service is first-come, first-served.

★ ㉛ Either ferry will leave you close to Mull's two best-known castles, **Torosay** and **Duart. Torosay Castle** is probably more fun. It also has the novelty of a steam-and-diesel service on a narrow-gauge railway, which takes 20 minutes to run from the pier at Craignure to Torosay's grounds. Scottish baronial in style, Torosay has a friendly air. Visitors have the run of much of the house, which is full of intrigue and humor by way of idiosyncratic information boards and informal family albums. The main feature of the castle's gardens—a gentle blend of formal and informal—is its Italian statue walk. *A849, 1½ mi southeast of Craignure,* ☎ *01680/812421. Admission to castle and gardens: £3.50 adults, £1.50 children, £2.75 students and senior citizens; admission to gardens: £1.50 adults, £1 senior citizens, children, and students. Castle open Easter and mid-Apr.–mid-Oct., daily 10:30–5:30 (last admission 5 PM); gardens open summer, daily 9–7; winter, daily sunrise–sunset.*

㉜ The energetic can walk along the shore from Torosay to **Duart Castle;** if you're driving use the A849. This ancient Maclean seat was ruined by the Campbells in 1691 but bought and restored by Sir Fitzroy Maclean in 1911. *Off A849,* ☎ *01680/812309.* ☛ *£3 adults, £2 senior citizens, £1.50 children, £7.50 family ticket.* ☉ *May–mid-Oct., daily 10:30–6.*

Beyond Duart Castle the double-lane road narrows as it continues southwest, touched by sea inlets at Lochs Don and Spelve. Gray and green are the most prevalent colors of the interior, with vivid grass and high rock faces in Glen More. These stepped rock faces, the by-product of ㉝ ancient lava flows, reach their highest point in **Ben More,** the only island *munro* outside Skye. (A munro is a Scottish mountain over 3,000 ft high.) Its high, bald slopes are prominent by the time you reach the road junction at the head of Loch Scridain. Stay on the A849 for a pleasant drive the length of the **Ross of Mull,** a wide promontory with scattered settlements. Look to the right for good views of the dramatic cliff ramparts of Ardmeanach, the stubbier promontory to the north. The National Trust for Scotland cares for the rugged stretch of coast known ㉞ as the **Burg,** which is home to a 40 million-year-old fossil tree (at the end of a long walk from the B8035, signposted left off the A849).

The well-used A849 continues through the village of **Bunessan** and eventually ends in a long car-park opposite the houses of **Fionnphort.** The vast parking space is made necessary by the popularity of the nearby ★ ㉟ island of **Iona,** to which visitors cannot bring cars. Ferry service is frequent in summer months.

The fiery and argumentative Irish monk Columba chose Iona for the site of a monastery in AD 563 because it was the first place he landed from which he could not see Ireland. Christianity had been brought to Scotland (Galloway) by Saint Ninian in 397, but until Saint Columba's church was founded, the word had not spread widely among the ancient northerners, called Picts. Iona was the burial place of the kings of Scotland until the 11th century. It survived repeated Norse sackings and finally fell into disuse around the time of the Reformation. Restoration work began at the turn of this century, and later, in 1938, the **Iona Community** was founded. Today the restored buildings serve as a spiritual center under the jurisdiction of the Church of Scotland. The ambience of the complex is a curious amalgam of the ancient and the earnest. But beyond the restored cloisters the most mystifying aspect of all is the island's ability to absorb visitors and still feel peaceful—a phenomenon often remarked upon by tourists; most folk only make the short walk from the ferry pier by way of the nunnery to the abbey. ☎ *01681/700404. Abbey gift and bookshop open Mon.–Sat. 10–5, Sun.*

noon–4; abbey coffeehouse open Apr.–Oct., Mon.–Thurs. and Sat. 11–4:30, Fri. and Sun. noon–4:30.

On your return to Mull retrace your route eastward and look for a sign on the right to Carsaig as you approach the head of Loch Scridain. This route takes you to the remote south coast. From the pierhead at the tiny settlement a rough path meanders west below lava cliffs to the impressive **Carsaig Arches.** Taking on the arches is a separate excursion reserved for the agile.

36

After your foray to the arches take the B8035 at Loch Scridain. The road rises away from the loch to the conifer plantations and green slopes of **Gleann Seilisdeir.** The main road through the glen breaches the stepped cliffs and drops to the shore, offering inspiring views of the island of Ulva guarding Loch na Keil. This stretch of the B8035, with splinters of rock from the heights strewn over it in places, feels remote. The high ledges eventually give way (not literally) to vistas of the screes of Ben More.

Continue to skirt the coast by way of the B8073, and you will enjoy a succession of fine coastal views with Ulva in the foreground. Beyond Calgary Bay the landscape is gentler, as the road leads to the village of **Dervaig.** Just before Dervaig the **Old Byre** is signposted. An audiovisual presentation on the history of Mull plays here. *Every hr on the half-hr, £2 adults, £1.50 senior citizens and students, £1 children.*

37

TIME OUT The wholesome catering at the restaurant at the **Old Byre** heritage center (signposted just before Dervaig, ☎ 01688/400229) certainly will be appreciated by weary travelers, particularly those who enjoy thick and hearty homemade soups. The restaurant is open Easter–Oct., daily 10:30–6:30 (last admission 6).

In Dervaig the Mull Little Theatre (*see* The Arts and Nightlife, *below*) offers a varied program and claims the record as the smallest professional theater in the United Kingdom. After the small town the road leads through woodlands to **Tobermory.** Founded as a fishing station, this community gradually declined, hastened by the arrival of the railroad station at Oban, which took away fishing traffic. However, the brightly painted crescent of 18th-century buildings gives Tobermory a Mediterranean look.

38

To return to the ferry, make your way southward on the A848, which yields pleasant, though unspectacular, views across to Morvern on the mainland. On the coast just beyond **Aros,** look back and across the river flats for a view of the ruined 13th-century **Aros Castle.** Continue through Salen to either Fishnish for Morven or Craignure for Oban.

What to See and Do with Children

The Argyll Wildlife Park has 60 acres with extensive collections of wildfowl and other Scottish wildlife. *Dalchenna, Inveraray on A83,* ☎ *01499/302284.* ☛ *£3.75 adults, £1.50 children, £3 senior citizens.* ☉ *Daily 9:30–dusk. (Tearoom open Apr.–Oct.)*

Auchindrain Old Farming Township (*see* Tour 1)

Cruachan Dam Power Visitor Centre and Tour (*see* Tour 1)

Ganavan Sands Leisure Centre (☎ 01631/564100) has sandy beaches, an outdoor play area, a boating pool, and donkey rides. To get there, follow the road from the center of Oban, where the promenade starts.

Inveraray Jail (*see* Tour 1)

Lady Rowena Steam Launch is an Edwardian peat-fired steamboat that cruises Loch Awe from BR station pier at Lochawe on A85. ☎ *01838/ 200440 or 01838/200449.* ☛ *£3.75 adults, £3 senior citizens, £2 children, £10 family ticket. Reservations can be made on the spot or in advance.*

Mull and West Highland Narrow Gauge Railway (*see* Tour 4)

The Sea Life Centre displays native marine life in a spacious aquarium. One of the most entertaining places in Argyll, the center also has a shop and a café. *On the A828, Barcaldine, 11 mi north of Oban,* ☎ *01631/ 72386.* ☛ *£4.35 adults, £3.25 senior citizens, £2.95 children.* ☉ *Mar.–June and Sept.–Nov., daily 9–6; July and Aug., daily 9–7; Dec.–Feb., weekends 9–5. Call to check opening hours in winter season.*

A World in Miniature displays hand-crafted miniature rooms and furniture made to a ½th scale. *North pier, Oban,* ☎ *01852/316272 or 01631/566300.* ☛ *£1.50 adults, £1 senior citizens and children, £4 family ticket.* ☉ *Easter–Oct., Mon.–Sat. 10–5, Sun. 2–5.*

Off the Beaten Path

Castle Sween, the oldest stone castle on the Scottish mainland (12th century), sits in a rocky sea-edge setting 15 miles southwest of Lochgilphead. The castle is reached by an unclassified road from Crinan yielding outstanding views of the Paps of Jura across the sound. There are also some attractive white sand beaches here.

Duncan Ban Macintyre Monument (Monument Hill) was erected in honor of the Gaelic poet Duncan Ban Macintyre (1724–1812), sometimes referred to as the Robert Burns of the Highlands. The monument is not far from the village of Dalmally, just east of the top end of Loch Awe in Argyll. From there, follow an old road running southwest toward the banks of Loch Awe. At the road's highest point, often called Monument Hill, the round, granite monument can be seen. The view from here is one of the finest in Argyll, taking in Ben Cruachan and the other peaks nearby, as well as Loch Awe and its scattering of islands.

Island of Gigha is a delectable Hebridean island, barely 5 miles long, sheltered in a frost-free, sea-warmed climate between Kintyre and Islay. The isle is noted for the **Achamore House Gardens.** It is possible to take the ferry (a 20-minute trip), walk to the gardens, and return to the mainland, all on a short day-trip, but there are good accommodations on the island. ☎ *01583/505254. Admission to gardens: £2 adults, £1 children.* ☉ *Daily 10–dusk.*

Famous in song, the **Mull of Kintyre** is, in reality, a road to the lighthouse beyond Campbeltown at the tip of Kintyre. The narrow road crosses moors and sheep pastures. There is a parking place before the road suddenly dips to reach the lighthouse tower, placed well down the steep slope that tilts toward the sea. Do not go down the hill; the best sunset views are from the adjacent moors, from which you can see Ireland quite clearly.

SHOPPING

The lure of great shopping is not what attracts visitors to this predominantly rural area, although the day-to-day needs of the local population are well cared for. Nonetheless, there are several interesting crafts outlets; the islands, in particular, offer many opportunities to sample and purchase fine island whiskies. Starting in **Oban,** the **Oban Glass**

Studio (part of Caithness Glass, Heritage Wharf, ☎ 01631/563386) offers self-guided factory tours (weekdays) and a well-stocked factory shop.

Also worth a visit is the **Highbank Porcelain Pottery** (Highbank Industrial Estate, Lochgilphead, ☎ 01546/602044), where visitors can watch slip casting, hand painting, and firing. Highbank also has a shop that sells pottery animals (including reasonably priced seconds).

East of Oban, in Taynuilt, stop at **Inverawe Fisheries and Smokery** (☎ 01866/822446; smokery open mid-Mar.–Dec., weekdays 8:30–4; shop open daily 8–6:30; call ahead in winter). The smoked salmon and other fish produced and served on the premises are impractical to take home (at least abroad), but they make a delicious picnic.

Also recommended are the products of **Loch Fyne Oysters** (Clachan Farm, on the A83, ☎ 01499/600264). You can sample them in the oyster bar, which serves all types of seafood and game products, before buying them in the adjacent Seafood Shop.

Farther down the A83, at Inveraray, you can buy Scottish crafts at the shop within **Inveraray Jail** (*see* Tour 1 in Exploring Argyll and the Isles, *above*). Campbeltown is the center for local shopping requirements on the Kintyre peninsula; here you will find **Oystercatcher Crafts and Gallery** (10 Hall St. and 2–4 Main St., ☎ 01586/553070), with original paintings, woodcarvings, and knitwear.

A few miles north, at Carradale, is **Wallis Hunter Design** (The Steading, ☎ 01583/431683), which makes gold and silver jewelry. Clachan is the home of **Ronachan Silks** (Ronachan Farmhouse, ☎ 01880/740242), which produces distinctive jewel-color scarves, cushion covers, and clothing.

On Islay you'll be spoiled by the sheer number of distilleries from which to choose. Most of them welcome visitors by appointment: **Caol Ila** (Port Askaig, ☎ 01496/840207), **Bunnahabhain** (Port Askaig, ☎ 01496/840646), **Isle of Jura** (Craighouse, Jura, ☎ 01496/820240), **Laphroaig** (Port Ellen, ☎ 01496/302418), **Bowmore** (School St., Bowmore, ☎ 01496/810441), and **Lagavoulin** (Port Ellen, ☎ 01496/302250). Their delicious products, characterized by a peaty taste, can be purchased at off-license shops on the island, at local pubs, or at those distilleries that have shops. **The Islay Woollen Mill** (Bridgend, ☎ 01496/810563) is also worth a visit, not only for its shop, but for its mill tour. Beside the usual tweed lengths, the mill has a distinctive range of hats, caps, and clothing made from its own cloth.

Arran's shops are particularly well stocked with island-produced goods. **Something Special** (The Pier, Brodick, ☎ 01770/302831), stocks soaps, creams, and other beauty products made on the island from natural ingredients. **Patterson Arran Ltd.** (The Old Mill, Lamlash, ☎ 01770/600606) is famous for its mustards, preserves, and marmalades. **Crafts of Arran** (Whiting Bay, ☎ 01770/700251) prides itself on stocking craftwork produced in Arran. **Corriecraft and Antiques** (Corrie, ☎ 01770/810661) sells craftwork (though it may come from different parts of Scotland), together with a carefully chosen mix of small antiques and curios. At Machrie (near the stone circles at Machrie Moor) shoppers frequent the **Old Byre Showroom** (Auchencar Farm, ☎ 01770/840227), which sells sheepskin goods, locally hand-knit "jumpers" (sweaters), leather goods, and tweeds.

The tiny island of Iona has one or two pleasant surprises for shoppers, the biggest being **The Old Printing Press Bookshop** (St. Columba Hotel, ☎ 01681/700304), an excellent antiquarian and secondhand bookshop.

The shop at the **Abbey** (☎ 01681/700404) is also worth a visit for its selection of Celtic-inspired gift items.

Near Dervaig, on the island of Mull, do not miss the **Old Byre Heritage Centre's craft shop** (signposted before Dervaig, ☎ 01688/400229), nor the restaurant with delicious home baking. The shop's inventory is definitely more extensive than most and includes locally made, as well as other Scottish-produced items.

SPORTS AND FITNESS

Bicycling

As a popular holiday destination and a ferry gateway, Oban gets a lot of traffic. Main routes to and from town are busy, and there are few side roads. Island roads may be single-track, so wear high-visibility clothing, especially in the busy summer months, and be *sure* to bring rain gear. Bicycles can be rented from **Tortoise Cycle Centre** (c/o Highland Stores, 152–156 Argyll St., Dunoon, ☎ 01369/5959), **Pedal Power** (Tobermory, ☎ 01688/302226), and **On Yer Bike** (Salen, ☎ 01680/300501), both on Mull, and **Oban Cycles** (9 Craigard Rd., Oban, ☎ 01631/566996). Arran is a popular island for cycling, with a large number of bicycle-rental shops, including **Brodick Boat and Cycle Hire** (The Beach, Brodick, ☎ 01770/302388), **Spinning Wheels** (The Trossachs, Corrie, ☎ 01770/810640), **Whiting Bay Cycle Hire** (☎ 01770/700382), and **Brodick Cycles** (Roselynn, Brodick, ☎ 01770/302460). In Rothesay, try **Calder Brothers** (7 Bridge St., Rothesay, Isle of Bute, ☎ 01700/504477).

Fishing

Local tourist information centers (*see* Important Addresses and Numbers in Argyll and the Isles Essentials, *below*) provide information. Local fishing literature identifies at least 50 fishing sites on lochs and rivers for game fishing and at least 20 coastal settlements suited for sea angling.

Golf

The area has about two dozen golf courses; notably scenic examples are the outstanding courses on Bute, as well as the fine coastal links, of which **Machrihanish** near Campbeltown is the most famous (☎ 01586/810213; 18 holes, 6,228 yards, SSS 70). The local tourist information centers can provide detailed leaflets.

Pony Trekking

Explorers can take off from riding outlets on the mainland and on the islands: **Ballivicar Pony Trekking** (Ballivicar Farm, Port Ellen, Islay, ☎ 01496/302251), **Castle Riding Centre and Argyll Trail Riding** (Brenfield, Ardrishaig, Argyll, ☎ 01546/603274), **Cairnhouse Riding Centre** (Blackwaterfoot, Arran, ☎ 01770/860466), **Cloyburn Trekking Centre** (Brodick, Arran, ☎ 01770/302108), and **Lettershuna Riding Centre** (Appin, Argyll, ☎ 01631/73227).

Water Sports

The assortment of sea, island, and sea-loch make this a popular area for a variety of water sports. Local operators include **Linnhe Marine Watersports Centre** (Lettershuna, Appin, Argyll, ☎ 01631/73227), though generally people bring their own equipment.

DINING AND LODGING

Dining

This part of Scotland is not usually considered a great gastronomic center; it has only a few restaurants of distinction. Still, the ingredients used in dishes are of good quality and are locally produced: Fish, fresh from the sparkling lochs and sea, could hardly be better. Beef, lamb, and game are also common. In the rural districts, your best bet is to choose a hotel or guest house that can provide a decent evening meal as well as breakfast.

WHAT TO WEAR
This is a relaxed area in terms of dress. Upscale hotel restaurants expect a smarter standard of dress—no T-shirts or shorts.

CATEGORY	COST*
$$$$	over £40
$$$	£30–£40
$$	£15–£30
$	under £15

per person for a three-course meal, including VAT and excluding drinks and service

Lodging

Accommodations in Argyll and the Isles range from châteaulike hotels to modest inns. The traditional provincial hotels and small coastal resorts have been modernized and equipped with all the necessary comforts, yet they retain their sense of personalized service and the charm that comes with older buildings. Away from these areas, however, your choices are more restricted, and your best overnight option, with some exceptions, is usually a modest guest house offering bed, breakfast, and an evening meal.

CATEGORY	COST*
$$$$	over £110
$$$	£80–£110
$$	£45–£80
$	under £45

All prices are for a standard double room, including service, breakfast, and VAT.

Aros

LODGING
$–$$ Kentallen Farm. This traditional stone farmhouse on a working farm serves as a high-standard bed-and-breakfast. Its unelaborate rooms with en suite facilities are a good value. Wonderful views across the Sound of Mull toward Ardnamurchan are a bonus. ⌖ *Aros, Isle of Mull,* ☎ *and fax 01680/300427. 3 rooms with bath. No credit cards.*

Ballygrant

LODGING
$$ Kilmeny Farmhouse. There are fine views over the surrounding countryside from this white-painted traditional farmhouse, also on a working farm. It offers bed-and-breakfast accommodations with evening meal if desired. Home baking and homemade preserves make breakfast special. ⌖ *Ballygrant, Isle of Islay PA45 7QW,* ☎ *01496/840668. 3 rooms with bath and shower. No credit cards.*

Brodick

DINING AND LODGING

$$–$$$ **Kilmichael Country House Hotel.** At the head of Glen Cloy, just out-
★   side of Brodick, is this 300-year-old mansion, built by the Fullerton
family on land granted to them by Robert the Bruce. Now an outstanding
small hotel, it is furnished in Georgian oak antiques, Sanderson fabrics, and light, sunny colors. At one end of the blue-and-yellow sitting
room, in what was once a private chapel, is a stained-glass window
showing the Fullerton family crest. Cuisine in the hotel's restaurant is
also exceptional: Salmon en croute with dill sauce, duck with kumquats,
and salad of pigeon with walnuts and smoked bacon are examples of
the marriage of fresh Scottish produce and international flair. ☎ *Brodick, Isle of Arran, KA27 8BY, ☎ 01770/302219. 8 rooms with bath.
Restaurant (reservations required, jacket and tie). V.*

Connel

LODGING

$ **Ronebhal Guest House.** Loch Etive and the mountains beyond can be
★   seen from this stone house near the busy town of Oban. Although
Connel is on the main road, Ronebhal is set back within its own
grounds. It offers bed-and-breakfast accommodation in spacious surroundings. ☎ *Connel, Argyll PA37 1PJ, ☎ 01631/71310. 6 rooms, 4
with shower. MC, V.*

Crinan

DINING AND LODGING

$$–$$$$ **Crinan Hotel.** This turn-of-the-century property overlooking the pic-
turesque Crinan Canal and the Sound of Jura has been extensively re-
furbished. The friendly and helpful present owner is an interior
decorator—hence the high standard of each room's decor. All are in-
dividually decorated with pine or oak furniture and soft pastel floral
fabrics and wallpapers. The hotel has two restaurants: **The Westward
Room** serves Scottish cuisine in a luxurious, country-mansion setting,
where you are surrounded by antiques and floral arrangements; the
rooftop **Lock 16** has a nautical theme, and superb sunsets accompany
the award-winning fresh seafood. ☎ *Crinan, near Lochgilphead (20
mi south of Oban on A816), Argyll, PA31 8SR, ☎ 0154683/261, FAX
0154683/292. 22 rooms with bath. 2 restaurants (reservations re-
quired; jacket and tie at Lock 16), coffee shop, sea fishing, boat trips.
AE, DC, MC, V. Lock 16 closed Sun., Mon.*

Dervaig

DINING AND LODGING

$–$$ **Druimard Country House.** From this attractive Victorian house on the
outskirts of the village, there are loch and glen views over the River
Bellart. The restaurant is elegantly furnished and offers an original menu
with several vegetarian options. Local prawns sautéed with mushrooms in a wine-and-cream sauce and Argyll lamb with red-wine-and-
rosemary sauce and apricot chutney tartlets are two popular dishes.
Rooms are individually decorated with Laura Ashley wallpapers and
fabrics and antique Victorian oak or mahogany furniture. Bed-and-breakfast accommodations are available. ☎ *Dervaig, Isle of Mull, Argyll,
☎ 01688/400345, FAX 01688/400291. 6 rooms, 4 with bath. Restaurant (reservations advised). MC, V. Closed Nov.–Mar.*

Dunoon

DINING AND LODGING

$$–$$$ **Ardfillayne Hotel.** Sixteen acres of wooded garden surround this 150-year-old mansion. The decor is Victorian in inspiration. Rooms have antique oak or mahogany furniture and striped or floral wallpaper. The owners clearly enjoy looking after their guests. The food is French, with a Taste of Scotland mixed in—local seafood, marinated and roasted venison, and smoked chicken on a bed of salad leaves are among the offerings. ⌸ *West Bay (3 mi west of Gourock across Firth of Clyde, Dunoon, Argyll) PA23 7QJ,* ☎ *01369/702267,* ℻ *01369/702501. 7 rooms with bath. Restaurant (reservations advised). AE, DC, MC, V.*

LODGING

$$ **Abbot's Brae.** This sizeable Victorian bed-and-breakfast is set in woodland but has sea and hill views. Its bedrooms are furnished to luxury-hotel standard, but its rates are still low. Three of the rooms have bay windows overlooking the sea. You can choose to eat dinner here; meals are prepared using fresh local ingredients in a straightforward style, and there's a carefully chosen wine list. Try the rack of local lamb with rosemary or the poached salmon. ⌸ *West Bay, Dunoon, Argyll PA23 7QJ,* ☎ *and fax 01369/705021. 4 rooms with bath, 3 with shower. DC, MC, V.*

Kentallen

DINING AND LODGING

$$$ **Holly Tree.** Railway buffs should enjoy this converted Edwardian rail-
★ way station, complete with some of its original fixtures and fittings, which have been carefully extended over the onetime platform to create a spacious restaurant. You may see seals in Loch Linnhe from your dinner table, along with memorable sunsets over the Ardgour mountains. The hotel's bedrooms are elegantly yet comfortably furnished—thick carpets, easy chairs, and good mattresses. The restaurant often has salmon, prawns, and venison on the menu; the homemade sorbets and ice creams are a delicious end to the meal. *Kentallen, Appin, Argyll,* ☎ *01631/740292,* ℻ *01631/740345. 10 rooms with bath or shower. Restaurant (reservations advised). AE, MC, V.*

Kilchrenan

DINING AND LODGING

$$$$ **Ardanaiseig House.** Set on the shores of Loch Awe and framed by rhodo-
★ dendron blossoms in May and June (the gardens are famous), this excellent, privately run hotel is worth the extra cost, especially when the rhododendrons are blooming. All the bedrooms, which vary in size, have been decorated individually in traditional style, and the public rooms, with an abundance of chintz and polished wood, are just as comfortable. The food more than matches the decor, featuring five imaginative courses prepared with local ingredients; home-smoked scallops, fresh fruit from the garden, pickled salmon, and wood pigeon are among the choices. ⌸ *Kilchrenan, near Taynuilt, Argyll,* ☎ *018663/333,* ℻ *018663/222. 14 rooms with bath. AE, DC, MC, V. Closed Oct.–mid-Apr.*

Kilmore

LODGING

$$$$ **Glenfeochan House.** This family-run Victorian mansion stands on 350-acre grounds and has tastefully decorated rooms with antique furniture and original plasterwork. The owner, once a teacher at the Cordon Bleu School in London, serves a home-cooked, four-course dinner to his lucky guests, using only local, fresh, seasonal ingredients—most of the produce comes from the walled garden on the estate, the venison comes from the island of Jura, and shellfish from local fishermen. *Kilmore (5 mi south of Oban on A816), Argyll, PA34 4QR, ☎ 01631/770273, ℻ 01631/770624. 3 rooms with bath. Restaurant, fishing. MC, V. Closed Nov.–Mar.*

Oban

DINING AND LODGING

$$$$ **Manor House Hotel.** Once the home of the Duke of Argyll, this 1780 stone house on the shore just outside Oban is now a hotel with great views of the sea. It's within easy walking distance of downtown Oban and the bus, train, and ferry terminals. The reception and public areas are furnished with many genuine antiques, and the bedrooms, with reproductions. Bed coverings and curtains are made of textured fabrics in warm colors such as gold, pink, and yellow. The restaurant serves both Scottish and French dishes, including lots of local seafood and game in season, complemented by a carefully chosen wine list. Dinner is included in the room rate. ☒ *Gallanach Rd., Oban, Argyll PA34 4LS, ☎ 01631/562087, ℻ 01631/563053. 11 rooms with bath. Restaurant (reservations advised, jacket and tie). MC, V. ☯ Feb.–Dec.*

LODGING

$–$$ **Kilchrenan House.** A fully refurbished Victorian house only a few minutes' walk from the town center, Kilchrenan offers high-grade bed-and-breakfast in rooms with views out to sea and to the islands. ☒ *Corran Esplanade, Oban, Argyll PA34 5AQ, ☎ and fax 01631/562663. 8 rooms with bath, 2 with shower. MC, V. Closed Nov.–Mar.*

$ **Dungrianach.** This aptly named bed-and-breakfast ("the sunny house on the hill") is set in woodland with superb views of the ocean and islands, yet it is only a few minutes walk from Oban's ferry piers and town center. All rooms in this late Victorian house have private facilities and are decorated with handsome period furniture. ☒ *Pulpit Hill, Oban, Argyll PA34 4LX, ☎ 01631/562840. 3 rooms with bath or shower. No credit cards. Closed Nov.–Mar.*

Port Appin

DINING AND LODGING

$$$$ **Airds Hotel.** This former ferry inn dating from the 17th century has some of the finest views in all of Scotland. Located in a peaceful village 24 miles north of Oban, the long white building, backed by trees, has a friendly feel to it. Quilted bedspreads and family mementos make guests feel right at home. Shooting and fishing trips can be arranged. The restaurant serves Scottish cuisine, including deer and grouse dishes. ☒ *Port Appin, Argyll PA38 4DF, ☎ 0163173/236, ℻ 0163173/535. 12 rooms with bath. Restaurant (reservations advised, jacket and tie). AE, MC, V.*

Port Askaig

DINING AND LODGING

$$ **Port Askaig Hotel.** This modernized drovers' inn by the roadside, with grounds extending to the shore, overlooks the Sound of Islay and the island of Jura and is conveniently located near the ferry terminal. Accommodations are comfortable without being luxurious, and the food is well prepared, using home-grown produce, but not very imaginative. ☒ *Port Askaig, Isle of Islay, Argyll PA46 7RD, ☎ 01496/840245, ℻ 01496/840295. 9 rooms, 5 with bath. 2 bars, dining room. No credit cards.*

Strachur
DINING AND LODGING

$$$ **Creggans Inn.** This traditional inn overlooking Loch Fyne dates to the
17th century. Visitors can enjoy an appetizing lunch in the bar or a
more formal dinner in the inn's attractive dining room, replete with
views of the water. Once again, local produce and seafood, including
Loch Fyne oysters, are staples on the menu. Accommodations are
available: The bedrooms vary in size from large to rather small, but
all are decorated in pastel shades. The staff is friendly and hospitable.
⌂ *Strachur, Argyll,* ☎ *01369/860279,* ℻ *01369/860637. 21 rooms,
17 with bath. Restaurant (reservations advised). AE, DC, MC, V.*

Tobermory
LODGING

$$ **Tobermory Hotel.** This 18th-century building by the quay on the northeastern tip of the island of Mull commands superb views. The ambi-
ence is crisp and bright, plants dot every windowsill, and the rooms
are spacious and sunny (weather permitting, of course). ⌂ *Tobermory,
Isle of Mull, Argyll PA75 6NT,* ☎ *01688/302091,* ℻ *01688/302254.
17 rooms, 9 with bath or shower. MC, V.*

THE ARTS AND NIGHTLIFE

The Arts

This predominantly rural area with a small population relies to a great
extent on touring companies and small local exhibitions and events for
its cultural fulfillment. Tourist information centers (*see* Important Addresses and Numbers in Argyll and the Isles Essentials, *below*) can supply an up-to-date events list.

Theater
Mull Little Theatre (Dervaig, Isle of Mull, ☎ 01688/400267) is Britain's
smallest professional playhouse (43 seats) and presents a number of
productions throughout the season. There is a restaurant nearby (*see*
Druimard Country House in Dining and Lodging, *above*).

Film
The **Highland Discovery Centre** (George St., Oban, ☎ 01631/562444)
shows feature films and also has a theater for plays.

Nightlife

Cabaret
The **Highland Discovery Centre** (*see above*) features a summer cabaret,
This Is Scotland.

ARGYLL AND THE ISLES ESSENTIALS

Arriving and Departing

By Bus
Daily bus service from Glasgow Buchanan Street Station to Mid-Argyll
and Kintyre is available through **Scottish Citylink** (☎ 0141/332–9191).

By Car

The A85 reaches Oban, the main ferry terminal for Mull, and the A83 rounds Loch Fyne and heads down Kintyre to reach Kennacraig, the main ferry terminal for Islay. Farther down the A83 is Tayinloan, the ferry departure point for Gigha. Brodick (Arran) is reached from Ardrossan on the Clyde coast (A8/A78 from Glasgow), and Rothesay (Bute) from Wemyss Bay (same roads from Glasgow). For information on ferry times contact **Caledonian MacBrayne** (*see* Getting Around by Car and Ferry, *below*).

By Plane

Although the nearest full-service airport for the entire area is in Glasgow (*see* Chapter 5), there are two airports within Argyll and the Isles. Both **Campbeltown** (on the mainland Kintyre peninsula) and the island of **Islay** are served weekdays (Islay also on Saturday) by **British Airways Express** (☎ 0345/222111) from Glasgow.

By Train

Oban (☎ 01631/563083) and Ardrossan (☎ 0141/204–2844) are the main rail stations. All trains connect with ferries.

Getting Around

By Bus

The following companies operate in the area: **Alexander Baird Ltd.** (Dunoon, ☎ 01369/3642), **B. Mundell Ltd.** (Islay, ☎ 01496/840273), **Bowman's Coaches** (Mull, ☎ 01680/812313), **C. MacLean** (Jura, ☎ 01496/820221), **Oban & District Buses** (Oban and Lorne, ☎ 01631/562856), **Stagecoach Western** (Arran, ☎ 01770/302000), and **West Coast Motor Service** (Mid-Argyll and Kintyre, ☎ 01586/552319).

By Car and Ferry

Negotiating this area can be quite easy, except in peak season, when the roads around Oban may be congested. There are some single-lane roads, especially on the east side of the Kintyre peninsula and on the islands. Car-ferry services to and from the main islands are operated by **Caledonian MacBrayne** (CalMac, main office is at the Ferry Terminal, Gourock, ☎ 01475/650100, FAX 01475/637607; for reservations, ☎ 01475/650000, FAX 01475/637607). A *CalMac Hopscotch* ticket reduces the cost of island-hopping excursions. **Western Ferries** (☎ 0141/332–9766) operates the Islay–Jura ferry service.

By Train

Aside from the main line to Oban, with stations at Dalmally, Loch Awe, Falls of Cruachan, Taynuilt, and Connel Ferry, there is no train service. You can travel from the pier head at **Craignure** on **Mull** to **Torosay** by narrow-gauge railway, a distance of about 1 mile.

Guided Tours

Orientation

The bus companies listed above offer orientation tours.

Special-Interest

Bowman's Coaches (*see above*) offers trips to Mull and Iona. **Gordon Grant Marine** (Staffa Ferries, Isle of Iona, ☎ 01681/700338) offers a "Three Isle" excursion to Mull, Iona, and Staffa, and also trips to the

Treshnish Isles and to Staffa, from Mull. Other boat cruises are available on **Loch Etive Cruises** (from Taynuilt near Oban, ☎ 01866/822430, or call the tourist information center at Oban). **Sea Life Cruises** on the MV *Alpha Beta* (from Dervaig on Mull, ☎ 01688/400223) offers four-hour day trips, and three-, five-, and seven-day packages where you can assist with an ongoing whale and dolphin survey. **MacDougall's Tours** (Oban, ☎ 01631/562133) runs half- and full-day touring and sailing expeditions to Mull and Iona. **Turas Mara** (Penmore Mill, Dervaig, Isle of Mull, ☎ and fax 01688/400242) runs daily excursions from Oban and Mull to Staffa, Iona, and the Treshnish Isles.

Important Addresses and Numbers

Emergencies

For police, fire, or ambulance, dial 999 from any telephone. No coins are needed for emergency calls from public telephone booths.

Doctors and Dentists

Information is available from your hotel, the local tourist information center, and the police, or look under "Doctors" or "Dentists" in the Yellow Pages telephone directory. There is an emergency room at **Lorne and Islands District General Hospital** (Glengallen Rd., Oban, ☎ 01631/567500).

Late-Night Pharmacies

Pharmacies are not found in rural areas. In an emergency the police will provide assistance in locating a pharmacist. In rural areas general practitioners may also dispense medicines.

Visitor Information

Local tourist information centers include the **Tourist Information Centre** in Argyll (7 Alexandra Parade, Dunoon, ☎ 01369/3785, FAX 01369/6085), the **Tourist Information Centre** in Arran (The Pier, Brodick, ☎ 01770/302140, FAX 01770/302395), the **Tourist Information Centre** on the Isle of Bute (15 Victoria St., Rothesay, ☎ 01700/502151), and the **Tourist Information Centre** in Oban (Boswell House, Argyll Square, ☎ 01631/563122, FAX 01631/564273). There are also information centers (some seasonal) at Bowmore (Islay), Campbeltown, Craignure (Mull), Inveraray, Lochgilphead, Lochranza (Arran), Tarbert, and Tobermory (Mull).

10 Around the Great Glen

Loch Ness, Speyside

The Great Glen cuts through the Southern Highlands from Inverness to Fort William and is surrounded by Scotland's tallest mountains and greatest lochs; it is considered by many to be the most dramatic, captivating landscape in Scotland. Of it lochs, the most famous is Loch Ness. East of Fort William, Glen Nevis is home to Ben Nevis, Britain's highest peak.

THE ANCIENT RIFT VALLEY of the Great Glen is a dramatic feature on the map of Scotland, giving the impression that the top half of the country has slid southwest. Geologists confirm that this actually occurred, having matched granite from Strontian in Morvern, west of Fort William, with the same rocks found at Foyers, on the east side of Loch Ness, some 65 miles away. The Great Glen, with its sense of openness, lacks the grandeur of Glen Coe or the Torridons, but the highest mountain in the United Kingdom, Ben Nevis (4,406 ft), looms over its southern portals, and spectacular scenery lies within a short distance of the main glen.

By Gilbert Summers

Though it's the capital of the Highlands, Inverness has the flavor of a Lowland town, its winds blowing in a sea-salt air from the Moray Firth. Inverness is also home to one of the world's most famous monster myths: In 1933, during a quiet news week for the local paper, the editor decided to run a story about a strange sighting of something splashing about in Loch Ness. More than 60 years later the story lives on, and the dubious Loch Ness phenomenon continues to keep cameras trained on the deep waters, which have an ominous tendency to create mirages in still conditions. The loch also has the distinction of being Scotland's largest body of water.

Fort William, without a monster on its doorstep, makes do with Ben Nevis and the Road to the Isles, a title sometimes applied to the breathtakingly scenic route to Mallaig, which is best seen by rail. On the way, road and rail routes pass Loch Morar, the country's deepest body of water, which laid claim to its own monster, Morag.

Away from the Great Glen to the north lie the heartlands of Scotland, a bare backbone of remote mountains. The great hills that loom to the south can be seen clearly on either side of Strathspey, the broad valley of the River Spey. The area is also commonly known as Speyside.

EXPLORING

Of the two tours described below, the first takes in some of the byways of both the Great Glen and Speyside, demonstrating that the best sights are hidden from the main road. However, the tour initially highlights some of the attractions within easy reach of Inverness along the inner Moray Firth. The second tour, originating in Fort William, takes in the special qualities of birch-knoll and blue island West Highland views. The tours also point out the romantic and historic associations of this area, where the rash adventurer Prince Charles Edward Stuart both arrived for and departed after the final Jacobite rebellion of 1745–46.

Tour 1: Speyside and Loch Ness

Numbers in the margin correspond to points of interest on the Great Glen Area map.

1 **Inverness** seems designed for the tourist, with its banks, souvenirs, high-quality woolens, and well-equipped tourist information center. Compared with other Scottish towns, however, Inverness has less to offer visitors with a keen interest in Scottish history. Frequently throughout its history Inverness was burned and ravaged by one or another of the restive Highland clans competing for dominance in the region. Thus a decorative wall panel here and a fragment of tower there are all that remain amid the modern shopping facilities and 19th-century down-town developments. One of the town's few historical landmarks is the **castle** (the local Sheriff Court), nestled above the river. The present structure is Victorian, built after a former fort was blown up by the Jacobites in the 1745 campaign. Because Jacobite tales are interwoven with landmarks throughout this entire area, you may enjoy your touring a little more if you first learn something about this thorny but colorful period of Scottish history. One of the best places to do this is at **Culloden,** just 5 miles east of Inverness on the B9006.

★ ❷ At **Culloden Moor,** on a sleety April day in 1746, an army of 5,000 Jacobites under Prince Charles Edward Stuart faced 9,000 well-armed British army troops at the command of the prince's distant cousin, General Cumberland. The latter became known in Scotland after the war as Butcher Cumberland because of the atrocities committed by his men after the battle ended. The story of the encounter, of how the ill-advised, poorly organized, and exhausted rebel army was swept aside by superior British firepower, is illustrated in the visitor center by a moving audiovisual presentation. *B9006, ☎ 01463/790607. Admission to visitor center £1.80 adults, 90p senior citizens, children, and students. Site open daily. Visitor center open Apr.–Oct., daily 9–6; Nov., Dec., Feb., and Mar., daily 10–4 (closed Christmas).*

Not far from Culloden, on a narrow road southeast of the battlefield,
❸ are the **Clava Cairns,** dating from the Bronze Age. In a cluster among the trees, these stones and monuments form a large ring with passage graves, which consist of a central chamber below a cairn of stone reached via a passage. On-site information placards explain the graves' significance.

To get to the next chapter of the Highlands' history, drive northeast
★ ❹ from Culloden. Use either the B9039 or B9006 to get to **Fort George,** a fortress that was started in 1748 and completed some 20 years later. As a direct result of the battle at Culloden, the nervous government in London ordered the construction of a large fort on this promontory reaching into the Moray Firth. It survives today as perhaps the best-preserved 18th-century military fortification in Europe. Because it is low lying, its immense scale can be seen only from within. The huge walls, as broad and high as harbor quays, are large enough to contain a complete military town. A walk along the wall-tops affords fine views of the Highland hills in the distance and of the firth immediately below. Even though no one has sighted a Jacobite here for more than 200 years, the army still uses the barracks. And if you happen to meet any of the fort's current military residents, you will find them unfailingly polite. A visitor center and a number of tableaux at the fort portray the 18th-century Scottish soldier's way of life, as does the **Regimental Museum of the Queen's Own Highlanders.** *B9039, off A96 west of Nairn, ☎ 0131/244–3101. Admission to fort: £2.50 adults, £1.50 senior citizens, £1 children; free admission to museum. Fort and museum open Apr.–Sept., Mon.–Sat. 9:30–6, Sun. 2–6; Oct.–Mar., Mon.–Sat. 9:30–4, Sun. 2–4. Last tickets sold 45 min before closing.*

❺ To the east is **Nairn,** which has the air of a Lowland town yet looks, administratively speaking, to Inverness as part of the Highlands. A once-prosperous fishing village, Nairn does in fact have something of a split personality. King James VI once boasted that there was a town in his kingdom so large that the residents at either end of town spoke different languages. He was referring to the fact that Nairn's fisherfolk spoke Lowland Scots by the sea, while the uptown farmers and crofters spoke Gaelic. The fishing boats have since moved to larger ports, but the town's historic flavor has been preserved in the **Nairn Fishertown Museum,** a hall crammed with artifacts, photographs, and model boats. This is an informal museum in the best sense, where the volunteer staff are full of information and eager to talk. *Laing Hall, King St.,* ☎ *01667/ 453331.* ☛ *30p adults, 15p children.* ☉ *June–Sept., Mon.–Sat. 2:30– 4:30, also Mon., Wed., and Fri. evenings 6:30–8:30.*

★ ⑥ Next head southwest to **Cawdor Castle.** Shakespeare's Macbeth was Thane of Cawdor, but the sense of history that exists within these turreted walls is more than fictional. Cawdor is a lived-in castle, not an abandoned, decadent structure to be preserved in aspic. The earliest part of the castle is the 14th-century central tower; the rooms contain family portraits, tapestries, fine furniture, and paraphernalia reflecting 600 years of history. Outside the castle walls there are sheltered gardens and walks. *B9090, 5 mi southwest of Nairn,* ☎ *01667/404615.* ☛ *£4.50 adults, £3.50 senior citizens, £2.50 children, £12.50 family ticket; garden and grounds only: £2.50.* ☉ *May–Sept., daily 10–5.*

If Cawdor has inspired you to seek the wild Highlands, make your way to the southeastern portion of the region, using either the unclassified roads southeast of Cawdor or heading northeast along the B9101 to pick up the A939 south. If you use the unclassified roads, you will find yourself in a classic Highland "edge" landscape, where the open moor contrasts with the improved upland pasture and thickets of birch and fir. (Clunas may be the first road sign you see, but reaching Dulsie is your first objective.) As you take to the higher ground, look for the longest views back over the Firth—you should still just barely be able to see Fort George in the distance. Follow what was the former military road built in the 1750s to service the garrison. Look for the point where the road crosses the River Findhorn by a narrow span, the ⑦ **Dulsie Bridge.** Just beyond the bridge, on the right, is a parking place and kissing gate. If you park and go through the gate, a walk of a few yards brings you to a viewpoint over the birch-scattered rocky confines of the river.

Shortly after Dulsie Bridge, turn right off the unclassified road onto the B9007. Shakespeare's Thane of Cawdor met the three prophesying witches on a bare moor very much like this one. Rolling folds of marbled purple and brown are broken here and there by a roofless cottage. You can either switch to the A938 and Carrbridge on Speyside heading south (*see below*), or if you have more time, you can take a ⑧ short diversion to the east for a view of the lonely ruin of **Lochindorb Castle.** What appears to be a walled enclosure fills and surrounds an entire island on Lochindorb loch. This 13th-century stronghold was the former power base of the Wolf of Badenoch (the marauding Earl of Buchan who damaged Elgin Cathedral). The castle was eventually dismantled by a 15th-century Thane of Cawdor, on the order of the king. (Lochindorb's iron *yett* [gate] is now on view at Cawdor.)

After you have viewed Lochindorb, drive farther south along the A939 ⑨ to **Grantown-on-Spey.** This sturdy settlement, set amid tall pines which flank the River Spey, gives visitors access to many points of interest, including a heavily stocked heather nursery at nearby **Skye of Curr.** The A95, which runs southwest along the river, is an attractive road, but you may wish to follow the more tranquil B970 via **Nethy Bridge.** Then ⑩ look for signs to the **Loch Garten Nature Reserve,** administered by the Royal Society for the Protection of Birds (RSPB). This sanctuary achieved fame when the osprey, a bird that was facing extinction in the early part of this century, returned to breed here. Instead of cordoning off the nest site, the RSPB encouraged visitors by constructing

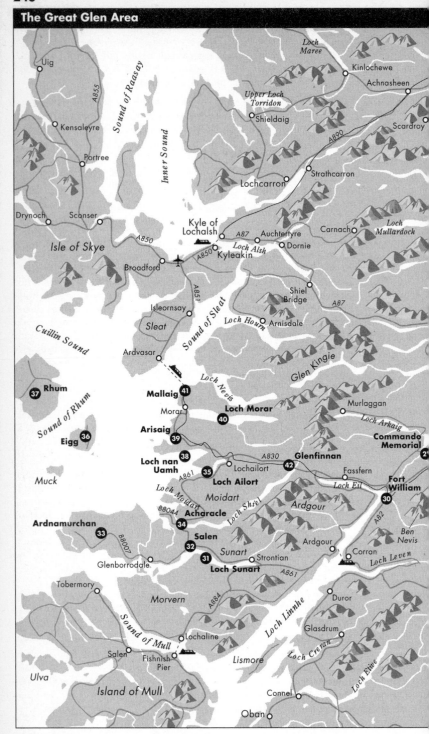

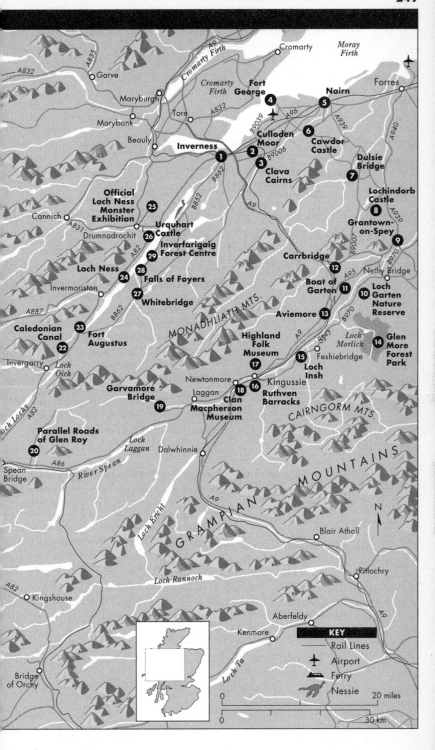

A835

A832 Garve

Maryburgh

Marybank

Beauly

Cromarty

Cromarty Firth

Cromarty Firth

A9

Tore

A832

Fort George

Nairn

Forres

Moray Firth

B9039

A96

A939

A940

Inverness ❶

❹

Culloden Moor ❷

B9006

❸ Clava Cairns

Cawdor Castle ❻

❺

B862

A9

Dulsie Bridge ❼

Official Loch Ness Monster Exhibition ㉕

A831

Cannich

Drumnadrochit

Urquhart Castle ㉖

Loch Ness ㉔

㉘

㉙ Inverfarigaig Forest Centre

Falls of Foyers

B852

Lochindorb Castle ❽

Grantown-on-Spey ❾

A939

A95

Carrbridge

❿

❶❷

B9007

B970

Nethy Bridge

Invermoristen

A82

㉗ Whitebridge

B862

MONADHLIATH MTS.

Boat of Garten ⓫

Loch Garten Nature Reserve ❿

A887

Caledonian Canal ㉓

㉒

Invergarry

Loch Oich

Fort Augustus

Highland Folk Museum ⓱

Aviemore ⓭

Glen More Forest Park ⓮

Loch Morlich

Spey

A9

Feshiebridge

Loch Insh ⓯

Kingussie

B970

och Locky

A82

Garvamore Bridge

⓳

Laggan

Newtonmore

⓲ ⓰

Clan Macpherson Museum

Ruthven Barracks

CAIRNGORM MTS.

Parallel Roads of Glen Roy ⓴

A86

Loch Laggan

Dalwhinnie

Spean Bridge

River Spean

Loch Ericht

GRAMPIAN MOUNTAINS

Blair Atholl

Pitlochry

A9

Loch Rannoch

A82 Kingshouse

Aberfeldy

A9

Kenmore

Loch Ta

Bridge of Orchy

a blind from which to watch the birds. Now thousands of bird lovers visit annually to get a glimpse of the domestic arrangements of this fish-eating bird, which has since been bred in many other parts of the Highlands. *Off B970, 8 mi northeast of Aviemore, ☏ 01479/821409 or 0131/557–3136. ☞ £2 adults, £1 senior citizens, 50p children. Osprey observation post open May–Aug. 10–6:30; other areas of reserve open daily year-round.*

⑪ Near Loch Garten is **Boat of Garten,** a peaceful village where the scent of pine trees is interrupted by an equally evocative smell. This is the terminus of the **Speyside Railway,** and the acrid scent of smoke and steam hang faintly in the air near the authentically preserved station next to the **Boat Hotel.** The 5-mile train trip to Aviemore not only offers a chance to wallow in nostalgia, but also yields superb views southward to the high and often white domes of the Cairngorms.

TIME OUT At the **Boat Hotel** (☏ 01479/831258), in Boat of Garten, you can have a friendly pub lunch while you wait for the train. The malt-whisky selection behind the bar may also be of interest.

⑫ In **Carrbridge,** just about 5 miles northwest of Boat of Garten (follow the A95 and then the B9153), you'll find the **Landmark Visitor Centre,** an early pioneer in the move toward more sophisticated visitor attractions. It has an audiovisual presentation on the history of the Scottish Highlands, a permanent exhibition, a display on forestry with working steam-powered sawmill and a Clydesdale horse to haul the logs, a forestry workshop where you can try out forest skills such as bark peeling, plus a bookshop and restaurant. Outdoors are nature trails, a treetop trail, and a viewing platform, as well as plenty of diversions for children, such as a Wild Forest maze and an adventure playground. *Old A9, 6 mi north of Aviemore, ☏ 01479/841613. ☞ £4.90 adults, £3.20 senior citizens and children, £14.95–£20.80 family ticket. ☉ Apr.–June, daily 9:30–6; July and Aug., daily 9:30–8; Sept. and Oct., daily 9:30–5:30; Nov.–Mar., daily 10–5.*

No matter which side of the Spey you choose to travel (the quiet B970 on the southeast side is recommended), signs will point you to **Aviemore.**
⑬ Once a quiet junction on the Highland Railway, Aviemore now possesses all the brashness and concrete boxiness of a year-round holiday resort. A resort environment certainly translates into a lot of things to do, however, and here you can swim, curl, skate, see a movie, dance, and shop. Signs will direct you to other sights, such as the **Cairngorm Whisky Centre,** which has one of the largest selections of malt whiskies in the world. *On the road to the Cairngorms, ☏ 01479/810574. ☉ Daily 9:30–4:30 (longer hrs in summer).*

The Aviemore area is a versatile walking base, but walkers must be properly dressed for high-level excursions onto the near-Arctic plateau. Visitors interested in skiing and rugged hiking can follow the B970 from
⑭ Aviemore past Loch Morlich in the **Glen More Forest Park** to the high car parks on the exposed shoulders of the **Cairngorm Mountains.** The chair lifts take you even higher, during and after the ski season, for extensive views of the broad valley of the Spey. But be warned: It can get very cold at over 3,000 feet, and weather conditions can change rapidly even in the middle of summer. *Off B9152, ☏ 01540/651223 or 01479/861261. ☉ Daily, weather permitting.*

While you are on the high slopes, you may sight the reindeer herd that was introduced here in the 1950s. In fact, by inquiring at the **Cairngorm Reindeer Centre,** by Loch Morlich, you can accompany the keeper on his daily rounds. *Loch Morlich, Glen More Forest Park,* ☎ *01479/861228.* ☞ *£3 adults, £2 children. Departures daily at 11 AM (subject to weather conditions); also at 2:30 PM in peak season. Visitor Centre admission: £1.50 adults, £1 children; open daily 10–6.*

★ The place that best sums up Speyside's piny ambience is probably **Loch an Eilean,** a mile or so south of Aviemore, signposted off the B970 (parallel with the main A9). A converted cottage on the **Rothiemurchus Estate** houses a visitor center (the area is a National Nature Reserve). Visitors should exercise care upon entering the cottage: It has an extremely low door and a very hard lintel! All around the loch you can still see some stands of old Scots pines; look for the characteristic red limbs high up. These are the descendants of the Caledonian Forest that once covered much of Scotland and now survives only in remnants. *Rothiemurchus Estate Visitor Centre,* ☎ *01479/810858.* ☞ *Free.* ⊙ *Daily 9–5.*

⑮ About a mile west of **Feshiebridge** is **Loch Insh.** Other lochs in the vicinity, notably Loch an Eilean and Loch Garten, are what geologists call kettle holes—round depressions that remained after huge blocks of ice melted at the end of the Ice Age. Loch Insh is thought to be the remains of a much larger loch, which, until recent geological times, filled the valley's floor. Loch Insh is known for its recreational diversions—sailing and canoeing—and is a popular water-sports center. Beyond the loch the valley floor broadens into marshland, the haunt of watery tribes of birds and hence bird-watchers. Look for ospreys here.

Gaunt against the rounded **Monadhliath Mountains** (*monadhliath* is Gaelic for gray moors) to the north is what appears, at first glance, to be a ruined castle on a mound. The remains are not of a castle, how-
⑯ ever, but of **Ruthven Barracks,** roofless and redolent with tales of the '45 (as the last Jacobite rebellion is often called). The defeated Jacobite forces rallied here after Culloden, but then abandoned and blew up the government outpost they had earlier captured. *B970, ½ mi south of Kingussie,* ☎ *0131/244–3101.* ☞ *Free.*

The barracks lie within a few minutes of the village of **Kingussie** (pronounced Kin-*yoo*-see) and can be seen clearly from the main A9. The
⑰ village is of interest primarily because of the **Highland Folk Museum.** The interior exhibits are housed in what was an 18th-century shooting lodge, its paneled and varnished ambience still apparent. Displays include 18th-century furniture, clothing, and implements, and, outside, various types of Highland buildings have been reconstructed. In summer, local weavers and other artisans demonstrate Highland crafts. Visitors can wander around the grounds freely or see the highlights of the museum on a guided tour. *A9 at Kingussie,* ☎ *01540/661307.* ☞ *£2.50 adults, £1.50 senior citizens and children.* ⊙ *Apr.–Oct., Mon.–Sat. 10–6, Sun. 2–6; Nov.–Mar., Mon.–Fri. 10–3.*

Down the road from Kingussie is neighborly **Newtonmore,** home of
⑱ the **Clan Macpherson Museum.** One of many clan museums scattered throughout the old homelands, the Macpherson Museum displays a number of interesting artifacts associated with the '45 rebellion, as well as of clan chiefs of the even more distant past. *A9/A86, Newtonmore,* ☎ *01540/673332.* ☞ *Free (donation box).* ⊙ *May–Sept., Mon.–Sat. 10–5:30, Sun. 2:30–5:30 (open at other times by appointment).*

At Newtonmore you will leave the great artery of the A9 behind. It veers off to the southeast for the Pass of Drumochter at this point. This tour continues westward on the A86 around the edge of the Monadhliath range, which separates Speyside from the Great Glen. The Monadhliath are less often explored by hill walkers than the Cairngorms, which form Speyside's southern side. At **Laggan,** where the main road crosses the young River Spey, an unclassified road runs west up the glen to **Garvamore.** If you are staying in the area and you are not pressed for time, **⑲** it's worth making this detour to view the **Garvamore Bridge** (about 6 mi from the junction, at the south side of the Corrieyairack Pass). This dual-arched bridge was built in 1735 by English General Wade, who had been charged with the task of improving Scotland's roads by a British government concerned that its troops would not be able to travel the Highlands quickly enough to quell an uprising.

If you opt not to take the Garvamore Bridge detour, you may continue south on the A86, which hugs the western shore of **Loch Laggan.** This was the route chosen by later road builders to avoid the high Corrieyairack Pass. Still quite narrow in a few places, this stretch of the A86 is a road to be enjoyed, offering superb views of the mountainous heartlands to the north, where high shoulders loom, and to the south, over the silvery spine of hills known as the **Grey Corries** and culminating with **Ben Nevis.**

In **Roybridge** you'll find the first of the Great Glen cul-de-sac diver- **⑳** sions. The so-called **Parallel Roads of Glen Roy** are three curious terraces, parallel and level, cut across the hillsides on both sides of the glen. Their levelness lends a clue to their origins as former shorelines of lochs dammed by ice that melted in stages at the end of the last Ice Age. *Unclassified road off A86 at Roybridge.*

Turn right and north at the junction with the main Great Glen road, the A82, to reach **Spean Bridge.** Uphill and beyond this little village, **㉑** easily visible from the road, is the arresting and dignified **Commando Memorial.** The rugged glens and hills of this area were a training ground for elite forces during World War II. Today, three battle-equipped figures on a high stone plinth overlook the panorama, while the veterans and younger generations who visit follow their gaze.

TIME OUT   If you're passing Invergarry (just east of Loch Lochy) around lunchtime, consider stopping at the rambling **Glengarry Castle Hotel** (☎ 01809/ 501254; open Apr.–Oct.), an interesting building with a pleasingly old-fashioned ambience. The hotel serves hearty soup-and-sandwich meals; more substantial fare is available in the evenings. The ruined **Glengarry Castle,** a seat of the MacDonnell Clan, can be seen on the grounds. The hotel entrance is south of the A82–A87 road junction.

Traveling north up the Great Glen by the A82 takes you parallel to **㉒** Loch Lochy (on the eastern shore) and over the **Caledonian Canal** at Laggan Locks. From this beautiful spot, which offers stunning vistas of lochs, mountains, and glens in all directions, you can look back on the impressive profile of Ben Nevis. The canal, which links the lochs of the Great Glen—Loch Lochy, Loch Oich, and Loch Ness—owes its origins to a combination of military as well as political pressures that emerged at the time of the Napoleonic Wars with France. (Mostly, the British needed a better and faster way to get naval vessels from one side of Scotland to the other.) The great Scottish engineer Thomas Telford surveyed the route in 1803. The canal, which took 19 years to complete, has 29 locks and 42 gates. Telford took advantage of the three lochs that lie in the Great Glen (which have a combined length of 45 miles), and only 22 miles of canal were constructed to connect the lochs and complete the waterway from coast to coast.

❷❸ The best place to see the locks in action is at **Fort Augustus,** at the southern tip of Loch Ness. (Fort Augustus itself was captured by the Jacobite clans during the 1745 rebellion. Later the fort was rebuilt as a Benedictine abbey.) The canal activity at a series of locks that rise from Loch Ness takes place in the village center.

❷❹ From the B862 just east of Fort Augustus you'll get your first good long view of the formidable and famous **Loch Ness,** which has a greater volume of water than any other Scottish loch and a maximum depth of more than 800 feet. Early travelers who passed this way included English lexicographer Dr. Samuel Johnson and his guide and biographer James Boswell, who were on their way to the Hebrides in 1783. They remarked at the time about the condition of the population and the squalor of their homes. Another early travel writer, Thomas Pennant, noted that the loch kept the locality frost-free in winter. Even General Wade came here, his troops blasting and digging a road up much of the eastern shore. None of these observant early travelers ever made mention of a monster. Clearly, they had not read the local guidebooks.

❷❺ If you're in search of the infamous beast Nessie, it's best to continue northward along the coast on the A82. At **Drumnadrochit** you will find the **Official Loch Ness Monster Exhibition,** which presents the facts and the fakes, the photographs, the unexplained sonar contacts, and the sincere testimony of eyewitnesses. It's then up to you to make up your own mind. *A831,* ☎ *01456/450573 and 01456/450218.* ☛ *£4 adults, £3 senior citizens and students, £2.50 children, £10.50 family ticket.* ☉ *Easter–May, daily 9:30–5:30; June and Sept., daily 9:30–6:30; July and Aug., daily 9–8:30; Oct.–Mar., daily 10–4 (last admission 1 hr before closing). Off-season opening times vary; call ahead.*

❷❻ **Urquhart Castle,** near Drumnadrochit, is another favorite monster-watching spot. This plundered fortress stands on a promontory overlooking the loch, as it has since the Middle Ages. Because of its central and strategic position in the Great Glen line of communication, the castle has a complex history involving military offense and defense, as well as its own destruction and renovation. The castle was begun in the 13th century and was destroyed before the end of the 17th century to prevent its use by the Jacobites. The ruins of what was one of the largest castles in Scotland were plundered for building material. Today swarms of bus tours pass through after investigating the Loch Ness phenomenon. *West shore of Loch Ness, 2 mi southeast of Drumnadrochit,* ☎ *0131/244–3101.* ☛ *£3 adults, £2 senior citizens, £1 children.* ☉ *Apr.–Sept., daily 9:30–6; Oct.–Mar., Mon.–Sat. 9:30–4, Sun. 11:30–4.*

The west-bank road, the A82, offers intermittent views of the loch, which often glitters hypnotically in the sun. You can be caught up in the fast-moving traffic on this busy road and find yourself in Inverness before you know it. Or you can choose a more leisurely alternative—combining monster watching with peaceful road touring—by taking the B862 from Fort Augustus and following the east-bank route to Inverness.

The B862 runs around the end of Loch Ness then climbs into moorland and forestry plantation. Fine views of Fort Augustus can be seen by climbing a few yards up and to the right, onto the moor; here you'll be able to see above the conifer spikes. The half-hidden track beside the road is a remnant of the military road built by General Wade. Loch Ness quickly drops out of sight, but is soon replaced by the peaceful, reedy **Loch Tarff.**

❷❼ The B862 continues along the line of the former military route and shows appropriate military precision nearly all the way to **Whitebridge,** where a handsome single-arch Wade bridge (look for it on your right) has been restored. Just before the bridge is the **Whitebridge Hotel,** a former Kingshouse, one of a chain of inns built by authorities in the 18th century to service the military roads. The Kingshouse name is still used by a few of Scotland's hotels. Beyond Whitebridge the small banks on either side of the road are thought to have survived from the military's original work in 1726; thus you find yourself traveling one of the earliest roads in the Highlands. Take the B852, left at the junction beyond Whitebridge, to regain the shores of Loch Ness by some fine woodlands.

Just before you reach the level of the loch at **Foyers,** a sign outside the general store will direct you to the **Falls of Foyers.** Steep, pinecone-strewn paths lead to a viewpoint where a thin waterfall streams into a dark pot and then down a ravine. The original volume of the falls was much reduced shortly before the turn of the century when the power generated here was harnessed for the first commercial application of hydroelectricity (1896), in an aluminum-smelting plant on a site by the loch.

The B852 meanders pleasantly from Foyers, offering some views of the loch on the way to **Inverfarigaig.** Just before the main road bridge is the **Inverfarigaig Forest Centre,** on the right. The center has several displays on forestry activities, and a number of trails lead from the center into the woodlands. *Off of B862, Inverfarigaig, 17 mi southwest of Inverness,* ☎ *01320/366322.* ☛ *Free.* ☉ *Easter–mid-Oct., daily 9:30–7.*

Tour 2: Toward the Small Isles

Fort William probably has enough points of interest for visitors—a museum, exhibits, and shopping—to compensate for its less-than-picturesque milieu. The town's primary purpose is to serve the west Highland hinterland; its role as a tourist stop is secondary. Since this is a relatively wet part of Scotland, and since Fort William itself can always be explored if it rains, strike west toward the coast if the weather looks settled: On a sunny day, the Small Isles—Rhum, Eigg, Canna, and Muck—look as blue as the sea and sky together. From here you could also visit Skye via the ferry at Mallaig, or take a day cruise (*see* Off the Beaten Track, *below*) from Arisaig to the Small Isles for a glimpse of traffic-free island life.

Begin your visit to Fort William by stopping by the helpful tourist information center in **Cameron Square.** Just a few doors down is the **West Highland Museum,** which explores the theme of Prince Charles Edward Stuart and the 1745 rebellion. Included in the museum's folk exhibits is a section on tartans. *Cameron Sq.,* ☎ *01397/702169.* ☛ *£1.50 adults, £1 senior citizens, 40p children.* ☉ *Mar.–Oct., Mon.–Sat. 10–1 and 2–5 (extended hours in summer).*

The ScotRail station in Fort William is the place to book your ticket for the train trip to Mallaig, along the beautiful West Highland line. If you visit Fort William by car, leave the car behind to take this trip. ☎ *01397/703791.*

If you're not reliant on public transportation, you can make an interesting West Highlands circuit by traveling down the eastern side of **Loch Linnhe** to **Corran,** where a frequent ferry shuttles autos and foot passengers across the loch to **Ardgour.** (From the map you will see you can avoid the ferry by driving around the head of Loch Eil, but it's not a very scenic route.) From Ardgour, a reliable two-lane road runs along Loch Linnhe before turning into Glen Sanda, crossing the watershed, and running down to the long shores of **Loch Sunart.** This is a typical West Highlands sea loch: Orange wrack marks the tide lines, and herons stand muffled and miserable, wondering if it is worth risking a free meal at the local fish farm. As for the fish farms themselves, visitors will become accustomed to their floats and cages turning up in the foreground of every sea-loch view. The farms were originally hailed as the savior of the Highland economy because of the number of jobs they created, but questions are now being raised about their environmental effects, and the market for their product is being threatened by Scandinavian imports.

32 33 At **Salen** you have a choice. The B8007 runs west, blind-bending partly through thickets of rhododendrons to **Ardnamurchan,** the most western point of mainland Scotland and a must-see for those who love unspoiled coastal scenery. Here you'll find crofting communities and holiday homes.

★ **34** If you are short on time, swing north instead from Salen along the B8044 and head for **Acharacle** (pronounced ak-*ar*-ra-kle). You'll pass through deep-green plantations and moorland lily ponds to reach this strungout settlement backed by the hills of Moidart and **Loch Shiel.** The south end of Loch Shiel is shallow and reedy. The north end is more dramatic and sits deep within the rugged hills. A few minutes beyond Acharacle—where the main road turns sharply right—take the narrow road to the left, overhung in places by mossy trees, to emerge at **Castle Tioram.** This ruined keep dominates a bracken-green islet, barely anchored to the mainland by a sand spit. The castle was once the home of the chief of the MacDonalds of Clan Ranald, but the last chief burned the castle to prevent its falling into the hands of his enemies, the Campbells, during the 1715 Jacobite rebellion. Conservation agencies do not yet require an admission charge to this fragment of Highlands history guarding the south channel of Loch Moidart. *Reached by an unclassified road north of A861.* ✆ *Daily.*

35 The upper sandy reached of **Loch Moidart** are reached by returning to the main road, climbing a high moorland pass and then dropping down to a two-lane road again. On the next ascent from the shores of Loch Moidart you'll be rewarded with stunning sea views. The coast is reached by the mouth of **Loch Ailort** (pronounced *eye*-ort), and there are plenty of places to pull off among the boulders and birch scrub and sort out the view of the islands. Offshore in the distance you'll be able

36 37 to spot **Eigg,** a low island marked by the dramatic black peak of An Sgurr. Beyond Eigg is the larger **Rhum,** with its range of hills, the Norse-named Rhum Coullin, looming cloud-capped over the island.

Loch Ailort itself is another picturesque inlet, now cluttered with the garish floats of fish cages. You meet the bustle of the main road again at its head, at the junction with the A830, the main road from Fort William to Mallaig. Turn left here to reach Mallaig.

The breathtaking seaward views continue to distract you from the road (hence the earlier recommendation to take the train) as you travel by

38 **Loch nan Uamh** (from the Gaelic meaning cave, and pronounced *oo*-am). This loch is associated with Prince Charles Edward Stuart's ninemonth stay on the mainland, during which he gathered a small army, marched as far south as Derby in England, alarmed the king, retreated to unavoidable defeat at Culloden in the spring, and then spent a few months as a fugitive in the Highlands. A cairn by the shore marks the spot where the prince was picked up by a French ship. Prince Charles never returned to Scotland.

39 **Arisaig,** signposted off the A830, offers many options for dining and lodging (*see* Dining and Lodging, *below*). Beyond this point the road cuts across a headland to reach a stretch of coastline where the silver sands around Loch Morar glitter with the mica in the local rock; clear water, blue sky, and white sand lend a tropical flavor to the beaches—when the sun shines.

40 A small, unclassified side road off to the right leads to an even smaller road that will bring you to **Loch Morar,** the deepest of all the Scottish lochs (over 1,000 ft); the next deepest point is miles out into the Atlantic, beyond the Continental Shelf. Apart from this short public road, the area around the loch is all but roadless; the area to the immediate north and west, beyond Loch Nevis, one of the most remote in Scotland, is often referred to as the Rough Bounds of Knoydart.

41 After the approach along the coast, the town of **Mallaig** itself is anti-climactic. It has a few shops, and there is some bustle by the quayside when fishing boats unload or the Skye ferry departs. Mallaig is also the starting point for day cruises up the Sound of Sleat, which separates Skye from the mainland and offers views into rugged Knoydart and its sea lochs (*see* Off the Beaten Track, *below*). You may want to visit the **Heritage Centre,** with exhibits, photographs, films, and models on all aspects of the local history. Beside the harbor, **Mallaig Marine World** shows you what goes on beneath the surface of the Sound of Sleat: live fish and shellfish, and a display on the local fishing tradition are among the attractions here. *Heritage Centre: Station Rd.,* ☎ *1687/462085.* ☛ *£1.50 adults, 75p senior citizens and children, £4 family ticket.* ⊗ *Mid-May–Sept., Mon.–Sat. 10–5 (also Sun. noon–5 in July and Aug.); call ahead for spring and fall hours. Mallaig Marine World: The Harbour, Mallaig,* ☎ *01687/462292.* ☛ *£2.50 adults, £1.50 children, £2 senior citizens and students, £7 family ticket.* ⊗ *Daily 10–5; closed Christmas, New Year's, and late Jan.–early Feb.*

42 You can get back to Fort William by retracing your route along the A830 to the **Lochailort** junction. From here, the road eastward to Fort William has many points of interest. **Glenfinnan,** perhaps the most visitor-oriented stop on the way, has the most to offer visitors interested in Scottish history. Here the National Trust for Scotland has capitalized on the romance surrounding the story of the Jacobites and their intention of returning a Stuart monarch and the Catholic religion to a country that had become staunchly Protestant. In Glenfinnan in 1745 the sometimes-reluctant clans joined forces and rallied to Prince Charles Edward Stuart's cause. The raising of the prince's standard is commemorated by the Glenfinnan Monument (an unusual tower on the banks of Loch Shiel), and the story of his campaign is told in the nearby visitor center. Note that the figure at the top of the monument is of a Highlander, not the prince. *A830,* ☎ *01397/722250.* ☛ *£1 adults, 50p children.* ⊗ *Apr.–mid-May and Sept.–late Oct., daily 10–5; late May–Aug., daily 9:30–6.*

The view down Loch Shiel from this point is one of the most-photographed views in Scotland. Equally impressive (for visitors who have tired of the Jacobite "Will He No Come Back Again" sentiment) is the curving railway viaduct that stretches across the green slopes behind. The **Glenfinnan Viaduct,** 21 spans and 1,248 feet long, was in its time the wonder of the Highlands. The railway's contractor, Robert MacAlpine, known as Concrete Bob by the locals, pioneered the use of mass concrete for viaducts and bridges when his company built the Mallaig extension, which was opened in 1901.

What to See and Do with Children

Darnaway Farm Visitor Centre, of the Moray Estates, has farm animals, a woodland walk, and a place where children can watch the cattle being milked. *Off A96, 3 mi west of Forres,* ☎ *01309/641469.* ☛ *£2 adults, £1.20 children.* ☉ *May–mid-Sept., daily 10–5.*

Fort George (*see* Tour 1)

Landmark Visitor Centre (*see* Tour 1)

The **Official Loch Ness Monster Exhibition** (*see* Tour 1)

Off the Beaten Path

Remote **Lochs Nevis and Hourn** are long, fjordlike sea lochs that can be seen from the Sound of Sleat between the mainland and Skye. Visitors can also reach the lochs by sea from Mallaig. Check the range of rail/cruise options promoted from Fort William by contacting the **Transport Centre** (☎ 01397/703791) at the Fort William Station or by calling **Bruce Watt Sea Cruises** (Western Isles Guest House, Mallaig, ☎ 01687/462320).

Anyone with a day to spend in Fort William can visit at least a couple of the **Small Isles: Rhum, Eigg, Muck,** and **Canna.** Caledonian MacBrayne ferries (*see* Guided Tours, *below*) connect from Mallaig, but a better option is to contact **Murdo Grant** (Arisaig Marine, Arisaig, Invernessshire, ☎ 01687/450224), who runs a service from the harbor at Arisaig. The MV *Shearwater,* a former naval inshore minesweeper, delivers supplies and mail as well as visitors to the diminutive island communities. What sets Grant's operation apart from the tourism-oriented excursions is that it offers visitors a glimpse of island life from a working vessel going about its summer routine. Also available for charter from Arisaig Marine is a fast twin-engine motor yacht, which can take up to 12 passengers for go-where-you-please cruises around the Small Isles and farther afield.

Two outstanding mountain landscapes, those of **Glens Affric and Cannich,** located toward the northern end and to the west of the Great Glen, can be viewed in one easy day from Inverness. For visitors who have limited time but wish to see the Scottish heartland, these two glens offer a cross section of landscape. Accessible by way of Beauly and Strathglass (A831), Glen Cannich is constricted by crags and birch-clad slopes before opening into a broad valley with a hydroelectric dam at its far end. Glen Affric is, if anything, even more aesthetically appealing, with oak woodlands and hayfields in the lower reaches and wild lochs (also dammed) and pine forests, similar to the Trossachs, but on a grander scale.

If you're touring the West Highlands, you can take the backdoor ferry route to the **island of Mull** (*see* Chapter 10) from Lochaline in Morven, southwest of Fort William. This route affords views of moorland and woodland scenery and has little traffic. (No need to book car space on this ferry—just show up.)

At Corpach, do not miss **Treasures of the Earth,** an exhibition of gemstones, crystals, and fossils that include a 26-pound uncut emerald. ☎ *01397/772283.* ☛ *£2.50 adults, £1.50 children.* ☉ *July, Aug., Sept., daily 9:30–7; Oct.–Dec., Feb.–June, daily 10–5 (open in Jan. by appointment only).*

SHOPPING

Aviemore

The **Cairngorm Whisky Centre** (☎ 01479/810574) at Rothiemurchus has one of the largest selections of malt whiskies in the world—more than 500. There is a tasting room to help you make your choice.

Fort William

The majority of the shops here are located along High Street, which in summer attracts ever-present, bustling crowds intent on stocking up for excursions to the west. **Ben Nevis Woollen Mill** (Belford Rd., ☎ 01397/704244), at the north end of town, is a major supplier of tartans, woolens, and tweeds and has a restaurant. **J & K Ness** (The Granite House, High St., ☎ 01397/703651) stocks Scottish jewelry (including some by local designer Pat Cheney), china and crystal giftware, wildlife sculptures, and other collectibles. **Scottish Crafts and Whisky Centre** (135–139 High St., ☎ 01379/704406) has the usual range of souvenirs, but also sells homemade chocolates and a vast range of malt whiskies, including miniatures and limited edition bottlings.

Grantown on Spey and Environs

Speyside Heather Centre (Skye of Curr, ☎ 01479/851359), not only has 200 varieties of heather for sale (some in sterile planting media), but also a crafts shop and floral-art sundries. **The Kist** (74 High St., Grantown on Spey, ☎ 01479/873043), is a well-stocked high-quality gift shop specializing in local and Scottish crafts.

Inverness

Although Inverness has the usual High Street chain stores and department stores—including **Arnott's** and **Marks and Spencer**—the most interesting goods are to be found in the various specialty outlets in and around town.

The Riverside Gallery (11 Bank St., ☎ 01463/224781) sells paintings and prints of Scottish natural history and sporting themes. For contemporary art there's the **Highland Printmakers Workshop and Gallery** (20 Bank St., ☎ 01463/712240). **Duncan Chisholm and Sons** (47–51 Castle St., ☎ 01463/234599) manufactures Highlands dress, tartans, and Scottish crafts. **James Pringle Ltd.** (Holm Woollen Mills, Dores Rd., ☎ 01463/223311) has a shop stocked with a vast selection of cashmere, lambswool, and Shetland knitwear, tartans, and tweeds. The **Scottish Kiltmaker Centre** (4/9 Huntly St., ☎ 01463/222781) explains the history of the kilt, shows them being made, and then gives you the opportunity to buy.

In a different vein entirely is **Highland Aromatics** (Drumchardine, Kirkhill, ☎ 01463/831625), where, in a converted church, sweet-smelling soaps with the scents of the Highlands are manufactured. **Highland Wineries** (Moniack Castle, Kirkhill, ☎ 01463/831283) makes wines from Scottish ingredients such as birch sap.

Nairn and Environs

In Nairn do not miss **Nairn Antiques** (St. Ninian Pl., near the traffic circle, ☎ 01667/453303) for a wide inventory of antique jewelry, glassware, furniture, pottery, and prints. **Culloden Pottery** (at Gollanfield, midway between Nairn and Inverness, ☎ 01667/463240) offers you the chance to throw your own pot (which is then fired, glazed, and mailed to your home) or to choose from an original and extensive selection of hand-thrown domestic stoneware. There is also a gift-and-crafts shop and a restaurant that prides itself on serving only fresh—never frozen—food; there are fine views from the restaurant as well. **Brodie Country Fare** (Brodie, east of Nairn, ☎ 01309/641555) is guaranteed to affect your wallet in a pleasant way. Unusual knitwear, quality clothing, gifts, toys, and a restaurant beckon from beyond the fare's foodstore and delicatessen. The fare is well worth a visit, which could be combined with a trip to nearby Brodie Castle.

SPORTS AND FITNESS

Beaches
The most extensive beaches are at **Nairn**, with miles of clean, golden sand. The best known are at **Morar**, home of the famous white-and-silver sands.

Bicycling
The Great Glen is a fairly rugged area, and there are only two routes that go through it. The B862/B852, which runs by the east side of Loch Ness, is the less-trafficked and therefore a better bet for cyclists.

Bicycles can be rented from **Lee's Cycle Hire** (Fort William, ☎ 01397/704204), and **Off Beat Bikes** (Fort William, ☎ 01397/704008). Near Arisaig, **Bespoke Highland Tours** (The Bothy, Camusdarach, Inverness-shire, ☎ 01687/450272) rents bicycles and arranges tours of the Great Glen and the Highlands. **Mountain Madness** (Ballachulish, ☎ 01855/811728) rents mountain bikes and can suggest tour routes in the Glen Coe area. Aviemore has a wide choice of bicycle rental outlets, among them **Inverdruie Mountain Bikes** (at Inverdruie, on the Cairngorms road out of Aviemore, ☎ 01479/810787), **Speyside Sports** (Main St., Aviemore, ☎ 01479/810656), and **Sporthaus** (Main St., ☎ 01479/810655). Drumnadrochit, beside Loch Ness, has **Glen Cycles** (The Green, ☎ 01456/450554), while Inverness outlets include **Thorntons Cycles** (23 Castle St., ☎ 01463/235078).

Fishing
The Great Glen offers many rivers and lochs where you can fly-fish for salmon and trout. Tourist information centers (*see* Important Addresses and Numbers in Around the Great Glen Essentials, *below*) can provide information on locations, permits, and fishing rights (which differ from those in England and Wales). The fishing seasons are as follows: salmon, depending on the area, early February through September or early October; brown trout, March 15 to September 30; sea trout, May through September or early October; rainbow trout, no statutory-close season. Sea angling from shore or boat is also possible.

Golf
As is the case with most of Scotland, there is a broad selection of courses, especially toward the eastern end of this area. Nairn, with two courses, is highly regarded among Scottish players. The following courses welcome visitors: **Inverness Golf Club** (☎ 01463/239882), **Nairn Dunbar Golf Club** (☎ 01667/452741), **Nairn Golf Club** (☎ 01667/453208), **Torvean Golf Course** (Inverness, ☎ 01463/711434).

Skiing
Aviemore is perhaps the most advanced ski resort in the area, though the word "resort" is only loosely applicable to skiing in Scotland. Sometimes lifts can't operate due to winds. **Nevis Range on Aonach Mor** (☎

01397/705825; ski hotline, ☎ 01898/654660), near Fort William, offers some long runs.

Walking

The Great Glen area is renowned for its hill-walking opportunities, but walkers should be fit and properly outfitted. Tourist information centers (*see* Important Addresses and Numbers in Around the Great Glen Essentials, *below*) can offer guidance on low-level routes, and several excellent hill-walking guides available locally can and should be consulted for high-level routes. Remember that on **Ben Nevis,** a popular route even for inexperienced hill-walkers, it can snow on the summit plateau at any time of the year. Ben Nevis is a large and dangerous mountain.

DINING AND LODGING

Dining
WHAT TO WEAR

As elsewhere in Scotland, the country house hotels in this area expect a high standard of dress in their public areas. However, the less grand hotels, guest houses, and bed-and-breakfasts are used to dealing with the needs of hillwalkers and other outdoor enthusiasts, and only ask that you arrive at table clean and fresh after your day enjoying this beautiful region.

CATEGORY	COST*
$$$$	over £40
$$$	£30–£40
$$	£15–£30
$	under £15

per person for a three-course meal, including VAT, excluding drinks and service

Lodging
CATEGORY	COST*
$$$$	over £110
$$$	£80–£110
$$	£45–£80
$	under £45

All prices are for a standard double room, including service, breakfast, and VAT.

Arisaig
DINING AND LODGING

$$$$ **Arisaig House.** This secluded and grand Victorian mansion offers tranquility and some marvelous scenery, including views of the Inner Hebrides. The bedrooms are plush and restful, with soft-pastel colors, original moldings, and antique furniture. The cuisine at the restaurant emphasizes fresh local produce; try the local scallops and prawns with fresh basil and coriander or the spring lamb with fresh herbs. Children may not feel comfortable at this hotel. ☒ *Beasdale (6 mi south of Mallaig on A830), Arisaig PH39 4NR, ☎ 01687/450622, FAX 01687/450626. 2 suites, 12 rooms with bath. Croquet, sailing, fishing, island trips, billiards, library, 9-hole golf course at Trigh. AE, MC, V. Closed Nov.–Mar.*

$$ **Arisaig Hotel.** An old coaching inn close to the water, with magnificent views of the Small Isles, this hotel offers a slightly more modest environment than Arisaig House. The inn has retained its provinciality with simple decor and home cooking. High-quality local ingredients are used here to good advantage; locally caught lobster, langoustines, and crayfish are specialties, as are proper puddings, such as fruit crumbles. ⊠ *PH39 4NH,* ☎ *01687/450210,* 🖷 *01687/450310. 15 rooms, 6 with bath. MC, V.*

$$ **Old Library Lodge and Restaurant.** This guest house, a converted barn situated on the waterfront, has a fine restaurant, giving visitors another reason to believe that the village of Arisaig is unusually well endowed with good places to eat at all price levels. It offers local produce prepared in a French bistro style, served in a whitewashed, airy dining room. The bedrooms are very comfortable, from the flowery duvets to the cozy armchairs. ⊠ *PH39 4NH,* ☎ *01687/450651. 6 rooms with bath or shower. Restaurant (reservations advised). AE, MC, V. Closed Nov.–Mar.*

Dalcross
LODGING
$ **Easter Dalziel Farm.** This working 210-acre livestock and arable farm offers plenty of interest for guests staying one night or longer. The Victorian farmhouse, with log fire, home baking, and pretty gardens, is a welcome change from an impersonal hotel. Rooms have antique mahogany, oak, or pine furniture and floral fabrics, and tapestries stitched by the owner are displayed throughout the house. ⊠ *Dalcross, Inverness,* ☎ *and fax 01667/462213. 3 rooms. MC, V.*

Daviot
LODGING
$ **Greystanes.** Situated in a pine wood, this modern bungalow has superb views up the glen of the River Nairn to the hills beyond. The friendly hosts are delighted to share their home with visitors and provide a high standard of bed-and-breakfast. Rooms have modern furniture and floral fabrics. Wholesome Scottish dinners are prepared on request. ⊠ *Daviot West, IV1 2EP,* ☎ *01808/521381. 4 rooms, 1 with shower. MC, V.*

Drumnadrochit
DINING AND LODGING
$$–$$$$ **Polmaily House.** This country house is located on the northern edge of Loch Ness amid lovely parkland. Books, log fires, and a helpful staff contribute to an atmosphere that is warmer and more personal than that found at grander, more expensive hotels. The restaurant is noted for its traditional British cuisine, which takes advantage of fresh Highland produce. Tay salmon in pastry with dill sauce, roast rack of lamb with rosemary, and cold smoked venison with melon are examples of some flavorful dishes. ⊠ *Drumnadrochit, near A82, 12 mi southwest of Inverness, IV3 6XT,* ☎ *01456/450343,* 🖷 *01456/450813. Restaurant reservations advised. 11 rooms with bath. Restaurant (reservations advised), outdoor pool, tennis court, croquet. MC, V.*

LODGING
$–$$ **Borlum Farmhouse.** Spectacular views over Loch Ness are the outstanding feature of this guest house on a working farm. The rooms are individually decorated, most with light colors and antique furniture, and the food is well cooked. No smoking is permitted. ⊠ *Drumnadrochit, Inverness IV3 6XN,* ☎ *and fax 01456/450358. 5 rooms, 2 with bath. MC, V.*

Fort William
DINING AND LODGING

$$$$ **Inverlochy Castle.** A red-granite Victorian castle, Inverlochy stands in
★ 50 acres of woodland in the shadow of Ben Nevis, with striking Highland landscape on every side. Queen Victoria stayed here and wrote,
"I never saw a lovelier or more romantic spot." Dating from 1863,
the hotel retains the splendor of its period, with a fine frescoed ceiling, crystal chandeliers, and a handsome staircase in the Great Hall;
paintings and hunting trophies everywhere; and plush, comfortable bedrooms. The restaurant is exceptional. Many of the specialties are made
from local produce; the changing menu may include roast breast of Gress-
ingham duck with wild mushrooms and crispy vegetables, or braised
escalope of turbot with leeks, black trompette, and a mousse of scallops. For those in search of some pampering, this is the place to stay—
Inverlochy Castle spares no expense to ensure the comfort of its guests.
Torlundy (3 mi northeast of Fort William on A82), Inverness-shire PH33
6BN, ☎ *01397/702177,* ⓕⓐⓧ *01397/702953. 16 rooms with bath.*
Restaurant (reservations essential, jacket and tie). AE, MC, V. Closed
Dec.–mid-Mar.

Invergarry
DINING AND LODGING

$$ **Glengarry Castle Hotel.** This rambling, pleasantly old-fashioned man-
sion makes a good touring base; Invergarry is just south of Loch Ness
and within easy reach of the Great Glen's best sights. Rooms have tra-
ditional Victorian decor, and many have superb views over Loch Oich.
The food is reliably well-cooked in traditional Scottish style; try the poached
salmon with hollandaise or the loin of lamb with rosemary. ☎ *Inver-*
ness-shire, PH35 4HW, ☎ *01809/501254,* ⓕⓐⓧ *01809/501207. 26 rooms*
with bath. Tennis court, trout and pike fishing. AE, MC, V.

Inverness
DINING AND LODGING

$$$$ **Bunchrew House.** This turreted mansion set on the banks of the Beauly
Firth abounds with handsome wood paneling. The dining room is
particularly attractive, with fine antique furniture, and the lounge and
comfortable bedrooms are decorated with velvet and chintz. The
restaurant serves French-influenced Scottish cuisine, using the best
Aberdeen Angus beef, local salmon, and game. The extensive grounds
are delightful for a predinner stroll, and the views of the Firth are su-
perb. ☎ *Bunchrew, Inverness-shire IV3 6TA,* ☎ *01463/234917,* ⓕⓐⓧ
01463/710620. 11 rooms with bath. AE, MC, V.

$$$$ **Kingsmills Hotel.** A rambling mansion set in four acres of gardens, on
the edge of a golf course, the Kingsmills is only one mile from the cen-
ter of Inverness and is a great place for families: children under 14 stay
for free, and the heated indoor pool and extensive leisure facilities offer
plenty to do. The bedrooms are particularly spacious, comfortable, and
well-equipped. The restaurant serves well-prepared and reliable dishes,
such as steak, seafood tagliatelle, and game pâté. ☎ *Culcabock Rd.,*
IV2 3LP, ☎ *01463/237166,* ⓕⓐⓧ *01463/225208. 84 rooms with bath.*
Restaurant (reservations advised), indoor pool, 3-hole golf course,
golf privileges, health club. AE, DC, MC, V.

$$–$$$$ **Dunain Park Hotel.** Guests receive individual attention in this 18th-
century mansion set in six acres of wooded gardens. A log fire awaits
you in the living room, where you can sip a drink and browse through
books and magazines. Antiques and traditional decor make the bedrooms equally cozy and attractive. You can enjoy French-influenced

Scottish dishes in the restaurant, where candlelight is reflected in bone china and crystal. Saddle of venison in port sauce and boned quail stuffed with pistachios are two of the specialties. ⌂ *Dunain (2½ mi SW of Inverness on A82) IV3 6JN,* ☎ *01463/230512,* FAX *01463/224532. 14 rooms with bath. Restaurant (reservations advised, jacket and tie), indoor pool, sauna. AE, DC, MC, V. Closed 2 weeks in Feb.*

LODGING

$$ Ballifeary House Hotel. This well-maintained Victorian property was redecorated in 1993 and is within easy reach of downtown Inverness. The particularly helpful proprietors offer high standards of comfort and service. Rooms are individually decorated with modern furnishings, while the downstairs has reproduction antiques. Smoking is not permitted throughout the hotel. ⌂ *10 Ballifeary Rd., IV3 5PJ,* ☎ *01463/ 235572,* FAX *01463/717583. 8 rooms with bath. MC, V. Closed Nov.–Feb.*

$ Atholdene House. This family-run, 19th-century stone villa offers a friendly welcome and modernized accommodations. Evening meals can be provided for guests on request. The bus and railway stations are a short walk away. ⌂ *20 Southside Rd., IV2 3BG,* ☎ *01463/233565. 9 rooms, 7 with shower. No credit cards.*

$ Clach Mhuilinn. This modern family home is set in a pretty garden and has good parking facilities. It offers bed-and-breakfast of very high standard in an entirely nonsmoking environment. ⌂ *7 Harris Rd., IV2 3LS,* ☎ *01463/237059. 3 rooms, 1 with shower, 1 with bath. MC, V. Closed Dec.–Feb.*

$ Daviot Mains Farm. A 19th-century farmhouse, 5 miles south of Inverness on the A9, provides the perfect setting for home comforts and ★ traditional Scottish cooking for guests only; lucky ones may find wild salmon on the menu. ⌂ *Daviot Mains,* ☎ *01463/772215. 3 rooms; 1 with bath, 1 with shower. MC, V.*

Kingussie

DINING AND LODGING

$$$$ The Cross. Meals are superb, and the wine list is even more extensive than Osprey's (*see below*). This is an award-winning "restaurant with rooms" in the French style. Dinner, which could be breast of wood pigeon with onion confit or mousseline of pike with prawn sauce, is included in the price of your room. Bedrooms—all with king-size beds—are individually decorated, and may have a balcony, canopied bed, or an antique dressing table. ⌂ *Tweed Mill Brae, Kingussie, Inverness-shire PH21 1TC,* ☎ *01540/661166,* FAX *01540/661080. 9 rooms with bath. MC, V. Closed Dec.–Feb. and Tues. dinner.*

$ Osprey Hotel. This friendly hotel in the village of Kingussie is ideally located for skiing and hill walking. Rooms have old or antique furniture and floral wallpaper. An impressive wine list complements the much praised cuisine, which might include such dishes as halibut with smoked salmon sauce, or fillet steak with Stilton blue cheese and port. ⌂ *Kingussie, Inverness-shire PH21 1HX,* ☎ *and fax 01540/661510. 7 rooms with bath. AE, DC, MC, V.*

Nairn

DINING AND LODGING

$$$ Clifton House. Here is an utterly unique hotel: original works of art cover the walls, antique furniture graces the rooms, and antique silver gleams in the dining room—you may even find a musical recital taking place during your visit. The cuisine is famed far and wide for its classic preparation of Scottish produce—the Beef Wellington, lamb cutlets, and duck à l'orange are particularly good—and the wine list is probably the longest in the area. ⌂ *Viewfield St., Nairn,* ☎ *01667/*

453119, ☒ *01667/452836. 12 rooms with bath. 2 restaurants. AE, DC, MC, V. Closed Dec. and Jan.*

Whitebridge

DINING AND LODGING

$$$$ **Knockie Lodge.** Set on rising ground not far from Loch Ness, this for-
★ mer shooting lodge has superb views over peaceful surroundings and
is especially popular with fishermen and other outdoor-sports enthusiasts. The hotel is decorated with traditional and antique furniture,
there's a restrained elegance throughout the hotel. The restaurant offers enticing fixed menus with a choice of desserts. The chef uses top-
quality produce and prepares everything with great care; try the chicken
and duck terrine, the beef fillet wrapped in bacon and herbs with red
wine sauce, or the salmon fillet in filo pastry with sole mousse. Bar
lunches are also wholesome. The dining room is quite small, so advance reservations are needed if you are not a guest of the hotel. Dinner is included in the price of rooms. Inverness is easily accessed from
the hotel. ☎ *Whitebridge IV1 2UP,* ☎ *01456/486276,* ☒ *01456/
486389. 10 rooms with bath. Restaurant (reservations required). AE,
DC, MC, V. Closed Nov.–Apr.*

THE ARTS AND NIGHTLIFE

Do not visit this area expecting to have a big-city choice of late-night
activities. With the exception of Inverness, evening entertainment revolves around pubs and hotels, with the ceilidh, a small, informal, musical get-together; and Scottish evening, a staged performance of
tartan-clad Highland dancers, being the most popular forms of entertainment offered to visitors.

The Arts

Theater

Eden Court Theatre (Bishops Rd., Inverness, ☎ 01463/221718) offers
not only drama, but also a program of music, film, and light entertainment, and an art gallery.

Clifton House (*see* Dining and Lodging, *above*) at Nairn runs a program of concerts, recitals, and plays.

Nightlife

Bars and Lounges

Inverness has an array of bars and lounges. Among the most popular
are **Gunsmith's** (Union St.), a traditional pub offering bar meals, and
DJ's Café Bar (High St.), which serves everything from breakfast to late-
night cocktails. **Fort William** has a similarly wide range, and the pubs
of **Aviemore** offer an après-ski ambience.

Cabaret

Scottish Showtime (Cummings Hotel, Church St., Inverness, ☎ 01463/
232531) and **McTavish's Kitchens** (High St., Fort William, ☎ 01397/
702406) are the two most popular choices in the region. They both
offer Scottish cabaret of the tartan-clad dancer and bagpipe/accordian
variety.

Discos

There are a number of places to go dancing, particularly in Inverness, some in local hotels. For example, the **Caledonian Hotel** (Church St., Inverness, ☎ 01463/235181) holds regular ceilidhs in the summer season. To obtain a complete list, it is best to consult the local tourist information center (*see* Important Addresses and Numbers in Around the Great Glen Essentials, *above*).

In Aviemore, **Crofters** (☎ 01479/810624) at the Aviemore Mountain Resort has a bar open all day, with dancing nightly until 1 AM.

AROUND THE GREAT GLEN ESSENTIALS

Arriving and Departing

By Bus

There is a long-distance **Citylink** service from Fort William to Glasgow (Glasgow coach station, ☎ 0141/332–9191). Inverness is also well served from the central belt of Scotland (Inverness coach station, ☎ 01463/233371).

By Car

As in all areas of rural Scotland, a car is a great asset for exploring the Great Glen and Speyside, especially since the best of the area is away from the main roads. The fast A9 brings you to Inverness in roughly three hours from Glasgow or Edinburgh, even if you take your time.

By Plane

Inverness Airport (Dalcross, ☎ 01463/232471) has flights from Glasgow operated by **British Airways** (☎ 0345/222111). Alternatively, Fort William has bus and train connections with Glasgow, so **Glasgow Airport** can be an appropriate access point. *See* Chapter 4, Glasgow, for further information.

By Train

The area is surprisingly well served by train. There are connections from London to Inverness and Fort William, as well as reliable links from Glasgow and Edinburgh. For information call **ScotRail** (Fort William, ☎ 01397/703791; Inverness, ☎ 01463/238924) or contact any mainline station in Scotland.

Getting Around

By Bus

There is limited service available in the Great Glen area and some local service running from Fort William. **Highland Bus and Coach Company** (☎ 01397/702373) operates buses down the Great Glen, and has local service around Fort William. GaelicBus (☎ 01855/811229) operates the local bus service in the Lochaber area, and also has service from Fort William, south to Oban. A number of post-bus services will help get you to the more remote corners of the area. The timetable is available from the **Head Post Office** (Edinburgh, ☎ 0131/550–8232) or the **District Head Post Office** (14–16 Queen's Gate, Inverness, ☎ 01463/234111, ext. 248).

By Car

You can use the main A9 Perth–Inverness road (via Aviemore) to explore this area or use one of the many other smaller roads (some of them old military roads) to explore the much quieter east side of Loch Ness. The same applies to Speyside, where a variety of options open up away from the A9, especially through the pinewoods by Coylumbridge and Feshiebridge, east of the main road. Mallaig, west of Fort William, also has improving road connections, but rail still remains the most enjoyable way to experience the rugged hills and loch scenery between these two places. In Morvern, the area across Loch Linnhe southwest of Fort William, you may encounter single-lane roads, which require slower speeds and concentration.

By Train

Though the Great Glen has no rail connection (in Victorian times Fort William and Inverness had different lines built by companies that could not agree), this area has the **West Highland line,** which links Fort William to Mallaig, a small fishing and ferry port on the west coast.

Guided Tours

Orientation

From Fort William, **Highland Bus and Coach Company** (Travel Centre, Fort William, ☎ 01397/702373) operates coach tours in the summer season. **ScotRail** (☎ 01397/703791) runs services on the outstandingly beautiful West Highland Line to Mallaig. **Caledonian MacBrayne** runs scheduled service and cruises to Skye, the Small Isles, and Mull from Mallaig (☎ 01475/650100, FAX 01475/637607). **Arisaig Marine** (☎ 01687/450224) operates highly recommended Hebridean day cruises on the MV (motor vessel) *Shearwater* to the Small Isles and Skye at Easter, and daily from May to September.

From Inverness, **Highland Bus and Coach Company** (Inverness bus station, ☎ 01463/233371) offers coach tours during the summer season, as do **Macdonald's Tours** (☎ 01463/240673), and **Spa Coaches** (☎ 01997/421311).

Special-Interest

From Inverness, **Highland Insight Tours and Travel** (☎ 01463/831403), offers personalized touring holidays and full-day or half-day tours that cater to any interest, with **James Johnson Chauffeur Drive** (☎ 01463/790179) offering a similar service. **Linnmhor Limousines** (Linnmhor, Strathpeffer, ☎ 01997/421528), has chauffeur-driven limousines for daily hire. **Jacobite Cruises Ltd.** (Tomnahurich Bridge, Glenurquhart Rd., Inverness, ☎ 01463/233999, FAX 01463/710188) runs morning and afternoon cruises to Loch Ness, morning and afternoon excursions to Urquhart Castle, and boat and coach excursions to the Monster Exhibition. **Macaulay Charters** (12 Pict Ave., Inverness, ☎ 01463/225398) provides trips by boat from Inverness to Nairn and the surrounding coastline, offering visitors the chance to see dolphins in their breeding area.

Important Addresses and Numbers

Emergencies

For police, fire, or ambulance, dial 999 from any telephone. No coins are needed for emergency calls from phone booths.

Hospitals

Emergency rooms are located at the following hospitals: **Belford Hospital** (Belford Rd., Fort William, ☎ 01397/702481), **Raigmore Hospital** (Perth Rd., Inverness, ☎ 01463/704000), and **Town and County Hospital** (Cawdor Rd., Nairn, ☎ 01667/452101).

Late-Night Pharmacies

Pharmacies are not common away from the larger towns. In an emergency, the police will assist you in locating a pharmacist. In Inverness, **Kinmylies Pharmacy** (1 Charleston Court, Kinmylies, ☎ 01463/221094) is open weekdays until 6 and Saturday until 5:30. The pharmacy at the **Scottish Co-op** superstore (Milton of Inshes, Perth Rd., outside Inverness, ☎ 01463/242525), is open Monday to Wednesday 9–8, Thursday and Friday 9–9, Saturday 8–6, and Sunday 10–5. In Fort William, **Boots the Chemist** (High St., ☎ 01397/705143) is open Monday to Saturday 8:45–6. A rotation system provides limited Sunday service—consult the list on any pharmacy door.

Visitor Information

The principal centers in the area are the **Tourist Information Centre** in Aviemore (Grampian Rd., ☎ 01479/810363, FAX 01479/811063), the **Tourist Information Centre** in Fort William (Cameron Centre, Cameron Sq., ☎ 01397/703781, FAX 01397/705184), and the **Tourist Information Centre** in Inverness (Castle Wynd, ☎ 01463/234353, FAX 01463/710609). Other tourist information centers open seasonally include those at Ballachulish, Carrbridge, Daviot Wood (A9), Fort Augustus, Grantown on Spey, Kilchooan, Kingussie, Mallaig, Nairn, Ralia (A9), Spean Bridge, and Strontian.

11 The Northern Highlands

The Highlands contain the country's most breathtaking scenery. In a couple of hours you pass from heather, bracken, and springy turf to granite rock and bog, to serrated peak and snow-water lake, to the red sandstone of Wester Ross, and the flowery banks of Lochs Ewe and Maree. The interior has forested glens, hills of heather, rocky waterfalls, and the Cuillin Mountains. The Outer Hebrides are the most rugged part of Scotland, with constant wind and rain, and an often inhospitable landscape where anything that grows seems a gift.

THE OLD COUNTIES of Ross and Cromarty (sometimes called Easter and Wester Ross), Sutherland, and Caithness constitute the most northern portion of mainland Scotland. The population is sparse, mountains and moorland limit the choice of touring routes, and distances are less important than whether the winding, hilly roads you travel are two lanes or one. On a map, this area seems far from major urban centers, but it is easy to get to. Inverness has an airport with direct links to Glasgow, and you can reach such destinations as the fishing town of Ullapool in about an hour by car from Inverness. In fact, much of the western seaboard is easily accessible from the Northern Highlands.

By Gilbert
Summers

The area contains some of Scotland's most fascinating scenery. Much of Sutherland and Wester Ross, for example, is comprised of a rocky platform of Lewisian gneiss, certainly the oldest rocks in Britain, scoured and hollowed by glacial action into numerous lochs. On top of this rolling wet moorland landscape sit strangely shaped quartzite-capped sandstone mountains, eroded and pinnacled.

Many of the place-names in this region reflect its early links with Scandinavia. Sutherland, the most northern portion of mainland Scotland, was once the "southern land" of the Vikings. Scotland's most northern point, Cape Wrath, got its name from the Viking's word *hvarth*, meaning a "turning point," and Laxford, Suilven, and dozens of other names in the area have Norse rather than Gaelic derivations.

The islands of Skye and especially the Outer Hebrides, which are now often referred to as the Western Isles, are the stronghold of the Gaelic language. Skye is famous for its misty mountains called the Cuillins, while the Outer Hebrides have some of Scotland's finest beaches.

EXPLORING

From Inverness, gateway to the Northern Highlands, roads fan out like the spokes of a wheel to join the coastal route around the rim of mainland Scotland. Most visitors tour from east to west, saving the best scenery for last. The first three tours described below take the visitor to the west, while the fourth explores up the east coast to John o'Groats, and to Duncansby Head in the far north.

Tour 1: The Northern Landscapes—
Wester Ross and Sutherland

Numbers in the margin correspond to points of interest on the Northern Highlands and Skye map.

It takes roughly one hour to travel from Inverness to Ullapool (on A9 and then A835), where you can catch a ferry to Stornoway on the isle of Lewis, part of the Outer Hebrides. If you're not rushing to catch a ferry, however, stop along the way in the former Victorian spa town of ❶ **Strathpeffer** on A834—where you can even taste the waters. Not far from Strathpeffer are the tumbling **Falls of Rogie** (signposted off the A835), where an alarmingly sagging suspension bridge leaves visitors with a fine view of the splashing waters below and an uneasy stomach.

★ ❷ If you really want to give yourself a touch of vertigo, however, the **Corrieshalloch Gorge** should be next on your sightseeing agenda. You can reach the gorge by following the A835 (to Ullapool) west of **Garve**, across the bare backbone of Scotland. As the road begins to drop down from the bleak lands of the interior, look for Braemore junction and continue on the A835. Shortly after, as you draw closer to the woods, you'll see the Corrieshalloch Gorge parking lot on the left. A burn draining the high moors plunges 150 feet into a 200-foot-deep, thickly wooded gorge. There is a suspension-bridge viewpoint and an atmosphere of romantic grandeur, like an old Scottish print come to life.

❸ The road then rolls down to **Ullapool** by the shores of salty **Loch Broom.** This community was founded in 1788 as a fishing station, to exploit the local herring stocks. In recent years the fishing activity here has included "klondyking," the direct purchase of fish from local boats by large, Eastern European factory ships. Ullapool has a cosmopolitan air and comes alive when the Lewis ferry docks and departs.

TIME OUT **Ceilidh Place** (W. Argyle St., ☎ 01854/612103) is a warm, friendly coffeehouse and restaurant where the prices are sensible, and there is a regular program of music and drama. Ceilidh Place also offers excellent, reasonably priced accommodation (*see* Dining and Lodging, *below*).

If you travel northward, you will take a two-lane road, the A835/A837, which takes you past the strange landscape of **Wester Ross.** Look westward for the little mountain **Stac Polly**—which resembles a ruined fortress—and the humps of **Suilven.** At **Knockan,** about 15 miles north of Ullapool, a nature trail along a cliff illuminates some of the interesting local geology, as well as the area's flora and fauna. If this jaunt sounds too energetic, a more restful alternative may be to enjoy the good **❹** views of the mountains from the **Inverpolly National Nature Reserve.**

Following the signs for Lochinver along Loch Assynt will bring you to **❺** the unattended ruins of **Ardvreck Castle,** on the edge of Loch Assynt. This was a clan MacLeod stronghold, built in the 15th century. From **❻** Ardvreck Castle it's only a 20-minute drive on a two-lane road to **Lochinver,** a charming community with a few choices of accommodations and places to eat. Behind the town the mountain Suilven rises abruptly. This unusual monolith is best seen from across the water, however: Take the cul-de-sac, **Baddidarach Road,** for the finest photo opportunity.

A single-lane unclassified road winds south from Lochinver, providing outstanding sea views within the first 5 miles. Do not fall victim to the breathtaking landscape, however: The road has several blind bends that demand special care. You will then be near what is perhaps Scotland's most remote bookshop. The road will swing left and inland immediately after **Loch Kirkaig;** nearby is a car park beside the River Kirkaig, and a short stroll away is **Achins Book and Craft Shop** (☎ 01571/844262, look for signs by the river bridge). Its pleasant coffee shop is open Easter through October, daily (except Sunday) 10–5.

This wild though harmonious landscape of bracken and birch tree, heather and humped hill horizons, prevails until you see signs for **❼** **Achiltibuie:** You'll then encounter a strung-out line of crofts, many now owned by incomers. Offshore are the **Summer Isles,** romantic enough in thought, but in reality bleak and austere. In Achiltibuie there's a smokehouse that serves succulent smoked cuts of venison and other delicacies, and the Hydroponicum, a huge glass house that certainly looks out of place but is effective in producing giant strawberries.

Return to Ullapool, then retrace your route as far as the Braemore Road junction, noted earlier, which juts above the Corrieshalloch Gorge. Take the A832 toward **Gairloch.** Soon you will once more be traversing wild country. The toothed ramparts of the mountain **An Teallach** (pronounced *tyel*-lach, with Scots *ch*, of course) can be seen on the horizon ahead. The moorland route you travel is known chillingly as **Destitution Road.** It was commissioned in 1851 to give the local folk (long vanished from the area) some way of earning a living following the failure of the potato crop; it is said the workers were paid only in food.

★ ❽ The road descends to the woodlands of **Dundonnell** and to Loch Broom. The coastal scenery hereabouts improves with views of **Gruinard Bay** and its white beaches, but the highlight for most travelers is **Inverewe Gardens,** another half hour to the south. The reputation of the gardens at Inverewe, in spite of their comparatively remote location, has grown steadily through the years. The main attraction lies in the contrast between the bleak coastal headlands and thin-soiled moors and the lush plantings of the garden behind the dense shelterbelts. These are proof of the efficiency of the warm North Atlantic Drift, part of the Gulf Stream, which takes the edge off winter frosts. (Inverewe is sometimes described as subtropical, but this is an inaccuracy which truly irritates the head gardener; do not expect coconuts and palm trees here.) *A832, 6 mi northeast of Gairloch,* ☎ *01445/781200.* ✔ *£3.50 adults, £1.80 children. Gardens open Apr.–late Oct., daily 9:30–9; late Oct.–Mar., daily 9:30–5. Visitor center open Apr.–mid-Oct., daily 9:30–5:30. Guided walks with the head gardener Apr.–mid-Oct., weekdays at 1:30.*

TIME OUT The National Trust for Scotland, which looks after the gardens, also runs an adequate **tearoom** (☎ 01445/781200; open 10–5) with a selection of cakes and biscuits.

❾ **Gairloch,** the region's main center, lies to the south of the gardens and has some shops and accommodations. The **Myrtle Bank Hotel** (☎ 01445/712004), for instance, serves cream-scone teas as well as bar meals. Also in the village is the **Gairloch Heritage Museum,** with exhibitions covering the area from prehistoric times to the present. Gairloch has one further advantage: Lying just a short way from the mountains of the interior, this small oasis often escapes the rain clouds that sometimes cling to the high summits. Guests can enjoy a game of golf here and perhaps stay dry, even when the nearby Torridon hills are deluged.

★ ❿ From Gairloch the road goes inland to one of Scotland's most scenic lochs, **Loch Maree.** Look for the sign, soon after the road reaches the loch side, for **Victoria Falls,** an attractive waterfall named after the queen who visited them. The harmonious environs of the loch, with its tall Scots pines and the mountain Slioch looming as a backdrop, witnessed the destruction of much of its tree cover in the 18th century. Iron ore was shipped in and smelted using local oak to feed the furnaces. Oak now grows here only on the northern limits of the range.

The Nature Conservancy Council has an information center and nature trails by the loch side. Red deer sightings are virtually guaranteed; locals say the best place to spot another local denizen, the pine marten, is around the trash containers in the parking turnoffs.

★ ⓫ The tall pines of Loch Maree prepare the visitor for the contrasting scenic spectacle of **Glen Torridon,** which you can reach by turning right at Kinlochewe. Some say that Glen Torridon has the finest mountain scenery in Scotland. It consists mainly of the long gray quartzite flanks of **Ben Eighe** (rhymes with *say*), which make up Scotland's oldest national nature reserve, and **Liathach** (pronounced *leea*-gach), with its distinct ridge profile that looks like the keel of an upturned boat.

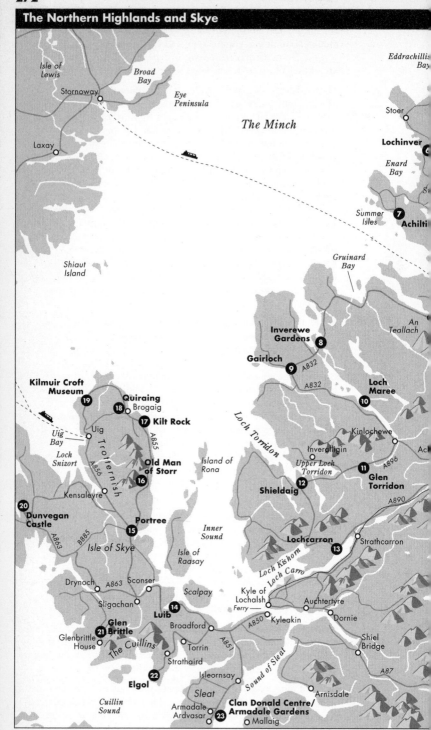

Isle of Lewis

Stornoway

Broad Bay

Eye Peninsula

Laxay

The Minch

Eddrachillis Bay

Stoer

Lochinver

Enard Bay

Summer Isles

7 **Achilti**

Shiant Island

Gruinard Bay

An Teallach

Inverewe Gardens **8**

Gairloch **9** A832

A832

Loch Maree

10

Kilmuir Croft Museum **19**

Quiraing **18**
Brogaig

Kilt Rock **17**

Uig Bay

Uig

A855

Loch Snizort

A856

Trotternish

Loch Torridon

Kinlochewe

Inveralligin

Upper Loch Torridon

11

Glen Torridon

A896

Ac

Old Man of Storr **16**

Island of Rona

Shieldaig

12

Kensaleyre

20
Dunvegan Castle

A863

B885

Portree **15**

Isle of Skye

Inner Sound

Isle of Raasay

Lochcarron

13

Strathcarron

A890

Loch Kishorn

Loch Carro

Drynoch

A863 Sconser

Scalpay

Sligachan

Luib **14**

Glen Brittle **21**

Glenbrittle House

The Cuillins

Broadford

Torrin

Strathaird

A851

Kyle of Lochalsh
Ferry

Kyleakin

A850

Auchtertyre

Dornie

Shiel Bridge

A87

Elgol **22**

Cuillin Sound

Isleornsay

Sleat

Armadale
Ardvasar

Clan Donald Centre/ Armadale Gardens **23**

Mallaig

Sound of Sleat

Arnisdale

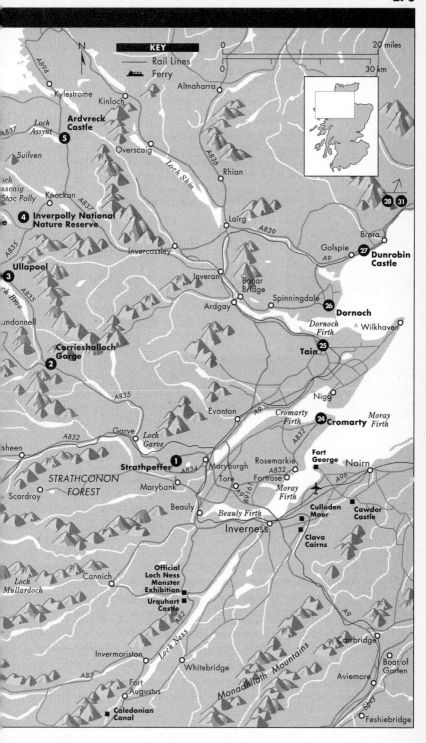

KEY

— Rail Lines

⛴ Ferry

0   20 miles

0   30 km

A894

Kylestrome

Kinloch

Altnaharra

Loch Assynt

A837

Ardvreck Castle

⑤

Suilven

Overscaig

Loch Shin

Rhian

A836

och uscaig Stac Polly

Knockan

A837

④ **Inverpolly National Nature Reserve**

Lairg

A839

Brora

A835

Golspie

A9

⑦ **Dunrobin Castle**

②⑧ ③①

③ **Ullapool**

A835

Invercassley

Inveram

Bonar Bridge

Spinningdale

②⑥ **Dornoch**

ch Broo

A835

undonnell

Ardgay

Dornoch Firth

Wilkhaven

Corrieshalloch Gorge

②

Tain

②⑤

A835

Nigg

Evanton

A9

Cromarty Firth

②④ **Cromarty**

Moray Firth

Garve

Loch Garve

A832

Strathpeffer ①

A834

Maryburgh

Rosemarkie

A832

Fort George

Nairn

sheen

A96

STRATHCONON FOREST

Marybank

Tore

Fortrose

A9/A96

Moray Firth

Scardroy

Beauly

Beauly Firth

Culloden Moor

Cawdor Castle

Inverness

Clava Cairns

Loch Mullardoch

Cannich

Official Loch Ness Monster Exhibition

Urquhart Castle

A82

Carrbridge

A9

Invermoriston

Loch Ness

Whitebridge

Monadhliath Mountains

Boat of Garten

A87

Aviemore

Fort Augustus

Caledonian Canal

Spey

Feshiebridge

At the far end of the glen the National Trust for Scotland operates a visitor center that explains the ecology and geology of the area.

⑫ Not too far from the southern coast of Upper Loch Torridon is **Shieldaig,** a village that sits in an attractive crescent over a loch of its own, **Loch Shieldaig.** For an atmospheric evening foray, walk north toward Loch Torridon at the northern end of the village, by the church. The path is fairly well made, though hiking shoes are recommended. You will find exquisite views and tiny rocky beaches.

You can then continue driving south by the A896, passing **Rassal Ash Wood** on your left. The lushness of the fenced-in area within this small nature reserve is a reminder of what Scotland might have been had sheep and deer not been kept here in such high numbers. The combined nibbling of these animals ensures that Scotland's natural tree cover does not regenerate without human intervention.

⑬ The road continues past **Kishorn** to **Lochcarron,** a village strung along the shore. Return toward Inverness on the A890, a single-lane road in some stretches, with plenty of open vistas across the deserted heart of northern Scotland.

Tour 2: Skye, the Misty Island

Skye ranks near the top of most visitors' priority lists: The romance of Bonnie Prince Charlie, the misty **Cuillin Mountains,** and its nearness to the mainland all contribute to its popularity. The following tour takes you around the island in two or three days. Orientation is easy: Follow the only roads around the loops on the northern part of the island. There are some stretches of single-lane road, but none pose a problem.

⑭ After crossing the bridge at Kyle of Lochalsh, follow the A850 along the coast. At **Luib,** note the **Old Skye Crofter's House,** with its traditional thatch and 19th-century furnishings. The hills ahead have a reddish hue—they comprise the **Red Cuillin,** the gentler companions of the Black Cuillins, which swing spectacularly into view on the approaches to **Sligachan.**

⑮ Turning away from the hills, the road goes north through tranquil scenery to **Portree,** the population center of the island. Not overburdened by historical features, Portree is a pleasant center clustered around a small and sheltered bay.

To see the northern peninsula of **Trotternish,** head out on the A855, noting the cliffs rising to your left. The cliffs are actually the edge of an ancient lava-flow that runs for miles as your rugged companion, set back from the road. In some places the hardened lava has created spectacular features. Soon you will see one of them on the horizon: a curious **⑯** pinnacle called the **Old Man of Storr.** Continue past neat white crofts **⑰** and forestry plantings until you reach **Kilt Rock.** Everyone on the Skye-tour circuit stops here to peep gingerly over the cliffs for a look at the curious geology of the cliff edge. Here, bands of two different types of rock have a folded, pleated effect just like the material of a kilt.

★ **⑱** Even more spectacular is the **Quiraing,** 5 miles farther. For a closer view of the strange pinnacles and rock forms, make a left onto a small road at **Brogaig** by **Staffin Bay.** There is a car park near the point where this road breaches the ever-present cliff line, though you will have to be physically fit to walk back toward the Quiraing itself, where the rock formations and cliffs are most dramatic. The trail is on uneven, stony ground, and it's a steep scramble up to the rock formations. In ages past, stolen cattle were hidden deep within the Quiraing's rocky jaws.

(19) Return to the main A855, continuing around the top end of Trotternish, to the **Kilmuir Croft Museum,** where you can see the old farming ways brought to life. Included in the displays and exhibits are documents and photographs, reconstructed interiors, and implements. Flora Macdonald, helpmate of Prince Charles Edward Stuart, is buried nearby.

(20) The west coast of Trotternish is pleasant, but this is probably all you could easily manage in one day. You may want to return to Portree and spend the night before making a separate expedition to **Dunvegan Castle.** In a commanding position above a sea loch, Dunvegan has been the seat of the chiefs of Clan Macleod for more than 700 years. Though greatly changed over the centuries, a gloomy ambience prevails, and there is plenty of family history on display, notably the fascinating "Fairy Flag"—a silk banner, thought to be originally from Rhodes or Syria and believed to have magically saved the clan from danger. The banner's powers are said to suffice for only one more use. ☎ 01470/521206. ☛ *£4 adults, £3.60 senior citizens and students, £2.20 children; garden only, £2.50 adults, £1.50 children.* ☉ *Mid-Mar.–Oct., Mon.–Sat. 10–5:30, Sun. 1–5:30 (last entry 5). Craft shop and restaurant open mid-Mar.–Oct., daily 10–5:30.*

★ (21) There are two other excursions to consider, both taking in spectacular mountain scenery. The first is to **Glen Brittle,** off the A863 on the west side of the island. This jaunt provides some fine views of the Cuillin ridges—not a place for the ordinary walker (there are many dangerous ridges and steep faces). The second suggestion follows a small road, a cul-de-sac resembling Glen Brittle, which leads you to one of the finest views in Scotland. At **Broadford,** take the A881 for Elgol. This road passes through **Strath Suardal** and little **Loch Cill Chriosd** (**Kilchrist**) by a ruined church. If there are cattle wading in the loch and the light is soft—typical of Skye—then this place takes on the air of a romantic Victorian oil painting. Mindful of the marble quarry at **Torrin** and the breathtaking

★ (22) views of the mountain **Blaven,** simply follow the road to **Elgol.** This is just a gathering of crofts along the suddenly descending road, which ends at a pier. You can admire the heart-stopping profile of the Cuillin peaks from the shore or, at a point about halfway down the hill, find the path that goes toward them across the rough grasslands.

(23) To leave the island you can take the alternative ferry running from **Armadale** to **Mallaig.** If you go this way, you can visit the popular **Clan Donald Centre** and **Armadale Gardens** on the A851. The center tells the story of the Macdonalds and their proud title: the Lords of the Isles. In the 15th century they were powerful enough to threaten the authority of the Stuart monarchs of Scotland. There is also a major exhibition in a restored part of the castle, as well as extensive gardens and nature trails. *A851 at Armadale, ½ mi north of Armadale Pier,* ☎ *01471/844305 or 01471/844227. Admission to center: £3.20 adults, £2.20 senior citizens and children, £9 family ticket. Center open Apr.–Oct., daily 9:30–6 (last entry 5). Gardens open at all times.*

Tour 3: The Road to John o'Groats

The essence of **Caithness,** the area at the top of Scotland (reached by Route A9, the main east-coast road), is space, big skies, and distant blue hills beyond endless rolling moors.

(24) From Inverness, cross the Beauly Firth on the Kessock Bridge, and follow the B9161/A832 in the direction of Cromarty, via Fortrose and Rosemarkie. You are now in the **Black Isle,** a pleasant mixture of woods and farmland. At the end of the A832, **Cromarty** is a good ex-

ample of a Scottish eastern seaboard town, with narrow, winding streets and old cottages interspersed with a few Georgian mansions, the town houses of landowners living 200 years ago. Thanks to the conversion of the **Cromarty Courthouse** into a visitor center, you can learn all about life in an 18th-century Scottish *burgh* (a town with trading rights); take a self-guided walking tour of the town—the center's cassette and headphones will keep you on track. *Church St.,* ☎ *01381/600418.* ☛ *£2.75 adults, £1.50 senior citizens and children.* ☉ *Apr.–Oct., daily 10–6; Nov.–Mar., daily noon–4.*

Hugh Miller's Cottage is nearby. Hugh Miller was a 19th-century stonemason, theologian, and self-taught geologist, who advanced the science of geology by his fossil discoveries in Scotland. The cottage itself is whitewashed, thatched, and dates from 1711, when it was built by Hugh Miller's great-grandfather. It contains an exhibition on Hugh Miller's life and work, and is decorated in period style. *Church St.,* ☎ *01381/600245.* ☛ *£1.50 adults, 80p children.* ☉ *May–Sept., Mon.–Sat. 10–1 and 2–5:30, Sun. 2–5:30.*

㉕ Return to the A9, and continue north to **Tain,** another attractive community and once a place of pilgrimage of the Scottish kings, as the local museum and visitor center will tell you. The ruins of St. Duthac's Chapel built from 1065 to 1256, mark the site of the birthplace of St. Duthac, an early missionary to the Picts. The chapel was a pilgrimage site for centuries. The **Pilgrimage Visitor Centre** (Tower St., ☎ 01862/894089) has displays on where pilgrimages were made and

㉖ why. Over the Dornoch Firth (there's a bridge) lies **Dornoch,** with its 13th-century cathedral. This town of mellow sandstone and tiny, rose-filled gardens is noted for its golf—you may hear it referred to as "the St. Andrews of the north." Visit the crafts center which now occupies the former town jail; here you can watch weavers at work weaving tartan cloth. *Castle St.,* ☎ *01862/810555.* ☛ *Free.* ☉ *Easter–Sept., daily 9–5; Oct.–Easter, weekdays 10–1 and 2–4.*

Continuing north on the A9, you'll see the controversial statue of the 1st Duke of Sutherland on Beinn a Bragaidh (Ben Braggie), the hilltop to the west. 1994 saw the initiation of a campaign to have it removed, as the Duke was partly responsible for brutality associated with the Sutherland Clearances of 1810–1820, when thousands of peasants were dislocated from crowded interior crofts to sites on the coast. His Scot-

㉗ tish home was **Dunrobin Castle,** one of the largest houses in the Highlands, which is open to visitors. *Golspie (on the A9),* ☎ *01408/633177.* ☛ *£3.70 adults, £1.90 children, £2.30 senior citizens, £9.40 family ticket.* ☉ *May and Oct., Mon.–Sat. 10:30–4, Sun. 1–4; June–Sept., Mon.–Sat. 10:30–5, Sun. 1–5.*

㉘ Stay on the A9 for **Helmsdale.** Here, the **Timespan Heritage Centre,** a thought-provoking mix of tableaux, artifacts, and audiovisual materials, portrays the history of the area, from the Stone Age to the 1869 gold rush in the Strath of Kildonan. *Helmsdale,* ☎ *01431/821327.* ☛ *£2.75 adults, £2.20 students and senior citizens, £1.65 children, £7.20 family ticket.* ☉ *Apr.–Oct., Mon.–Sat. 10–5, Sun. 2–5 (closes at 6 PM in summer).*

Nearby, at **Baile an Or,** on the site of the 1869 gold rush (*baile an or* means gold town), panning is still possible, using pans supplied by Strathullie Local and Scottish Crafts. *Helmsdale,* ☎ *01431/821343.* ☛ *£1.50/day to hire pan, riddle, and trowel.*

The scenery changes, growing wilder as the moors of Caithness roll
㉙ down to the sea. At **Dunbeath,** the **Dunbeath Heritage Centre** is an old

school that the local community—concerned that their past should be recorded—turned into a museum. It displays photographs, and domestic and crofting artifacts which relay the history of the area from the Bronze Age to the oil age, and is particularly helpful to those researching their family history. Nearby, the **Lhaidhay Croft Museum** feels, appropriately, more like a private home than a museum. It was built around 1842, comprising a longhouse and barn—animals and people lived under the same long roof—furnished as it would have been during its working life. *Dunbeath Heritage Centre: Dunbeath,* ☎ *01593/731233.* ☞ *£1.50 adults, 50p children and senior citizens, £3.50 family ticket.* ☺ *May–Sept., Mon.–Sat. 10–5, Sun. 11–6. Lhaidhay Croft Museum: Dunbeath,* ☎ *01593/731244.* ☞ *£1 adults, 20 p children.* ☺ *Easter–mid-Oct., daily 10–6.*

㉚ Continue on the A9 to **Wick,** a substantial town that was built on its fishing industry. Visit the **Wick Heritage Centre** for details on how this town grew—it's run by local people for the local community, and they are real enthusiasts. *18 Bank Row,* ☎ *01955/605393.* ☞ *£1.50 adults, 50p children.* ☺ *June–Sept., Mon.–Sat. 10–5.*

Our tour stops here, but you might wish to continue your trek north: The gaunt, bleak ruins of Castle Sinclair and Castle Girnigoe teeter on a clifftop to the north of Wick, while farther north is the Northlands Viking Centre (open June–Sept., daily 10–4), reminding us of the role of Scandinavian settlers in this area. From here it is only minutes to **㉛** **John o'Groats,** a windswept little outpost—the most northerly town on the Scottish mainland—with some high-quality crafts shops. Go east to **Duncansby Head** for spectacular views of cliffs and sea-stacks by the lighthouse—and puffins, too, if you know where to look. If you have time, turn west to explore the whole of Scotland's topmost coast; if not, return to Inverness on the A9.

Tour 4: The Outer Hebrides (Western Isles)

Numbers in the margin correspond to the points of interest on the Outer Hebrides map.

The Outer Hebrides—in common parlance also known as the Western Isles—stretch about 130 miles from end to end and lie about 50 miles from the Scottish mainland. This splintered archipelago extends from the pugnacious Butt of Lewis in the north to the 600-foot Barra Head on Berneray in the south, whose lighthouse has the greatest arc of visibility in the world. The **Isle of Lewis and Harris** is the northernmost and largest of the group. The island's only major town, **Stornoway,** is situated on a big, nearly landlocked harbor on the east coast of Lewis.

Just south of the Sound of Harris is **North Uist,** rich in monoliths and chambered cairns and other reminders of a prehistoric past. Though it is one of the smaller islands in the chain, **Benbecula,** sandwiched between North and South Uist and sometimes referred to as the Hill of the Fords, is in fact less bare and neglected looking than its bigger neighbors to the north. **South Uist,** once a refuge of the old Catholic faith, is dotted with ruined forts and chapels; in summer its wild gardens burst with riots of Alpine and rock plants. **Eriskay** and a scattering of islets almost block the 6-mile strait between South Uist and **Barra,** the southernmost major formation in the Outer Hebrides, an isle you can walk across in an hour.

Lewis and Harris

32 The port capital for the Outer Hebrides is **Stornoway** on Lewis, which can be reached by car ferry from Ullapool on the mainland. This is probably the most convenient starting point for a driving tour of the islands if you're approaching the Western Isles from the Northern Highlands. In Stornoway itself, the **An Lanntair Gallery** offers a varied program of contemporary and traditional exhibitions that change monthly, as well as frequent musical and theatrical events emphasizing traditional Gaelic culture. *Town Hall, S. Beach St., Stornoway,* ☎ *01851/703307.* ☛ *Free.* ◎ *Mon.–Sat. 9–5:30.*

The best road to use to explore the territory north of Stornoway is the A857, which runs first across the island to the northwest and then to the northeast all the way to Port of Ness (about 30 miles). At the northernmost point of the island—just a few minutes northwest of **33** **Port of Ness** along the B8014—stands the **Butt of Lewis lighthouse,** designed by David and Thomas Stevenson (of the prominent engineering family, whose best-known member was, ironically, the novelist Robert Louis Stevenson). The lighthouse was first lit in 1862. The adjacent cliffs provide a good vantage point for viewing seabirds, whales, and porpoises.

Go back south on the A857 and pick up the A858 at Barvas. From there it's about a 10-minute drive to the small community of **Arnol.** **34** Look for signs off the A858 for the **Arnol Black House,** a well-preserved example of an increasingly rare type of traditional Hebridean home. Once in common use throughout the islands (as recently as 50 years ago), these dwellings were built without mortar and thatched on a timber framework without eaves. Other characteristic features include an open central peat hearth and the absence of a chimney—hence the sooty atmosphere and the designation "black." On display inside are many of the house's original furnishings. *Off A858, Arnol,* ☎ *0131/244–3101.* ☛ *£1.50 adults, £1 senior citizens, 75p children.* ◎ *Apr.–Sept., Mon.–Sat. 9:30–6; Oct.–Mar., Mon.–Sat. 9:30–4.*

Continue south on A858 another 5 miles or so to reach **Shawbost,** home **35** of the **Shawbost School Museum.** This museum came to life as a result of the so-called Highland Village Competition in 1970, during which school pupils gathered artifacts and contributed to displays aimed at illustrating a past way of life in Lewis. Though it has, sadly, become a bit dog-eared and dusty, the museum does provide a glimpse at the old life and customs of the island. *A858,* ☎ *01851/710213.* ☛ *Voluntary donation.* ◎ *Apr.–Nov., Mon.–Sat. 10–6.*

36 Approximately 8 miles farther south on A858, at **Dun Carloway,** you can see one of the best preserved Iron Age brochs in Scotland. The mysterious circular defensive towers of the Dun Carloway broch, built about 2,000 years ago possibly as protection against seaborne raiders, provide fine views of a typical Lewis landscape. Parts of the storied walls still stand as high as 30 feet. *A858,* ☎ *0131/244–3101.* ☛ *Free.* ◎ *24 hrs.*

Follow A858 about 10 miles to the southeast, along the inlet called East Loch Roag, to reach **Callanish.** A few miles west of the village **37** (along B8012) are the **Callanish Standing Stones,** a setting of megaliths rated second only to Stonehenge in England. Probably positioned in several stages between 3,000 and 1,500 BC, this grouping is made up of an avenue of 19 monoliths extending northward from a circle of 13 stones, with other rows leading south, east, and west. It's believed

they may have been used for astronomical observations. The site is accessible at any time.

TIME OUT   **Callinish Stone's Tearoom** (☎ 01851/621373) has an interesting craft shop with locally woven tweeds in the restored black house beside the gate leading to the Standing Stones. The tearoom serves home-baked scones, cakes, and shortbread, and hearty soups.

㊳ To reach **Tarbert,** the main port of Harris, head back east toward Stornoway on the A858 and pick up the A859 south (a distance of some 50 miles). If you want to break up the ride south, you could make a slight detour about two-thirds of the way down A859 to explore the
㊴ area around **Rhenigidale.** Considered to be the most isolated inhabited village in Harris, Rhenigidale was for a long time accessible only by sea or via a rough hill path. A road completed in the early 1990s, which offers fine views high above Loch Seaforth, has now linked the village with the rest of Scotland.

㊵ About 10 miles northwest of Tarbert on the B887 stands **Amhuinnsuidhe Castle** (the name is almost impossible to pronounce—try *avun-shooee*), a turreted structure built in the 1860s by the earls of Dunmore as a base for fishing and hunting in the North Harris deer forest.

㊶ **Traigh Luskentyre,** roughly 5 miles southwest of Tarbert, is a spectacular example of Harris's tidy selection of beaches—2 miles of yellow sands adjacent to **Traigh Seilebost** beach, where there are superb views northward to the hills of the Forest of Harris.

At the southernmost point of the island, about a 20-mile drive from
㊷ Tarbert, is the community of **Rodel.** Here you'll find **St. Clement's Church,** a cruciform church standing on a prominent site right on route A859. It was built around 1500 and contains the magnificently sculptured tomb of the church's builder, Alasdair Crotach, eighth chief of Dunvegan Castle.

North Uist
㊸ At **Newtonferry (Port nan Long),** the port of entry for ferries coming from Harris (via Berneray), stand the remains of what was reputed to be the last inhabited broch in North Uist, **Dun an Sticar.** This defensive tower, approached by a causeway over the loch, was occupied by Hugh MacDonald, a descendant of MacDonald of Sleat, until 1602.

㊹ Eight miles southwest of Lochmaddy, off the A865, are the ruins of **Trinity Temple (Teampull na Trionaid),** a medieval college and monastery said to have been founded by Beathag, daughter of Somerled, progenitor of the Clan Donald, in the 13th century. ☛ *Free.*

Sitting very close to the A867 on the stretch between Lochmaddy and
㊺ Clachan is the **Barpa Langass Chambered Cairn.** Dating from the third millennium BC, this is the only chambered cairn in the Western Isles known to have retained its inner chamber fully intact.

On the western side of North Uist, about 3 miles northwest of Bay-
㊻ head, which you can reach via A865, is the **Balranald Nature Reserve,** administered by the Balranald branch of the Royal Society for the Protection of Birds. Large numbers of waders and seabirds, including rednecked phalarope, can be seen here in a varied habitat of loch, marsh, machair (grasslands just behind the beach), and sandy and rocky shore. The reserve can be viewed anytime, but visitors are asked to keep to the paths during breeding season (March to July) so as not to disturb

the birds. *Reception cottage at Goular,* ☎ *01463/715000 or 0131/557-3136.* ☛ *Free.* ⏲ *Daily.*

South Uist

South Uist is connected to North Uist via Grimsay, Benbecula, and three causeways. You can travel the length of South Uist along route A865, making short treks off this main road on your way to Lochboisdale on the southeastern coast of the island; at Lochboisdale you can get ferries to Barra, the southernmost principal island of the Outer Hebrides, or to Oban on the mainland.

About 5 miles south of the causeway from Benbecula, atop Reuval Hill, stands the 125-foot-high statue of the Madonna and Child known as
㊼ **Our Lady of the Isles.** The work of sculptor Hew Lorimer, the statue was erected in 1957 by the local Catholic community. A few miles far-
㊽ ther south, to the west of A865, you will come to the **Loch Druidibeg National Nature Reserve.** One of only two remaining British native—nonmigrating—populations of greylag geese make their home here in a fresh and brackish loch environment. (Stop at the warden's office for full information about access.)

A few miles south of Howmore, just west of A865, stand the ruins of
㊾ **Ormaclete Castle,** which was built in 1708 for the chief of the Clan Ranald, but was accidentally destroyed by fire in 1715 on the eve of the Battle of Sheriffmuir, during which the chief was killed. At Gearraidh Bhailteas (just west of A865 near Milton), you can see the ruins
㊿ of **Flora Macdonald's birthplace.** South Uist's most famous daughter, Flora helped the Young Pretender Prince Charles Edward Stuart avoid capture and was feted as a heroine afterward.

Barra

Barra is an island with a rocky east coast and a west coast of sandy
(51) beaches. **Kisimul Castle,** the largest ancient monument in the Western Isles, is situated on an islet in Castlebay, Barra's principal harbor. Kisimul was the stronghold of the Macneils of Barra, noted for their lawlessness and piracy. The main tower dates from about AD 1120. A restoration that was completed in 1970 was started by the 45th clan chief, an American architect. *Contact tourist information center for opening times and admission prices.*

Craigston Museum, in a thatched cottage at Baile ne Creige (Craigston), displays artifacts of local crofting life. (It's open only during the main summer season.) At Eolaigearraidh (Eoligarry), the departure point for
(52) the passenger ferry to South Uist, you can view **Cille Bharra,** the ruins of the church dedicated to the saint who gave his name to the island. Also nearby is the restored **chapel of St. Mary** and part of a medieval monastery and cemetery.

Barra's airport is at the north end of the island on a simple stretch of sand known as **Traigh Moor** (the Cockle Strand)—which is washed twice daily by the tides. The departure and arrival times for the daily flights to and from Glasgow, Benbecula, and Stornoway are scheduled to coincide with low tide.

What to See and Do with Children

Baile an Or (*see* Tour 4)

Timespan (*see* Tour 4)

Off the Beaten Path

It can be argued that all of the Northern Highlands are off the beaten track. Below are some examples of the peerless views and open countryside for which the area is renowned.

Applecross. The tame way to reach this little community facing Skye is by a coastal road from near Shieldaig; the exciting way is by a series of hairpin turns up the steep wall at the head of a corrie (a glacier-cut mountain valley), approached from the A896 a few miles farther south. There are spectacular views of Skye from the bare plateau on top, and you can boast afterward that you have been on what is probably Scotland's highest motorable road. The town of Applecross itself is pleasant but not riveting.

Cape Wrath. Those that tour far to the north will want to go all the way to the northwest tip of Scotland. You can't drive the entire way in your own car; a ferry carries you across the Kyle of Durness, a sea inlet, then a minibus takes you to the lighthouse. The highest mainland cliffs in Scotland lie between the Kyle and Cape Wrath. These are the 800-foot **Cleit Dubh** (the name means "black cleft" in Gaelic and comes from the Old Norse *klettr,* or crag).

Drumbeg loop from Lochinver. Bold souls spending time at Lochinver may enjoy the interesting single-lane B869 Drumbeg loop to the north of Lochinver—it has several challenging hairpin turns along with breathtaking views. (The junction is just north of the River Inver bridge on the outskirts of the village, signed Stoer and Clashnessie.) Just beyond the scattered community of Stoer, a road leads west to **Stoer Point Lighthouse.** Energetic walkers can hike across the short turf and heather along the cliff top for fine views east toward the profiles of the northwest mountains. There is also a red-sandstone sea-stack to view: the **Old Man of Stoer.** This makes a pleasant excursion on a long summer evening. If you stay on the Drumbeg section, there is a particularly tricky hairpin turn in a steep dip that may force you to take your eyes off the fine view of Quinag, yet another of Sutherland's shapely mountains.

Eas Coul Aulin waterfall. This is the longest waterfall in the United Kingdom. Located east of the Kylesku Bridge on the A894, these falls have a 685-foot drop. A rugged walk that leads to the falls is popular with hikers; in summer, cruises offer a less taxing way to view the falls. *At the head of Loch Glencoul, 3 mi west of A894; contact the tourist information center in Ullapool or Lochinver for more information.*

SHOPPING

Northern Highlands

As in Argyll and the Western Isles, shopping in the Northern Highlands tends to be more interesting for the variety of crafts available rather than for the number and types of shops. After all, the population of the area is scattered, and if the locals have any special needs, they can travel to the larger population centers, as well as to Inverness. Perhaps the best-known purveyor of crafts in the northeastern corner of the area is **Caithness Glass** (Wick Industrial Site, Wick Airport, ☎ 01955/602286), also with branches at Oban and Perth. Producing a distinctive style of glassware and paperweights familiar to those traveling around Scotland (most of the better gift shops stock Caithness Glass), the factory has tours of the glassblowing workshops and a shop stocking the full product range.

There are two other interesting crafts outlets farther south: At Golspie the **Orcadian Stone Company** (Main St., Golspie, ☎ 01408/633483) makes stone products (including items made from local Caithness slate and modern versions of the carpet bowls, beloved of the Victorians and of today's interior designers), jewelry, incised plaques, and prepared mineral specimens. There is also a geological exhibition on site.

The former **town jail of Dornoch** (Castle St., Dornoch, ☎ 01862/810555) is now a textile-and-crafts center where tartans are woven. There's also an exhibition of prison life in past times just to remind you of the building's origins.

At Lochinver, on the west coast, **Highland Stoneware** (Baddidarroch, Lochinver, ☎ 01571/844376) manufactures tableware and decorative items with hand-painted designs of Highland wildflowers, animals, and landscapes. There is a showroom where you can browse and purchase wares.

At Inverkirkaig, just south of Lochinver, do not miss **Achins Book and Craft Shop** (Inverkirkaig, ☎ 01571/844262) for Scottish books on natural history, hill walking, fishing, and crafts as well as a well-chosen variety of craftware: knitwear, tweeds, and pottery.

There are also several well-stocked gift shops south of Lochinver, at Ullapool. In Lochcarron, the premises of **Lochcarron Weavers** (North Strone, Lochcarron, ☎ 01520/722212) are open to the public: Weavers can be seen at work, producing pure-wool worsted tartans that can be bought on site or at the firm's other outlets in the area.

East of Lochcarron, at Achnasheen, is the **Highland Line Craft Centre** (center of Achnasheen, ☎ 01445/720227), where silver and gold jewelry is made, and you can watch the silversmiths; products are available in the shop on the premises.

Skye
Shopping is limited on Skye, although there are quite a few gift outlets—as well as more crafts businesses—that cater to visitors. **Ragamuffin** (Armadale Pier, ☎ 01471/844217) specializes in designer knitwear and clothing. **Skye Batiks** (Armadale, ☎ 01471/844396) has designs influenced by Celtic motifs, and sells wall hangings and cotton, silk, and linen clothing at reasonable prices. **Harlequin Knitwear** (Duisdale, Sleat, ☎ 01471/833321) sells colorful wool sweaters created by local designers. **Skye Silver** (The Old School, Colbost, ☎ 01470/511263) makes gold and silver jewelry with a Celtic theme. **Craft Encounters** (Broadford, ☎ 01471/822201) stocks an array of Scottish crafts, including marquetry and jewelry. For wood-fired stoneware, try **Edinbane Pottery** (Edinbane, ☎ 01470/582234). There are also several art galleries and studios of interest on Skye, among them **Skye Original Prints** (Portree, ☎ 01478/612388), which stocks original works by local artists, together with a good range of original greeting cards.

Outer Hebrides
At the **Callanish Tearoom** (18 Callanish, ☎ 01851/621373), Beatrice Schulz sells craft items, knitwear, and tweed lengths in a kaleidoscopic range of colors. She also has a shop in Stornoway, **Gifts Unlimited** (9 Bayhead St., ☎ 01851/703337) with a similar range of stock. At **Borve Pottery** (on the road to Ness, ☎ 01851/850345) you can buy an attractive range of items made on the premises—platters, mugs, dishes, and candleholders. Harris tweed is available at many outlets on the is-

lands, including some of the weavers' homes; try **Alistair Campbell** (4 Plocrabol, Isle of Harris, ☎ 01859/511217). On South Uist, **Hebridean Jewelry** (Garrieganichy, Lochdar, ☎ 01870/610288) makes decorative jewelry and framed pictures; the owners also run a crafts shop.

SPORTS AND FITNESS

Bicycling

Be prepared to meet holiday traffic at peak season. Some side roads (and even, in the far northwest, some main roads) are single track and narrow, meaning there will be traffic coming the other way between passing places. High-visibility clothing is advised.

Bicycles may be rented from **The Bike Shop** (35 High St., Thurso, ☎ 01847/66124 or 01847/64223), **Island Cycles** (The Green, Portree, ☎ 01478/613121), **Alex Dan Cycle Centre** (67 Kenneth St., Stornoway, ☎ 01851/704025), **MacDougall Cycles** (29 St. Brendan Rd., Castlebay, ☎ 01871/810284), **Skye Bike** (The Pier, Kyleakin, ☎ 01599/534795), **The Ferry Filling Station** (Ardvasar, Skye, ☎ 01471/844249), and **Broadford Bicycle Hire** (Fairwinds, Elgol Rd., Broadford, ☎ 01471/822270), **Kintail Crafts** (Glenshiel, ☎ 01599/511345), **Raasay Outdoor Centre** (Raasay House, Isle of Raasay, ☎ 01478/660266).

Fishing

The possibilities for fishing are endless here, as a glance at the loch-littered map of Sutherland suggests. As in other parts of Scotland, post offices, local shops, and hotels usually sell permits to fish in local waters, and tourist information centers carry lists of the best locales for fishing.

Golf

There are only about 15 courses in the area—a low number compared with other regions of Scotland—with almost no courses on the west coast, though **Gairloch Golf Club** has its enthusiasts. *60 mi west of Dingwall,* ☎ *01445/712407. 9 holes, 1,942 yards, SSS 71.*

The best-known club in the area is **Royal Dornoch.** Were it not for its northern location, the club would undoubtedly be a candidate for the Open Championship. *40 mi north of Inverness,* ☎ *01862/810219. 18 holes, 6,581 yards, SSS 72.*

Pony Trekking

Pony trekking was invented to give the sturdy highland ponies a job to do when they weren't carrying dead deer off the hills during the "stalking" (deer-hunting) season. Treks last from two hours to a whole day, and ponies can be found to suit all ages and levels of experience.

Contact one of the following centers for information about specific opportunities and costs: **The Black Isle Riding Centre** (☎ 01463/731707), **Uig Pony Trekking** (Skye, ☎ 01470/542205), and **Latheron Pony Centre** (☎ 01593/741224).

Water Sports

Raasay Outdoor Centre (Raasay House, Isle of Raasay, near Kyle, Wester Ross, ☎ 01478/660266) offers a variety of courses in canoeing, sailing, windsurfing, and navigation skills.

DINING AND LODGING

Dining

In an area with such a low population, the choice of restaurants is inevitably restricted. The places selected below can be relied upon for both accommodations and acceptable standards in the dining room.

WHAT TO WEAR

In mainland hotels and guesthouses in the northern Highlands, your fellow guests will be walkers and fishermen, and the dress code will be relaxed. At upscale country houses you'll be more comfortable if you dressed up a bit.

CATEGORY	COST*
$$$$	over £40
$$$	£30–£40
$$	£15–£30
$	under £15

per person for a three-course meal, including VAT and excluding drinks and service

Lodging

This region of Scotland has some good modern hotels and some charming inns but not many establishments in the more expensive categories. Travelers often find that the most enjoyable accommodations are low-cost guest houses (often family-run), offering bed-and-breakfast. Dining rooms of country-house lodgings frequently reach the standard of top-quality restaurants.

CATEGORY	COST*
$$$$	over £110
$$$	£80–£110
$$	£45–£80
$	under £45

All prices are for a standard double room, including service, breakfast, and VAT.

Dundonnell

DINING AND LODGING

$$–$$$ **Dundonnell Hotel.** Set on the roadside by Little Loch Broom, just south of Ullapool, this hotel has been a family-run enterprise since 1962 and has cultivated a solid reputation for hospitality and cuisine. The bedrooms are decorated in a fresh, modern style, with light, floral curtains and bedspreads, contemporary furnishings, and modern comforts including tea- and coffee-making equipment, and many have stunning views over pristine hills and lochs, as do the public rooms. The Taste of Scotland menu features homemade soups, fresh seafood, and desserts well worth leaving room for. ☎ *Dundonnell, near Garve, Ross-shire,* ☎ *01854/633204,* FAX *01854/633366. 30 rooms with bath. Restaurant (reservations advised), bar. AE, MC, V.*

Harris

DINING AND LODGING

$$–$$$ **Ardvourlie Castle.** A former Victorian hunting lodge that still retains
★   its character, Ardvourlie is set in splendid isolation amid the dramatic mountain scenery of Harris, an ideal habitat for hill walking. The bathrooms are magnificent, with mahogany paneling and Victorian-style fixtures, and the decor of the bedrooms and public rooms is bold, idiosyncratic, and entirely in keeping with the High Victorian atmosphere

of the castle. The country-house hospitality is perpetuated by the well-stocked library and roaring fires. The cooking is along traditional lines and is of a high standard, favoring fresh local produce and, often, wild game. The portions are generous. *Isle of Harris,* ☎ *01859/502307. 4 rooms with bath. Restaurant (reservations essential). No credit cards.*

Kylesku

DINING AND LODGING

$ **Linne Mhuirich.** This modern croft house bed-and-breakfast offers cooking with a Taste of Scotland theme. The evening meal may consist of salmon with lime and almonds, local mussels and prawns in garlic butter, or cashew-and-mushroom flan. The property is set in the middle of open country surrounded by superb mountain scenery. Rooms have pine furniture and tartan or floral fabrics. No smoking is permitted throughout the property. ☎ *Unapool Croft Rd., Kylesku, via Lairg, Sutherland IV27 4HW,* ☎ *01971/502227. 3 rooms, 1 with bath. No credit cards.* ☺ *May–Oct.*

Scourie

DINING AND LODGING

$$ **Eddrachilles Hotel.** This old, established traditional inn has one of the best views of any hotel in Scotland—across the islands of Eddrachillis Bay (which can be explored by boat from the hotel). The hotel sits on 320 acres of private moorland and is just south of the Handa Island bird sanctuary. Inside and outside, the hotel is well preserved. The bedrooms are modern and comfortable, and each is outfitted with tea- and coffee-making facilities. The chef uses local produce to prepare meals cooked in straightforward Scottish style, with the emphasis on fish and game; try the saddle of venison or the poached salmon. ☎ *Badcall Bay, Scourie,* ☎ *01971/502080,* FAX *01971/502477. 11 rooms with bath or shower. Restaurant (reservations essential), bar. MC, V. Closed Nov.–Feb.*

Skye

DINING AND LODGING

$$$–$$$$ **Kinloch Lodge.** This hotel offers elegant comfort on the edge of the world. Run by Lord and Lady MacDonald with flair and considerable professionalism, Kinloch Lodge is a supremely comfortable country house, with warm, restful lounges with antique furnishings, chintz fabrics, and family photographs; snug bedrooms individually decorated with quilted bedspreads and pastel wallpaper; and a handsome dining room that serves imaginative cuisine such as warm chicken-liver salad with croutons, herb crepe filled with smoked trout and cucumber, and monkfish stir-fried with tomatoes and garlic. ☎ *Sleat IV43 8QY,* ☎ *01471/833333,* FAX *01471/833277. 10 rooms with bath. Restaurant (reservations advised), fishing. MC, V. Closed Dec.–early May.*

$$–$$$ **Cuillin Hills Hotel.** Situated on lovely grounds just outside Portree, this gabled hotel is within easy walking distance of the town center. Many of the rooms have outstanding views over Portree Bay toward the Cuillin Hills. Bedrooms are reasonably spacious and well equipped, and individually decorated in bold floral patterns. The public rooms give you a choice of sitting areas and a friendly bar. The meals, especially seafood dishes, are prepared in straightforward fashion, with few gimmicks and a lot of flavor—try the local prawns, lobster, or scallops, or glazed ham carved from the bone. ☎ *Portree, Isle of Skye,* ☎ *01478/612003,* FAX *01478/613092. 25 rooms with bath and/or shower. Restaurant (reservations advised, jacket and tie), bar. AE, MC, V.*

Torridon

DINING AND LODGING

$$ **Loch Torridon Hotel.** Once a shooting lodge, and right on the shore of Loch Torridon with forest and mountains rising behind, the hotel provides a real Highland welcome. Log fires, handsome plasterwork ceilings, mounted stag heads, and traditional furnishings set the mood downstairs, while bedrooms are decorated in restrained pastel shades with antique mahogany furniture. The restaurant makes elaborate use of local seafood, salmon, beef, lamb, and game, and the cellar includes many fine wines. ✉ *By Achnasheen, Wester Ross IV27 2EY,* ☎ *01445/791242,* FAX *01445/791296. 19 rooms, 18 with bath, 1 with shower. Restaurant (reservations essential, jacket and tie). AE, MC, V.*

Ullapool

DINING AND LODGING

$–$$$ **Ceilidh Place.** This hostelry is extremely comfortable; guests can while away the hours on deep luxurious sofas in the first-floor sitting room—which overlooks the bay—or borrow one of the many books scattered throughout the inn to read back in the room or over breakfast. About as far away in style as you can get from a major chain hotel, the Ceilidh Place must be taken strictly on its own terms—relax and fit in and you will thoroughly enjoy a stay here. Rooms have cream bedspreads and rich, warm color schemes. The inn's restaurant specializes in seafood and vegetarian cooking (try the mushroom-and-walnut pâté, poached wild salmon, monkfish and prawn brochettes, or venison casserole) and ceilidhs and other musical events are held here frequently. There is a bunkhouse across the road for guests desiring less expensive accommodations. ✉ *W. Argyle St., Ullapool IV26 2TY,* ☎ *01854/612103,* FAX *01854/612886. 26 rooms, 20 with bath and showers. Restaurant (reservations essential). AE, DC, MC, V.*

Wick

LODGING

$ **Greenvoe.** This is perhaps one of the best value bed-and-breakfasts anywhere in Scotland. A well-appointed modern house, fresh and beautifully maintained, Greenvoe has unfussy, functional, and comfortable bedrooms. It's the ideal base for touring the far north of Scotland around John o'Groats, or for catching the Orkney ferry. A delicious substantial breakfast is included in the room rate, and late-night snacks are a hospitable touch. Smoking is prohibited. ✉ *George St., Wick, Caithness KW1 4DE,* ☎ *01955/603942. 3 rooms with shared bath. No credit cards.*

THE ARTS AND NIGHTLIFE

The Arts

The **Lyth Arts Centre,** between Wick and John o'Groats on the A9, is set in an old country school. From April to September each year, it hosts frequent performances by quality touring music and theater companies (admission: £7 adult, £4 concessions; part of the circuit of British Arts Centres). In July and August there are also local and touring exhibitions of contemporary fine art (small admission charge). *4 mi off A9,* ☎ *01955/641270.* ☉ *Apr.–Sept. daily 10–6.*

The **Ceilidh Place** in Ullapool (*see* Dining and Lodging, *above*) frequently presents ceilidhs and has a regular program of musical and dramatic productions—chamber music, folk music, and opera all find a place here. **An Lanntair,** in the Stornoway town hall (Isle of Lewis and Harris), also conducts an eclectic program of monthly exhibitions and evening events. Various Scottish ballet- and opera-touring companies perform in local halls. Consult tourist information centers' event lists for details.

Nightlife
The nightlife here is confined mainly to hotels and pubs. Ceilidhs, dances, and concerts are performed on a sporadic basis and advertised locally.

NORTHERN HIGHLANDS ESSENTIALS

Arriving and Departing

By Bus
National Express/Scottish Citylink (☎ 0141/332–9191) runs buses from England to Inverness, Ullapool, and Dingwall. There are also coach connections between the ferry ports of Tarbert and Stornoway.

By Car and Ferry
The fastest route to this area is the A9 to the gateway town of Inverness. The ferry services run by **Caledonian MacBrayne,** called CalMac, link the Outer Hebrides: Ferries run from Ullapool to Stornoway (☎ 01854/612358), from Oban to Castlebay and Lochboisdale (☎ 01631/562285), and from Uig on the island of Skye to Tarbert and Lochmaddy (☎ 01470/542219). Causeways link North Uist, Benbecula, and South Uist.

By Plane
The main airports for the Northern Highlands are **Inverness** and **Wick** (both on the mainland). There is direct air service from Edinburgh and Glasgow to Inverness and Wick. Contact **British Airways** (☎ 0345/222111). **Gill Air** (☎ 0191/286–2222) operates the Aberdeen–Wick service. There are island flight connections to Stornoway (Lewis), and Barra and Benbecula in the Outer Hebrides; contact British Airways for details.

By Train
Main railway stations in the area include Oban (for Barra and the Uists) and Kyle of Lochalsh (for Skye) on the west coast or Inverness (for points north to Thurso and Wick). There is direct service from London to Inverness and connecting service from Edinburgh and Glasgow.

Getting Around

It is in the Highlands and Islands that the **Freedom of Scotland Travelpass** really becomes useful, saving you money on ferries, trains, and some buses. *See* the Gold Guide for details.

By Bus
Highland Bus and Coach Company (mainland and Skye, ☎ 01463/233371) provides bus service in the Highlands area. On the Outer Hebrides a number of small operators and post buses—which also deliver mail—run regular routes to most towns and villages. The postbus service becomes increasingly important in remote areas; it supplements the regular bus service, which runs only a few times per week because of the small population on the islands. A full timetable

of services for the Northern Highlands (and the rest of Scotland) is available from the **District Head Post Office** (14–16 Queensgate, Inverness, ☎ 01463/234111, ext. 248) or from the **Head Post Office** (2–4 Waterloo Pl., Edinburgh, ☎ 0131/550–8232).

By Car

Note that in this sparsely populated area, distances between gas stations can be considerable. Although getting around is easy, even on single-lane roads, the choice of routes is restricted by the rugged terrain.

An important caveat for visitors driving in this area: There are still some single-lane roads in this part of Scotland. These twisting, winding thoroughfares demand a degree of driving dexterity. Local rules of the road require that when two cars meet, whichever driver reaches a passing place first must stop in it or opposite it and allow the oncoming car to continue. Small cars tend to yield to large commercial vehicles. Never park in passing places, and remember that these sections of the road can also allow traffic behind you to pass; don't hold up a vehicle trying to pass you—in the northwest, tempers flare over such discourtesies.

By Plane

British Airways (☎ 0345/222111) operates flights between the islands of Barra, Benbecula, and Stornoway in the Outer Hebrides.

By Train

Stations on the northern lines (Inverness to Thurso/Wick and Inverness to Kyle of Lochalsh) include Muir of Ord, Dingwall; on the Thurso/Wick line, Alness, Invergordon, Fearn, Tain, Ardgay, Culrain, Invershin, Lairg, Rogart, Golspie, Brora, Helmsdale, Kildonan, Kinbrace, Forsinard, Altnabreac, Scotscalder, and Georgemas Junction; and on the Kyle line, Garve, Lochluichart, Achanalt, Achnasheen, Achnashellach, Strathcarron, Attadale, Strome Ferry, Duncraig, Plockton, and Duirinish.

Guided Tours

Orientation

The bus company named above also operates orientation tours in summer, as does **Spa Coach Tours** (Strathpeffer, ☎ 01997/421311), which covers a large portion of the Northern Highlands and Skye.

Special-Interest

Dunvegan Sea Cruises, at Dunvegan Castle (☎ 01470/521206; *see* Tour 2: Skye, *below*) offers a boat trip to the nearby seal colony (£3.50 adults, £2.50 children) and also a spectacular trip up Loch Dunvegan to see seals and many different kinds of birds (£6.50 adults, £4.50 children). A number of small firms run boat cruises along the spectacular west-coast seaboard. Contact the local tourist information center for details of local operators. On Skye there is also a broad selection of mountain guides. A list can be obtained from Skye's tourist information center (*see* Important Addresses and Numbers, *below*). **Cycle Caithness** (Thurso, ☎ 01847/66124 or 01847/64223) organizes cycling and accommodation packages in ideal, flat, cycling territory.

Important Addresses and Numbers

Emergencies

For police, fire, or ambulance, dial 999 from any telephone. No coins are needed for emergency calls from public telephone booths.

Late-Night Pharmacies

These are not found in rural areas. In an emergency the police will provide assistance in locating a pharmacist. General practitioners may also dispense medicines.

Visitor Information

Tourist Information Centres are located in **Caithness** (Whitechapel Rd., off High St., Wick, ☎ 01955/602596, FAX 01955/604940), the **Western Isles** (**Outer Hebrides**) 4 S. Beach St., Stornoway, ☎ 01851/703088, FAX 01851/705244), **Isle of Skye and South West Ross** (Portree, Isle of Skye, ☎ 01478/612137, FAX 01478/612141), **Ross and Cromarty** (North Kessock, ☎ 01463/731505, FAX 01463/731701), **Gairloch** (Auchtercairn, ☎ 01445/712130), and **Sutherland** (The Square, Dornoch, ☎ 01862/810400, FAX 01862/810644). Seasonal tourist information centers can be found at Bettyhill, Broadford (Skye), Castlebay (Outer Hebrides), Durness, Glen Shiel, Helmsdale, John o' Groats, Kyle of Lochalsh, Lairg, Lochboisdale (Outer Hebrides), Lochcarron, Lochinver, Lochmaddy (Outer Hebrides), Strathpeffer, Tarbert (Outer Hebrides), Thurso, Uig, and Ullapool.

12 The Northern Isles

Orkney, Shetland

The nearly unceasing wind and rain in the Northern Isles create a challenging climate that contributes to the feeling that you've reached the end of the world. Orkney, a grouping of almost 70 islands, 20 of them inhabited, has the greatest concentration of prehistoric sites in Scotland. Shetland's islands, with their dramatic vertical cliffs on the coastline and barren moors in the interior, are protected from winter by the Gulf Stream.

By Gilbert
Summers

BOTH ORKNEY AND SHETLAND possess a Scandinavian heritage that gives them an ambience different from any other region of Scotland. For mainland Scots, visiting this archipelago is a little like traveling abroad without having to worry about a different language or currency. Both of these isles are bound by the sea, and both are essentially bleak and austere, with awesome seascapes and genuinely warm, friendly people. Neither island has yet been overrun by tourists. Orkney is the greener of the two island groupings, which number 200 islets between them.

There are more prehistoric sites in Orkney than anywhere else in the United Kingdom, although Shetland also has a few historic sites of great interest. Orkney's wealth of sites includes stone circles, burial chambers, ancient settlements, and fortifications that emphasize many centuries of continuous settlement. Most of the sites are open to view, offering an insight into the life of bygone eras. At Maes Howe, for example, visitors will discover that graffiti is not solely an expression of today's youths: The Vikings left their marks here in the 8th century.

The differences between Orkney and Shetland can be summed up with the description that an Orcadian is a farmer with a boat, while a Shetlander is a fisherman with a croft (small farm). Shetland, rich in ocean views and sparse landscapes, is endowed with a more remote atmosphere than its neighbor Orkney. However, don't let Shetland's bleak countryside fool you—it's far from being a backwater island. Oil money from the mineral resources around its shores and the fact that it has been a crossroads in the northern seas for centuries have helped make it a cosmopolitan place.

EXPLORING

Tour 1: Around Shetland

Numbers in the margin correspond to points of interest on the Shetland Islands map.

The Shetland coastline is an incredible 900 miles due to all the indentations, and there isn't a point on the island farther than 3 miles from the sea. Settlements away from Lerwick, the primary town, are small and scattered—ask the friendly locals for directions.

❶ Visitors would be remiss if they failed to explore some of **Lerwick**'s nearby diversions before venturing beyond it. **Fort Charlotte** is a 17th-century Cromwellian stronghold, built to protect the Sound of Bressay. ☎ *0131/244–3101. ☛ Free. ☉ Apr.–Sept., Mon.–Sat. 9:30–6, Sun. 2–6; Oct.–Mar., Mon.–Sat. 9:30–4, Sun. 2–4.*

The **Shetland Museum** in Lerwick gives an interesting account of the development of the town and includes displays on archaeology, art and textiles, shipping, and folk life. *Lower Hillhead, ☎ 01595/695057. ☛ Free. ☉ Mon., Wed., Fri. 10–7, Tues., Thurs., Sat. 10–5.*

TIME OUT   Near the harbor in Lerwick, the **Kvelsdro House Hotel** (☎ 01595/ 692195) serves hearty pub grub meals; try the breaded haddock or steak pie.

❷ **Clickhimin Broch,** on the site of what was originally an Iron-Age fortification, can be your introduction to the mysterious Pictish monuments, whose meaning is still largely obscure. *1 mi south of Lerwick,*

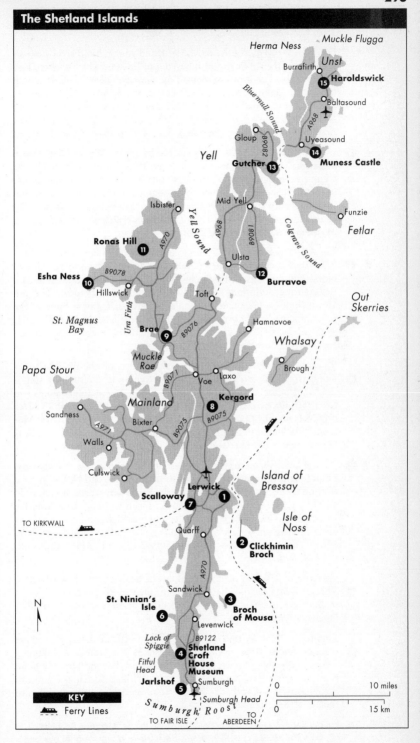

The Shetland Islands

Muckle Flugga

Herma Ness

Burrafirth *Unst*

15 **Haroldswick**

Baltasound

A968

Blaemull Sound

Gloup

B9082

Uyeasound

14

Muness Castle

Yell

Gutcher 13

Isbister

Yell Sound

Mid Yell

Ronas Hill

11

A970

A968

B9081

Funzie

Fetlar

Esha Ness

10

B9078

Hillswick

Ulsta

12

Burravoe

Colgrave Sound

Toft

Out Skerries

St. Magnus Bay

Ura Firth

Brae

9

B9076

Hamnavoe

Whalsay

Papa Stour

Muckle Roe

B9071

Voe

Laxo

Brough

Sandness

A971

Mainland

Bixter

B9075

B9075

8

Kergord

Walls

Culswick

Lerwick

7

1

Island of Bressay

Scalloway

Quarff

Isle of Noss

TO KIRKWALL

2 **Clickhimin Broch**

Sandwick

A970

3

St. Ninian's Isle

6

Broch of Mousa

Levenwick

Loch of Spiggie

B9122

Shetland Croft House Museum

4

Fitful Head

Jarlshof

5

Sumburgh

Sumburgh Head

N

Sumburgh Roost

TO FAIR ISLE

TO ABERDEEN

0   10 miles

0   15 km

KEY

Ferry Lines

☎ *0131/244–3101.* ☛ *Free.* ◔ *Apr.–Sept., Mon.–Sat. 9:30–6, Sun. 2–6; Oct.–Mar., Mon.–Sat. 9:30–4, Sun. 2–4.*

★ ❸ From the broch go south on the A970, and you will find vivid views of the cliffs at the south end of the island of Bressay, which shelters Lerwick harbor. The **Broch of Mousa,** the most complete of all the broch towers remaining in Scotland, can be reached by boat from Sandwick, just off the main road. *Mousa,* ☎ *0131/244–3101.* ☛ *Free.* ◔ *Apr.–Sept., Mon.–Sat. 9:30–6, Sun. 2–6; Oct.–Mar., Mon.–Sat. 9:30–4, Sun. 2–4. Boat for hire May–Sept. afternoons, Sat., Sun. mornings, some evenings.*

★ ❹ Continue south on A970 until you see a sign for the **Shetland Croft House Museum.** This traditionally constructed 19th-century thatched house contains a broad range of artifacts that depict the former way of life of the rural Shetlander, which the museum attendant will be delighted to discuss with you. *Voe, Dunrossness, unclassified road east of A970,* ☎ *01595/695057.* ☛ *£1.50 adults, £1 senior citizens and children.* ◔ *May–Sept., daily 10–1 and 2–5.*

★ ❺ The A970 then continues south to **Sumburgh.** The big attraction here is **Jarlshof,** a centuries-old site that includes the extensive remains of Norse buildings, as well as prehistoric wheel houses and earth houses representing thousands of years of continuous settlement. The site also includes a 17th-century laird's (landowner's) house built on the ruins of a medieval farmstead. *Sumburgh Head,* ☎ *0131/244–3101.* ☛ *£2 adults, £1.25 senior citizens, 75p children.* ◔ *Apr.–Sept., Mon.–Sat. 9:30–6, Sun. 2–6. Closed Oct.–Mar.*

❻ Retrace your route to **Skelberry,** making a left on the B9122. It was on nearby **St. Ninian's Isle**—actually a "tombolo," a term for a spit of sand that moors an island to the mainland—where archaeologists in the 1950s uncovered the St. Ninian treasure, a collection of 28 silver objects from the 8th century. This Celtic silver is now in the Royal Museum of Scotland in Edinburgh (*see* Chapter 3), though good replicas are on view in the Shetland Museum in Lerwick (*see above*).

❼ West of Lerwick, on the western coast of Mainland Island, is **Scalloway.** Look for the information board just off the main road (A970), which overlooks the settlement and its castle. **Scalloway Castle** was built in 1600 by Earl Patrick, who coerced the locals to build it for him. He was executed in 1615 for his cruelty and misdeeds, and the castle was never used again. *6 mi west of Lerwick,* ☎ *0131/244–3101.* ☛ *Free.* ◔ *Apr.–Sept., Mon.–Sat. 9:30–6, Sun. 2–6; Oct.–Mar., Mon.–Sat. 9:30–4, Sun. 2–4.*

❽ Take the B9075 east off the A970, at the head of a narrow sea inlet. This leads into the unexpectedly green valley of **Kergord,** noted for its thick carpet of trees. This would be unremarkable farther south, but here it is a novelty.

❾ Rejoin the A970 by making a left off the B9075 at Laxo, then drive through Voe to **Brae,** home of the Busta House Hotel (*see* Lodging, *below*), probably the best hotel on the island. Beyond Brae the main road meanders past **Mavis Grind,** a strip of land so narrow you can throw a stone—if you are strong—from the Atlantic, in one inlet, to the North Sea, in another.

TIME OUT   Follow the A970 left for Hillswick to reach the **St. Magnus Bay Hotel** (☎ 01806/503371), which serves fresh fish in a wood-panel bar and dining room.

★ ⑩ For outstanding views of the rugged, forbidding cliffs around **Esha Ness,** return to the A970 and drive a few miles north, then turn left onto the B9078. On the way, look for the sandstone stacks in the bay that resemble a Viking galley under sail. After viewing the cliffs at Esha Ness, return to join the A970 at Hillswick and follow an ancillary road from the head of Ura Firth. This road provides vistas of rounded, bare

⑪ **Ronas Hill,** the highest hill in Shetland. Though only 1,468 feet high, it is noted for its arctic-alpine flora growing at low levels.

To visit Yell and Unst, the two main northern islands, go south as far as Brae and take the B9076. After crossing over from the Shetland port

⑫ of Toft to Ulsta, on the island of **Yell,** take the B9081 east to **Burravoe.** There's not a lot to say about the blanket bog that covers two-thirds of Yell, but the **Old Haa** (hall) of Burravoe, the oldest building on the island, is architecturally interesting and has a museum upstairs. One of the displays tells the story of the wrecking of the German sailship, the *Bohus,* in 1924. A copy of the ship's figurehead is displayed outside the Old Haa itself; the original is at the shipwreck site overlooking Otters Wick, along the coast on the B9081. ☎ *01957/722339 or 01957/702127. ☛ Free. ☉ Apr.–Sept., Tues., Wed., Thurs., and Sat. 10–4, Sun. 2–5.*

TIME OUT The **Old Haa,** formerly a merchant's house, serves light meals with home-baked buns, cakes, scones, and other goodies; has a craft shop; and acts as a kind of unofficial information point. The staff are friendly and give advice to sightseers.

⑬ Rejoin the main A968 at Mid Yell to reach **Gutcher,** the ferry pier. If time permits, turn left on the B9082 for a pleasant drive to **Gloup,** a cluster of houses at the end of the road. Behind a croft, in a field overlooking a long voe (sea inlet) is the **Gloup Fisherman's Memorial,** which recalls an 1881 tragedy involving all hands of 10 six-oared local fishing boats.

Take the ferry to the other side of the Bluemull Sound to **Unst,** the northernmost inhabited island in Scotland. Because of its strategic location— it protrudes well into the northern seas—Unst is inhabited by the military. Follow the A968 until you reach the right turn on the B9084

⑭ for **Muness Castle.** Scotland's northernmost castle, it was built just before the end of the 16th century. Those visiting the castle will be pleasantly surprised to find some photogenic Shetland ponies in the field nearby. *Southeast corner of Unst, ☎ 0131/244–3101. ☛ Free. Ask for the key-keeper. ☉ Apr.–Sept., Mon.–Sat. 9:30–6, Sun. 2–6; Oct.–Mar., Mon.–Sat. 9:30–4, Sun. 2–4.*

Just to the north is the **Keen of Hamar** national nature reserve. Far-

⑮ ther north is **Haroldswick,** with its post office and heritage center. If you take the B9086 at Haroldswick you will go around the head of **Burrafirth** (a sea inlet) and eventually reach a parking lot. From there a path goes north across moorland and up a gentle hill. Bleak and open, this is bird-watchers' territory and is replete with diving skuas—single-minded sky pirates that attack anything that strays near their nest sites. Gannets, puffins, and other seabirds nest in spectacular profusion by the cliffs on the left as you look out to sea. Visitors should make sure they keep to the path; this is a national nature reserve.

At the top of the hills, amid the windy grasslands, you can see **Muckle Flugga** to the north, a series of tilting offshore rocks; the largest of these sea-battered protrusions has a lighthouse. This is the northernmost point in Scotland; the sea rolls out on three sides, no land lies beyond.

Tour 2: Around Orkney

Numbers in the margin correspond to points of interest on the Orkney Islands map.

Orkney has the greatest concentration of prehistoric sites in Scotland. Visitors traveling to Orkney from the mainland can take a ferry from Scrabster—located roughly 2 miles northwest of Thurso off the A836—**⓰** to **Stromness** on Mainland. You will find two points of interest in Stromness as soon as you arrive. The **Pier Arts Centre** is a former Stromness merchant's house (circa 1800) and has adjoining buildings that now serve as a gallery with a permanent collection of 20th-century paintings and sculptures. *Victoria St.,* ☎ *01856/850–209.* ☛ *Free.* ⊙ *Tues.–Sat. 10:30–12:30 and 1:30–5; also Sun. in July and Aug. 2–5.*

Nearby, the **Stromness Museum** has a varied collection of natural-history material on view, including preserved birds and Orkney shells. The museum also displays exhibits on fishing, shipping, whaling, and the Hudson Bay Company, as well as ship models and a feature on the German fleet that was scuttled on Scapa Flow. *Stromness,* ☎ *01856/850025.* ☛ *£1 adults, 50p children.* ⊙ *Mon.–Sat. 10:30–12:30 and 1:30–5.*

★ **⓱** Located just off the A965, 5 miles northeast of Stromness, the **Ring of Brogar** is a magnificent circle of 36 stones (originally 60) surrounded by a deep ditch. When the fog descends over the stones—a frequent occurrence—their looming shapes seem to come alive. Though their original use is uncertain, it is not hard to imagine strange rituals taking place here in the misty past. *Between Loch of Harray and Loch of Stenness, 5 mi northeast of Stromness,* ☎ *0131/244–3101.* ☛ *Free.* ⊙ *At all times.*

★ **⓲** One mile farther on the A965 brings visitors to another ancient site, the huge burial mound of **Maes Howe** (circa 2,500 BC), which measures 115 feet in diameter and contains an enormous burial chamber. It was raided by Vikings in the 12th century, and Norse crusaders sheltered here, leaving a rich collection of runic inscriptions. *Off A965, 9 mi west of Kirkwall,* ☎ *0131/244–3101.* ☛ *£2 adults, £1.25 senior citizens, 75p children, or joint entry ticket to all Historic Scotland's Orkney sights.* ⊙ *Apr.–Sept., Mon.–Sat. 9:30–6, Sun. 2–6; Oct.–Mar., Mon.–Sat. 9:30–4, Sun. 2–4.*

★ **⓳** To reach the neolithic village of **Skara Brae,** take the A965 west to the B9056. Here you will find houses, joined by covered passages, with stone beds, fireplaces, and cupboards that have survived since the village was first occupied around 3,000 BC. The site was preserved in sand until it was uncovered in 1850. *19 mi northwest of Kirkwall,* ☎ *0131/244–3101.* ☛ *£2.50 adults, £1.50 senior citizens, £1 children, or joint entry ticket to all Historic Scotland's Orkney sights.* ⊙ *Apr.–Sept., Mon.–Sat. 9:30–6, Sun. 2–6; Oct.–Mar., Mon.–Sat. 9:30–4, Sun. 2–4.*

⓴ To the north of Skara Brae, up the B9056, sits the **Marwick Head Nature Reserve,** with its spectacular seabird cliffs, tended by Scotland's Royal Society for the Protection of Birds. The **Kitchener Memorial,** which recalls the sinking of the cruiser HMS *Hampshire* with Lord Kitchener aboard in 1916, can also be seen in the reserve, on a cliff-top site. *Access to reserve along path north from Marwick Bay,* ☎ *01856/850176.* ☛ *Free.* ⊙ *At all times.*

㉑ Just beyond Marwick at Birsay (25 mi northwest of Kirkwall) is **Earl's Palace,** the impressive remains of a 16th-century palace built by the earls of Orkney. *Birsay,* ☎ *0131/244–3101.* ☛ *Free.* ⊙ *At all times.*

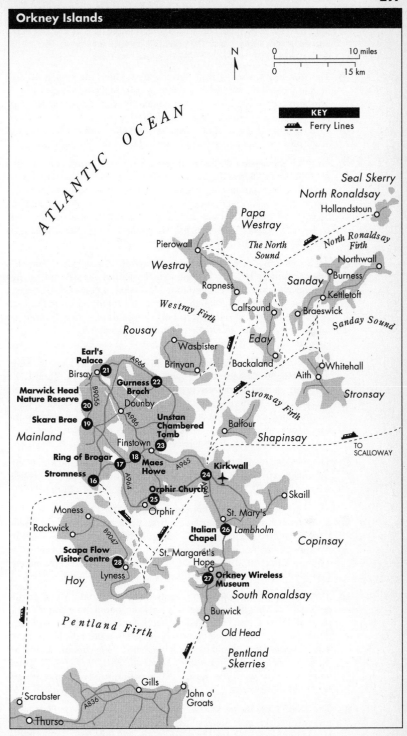

Orkney Islands

N

0 ——— 10 miles
0 ——— 15 km

KEY
🚢 Ferry Lines

ATLANTIC OCEAN

Seal Skerry
North Ronaldsay
Hollandstoun

Papa
Westray
The North
Sound

Pierowall
Westray

North Ronaldsay
Firth

Northwall
Burness
Sanday

Rapness
Kettletoft

Calfsound
Braeswick

Westray Firth
Sanday Sound

Rousay
Wasbister
Eday
Whitehall
Aith
Stronsay

Brinyan
Backaland

Stronsay Firth

**Earl's
Palace**
Birsay ㉑

A966

**Gurness
Broch** ㉒
Dounby

**Marwick Head
Nature Reserve** ⑳

B9056

A986

Skara Brae ⑲

**Unstan
Chambered
Tomb**

Balfour

Mainland

Finstown

Shapinsay

TO
SCALLOWAY

Ring of Brogar ⑰ ⑱

**Maes
Howe** ㉓

A965

Kirkwall ㉔ ✈

Skaill

Stromness ⑯

A964

Orphir Church ㉕
Orphir

St. Mary's

Moness

Rackwick

B9047

**Italian
Chapel** ㉖
Lambholm

Copinsay

**Scapa Flow
Visitor Centre** ㉘
Lyness

St. Margaret's
Hope

**Orkney Wireless
Museum** ㉗

Hoy

South Ronaldsay

Burwick

Old Head

Pentland
Skerries

Pentland Firth

Gills

John o'
Groats

Scrabster

A836

Thurso

Nearby is the **Brough of Birsay,** the remains of a Romanesque church (and a Norse settlement) on an island accessible only at low tide. Lest you are swept away, check the tide tables before setting out. *Birsay,* ☎ *0131/244–3101.* ☛ *Free.* ☉ *Daily, subject to tides.*

❷❷ The **Gurness Broch,** an Iron-Age tower standing more than 10 feet high, is located off the A966, about 8 miles from Birsay along Orkney's northern coast. The broch is surrounded by stone huts. *Off A966 at Aikerness, 14 mi northwest of Kirkwall,* ☎ *0131/244–3101.* ☛ *£2 adults, £1.25 senior citizens, 75p children, or joint entry ticket to all Historic Scotland's Orkney sights.* ☉ *Apr.–Sept., Mon.–Sat. 9:30–6, Sun. 2–6.*

❷❸ To reach the **Unstan Chambered Tomb** from the Gurness Broch, simply follow the A966 south for about 10 miles to Finstown. This 5,000-year-old cairn containing a chambered tomb is midway between Stromness and Kirkwall: roughly 3.5 miles from each. Pottery that has been found within the tomb is now known as Unstan ware. ☎ *0131/ 244–3101.* ☛ *Free.* ☉ *Apr.–Sept., Mon.–Sat. 9:30–6, Sun. 2–6; Oct.– Mar., Mon.–Sat. 9:30–4, Sun. 2–4.*

❷❹ Take the A965 east, straight into **Kirkwall,** to reach **Earl Patrick's Palace,** built in 1607 and perhaps the best surviving example of Renaissance architecture in Scotland. The **Bishop's Palace** nearby dates from the 13th century, though its round tower was added in the 16th century. *Kirkwall. Admission to both: £1.20 adults, 75p children, or joint entry ticket to all Historic Scotland's Orkney sights. Both open Apr.–Sept., Mon.–Sat. 9:30–6, Sun. 2–6.*

★ Founded by Jarl Rognvald in 1137 and dedicated to his uncle St. Magnus, **St. Magnus Cathedral** in Kirkwall was built between 1137 and 1200; however, additional work was carried out during the following 300 years. The cathedral is still in use and contains some of the best examples of Norman architecture in Scotland. The ornamentation on some of the tombstones is particularly striking. ☉ *May–Aug., Mon.–Sat. 9–5; Sept.–Apr., Mon.–Sat. 9–1 and 2–5, open Sun. for services and 2–6.*

❷❺ The remains of the 12th-century **Orphir Church,** Scotland's only circular medieval church (12th century), lie near the A964, 8 miles southwest of Kirkwall. ☎ *0131/244–3101.* ☛ *Free.* ☉ *At all times.*

★ ❷❻ Travelers can reach **South Ronaldsay** via the A961 causeway heading south from Kirkwall. The island's first distinctive point is the **Italian Chapel,** located below the small village of St. Mary's. It was here, by the shore at Lambholm, in 1943, that Italian prisoners of war, using a Nissen hut, created a beautiful chapel from scrap metal and concrete. *Lambholm.* ☛ *Free.* ☉ *At all times.*

❷❼ The **Orkney Wireless Museum,** located about 10 miles south on the A961 at St. Margaret's Hope, is a museum of wartime communications at Scapa Flow. Thousands of service men and women were stationed here and used the equipment displayed to protect the Home Fleet. The museum also contains many handsome 1930s wireless radios. *St. Margaret's Hope, 11 mi south of Kirkwall,* ☎ *01856/874272. Small admission charge.* ☉ *June–Aug.; check with tourist information center for opening hours.*

❷❽ The **Scapa Flow Visitor Centre,** off the B9047 at Lyness on Hoy, has a growing collection of material portraying the strategic role of the sheltered anchorage of Scapa Flow (said to be Britain's best diving site) in two world wars. *Lyness,* ☎ *01856/791300.* ☛ *£1.50 adults, 80p senior citizens and children.* ☉ *May–Sept., Mon.–Fri. 9–4, Sat. 9–3:30, Sun. 9–6; Oct.–Apr., Mon.–Fri. 9–4.*

Off the Beaten Path

Tended by the Royal Society for the Protection of Birds, the **North Hoy Nature Reserve,** home to vast numbers of land birds and seabirds, is comprised of high ground and moor. Huge cliffs nearby include the Old Man of Hoy, a 450-foot sea stack. Visitors can access the reserve any time by boat from Stromness. ☎ *01856/791298.* ☛ *Free.* ☉ *At all times.*

The **Knap of Howar** is one of the oldest inhabited sites in Europe. Its two 5,000-year-old dwellings—which have yielded some unusual artifacts, such as whalebone mallets, a spatula, and stone grinders—can be found on the west side of Papa Westray, off the island of Westray. *West of Holland House,* ☎ *0131/244–2903.* ☛ *Free.*

SHOPPING

Neither Orkney nor Shetland is visited expressly for shopping. However, both have attracted high-quality crafts workers, and, in the United Kingdom, Shetland is almost synonymous with distinctive knitwear.

On Shetland, **Hjaltasteyn** (161 Commercial St., ☎ 01595/696224) handcrafts gems and jewelry. **Shetland Jewelry** (Sound Side, Weisdale, ☎ 01595/830275) makes jewelry and other small goods, which are stocked at J. G. Rae in Lerwick (*see below*). In Scalloway the **Shetland Woollen Company** (Castle St., ☎ 01595/880243) is one of many operators with a selection of Shetland knitwear. Other places for knitwear and woolen goods in Lerwick include **The Spider's Web** (41 Commercial St., ☎ 01595/693299), selling handspun and handknitted goods in neutral earthtones, as well as pottery made in Shetland. **Anderson & Co.** (The Shetland Warehouse, Commercial St., ☎ 01595/693714) sells handmade knitwear and a has a small stock of machine-made items and tourist souvenirs. **Millers** (108–110 Commercial St., Lerwick, ☎ 01595/692517) stocks machine-made knitwear in Shetland and Argyle patterns, Aran sweaters, and capes, rugs, and scarves made elsewhere in Scotland. **J. G. Rae Limited** (92 Commercial St., ☎ 01595/693686) stocks Shetland Silvercraft and gold and silver jewelry with Norse and Celtic motifs. **Shetland Workshop Gallery** (Burns La., ☎ 01595/693343) has a good selection of pottery, knitwear, and crafts. In Sandwick you'll find **Lawrence J. Smith Ltd.** (Hoswick, ☎ 01950/431215), selling Shetland knitwear—both hand- and machine-made—at all prices and for all ages, in a wide range of colors.

On Orkney, Kirkwall is the main shopping hub. Do not miss **Ola Gorrie at the Longship** (7–9 Broad St., ☎ 01856/873251). The shop designs gold and silver jewelry with Celtic and Norse themes, including a delightful representation of a dragon, originally drawn on the wall of the burial chamber at Maes Howe. Also in Kirkwall is **Ortak Jewelry** (10 Albert St., ☎ 01856/873536), which stocks a potpourri of gifts. At **Judith Glue** (25 Broad St., ☎ 01856/874225) visitors can purchase designer knitwear with traditional patterns, as well as watercolors, prints, and Orkney-made crafts. **Fursbreck Pottery** (Harray, ☎ 01856/771419) offers an unusual range of ceramics. **Joker Jewelry** (East School, Holm, ☎ 01856/781336) makes eye-catching and whimsical clocks, brooches, and other jewelry using animal motifs (especially puffins).

SPORTS AND FITNESS

Bicycling

The islands do not have much traffic, but the ever-present wind is a factor to be considered when making cycling plans. Bicycles can be rented on Shetland from **Puffins Pedals** (Mounthooly St., Lerwick, ☎ 01595/695065) or **Eric Brown Cycles** (Grantfield Garage, Grantfield, Lerwick, ☎ 01595/692709); on Orkney from **Patterson's Cycle Hire** (Kirkwall, ☎ 01856/873097), or the **Baby Linen Shop** (Stromness, ☎ 01856/850255).

Diving

Orkney, especially the former wartime anchorage of Scapa Flow, claims to have the best dive sites in Britain. Part of the attraction is the remains of the German navy, scuttled here in 1919. Consult the Orkney Tourist Board (*see* Important Addresses and Numbers in Northern Isles Essentials, *below*) for information on the many boat rental firms offering diving charters. Shetland also has exceptional underwater visibility, perfect for viewing the treasure wrecks and abundant marine life. The Shetland Isles tourist information center (*see* Important Addresses and Numbers in Northern Isles Essentials, *below*), as well as the **Skolla Diving Centre** (Gulberwick, ☎ 01595/694175), can provide the necessary information.

Fishing

Sea angling is such a popular sport in Orkney that the local tourist boards advise fishermen to book early. There are at least seven companies offering sea-angling boat rentals, with fishing rods available in most cases. Loch angling in Orkney is also popular; Loch of Harray and Loch of Stenness are the best-known spots. Contact the Orkney Tourist Board (*see* Important Addresses and Numbers in Northern Isles Essentials, *below*) for information. Shetland, also renowned for sea angling, holds several competitions throughout the year. Contact the **Shetland Association of Sea Anglers** via the tourist information center (*see* Important Addresses and Numbers in Northern Isles Essentials, *below*) for further information.

Pony Trekking

There is only one riding center on Shetland: **Broothom Ponies** (Braeside, Dunrossness, ☎ 01950/460556). There are no riding centers on Orkney.

Water Sports

There are good anchorages among Orkney's many islands. Contact the tourist information centers for details. There are also sailboats available from Shetland. Details may be obtained from the **Lerwick Boating Club,** which can be contacted through the tourist information center (*see* Important Addresses and Numbers in Northern Isles Essentials, *below*).

DINING AND LODGING

Dining

CATEGORY	COST*
$$$$	over £25
$$$	£15–£25
$$	£10–£15
$	under £10

per person for a three-course meal, including VAT and excluding drinks and service

WHAT TO WEAR
Casual attire is acceptable at all but the most expensive esblishments. At country-house hotels you may wish to dress up for dinner.

Lodging

CATEGORY	COST*
$$$$	over £110
$$$	£80–£110
$$	£45–£80
$	under £45

*All prices are for a standard double room, including service, breakfast, and VAT

Orkney

DINING AND LODGING

$$–$$$ **The Creel Restaurant.** This seafront restaurant with a cottage-style interior serves local seafood (including lobster) as its specialty, prepared personally by the owner/chef. The Creel also has some modest accommodations: Three spacious rooms with sea views are offered in an inexpensive bed-and-breakfast style. ☎ *Front Rd., St. Margaret's Hope,* ☎ *01856/831311. 1 room with bath, 2 with shower. Restaurant (reservations required). MC, V. Closed Jan.*

$$–$$$ **Foveran Hotel.** Surrounded by 34 acres of grounds and overlooking Scapa Flow, this warm hotel has an attractive light-wood, Scandinavian-style dining room and an open fire in its sitting room. The menu features Taste of Scotland, and the homemade soups, pâtés, and seafood have helped secure the restaurant's reputation as a very dependable place to eat. ☎ *St. Ola, Orkney KW15 1SF,* ☎ *01856/872389,* FAX *01856/ 876430. 8 rooms with bath. Restaurant, 2 lounges. MC, V.*

LODGING

$ **Polrudden Guest House.** Quietly situated yet close to the town center and public parks, this modern guest house offers a high standard of accommodation for the price. Multi-colored, matching curtains and quilt covers complement the cream-color rooms and pine furnishings. ☎ *Pickaquoy Rd., Kirkwall,* ☎ *and fax 01856/874761. 7 rooms with shower. No credit cards.*

Shetland

DINING AND LODGING

$$–$$$ ★ **Busta House.** Probably the best hotel in Shetland, the Busta House dates in part from the 16th century and is surrounded by terraced grounds. Bedrooms are well furnished in traditional style—floral chintzes and antique furniture—and the 16th-century Long Room is a delightful place to sample the hotel's selection of malt whiskies while sitting beside a peat fire. The dining room features a Taste of Scotland menu, with Shetland salmon and lamb usually available. ☎ *Brae, Shetland ZE2 9QN,* ☎ *0180622/506,* FAX *0180622/588. 20 rooms with bath or shower. Restaurant, bar. AE, DC, MC, V.*

$$–$$$ **Shetland Hotel.** Modern and well appointed (a result of the oil boom in the area and the needs of high-flying oil executives), the Shetland is located directly opposite the ferry terminal in Lerwick. The hotel is decorated in an attractive blend of peach, burgundy, and blue color schemes. The food is rich and filling, with sometimes wildly clashing flavors. One entrée consists of a folded fillet of beef with Stilton cheese inside, coated in oatmeal and served with a rich red-currant sauce: enough of a meal to sink the Shetland ferry! ☎ *Holmsgarth Rd., Lerwick ZE1 0RB,* ☎ *01595/695515,* FAX *01595/695828. 66 rooms with bath. 2 restaurants, 2 bars. AE, DC, MC, V.*

<u>LODGING</u>

$ **Bremner's Guest House.** Comfortable and relaxed, this modern house boasts stunning sunset views which rival those anywhere in the United Kingdom. The rooms are clean and functional, much like the rest of this family-run bed-and-breakfast inn. ☎ *Barns, Newgord, Westing, Uyeasound, Unst,* ☎ *01957/755249. 2 twin rooms share 1 bath. AE, MC, V.*

$ **The Old Manse.** The oldest inhabited building in Lerwick is now a friendly guest house, located on a quiet side street in the town center. The house dates from 1685 and was built for Lerwick's first minister. Furnishings are traditional, in keeping with the pleasantly aged feel of the house. Dinners are also traditional Scottish, mostly fish, beef, and stews. ☎ *9 Commercial St., Lerwick,* ☎ *01595/696301. 1 room with shower, 2 with shared bath. No credit cards.*

THE ARTS AND NIGHTLIFE

The Arts

Shetland has quite a strong cultural identity, thanks to its Scandinavian heritage. There are books of local dialect verse, a whole folklore contained in knitting patterns, and a strong tradition of fiddle-playing, for example. In the middle of the long winter, at the end of January, the Shetlanders celebrate their Viking culture with the **Up-Helly-Aa festival,** which involves much merrymaking, dressing up, and the burning of a replica of a Viking longship. The end of January, however, is hardly a peak time for tourists. The **Shetland Folk Festival,** held in April and May, and the **Shetland Accordian and Fiddle Festival,** in October, both attract large numbers of visitors. The tourist information center (*see* Important Addresses and Numbers in Northern Isles Essentials, *below*) can provide details on both festivals.

Orkney's cultural highlight is the **St. Magnus Festival,** a festival of music based in Kirkwall and usually held the third week in June (☎ 01856/ 872669 for details). Orkney also has an annual folk festival at the end of May. The Orkney Tourist Board (*see* Important Addresses and Numbers in Northern Isles Essentials, *below*) carries a full events list. **The Pier Arts Centre** (Victoria St., ☎ 01856/850209) focuses on artistic life in Stromness, with an eclectic display of paintings and sculptures and changing exhibitions, often by local artists.

Nightlife

No one goes to Orkney or Shetland for the nightlife, although there are bars and lounges with live entertainment in Lerwick on Shetland, thanks to the fluctuating population of oil workers and boat crews. The same is true in Kirkwall. Tourist information centers (*see* Important Addresses and Numbers in Northern Isles Essentials, *below*) will provide details on local concerts and summer programs for visitors.

NORTHERN ISLES ESSENTIALS

Arriving and Departing

By Bus
Aberdeen and Thurso have reliable bus links to and from all over Scotland: **Scottish Citylink** (☎ 0141/332–9191).

By Car and Ferry

To get to Lerwick, Shetland, take the ferry from the port in Aberdeen. To reach Stromness, Orkney, take the ferry from the port in Scrabster. Contact **P & O Ferries** (Orkney and Shetland Services, Jamieson's Quay, Aberdeen, ☎ 01224/572615, FAX 01224/574411) for reservations.

By Plane

British Airways (☎ 0345/222111) provides regular service to **Lerwick** (in Shetland) and **Kirkwall** (in Orkney) from Edinburgh, Glasgow, Aberdeen, and Inverness. **Business Air** (☎ 01382/566345) operates flights to **Lerwick** from Edinburgh and Aberdeen.

By Train

There are no trains on Orkney or Shetland, although Aberdeen (which has a ferry to Shetland) is well served by train, and Thurso is the terminus of the far-north line. For information, contact the British Rail information line (☎ 0345/212282). From Thurso a bus connects to Scrabster for Orkney.

Getting Around

By Bus

The main bus services on Orkney are operated by **James D. Peace & Co.** (☎ 01856/872866), **Causeway Coaches** (☎ 01856/831444), and **Shalder Coaches** (☎ 01856/850809); on Shetland by **Shalder Coaches** (☎ 01595/880217) and **J. Leask** (☎ 01595/693162).

By Car

Because of the oil wealth, the roads on Shetland are in very good shape. Both Orkney and Shetland are part of a network of islands with interconnecting ferries that are heavily subsidized. It's a good idea to book ferry tickets in advance. For information, contact the tourist information center in Shetland (*see* Important Addresses and Numbers, *below*) or ☎ 01957/722259 or 01957/722268 if you are visiting during peak season. Shetland visitors who want to get to Orkney can do so by way of ferry from Lerwick on Shetland to Stromness, in Orkney (*see* P & O Ferries, *above*).

Orkney also has causeways connecting some of the islands, but using these roads will, in some cases, take you on fairly roundabout routes, thus making for a longer journey than you might have if you took a ferry.

CAR RENTAL
Although Shetland has a number of car-rental firms, you have the option of taking your car from Aberdeen by sea. The rule of thumb is that for any visit under five days it is cheaper to rent a car in Shetland. Most of the rental companies are based in Lerwick; they include **Star Rent-a-Car** (22 Commercial Rd., Lerwick, ☎ 01595/692075, FAX 01595/693964) and **Bolts Car and Minibus Hire** (26 North Rd., Lerwick, ☎ 01595/692855, FAX 01595/693463). On Orkney try **J & W Tait** (Sparrowhawk Rd., Hatston Industrial Estate, Kirkwall, ☎ 01856/872490) or **James D. Peace & Co.** (Junction Rd., Kirkwall, ☎ 01856/872866).

By Plane

Note that because of the isolation of Orkney and Shetland there is a network of inter-island flights. Tourist information centers (*see* Important Addresses and Numbers, *below*) will provide details, or call British Airways (*see* Arriving and Departing by Plane, *above*).

By Train

There are no trains on Shetland or Orkney.

Guided Tours

Orientation

In addition to the bus companies mentioned above, well-run personally guided tours are offered in Orkney by **Go-Orkney** (☎ 01856/874260). Other companies that schedule general orientation tours include **Causeway Coaches** (☎ 01856/831444) and **Shalder Coaches** (☎ 01856/850809). The tour companies that service Shetland are **J. Leask** (☎ 01595/693162) and **Shalder Coaches** (☎ 01595/880217).

Special-Interest

All the above companies run special-interest tours to specific places of interest on the islands, and most can also tailor tours to your interests. Guided walks are available on Orkney: Contact **Wildabout** (through Orkney Tourist Board) for details of early morning, late evening, and all-day walks with an environmental theme. In Shetland, several companies tour the spectacular Noss Bird Sanctuary—a National Nature Reserve—in the summer, weather permitting. The tourist information center can provide details and take reservations.

Important Addresses and Numbers

Emergencies

For police, fire, or ambulance, dial 999 from any telephone. No coins are needed for emergency calls from public telephone booths.

Doctors and Dentists

Most general practitioners will see visitor patients by appointment or immediately in case of emergency. Your hotel or local tourist information center can advise you accordingly. You can also consult the Yellow Pages of the telephone directory, under "Doctor" or "Dentist." Hospitals with emergency rooms are **Gilbert Bain Hospital** (South Rd., Lerwick, Shetland, ☎ 01595/695678) and **Balfour Hospital** (New Staffa Rd., Kirkwall, Orkney, ☎ 01856/872763).

Late-Night Pharmacies

There are no late-night pharmacies on the islands. In case of emergency, police can provide assistance in locating pharmacists. Doctors in rural areas also dispense medication.

Discount Pass

A joint entry ticket to all of Historic Scotland's Orkney sights is available from the sights themselves. The ticket lasts until you've seen all the sights and costs £6 adults, £3 senior citizens, £2 children.

Visitor Information

The main **Tourist Information Centres** in the area are in **Orkney** (6 Broad St., Kirkwall, ☎ 01856/872856, FAX 01856/875056; and Ferry Terminal Building, Stromness, ☎ 01856/850716) and **Shetland** (Market Cross, Lerwick, ☎ 01595/693434, FAX 01595/695807).

13 Portraits of Scotland

Scotland at a Glance:
A Chronology

The Story of Scotland

Robert Burns,
Scotland's Eternal Laureate

SCOTLAND AT A GLANCE:
A CHRONOLOGY

c 3000 BC Neolithic migration from Mediterranean: "chambered cairn" people in north, "beaker people" in southeast.

c 300 BC Iron Age: infusion of Celtic peoples from the south and from Ireland; "Gallic forts," "brochs" built.

AD 79–89 Julius Agricola, Roman governor of Britain, invades Scotland; Scots tribes defeated at Mons Graupius (Grampians): "they make a desert and call it peace." Roman forts built at Inchtuthil and Ardoch.

142 Emperor Antoninus Pius orders Antonine Wall built between the Firths of Forth and Clyde.

185 Antonine Wall abandoned.

367 Massive invasion of Britain by Picts, Scots, Saxons, Franks.

392 Ninian's mission to Picts: first Christian chapel at Whitehorn.

400–1000 Era of the Four Peoples: red-haired Picts in the north, Gaelic-speaking Scots and Britons in the west and south, Germanic Angles in the east. Origins of Arthur legend (Arthur's Seat, Ben Arthur). Picts, with bloodline through mothers, eventually dominate.

563 Columba establishes monastery at Iona.

780–1065 Scandinavian invasions; Hebrides remain Norse until 1263, Orkney and Shetland until 1472.

1005–1034 Malcolm II unifies Scotland and (temporarily) repels the English.

1040 Malcolm's heir, Duncan, is slain by his rival, Macbeth, whose wife has a claim to the throne.

The House of Canmore

1057 Malcolm III, known as "Canmore" ("Big Head"), murders Macbeth and assumes the throne.

1093 Death of Malcolm's queen, St. Margaret, founder of modern Edinburgh.

1124–1153 David I, "soir sanct" (sore saint), builds the abbeys of Jedburgh (1118), Kelso (1128), Melrose (1136), and Dryburgh (1150) and brings Norman culture to Scotland.

1290 The first of many attempts to unite Scotland peacefully with England fails when the Scots queen Margaret, "the Maid of Norway," dies on the way to her wedding to Edward, son of Edward I of England. The Scots naively ask Edward I (subsequently known as "the hammer of the Scots") to arbitrate between the remaining 13 claimants to the throne. Edward's choice, John Balliol, is known as "toom tabard" (empty coat).

1295 Under continued threat from England, Scotland signs its first treaty of the "auld alliance" with France. Wine trade flourishes.

1297 Revolt William Wallace, immortalized by Burns, leads the Scots against the English.

1305 Wallace captured by the English and executed.

1306–29 Reign of Robert Bruce (Robert I). Defeats Edward II at Bannockburn, 1314; Treaty of Northampton, 1328, recognizes Scottish sovereignty.

1368 Edinburgh Castle rebuilt.

The House of Stewart

1371 Robert II, son of Robert Bruce's daughter Marjorie and Walter the Steward, is crowned. Struggle (dramatized in Scott's novels) between the crown and the barony ensues for the next century, punctuated by sporadic warfare with England.

1411 Founding of University of St. Andrews.

1451 University of Glasgow founded.

1488–1515 Reign of James IV. The Renaissance reaches Scotland. The "Golden Age" of Scots poetry includes Robert Henryson, William Dunbar, Gavin Douglas, and the king himself.

1495 University of Aberdeen founded.

1507 Andrew Myllar and Walter Chapman set up first Scots printing press in Edinburgh.

1513 At war against the English, James is slain at Flodden.

1542 Henry VIII defeats James V at Solway Moss; the dying James, hearing of the birth of his daughter, Mary, declares: "It came with a lass [Marjorie Bruce] and it will pass with a lass."

1542–67 Reign of Mary Queen of Scots. Romantic, Catholic, and with an excellent claim to the English throne, Mary proved to be no match for her barons, John Knox, or her cousin, Elizabeth of England.

1560 Mary returns to Scotland from her childhood in France, at the same time that Catholicism is abolished in favor of Knox's Calvinism.

1565 Mary marries Lord Darnley, a Catholic.

1567 Darnley is murdered at Kirk o' Field; Mary marries one of the conspirators, the earl of Bothwell. Driven from Scotland, she appeals to Elizabeth, who imprisons her. Mary's son, James (1566–1625), is crowned James VI of Scotland.

1582 University of Edinburgh is founded.

1587 Elizabeth orders the execution of Mary.

1603 Elizabeth dies without issue; James VI is crowned James I of England. Parliaments remain separate for another century.

1638 National Covenant challenges Charles I's personal rule.

1639–41 Crisis. The Scots and then the English Parliaments revolt against Charles I.

1643 Solemn League and Covenant establishes Presbyterianism as the Church of Scotland ("the Kirk"). Civil War in England.

1649 Charles I beheaded. Cromwell made Protector.

1650–52 Cromwell roots out Scots royalists.

1658 First Edinburgh—London coach: the journey took two weeks.

1660 Restoration of Charles II. Episcopalianism reestablished in Scotland; Covenanters persecuted.

1688–89 Glorious Revolution; James VII and II, a Catholic, deposed in favor of his daughter Mary and her husband, William of Orange. Supporters of James ("Jacobites") defeated at Killiecrankie. Presbyterianism reestablished.

1692 Highlanders who refuse oath to William and Mary massacred at Glencoe.

1698–1700 Attempted Scottish colony at Darien fails.

1707 Union of English and Scots Parliaments under Queen Anne; deprived of French wine trade, Scots turn to whisky.

The House of Hanover

1714 Queen Anne dies; George I of Hanover, descended from a daughter of James VI and I, crowned.

1715 First Jacobite Rebellion. Earl of Mar defeated.

1730–90 Scottish Enlightenment. The Edinburgh Medical School is the best in Europe; David Hume (1711–1776) and Adam Smith (1723–1790) redefine philosophy and economics. In the arts, Allan Ramsay the elder (1686–1758) and Robert Burns (1759–1796) refine Scottish poetry; Allan Ramsay the younger (1713–1784) and Henry Raeburn (1756–1823) rank among the finest painters of the era. Edinburgh's New Town, begun in the 1770s by the brothers Adam, provides a fitting setting.

1745–46 Last Jacobite Rebellion. Bonnie Prince Charlie, grandson of James VII and II, is defeated at Culloden; wearing of the kilt is forbidden until 1782. James Watt (1736–1819) of Glasgow is granted a patent for his steam engine.

1771 Birth of Walter Scott, Romantic novelist.

1778 First cotton mill, at Rothesay.

1788 Death of Bonnie Prince Charlie.

1790 Forth and Clyde Canal opened.

1800–1850 Highland Clearances: overpopulation, increased rents, and conversion of farms to sheep pasture leads to mass migration, sometimes forced, to North America and elsewhere. Meanwhile, the lowlands industrialize; Catholic Irish immigrate to factories of southwest.

1828 Execution of Burke and Hare, who sold their murder victims to an Edinburgh anatomist, a lucrative trade.

1832 Parliamentary Reform Act expands the franchise, redistributes seats.

1837 Victoria accedes to the British throne.

1842 Edinburgh–Glasgow railroad opened.

1846 Edinburgh–London railroad opened.

1848 Queen Victoria buys estate at Balmoral as her Scottish residence. Andrew Carnegie emigrates from Dunfermline to Pittsburgh.

1884–85 Gladstone's Reform Act establishes manhood suffrage. Office of Secretary for Scotland authorized.

1886 Scottish Home Rule Association founded.

1901 Death of Queen Victoria.

The House of Windsor

1928 Equal Franchise Act gives the vote to women. Scottish Office established as governmental department in Edinburgh. Scottish National Party founded.

1931 Depression hits industrialized Scotland severely.

1945 Two Scottish Nationalists elected to Parliament.

1959 Finnart Oil Terminal, Chapelcross Nuclear Power Station, and Dounreay Fast Breeder Reactor opened.

1964 Forth Road Bridge opened.

1970 British Petroleum strikes oil in the North Sea; revives economy of northeast.

1973 Britain becomes a member of the European Economic Community ("Common Market").

1974 Eleven Scottish Nationalist MPs elected. Old counties reorganized and renamed new regions.

1979 Referendum on "devolution" of a separate Scotland: 33% for, 31% against; 36% don't vote.

1981 Europe's largest oil terminal opens at Sullom Voe, Shetland.

1988 Revival of Scots nationalism under banner of "Scotland in Europe," anticipating 1992 economic union.

1992 Increasing attention focused on Scotland's dissatisfaction with rule from London, England. Poll shows 50% of Scots want independence.

1995 In the face of a Tory Government increasingly looking like a "lame duck" and divided on the issue of Europe, Scotland continues to argue its own way forward. The Labour Party promises a Scottish Parliament but wants to keep Scotland within the United Kingdom; the Scottish National Party still wants independence and sees Labour's Scottish Parliament as a stepping-stone to full autonomy.

THE STORY OF SCOTLAND

By Gordon Donaldson

Professor Gordon Donaldson of Edinburgh University was Her Majesty's Historiographer Royal in Scotland and the author of more than 30 books, mainly on Scottish history. He died in 1993.

SCOTLAND ALMOST DEFIES classification. It is no longer an independent country and it has no legislative organ of its own, for the United Kingdom Parliament at Westminster legislates for it. Yet it has a distinct executive, with a Secretary of State and a number of ministers; its own legal system and its own law courts, different and separate from those of England (the British House of Lords, however, is the final court of appeal in civil cases). There is a Church of Scotland whose government is Presbyterian and totally separate from the Episcopalian Church of England. The local government system is now constructed not (as in England) of counties, but of single-tier authorities, each covering quite a wide area, and one still finds "burghs" (not boroughs) and "provosts" (not mayors). Scottish sheriffs are salaried judges and therefore different from the sheriffs of either England or the United States. Scotland has its own banks and banknotes.

It is arguable whether there is a Scottish nation. The Scots of today are descended from Scandinavians, Irish, English, Welsh, French, and Flemings, who immigrated in earlier centuries and obliterated traces of more primitive inhabitants. The whole of Britain has a Celtic fringe, which in the south consists of Wales and Cornwall and in Scotland consists of the central and west Highlands. A new factor entered in the 19th century with a massive immigration from Ireland, which has left conspicuous features, not least a very large Roman Catholic element.

If there is no Scottish race, it is equally true that there is no Scottish language. The speech of the earliest known inhabitants has long vanished, leaving two tongues, which arrived about 500 BC. A people from Ireland calling themselves Scots settled in Argyll and brought with them the Gaelic language of Ireland, which used to be known in Scotland, quite accurately, as Irish. The fact that the name is sometimes pronounced *Gallic* must not mislead the unwary into thinking that there is anything French about it. From the European continent came the Angles or English, who settled in northeastern England and southeastern Scotland, introducing what became the speech of England and most of Scotland. The area where Irish or Gaelic was spoken shrank steadily until it was confined to the western fringe of the mainland and some of the Hebrides. The Scandinavian tongue, which was brought by immigrants from Norway—some of them Vikings—to Orkney and Shetland, has left many traces in the speech of the people there. French was spoken by the Norman immigrants of the 12th century (who introduced many familiar Scottish surnames, such as Bruce, Cumming, Fraser, Hay, Somerville, Colville, Mowat, Menzies, and Stewart), but it hardly extended much beyond the aristocracy and probably died out in the 14th century.

The Lowlands must be considered to include the Orkney and Shetland islands and to continue along a coastal plain stretching from Caithness down nearly the entire eastern seaboard, extending various distances inland, and finally crossing the country from the Firth of Forth to the River Clyde. The southern uplands, that is, the hills between the Forth–Clyde line and the Border, while not Lowland in a physical sense, are racially and linguistically part of the Lowlands. Thus the Highlands lie to the west rather than to the north of the Lowlands and include the mountainous center of Scotland and the entire west coast. There is a Highland town south of Berwick in England: Campbeltown in Kintyre.

The fertile lowlands were suitable for arable farming, although also with good grazing on hill slopes, while the Highlands lent themselves to a mainly pastoral economy in the glens or valleys, which ran through the barren wastes of the mountains. In later times it was chiefly in the Lowlands that industries developed. The eastern Lowland areas have a fairly dry and temperate climate; in the central Highlands there are severe winters, whereas the western seaboard has in general mild conditions, usually kind to both plant and animal life, but the area is apt to be lashed by tempests of wind and rain. Few activities are more dispiriting than farming in the west Highlands, but there was little else to provide a livelihood. The Highlands could hardly ever have been economically viable without outside subsidies. For centuries these took the shape of raids by Highlanders on their Lowland neighbors, who despised and hated the westerners. It was said that after God created the first Highlander (out of a piece of horse manure),

Quoth God to the Highlander, "What will you now?"

"I will down to the Lowland, Lord, and there steal a cow."

The tourist's image of the Scot is of a bagpipe-playing figure in what is called Highland dress and sometimes miscalled Scottish national dress. In fact, if anyone arrayed in Highland dress had turned up in the Lowlands three or four hundred years ago, he would probably have been shot on sight.

The many peoples who inhabited early Scotland were gradually brought under the rule of a single king. The lands north of the Forth and Clyde were united in 844 in the kingdom of Alba—in or about 1018 the king of Alba established control over the country between those rivers and the present border. In 1266 the western isles were ceded by Norway, and in 1468–69 Orkney and Shetland, too, came under Scottish rule.

The geography of the country presented so many obstacles to communications that, until a relatively late date, order could not be maintained everywhere, especially in the Highlands and the Borders. It is noticeable that the cathedrals for the dioceses that covered the Highlands were in towns situated in or near the Lowlands—Dunblane, Dunkeld, Elgin, Dornoch, and Fortrose. Similarly, the sheriffs who were supposed to administer jus-

tice in the Highlands sat in Dingwall, Inverness, Banff, and Perth. They were safer there! Highland chiefs often allied with the English against their own kings. It was not until after James VI became king of England in 1603 that joint Anglo-Scottish action could be taken against disorderly Borderers who sought refuge across the frontier and against disorderly Highlanders who sought refuge in Ireland.

THERE WERE strong local loyalties, arising partly from the fact that even in the Lowlands one fertile and populous area was often separated from another. Thus the Tweed valley was cut off by bleak hills from Edinburgh and its hinterland, while Angus and Kincardinshire were isolated from Aberdeenshire by mountains thrusting eastward to the sea near Stonehaven. Then there were elements in Scottish society that made the task of government difficult. The head of a great family was acknowledged as the leader of his own blood relations, of collateral branches of the family descended from a common ancestor, of tenants and vassals whose links with him sprang from land tenure and not from blood, of men who contracted to serve him, and of men who simply happened to share his surname. Very much the same kind of social organization existed throughout the whole country in the Middle Ages.

In the Highlands, the practice of accepting the leadership of a chief persisted until well into the 18th century. The "clan" has somehow captured the imagination of those who have no idea what a clan was. The historic Highland clan did not consist of people with the same surname, and indeed until the 18th century few Highlanders had surnames at all. The Highland clan comprised people associated for much the same reasons as the Lowland groupings just described. The modern clan, composed on the basis of surnames, has little historical foundation. It may be added that nearly all the clan tartans were devised by manufacturers in the 19th or 20th century and are simply big business.

While the government of Scotland involved many internal problems, the country was fortunate to escape the kind of competition for the throne that led to the Wars of the Roses in England: The succession in the house of Stuart proved so stable that for three centuries (1371–1649) the crown passed from father to child without deviation. This did mean, however, that at a time when almost everything depended on the ability of the monarch in person, the throne was frequently occupied by minors and government was weak.

The great external problem was relations with England. In the 12th and 13th centuries the ruling families of the two countries frequently intermarried and peace generally prevailed, but at the end of the 13th century there was a disputed succession in Scotland that gave Edward I of England an opportunity to attempt conquest. The Scots resisted, at first unsuccessfully under William Wallace (who was victorious at Stirling in 1297, but defeated at Falkirk in 1298) and then successfully under Robert the Bruce (who defeated the English at Bannockburn in 1314). In 1320 the Scottish nobles put their seals to a Declaration of Independence, dated at Arbroath, in which they declared: "As long as a hundred of us remain alive, we will never be subject to the English king; because it is not for riches, or honors, or glory that we fight, but for liberty alone, which no worthy man loses save with his life." But war went on intermittently for more than another two centuries, with many Scottish defeats like Flodden (1513) and Pinkie (1547). Yet the Scots succeeded in preserving their independence against their mighty neighbor.

As a result of the marriage in 1503 of James IV, king of Scots, to Margaret Tudor, daughter of Henry VII of England, their great-grandson, James VI, became king James I of England in 1603 on the death of Elizabeth, the last of the Tudors. Scotland and England were still distinct kingdoms, each with its own parliament and its own administration. Such an arrangement could work only if there were no conflicts of interest or if the Crown was more powerful than the parliaments. In the middle of the century, as a result of the civil war occasioned by the unpopular policies of Charles I, the union broke down, for after the execution of the king, the English declared a republic while the Scots proclaimed their allegiance to Charles II;

the result was the conquest of Scotland by the armies of Oliver Cromwell. In 1660, when the monarchy was restored, there were again two kingdoms, separate but under the same king.

THE NEXT CRISIS AROSE in the 1690s, after James VII (of Scotland) and II (of England) had been deposed in favor of William of Orange. This revolution increased the powers of the two parliaments and made friction more likely. The Scottish parliament adopted independent economic policies that threatened to lead to separate foreign policies. It became clear that either the existing union might have to be dissolved (which would probably have led to war) or the countries would have to be more closely united. It was the latter course that prevailed, when the two parliaments agreed on May 1, 1707, that the kingdom of Scotland and the kingdom of England alike should come to an end and be replaced by a United Kingdom of Great Britain, with one parliament.

William of Orange was followed by Anne and then by the house of Hanover, beginning with George I (1714), but James (VII and II) left a son, "the Old Pretender," and had two grandsons, the elder of them Charles Edward, "Bonnie Prince Charlie," and the claims of this line were supported by the Jacobites, who raised two serious rebellions, in 1715 and 1745. The "Fifteen" was a dull affair led by dull men and ended in an indecisive battle at Sheriffmuir. But the "Forty-Five" was a dashing affair led by the glamorous Prince Charlie and supported mainly by gallant Highlanders. They gained a brilliant victory at Prestonpans and made a spectacular dash into the heart of England before suffering a disastrous defeat at Culloden (1746).

The union preserved Scots law and the existing Scottish church system, which had characteristics rooted in a long history. In simple terms, whereas in England the more extreme reformers, the Puritans, failed, in Scotland they succeeded. In the course of opposition to Charles I, the Scots adopted a manifesto called the National Covenant (1638), from which developed the concept of a "covenanted nation," or Chosen People, comparable to the Jews. After parliament finally decided in 1690 that the Church was to be Presbyterian, there were many divisions within it, especially the Disruption of 1843, which founded the Free Church, and although there have been many reunions, some small dissenting Presbyterian churches still exist, especially in the west Highlands.

PERHAPS THE ecclesiastical disputes were related to the fact that the Scots were not only argumentative, but sufficiently well educated to grasp the finer points that were at issue. From its earliest days the reformed church had stressed the need for education, and already in the 17th century it was normal for a parish in Lowland Scotland to have a school, although the Highlands were not adequately served until later. One looks in vain in Scottish literature for the "ignorant yokel" so familiar in English literature, and for generations Scotland was far ahead of England in its educational standards. Scots like to boast that they had five universities when England had only two, and it was claimed that higher education and a successful career were always open to a "lad o' pairts" (a boy with the ability to make his way in the world).

In the Middle Ages Scotland was not alone in being constantly under threat from England. France also faced English aggression, and it was natural that France and Scotland should form The Auld Alliance, first formulated in 1295 and continuing to the reformation and even after it. In the 16th century it was agreed that the two peoples should have joint nationality. There was thus a strong Continental influence on Scottish law, universities, and architecture, and French words found their way into Scottish speech. Scotland, although more physically remote, was a less insular, more Continental country than England, where the law in particular followed its own unique development. Apart from the French connection, Scotland had close ties with the Low Countries, Denmark, and the Baltic, so that she was not isolated in a distant northern backwater but drew cultural inspiration from the mainstream of European civilization.

Partly because resources at home were limited and the ambitious saw better prospects abroad, already in the Middle Ages Scots were to be found all over Europe as merchants, soldiers, and scholars. With the development of colonization, new fields opened up, and Scots peopled lands overseas in numbers far out of proportion to the population of their own country. There are some common misconceptions about the causes. Many inhabitants of the American continent are convinced that their ancestors were Jacobites who had to flee after Culloden. It is true that a small number of rebels were deported to America as their punishment, but there is little evidence of involuntary flight. Others see the Highland Clearances as a main reason for emigration; in the Highlands, as elsewhere, the population had so increased as to outstrip subsistence by about 1800, and people were trying to live on tiny holdings, precariously dependent on the potato crop, which sometimes failed. Some landlords decided to turn their estates over to sheep farming and to develop fishing, which meant displacing tenants. However, few of those tenants went overseas immediately, and the population of the Highlands actually increased during that period. Curiously, it was only after tenants gained protection against arbitrary eviction in 1886 that the Highland population fell disastrously.

Whatever the causes, there was not a part of the world in which Scots were not to be found, and they gained a reputation for success. An observer in 1888 remarked that "from Canada to Ceylon, from Dunedin to Bombay, for every Englishman that you meet who has worked himself up to wealth from small beginnings without external aid, you find ten Scotchmen. . . . Wherever abroad you come across a Scotchman, you invariably find him prosperous and respected." It was put more briefly: "You never find a foolish Scot abroad; all the fools stay at home."

Thomas Edison; Samuel Morse; Edgar Allan Poe; Washington Irving; Robert E. Lee; Presidents Jefferson, Monroe, Jackson, Grant, and Polk; Patrick Henry; and James McNeil Whistler all claimed Scottish ancestry. Allan Pinkerton of the detective agency was born in Glasgow; John Paul Jones, founder of the U.S. Navy, came from the Solway shore. Samuel Wilson, whose parents sailed to America from Greenock on the Clyde, has been officially recognized as the original Uncle Sam.

The Scottish John Macdonald and Alexander Mackenzie were Canada's first and second prime ministers. That country's Fraser and Mackenzie rivers are named for Scottish pioneers, as is her leading university, McGill.

Some pioneers carried royal blood to the New World, if the genealogists are to be believed. Jimmy Carter, through his alleged descent from King Henry III, must be linked with the Stuarts; the Irish Kennedys' Scottish cousins went back to Robert the Bruce, as did those of Thomas Jefferson, James Monroe, and James Buchanan; Ulysses S. Grant claimed descent from an earlier king, David I; and Theodore Roosevelt boasted three clan chieftains—a Stuart, a Drummond, and a Douglas—in his ancestry.

Perhaps the most famous American Scot was Andrew Carnegie, steel baron and multimillionaire, who started work as a bobbin boy in a Pittsburgh mill. When he was a baby in Dunfermline (Fife), his parents sold everything they had to raise the fare for the passage to New York.

While it was often the enterprising rather than the economically depressed who emigrated, periods of slump usually saw heavy emigration: During the 1920s, when Scotland's heavy industries felt the full blast of depression, nearly 400,000 people left the country, and its population fell for the first time.

Although the Union of 1707 gave Scotland and England a single parliament, there was at first little to stimulate the Scots to an interest in British politics. The Liberal party had a majority of Scottish seats at almost every election between 1832 and 1914, and sometimes the Scottish Liberal vote ensured a Liberal government in London for which the majority of the English had not voted. In the past few decades the Labour party began to take the place of the Liberals in Scottish attachment, with the result that, in a reversal of the earlier situation, the Scots have had Conservative governments sitting in Westminster for which they did not vote. (On the other hand, it should be remembered that out of nine successive prime ministers between 1892 and 1924, six were Scots.)

For over a century now there have been intermittent demands for legislative devolution, and Home Rule was proposed several times before 1914. In recent years anxiety over the poor state of the Scottish economy has led to renewed agitation for Home Rule, though its cause usually makes a poor showing at general elections, and in a referendum on the subject in 1979, Home Rule did not raise the required 40% of the votes needed. However, an election in Govan, a Glasgow constituency, was won overwhelmingly by a Scottish Nationalist candidate at the end of 1988; since then the cause of Scotland for the Scots has been firmly back on the agenda, although endless arguments rage as to whether the answer is devolution (with the formation of a Scottish parliament, yet still subject to Westminster in England) or complete independence.

ROBERT BURNS, SCOTLAND'S ETERNAL LAUREATE

By Holly Hughes

Holly Hughes has written books on Dickens and Eliot and is a contributing editor to *Literary Cavalcade* magazine.

BEFORE I EVER VISITED Scotland, I had only a foggy sort of notion of who Robert Burns was. Then I traveled to Edinburgh one summer for the arts festival and discovered Burns everywhere. His rakish dark eyes and bold features peered skeptically from portraits and monuments and even biscuit tins; phrases from his poems popped up in advertising jingles and newspaper headlines and in the names of tea shops and bed-and-breakfasts.

On subsequent trips, I discovered that Scotland's map is covered with places that claim an association with Burns—not just his own homes (and there are plenty, for he was constantly on the move, leaving behind him a trail of debts and lovelorn lasses), but pubs where he drank, landscapes he praised, cemeteries where his lovers and enemies were buried—it's almost like the proliferation of historic homes in the eastern United States that claim "Washington slept here."

Ayrshire is officially Burns country, beginning with the thatched cottage in Alloway, near Ayr, where Burns was born in 1759, and ending with Dumfries, where Burns was buried in St. Michael's churchyard in 1796 (the very same day his youngest son, Maxwell, was born). Tarbolton was the village where young Burns enjoyed many a late evening drinking with the Bachelor's Club and where he fell in love with Mary Campbell, the subject of some of his finest love lyrics ("Ye banks and braes and streams around/The castle o' Montgomery!/Green be your woods, and fair your flowers,/Your waters never drumlie./There Simmer first unfald her robes,/And there the langest tarry;/For there I took the last fareweel/O' my sweet Highland Mary"). At the Burns farm in Mossgiel, visitors can see the field where he ploughed up the "Wee, sleekit, cowrin, tim'rous beastie" eulogized in "To A Mouse." Kilmarnock, with its Burns monument and museum, was where his first book of poetry, *Poems Chiefly in the Scottish Dialect,* was printed in 1786. Mauchline was where Burns and his wife, Jean Armour, married and had their first home together, and its churchyard's graves are covered with names familiar from his poems. Moffat, Lochlea, Kirkoswald, and many other Ayrshire towns all boast some kind of Burns connection, often of a purely imaginative provenance: Grey Mare's Tail, near Moffat in Galloway, is simply a magnificent cascade that has been named after the tail of Tam O'Shanter's horse, Meg, who was pursued by a horde of witches in one of Burns's most famous comic ballads.

Even the Highlands boasts Burns associations, quoting his song "My heart's in the Highlands" ("Wherever I wander, wherever I rove/The hills of the Highlands forever I love"). Burns traveled there in 1787, following what was probably a fairly typical tourist's itinerary. He began in Stirling, where he visited the battlefield of Bannockburn, then up the north road to Inverness, with side trips to Culloden Moor and to Cawdor, with its Macbeth associations. From there he went east along the Moray Firth, down to Peterhead, and along the coast to Aberdeen, Dundee, and Perth, where there were side trips to Scone Palace and to Ossian's grave at Crieff.

Wherever you go throughout Scotland, it's easy to believe that Robert Burns must be as important a poet as Shakespeare or Milton or Keats or any of those English scribblers. Burns didn't just spring out of nowhere, of course. He was one of the many fruits of the Scottish Enlightenment, that glorious era of the 18th century when Scotland, seeking its own identity after being swallowed up in a political union with England, suddenly produced an astonishing crop of scientists, philosophers, and writers. Scotland's literary history up to that point could boast only of the 15th century's so-called Scottish Chaucerians, William Dunbar and Robert Henryson, and Gavin Douglas, who translated the *Aeneid* into Scots in 1513. The earliest lights of the 18th-century Scottish literary renaissance had to prove themselves by writing in English and hobnobbing in London, as did Edinburgh-born James Thomson, who published the first book of the immensely popular poem *The Seasons* in 1726, and James Boswell, whose *Journal of a Tour of the Hebrides,* documenting his travels with the sage Samuel Johnson, appeared in 1785. In midcentury, two somewhat more homegrown talents, Allan Ramsay and Robert Fergusson, brought forth some rather good poetry written in a literary mixture of Scots (the dialect of the Lowlands) and English, and Invernesshire's James Macpherson published several volumes of Gaelic epic poems supposedly written by Ossian, the son of the ancient Scottish hero Fingal, which Macpherson said he had simply translated into modern English. This turned into a scandal, however, when Macpherson, encouraged by his success, kept "discovering" more lost poems to translate and couldn't even produce authentic manuscripts for them.

Although this hoax tarnished Scotland's reputation in London, Edinburgh was still a flourishing cultural capital in 1786 when the first edition of Robert Burns's poetry appeared. Intellectuals and wealthy patrons of the arts in Edinburgh were quick to seize upon this Ayrshire farmer's son, praising his portraits of rural Scotland and extolling the vigor and grace of his use of Scots dialect, much the same way as music critics in the early 1960s rushed to praise the Beatles as natural untutored geniuses. And like the Beatles, Burns came equipped with dashing good looks, a way with the ladies, dangerously radical political views, and a taste for hard liquor. Though not conventionally handsome, with his stocky build, thick features, and thin dark hair, he managed to cut quite a figure at fashionable Edinburgh soirees during the year and a half, from 1786 through 1788, after the phenomenal success of his first volume. Perhaps it helped that everyone, expecting to meet a clownish Ayrshire farmer with clods of mud still sticking to his boots, found instead a literate, intelligent fellow in a genteel dark jacket, light-colored waistcoat, and modestly ruffled linen shirt.

YET WHILE Edinburgh's elite pursued this new prodigy, Burns himself seemed uncomfortable with all this lionizing, asserting himself with a forthright honesty that all too often bordered on rudeness. He became increasingly restless as his stay in the capital dragged on (and his debts piled up and his love affairs grew more entangled), and one senses in his letters a note of relief once he cut himself free and returned to Ayrshire and to the uncertain prospect of life as a farmer and, after the failure of his crops, as an excise collector. Centuries later, this is the image of Burns his fans treasure most: riding about the countryside, singing to himself as he molded random bits of song into polished poems, or hunkering down with a congenial group of local wits at a country pub.

Neither of Scotland's other two great literary figures, Sir Walter Scott (1771–1832) and Robert Louis Stevenson (1850–94), have remained as firmly lodged in the hearts of their countrymen as Burns has. Scott, who celebrated Scotland in both poetry (*The Lay of the Last Minstrel, Marmion,* and *The Lady of the Lake*) and novels (*Ivanhoe, The Heart of Midlothian,* and *Waverly*) was enormously popular throughout the 19th century, and his career was longer and his output greater than Burns's. Stevenson, although born in Edinburgh, was never associated as closely with Scotland as Burns and Scott were, since frail health, poverty, and a roaming spirit conspired to make him live abroad from the age of 23 on. Except for a handful of Scottish historical novels—*The Master of Ballantrae, Kidnapped, David Balfour,* and *Weir of Hermiston*—Stevenson's best-known works (*Dr. Jekyll and Mr. Hyde, Treasure Island*) are not even set in Scotland.

As an English major whose professors never bothered to teach me about Burns, after my travels I became curious to reread his poetry, and I discovered that it really is wonderful. And looking back at my old school anthologies, I see that, with the exception of "To A Mouse," almost every one had a different selection of Burns's poems to include, which is a clue to just how many good things he really wrote. Of course, Robert Burns has never really faded from the general public's literary consciousness. For instance, just about every song that we associate with Scotland turns out to have lyrics by Burns: "My Love Is Like a Red, Red Rose," "Auld Lang Syne," "Flow Gently, Sweet Afton," "Green Grow the Rushes," "My Heart's in the Highlands," "The Banks O' Doon." *Bartlett's Quotations* devotes several pages to Burns, listing such well-known phrases as "the best-laid schemes of mice and men," "man's inhumanity to man," "to see ourselves as others see us," "death's untimely frost," "a man's a man for all that," "nursing her wrath to keep it warm," and "nae man can tether time or tide."

ISUPPOSE THE MAIN BARRIER for modern readers is the unfamiliar Scots dialect that peppers Burns's poems, but it is nowhere near as incomprehensible as, say, Chaucer's Middle English. And if you read the verses out loud—the best way to enjoy those lilting stanzas anyway—many of the oddly spelled Scots words are perfectly easy to understand. After all, Burns was not writing in some kind of primitive, substandard rural slang. He was following a very specific literary style, following the precedent of Allan Ramsay and Robert Fergusson. Despite his rural upbringing, Burns had enough education to write perfectly standard English, as shown by all his personal correspondence and a good number of his poems (though, tellingly, these are usually not his most successful verses). Burns himself, teetering precariously between social classes, probably shifted in conversation from correct English—which he would have spoken at dinner parties thrown by his wealthy Edinburgh patrons—to broad Scots dialect, which would have been useful when he took his farm produce to market or set about wooing local peasant girls. (Scots was the everyday speech of Lowland Scotland, as opposed to the Highlands' Gaelic dialect, and therefore it is also sometimes called Lowlands, or Lallans.) In his poems, he inserted dialect where any good poet uses his or her most unusual vocabulary—as intensifying adjectives, line endings, and rhymes. The result is an extraordinarily effective poetic language, with a wide range of emotion and humor.

There are other reasons, though, apart from the quality of his verse, why Robert Burns has become enshrined as Scotland's national bard and why his birthday, January 25, is still celebrated with formal dinners (called Burns Suppers) around the globe. Burns's personality somehow speaks to us across the ages, corny as that may sound. People who knew him wrote invariably of his personal magnetism—his dark, flashing eyes; his lively wit; his zest for living—and what has survived of his correspondence suggests that he must have been one of those people you can't help being fond of. He also embodies something that is very near and dear to the Scottish national character: He had a wonderful common touch. He felt at home with ordinary village life; loved bawdiness and roistering; and was deeply suspicious of authority, especially as it was vested in the Scottish kirk, with all its dour piety. Instinctively he was a hardy partisan of individual liberty, though his political convictions were inconsistent—he also nursed a sentimental fondness for Scottish royalty, especially the romantic figure of Mary Queen of Scots. Sentimentality, indeed, was curiously mixed with cynicism in his emotional makeup. Burns was capable of writing both achingly romantic love poetry and bawdy verses about lust; while poems such as "The Cotter's Saturday Night" mawkishly extol the virtues of humble poverty, in other poems Burns is just as likely to lament how hard it is to eke out a living, as in the poignant last stanza of "To A Mouse": "Still thou are blest, compar'd wi' me;/The present only toucheth thee,/But och! I backward cast my e'e,/On prospects drear!/An' forward, tho' I canna see,/I guess an' fear!"

Burns's myth, in truth, has been distorted a bit to make him even more glamorous to 20th-century fans. For example, popular imagination wants to believe that Burns drank himself to death. There's no question that Burns enjoyed a good carouse as well as the next Scotsman—after all, this is the man who wrote, in "Scotch Drink," "O whisky! soul o' plays and pranks!/ Accept a bardie's gratefu' thanks!/ When wanting thee, what tuneless cranks/ Are my poor verses!" Contemporary accounts, however, confirm that he was only a social drinker. His death was most probably a result of bacterial endocarditis, brought on by rheumatic fever, although he didn't help matters any by going out one night to a local tavern, getting roaring drunk, and passing out in the January cold on his way home. Never really robust, he had been subject to periods of weakness and depression ever since he was a teenager working long, hard days on his father's Ayrshire farm.

Another indelible part of the Burns myth is the image of him as a great womanizer, seducing well-born ladies, making peasant girls swoon wherever he went, and scattering bastard bairns around the countryside. It's true that his first children with Jean Armour were born out of wedlock, and one of his finest poems is written to the illegitimate child he fathered on Elizabeth Paton ("Welcome! my bonie, sweet, wee dochter,/Tho' ye come here a wee unsought for,/And tho' your comin' I hae fought for,/Baith kirk and queir;/Yet, by my faith, ye're no unwrought for,/Thast I shall swear!"). But Burns was no mere rake—he was usually romantically in love with whatever girl he was chasing, and when it came down to it, he was a loyal (if not entirely faithful) husband to Jean. She herself seemed calmly resigned to his ardent nature, saying philosophically, "Our Robbie should ha' had twa wives."

INDEX

NOTES

NOTES

NOTES

NOTES

NOTES

Escape to ancient cities and

journey to   *exotic islands with*

CNN *Travel Guide, a wealth of valuable advice. Host*

Valerie Voss will take you to

all of your favorite destinations,

including those off the beaten

path. Tune-in to your passport to the world.

CNN TRAVEL GUIDE
SATURDAY 12:30 PMᴇᴛ   SUNDAY 4:30 PMᴇᴛ

CNN

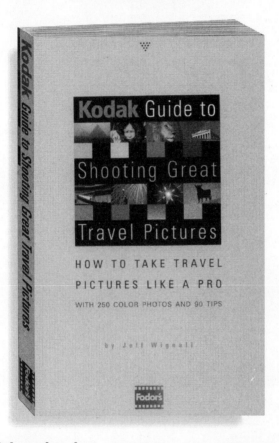

Fodor's Travel Publications

Available at bookstores everywhere, or call 1–800–533–6478, 24 hours a day.

Gold Guides

U.S.

Alaska	Florida	New Orleans	Santa Fe, Taos, Albuquerque
Arizona	Hawaii	New York City	
Boston	Las Vegas, Reno, Tahoe	Pacific North Coast	Seattle & Vancouver
California		Philadelphia & the Pennsylvania Dutch Country	The South
Cape Cod, Martha's Vineyard, Nantucket	Los Angeles		U.S. & British Virgin Islands
	Maine, Vermont, New Hampshire		
The Carolinas & the Georgia Coast	Maui	The Rockies	USA
Chicago	Miami & the Keys	San Diego	Virginia & Maryland
Colorado	New England	San Francisco	Waikiki
			Washington, D.C.

Foreign

Australia & New Zealand	Egypt	Madrid & Barcelona	Provence & the Riviera
Austria	Europe	Mexico	Scandinavia
The Bahamas	Florence, Tuscany & Umbria	Montréal & Québec City	Scotland
Bermuda	France	Moscow, St. Petersburg, Kiev	Singapore
Budapest	Germany	The Netherlands, Belgium & Luxembourg	South Africa
Canada	Great Britain		South America
Cancún, Cozumel, Yucatán Peninsula	Greece	New Zealand	Southeast Asia
Caribbean	Hong Kong	Norway	Spain
China	India	Nova Scotia, New Brunswick, Prince Edward Island	Sweden
Costa Rica, Belize, Guatemala	Ireland		Switzerland
	Israel	Paris	Thailand
Cuba	Italy	Portugal	Tokyo
The Czech Republic & Slovakia	Japan		Toronto
	Kenya & Tanzania		Turkey
Eastern Europe	Korea		Vienna & the Danube
	London		

Fodor's Special-Interest Guides

Branson	Fodor's London Companion	Shadow Traffic's New York Shortcuts and Traffic Tips	Where Should We Take the Kids? California
Caribbean Ports of Call	Gay USA	Sunday in New York	Where Should We Take the Kids? Family Adventures
The Complete Guide to America's National Parks	France by Train	Sunday in San Francisco	
	Halliday's New England Food Explorer	Walt Disney World, Universal Studios and Orlando	Where Should We Take the Kids? Northeast
Condé Nast Traveler Caribbean Resort and Cruise Ship Finder	Healthy Escapes		
Cruises and Ports of Call	Italy by Train	Walt Disney World for Adults	
	Kodak Guide to Shooting Great Travel Pictures		

Fodor's

Special Series

Affordables
Caribbean
Europe
Florida
France
Germany
Great Britain
Italy
London
Paris

Fodor's Bed & Breakfasts and Country Inns
America's Best B&Bs
California's Best B&Bs
Canada's Great Country Inns
Cottages, B&Bs and Country Inns of England and Wales
The Mid-Atlantic's Best B&Bs
New England's Best B&Bs
The Pacific Northwest's Best B&Bs
The South's Best B&Bs
The Southwest's Best B&Bs
The Upper Great Lakes' Best B&Bs

The Berkeley Guides
California
Central America
Eastern Europe
Europe
France
Germany & Austria
Great Britain & Ireland
Italy
London
Mexico
Pacific Northwest & Alaska
Paris
San Francisco

Compass American Guides
Arizona
Chicago
Colorado
Hawaii
Idaho
Hollywood
Las Vegas
Maine
Manhattan
Montana
New Mexico
New Orleans
Oregon
San Francisco
Santa Fe
South Carolina
South Dakota
Southwest
Texas
Utah
Virginia
Washington
Wine Country
Wisconsin
Wyoming

Fodor's Citypacks
Atlanta
Hong Kong
London
New York City
Paris
Rome
San Francisco
Washington, D.C.

Fodor's Español
California
Caribe Occidental
Caribe Oriental
Gran Bretaña
Londres
Mexico

Nueva York
Paris

Fodor's Exploring Guides
Australia
Boston & New England
Britain
California
Caribbean
China
Egypt
Florence & Tuscany
Florida
France
Germany
Ireland
Israel
Italy
Japan
London
Mexico
Moscow & St. Petersburg
New York City
Paris
Prague
Provence
Rome
San Francisco
Scotland
Singapore & Malaysia
Spain
Thailand
Turkey
Venice

Fodor's Flashmaps
Boston
New York
San Francisco
Washington, D.C.

Fodor's Pocket Guides
Acapulco
Atlanta
Barbados

Jamaica
London
New York City
Paris
Prague
Puerto Rico
Rome
San Francisco
Washington, D.C.

Rivages Guides
Bed and Breakfasts of Character and Charm in France
Hotels and Country Inns of Character and Charm in France
Hotels and Country Inns of Character and Charm in Italy

Short Escapes
Country Getaways in Britain
Country Getaways in France
Country Getaways in New England
Country Getaways Near New York City

Fodor's Sports
Golf Digest's Best Places to Play
Skiing USA
USA Today The Complete Four Sport Stadium Guide

Fodor's Vacation Planners
Great American Learning Vacations
Great American Sports & Adventure Vacations
Great American Vacations
National Parks and Seashores of the East
National Parks of the West

Before Catching Your Flight, Catch Up With Your World.

Fueled by the global resources of CNN and available in major airports across America, CNN Airport Network provides a live source  of current domestic and international news,  sports, business, weather and lifestyle programming. Plus two daily Fodor's features for the facts you need: "Travel Fact," a useful and creative mix of travel trivia; and "What's Happening," a comprehensive round-up of upcoming events in major cities around the world.

With CNN Airport Network, you'll never be out of the loop.

HERE'S YOUR OWN PERSONAL VIEW OF THE WORLD.

Here's the easiest way to get up-to-the-minute, objective, personalized information about what's going on in the city you'll be visiting—before you leave on your trip! Unique information you could get only if you knew someone personally in each of 160 destinations around the world. Everything from special places to dine to local events only a local would know about.

It's all yours—in your Travel Update from Worldview, the leading provider of time-sensitive destination information.

Review the following order form and fill it out by indicating your destination(s) and travel dates and by checking off up to eight interest categories. Then mail or fax your order form to us, or call your order in. (We're here to help you 24 hours a day.)

Within 48 hours of receiving your order, we'll mail your convenient, pocket-sized custom guide to you, packed with information to make your travel more fun and interesting. And if you're in a hurry, we can even fax it.

Have a great trip with your Fodor's Worldview Travel Update!

Fodor's WORLDVIEW TRAVEL UPDATE

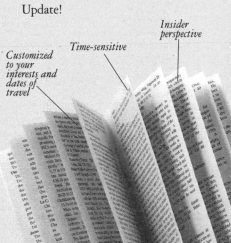

Customized to your interests and dates of travel

Time-sensitive

Insider perspective

DESTINATIONS

Worldview covers more than 160 destinations worldwide. Choose the destination(s) that match your itinerary from the list below:

Europe
Amsterdam
Athens
Barcelona
Berlin
Brussels
Budapest
Copenhagen
Dublin
Edinburgh
Florence
Frankfurt
French Riviera
Geneva
Glasgow
Lausanne
Lisbon
London
Madrid
Milan
Moscow
Munich
Oslo
Paris
Prague
Provence
Rome
Salzburg
Seville
St. Petersburg
Stockholm
Venice
Vienna
Zurich

United States (Mainland)
Albuquerque
Atlanta
Atlantic City
Baltimore
Boston
Branson, MO
Charleston, SC
Chicago
Cincinnati
Cleveland
Dallas/Ft. Worth
Denver
Detroit
Houston
Indianapolis
Kansas City
Las Vegas
Los Angeles
Memphis
Miami
Milwaukee
Minneapolis/St. Paul
Nashville
New Orleans
New York City
Orlando
Palm Springs
Philadelphia
Phoenix
Pittsburgh

Portland
Reno/Lake Tahoe
St. Louis
Salt Lake City
San Antonio
San Diego
San Francisco
Santa Fe
Seattle
Tampa
Washington, DC

Alaska
Alaskan Destinations

Hawaii
Honolulu
Island of Hawaii
Kauai
Maui

Canada
Quebec City
Montreal
Ottawa
Toronto
Vancouver

Bahamas
Abaco
Eleuthera/
 Harbour Island
Exuma
Freeport
Nassau &
 Paradise Island

Bermuda
Bermuda Countryside
Hamilton

British Leeward Islands
Anguilla
Antigua & Barbuda
St. Kitts & Nevis

British Virgin Islands
Tortola & Virgin
 Gorda

British Windward Islands
Barbados
Dominica
Grenada
St. Lucia
St. Vincent
Trinidad & Tobago

Cayman Islands
The Caymans

Dominican Republic
Santo Domingo

Dutch Leeward Islands
Aruba
Bonaire
Curacao

Dutch Windward Island
St. Maarten/St. Martin

French West Indies
Guadeloupe
Martinique
St. Barthelemy

Jamaica
Kingston
Montego Bay
Negril
Ocho Rios

Puerto Rico
Ponce
San Juan

Turks & Caicos
Grand Turk/
 Providenciales

U.S. Virgin Islands
St. Croix
St. John
St. Thomas

Mexico
Acapulco
Cancun & Isla Mujeres
Cozumel
Guadalajara
Ixtapa & Zihuatanejo
Los Cabos
Mazatlan
Mexico City
Monterrey
Oaxaca
Puerto Vallarta

South/Central America
Buenos Aires
Caracas
Rio de Janeiro
San Jose, Costa Rica
Sao Paulo

Middle East
Istanbul
Jerusalem

Australia & New Zealand
Auckland
Melbourne
South Island
Sydney

China
Beijing
Guangzhou
Shanghai

Japan
Kyoto
Nagoya
Osaka
Tokyo
Yokohama

Pacific Rim/Other
Bali
Bangkok
Hong Kong & Macau
Manila
Seoul
Singapore
Taipei

INTERESTS

For your personalized Travel Update, choose the eight (8) categories you're most interested in from the following list:

1.	**Business Services**	Fax & Overnight Mail, Computer Rentals, Protocol, Secretarial, Messenger, Translation Services

Dining

2.	**All-Day Dining**	Breakfast & Brunch, Cafes & Tea Rooms, Late-Night Dining
3.	**Local Cuisine**	Every Price Range — from Budget Restaurants to the Special Splurge
4.	**European Cuisine**	Continental, French, Italian
5.	**Asian Cuisine**	Chinese, Far Eastern, Japanese, Other
6.	**Americas Cuisine**	American, Mexican & Latin
7.	**Nightlife**	Bars, Dance Clubs, Casinos, Comedy Clubs, Ethnic, Pubs & Beer Halls
8.	**Entertainment**	Theater — Comedy, Drama, Musicals, Dance, Ticket Agencies
9.	**Music**	Classical, Opera, Traditional & Ethnic, Jazz & Blues, Pop, Rock
10.	**Children's Activites**	Events, Attractions
11.	**Tours**	Local Tours, Day Trips, Overnight Excursions
12.	**Exhibitions, Festivals & Shows**	Antiques & Flower, History & Cultural, Art Exhibitions, Fairs & Craft Shows, Music & Art Festivals
13.	**Shopping**	Districts & Malls, Markets, Regional Specialties
14.	**Fitness**	Bicycling, Health Clubs, Hiking, Jogging
15.	**Recreational Sports**	Boating/Sailing, Fishing, Golf, Skiing, Snorkeling/Scuba, Tennis/Racket
16.	**Spectator Sports**	Auto Racing, Baseball, Basketball, Golf, Football, Horse Racing, Ice Hockey, Soccer
17.	**Event Highlights**	The best of what's happening during the dates of your trip.
18.	**Sightseeing**	Sights, Buildings, Monuments
19.	**Museums**	Art, Cultural
20.	**Transportation**	Taxis, Car Rentals, Airports, Public Transportation
21.	**General Info**	Overview, Holidays, Currency, Tourist Info

Please note that content will vary by season, destination, and length of stay.

Name
Address
City   State   Country   ZIP
Tel #   (   )   -   Fax #   (   )   -
Title of this Fodor's guide:
Store and location where guide was purchased:

INDICATE YOUR DESTINATIONS/DATES: You can order up to three (3) destinations from the previous page. Fill in your arrival and departure dates for each
destination. **Your Travel Update itinerary (all destinations selected) cannot exceed 30 days from beginning to end.**

			Month	Day	Month	Day
(Sample) **LONDON**	From:	**6**	/	**21**	To: **6** / **30**
1	From:		/		To:	/
2	From:		/		To:	/
3	From:		/		To:	/

CHOOSE YOUR INTERESTS: Select up to eight (8) categories from the list of
interest categories shown on the previous page and circle the numbers below:

1 2 3 4 5 6 7 8 9 10 11 12 13 14 15 16 17 18 19 20 21

CHOOSE WHEN YOU WANT YOUR TRAVEL UPDATE DELIVERED (Check one):
❑ Please send my Travel Update immediately.
❑ Please hold my order until a few weeks before my trip to include the most up-to-date
information.
Completed orders will be sent within 48 hours. Allow 7–10 days for U.S. mail delivery.

ADD UP YOUR ORDER HERE. SPECIAL OFFER FOR FODOR'S
PURCHASERS ONLY!

	Suggested Retail Price	Your Price	This Order
First destination ordered	$ 9.95	$ 7.95	$ 7.95
Second destination (if applicable)	$ 6.95	$ 4.95	+
Third destination (if applicable)	$ 6.95	$ 4.95	+

DELIVERY CHARGE (Check one and enter amount below)

	Within U.S. & Canada	Outside U.S. & Canada
First Class Mail	❑ $2.50	❑ $5.00
FAX	❑ $5.00	❑ $10.00
Priority Delivery	❑ $15.00	❑ $27.00

ENTER DELIVERY CHARGE FROM ABOVE: +
TOTAL: $

METHOD OF PAYMENT IN U.S. FUNDS ONLY (Check one):
❑ AmEx ❑ MC ❑ Visa ❑ Discover ❑ Personal Check (U. S. & Canada only)
❑ Money Order/International Money Order

Make check or money order payable to: Fodor's Worldview Travel Update

Credit Card __/__/__/__/__/__/__/__/__/__/__/__/__/__/__/__/ **Expiration Date:** __/__

Authorized Signature

SEND THIS COMPLETED FORM WITH PAYMENT TO:
Fodor's Worldview Travel Update, 114 Sansome Street, Suite 700,
San Francisco, CA 94104

OR CALL OR FAX US 24-HOURS A DAY
Telephone **1-800-799-9609** • Fax **1-800-799-9619** (From within the U.S. & Canada)
(Outside the U.S. & Canada: Telephone 415-616-9988 • Fax 415-616-9989)

(Please have this guide in front of you when you call so we can verify purchase.)
Code: FTG   Offer valid until 12/31/97